Leibniz: Critical and Interpretive Essays

Leibniz: Critical and Interpretive Essays

Michael Hooker
Editor

University of Minnesota Press
Minneapolis

Published by the University of Minnesota Press,
2037 University Avenue Southeast, Minneapolis, MN 55414
Printed in the United States of America.

Library of Congress Cataloging in Publication Data
Main entry under title:

Leibniz: critical and interpretive essays.

    Bibliography: p.
    Includes indexes.
    1. Leibniz, Gottfried Wilhelm, Freiherr von,
1646-1716 – Addresses, essays, lectures.
I. Hooker, Michael.
B2598.L425   193   82-7010
ISBN 0-8166-1020-7   AACR2
ISBN 0-8166-1023-1 (pbk.)

List of Contributors

Robert Merrihew Adams, Dept. of Philosophy, University of California-Los Angeles, Los Angeles, CA 90024

David Blumenfeld, Dept. of Religion and Philosophy, Southwestern University, Georgetown, TX 78626

Hector-Neri Castañeda, Dept. of Philosophy, Indiana University, Bloomington, IN 47401

Edwin Curley, Dept. of Philosophy, Northwestern University, Evanston, IL 60201

Daniel Garber, Dept. of Philosophy, University of Chicago, Chicago, IL 60637

Martial Gueroult, formerly a member of the Institut and Professor of Philosophy at the College de France. The translation of the Gueroult essay is by Professor Roger Ariew, Dept. of Philosophy and Religion, Virginia Polytechnic Institute and State University, Blacksburg, 24061

Ian Hacking, Dept. of Philosophy, Stanford University, Stanford, CA 94305

Michael Hooker, Office of the President, Bennington College, Bennington, VT 05201

Hidé Ishiguro, Dept. of Philosophy, University of London-University College, London WC1E 6BT, England

Nicholas Jolley, Dept. of Philosophy, University of California-San Diego, La Jolla, CA 92093

Mark Kulstad, Dept. of Philosophy, Rice University, Houston, TX 77001

Robert McRae, Dept. of Philosophy, University of Toronto, Toronto, Ontario M5S 1A1 Canada

Fabrizio Mondadori, Dept. of Philosophy, Princeton University, Princeton, NJ 08540

G. H. R. Parkinson, Dept. of Philosophy, University of Reading, Reading, Berkshire RG6 2AH England

Mark Pastin, Dept. of Philosophy, Arizona State University, Tempe, AZ 85281

Robert Sleigh, Dept. of Philosophy, University of Massachusetts, Amherst, MA 01003

R. S. Woolhouse, Dept. of Philosophy, University of York, Derwent College, Heslington, York YO1 5DD England

Preface

The last two decades have seen an enormous increase in the attention paid by philosophers to the history of their discipline, especially to the seventeenth century. This is not surprising, since many of the themes of contemporary philosophical concern and much of the style of treating those themes are found to have their roots in Descartes and Leibniz. For that reason, any effort to come to grips with the metaphysics and epistemology of the seventeenth century will enhance our understanding of contemporary philosophy, and in turn historical understanding is augmented by the tools and results of contemporary philosophical endeavor. This symbiotic relationship is probably clearest in the case of Leibniz, as can be seen in the essays collected in this volume.

Of the sixteen essays contained here, all but two are previously unpublished. The essay by Robert Adams appeared first in *Rice Studies*. The essay by Martial Gueroult, though previously published in French, has been translated for this collection by Roger Ariew, and it appears in English for the first time. All the Leibniz scholars who have contributed to the volume are conversant with the tools of contemporary philosophical analysis and sensitive to the importance of historical integrity. The essays will do much to advance the state of Leibniz scholarship and to further current work in philosophy.

I am grateful to John Kish for invaluable assistance in the preparation of this manuscript, especially the bibliography and indexes.

Contents

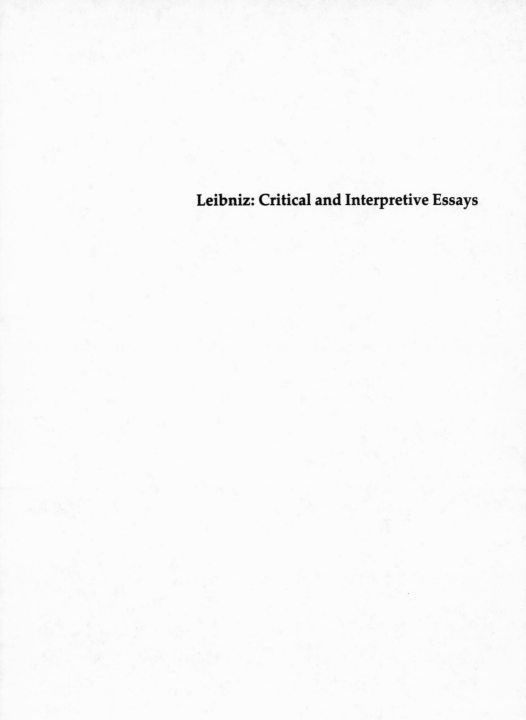

Leibniz: Critical and Interpretive Essays

The "Intellectualization of Appearances": Aspects of Leibniz's Theory of Sensation and Thought

G. H. R. Parkinson

I

Kant's assertion that Leibniz "intellectualized appearances" (*Critique of Pure Reason*, A 271, B 327) is often quoted, and seems often to be regarded as authoritative. That is to say, it is widely held that Leibniz recognized no difference in kind between sense perception and thinking; sense perception, according to this view, is for Leibniz a *kind* of thinking, whose difference from abstract thought is merely one of degree.[1] However, in his recent study of Leibniz's theory of knowledge, *Leibniz: Perception, Apperception and Thought* (Toronto, 1976), Robert McRae argues that this view of Leibniz is wrong, and offers another interpretation of what Leibniz says about the relations between sensation and thought. In this paper, I propose to reexamine the issue. I shall argue that McRae's interpretation is broadly correct, but that it requires some supplementation and modification.

As McRae points out (pp. 126-27), there is evidence that appears to support the Kantian interpretation. For example, in his *Addition à l'explication du système nouveau* (after 1698: GP IV 574-75[2]), Leibniz writes:

> Normally, we conceive confused thoughts as being generically quite different from distinct thoughts. . . . Basically, however, confused thoughts are simply a multitude of thoughts which, in themselves, are like distinct thoughts, but which are so small that each one taken separately does not attract our attention and cause itself to be distinguished. It can even be said that there is, at the same time, a truly infinite number of these contained in our sensations.

Again, in his *Réponse aux réflexions . . . de M. Bayle* (1702: GP IV 563, L 944) Leibniz says: "It has been believed that confused thoughts differ *toto genere* from distinct ones; in fact, however, they are merely less distinct and less

3

developed, by virtue of their multiplicity." Leibniz gives as examples of confused thoughts "those of colors, odors, tastes, heat, cold, etc.," which "always
involve the infinite, and not only that which happens in our body but also, by its
means, what happens elsewhere" (*ibid.*).

These passages may well be regarded as showing that Leibniz believed
sense perception to be confused thought. To see if this really was his view, let us
first examine what he says about sense perception.

II

We understand the term 'sense perception' in what seems to be a standard way;
as referring to seeing, hearing, touching, smelling, and tasting, where what are
seen, heard, and so on, are physical things or events — a cloud, say, or a clap of
thunder. Leibniz's theory of sense perception is not readily available, since he
wrote no detailed treatise on the subject; his views have to be pieced together
from scattered references in a number of papers.[3] Here, we will take as a starting
point his views about truths of fact. Such truths, he says, are the following: that
I think (*ego cogito*) and that various things are thought by me (*varia a me cogi-
tantur*) (*Animadversiones in partem generalem Principiorum Cartesianorum*, GP
IV 357, L 632-33). The second of these truths is the one that is important here.
Taken by itself, Leibniz's assertion might mislead, in that it might be thought to
mean that I perform a number of successive acts of thought. What Leibniz has in
mind, however, is something else, as his *De Synthesi et Analysi Universali* (GP
VIII 296, L 357, MP 15) indicates. Here he says, "I perceive . . . that there
are many differences in my thoughts, from which I infer that other things besides myself exist." This would make no sense if Leibniz simply meant that he
has a series of thoughts. What he does mean is shown by a passage from the *De
modo distinguendi phaenomena realia ab imaginariis* (GP VII 319, L 603):

> I judge to exist — without proof, from simple perception of experi-
> ence — that of which I am conscious within myself: that is, first myself as
> thinking various things (*me varia cogitantem*), and then the various phe-
> nomena or appearances that exist in my mind. For . . . it is as certain
> that there exists in my mind the appearance (*speciem*) of a golden moun-
> tain or a centaur, when I dream of them, as it is certain that I, the dreamer,
> exist; for each is contained in the single fact that it is certain that a centaur
> appears to me.

This passage clearly shows that, in Leibniz's view, to say "Various things
are thought by me," or "There are many differences in my thoughts," is to say
that phenomena of various kinds exist in my mind. Some of these, such as the
phenomenon of a centaur, exist in my mind only when I am dreaming or imagining, but others exist when I am awake and perceiving things by my senses. The
"truth of sensible things," Leibniz says in the *Nouveaux Essais* (NE IV.2.14, GP
V 355), consists simply in the connection of phenomena, which is what dis-

tinguishes them from dreams.[4] It now has to be asked how Leibniz conceives the relation between phenomena and a physical thing in such a case. On this topic I will be brief, as I have discussed the matter elsewhere.[5] When Leibniz says that the "truth of sensible things" consists solely in the connection of phenomena, he is speaking about the criteria by which we distinguish between sense-illusion and the genuine sense perception of physical reality; he is not upholding phenomenalism, i.e., a theory about the nature of physical things. As he says in the section of the *Nouveaux Essais* just quoted, "In the matter of the objects of the senses, the true criterion is the connection of phenomena."[6] He did indeed toy with phenomenalism for a while, but came to reject it; his reason seems to have been that to deny the existence of physical things, as entities that are independent of the existence of minds, is incompatible with the principle of the best (*Eclaircissement* . . . (1696), GP IV 495). His positive view about the relation between phenomena and physical things can be regarded as a version of the causal theory of sense perception. His theory has in effect two levels, the scientific and the metaphysical. He would say that on the scientific level, it is correct to assert that for an observer O to have a sense perception of a physical object X is for there to be in O's mind phenomena that are caused by X. But he would add that such language is not strictly accurate; for accuracy, we must move to the metaphysical level, where it is untrue to say that any created substance acts on any other. What was stated inaccurately in terms of causation must be restated in terms of the concept of expression, and it must be said that when one has a sense perception of a physical object X the phenomena in one's mind *express* X in a certain way, that is, there is "a constant and regular relation between what can be said of the one and of the other" (to Arnauld, 9 Oct. 1687; GP II 112, L 521, MP 71-72).

What concerns us here is only a part of the theory that has been sketched: namely, the precise nature of the 'phenomena' that have been mentioned. To clarify their nature, it is necessary to introduce two of the technical terms of Leibniz's philosophy of sense perception, the terms 'perception' and 'sensation.' It is important to be quite clear that Leibniz distinguishes between perception and sensation. Not all perception is sensation, he says (to Wagner, 1710; GP VII 529); a sensation is something that is more than a simple perception (Mon. par. 19, MP 182). According to Leibniz, perception[7] is a substance's interior state that 'represents' (i.e., expresses) external things (PNG par. 4, MP 197; Mon par. 14, MP 180). The term 'sensation' renders a group of equivalent words Leibniz uses— 'la sensation,' 'le sentiment,' and 'sensio.'[8] Sensation is the type of perception that is peculiar to individuals who have sense-organs (PNG par. 4, MP 196). To be more specific, a sensation is that perception that a percipient has when he actually perceives some external object by the senses, as distinct from merely imagining it; in the latter case Leibniz speaks of an 'imagination' rather than of a 'sensation.'[9] The question now arises, whether the term 'phenomenon' is equivalent to 'perception' in Leibniz's sense of the term, or whether it refers exclusively to sensations or imaginations. In the *Discourse on Metaphysics*,

Leibniz seems to equate phenomena (or more exactly, appearances) with perceptions, in that he refers to 'appearances or perceptions' (*apparences ou perceptions*; DM par. 33). But in the passages that chiefly concern us — those quoted in the last paragraph — 'phenomena' must refer to sensations and imaginations. It will be noted later in this section that there are, according to Leibniz, perceptions that are not noticed; but we could not possibly use such perceptions as criteria by which to distinguish our experience of real things from dreaming or imagination. Again, in the *De Synthesi et Analysi Universali* (*loc. cit.*) Leibniz speaks of constructing a "record of phenomena" (*Historia phaenomenorum*), and such a record must be of what human beings have noticed.

We can now leave aside the term 'phenomenon,' and concentrate on the terms 'sensation' and 'perception.' The question is, how exactly a sensation differs from a perception; what that "something more" is (*quelque chose de plus*; Mon. par. 19) that a sensation has. Leibniz's view is that although every substance has perceptions, the only substances that have sensations are those that have what he calls 'distinct' perceptions.[10] The opposite of 'distinct' is 'confused;' so the soul after death, for example, has no sensations, but still has perceptions — perceptions that are highly confused. As Leibniz says in a paper on the metaphysical consequences of the principle of reason (c. 1712: C 15, MP 177): "If it" (sc. the soul) "should arrive at that state in which it has perceptions that are almost all confused, we call this 'death'; for then a stupor arises, as in a profound sleep or in apoplexy" (Cf. Mon. par. 21, MP 182; PMG par. 4, MP 197; NE II.1.11, GP V 103). This does not mean that confused perceptions are irrelevant to the topic of sensation. Beings that have sensations, Leibniz asserts, have confused perceptions also, and it will be seen shortly that in his view, confused perceptions are involved in all sensation.

In trying to clarify what Leibniz means by all this, let us begin with the notion of confused perception. This notion is dependent on one of Leibniz's metaphysical theses: namely, that each substance expresses the whole universe by perceiving it.[11] Leibniz's argument may be stated as follows: At each moment of its history, every substance perceives the whole universe; further, what it perceives is of infinite complexity, since the universe is infinite. In perceiving the universe at any given moment it has an infinity of perceptions, for only in this way can it be said to express the whole universe, that is, only in this way is it in principle possible to infer from its states to the states of all other substances. Now, human souls are substances; but it is obvious that at any given time such a soul does not *notice* everything that occurs in the universe. Leibniz puts this by saying that although the human soul perceives the whole universe, the perceptions that it (and indeed, every created substance) has are 'confused.' Let us now apply this to the sensations that a soul has. Suppose that someone is looking at a tree. The tree is only a minute portion of the universe, yet (Leibniz would say) the sensation that the observer's soul has must include an infinity of confused perceptions (PNG par. 13, MP 201).[12]

In calling perceptions 'confused' in this and similar contexts, Leibniz seems to have in mind a standard sense of the term. In this sense, something is called 'confused' if it is a mixture whose elements cannot be distinguished. Similarly, in calling perceptions confused, Leibniz means that because of their infinity, the percipient cannot distinguish each one separately. Confusedness, then, is not a property that belongs to perceptions *in themselves*; to call perceptions 'confused' is to say that, because of their infinity, they cannot be distinguished by the percipient.

When Leibniz speaks of the way in which a substance perceives the whole universe, he often illustrates this by the example of our perception of the waves of the sea, where "the confused murmur that is heard by those who approach the sea-shore comes from the accumulation of the repercussions of innumerable waves" (DM par. 33, MP 43; cf. to Arnauld, 30 April 1687, GP II 91; 9 Oct. 1687, GP II 113, MP 72). The sound of the sea is also mentioned as an example of what he calls 'little perceptions,' and indeed it is clear that 'confused perceptions' are closely related to little perceptions, that is, to perceptions that we do not notice.[13] As Leibniz explains (NE Pref., GP V 47, MP 155), the failure to notice such perceptions may be because of their great number (as in the case of the waves of the sea), or their smallness (Leibniz speaks of the 'little noise' of each wave), or their monotony (as in the case of a waterfall, whose noise is not noticed by those who live near it). Leibniz does not suggest that such little perceptions are *unnoticeable*; obviously the waterfall can be heard, and in the case of the other kinds of little perceptions Leibniz says that we could notice them, if we were not distracted by their multitude, or if they were not obscured by bigger perceptions (NE II.1.9, GP V 121). He does seem to think that a confused perception, which is one of an infinity of perceptions that a percipient has at a given time, cannot be noticed. However, since what cannot be noticed certainly is not noticed, a confused perception may be regarded as a type of little perception — though it should clearly be understood that not every little perception is confused, in the sense defined.

III

There will be more to say about Leibniz's use of the term 'confused perception' later; now, however, it is time to consider his views about distinct perception. A distinct perception is contrasted with a confused perception as just defined: that is, with a perception that is not noticed, and that indeed (it appears) cannot be noticed. This at once suggests two possibilities: a distinct perception may be (a) a perception that is noticed, or (b) a perception that, whether or not it is noticed, *can be* noticed. But there are other possibilities as well. A distinct perception may be, not something that is or can be noticed, but either (c) a noticing of something, or (d) the capacity to notice something. It cannot be said that Leibniz makes very clear just what he has in mind here; however, it is most important to try to see what he means, because, as noted in Section II, only those substances that have distinct perceptions have sensations. More than this: having distinct perceptions is not just a necessary condition of having sensations, but is both necessary and sufficient. As Leibniz remarks (GP VII 317, quoted in note 10), "If the perception is more distinct, it makes a sensation." If, then, we can explain the nature of distinct perception, we shall at the same time be explaining what Leibniz thinks about the nature of sensation.

In using the term 'distinct,' Leibniz seems in part to be calling attention to the part played in sensation by the sense-organs. He says that the soul recognizes (*connaît*) the things that it perceives only insofar as it has sensations that are "distinct and heightened" (*relevées*: PNG par. 13, MP 201; cf. Mon. par. 24, MP 182). In explaining this, Leibniz begins by saying (PNG par. 4, MP 196; Mon. par. 25, MP 183; C 15, MP 177) that the function of the sense-organs is as it were to concentrate the infinity of physical stimuli that act on the percipient's body; for example, in the case of sight, rays of light are concentrated by the eye and act with more force, producing on the organs physical impressions that are "distinct and heightened" (PNG par. 4). Now, the impressions on the sense-organs are 'represented' (sc. expressed) by perceptions, so just as the impressions are distinct, so too are the corresponding perceptions (*ibid.*; cf. Mon. par. 25). But this does not explain *in what sense* a perception is 'distinct'; it merely explains the physical conditions that make distinct perception possible. We must, then, look further if we are to answer the question "Which, of the four alternatives mentioned earlier, represents Leibniz's view of the nature of distinct perception?" and so throw light on his theory of sensation.

We may begin by noting that to have a sensation is to notice something. To ask someone, "What do you notice here?" is to ask him to look, listen, and so on. The question is what Leibniz believes to be involved in noticings of this kind. It has already been seen that in his view, a confused perception is a perception that is not noticed; conversely, it can be seen that for Leibniz, to have a sensation involves a noticing of *perceptions*. When one is said to see a tree, for example, the situation according to Leibniz is that one notices a perception that expresses (or group of perceptions that express) the tree. That this is Leibniz's view is shown by what he says about 'apperception.' By this term, Leibniz understands self-consciousness; apperception is a substance's reflection on its own inner states (PNG par. 4, MP 197; Mon. par. 23, MP 182). The part that apperception plays in sense perception is shown by the following passage from the *Nouveaux Essais* (NE II.9.4, GP V 121):

> The perception of light or color, for example, that we apperceive is composed of a number of little perceptions that we do not apperceive, and a noise of which we have a perception, but do not notice, becomes apperceptible by a little addition or augmentation.

It is clear that Leibniz holds that when we are said to see a color, we *apperceive* a perception or perceptions. What is not immediately clear is exactly *what* we apperceive. Do we (a) apperceive a sensation? Or is it that (b) to have a sensation is to apperceive confused perceptions? In seeking an answer, we must first examine the relations between sensations and confused perceptions.

Leibniz often says that our sensations are the *result* of an infinite variety of perceptions;[14] they are, moreover, results of a special kind. They result from confused perceptions, not as a chemical compound results from the mixing of several substances, but rather as a rainbow results from light rays and droplets of water; sensations, Leibniz says in the *Nouveaux Essais*, are mere appearances, 'phantoms' (NE IV.6.7, GP V 384). It is easy to reconstruct Leibniz's reasoning here. Suppose that I have a sensation — say, of an expanse of green. Really, I am having an infinity of confused perceptions, yet what I sense is a single expanse of color (cf. NE II.2.1, GP V 109). It cannot be that what I sense is both one and many; it must be, then, that the confused perceptions that I have appear to be what they are not.

Despite this, Leibniz often says that sensations are *composed of* confused perceptions. One such passage (NE II.9.4) has already been cited in this section, and several others could be mentioned.[15] There are too many such passages for them to be discounted as mere mistakes, and one is therefore faced with the problem of reconciling them with the passages that state that a sensation is not composed of confused perceptions, but results from them. Perhaps Leibniz reasoned that if a sensation is a mere 'phantom,' resulting from confused perceptions, then these confused perceptions are what really exist in us when we sense something. In this sense, they may be said to "compose" the sensation; not in the way in which a crowd is composed of people, but in the way in which a rainbow is composed of drops of water.

Let us now see what light this throws on our problem. This was: Is it Leibniz's view that when we sense something, a sensation is what is noticed, or is it his view that to have a sensation is to *notice* confused perceptions? It can now be seen that if Leibniz held the first view, he would have to say that confused perceptions produce sensations, which are noticed by the self. But this is not what he would say. This interpretation would make of a sensation something rather like a physical object, something that does not depend for its existence on being noticed. But, as has just been seen, Leibniz did not reify sensations in this way, but regarded them as mere appearances. A sensation does not have an existence that is logically independent of its being noticed; rather, it is generated by the act of noticing. The second view, then, seems the more likely; is there any positive evidence in its favor? If Leibniz is to hold such a view — if he is to say that the soul notices confused perceptions insofar as it has sensations — then he must say that it notices them *confusedly*; not as a friend, say, is noticed in a crowd, but in the way that a crowd, which is really a large number of individuals, is seen from a distance as one expanse. This is indeed the kind of thing he does say. In several passages he speaks of sensations, not as resulting from confused perceptions, but as themselves being confused perceptions.[16] He speaks, for example, of the "insensible ingredients of confused perceptions" (GP VII 501), where confused perceptions are not regarded as the "insensible ingredients" of sensations, but are equated with sensations, in that they are said to have little perceptions as ingredients. Essentially the same is said in the *Principles of Nature and of Grace*, though here sensations are regarded as the results of, rather than composed of, little perceptions, Leibniz saying that our confused perceptions are the result of the impressions that the whole universe makes on us (PNG par. 13, MP 201). Similarly, in the *Discourse on Metaphysics* (DM par. 33, MP 43) Leibniz says that 'confused sensations' are the result of an infinite variety of perceptions.[17] This ambiguity in the term 'confused perception' leads to a paradox, in that there is a sense in which a sensation is both a distinct perception and a confused perception. But the paradox disappears when it is remembered that the sense of 'confused' to which 'distinct' is opposed is different from that in which a sensation is called 'confused.'

In sum, it appears to be Leibniz's view that to have a sensation is to notice confused perceptions. With this in mind, let us return to the problem stated at the beginning of this section. There, four possible interpretations of the term 'distinct perception' were suggested. What has just been said disposes of (a) (a distinct perception is a perception that is noticed) in favor of (c) (a distinct perception is a noticing of something). As to (b) and (d), which interpret distinct perception in terms of (b) what can be noticed, or (d) of a capacity to notice, (b) is ruled out for the same reason as (a) — a distinct perception is *a noticing*, not what is or can be noticed. (d) is eliminated in that a distinct perception is an *act* of noticing, not a capacity to notice.

To conclude this section, we must note a difficulty that arises from Leibniz's views about the part played by apperception in sensation. The difficulty is obvious. When one perceives a physical object, one is not necessarily aware that one is having a certain sensation; rather, one perceives the object *in having* the sensation. The point may be brought out in another way. To scrutinize one's mental state when one perceives — to consider, as Locke and Berkeley would have us do, what is immediately present to the mind in such a case — requires a deliberate act of introspection. This clearly differs from those cases in which one is not considering the philosophy of sense perception, but is simply perceiving things. Yet Leibniz seems to be saying that all sense perception is introspective.

Essentially the same problem arises from what Leibniz says about animal sensations. The Cartesians had denied that animals have sensations; Leibniz says that this was an error, and that it arose because the Cartesians failed to distinguish perception from apperception (PNG par. 4, MP 197; cf. Mon. par. 14, MP 180). He means that the Cartesians were right in denying apperception to animals; the animals do indeed lack any consciousness of self (cf. PNG par. 5). But the Cartesians wrongly identified perception with apperception, and so were led to the false conclusion that animals have no perceptions, or more precisely no sensations. So much is clear; the problem is that Leibniz has also said that sensation involves apperception. How can this be, if the animals have sensations, but lack apperception?

McRae (p. 30) finds a contradiction here. Perhaps, however, there is no real contradiction in Leibniz's thought, but only an ambiguity in the term 'apperception.' Leibniz may mean by it: (i) An awareness of one's own perceptions. In this sense, Locke and Berkeley would ascribe apperception to the mind, when they speak of ideas as being the immediate objects of the mind. (ii) An awareness of one's perceptions *as one's own*. This would correspond to Locke's 'ideas of reflection,' as opposed to his 'ideas got by sensation' (*Essay*, II.1.24). To apply this to the problem under consideration: The animals have apperception in sense (i), and so have sensation; they do not, however, have apperception in sense (ii), in that they are unable to introspect.

McRae considers this possibility (p. 33), but rejects it. He relies on a passage[18] quoted early in Sec. II above, which runs:

> It is as certain that there exists in my mind the appearance of a golden mountain or a centaur, when I dream of them, as it is certain that I, the dreamer, exist; for each is contained in the single fact that it is certain that a centaur appears to me.

According to McRae, this shows that to be conscious of the *I*'s perceptions is to be conscious of the *I*; separation of the apperception of perceptions from apperception of the *I* is therefore impossible. Against this, it may be argued that Leibniz does not say in this passage that sensation implies self-awareness. What he says is that a certain *proposition* ("A centaur appears to me") has certain logical consequences. This assertion has no relevance to animals, which do not frame propositions, nor is there any reason to suppose that Leibniz intends it to have such relevance.

It seems, then, that Leibniz could avoid the contradiction into which he seems to fall. But it cannot be said that Leibniz was clear about the distinction suggested; certainly, if this distinction is sound, then he failed to locate the precise point at which the Cartesians went wrong. They did not err in that they failed to distinguish between perception and apperception, in the sense of self-consciousness; they erred in that they failed to make the more subtle distinction between two kinds of apperception.

The argument of the last two sections has been complex, and before we go further it may be helpful to give a short review of its course. Our concern is with Leibniz's theory of what may be called either 'sense perception' or 'sensation'; in particular, we wish to decide whether (as some have supposed) he believed that sensation is a kind of thinking. We began with a sketch of his account of 'phenomena.' For Leibniz, it is a primitive truth of fact that phenomena exist in the mind. The term 'phenomenon' covers both sensations and imaginations, which we distinguish by virtue of their greater or lesser coherence. What exactly, then, is a sensation? Leibniz answers that a sensation is a perception, but not a perception of absolutely any kind. To have a sensation is to have a perception that is 'distinct', that is, not 'confused.' Leibniz's point is that even in death or deep sleep, the soul has some perceptions, but these perceptions are confused—they are such that, because of their infinity, they cannot be discerned separately.

Such confused perceptions appear to be a subclass of what Leibniz calls 'little perceptions,' perceptions that *are not* noticed; for what cannot be noticed certainly is not noticed. Turning next to distinct perceptions, we noted that a condition of a percipient's having these is the possession of sense-organs. But in what sense are the perceptions 'distinct?' The answer is that to have a distinct perception is to *notice* a perception or perceptions; that is, it is to be *aware of* a perception, to 'apperceive.' Does Leibniz mean, then, that to have a distinct perception is (a) to apperceive a sensation, or does he mean that (b) in sensing, we apperceive confused (i.e., not separately discernible) perceptions? It is clear that the answer cannot be (a), because Leibniz says that our sensations result from confused perceptions, as a rainbow results from light-rays and water-drops. He must mean, then, that a sensation is *generated by* the act of noticing. The soul notices its infinite perceptions only confusedly, so Leibniz sometimes says that sensations are confused perceptions. This leads to the apparently paradoxical conclusion that a sensation (a *distinct* perception) is a *confused* noticing. We noted finally that what Leibniz says about apperception has been thought to lead to a contradiction. He insists that animals have sensations, yet he also says that they lack apperception. But perhaps what he means is that they have no concept of '*I,*' and so cannot recognize perceptions *as their own.*

IV

It is now time to turn from Leibniz's views about confused perception to his views about confused thought. Let us begin by looking again at the passages about 'confused thoughts' (GP IV 574-75, 563) that were quoted in Section I as appearing to support Kant's view that for Leibniz, sensation is confused thought. What is striking about them is that, when seen in the light of what has already been established about confused perception, they do not seem to present anything new. They seem to express in other words what has already been seen about the relations between sensations and little perceptions — that sensations are "more distinct" than little perceptions, of which they contain an infinity. The only apparent difference is that, instead of using the term 'perception,' Leibniz uses the term 'thought' (*pensée*). The question is, whether Leibniz is here using the term 'thought' in a sense so wide as to cover perceptions and sensations, so that he really is saying nothing new. There would be a Cartesian precedent for doing this,[19] but it cannot be assumed without further argument that Leibniz is following Descartes here. However, it is significant that (cf. the beginning of Section II) when Leibniz declares it to be a basic truth of fact that various things are 'thought' by me, or that there are many differences in my 'thoughts,' he means that various phenomena exist in my mind.

It seems, then, that the passages quoted in support of the Kantian interpretation of Leibniz's views about sensation and thought do not, in fact, support it. However, this conclusion does not of itself dispose of the Kantian interpretation; we need to see how Leibniz did view the relations between sensation and thought. We need to examine Leibniz's discussions of the nature of confused and distinct concepts, during which he often refers to sense perception. The most authoritative source of his views on these topics is the *Meditationes de Cognitione, Veritate et Ideis* (GP IV 422 ff., L 351 ff.), published in November 1684. This exposition can be supplemented by passages from other works: e.g., the *Discourse on Metaphysics* (par. 24, MP 33-34), the *Nouveaux Essais* (NE II.29.2 ff., GP V 236 ff.; NE IV.4.4-7, GP V 275), and two works that may precede the *Meditationes*—*Introductio ad Encyclopaediam Arcanam* (C 512, MP 6) and *De Synthesi et Analysi Universali* (GP VII 293-94, MP 11-12).

In the *Meditationes*, Leibniz distinguishes between 'obscure' and 'clear' knowledge; the latter is divided into 'confused' and 'distinct' knowledge, and distinct knowledge is in turn subdivided into 'adequate' and 'inadequate,' and also into 'symbolic' and 'intuitive' knowledge (GP IV 422). This classification of types of knowledge is paralleled by corresponding distinctions between types of concept; Leibniz speaks, for example, of 'obscure' and 'distinct' concepts. He does not explain how knowledge and concepts are linked, but it appears that his line of thought is as follows. Knowledge is expressed in the form of propositions;[20] that is, the man who has knowledge of X can state propositions about X. Now, a proposition contains concepts, and if the concept of X is of a given type, then the knowledge of X that is expressed by the propositions in which this concept appears will be of the same type. To illustrate: an 'obscure' concept, according to Leibniz, is one that does not suffice for the thing that it represents to be recognized. Now, if an obscure concept of X is part of a proposition entertained by A, then the knowledge of X that A has, as expressed by this proposition, is obscure. It does not seem to matter whether the obscure concept occurs as subject or predicate; if my concept of (say) an Eschscholtzia is obscure, then whether I say "This flower is an Eschscholtzia," or "This Eschscholtzia is orange," my knowledge of an Eschscholtzia is obscure also.

Our concern here is not with obscure concepts but with clear concepts— concepts that do enable the thing represented to be recognized — and more specifically with their two main subforms, confused and distinct concepts. A concept is confused if the person who has it "cannot list separately the marks which are sufficient to distinguish the thing from others, even though it has such marks and requisites,[21] into which its concept can be analyzed" (GP IV 422, L 449). Leibniz illustrates this by the example of colors, smells, tastes," and the other peculiar objects of the senses." He distinguishes these (GP IV 423) from "concepts common to several of the senses," such as those that we have of number, magnitude, and shape, and also of many "affects of the mind," such as hope and fear. The "peculiar objects of the senses," which Leibniz also calls 'qualities' (sc. of things), we can recognize and distinguish from each other; but we do so "solely by the evidence of the senses, and not by marks that can be stated." Yet, Leibniz goes on, "the concepts of these qualities are composite and can be analyzed, in that they have their causes.

It is not clear from the text whether it is the concepts or the qualities that are said to have causes. But it is hard to see what Leibniz could mean by saying that a concept has a cause,[22] and in fact at the end of the *De Organo sive Arte Magna Cogitandi* (C 432, MP 4) he clearly means that it is the quality, not the concept, that has a cause. Speaking here of the concept of heat, which he would regard as a confused concept, he says, "But no one doubts that there is some cause of heat, and if this were known perfectly, there would be a definition of heat" — that is, in the language of the *Meditationes*, the concept of heat is analyzable.[23] It may be asked why Leibniz should argue that to say that (for instance) heat has a cause means that its concept must be complex. The answer is to be found in Leibniz's theory of the 'full' concept (*notio plena*). The full concept of heat[24] contains all that can truly be said of heat; it must therefore contain the concept of the cause of heat. More exactly (since no created substance really acts on any other) the full concept of heat must be such that it is possible to derive from it the concepts of those states of other substances that are called the 'cause' of heat.

What Leibniz thinks about the exact nature of such causes can be seen from what has already been said about sensations. Consider, for example, the case of color. Leibniz would assert that the colors that we sense have no objective existence; this is because anything colored is extended, and no Leibnizian substance is extended. In saying that color has a cause, then, Leibniz must mean that our *sensations* of color have a cause. He would argue (cf. Sec. III) that A's sensation of color is the result of an infinity of A's little perceptions. These little perceptions are perceptions of every other substance in the universe; but if we say no more than this, then (since the same can be said of any of A's sensations) we do not explain what makes it a sensation of color and not of something else. Leibniz must therefore have recourse to what he has said about 'distinct perceptions': namely, that every sensation is the accompaniment of, and expresses, certain processes in the sense-organs of the individual who has the sensation, produced by the activity of external objects.[25] This is why he says sometimes that the little perceptions are of "the most minute motions and shapes" (GP IV 426), or again that the ideas of sense (*idées sensitives*) depend on shapes and motions (NE IV.6.7, GP V 383-84).[26] It should be stressed that Leibniz is here speaking on a scientific and not on a metaphysical level; as already noted, no substance is really extended, and no created substance really acts on another.

A concept that did offer an accurate analysis of color would be a 'distinct' concept of color. Leibniz's favorite example of a distinct concept is the concept that assayers have of gold (GP IV 423). The assayer distinguishes true from false gold "by means of certain tests or marks that constitute the definition of gold" (DM par. 24, MP 33), marks that he can "state and describe" (*Introductio ad Encyclopaediam Arcanam*: C 512, MP 6). Leibniz does not mean that an assayer can state *all* the marks that constitute the definition of gold, i.e., that he can analyze the concept of gold into all its component concepts. If he could do this, he would have an 'adequate' knowledge of gold; but as he can state only some of the marks of gold, his knowledge of gold, though distinct, is 'inadequate' (cf. GP

IV 423). It should be added that distinct knowledge does not always imply the capacity to analyze a concept; there is distinct knowledge of concepts that are primitive, that is, unanalyzable (*ibid.*). This means, then, that the mere inability to analyze a concept does not necessarily imply that one's concept is confused. Rather, one's concept of X is confused if one is able to identify instances of X but is unable to give any analysis of the concept of X, though that concept is in fact analyzable.

V

We are now in a position to compare the confusedness and distinctness of concepts with the confusedness and distinctness of perceptions. The way in which Leibniz distinguishes a concept from a perception is easily seen. As already noted (Sec. II, quoting PNG par. 4 and Mon. par. 14), a perception is a state of a substance. Concepts, on the other hand, have to do with meaning; a noun or noun phrase, according to Leibniz, has meaning insofar as it is the sign of a concept.[27] McRae argues (p. 128) that as both perceptions and concepts are called 'distinct' and 'confused,' distinctness and confusedness cannot be used to distinguish them from each other. Perception and thought must therefore (contrary to Kant's interpretation of Leibniz) differ generically; it makes no sense to say that perception is confused thinking. The argument is neat, but not conclusive, in that there could be an ambiguity in Leibniz's terminology, such that perceptions are distinct and confused in a different sense from that in which thoughts are distinct and confused. We need, therefore, to look further into Leibniz's views about thought and perception before Kant's interpretation can safely be rejected.

Now, it is clear that the distinctness that is ascribed to a sensation is not the same as that which is ascribed to a concept. A sensation is a distinct perception in that to have a sensation is to notice something; this noticing is the result of an infinity of confused (sc. 'little') perceptions, which are not noticed individually. But, as pointed out at the end of Section IV, to have a distinct concept is to have a concept that is either primitive, i.e., unanalyzable, or that is analyzable and that one is able to analyze, at least in some measure. In short, to have a distinct concept presupposes the capacity to analyze, where analysis is possible; to have a distinct perception presupposes the lack of such a capacity.

Leibniz, then, can consistently say that a perception may be either confused or distinct (i.e., either a little perception or a sensation), but that neither type of perception is a distinct thought. This leads to a vital question. Is a perception a thought that is not distinct (i.e., is it a confused thought?), or is it not a thought at all? When we talk of perception in this context, we are talking of sense perception, and not of little perceptions; it will therefore be better to use, in what follows, the less ambiguous term 'sensation.' Now, there does seem to be a certain correspondence between confused concepts and sensations—that is, perceptions that are 'confused' in the sense recognized in Section III. At first sight, there might not seem to be any correspondence between the two, in that sensations *result from* little perceptions, whereas a confused concept *consists of* the concepts into which it can be analyzed. It is true that there is a suggestion in Leibniz that concepts of the latter kind can be called causes of confused concepts, but it has already been argued in Section IV that this is not his real meaning. However, the difference between a sensation and a confused concept may not be as great as at first appears. Consider, as an example, the concept of color. According to Leibniz, this concept is analyzable, because color has causes. Precisely *what* concept is analyzable? It can hardly be the concept of color that is possessed by the "plain man," ignorant of the causes of color; for the concept that he has is of something simple. In saying, then, that the concept of color is analyzable, Leibniz is not referring to the plain man's concept of color; he is not talking about the rules according to which the plain man uses words. What he declares to be analyzable is *the concept* of color — understanding by this the concept that would be had of color by someone who understood color perfectly, and not the concept that is possessed by this or that human being, or, it may be, by this or that nation, or this or that epoch.[28] So it could be said that the plain man's confused concept of color obscures the real nature of the concept of color, much as a confused perception (i.e., a sensation) obscures the real nature of the little perceptions of which it is the result.

There is, then, a correspondence between confused perceptions (understanding by these, sensations) and confused concepts. But does this mean that a sensation *is* a confused thought? Clearly it does not entail it; to say that perceptions and thoughts are both instances of confusedness does not imply that a perception *is* a thought. To find an answer to the question, we must look elsewhere — namely, at what Leibniz says about the relations between sensations and concepts.

McRae points out (p. 129) that sense experience can provide concepts with a *sanction*. Leibniz insists that a concept must be shown to be possible, i.e., not to involve a contradiction. This can in principle be done either a priori or a posteriori. The a priori method would consist in analyzing a concept into its requisites, whose possibility is known, and showing that these concepts are compatible with each other. To do this, the analysis must be taken as far as primitive concepts, i.e., the knowledge involved must be what Leibniz calls 'adequate.' In the *Meditationes*, Leibniz says that he is not confident that human beings have such knowledge (GP IV 423, 425); as far as we are concerned, then, the a priori method seems to be possible in principle rather than in practice. The a posteriori method, however, is within our power. This method does not involve any analysis of concepts; instead, the possibility of a concept is shown by establishing, by means of sense experience, the existence of an instance of the concept (GP IV 425; DM par. 24, MP 34).

But this does not exhaust the relations between sensations and concepts. Sensations do not only sanction concepts; they are also a *source* of some of our concepts, namely, confused concepts. That they can be such a source is a consequence of Leibniz's views about truth. It is well known that Leibniz held that to say that S is P is to say that the concept of P is included in the concept of S. If one can establish that the concept of P is in the concept of S, one proves that S is P. Conversely, if one can establish that S is P, one thereby establishes the inclusion of the concept of P in the concept of S. In many cases, one can establish that S is P by means of sense experience, and in such cases sense experience will have been the source of one's concept of S as being P; or, in other words, it is by virtue of sense experience that one's concept of S will contain the concept of P. Clearly, such a concept of S must be confused. Suppose, for example, that on the basis of experience I form the concept of gold as of something yellow; that is, my concept of gold includes the concept of yellow. The concept of gold that I form in this way must be confused, in that it involves a concept of something (here, of yellow) that represents that something as simple when in fact it is analyzable. This is because this concept is based on sensations, and sensations are confused perceptions, in the sense that they do not enable the percipient to discriminate any of the infinity of little perceptions from which each sensation results.

But though sensation may *provide* us with concepts, this does not mean that a sensation *is* a concept, or that Leibniz thought that it is. The point may be put in this way. A sensation is confused in that when one has a sensation, what is not really simple *appears to* the percipient as simple. To have a confused concept, on the other hand, is to *think that* a word stands for something simple (or, it is to take the word as meaning something simple) when in fact it stands for something complex. It is true that the way in which we think about things depends, to some extent, on our sensations; but this does not commit one to the view that sensing is thinking, nor is there any firm evidence that Leibniz held such a view.

Let us now conclude. Our inquiry, though disagreeing with McRae's in some respects, has reached the same general conclusion: that Kant was mistaken in his belief that Leibniz viewed sense perception as a kind of confused thought. It is worth adding that the issue is not a merely marginal one where Leibniz's philosophy is concerned. In the passage in which he accuses Leibniz of intellectualizing appearances, Kant says that Leibniz regarded sensibility as serving only to confuse the representations that understanding yields (*Critique of Pure Reason*, A 271, B 327). The implication is that Leibniz viewed sense experience as not only a superfluity, but a harmful one, and thought that the person who wants to understand nature ought not to observe or experiment, but should confine himself to a priori thought. In other words, Kant seems to take the view that Leibniz was one of those who (in R. M. Harré's phrase) have "hoped to get to know the truth about Nature without going through the often tedious process of consulting her."[29] In fact, however, this is not true of Leibniz as a scientist,[30] and it has been the argument of this paper that nothing in Leibniz's theory of knowledge would oblige him to slight experience in this way.

NOTES

1. See, e.g., J. Bennett, *Kant's Analytic* (Cambridge, 1966), p. 55; W. H. Walsh, *Kant's Criticism of Metaphysics* (Edinburgh, 1975), p. 15.

2. The following abbreviations of Leibniz's works are used in this paper:

A   *Gottfried Wilhelm Leibniz: Sämtliche Schriften und Briefe*, Academy edition (Darmstadt and Berlin, 1923-   ). References are to series and volume.

C   *Opuscules et fragments inédits de Leibniz*, ed. L. Couturat (Paris, 1903).

DM   *Discours de Métaphysique*.

GP   *Die philosophischen Schriften von Gottfried Wilhelm Leibniz*, ed. C. I. Gerhardt, 7 vols. (Berlin, 1875-1890).

L   *Gottfried Wilhelm Leibniz: Philosophical Papers and Letters*, ed. and trans. L. E. Loemker, 1st ed. (Chicago, 1956).

Mon.   *Monadologie*.

MP   *Leibniz: Philosophical Writings*, ed. G. H. R. Parkinson, trans. Mary Morris and G. H. R. Parkinson (London, 1973).

NE   *Nouveaux Essais*. (This is contained in A VI.6. I have given page references to the text contained in GP V, which, despite its deficiencies, is more generally accessible).

PNG   *Principes de la Nature et de la Grace*.

All translations from Leibniz cited in the text are my own.

3. It should be added that this paper is concerned only with Leibniz's mature philosophy. The passages to be discussed will therefore either date from the period 1686-1716, or be in accordance with the views expressed during this period.

4. Cf. *De modo distinguendi* (GP VII 319-20, L 603-4); we judge what phenomena are real (*sc.* what phenomena are appearances of real things, and not dreams or illusions) by their vividness, multiplicity, and congruity.

5. G. H. R. Parkinson: *Logic and Reality in Leibniz's Metaphysics* (Oxford, 1965), pp. 179-80.

6. That this is his concern is also shown by the very title of the *De modo distinguendi*—"Of the method of distinguishing real from imaginary phenomena."

7. It should be added that when Leibniz refers to 'perception' he sometimes refers to a faculty of the mind (GP II 112; II 311; III 574-75, L 1077; VII 317, MP 85) and sometimes to *a* perception or perceptions (DM par. 33, MP 43; GP II 121; Mon. par. 14, MP 180; GP VII 311, MP 77).

8. 'La sensation': Mon. par. 19; GP VII 535. 'Sensio': GP VII 529; C 10; C 188. 'Le sentiment': GP IV 575; Mon. par. 19; PNG par. 4; DM par. 33.

9. Cf. NE IV.2.14, GP V 355, where Leibniz says that the difference between sensations and imaginations is to be found in the connection of phenomena. This implies that both sensations and imaginations *are* phenomena.

10. GP VII 317, MP 85: "If the perception is more distinct, it makes a sensation."

11. For statements of this dependence, see DM par. 14, MP 26; to Arnauld, 9 Oct. 1687, GP II 112; GP IV 523, L 806; GP VII 311, MP 77.

12. To be exact, Leibniz says that each 'distinct perception' of the soul must include an infinity of confused perceptions, but it will be seen later that we can substitute 'sensation' for 'distinct perception.'

13. For Leibniz's theory of little perceptions, see NE Pref. (GP V 47, MP 155-56), NE II.9.1, GP V 121; GP III 657; GP IV 523, L 806; GP VII 501.

It should be noted that the arguments for the existence of little perceptions advanced in the Preface to the *Nouveaux Essais* differ from the argument stated above, which is based on the thesis that each substance expresses the whole universe. In this Preface, Leibniz advances two arguments. One is reminiscent of an argument advanced by Zeno of Elea (cf. K. Freeman, *The Pre-Socratic Philosophers*, Oxford, 1949, p. 163) and states that if we do not perceive each individual wave of the sea, we cannot perceive their aggregate, since "a hundred thousand nothings cannot make something" (GP V 47, MP 156). The other argument is more distinctively Leibnizian, being based on a principle that Leibniz calls the 'law of continuity' (GP V 49, MP 158) and elsewhere the 'principle of general order' (e.g., *Extrait d'une lettre*, GP III 51 ff.). Leibniz argues (GP V 47, MP 156) that we should never be awakened, even by the loudest noise, if we did not have some little perception of its beginning. Just as the breaking of a rope is the final, perceptible stage of a succession of imperceptible stretchings, so our becoming aware of the noise is the final stage of a succession of unnoticed perceptions.

It is obvious that these arguments do not establish the conclusion that the unnoticed perceptions are perceptions of the whole universe; but this is not Leibniz's intention in this part of the *Nouveaux Essais*. All that he wishes to prove is that there *are* little perceptions.

14. DM par. 33, MP 43; PNG par. 13, MP 201. Cf. GP II 91, 113; GP VII 529; NE IV.17.9-13; GP V 469-70.

15. GP IV 426, L 454; to Remond, 4 Nov. 1715, GP III 657; PNG par. 13, MP 201.

16. This ambiguity in the term 'confused perception' has been noted by Margaret Wilson, in her paper "Confused Ideas" (*Rice University Studies* 63, No. 4 (1977): 126-27).

17. Cf. GP VII 311, MP 77: those of our perceptions (such as those of color, heat, etc.) that involve an infinity of things are confused. See also *Theodicy* par. 124, GP VI 179: confused 'thoughts' (here related to the senses) "come from the inter-relation of all things."

18. GP VII 319, disucssed by McRae on pp. 25-26.

19. Descartes, *Meditations*, II (*Descartes, Philosophical Writings*, trans. Anscombe and Geach, London, 1954, pp. 70-71). Cf. the Introduction to the same translation, pp. xlvii-viii.

20. This is implicit in a passage (GP IV 422; "unde propositio quoque . . .") in which Leibniz, after speaking of an obscure concept, says "hence the proposition into which such a concept enters is obscure also."

21. Cf. *Elementa Calculi* (1679), C 50: requisites are "simply the terms whose concepts compose the concept which we have of the thing."

22. It is true that in *De Synthesi et Analysi Universali* (GP VII 293, MP 12) Leibniz speaks of the "cause or analysis" ('causam sive resolutionem') of confused concepts. Here, however, 'cause' seems to be used as equivalent to 'analysis,' as it is not in the *Meditationes*. There would be little point in Leibniz's saying, in the *Meditationes*, that concepts "can be analyzed, in that they have an analysis."

23. Cf. NE III.4.4-7, GP V 275, where Leibniz expounds the views expressed earlier in the *Meditationes*: a 'real definition' of green would explain its cause, namely its being composed of blue and yellow, well intermixed.

24. 'Full,' not 'complete' ('completa'). A *complete* concept would be of an individual substance, such as 'this hot thing' (GP II 49 n. Cf. my *Logic and Reality in Leibniz's Metaphysics*, pp. 126-27).

25. Cf., e.g., NE II.8.13, GP V 118; NE IV.6.7, GP V 384.

26. In a letter to Sophie Charlotte, 1702 (GP VI 499, L 889) Leibniz seems to suggest that a color *is* certain corpuscular motions. It is clear from the context, however, that he is speaking in an abbreviated way of those physical motions that produce just those perceptions (*justement ces perceptions*) that we have of color. The suggestion made in this letter, that red is a whirling of certain small globes, is a description of the physical aspects of the perception of color; it is not the assertion that these aspects are all that there is to such perception. It seems, then, that Margaret Wilson ("Leibniz and Materialism," *Canadian Journal of Philosophy*, III, 1974, pp. 503-5) is mistaken in taking this passage as indicating that Leibniz flirted with materialism toward the end of his life. The same can be said of another passage cited by Professor Wilson (p. 502). This is from Leibniz's late dialogue *Entretien de Philarète et d' Ariste* (1713?), GP VI 587, L 1014. Here Philarète, who presents Leibniz's views, suggests that qualities such as color can be reduced to "something measurable, material, mechanical." But Philarète is saying here that his opponent, who supports Malebranche,

cannot refute Epicurean materialism by the arguments that he has brought. This does not mean that Leibniz thought that materialism was irrefutable; it means only that he thought that Malebranche had not refuted it.

Leibniz's views about the relations between confused concepts and the distinct concepts to be found in physics are stated clearly in an undated paper about "The secret of analysis in physics" ("Analyseos physicae arcanum . . . '," C 190). Although Leibniz speaks here of the 'reduction' (*revocatio*) of 'confused qualities' to 'distinct qualities,' it is clear that he means, not that confused qualities really are distinct qualities—e.g., that colors are really motions—but that they result from them. As there appears to be no English version of this short paper, I append a translation.

> The secret of analysis in physics consists in this one device: the reduction of the confused qualities of the senses (namely, heat and cold in the case of touch, flavors in the case of taste, odors in the case of smell, sounds in the case of hearing, and colors in the case of sight) to the distinct qualities that accompany them, namely number, size, shape, motion, and cohesion (*consistentia*), of which the last two are proper to physics. Therefore, if we discover that certain distinct qualities always accompany certain confused ones (e.g., that all color arises from the refraction of a ray, but not from its reflection), and that with the help of these distinct qualities we can explain precisely the entire nature of certain bodies, in such a way that we can demonstrate that it is of such and such a size, figure and motion—then it is necessary that these confused qualities also result from such a structure, though we cannot demonstrate the confused qualities in any other way from the distinct qualities. For there is no definition of confused qualities, and therefore demonstration does not apply in their case. It is enough, therefore, that by means of consistent inferences, which agree with experience, we can explain all those things that can be thought distinctly and that accompany the confused qualities. For with the aid of certain qualities that are sufficient to determine the nature of bodies, we can discover their causes, and from these causes we can demonstrate their other affects, i.e. the rest of their qualities, and so in a roundabout way we discover what is real and distinct in confused qualities. For that remainder that cannot be explained (as, for example, the way in which the appearance that we call yellowness arises out of that in which we have shown yellowness to consist objectively) must be known to depend, not on the thing itself, but on the disposition of our organs and on the most minute structure (*constitutionibus*) of things. But it is enough for us to show what exists objectively in the bodies from which yellowness arises, and that is sufficient for the needs of life. Thus we shall have a means of producing confused qualities.
>
> It is also useful for lessening labor if we reduce confused qualities to other simpler ones—e.g., if we reduce greenness to the compounding of yellow and blue. If we can show that certain flavors and odors go with certain colors, etc. [sc. "this will also be useful"—Translator] ; for we can reduce colors to distinct qualities more easily than we can reduce flavors.

27. *Characteristica verbalis*, C 432. Cf. C 286, 351, 497; GP VII 204; A II.1, 228. This is not to say that every being who has concepts is a word user. Leibniz does indeed believe that human beings cannot think or reason without the help of symbols such as words (GP VII 191, L 281; GP VII 204), but he also believes that God has concepts, and God does not use words.

28. For this distinction, compare Parkinson, *Logic and Reality in Leibniz's Metaphysics*, pp. 12-13.

29. R. M. Harré, *The Anticipation of Nature* (London, 1965), p. 7. 30. I have argued for this conclusion in my article "Science and Metaphysics in Leibniz's *Specimen Inventorum*," *Studia Leibnitiana* 6 (1974): 1-17.

Solipsistic Perception in a World of Monads

Fabrizio Mondadori

"To be joyous in the full acceptance of this *dénouement* is surely to possess a treasure, the key to which is the understanding that Key and Treasure are the same. There (with a kiss, little sister) is the sense of our story, Dunyazade: The key to the treasure is the treasure." J. Barth, *Chimera.*[1]

What I offer below is a *dénouement* of sorts to a story that I claimed in an earlier paper of mine[2] might have no dénouement at all: "of sorts," that is, since this paper, instead of offering an expected dénouement, very likely will turn out to provide some more evidence in favor of that claim. Indeed the expected dénouement leads to its own reversal, explains itself away, as we shall have occasion to see: what we get is a dénouement, but not quite—the dénouement of the story being precisely that the story has no dénouement. The reasons for this, however, are well worth some analysis. I shall deal, then, with monads, the nature of what they perceive, what it is for a given monad to perceive—more or less distinctly, more or less confusedly—the entire universe from its own point of view, and the relation between (solipsistic) perception and preestablished Harmony.

Now the dénouement, if any, would consist in this: that each monad perceives the entire universe from its own point of view is both what provides some sort of "foundation" for the Leibnizian "circle" (as outlined in section 0 below), *and* an irreducible relational fact (which, if true, would indeed be the ultimate irony). By "foundation," I mean nothing bolder or haughtier than "natural starting point" (metaphysically, not chronologically, speaking of course); and by "natural starting point" I mean nothing bolder or haughtier than that the notion

---

I wish to thank Adam Morton for helping me to bring out the sense of this vaguely chimerical story; also Jean and David Blumenfeld, for a number of discussions on Leibniz's views on perception.

of perception (of the entire universe on the part of each monad) may well be the intuitively most plausible motivation for the entire metaphysical "system" — conceived of, as I conceive of it, as a grand circular design.

The reversal of the dénouement, on the other hand, consists in this: as we shall see below, perception (of the entire universe on the part of each monad) is essentially a kind of *generalized* preestablished Harmony hold; and whereas the letter, and hence perception itself, may indeed be regarded as the key to the Leibnizian "circle," the real key to the "circle" is the "circle" itself. (Precisely in the same way that the real dénouement to the story is that it has no dénouement at all — or not quite.) The kind of generalized preestablished Harmony I have just alluded to, in other words, not unlike the view that each monad perceives the entire universe, is a sort of representation on a reduced scale of the "circle," which — the "circle," I mean — is needed in order to provide some sort of account or explanation of and justification for that doctrine and, hence, that view. Thus does the dénouement lead to its own reversal.

Dénouement or no dénouement, however, it appears that there are at least two models (complementary, as it turns out — definitely not competing) for representing the relation between perception and preestablished Harmony. On the one hand, following Russell,[3] we may take perception as basic, and derive preestablished Harmony from it: first model, more or less. On the other hand, we can take preestablished Harmony as basic, and characterize perception in terms of it: second model, more or less.

Whatever their differences, these two models have something quite important in common: in both of them (the notion of) perception is intimately associated (how intimately, we shall see below) with (the notion of) expression, in Leibniz's sense of "expression"; and in neither of them, as far as I can see, is any overt commitment made as to what, if anything, it is that monads can be said to perceive. Further, both models implicitly assume that there is an independently existing universe of *monads*: the latter being the "stuff" the former is made on, so to say. These are the main outlines of the present story. Let me now set the stage for the story itself.

0. Leibniz's Goldberg Variations

In an earlier paper (referred to in fn. 2 above) I claimed and attempted to show that Leibniz's metaphysical "system" is best regarded as a grand *circular* design; perception and preestablished Harmony, however, were left out of the picture, since, until this paper was actually completed, I regarded as positively entertainable the possibility that one of them should prove to be an appropriate "foundation" for the design. The natural questions accordingly arise, at this point, whether — and if so, how — they fit into that design; and whether that possiblility is indeed *positively* entertainable. Before answering the two questions I just raised, however, it is perhaps appropriate to say a few words on the circular design itself.

First, its components: the theory of complete concepts and the notion of a complete concept; the mirroring principle; the notion of compossibility; the notion of expression; the notion of connection; and the doctrine of (universal) Harmony. (*En passant*, I should also mention that I take the view that individual substances, or monads, are the "stuff" our universe is made on, to be part and parcel of the theory of complete concepts. It is also an essential feature of the latter the fact that a one-one correspondence holds between the set of individual substances and the set of exemplified complete concepts.)

Second, a fundamental distinction: not all of the notions, doctrines, theories, I have enumerated in the previous paragraph belong to the same (metaphysical) "level." Thus the notion of a complete concept, the mirroring principle, and the notion of compossibility all belong to what we might call the "level" of possibility—think of our own world as a set s of nonexemplified mutually compossible complete concepts; whereas the doctrine of (universal) Harmony, the notion of expression, and the notion of connection, all belong to what we might call the "level" of actuality—think of our own world as a set of individual substances exemplifying the concepts that are members of s.

Now what makes Leibniz's metaphysical "system" into a grand circular design is essentially a combination of two factors. First, there is no reason whatsoever to regard either of the two "levels" as metaphysically primary with respect to the other. Although what is true of the "level" of possibility determines, and necessarily so, what is true of the "level" of actuality,[4] one's conception of what is true of the "level" of actuality (i.e., one's conception of the metaphysical structure of actuality) may—indeed does—influence one's conception of the structure of the "level" of possibility. And conversely (in some loose sense of "conversely"), of course, if what is true of the "level" of possibility determines, and necessarily so, what is true of the "level" of actuality, the latter—actuality—must be structured in such a way as to "mirror" almost point-by point the "level" of possibility. Thus, given the view that, for instance, the set of concepts exemplified by individual substances is a set of compossible complete concepts, it follows immediately that each individual substance expresses the same universe, and that all things are connected—and conversely, as can easily be proved. (I leave this as a task to the skeptical reader.)

So much for the first of the two factors I mentioned in the previous paragraph. There is no more to the second factor than this—that all of the notions, doctrines, etc., that make up the circular design are tightly interconnected, in such a way, indeed, that virtually each of them, if taken as "primitive," will send you around to most if not all of the remaining ones—and ultimately to itself. Thus, just to give a simple example, the mirroring principle (see fn. 8 below) sends you around to the notion of compossibility; which in turn sends you around to that of expression; which in turn sends you around to that of connection; which in turn sends you around to the mirroring principle (see fn. 8 below); . . . and so on. . . . It is precisely at this point that what we might well call Leibniz's Goldberg Variations enter the picture: I mean, it is precisely at this point that a number of variations on the same theme, more or less, become possible.

For instance, take the view that all things are connected, and the view that each individual substance exemplifies a complete concept—given those views, it is no problem to derive the doctrine of (universal) Harmony, i.e., the view that each individual substance expresses the same universe from its own point of view.[5] (Notice: that each individual substance expresses the *whole* universe is a consequence of the fact that it exemplifies a complete concept: whereas what makes the *whole* universe into the *same* universe is the circumstance that all things, and in particular all substances, are connected.)[6]

Or else, take the view that each individual substance expresses the same, and hence the whole,[7] universe, and the attendant view that each individual substance exemplifies a concept compossible with the concepts exemplified by all other substances—given those views, it is no problem to derive the further view that the concepts in question are complete. (This follows from the fact that, in order for a given individual substance to express the same universe that is expressed by all other substances, the concept exemplified by it must at least be *complete*. Notice, further, that the notion of completeness is virtually "built into" that of compossibility. I spare you the details of the derivation, which, in view of what I have just said and of fn. 7, should be fairly obvious.)

Or else, take the mirroring principle (as applied to complete concepts)[8] and and the view that each individual substance exemplifies a complete concept—given that principle and that view, it is no problem to derive the further view that all things, and in particular all substances, are connected. (This assumes, of course, that for any two individual substances α and β to be connected—in what I take to be Leibniz's, or an essentially Leibnizian, sense of "connected"—it must be possible to deduce from α all the properties of β, and conversely—and conversely. But for it to be possible to deduce from α all the properties of β, and conversely, the concepts exemplified by α and β must be complete *and* mutually compossible. But since, via the mirroring principle and the view that each individual substance exemplifies a complete concept, we get completeness and compossibility, we are led right away precisely to the view that all things are connected.)

Or else, take the view that all things are connceted and the view that each individual substance expresses the whole universe—given those views, it is no problem to derive not only the further view that each individual substance exemplifies a complete concept, but also the notion of compossibility. (How? Well, to put it rather bluntly: connection and expression of the whole universe jointly entail expression of the *same* universe; expression, in turn, entails completeness, whereas *sameness* of universe entails compossibility. This is just one of the various possible ways of getting the desired result, of course.)

So much for Leibniz's Goldberg Variations; the ones I have just described constitute just a representative sample of the entire set of actual (as well as possible) variations; and a few more are forthcoming (see sections 2 and 3 below).

We also have a sort of *meta*-variation, so to say, which brings together the distinction between the two "levels" I have discussed a few paragraphs back, and the tight interconnection between the various notions, doctrines, etc., making up the grand circular design I have been talking about so far. Thus consider again the view that all things (and in particular, individual substances) are connected: it can plausibly be regarded as the analogue in actuality (or at the "level" of actuality) of the view that the concepts exemplified by the individual substances in question are mutually compossible. And conversely: the compossibility between the concepts exemplified by individual substances can plausibly be regarded as the analogue at the "level" of possibility of the connection between individual substances at the "level" of actuality.

Alternatively, consider the view that (universal) Harmony holds, i.e., as we have seen, that each individual substance expresses the same universe: it can plausibly be regarded as the analogue at the "level" of actuality of the view that the mirroring principle holds for sets of mutually compossible complete concepts. And conversely: that the mirroring principle holds, in particular, for the set of *exemplified* mutually compossible complete concepts can plausibly be regarded as the analogue at the "level" of possibility of the view that each individual substance expresses the same universe.

I shall spare you a description of the remaining "analogues": let me only say, by way of conclusion of the present section, that by "meta = variation" all I have in mind is a statement concerning "analogues." Without further beating about the bush, then, I shall now move on to a discussion of the main topic of this paper: solipsistic perception in a world of monads, and its relation to pre-established Harmony.

1. THE DÉNOUEMENT

According to Russell, that "Perception yields knowledge of an external world, i.e., of existents other than myself and my states," is one of the five "principal premisses of Leibniz's philosophy."[9] At the risk of explaining myself away, later on, I shall indeed claim, and attempt to show in the next couple of sections, that something pretty much like the premise in question can plausibly be regarded either as that to which the Leibnizian "circle" ultimately leads (its metaphysical terminus, as it were), or as what lies behind, provides some sort of "foundation" for, the "circle" itself.

This can be argued for roughly as follows. To begin with, let me draw a distinction between two sublevels, so to speak, within the "level" of actuality and let me refer to them as the metaphysical "sublevel" and the phenomenal "sublevel," respectively. The former is the realm to which talk of individual substances, real unities, mirrors of the entire universe—in a word: *monads*—strictly pertains: and all of the notions, doctrines, etc., belonging to the "level" of actuality ought to be regarded as strictly applying to the metaphysical "sublevel"— and therefore to monads and only to monads (although they may be applied, somewhat indirectly and by analogy and extension to the more mundane and vulgar phenomenal "sublevel").

The phenomenal "sublevel", on the other hand, is the realm of what Leibniz is often fond of referring to as *phenomena bene fundata*: the realm of bodies; of so-called corporeal substances; the realm of compounds; the realm of non substances; and so on. But, you may say, why "so-called"? And why "phenomena bene fundata"? At the cost of oversimplifying (perhaps even trivializing) one of the many celebrated *noli-me-tangere*s in Leibniz scholarship, I am somewhat tempted to say that what is at stake here is in all likeihood no more than a purely verbal issue, which underlies, to be sure, a fundamental ontological distinction—the distinction between substances (i.e., simple substances) and non-substances (i.e., what Leinbiz sometimes refers to, rather condescendingly, as "compound substances"). All and only *truly* simple and indivisible "entities" qualify as substances, according to Leibniz: or, to make the same point in the formal mode in order to bring out the essentially verbal nature of the issue, all and only *truly* simple and indivisible "entities" can be referred to by means of the common noun "substance" (this appears to be the moral of *L*, 539, 643; *G*, 557; *C*, 13-14).

This of course leads right away to the view that what is not simple and indivisible can neither possibly qualify as a substance proper, nor be referred to by means of the common noun "substance": and in this sense a body, for instance, is a nonsubstance—just a well-founded *phenomenon*, as opposed to *real* (i.e., simple and indivisible) substance. Clearly this is not to claim, or otherwise imply, that there are no bodies, no *so-called* corporeal substances—as the unhappy but suggestive phrase "phenomena bene fundata" is sometimes taken to suggest. It is just to claim (*a*) that bodies are not substances proper and hence can only be referred to by means of the disqualifying term "phenomenon"; (*b*) that the ultimate "constituents" of the universe, the "stuff" it is made on, for the better or for the worse, are monads or simple substances; and (*c*) that the well-foundedness of phenomena (i.e., nonsubstances) consists in their being (adjectives) *of* something truly substantial. To adapt a happy and suggestive phrase of Austin's, phenomena—i.e., nonsubstances—are substance-hungry. (Cf., "Substantial unities are not parts but foundations of phenomena," *L*, 536; i.e., I take it, the "reality" of bodies, nonsubstances, is merely *relative*, in the sense that bodies acquire whatever "reality" they have as fleeting "substances" from "simple substances, which alone have unity and *absolute* reality,"[10] *GP* II, 275—italics mine. See also *L*, 624-25; *GP* VIII, 31.)

But to revert to the safer metaphysical "sublevel." As I have pointed out above, it is the realm of substances proper, or monads—and the realm of perception as well (which is not to say, of course, that there is no perception of, or on the part of, nonsubstances, even given Leibniz's rather outlandish way of understanding the notion of perception):

one monad by itself and at a single moment cannot be distinguished from another except by its internal qualities and actions, and these can only be its *perceptions*—that is to say, the representations of the compound, or of that which is without, in the simple— . . . the simplicity of a substance does not prevent the plurality of modifications which must necessarily be found together in the same simple substance; and these modifications must consist of the variety of relations of correspondence which the substance has with things outside. (*L*, 636; see also *L*, 599, 643-44)

since the nature of a simple substance consists of perception and appetite, it is clear that there is in each soul a series of appetites and perceptions, through which it is led from the end to the means, from the perception of one object to the perception of another. (*C*, 14)

I am further asked how it happens that God is not content to produce all the thoughts and *modifications* of the soul, without these *useless* bodies which the soul (it is said) can neither *move* nor *know*. The answer is easy. It is that it was God's will that there should be a greater rather than a lesser number of substances, and he found it good that these *modifications* should correspond to something outside. (*GP* IV, 49; see also *L*, 636, 663)

It is therefore these present perceptions, along with their regulated tendency to change *in conformity to what is outside*, which form the musical score which the soul reads. . . . confused perceptions include all *external things* and contain an infinity of relations. (*L*, 580, 581—italics mine)

Two points ought to be made concerning the passages I have just quoted. First, on Leibniz's view it is essential to simple substances, or monads, that, in particular, they should *perceive* (and hence be in a given perceptual state at a given time); and second, perhaps more significantly (and somewhat surprisingly, the sudden dash into the unexpected), he appears to hold, especially in the third and fourth of the four passages quoted above, that what monads perceive is (part of) an *independently* existing world (universe)—at the phenomenal "sublevel," that is (recall my remarks above on the "reality" of bodies or nonsubstances). Let me take up the first point first, and then proceed to a discussion of the second—which, as I have vaguely intimated a few lines back, does not have *that* much textual evidence for it, and is indeed a point to which Leibniz does not appear to be willing to commit himself *too* definitely (as we shall see below).

Well, then: perception. What is perception, according to Leibniz? And what is it that monads do perceive? Perception, according to Leibniz, is "the expression of many things in one" (*L*, 91), or, equivalently, "the representation[s] of the compound, . . . in the simple" (*L*, 636; see also *L*, 644, 663; *CA*, 155)— that is, of a body, a corporeal "substance" ("many things," "the compound") in a monad, a simple substance ("one," "the simple"). The key notion in this definition (which Leibniz never changed or revised or abandoned in favor of a different one) is obviously that of expression (or representation); and indeed, in *CA*, 144 Leibniz says quite explicitly that perception is a "species" of expression— that is, I take it, to claim that α perceives b (whatever b may be: a body, the entire universe, . . .) is to claim that "there exists a fixed and constant relationship between what can be said of one and of the other" (*ibid.*).

That is to say, since (*a*) expression is essentially a question of deducibility via the completeness of concepts,[11] and (*b*) perception is a species of expression, perception will also turn out to be—if not essentially, at least in part—a question of deducibility (presumably, I should think, of the properties of a given compound, be it a body or the entire universe) from the appropriate state of a given simple (substance), or monad, via the complete concept exemplified by it. (Cf. also the following passage: "when I consider only distinct notions, it seems to me possible to conceive that phenomena that are divisible or made up of many entities can be expressed or represented in a single indivisible entity [i.e., a simple substance or monad], and this is enough for conceiving of a perception," *CA*, 155.)

As I have pointed out a few pages back, this way of characterizing perception is common to the two (complementary) ways of picturing the relation between perception and preestablished Harmony I have briefly outlined at the beginning. Notice, however, that perception cannot be regarded *purely*, or even essentially, as a question of deducibility, at least in view of the rather crucial fact that deducibility does *not* guarantee—indeed, assumes—that what is deduced via the complete concept is correlated in the *appropriate* way with the simple substance exemplifying the concept.

In other words: that perception is a species of expression, and hence in part a question of deducibility of the properties (or states) of what is perceived from those of the percipient, leaves open the question of how the properties of the former and those of the latter are so correlated that the former are indeed deducible from the latter. As Leibniz himself puts it, "there would be no order between simple substance, . . . unless they mutually corresponded" (*C*, 14): now it is precisely this "correspondence" that, as we shall see below, guarantees the appropriateness of the correlation, thereby making the required deduction possible.

(To characterize perception in terms of deducibility is, of course, consistent with, does full justice to, and is an obvious consequence of, Leibniz's well-known view that "every simple substance . . . must be the immediate cause of all its actions and inward passions; and, speaking strictly in a metaphysical sense, it has none other than those which it produces," *GP* VI, 351; see also *DM*, 56; *GP* IV, 484— the "actions and inward passions" of a given substance include its perceptions: see *L*, 644; or that "since they [= perceptions] are not miraculously induced by God, and cannot be imparted naturally by the body, it follows that they arise within the soul by a definite law," *L*, 593; see also *L*, 496.)

Let me now turn to an analysis of the second of the two questions I raised a couple of paragraphs back: What is it that monads perceive? Leibniz's usual, celebrated, and somewhat mind-boggling answer is: the entire universe—each monad not unlike a mirror with a definite perspective or point of view on the universe it is said to perceive:[12]

every simple substance is by its nature . . . a concentration and a living mirror of the whole universe according to its point of view. (*L*, 711)

since every monad is a mirror of the universe in its own way, and the universe is regulated in perfect order, there must also be an order in the being which represents it, that is to say, in the perceptions of the soul and therefore also in the body, according to which the universe is represented in it. (*L*, 649)

There are as many mirrors of the universe as there are minds, for every mind perceives the whole universe. (*L*, 279)

If to the view that each monad perceives the entire universe we now add the further view that the universe perceived by each monad is an *independently* existing universe (this, it will be recalled, was the second of the two points I made a few paragraphs back), we get as an obvious result that the analogy with mirrors Leibniz is so fond of must be taken *literally*. Indeed, the universe had better be regarded as quite literally an independently existing reality for monads to have "perspectives" *on*—indeed, perception is perception *of* an independently existing universe. (Cf. "perception . . . is the inner state of the monad representing external things," *L*, 637. In the Preface to the *Nouveaux Essais*, Leibniz appears to be even more uncompromising: he speaks of the "essential relation between perceptions and their objects", *GP* V, 50, and the context makes quite clear that there is more to objects than is ever dreamt of in any phenomenalistic, or intentional, reduction.)

If this is so, however, it follows that the mirroring principle (as applied to complete concepts) has a natural counterpart in the realm, or at the "level," of actuality: to say that (something like) the mirroring principle holds for monads is just to say that each monad perceives the entire universe (= is a mirroring principle as applied to monads) as "primitive" or metaphysically ultimate; we are forced, in view of the trade-off between the "level" of possibility and that of actuality, to extend the mirroring principle (as applied to monads) to complete concepts as well—specifically, to sets of mutually compossible complete concepts.

Thus do we finally break into the magic Leibnizian "circle." What else can we get (besides the mirroring principle for sets of mutually compossible complete concepts, that is)? Just about everything, I dare say: and here is how. To begin with, we get completeness: this follows immediately, in a rather uninteresting way, from the fact that perception is a species of expression, hence, as I have pointed out above, a question of deducibility via the *completeness* of concepts.

Next, we get the doctrine of (universal) Harmony, provided "whole" in "each monad perceives the whole universe from its own point of view" is replaced by "same." Surprising or unbelievable though this may appear to be at first sight, it is a pretty trivial and remarkably undistinguished result: for to say that (universal) Harmony holds is to say precisely that each monad expresses the same universe from its own point of view (and conversely); and perception be-ing, as we have seen above, a species of expression, we have all we need in order to get from perception of the same universe to (universal) Harmony.

Next, we get compossibility, as follows. In order for it to be possible for each monad to perceive the *same* (and not just, mind you, the whole) universe, the concepts exemplified by it must be *compossible* with all the concepts exem-plified by the remaining monads. In other words, the view that each monad per-ceives the same universe requires that the set of exemplified complete concepts be a set of mutually compossible complete concepts. Once we have compossi-bility and completeness, we also have connection (or the view that all things are connected); for, as I have already pointed out, connection turns out to be purely a question of the completeness and mutual compossibility of individual con-cepts.

At this point virtually the entire "circle" is at our disposal, so to say: and it appears that the promised dénouement has finally taken place—especially if we realize that the view that each monad perceives the same universe is presup-posed by the entire "circle," as I have just tried to show, and in turn presupposes it. Before getting to the reversal of the dénouement, however, a rather crucial point has to be settled. It concerns my remark early in the paper that perception (or perhaps better, the fact that it perceives) is an irreducible relational property of each monad—which, it will be recalled, was also supposed to be part of the expected dénouement. To show that this is indeed the case, a sharp distinction must be drawn between the claim that each monad *perceives* the entire universe, on the one hand, and the claim that a given monad is in a certain *perceptual state*, on the other: or between the *perceiving* of a monad, on the one hand, and its being in a certain *perceptual state*, on the other. In other words, to provide an account of what it is for a monad to be in a certain perceptual state is clearly *not* to provide an account of what it is for that monad to perceive—for, in particu-lar, the former account will always presuppose the latter, and hence could in no way be regarded as an appropriate substitute for it.

Thus, for instance, it may well be possible to describe, and in a sense ac-count for, the entire sequence or series of perceptual states of a given monad by just "looking into" the complete concept exemplified by that monad. In this way, given the distinction I have drawn in the previous paragraph, no reference need be made to, nor use need be made of the notion of, an independently exist-ing universe; and I suppose this is more or less what Leibniz means when he says that the present state (in particular, I take it, the present *perceptual* state) of a given monad "is always a natural consequence of its preceding state" (*CA*, 145-46; see also *L*, 496, 513, 531, 533, 539, 580, 711-12; and the following pas-sage: "every present state of a substance occurs to it spontaneously and is only a consequence of its preceding state," *CA*, 51).

When it comes to the *perceiving* of (that is, on the part of) a monad, how-ever, things are not so obvious (assuming for the sake of argument they were ob-vious in the previous case). Whereas particular perceptual states need not be treated as inherently or implicitly, and irreducibly, relational, *perceiving* (or: *that* a monad perceives) appears to be explicitly, and irreducibly (from Leibniz's point of view, in particular), relational. The contrary view, that perceiving is not irreducibly relational and is amenable to an analysis in which no reference is made to an independently existing universe, probably stems from a confusion— of which Leibniz himself was sometimes guilty—between *perceiving* itself and *perceptual states*: that the latter need not be inherently relational, or need not involve in their analysis any reference to an independently existing reality, is clearly no argument for the claim that the same is true of the former.

Specifically, what Leibniz appears to have overlooked is the rather critical distinction between (*a*) and the view that the *sequence* of (perceptual) states of a given monad is so to say self-contained, i.e., purely a function of the complete concept exemplified by that monad, and (*b*) the view that *perception* is a species of expression ("the expression of many things in one," *L* 91), and hence in part a question of deducibility. There are obvious differences between (*a*) and (*b*); and they cannot be explained away so as to make perception into a nonrelational property of each monad. To begin with, notice that (*a*) strictly speaking not only presupposes (the notion of) perception, but in effect does not bear on perception at all—perception, that is, *qua* "expression of many things in one." Second, what is equally significant, (*b*), unlike (*a*), requires that something like the notion of an *appropriate correlation* between properties or states of different "entities" be brought into the picture. I return to this topic below.

Once (*a*) and (*b*) of the previous paragraph are properly distinguished, it becomes extremely difficult to see how (the notion of) *perceiving*, even conceived of in the slightly eccentric way Leibniz conceives of it, can be handled in a nonrelational way. How it can be true *of* a given monad that it *perceives*, without there being something or other (bodies, the entire universe, or what not) it does perceive, appears to be inexplicable even in the framework of Leibniz's metaphysics. (Notice that it may well be true of a given monad that its present perceptual state is purely a consequence of the preceding one, or that the total sequence of such states is self-contained, without its being true of that monad that it perceives without there being something or other it does perceive: for to perceive is clearly not to be in a certain perceptual state, although of course to be in a certain perceptual state usually is, among other things, to have perceived. A separate argument is needed for the nonrelationality, so to say, of perception; and the one Leibniz seems to give is based on the confusion I described in the previous paragraph.

And here we have the ultimate irony: one of the basic notions of a metaphysical "system" in which relational properties, as well as relations, are claimed to be reducible is itself an irreducibly relational property, and can in no way be dispensed with in favor of nonrelational notions. Indeed, as we shall see below, the very doctrine of preestablished Harmony makes perception into an irreducible relation between the states of qualitatively different substances.

This completes, at least for the next couple of sections, my discussion of the (alleged) dénouement. Let me now turn to an analysis of its reversal; of why the story may plausibly be said to have no dénouement at all—or why its dénouement consists precisely in the story's not having any dénouement whatsoever.

2. REVERSAL OF THE DÉNOUEMENT; SOLIPSISTIC PERCEPTION

What makes Leibniz's notion of perception so peculiar and, so to say, nonstandard, is Leibniz's flat and often puzzling denial of (causal) interaction between simple substances (cf. "since our thoughts are only consequences of the nature of our soul, and are born in it by virtue of its concepts, it is useless to require the influence of another particular substance," CA, 84; see also L, 269; DM, 24)—so that even on the assumption of an independently existing universe, the latter plays absolutely no role (causal or whatever) in any account of what it is for a given monad to perceive (which may seem to make perceiving into a nonrelational property of each monad, after all). As Russell, somewhat baffled, put it, "Perception is marvellous, because it cannot be conceived as an action of the object on the percipient, since substances never interact."[13]

The problem we are faced with can be stated very simply and directly: given (1) that perception is perception of an independently existing universe (or that it is essentially and irreducibly relational), and (2) that perception in no way be due to an action of the action of the object on the percipient, in view of Leibniz's denial of causal interaction, how does one go about explaining the fact that a given monad can still be said to *perceive* (the entire universe, or any part thereof)? Or, more simply: how can perception be explained in a universe wherein no causal interaction between substances is allowed?[14] Or, even more simply: is there any way of explaining (or accounting for) solipsistic perception (that is, roughly, perception in a universe wherein substances do not causally interact)?

(Notice that reference to the fact that perception is a species of expression, appealing though it may appear to be at first sight, simply leads nowhere: that perceiving amounts more or less to expressing or representing a multiplicity in a unity, i.e., in a simple substance or monad, and that expressing or representing can be accounted for in terms of deducibility via complete concepts, only takes for granted what has to be explained—solipsistic perception itself. Specifically, what is taken for granted is *at least* that the state of the world at a given time and the (perceptual) state of a given monad at that very time are simultaneous,[15] and correlated in such a way that the former is deducible from the latter. There is more to perception, then, than mere deducibility via the completeness of concepts—herein, also, lies the beginning of the reversal of the dénouement.)

Partly following a suggestion of Russell's,[16] I should like to propose that the question I raised in the previous paragraph be answered by employing (a generalized version of) the doctrine of preestablished Harmony. To begin with, consider the following passages:

the perceptions which are found together in one soul at the same time include a veritable infinite multitude of little indistinguishable feelings, which the subsequent series must develop . . . . All this is only a consequence of the representative nature of the soul, which must express what happens, and even what will happen in its body and in some way in all other bodies, *through* the connection *or correspondence* between all the parts of the world. (*L*, 496 — italics mine)

the simplicity of a substance does not prevent the plurality of modifications which must necessarily be found together in the same simple substance; and these modifications must consist of the variety of *relations of correspondence* which the substance has with things outside. (*L*, 636 — italics mine)

There is a perfect *harmony* between the perceptions of the monad and the motions of the body, preestablished from the beginning between the system of efficient causes and that of final causes. (*L*, 637)

this mutual connection or accommodation of all created things to each other and of each to all the rest *causes* each simple substance to have relations which express all the others and consequently to be a perpetual living mirror of the universe. (*L*, 648 — italics mine)

[Human souls] perceive what passes without them by what passes within them, *answering* to the things without, in virtue of the *harmony* which God has preestablished . . . whereby each simple substance is by its nature . . . a living mirror of the whole universe. (*L*, 711)

when I wish to raise my arm, it is precisely at the moment when everything is arranged in the body so as to carry this out, in such a manner that the body moves by virtue of its own laws although it happens through the wonderful but unfailing harmony between things that these laws conspire towards that end precisely at the moment when the will is inclined to it. (*CA* 92; see also *CA*, 117)

(Incidentally, it is interesting to notice that Leibniz remarks, concerning the passages just quoted, "All these are merely consequences of the concept of an individual substance which embraces all its phenomena, in such a way that nothing can happen to a substance which is not born to it in its own depths, but in conformity with what happens to another," *ibid*. This is not *quite* right, however. Even assuming that "nothing can happen to a substance which is not born to it in its own depths," it would still *not* follow that substances, or the mind and the body, for that matter, are *correlated* in the *appropriate* way. For this to be the case, preestablished Harmony, or, more accurately, universal Harmony, must be supposed to hold: and indeed Leibniz himself tacitly concedes the point by his use of the notion of "conformity," which is simply a somewhat unpretentious synonym for the more sophisticated notion of "Harmony." What I have just said applies also to *L*, 457. See also *CA*, 148; 170-71.)

this correspondence (corresponsus) of the internal and the external, or representation of what is external in what is internal, of what is compounded in what is simple, of multiplicity in unity, constitutes perception. (*GP*, VII 529)

I shall not attempt to provide a full-fledged analysis of the passages I have just quoted (the most important one, to be sure, has been taken care of); all I need at this stage is just to draw the appropriate moral, if any, from them. Early in the paper I claimed that perception (of the entire universe on the part of each simple substance or monad) may plausibly be conceived of as a sort of *generalized* preestablished Harmony (more properly, it may be taken to *require* that something like the latter hold); and the moral I intend to draw from the passages in question is meant to throw some light on, and to provide some evidence for, that very claim.

Two points are noteworthy in the passages quoted above: first, Leibniz's implicit, but all the same quite definite, denial of causal interaction; and second, the almost explicit view, which is after all part and parcel of the doctrine of preestablished Harmony (as well as of that of universal Harmony), that the state (at a given time) of a given monad is in perfect correspondence—"conformity," to use Leibniz's term—with the state of the world (at that very time); or, to make the same point in a slightly *simpliste* way, that there is a perfect—perfect timingwise that is—correlation between mental and bodily states (see for instance the passages about raising one's arm I have quoted above).

The two points I have just made constitute, to a degree, the moral I said earlier I intended to draw from the passages quoted a few paragraphs back. How do they bear on my claim that perception is a kind of generalized preestablished Harmony (or requires that a kind of generalized preestablished Harmony hold)? Roughly as follows. Take the denial of causal interaction first: there being no (causal) interaction between percipients and what they perceive (which, and this is the crucial point, does *not* entail that no relation whatsoever holds between the former and the latter), a way must be found of accounting for the apparently incoherent view that simple substances (or monads) can coherently be said to perceive, after all (whatever it is that they may coherently be said to perceive). For, in a sense, it is *as if* what is perceived (whatever it may be) were not there at all: given the denial of causal interaction, what is (said to be) perceived might as well melt into thin air, as far as the (now alleged) percipient is concerned.

At this rather crucial juncture, in a misguided attempt to solve the problem we might try to bring into the picture Leibniz's view that all the states (including the perceptual ones) of a given simple substance are a consequence of the (complete) concept it exemplifies. We would get nowhere; for, as we have already seen, that view still leaves open the question of how it is that the perception(s) of a given monad and its (their) object(s) are correlated so as to make possible the deduction of the latter from the former—which brings me to the second of the two points I made a couple of paragraphs back. Here is the solution to the problem: what guarantees that the correlation not only obtains, but is of the *appropriate* kind, is (preestablished, or universal, as the case may be) Harmony.

In other words (preestablished, or universal, as the case may be) Harmony guarantees that the sequence of states of the universe and the sequence of any given monad's perceptual states are in perfect correspondence, which guarantees, in turn, that the correlation between perceptions and their objects is of the appropriate kind — timingwise and deducibilitywise, that is (see also *L*, 458). In this sense perception is indeed a kind of generalized preestablished Harmony, or otherwise requires that something like the latter hold: the intuition underlying both preestablished Harmony *and* generalized preestablished Harmony is the same — in both cases a correspondence between states is involved. (I assume here, for the sake of simplicity, that perception is a state. Think of this as a terminological aberration, if need be; but notice that this usage comes straight from Leibniz — cf. *L*, 644.)

What is perhaps equally significant, the generalized version of preestablished Harmony I have been talking about may be regarded as a sort of replacement, so to say, of causal interaction itself. In a sense, that is, it is indeed *as if* there were causal interaction between simple substances, although of course we know that could not be the case. (This is almost explicitly recognized by Leibniz in *CA*, 148, and *GP* IV, 49. The "as if" theme is most prominent in *GP* VII, 31: "yet all things agree with each other as if the soul could move the body or the body the soul"; see also *L*, 269, 460.)

It is no intention of mine, of course, to understate the importance of Leibniz's view that the state (perceptual or otherwise) of any given monad at a given time is a consequence of the preceding one — via the completeness of the concept exemplified by the monad in question: a view which is of a piece with the twin view that perception is a species of expression. But this is only an aspect — crucial though it may be — of Leibniz's theory of perception: and it is a matter of understanding (the theory itself), and not at all one of understating (this or that aspect of the theory). At any rate, the other aspect, which I regard as equally crucial, and which complements the first, deals with the perfect correspondence, and hence simultaneity as well as appropriate correlation, of states (of a given monad and of the entire universe, respectively).

This is not the whole story, however. For a perfect correspondence holds also between what I referred to above as the metaphysical and the phenomenal "sublevels." Consider the following passages:

> The souls follow their laws, which consist in a definite development of perceptions according to good and evils, and the bodies follow theirs, which consist in the laws of motion; nevertheless, these two beings of entirely different kind meet together and correspond to each other like two clocks perfectly regulated to the same time. (*L*, 587; see also *L*, 602-3)

there is a perfect *harmony* between the perceptions of the monad and the motions of the body, preestablished from the beginning between the system of efficient causes and that of final causes. (*L*, 637)

Strictly speaking, then, perception is nothing other than a perfect correspondence, timingwise (simultaneity) and deducibilitywise (expression), between the (so-called perceptual) state of a given monad at a given time (metaphysical "sublevel") and the appropriate state of the universe (in particular, of the body—or "phenomenon"—that is said to be perceived) at that same time. This is the kind of extended preestablished I referred to earlier, and it is strangely reminiscent of Spinoza's famous proposition, "The order and connection of ideas is the same as the order and connection of things" (*Ethics* II.vii)—provided by "ideas" we understand "perceptual states," by ,,things" we understand "perceived things," and by "the same as" we understand "corresponds to." (In this connection, it is interesting to notice that, in his 1678 notes on Spinoza's Ethics, Leinbiz remarked that the series (or connection) of ideas is distinct from the series (or connection) of bodies, and that they are only in reciprocal or mutual correspondence—see *G*, 282.)

Again, however, this is not the whole story. For we *also* want a perfect correspondence to hold at the metaphysical "sublevel" as well, that is, between the states of *all* monads *qua* percipients. In other words, we want *each* monad to mirror—from a different point of view, and hence with varying degrees of distinctness and confusion—the *same* (present state of the) universe. This we can easily get, once we have universal Harmony at our disposal: for to claim that universal Harmony holds is to claim, we have seen above, that each monad perceives the same universe from its own point of view, and conversely. (Notice that no such thing is implied by preestablished Harmony, or by the generalized version thereof. Both of them may indeed hold *without* its being the case that each monad perceives the *same* universe. This is essentially what distinguishes preestablished Harmony, and the generalized version thereof, from universal Harmony.) Do we really get the desired result? Somewhat boldly, I should be inclined to assert that we do—and leave to Russell the unpleasant task of explaining why: "Each monad always represents the whole universe, and therefore the states of all monads at every instant correspond, in that it is the same universe they represent."[17]

Can we put together all the pieces of the puzzle, so as to get a reasonably complete and coherent picture of the whole? Well, consider the following passage:

Monads perceive what passes without them by what passes within them, answering to the things without, in virtue of the harmony which God has preestablished by the most beautiful and the most admirable of all his productions, whereby every simple substance is by its nature . . . a concentration and a living mirror of the whole universe. (*L*, 711)

The main outlines of Leibniz's theory of perception can easily be found in the passage I have just quoted. First, the Harmony, or correspondence, between the metaphysical ("within them") and the phenomenal ("the things without") "sublevels," and hence, by implication, the unfailing and unfaltering correspondence not only between a given (perceptual) state of a given monad at a given time and the state of the universe at that very time ("generalized" preestablished Harmony), but also between all the (perceptual) states of all monads at a given time (universal Harmony).[18] And second, the view that each monad is a "mirror" of the entire universe as a result of the fact that it exemplifies a complete concept (which is what I take Leibniz to mean by the phrase, "by its nature").

At this point we have all we need to answer our original question—namely, how can we explain solipsistic perception? Very simply, we can explain it by saying that it is question (a) of the fact that each simple substance exemplifies a complete concept (or of the fact that "every present state of a substance occurs to it spontaneously and is only a consequence of its preceding state" (CA, 51)—which neatly takes care of Leibniz's view that perception is a species of expression; and (b) of the fact that universal Harmony, and, in particular, generalized preestablished Harmony both hold—which neatly takes care of the problems associated with the notion of expression qua deducibility. Solipsistic perception, in a word, is (the result of) a very delicate balance between, and combination of, the kind of generalized preestablished Harmony described above and universal Harmony. It may be characterized as ultimately consisting in an "exact correspondence of unities [= monads] with one another through their own laws" (GP IV, 49).

But what about the reversal of the dénouement? Do we indeed have a reversal here? I think we do, for the following reason: that we need virtually the entire Leibnizian "circle" to explain, or account for, or make sense of, preestablished Harmony—a generalized version of which played, it will be recalled, a crucial role in the analysis of perception I have suggested above.[19] Only in a "system" in which causal interaction between substances is denied; in which each simple substance is said to exemplify a complete concept; in which the set of exemplified complete concepts is claimed to be a set of mutually compossible complete concepts; in which all things are said to be connected; and so on—in a "system" of this kind does a doctrine such as that of preestablished Harmony (which for the sake of simplicity I take to include, here and below, its own generalized version) make sense, and only in terms of it can it be accounted for. (In GP IV, 49, Leibniz goes so far as to claim that "my hypothesis of harmony or concomitance follows from my view of unities, and . . . my whole contention stands or falls together.") If some more textual evidence is wanted for what I have just said, the following passages spring naturally and quite appropriately to mind:

according to [the way of preestablished Harmony] God has made each of the two substances from the beginning in such a way that though each follows only its own laws which it has received with its being, each agrees throughout with the other, entirely as if they were mutually influenced. (*L*, 460)

This hypothesis [namely, that of preestablished Harmony] is entirely possible. For why should God be unable to give to substance in the beginning a nature or internal force which enables it to produce in regular order . . . everything which is to happen to it, that is, all the appearances or expressions which it is to have? . . . And since it is the nature of the soul to represent the universe in a very exact way, . . . the sequence of representations which the soul produces will correspond naturally to the sequence of changes in the universe itself. So the body, in turn, has also been adapted to the soul to fit those situations in which the soul is thought of as acting externally. (*L*, 458)

It should not take *too* long, or *too* much philosophical insight, to realize that the main features of the Leibnizian "circle" are contained in, and can effortlessly be extracted from, the two passages I have just quoted—which is precisely the sort of evidence I need for my claim that (the doctrine of) preestablished Harmony presupposes for its intelligibility virtually the entire "circle" (by which I do *not* mean, mind you, that it would be unintelligible without the latter). To begin with, both passages implicitly deny any such thing as causal interaction ("influence") between substances. Second, the "laws" referred to in the first of the two passages, as well as the "nature or internal force" referred to in the second of the two passages, can plausibly be regarded as some sort of analogue, in the realm of actuality, of complete concepts in the realm of possibility. And third, we even have (the notion of) compossibility: artfully (or perversely, if you prefer) disguised though it may be, it *is* there—an especially tricky system of Chinese boxes, more or less as follows.

The notion of correspondence, as it occurs in Leibniz's remark (in the second of the two passages quoted above) that "the sequence of representations which the soul produces will *correspond* . . ." to the sequence of changes in the universe itself" (italics mine), presupposes the doctrine of (universal) Harmony. It presupposes it, that is, assuming "represents the universe" (as the latter occurs in the second of the two passages quoted a couple of paragraphs back) is taken to be shorthand for "represents the same universe that is represented by all other souls"; which involves a certain amount of reading between the lines, to be sure, but which is not (I trust) a wholly implausible assumption to make.

The doctrine of universal Harmony, in turn, presupposes the notion of compossibility: at least in view of the fact that to say that (universal) Harmony holds is to say that each simple substance expresses the same universe from its own point of view (and conversely, as we have seen)—and there is no way that I can think of, anyway) of explaining the notion of sameness of universe without that of compossibility. More or less, this is the system of Chinese boxes I referred to two paragraphs back: the complete system we get if we reverse the "direction" of containment of box within box, or of presuppositions. But there

would not be much point to doing that: for in a sense we have reached the desired terminus—compossibility. (Cf. also fn. 21).

So much, then for the dénouement. This is not the end of the story, however—not yet. Something remains to be said about the two models for representing the relation between perception and preestablished Harmony I have
briefly outlined at the beginning of the paper—which should throw some more
light, if need be, on what it is for the story to have no dénouement after all.

3. THE TWO MODELS

Let me start (or should I say, conclude) with a word of caution: the two models
are not incompatible; nor are they competing; nor is either of them complete—
indeed, the best proof, if I may say so, that the story has no dénouement consists precisely in the fact that both models are needed for a full account of Leibniz's theory of perception. In other words, it is true both that if we take perception as basic, preestablished Harmony is derivable from it (first model); *and* that
if we take preestablished Harmony as basic, perception can be characterized in
terms of (and not, mind you: derived from) it (second model).

Well, then: the first model. According to Russell,

> The preestablished harmony is an immediate result of perception and the
> mutual independence of monads. . . . It is better . . . to start with per-
> ception, and deduce the preestablished harmony. For some arguments can
> be adduced, if it be admitted that *we* have perceptions of an external
> world, to show that this is also true of other substances; and hence pre-
> established harmony follows.[20]

Let me first get rid of a potential source of misunderstanding: what
Russell in the passage just quoted refers to as "preestablished harmony" is not
what I have called so far "preestablished harmony"—rather, it is what I have
been calling all along "universal Harmony." This potential source of misunderstanding out of the way, two rather obvious questions arise: first, is Russell
correct in claiming that *universal* Harmony follows from "perception and the
mutual independence of monads"? And second, assuming the claim is correct,
would it still be correct if "universal Harmony" were replaced by "preestablished Harmony"? Let us see.

As for the first question, my answer is affirmative: Russell's claim is absolutely correct. For, if it be conceded (a) that we as well as other substances have
perceptions of an external world, and (b) that there is no such thing as causal
interaction between substances, the only way we have of explaining not only
how we have *perceptions* of an external world, but also how our perceptions are
perceptions *of* the *same* external world is by means of universal Harmony.[21] In
other words, (a) and (b) lead quite naturally—and so to say inevitably—to the
doctrine of (universal) Harmony.

Can we also deduce preestablished Harmony? I think we can, provided (a) of the previous paragraph is restricted to the perceptions of a *single* simple substance, that is, without any presumption as to whether or not other simple substances do have perceptions (of the same external world). The idea is simple: what holds for the whole (= the totality of simple substances involved in (*a*), holds for the parts as well. That is, (*a*), qualified in the way I have just suggested, and (*b*) lead to *a sort of* universal Harmony—what we might call a *particular* Harmony between the perceptual state of a given monad at a given time and the appropriate state of the world at that very time. As is easily seen, this is just a kind of generalized preestablished Harmony—and it enables us to answer the rather annoying question: what is perception perception *of*, what is perception anyway, since it is as if the object of perception *were not* there? by saying, it is perception *of* a given object (given a given state of the universe at a given time). It is *perception,* to be sure, precisely because it is *as if* the object *were* out there playing whatever role it plays in nonsolipsistic perception—as a result of the kind of generalized preestablished Harmony I have been talking about. And its being as if the object were out there amounts to its being the case that whatever manifest properties the object has when it is said to be perceived, those very properties are deducible from the complete concept exemplified by the "entity" perceiving the object in question. (We say "as if" purely on account of the fact that the object has no causal efficacy, so to speak, on the percipient: Harmony, whether preestablished, generalized, or universal, guarantees precisely that the deducibility of properties I have just alluded to gives us the right properties of the right object, and not accidentally—see *CA,* 147-48.)

So much for the first model. Taking perception (in some intuitive sense) as basic, we are naturally led to some sort of generalized preestablished Harmony—and to universal Harmony as well. Or, equivalently: perception (in some intuitive sense) requires that the generalized kind of preestablished Harmony, and universal Harmony, both hold. What about the other way round? Less misleadingly: do we have to use preestablished Harmony (or something pretty much equivalent to it) in order to characterize solipsistic perception? The answer is fairly obvious—we definitely do—and the reason for it is equally obvious. Without preestablished Harmony (or something pretty much equivalent to it) solipsistic perception would not get off the ground, so to say. That solipsistic perception is indeed perception, and not something else with the wrong tag attached to it, follows from the fact that it presupposes, or can—perhaps, must—be conceived of as a kind of, generalized preestablished Harmony—and ultimately as a species of universal Harmony.

Here the starting point is (1) preestablished Harmony; to it we add (2) the view that perception is a kind of expression (which gives us "solipsism" but not perception itself); finally, we bring into the picture (3) the kind of generalized preestablished Harmony I have introduced above; and this, together with (2) of a few lines back, gives us solipsistic *perception.*

This much ground, and more, we have already covered in the previous sections and I will not go through it again. Suffice it to repeat at this point that the two models are not competing models at all; they are complementary, in a rather one-sided way. Thus, that the first of them is correct (but not complete), comes of the simple fact that preestablished Harmony (or something pretty much like it) is virtually "built into" the notion of solipsistic perception—and even in that of perception understood in some intuitive sense. No wonder, therefore, that the latter (taken together with Leibniz's denial of causal interaction) leads right away to the former—as Russell quite rightly (but for different reasons than mine) pointed out.

We can have it both ways, then: start from perception (in some intuitive sense) as primitive; add to it the denial of causal interaction; and get to preestablished Harmony—and to universal Harmony as well. Or else, start from preestablished Harmony (and eventually universal Harmony as well), and characterize perception—that is, solipsistic perception—in terms of something pretty much like preestablished Harmony (and eventually in terms of universal Harmony as well). And both ways we are back to the "circle." This is precisely why the view that each simple substance perceives the entire universe from its own point of view is not after all the kind of dénouement (or "foundation") one should intuitively expect it to be—although it has to be conceded that if dénouement there must be, it is intimately related, if not indentical, to the view I have just described.

So this is how the view that each (simple) substance perceives the whole universe fits into the "circle": as its texture? its connecting tissue? its spread along a closed curve in space—but certainly not as its "foundation," not even, I suspect, in the sense of "foundation" I have described at the beginning of the paper. The same holds, to a degree, for the generalized kind of preestablished Harmony I have been talking about so far. The same holds, to a lesser degree, for preestablished Harmony itself: for it guarantees that, even in a universe consisting of as many mutually disjoint universes as there are simple substances, perception will run its usual course—unusual though it may be from the point of view of a universe like ours.

4. SOLIPSISTIC PERCEPTION AND SOLIPSISM

By way of conclusion, I should like to say a few words on the notion of solipsistic perception and its relation, if any, to solipsism. In a number of superficially rather puzzling passages, Leibniz appears to take the view that things would be just the same, no dramatic adjustments—actually, no adjustments at all—would be required, if all there was to the universe were God and, I trust you will excuse *my* audacity, me—which may be taken by some to be a somewhat disturbing and alarming symptom of solipsism. Here are some of the passages in question:

the perceptions of expressions of external things reach the soul at the proper time by virtue of its laws, as in a world apart, as if there existed nothing but God and itself. (*L*, 457) each substance is like a world apart, independent of any other things save God. (*DM*, 23)

each individual substance or complete entity is like a world apart, independent of everything except God. (*CA*, 64)

Before proceeding to a discussion of the view put forth in the passages just quoted, let me quickly (but more fully than I have done in section 2 above) characterize (the notion of) solipsistic perception: solipsistic perception is perception in a world (universe) wherein (1) no causal interaction between substances obtains, (2) "every present state of a substance occurs to it *spontaneously* and is *only* a consequence of its preceding state" (*CA*, 51—italics mine), and (3) both preestablished and universal Harmony hold. Now the sort of solipsism Leibniz appears to defend in the passages quoted above is an immediate consequence of solipsistic perception minus (3). In a word: to claim that "each substance is like a world apart" is just to claim that (1) and (2) above hold—for obvious reasons, (3) must be left out of the picture altogether. (Notice that the same account applies to Leibniz's well-known and somewhat extravagant metaphor of the windowlessness of monads.)

No cause for alarm, therefore: Leibniz' "solipsism" is perfectly consistent with the view that perception is perception *in*, and *of*, an in independently existing universe of simple substances. No question, either, that Leibniz regarded "solipsism" as a consequence (and a perfectly harmless one, for that matter) of solipsistic perception minus (3) of the previous paragraph: indeed, in response to Bayle's unusually well-taken point, "I am unable to understand the chain of internal and spontaneous actions which would cause the soul of a dog to feel pain immediately after having felt joy, even if it were alone in the universe" (*L*, 492), Leibniz politely remarks that

when I said that even if only it and God existed in the world, the soul would feel all that it feels now, I was merely using a fiction, assuming something which cannot happen naturally, in order to show that the feelings of the soul are entirely a result of what is already in it. (*L*, 492)

So much, I should think and hope, for Leibniz's alleged solipsism—there is so much less to it than actually meets the eye. To see this even more clearly, however, consider Furth's remark that "the world of each [monad] is wholly self-contained ('windowless'), necessarily unaffected by what is going on in any other, or by whether any others exist at all."[22] This is not *quite* right, however.

To begin with, a distinction (super-subtle though it may seem to be) ought to be drawn between the claim that the world of each monad is "necessarily unaffected by what is going on in any other," and the claim that it is "necessarily unaffected . . . by whether any others exist at all": self-containedness ("windowlessness") may well imply, or be equivalent to, the former claim; it certainly does not imply, nor is it equivalent to, the latter. For notice that (universal) Harmony (or what Leibniz in *CA*, 92, refers to as "conformity," or what in *L*, 493, he refers to as "agreement") would become utterly trivial, if not plainly

grotesque or pathetically pointless, if the world of each monad were "unaffected . . . by whether any others exist"; whereas the fact that the world of each
monad is "unaffected by what is going on in any other" *requires* precisely that
something pretty much like (universal) Harmony hold—if something pretty
much like ordinary perception is to be possible. But to say that Harmony holds
is equivalent to saying that the world of each monad is affected, after all, by
"what is going on in any other," in a somewhat Pickwickian—I am willing to
concede—sense of "affected": but I take it that the doctrine of Harmony was
also meant by Leibniz to explain how a monad could coherently be said to be
affected by all other monads, and hence to perceive, without in effect being
affected by any monad at all, and hence without perceiving anything at all in
any ordinary sense of "perceive."[23]

Notes

The following abbreviations are used in the text: *GP* for *Die philosophischen Schriften von Gottfried Wilhelm Leibniz*, ed. C. I. Gerhardt, 7 vols. (Berlin, 1875-1890); *C* for *Opuscules et fragments inédits de Leibniz*, ed. L. Couturat (Paris, 1903); *G* for *Textes inédits*, ed. G. Grua (Paris, 1948); *CA* for *Correspondence with Arnauld*, trans. H. T. Mason (Manchester, 1967); *DM* for Leibniz, *Discourse on Metaphysics*, trans. Lucas and Grint (Manchester, 1953); *L* for *Leibniz: Philosophical Papers and Letters*, ed. and trans. L. E. Loemker (Dordrecht, Holland, 1968).

1. This quotation from Barth is so obviously unscholarly, that it may even appear to the rare few to represent the peak of scholarship—or pretended scholarly *hauteur*, as they who are "out of it" might put it. It also appears to almost directly contradict something I said in the last few lines of the article referred to in fn. 2 below, which—particularly in view of this very footnote—may appear to some to be just another piece of lamentable *hauteur* on my part. Be that as it may, this article was written for, and with, a different kind of chimera, in mind—James Whistler's butterfly.

2. "The Leibnizian 'Circle,'" in *Essays on the Philosophy of Leibniz*, ed. Mark Kulstad, *Rice University Studies* 63, No. 4 (1977).

3. In *A Critical Exposition of the Philosophy of Leibniz* (London, 1900), p. 138.

4. For instance, all the properties entailed by the complete concept of a given individual substance *s* are essential to *s*; the fact that any two exemplified complete concepts are mutually compossible makes it true, so to say, that in the actual world all things are connected; the fact that any two exemplified individual concepts are complete and mutually compossible makes it true, so to say, that each individual substance expresses the same universe from its own point of view; and so on; and so forth; and conversely (as I show in the main text). See my "Leibnizian 'Circle.'"

5. Here I am just taking for granted something that I have shown in some detail in my "The Leibnizian 'Circle,'" that to say that (universal) Harmony holds is to say that each individual substance expresses the same universe—and conversely.

6. Let me explain. To claim that all things are connected is to exclude the possibility that each substance should express a different universe than the universe expressed by all other substances, or that there should be as many mutually *disjoint* universes as there are individual substances. In a sense, therefore, "sameness of universe" is "built into" the view that all things are connected, which is an obvious consequence of the fact that our own actual world is a set of exemplified mutually *compossible* complete concepts—which, of course, leads right away to "sameness of universe."

7. Why "hence"? Well, because, as I have pointed out in fn. 6 above, compossibility

guarantees "sameness of universe," and its characterization, involving as it does the notion of completeness (hence of deducibility from a given complete concept of all the properties of the concepts compossible with it), immediately entails that "same" entails "whole."

8. The mirroring principle, as applied to complete concepts, says, more or less, that each concept in a given possible world w mirrors all the other concepts belonging to w, that is, less metaphorically, that from the properties included in a given complete concept c it is possible (objectively, I mean) to deduce all the properties included in the complete concepts that are *compossible* with c. The analogue of the mirroring principle at the "level" of actuality is the view that the universe expressed by each individual substance is the same, or the view that all things are connected.

9. *A Critical Exposition*, p. 4.

10. The question we must ask here is not, Are bodies real? but, more specifically, are bodies *really* substances? or, Are bodies *real* substances? And the answer, of course, is, No, they are not—which of course does not entail that there are no such things as bodies, or that there is no reality *to* bodies. In other words, something may be both a real body and not a real substance (in Leibniz's sense of "substance"). This use, and treatment, of "real" derives from J. L. Austin, *Sense and Sensibilia* (Oxford, 1962), pp. 68 ff.

11. As I have suggested in "The Leibnizian 'Circle'"

12. The point of view of perspective of a monad I take to be something pretty much like the series or sequence of perceptual states of the monad itself.

13. *A Critical Exposition*, p. 132.

14. An analogous question was raised, and answered, by Russell: "To explain how perceptions give knowledge of present external things, though not due to these things, Leibniz invented the crowning conception of his philosophy, the conception by which he denoted his system namely, the doctrine of pre-established Harmony, "*A Critical Exposition*, p. 136.

15. See *A Critical Exposition*, p. 52. I should also point out that my talk of "state(s) of the world" and "state(s) of a monad," here and elsewhere in the paper, comes from Leibniz—in particular, from the following passage: "states of the soul are naturally and essentially expressions of the corresponding states of the world." *CA*, 146.

16. *Ibid.*, p. 136.

17. *Ibid.*, p. 138.

18. Very likely, Leibniz had precisely this in mind when he remarked that "each individual substance, which expresses the same universe in its own measure according to the laws of its own nature, is such that its changes and states correspond perfectly to the changes and stages of other substances, but the soul and the body correspond to one another most." *GP* VII, 31. See also *DM*, 23-24; *CA*, 170-71.

19. In the Preface to the *Nouveaux Essais*, Leibniz claims that his "theory" of *petites perceptions* accounts, among other notable things, for "that wonderful pre-established harmony of soul and body, and indeed of all monads or simple substances," *GP* V, 48. This goes a long way beyond, although it is certainly consistent with, the first of the two models for describing the relation between perception and preestablished Harmony I discuss in section 3 below.

20. *A Critical Exposition*, pp. 137, 138.

21. This assumes, of course, that all monads perceive the same universe as a result of the fact that (universal) Harmony holds. In my "The Leibnizian 'Circle,'" I have argued that the converse is true too: (universal) Harmony holds as a result of the fact that all monads perceive the same universe, "sameness of universe" being accounted for in terms of (the notion of) compossibility.

22. "Monadology," reprinted in *Leibniz: A Collection of Critical Essays*, ed. H. Frankfurt (New York, 1972), p. 117. fn. 23.

23. This, given a considerable amount of reading between the lines, I believe is the import of Leibniz's remark that "God could give to each substance its own phenomena independent of those of others, but in this way he would have made as many worlds without connection, so to speak, as there are substances," *L*, 493. See also *DM*, 27; *GP* III, 72.

The Nature
of an Individual Substance

R. S. Woolhouse

Predicting universal rejection of Leibniz's *Discourse on Metaphysics* and confessing himself shocked and frightened, Arnauld picked out for particular mention the thirteenth article of its summary, "That the individual concept of each person contains once for all everything that will ever happen to him" (M9:G.ii.15).[1] It would have been ironic if, because of its ill reception by Arnauld, Leibniz had really done as Russell believed and "carefully refrained from making . . . [this] idea public."[2] For precisely one of the ideas Leibniz is commonly known for is his view that "since Julius Caesar will become perpetual dictator and master of the republic and will overthrow the liberty of the Romans, this action is comprised in his notion" (LG.20:G.iv.437). Yet despite its being common knowledge that, according to Leibniz, individual substances have complete concepts there is not, it seems to me, a common understanding about what he meant. What follows is an outline of a suggested explanation of some features of Leibniz's conception of individual substance.

The very having of a complete concept is part of what it is to be a Leibnizian individual substance: "The nature of an individual substance or of a complete being is to have a notion so complete that it is sufficient to comprise and to allow the deduction from it of all the predicates of the subject to which this notion is attributed." (LG.13:G.iv.433).[3] But individual substance is not simply what Leibniz thought about it, and it is possible to approach his account in other than a head-on fashion. For one thing, he sees himself, rightly or wrongly, not as initiating but as clarifying an account, one that goes back to Aristotle (LG.12:G.iv.432-33). He assumes, as Parkinson points out, that the reader will be familiar with the notion of individual substance and will accept Julius Caesar, Alexander the Great, and the sphere that Alexander had placed on his tomb, as examples of it.[4] Moreover, quite apart from the detail of some tradition, it is clear enough what it is about these things that forms the focus of Leibniz's interest.

First, they all had an existence in time: Alexander was born, and lived for a certain time; whether or not it has since been destroyed, the sphere he had placed on his tomb came into temporal existence on being hewn out of the rock. Second, they all had properties, qualities, and entered into relations with other things; and at least some of these properties varied with time. Shortly after his birth Alexander was (perhaps) lying mewling, his two legs kicking, in his mother's arms. But though two-legged, it was not a mewling Alexander who later conquered Darius and Porus; and the stone sphere he had placed on his tomb doubtless suffered changes at the hands of time and weather. Third, given that Alexander (unlike his stone sphere) is the sort of thing that might, say, sit down, there would always have been a determinate answer to the question, had it been put, "Is Alexander sitting down now?" In short, quite apart from *Leibniz*'s views *about* it, we may suppose that an individual substance "persists for a finite time, however short; . . . [and] is in a perfectly determinate state in respect of each of its determinable characteristics at each moment of its history. Its states at every moment between two assigned moments may be all exactly alike, or they may not."[5]

So far we have envisaged that at any moment in Alexander's life answers were possible to questions like "Is Alexander sitting?" We have not envisaged that at his death answers were possible to questions like "Was Alexander sitting?" asked about moments of his past life. Nor have we envisaged that at his birth answers were possible to questions like "Will Alexander be sitting?" asked about moments of his future life. To suppose that the present is determinate, to suppose that it is true or false of a person that he is sitting, is not to suppose that the past and future are. It is not to suppose that it must be true or false of a person that he was sitting yesterday and that he will be sitting tomorrow. Of course the first of these further suppositions is rarely denied[6] and the second often admitted. Nevertheless, they need explicit mention, for they take us some considerable way toward the specifically Leibnizian conception of individual substance.

According to one interpretation, indeed, they take us *all the way* to his view that individual substances have complete concepts. On one interpretation, that is, Leibniz is taken to be saying that to have a complete concept just is to have a determinate past, present, and future; it is for propositions about one's past, present, and future alike, to be either true or false. Thus, according to Russell, that

> all the states of a substance are contained in its notion . . . as Leibniz means it, amounts to little more than the law of identity. Whatever my future actions may be, it must be true now that they will be such as they will be. . . . That is to say, whoever did otherwise would not be the same person. This really amounts to no more than (1) the assertion of permanent substances, (2) the obvious fact that every proposition about the future is already determined either as true or as false, though we may be unable to decide the alternative.[7]

Unlike Russell, Charles Hartshorne does not find the determinacy of the future so "obvious" but his interpretation of Leibniz is the same:

> the thing which continues to exist through change of states of itself . . . is never complete or fully determinate until it ceases to endure through change—until it is dead in fact. The predicational completeness is present and retrospective only, never prospective. Leibniz was trying to identify the predicationally complete with the individual as having a future, whereas the latter is essentially incomplete, with an element of indeterminacy or generality or abstractness.[8]

An elaboration of this interpretation of Leibniz attributes to him a purported explanatory justification of the claim that its being about the past, or about the present, or about the future, is irrelevant to a proposition's having a determinate truth-value. Thus (freely to adapt what C. D. Broad says about him[9]) Leibniz is sometimes supposed to have argued somewhat as follows: If Julius Caesar crossed the Rubicon at a certain time (say t_2) then at t_3 it would have been true to say that Julius Caesar crossed the Rubicon at t_2, and at t_1 it would have been true to say that Julius Caesar will cross the Rubicon at t_2. Now neglecting the complication that part of what is involved in the truth of what was said at t_1 (". . . will . . . at t_2") is that t_2 is later than t_1, and that part of what is involved in the truth of what was said at t_3 (". . . crossed . . . at t_2") is that t_2 is earlier than t_3, what was said on each occasion is made true by the same thing, namely by corresponding with a tenseless, changeless fact about Julius Caesar, viz. that he is tenselessly characterized by crossing the Rubicon at t_2. Along some such lines Wilfrid Sellars says that

> In effect . . . Leibniz suppose[s] that there is a timeless set of entities, i.e., facts, which are about what happens to a substance at different times, and such that it is by virtue of corresponding to these entities that our statements and judgements about the substance are true,[10]

and that there being this set of facts constitutes an individual substance's having a complete concept. And according to Russell, Leibniz's thought is that

> the different attributes which a substance has at different times are all predicates of the substance, and though any attribute exists only at a certain time, yet the fact of its being an attribute at that time is eternally a predicate of the substance in question. (P. 43)

Some passages might seem directly to support, perhaps even to engender, the idea that Leibniz really is thinking along these lines; for example, where he says that

> *The complete or perfect concept of an individual substance involves all its predicates, past, present, and future.* For certainly it is already true now that a future predicate will be a predicate in the future, and so it is contained in the concept of the thing. (L.268:C.520)

But there is much that counts against this *timeless fact interpretation* (as I shall call it). It will pave the way for an appreciation both of this counter-evidence and of a more satisfactory interpretation if we look now at what Leibniz says about possible and actual substances.

As is well known, Leibniz thinks of this actual world as being merely one of many possible worlds: "In the Ideas of God there is an infinite number of possible universes" (Lt.247:G.vi.615-16). God reviews the possible worlds and creates, actualizes the best of them. Now a good way of understanding this is, I suggest, to think of Leibniz's God as the producer of a company of actors who wishes to put on a play. He considers the various possibilities, decides on one, hands out the scripts, and the show begins. We need not wonder whether "the various possibilities" should cover only all actual plays of which the company has scripts or extends to as yet incompletely written, or even unthought of plays; and we may ignore the fact that the "possibilities" are anyway going to be restricted by the number, quality, and characteristics of the available actors. But one respect in which the analogy needs remedial attention stems from the supposition that the actual world of Alexander the Great is fully determinate, whereas a fictional world, say "The World of Suzie Wong," as portrayed in a play, is not. There being a determinate answer to the question of whether Alexander took his grandfather's name is not matched by there being one to the question of whether Suzie took her grandmother's. Though a play script and its associated stage directions specify a world and its history, a course of events that may be enacted on a stage, it specifies it only incompletely and with an amount of indeterminacy. So if the analogy is to serve it must be supposed that the scripts from which the producer chooses fully specify a complete and determinate course of events; it must be supposed that the stage instructions and background information are given down to the last possible detail.

Does the analogy *really* need refinement in this way? Even given that the actual world is fully specific in all its detail, does it follow that the scripts in the analogy need be; doesn't it perhaps follow that they need *not*? For even if the stage directions specify nothing about, say, the precise angle at which a fatal blow is struck, chance will make this determinate in any enactment of the play. But even though not all indeterminacies (e.g., that of whether Suzie has or has not a living third cousin) could be resolved in this way, the situation Leibniz faces us with is explicitly not one in which God leaves to chance how some indeterminacies become determinate on actualization: "One must not suppose that any event, however small it be, can be regarded as indifferent in respect of his wisdom and goodness. Jesus Christ has said divinely well that everything is numbered, even to the hairs of our head" (H.235:G.vi.218).[11] "God," Leibniz makes a point of saying, "is incapable of being indeterminate in anything whatsoever" (H.328:G.vi.315).

Looking at what Leibniz says about possible and actual worlds in terms of plays and their enactments may seem actually to encourage the very interpretation of his account of individual substances and their complete concepts that I want to contest. For it is quite natural to think of a play in a timeless, atemporal way. Whatever the case with people in the real world, characters in a play really are tenselessly characterized by doing such and such things at such and such a time. We might ask, not "What *did* Suzie do when her lover *discovered* she has a child?" but rather "What *does* she do when he *discovers* . . . ?" But this ought not to lead us to think that being an actual substance with a complete concept has to do with there being a timelessly true biographical account. If it does, it is because of confusion and unclarity about the relationship between possible and actual substances. We can get clearer here if we consider what it is for some events to be the enactment of a play; and we shall do this after, and in the light of, consideration of some textual evidence against thinking of complete concepts in terms of timeless facts.

It is going to be important here that not all truths about the world report on the present state of affairs. It is, for instance, true that Gaius Julius was Caesar, that Elizabeth is Queen, and (let us suppose) that Prince Charles will be the father of three. But only the second of these truths relates to the present state of affairs.[12] No features of the world as it presently is constitute Julius's having been Caesar, and Charles's future having of three children. So if at any time a list of truths were drawn up about the substances of this world, it would fall into two parts. First there would be propositions reporting on the state current at that time, and then there would be the rest—propositions reporting on the past and future state of affairs. In its first part, such a list for one time will of course differ from that for another. The first part of a list for the present time says that Elizabeth is Queen, but not that her son is King; whereas, we may suppose, at some future time the first part of the list reverses this situation. But when there are these differences, a proposition in the first part of a list for one time (e.g., Elizabeth is Queen) will reappear as a proposition in the second part of that for another (e.g., Elizabeth was Queen) and vice versa.

If we let 'p,' 'q,' 'r' and so on stand for propositions that might figure on the first part of such a list (e.g., Elizabeth is Queen) there is a choice how to handle propositions of the second sort (e.g., Elizabeth was a Princess; Elizabeth will be Queen Mother). One might take from tense-logic the propositional operators 'F' ("It will be the case that. . . .") and 'P' ("It has been the case that. . . .") so that the list for the present time would contain 'p' for "Elizabeth is Queen" and 'Pq' for "Elizabeth was a Princess;" the list for an earlier time would contain 'q' for "Elizabeth is a Princess" and 'Fp' for "Elizabeth will be Queen."[13] Finding it easier, however, I shall take from chronological logic the propositional operator 'R' ("It is the case at . . . that. . . ."), which produces out of our elementary present-reporting propositions (p, q, r) and times (t_0, t_1, t_2) what might be called dated propositions $(Rt_1 p)$.[14] Thus a list for one time, t_1, will be of the sort 'p, $Rt_0 q$, $Rt_2 r$,' and for another, t_0, will be 'q, $Rt_1 p$, $Rt_2 r$.' Besides those of the propositional calculus and some elementary quantification theory, rules governing this operator are: $Rt\text{-}p \equiv \text{-}Rtp$; $Rt(p \supset q) \supset (Rtp \supset Rtq)$; $(t)Rtp \supset p$; and $Rt' Rtp \supset Rtp$.

It is important to note that there are various ways in which a truth that does not report on a present state of affairs may yet be related to it. Aquinas says that

> when something is in the present it exists in itself, and hence it can be truly said of it that it is. But as long as something is future, it does not yet exist in itself, but it is in a certain way in its cause,[15]

and this reminds us that even though no feature of the world as it presently is constitutes Charles' future fatherhood, we might nevertheless suppose (perhaps falsely) that features exist that constitute sufficient causal conditions for that fatherhood. Similarly, even though no feature of the world as it presently is constitutes Julius' having been Caesar features exist that constitute effects of his having been: the present state of affairs contains much evidence that he was.

Now it is as much a feature of the present state of affairs that it contains Elizabeth's being Queen as that it contains evidence about certain past states and sufficient causal conditions for certain future ones. To take formal account of these ways in which the future and the past may be related to the present, we could use operators (e.g., 'E' read as "There is evidence that. . . ."; 'C' read as "There are causal conditions sufficient to bring it about that. . . .") that produce from dated propositions (e.g., Rt_0q) other propositions (e.g., ERt_0q) that are like the elementary nondated propositions (e.g., p, q, r) in that they too can be used to report on a current state of affairs. Thus if the second part of a list for a certain time, t_1, contains Rt_0q and Rt_2r, the first part might contain, besides p, also ERt_0q and CRt_2r.

Two ways may be shown in which there may be redundancies among the propositions in an extended list of this sort. First, it may well be that the features of the world at t_1 reported on by a proposition p are the same as those reported on by a proposition ERt_0q. Thus, for example, that there are now documents of a certain sort might be evidence that Gaius Julius was Caesar. Second, anyone who wishes to "reduce" the past to the present and to claim that statements about it are equivalent to statements about evidence would hold that a proposition of the sort ERt_0q and one of the sort Rt_0q simply repeat each other. Similarly Aquinas, in the above quoted passage, could be seen as saying that the future has existence only in its present causes, that statements about it are reducible to statements about present causal conditions, that the future is determinate only to the extent that it is determined (see notes 7 and 29) and that the list for time t_1 need not contain Rt_2r as well as CRt_2r. The possibility of a redundancy of this first kind, one among the different sorts of proposition in the first, the present-reporting part of a list, is harmless. Potentially more troublesome, however, is the possibility of redundancy of the second kind amongst the more complex propositions on the first part of a list (e.g., ERt_0q, CRt_2r) and the dated ones on the second part (e.g., Rt_0q, Rt_2r). For it would cast doubt on my initial distinction between what is true of the present state of affairs of the world as opposed to what is true of it in general.

So far I have been distinguishing between truths that, though about the world and its substances, do not report on their present state and truths that do. But it is important further to distinguish between the present state of the world as a whole and that of some particular individual substance. For even if the truth about the future or past of some substance is related to the present state of affairs of the world as a whole, it may or may not be related, either wholly or partially, to the present state of *that same* substance. Thus, for example, there is evidence of a person's earlier appendicitis both in his present scar and also in the hospital records. Similarly, the present causal conditions for someone's future fatherhood may lie in his intentions in that direction or in someone else's pregnancy. So instead of understanding a formula like CRtp along the lines of "The state of the world as a whole is such as to be causally sufficient to bring it about that so and so is a father at t" we might read it along those of "The state of so and so is such as to be causally sufficient to bring it about that he is a father at t."

Now if, armed with these distinctions, we turn back to Leibniz, we immediately see that the "timeless truth" interpretation of his idea that individual substances have complete concepts makes no particular use of them. It attributes to Leibniz the simple view that truths about the course (past, present, future) of an individual substance's life are backed by a set of timeless entities, an array of facts. Any question whether he holds that all such truths report on the present state of affairs (either of it or of the world as a whole), or that they are all related to it in some way (for example via present evidence or sufficient causal conditions) just does not arise. Any considerations of the sort I have been discussing just are not material to this interpretation.

It is more than plain, however, that a correct account of Leibniz must make use of the idea of a present state, the present state moreover, not merely of the world as a whole, but of specific individual substances. For, as the claim that substances have complete concepts is often put, "every substance contains in *its present state* all its states past and future" (M.161:G.ii.126, my italics).[16] There are, it is true, passages in which Leibniz says simply that the future states of each thing follow *from its own concept* (L.269:C.521, my italics);[17] and taken by themselves these perhaps do not upset the suggestion that having a complete concept has to do with there being a collection of facts, including ones about one's future. Perhaps too it is conceivable that the just stressed reference to a "present state" is *not* to anything more specific than the totality of truths about a substance's past, present, and future. But the picture must change when we read that "if I were capable of considering distinctly everything that is happening or appearing to me at this moment, I should be able to see therein everything that will happen or appear to me for ever after" (LG.24:G.iv.440).[18] It cannot be seriously supposed that "everything that is happening to me" is to be equated with "everything that was, is, and will be true of me," that the fact that Charles will be a father is to be counted as part of what is happening to him now.

So passages like this show that "present state" is to be distinguished from and not understood simply as the totality of truth. But if they show that Leibniz's view involves a distinction between what is true about a substance's present state as opposed simply to what is true of the substance, they also show it to be that all those truths that do not report on a substance's present state are nevertheless *related to it*. They show that for an individual substance to have a complete concept is, for Leibniz, for it to be such that every truth that is about or reports on its future and past states are related to its present state.

In fact, Leibniz's position is more extreme than I have just stated it to be. Though it is not clear from the passages cited, he believes not simply that every truth that is about or reports on the *future state of a substance* is related to its present state, but rather that every truth about the *substance's future* is so related. The difference between these two positions may be seen in the fact that even were it to be true of the Queen that she will be thought about by me on her Jubilee Day (and true of me that I will think of her), it would not be a truth about *her* future *state*, but rather one about mine. And it would be one thing to suppose that my future thinking about her is related to my present state, but quite another to suppose that her future being thought of by me is related to hers. However, in order that I might avoid discussion of Leibniz's views about relations and the mirroring of the *whole* world by a substance,[19] I shall in effect suppose that his position involves less than it in fact does, and speak indifferently of "a substance's future" and "a substance's future state."

It is clear, then, that the idea of timeless truth is not the key to Leibniz's very suggestive phrases about the present being "big with the future and laden with the past" (Lg.48:G.v.48).[20] What is the key is rather the idea that though truths about the future and past of a substance form no part of its present state (since its present state is carefully to be distinguished from the totality of truths about the substance), nevertheless such truths are related to its present state in some as yet undiscussed way. Clearly, the question needs to be faced as to the precise way in which, for Leibniz, the past and future are related to the present. He speaks of 'des suites' and 'des traces,' of 'praedeterminatio' and 'deductio';[21] and the already mentioned ideas of the present containing evidence for the past and sufficient causal conditions for the future immediately suggest themselves as bases for a possible interpretation of what he means. But the question should not be faced yet for, as was said earlier, the next task must be to get clearer about what it is for some events to be the enactment of a play. Moreover, what is said about this will turn out to provide an answer.

For certain events to embody a script, for them to be the enactment of a play, it is necessary that there be a correspondence between them and the script. This is not sufficient for it is also necessary that the events are as they are *because of* the script; not merely must things happen as in the script but also because they are scripted so to happen. Now given that we understand, as I have suggested we do, God's creation of the world as his bringing about the enactment of some one of many possible plays, it is important to see that there is more than one way that God might be supposed to ensure that things are happening because of and according to a certain script. God might be seen as retaining the chosen script and manipulating his actors, as a puppeteer his puppets, into doing at each moment what the script requires. Alternatively, he might hand scripts out to his actors who, unlike puppets, are seen as having "the power of acting" (PM.80:G.vii.313) accordingly. It is clear that it is something like this second possibility, not the first, that Leibniz favors.

"Why," he asks, "should God be unable to give to substance in the beginning a nature or internal force which enables it to produce in regular order . . . everything which is to happen to it?" (L.458:G.iv.485) Why, that is, might not a substance be such that it will act according to any script with which it is provided, and why may not God, on creating a substance, provide it with such a script? "The natures which God has established in things" (L.587:G.vi.541) are thus like the scripts for a play, and that God has established them in things is like his having handed them out to actors who will follow them. Leibniz himself on occasion uses the closely connected metaphor of a musical score[22] and it is clear from many other passages of which the following are merely three that Leibniz's view is (in effect) that from the outset substances are provided by God with a script and that they are merely carrying out their lines:[23]

God created the soul in the first place in such a way that ordinarily it has no need of . . . alterations. Whatever happens to the soul arises out of its own depths. (L.338:G.ii.58)

Each of these substances contains in its own nature *a law of the continuation of the series of its own operations* and everything that has happened and will happen to it . . . all its actions come from its own depths. (L.360:G.ii.136)

They [substances] have a certain self-sufficiency which makes them the sources of their internal activities and, so to speak, incorporeal automata. (Lt.229:G.vi.609-10)

Leibniz does not deny, indeed he insists, that just as God first causes substances, so He keeps them in existence: "Created substances depend on God, who preserves them and indeed even produces them continually by a kind of emanation, as we produce our thoughts" (L.311:G.iv.439).[24] But this is not to say that God is responsible for what substances do, in any way other than having at the start "established natures" in them:

Everything occurs in every substance as a consequence of the first state which God bestowed upon it when he created it, and, extraordinary concourse excepted, his ordinary concourse consists only of preserving the substance itself in conformity with its preceding state and the changes that it bears. (M.115:G.ii.91-92; see also L.593:D.ii.223)

From moment to moment He is responsible for substances being there to do anything at all but not responsible, from moment to moment, for what they do.

He is not responsible "in some other way than by preserving each substance in its course and in the laws established for it" (L.338:G.ii.58).

The "other way" that Leibniz has in mind here is what he calls "the hypothesis of occasional causes,"[25] which is precisely the first of the two above mentioned ways in which God might ensure that things are happening as it were because of and according to a certain script. It is the way of a Divine Puppeteer, or "perpetual supervisor" (L.494:G.iv.520) who manipulates his puppets according to a script which He Himself holds and follows; and it is a way that Leibniz firmly rejects.[26] Besides being unworthy of Him it would involve a perpetual miracle, or at least the help of angels, for God to be "the executor of his own laws" (L.580:G.iv.563) in this way.[27]

The contrast between these two ways in which the desired course of the world might be brought about, comes out at length in Leibniz's article "On Nature Itself, or on the Inherent Force and Actions of Created Things," which arose out of a controversy between J. C. Sturm and G. C. Schelhammer on matters raised by Robert Boyle's "A free inquiry into the vulgarly received notion of nature."[28] Given that what happens in the world now is what God all along wanted to happen (given, that is, "that motions now taking place result by virtue of an *eternal law* once established by God" [L.500:G.iv.506]) and given that the reason things thus happen in accord with a script God has chosen is not that God follows the script Himself (is not, that is, "that God moves things as a woodchopper moves his ax or a miller controls his mill by shutting off the water or turning it into the wheel" [L.500:G.iv.506]) then we have to suppose that the initially chosen script for the way of the world is actually handed out to or embodied in things as God created them:

> since this command in the past no longer exists at present, it can accomplish nothing unless it has left some subsistent effect behind which has lasted and operated until now. . . . It is not enough, therefore, to say that in creating things in the beginning, God willed that they should observe a certain law in their progression, if his will is imagined to have been so ineffective that things were not affected by it and no durable result was produced in them. . . . If . . . [then] the law set up by God does in fact leave some vestige of him expressed in things, if things have been so formed by the command that they are made capable of fulfilling the will of him who commanded them, then it must be granted that there is a certain efficacy residing in things, a form or force such as we usually designate by the name of nature, from which the series of phenomena follows according to the prescription of the first command. (L.500-1:G.iv.507)

The importance that Leibniz attaches to the idea that substances are following of their own accord scripts given them by God and are not, puppetlike, being manipulated by Him comes out in his testy reply to des Bosses:

> you say that it is gratuitous to assume monads which receive their modifications from their own resources. . . . But your point here is not merely

an addition; it is primary. If you think this, we must go back to the beginning, as if I had written nothing. (L.613:G.ii.503)

Now we saw earlier that the idea of timeless truth was not the key to the Leibnizian account of individual substances. We began to see that the essence of that account was the idea that though truths about the future and past of a substance formed no part of its present state, nevertheless such truths are related to its present state in some way. And we can now see that the understanding of complete concepts as akin to scripts for a part in a play fits perfectly well with this. So long as we take care to distinguish between on the one hand the events and actions specified and laid down in a script, and on the other hand the fact of somebody's actually following that script and carrying it out, then although we can still conceive of a complete concept as a script, specifying a life in an atemporal tenseless way, we will not think that some substance's having a complete concept has to do with there being a set of timeless facts about it. It is rather that, a complete concept being a script, the having of a complete concept is the following of a script—a script that lays down a complete course of events and actions that some actual substance (given that there *is* one with that concept) has been following from its creation. Thus we are provided here with an interpretation of the relation between the future and past of a substance and its present. A substance's future (and past) are, it can be said, "scripted by" its present state. That is to say, though Julius Caesar's future crossing of the Rubicon is not itself part of his present state, what is, is something having to do with this future crossing, viz. that Caesar is now following a script that includes it. It is no part of his present state that Caesar will cross the Rubicon. It is part of it that he is following a script that specifies his doing so.

This picture of substances—as actors following scripts handed out to them by their Producer—fulfills the minimum condition for an interpretation of Leibniz of providing a relation (that of "being scripted by") that relates a substance's future (and past) to its present; but is there anything else to be said in its favor? After all, we have noted other possible relations (for example, that of containing sufficient causal conditions) that, because of their nonmetaphorical quality, if for no other reason, may suit better. May it not be, indeed, that these come down in the end to the same thing? To answer these questions, let us begin by looking more closely at this alternative.

The adaptation (but not, I hope, distortion) of some ideas developed by Storrs McCall[29] would lead naturally to the suggestions that

A proposition of the form CRtp (i.e., "there exist causal conditions sufficient to bring it about at t that p") is true at some earlier time t' if and only if at t' causal conditions exist sufficient to bring it about at t that p,

and that

If a proposition of the form CRtp is true at some earlier time t' then it is true at all times between t' and t.

It follows from these suggestions that if CRtp is true at some earlier time t' then CRt−p is not true at t', i.e., CRtp $\supset$ −CRt−p is a necessary truth. But, it should be noted, the converse does not follow. It does not follow that if CRtp is not true at some earlier time t' then CRt−p is true at t', i.e., −CRtp $\supset$ CRt−p is *not* a necessary truth. That is, these suggestions leave open the possibility that at a given time t' neither CRtp nor CRt−p is true. This is an attractive feature when we remember that, as discussed earlier, Leibniz makes a point of saying that "God is incapable of being indeterminate in anything whatsoever."

At first sight this might seem not to be so. It may seem that this Leibnizian claim is missed rather than captured if it may be that at a given time t' neither CRtp nor CRt−p holds. It may even seem that in this respect the original timeless fact interpretation of Leibniz fares better. For in connection with it there are no formulas like CRt−p and CRtp to consider, but only the simple Rt−p and Rtp; and since, we have been supposing all along, at any given time t' either Rt−p or Rtp holds, it appears to capture the requisite determinacy. But precisely because the notion of prior causal sufficiency by itself leaves *open* the possibility that at a certain time neither CRtp nor CRt−p holds, it leaves room for a *subsequent closing* of this possibility to appear as a significant and substantive Leibnizian doctrine. If it were built into the interpretative framework that at any time t' either CRt−p or CRtp holds (as it is built into the framework of the timeless fact view that at any time either Rt−p or Rtp holds) then within its terms it would be impossible to see the Leibnizian view, according to which a determinate future is contained in the present, as a substantial view contrasting with the possible view that a semi-determinate future is contained there (or the view that nothing of the future is). An interpretative framework needs to leave room, which that of the timeless view does not, for a God who *is* capable of being indeterminate or, more strongly, one incapable of being determinate. Otherwise it cannot explicitly appear as a significant fact that Leibniz's God is not like those.

So far there is nothing to choose between an interpretation in terms of sufficient causal conditions and one in terms of scripts. For just as the one idea, taken by itself, does not assert that for any time and any future event there must exist causal conditions sufficient either to bring it about or to prevent it, so it is no part of the other, taken by itself, to assert that a script that is being followed must either specify some future thing's being done or specify its not being done. But a further feature of the ideas derived from McCall is that though at some time there may not yet be causal conditions sufficient to bring about (or to prevent) some future event, once there are such conditions there must continue to be, and the future event must come about (TF.276,TPM.434,441). And at this point, the two interpretations begin to diverge. For it is not incoherent to suppose that at one time t' a person is following a script that involves p's later being the case at t and that at an intermediate time the person is following another that involves p's not being the case at t. Nor is it incoherent to suppose that even if the person does not change scripts, he might, when the time comes, be prevented from doing what he should.

In this respect an interpretation of Leibniz in terms of the metaphor of scripts is to be preferred to one in terms of the idea (at least as conceived by McCall) of sufficient causal conditions. The reason is not, of course, that Leibniz envisages that individual substances might have one complete concept (be following one script) at one time, another at another; nor is it that he envisages that mutual interaction might prevent their properly playing their parts. The reason is, again, the very opposite: since, as we shall see, Leibniz so evidently does *not* envisage these things, it is an advantage if our interpretative framework allows us *explicitly* to say so, and affords the opportunity of a contrast between Leibniz and some other possible philosopher for whom substances can interact.

Even apart from the fact that Leibnizian exegesis is not McCall's aim in the work from which I have borrowed, it is not clear why he accepts what he calls "The Principle of the Continuity of Sufficient Conditions" (TPM.434), why he supposes impossible the existence at one time of sufficient causal conditions for some future event that fails to materialize. Indeed one of his own examples (TF.274), that of a doctor giving a patient a pill, lends itself easily and naturally to a development—suppose the pill later rendered ineffective by some further drug—that would illustrate the falsity of that Principle. The supposed impossibility hardly follows directly from the very idea of causal sufficiency, for the traditional talk of impedible causes as in the following passage from Aquinas is hardly obvious nonsense:

> It is . . . false that when a cause has been posited—even a sufficient one—the effect must be posited, for not every cause (even if it is sufficient) is such that its effect cannot be impeded. For example, fire is a sufficient cause of the combustion of wood, but if water is poured on it the combustion is impeded.[30]

Indeed, "if the drinking of poison were a nonimpedible cause of death it would be idle to seek advice about medicine."[31]

It may be that the idea of an impedible cause can get no grip if the world is conceived of as *one* causal system. As was noted earlier, "There exist causal conditions sufficient to bring it about that this man dies next week" might be read as "The state of the world as a whole is such as to be causally sufficient. . . ." or as "The state of this man. . . ." and though the man's state can be altered and interfered with from outside, it is difficult to see how that of the world as a whole can. Perhaps it is this that lies behind McCall's acceptance of the Principle, but be that as it may, the Principle is not something that, from the point of view of the standard branching-time semantics,[32] could easily be given up. For according to a formal semantics of this sort, the basic possibility that the future be "open," that there be no necessity for there to exist at a time either conditions sufficient to bring about a certain future event or conditions sufficient to prevent it, is represented by a tree branching out into the future (see figure on p. 58). Thus, there existing at time t casual conditions sufficient to bring it about that p at the later time t'' is represented by giving p the value 1 on every branch at t''. (Similarly, there not existing at t conditions sufficient

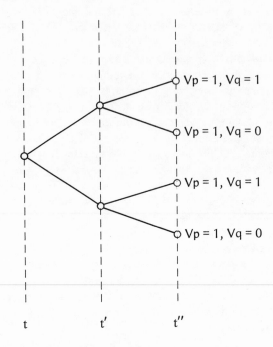

$Vp = 1, Vq = 1$

$Vp = 1, Vq = 0$

$Vp = 1, Vq = 1$

$Vp = 1, Vq = 0$

t   t′   t″

either to bring about or prevent q at t″ is represented, as above, by q's having the value 1 on some branches at t″ and the value 0 on others.) But now since p has the value 1 at t″ on every branch in the future of t, it equally (no matter by which branch the world moves from t to t′) has the value 1 at t″ on every branch in the future of t′. Hence such a semantics forces one to suppose that if there exist at t conditions sufficient to bring about p at t″ then there must exist at the intermediate time t′ conditions sufficient to bring about p at t″ (and also, of course, when t″ comes, p must be the case).

So the idea of the present's containing sufficient conditions for the future, at any rate in this development of it, has as part of its basic shape that RtCRt″p ⊃ Rt′CRt″p and that RtCRt″p ⊃ Rt″p. But, we have seen, Leibniz needs to be interpreted in some other terms (e.g., those of "following a script to the effect that. . . . ") that do not have this formal shape. And it is not difficult to construct the required formal semantics.[33] What is needed is a structure such that if p is the case at t″ so far as t is concerned (e.g., "At t Caesar is following a script to the effect that he later crosses the Rubicon at t″''"), this does not have the consequence that p is the case at t″ so far as some intermediate time t′ is concerned, or indeed so far as t″ itself is concerned. Thus rather than, as before, having the actual course of the world take place along some route up a branching tree, we must let it take place along a ribbed spine (see figure below). Any point in this structure can be specified by an ordered pair, the points on the spine being ⟨t, t⟩, ⟨t′, t′⟩, ⟨t″, t″⟩, . . . , and those on the first vertical rib being ⟨t, t′⟩,

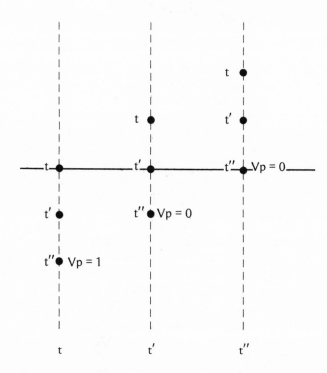

$\langle$t, t$\rangle$, $\langle$t, t''$\rangle$. Thus the supposition that $-$p is the case at t'' (i.e., Rt''$-$p) is repre-sented by giving p the value 0 (or $-$p the value 1) at the spinal point $\langle$t'', t''$\rangle$— which means that Rt''$-$p has the value 1 at $\langle$t, t$\rangle$ or any other spinal point. And the supposition that this future state is "scripted by" the present state at t is represented by p having the value 1 at the rib point $\langle$t, t''$\rangle$— which means that SRt''p has the value 1 at the adjoining spinal point $\langle$t, t$\rangle$. It is then quite possible, as shown by the above diagram, for RtSRt''p to be true and for each of Rt'SRt''p and Rt''p to be false. (The rules given earlier as governing the Rt-operator will all be validated.)

The reason I have given for interpreting Leibniz in terms allowing the formal possibility that what is specified in a substance's complete concept might fail to come about is that only then has one room for dealing with those of Leib-niz's remarks that rule the possibility out. Thus, that substances might follow one script at one time, another at another, is ruled out by his making it clear that their natures are permanent;[34] and that there is no mutual interaction between substances that might prevent their properly playing their parts is of central importance to him. In the article "On Nature itself" Leibniz recognizes as a formal possibility that a substance might fail to play its role when he ex-plains that created things have "a fruitfulness or an impulse to produce their actions and to operate, from which activity follows *if nothing interferes*" (L. 501-2:G.iv.508, my italics). And in a similar fashion he writes to Bourguet that a created being "pregnant with its future state . . . naturally follows a certain course, *if nothing hinders it*" (Lt.44:G.iii.566, my italics). But, having recognized it, he makes a point of ruling it out, for—apart from some suggestion about the intervention of God (L.613:G.ii.503)—"one created substance does not act upon another" (M.167:G.ii.133); they "cannot be naturally hindered in their inner determinations" (Lt.44:G.iii.566).[35]

So to the idea that the complete concepts of created substances are like scripts that lay down a part, complete to the last detail, for them to follow, it must be added that, because they do not interact or interfere with each other, the actual course of their lives is in complete agreement with that projected by their scripts. But at least at first sight it is not clear just what part is occupied in the whole body of Leibniz's thought by this view that substances do not interact and hence that everything that happens to them happens out of their own depths. It can appear that it has to do, not so much with his notion of individual substance as such, but rather with difficulties he antecedently finds in the notion of transient causation itself. Thus in "A new system of the nature and the communication of substances" he reports that though for a time he "found no way to explain . . . how one substance can communicate with another created substance" he was certain that the "common opinion is inconceivable" (L.457: G.iv.483): "The action of one substance upon another is not an emission or a transplanting of some entity, as is commonly supposed" (L.459:G.iv.486).[36] Just what this (apparently Scholastic) view of "the common run of philosophers" (L.457-8:G.iv.484) amounts to stands in need of historical investigation.[37] But, leaving aside the complicating insistence that "ordinary ways of speaking can still be preserved" (L.459:G.iv.486), there is room for the suspicion that Leibniz fails to distinguish between rejecting transient causation itself and rejecting a particular objectionable account of it.[38]

On the other hand, in many passages, including some of those just cited, Leibniz seems to have in mind that substances do not interact, not because of the impossibility of transient causation as such, but rather because of what it is to be created substance. Thus on closer scrutiny it appears that what he found no way to explain was "how one *substance* can communicate with another *created substance*" (L.457:G.iv.483, my italics),[39] and that, as though other things might interact, what is said to be impossible is "for the soul *or any other true substance* to receive something from without" (L.457:G.iv.484, my italics).[40] Whether or not it can really be seen in *these* passages, there are others where it could not be clearer that noninteraction between substances follows from the notion of substance itself.[41] Indeed this seems to be Leibniz's final view. He explains to Arnauld that the claim that individual substances have complete concepts is "of very great importance and merits a clear demonstration, for it follows that every soul is like a world apart independent of everything except God; . . . so to speak, incapable of being acted upon, [and] it retains in its substance indications of everything that happens to it" (M.51: G.ii.46-7).[42]

But what reasons and arguments has Leibniz for saying that an individual substance is such that *everything* that happens to it happens "out of its own depths"? It is certainly true that according to traditional conceptions something would not be a substance unless the reason for at least *some* of what is true of it lies within itself, unless at least some of what is true of it is an expression of *its* nature. And sometimes Leibniz claims no more than this, as on the occasions when he explains that if the happenings in the world resulted as from the actions of a Divine Puppeteer then only He, not also his "puppets" would be a substance:

> the doctrine of occasional causes . . . is fraught with dangerous consequences. . . . So far is this doctrine from increasing the glory of God by removing the idol of Nature that it seems rather, like Spinoza, to make out of God the nature of the world itself, by causing created things to disappear into mere modifications of the one divine substance, since that which does not act, which lacks active force, and which is despoiled of all distinctiveness and even of all reason and ground for subsistence can in no way be a substance. (L.506-7:G.iv.515)[43]

> It does not seem necessary to me to deny action or force to creatures on the pretext that they would be creators if they produced their modifications. For it is God who . . . establishes a source of changing modifications in the creatures . . . otherwise there would be no substances beyond his own. (L.583:G.iv.567-8)

But it is a further step from this to claim that *all* of what happens to a substance happens because of its own nature. At one point Leibniz appears to justify this step by appeal to the principle of sufficient reason (L.538:G.ii.271), but I imagine that what lies at the root of the matter is the idea, which I have not discussed, that the complete concept of a substance contains not only reference to the whole of its life but also to that of the whole world (see note 19)—so that the script that each substance enacts and follows is not only for its part in the course of events but somehow for the whole course of events itself. Given that an individual substance thus contains the whole world, one might wonder why the whole world is not a substance (L.532:G.ii.257), or how to understand there being more than one such substance (L.607:G.ii.460).[44] But, as I said at the outset, this essay attempts to explain only *some* features of Leibniz's conception of an individual substance.

What, finally, must be said is this. I have argued that Leibniz's account of actual individual substances' having complete concepts is usefully to be understood in terms of their following scripts. But talk of scripts here is, undeniably, highly metaphorical. What in literal terms would be meant by saying that Julius Caesar was all along, following a script that involved his later crossing the Rubicon? "Plans" and "programmed instructions" would still be metaphors even though computers and developing organisms are quite freely explained in those terms.[45] The whole matter could be put, as I have tried elsewhere to put it,[46] in the nonmetaphorical terms of the going-to-be future, since, as Aristotle remarks, "that which *shall* hereafter be (*to esomenon*) [is not in every case] identical with that which *is* now *going to be* (*to mellon*).[47] But even then one might wonder just what makes statements about what is going to happen true. Could it be explained in terms of the idea of some part of the world, rather than the world as a whole, containing causal conditions sufficient to bring something about? The problems here are, of course, basic ones of teleology: What is it for the present state of something to point beyond itself to the future, to some goal, to some planned, intended, programmed, encoded, or desired end, to something that is going to happen? And what is it for something to have come about *because* it was planned, programmed, intended, or going to?

Notes

1. Reference to Leibniz passages is made via the pages of the following English translations. Abbreviations are shown in brackets. *Leibniz's Theodicy*, trans. E. M. Huggard (London, 1951) [= H]; *Leibniz: Philosophical Papers and Letters*, trans. L. E. Loemker, 2nd ed. (Dordrecht, Holland, 1969) [= L]; *New Essays Concerning Human Understanding* by Gottfried Wilhelm Leibniz, trans. A. G. Langley, 3rd ed. (La Salle, Illinois, 1949) [= Lg]; *Leibniz: The Monadology and other Philosophical Writings*, trans. R. Latta (London, 1898) [= Lt]; *Leibniz: Discourse on Metaphysics*, trans. P. G. Lucas, L. Grint (Manchester, 1953) [= LG]; *The Leibniz-Arnauld Correspondence*, trans. H. T. Mason (Manchester & New York, 1967) [= M]; *Leibniz: Philosphical Writings*, ed. G. H. R. Parkinson, trans. Mary Morris and G. H. R. Parkinson (London, 1973) [= PM]. The following original sources are used: *Opuscules et fragments inédits de Leibniz*, ed. L. Couturat (Paris, 1903) [= C]; *Leibnitii: Opera omnia*, ed. L. Dutens (Geneva, 1768) [= D]; *Die philosophischen Schriften von Gottfried Wilhelm Leibniz*, ed. C. I. Gerhardt (Berlin, 1875-1890) [= G]; *Leibniz: Mathematische Schriften*, ed. C. I. Gerhardt (Berlin & Halle, 1849-55) [= GM]; *Leibniz: Sämtliche Schriften und Briefe*, ed. Preussische/Deutsche Akademie der Wissenschaften (Darmstadt & Leipzig, 1923-) [=PA].

2. B. Russell, *History of Western Philosophy*, etc. (London, 1946), p. 616; see also his *Philosophy of Leibniz*, new ed. (London, 1937), p. 44, note 1. To E. M. Curley's submission ("The root of contingency," *Leibniz*, ed. H. G. Frankfurt [New York, 1972], pp. 79-83 that Leibniz did not do as Rusell said, it may be added that the *Principles of Nature and Grace* (see para. 13 [L.640:G.vi.604]) and the *Monadology* (see para. 22 [Lt.231:G.vi. 610]), which, though not formally published, were informally promulgated by Leibniz (see L.636), at any rate echo the idea.

3. According to PM.95:C.403, having a complete concept is not merely part but the whole of being an individual substance.

4. G. H. R. Parkinson, *Logic and Reality in Leibniz's Metaphysics* (Oxford, 1965), p. 124.

5. C. D. Broad, *Leibniz*, ed. C. Lewy (London & New York, 1975), p. 20.

6. For a discussion see M. Dummett, "The Reality of the Past," *Proceedings of the Aristotelian Society* 69 (1968-1969).

7. *Philosophy of Leibniz*, p. 46 (see also Parkinson, *Logic and Reality in Leibniz's Metaphysics*, p. 128). Though Russell actually speaks of the future's being 'determined,' the evidence is that all he means is 'determinate' (see note 29).

8. "Leibniz's greatest discovery," *Journal of the History of Ideas* (1946): 420-21. For a similar interpretation of and attitude toward Leibniz see G. Buchdahl, *Metaphysics and the Philosophy of Science* (Oxford, 1969), p. 454.

9. *Leibniz*, pp. 22-24. Though this is his explicit interpretation of Leibniz, Broad ap-

pears to have had somewhere at the back of his mind another interpretation (akin to the one I shall propose). See my discussion of Broad in "Leibniz's Principle of Pre-Determinate History," *Studia Leibnitiana*, 7 (1975): 210 ff., and review of his *Leibniz* in *Philosophical Quarterly* 26 (1976): 267-68.

10. "Meditations Leibniziennes," *American Philosophical Quarterly* 2 (1965): 110. Though he does claim that the notion of timeless truth guided Leibniz's thinking (p. 110) he is clear (pp. 105-10 *passim*) that Leibniz needs to be approached also by another route (in effect the one I shall take).

11. See also M.19-20, 39-40 (G.ii.23,37-38).

12. For further discussion of this matter see A. N. Prior, *Past, Present and Future* (Oxford, 1967), pp. 79 ff., 121; and N. Rescher, A. Urquhart, *Temporal Logic* (New York, 1971), chap. 13, chap. 15, sect. 2.

13. See, for example, A. N. Prior, *Time and Modality* (Oxford, 1957), chap. 2; Rescher and Urquhart, *Temporal Logic*, chap. 5.

14. See, for example, Prior, *Time and Modality*, pp. 18-20; Rescher and Urquhart, *Temporal Logic*, chaps. 2-4; Rescher, "On the logic of chronological propositions," *Mind* 75 (1966): 75-96.

15. *Aristotle: 'On Interpretation,'* commentary by St. Thomas and Cajetan, trans. J. T. Oesterle (Milwaukee, WI, 1962), xiii.11 (p. 107); see also xiv.19 (p. 118), and Aquinas' *The Disputed Questions on Truth*, trans. R. W. Mulligan (Chicago, 1952), General reply and answer to ninth difficulty to Q.2, art. 12 (vol. i, pp. 118, 123).

16. See also L.493, 531, M.51, 64 (G.iv.518, ii.252, 47, 57).

17. See also LG.24, M.63 (G.iv.440, ii.56).

18. See also L.495, 576, 593 (G.iv.521, 557, D.ii.223).

19. L.269, LG.13, 24, 44, Lt.253, M.63, 64 (C.520, G.iv.433, 440, 451, vi.617, ii.56, 57).

20. See also L.580, 613, Lt.231 (G.iv.563, ii.503, vi.610).

21. See G.ii.47, 57, 252, D.ii.224. For various translations see L.337, 531, 593, M.51, 64.

22. L.580, M.119 (G.iv.564, ii.95).

23. See also L.576, 593, M.51, 92, 115-16, 161, 170 (G.iv.557-58, D.ii.223, G.ii.46-47, 74-75, 91-93, 126, 136).

24. See also L.312, 360, 441, 535, M.51, 161, 167, 170 (G.iv.439-40, ii.136, GM.vi.242, G.ii.264, 47, 126, 133, 136). But compare L.387 (G.iv.360).

25. M.51, 65 (G.ii.47, 58). Leibniz discusses the view more often in the specific context of God's bringing about changes in the mind (or body) on the occasion of changes in the body (or mind), e.g., L.457, 587 (G.iv.483, vi.540).

26. L.441, M.51-52, 114-19 (GM.vi.242, G.ii.47, 91-95).

27. See especially L.494-95, M.114-18 (G.iv.520-21, ii.91-94) and also L.441, 457, 501, 587, 593, M.65 (GM.vi.242, G.iv.483-84, 507-8, vi.540-41, D.ii.223).

28. For some historical details see Loemker's notes and references at L.498 and 508.

29. "Temporal Flux," *American Philosophical Quarterly* 3 (1966) [= TF] . See also "Time and the Physical Modalities," *The Monist* 53 (1969) [= TPM] , "Ability as a species of possibility," *The Nature of Human Action*, ed. Myles Brand (Glenview, IL, 1970). I speak of 'adaptation' because in fact McCall is developing a theory of dated propositions of the form Rtp. He would deny my distinction between these and those of the form CRtp and say that, *as I have explained them here*, there are no propositions of the former sort. He would hold that the future is determinate only to the extent that it is determined (cf. note 7).

30. Commentary on Aristotle's *On Interpretation*, xiv.11 (p. 114); see also xiii.9, xiv. 19, and *Disputed Questions on Truth*, Gen. reply and ans. to seventh diff. to Q.2, art. 12 (vol. i, pp. 118, 121).

31. Siger of Brabant, "On the necessity and contingency of causes," in *Medieval Philosophy: selected readings*, ed. H. Shapiro (New York, 1964). p. 430.

32. See TPM, p. 437 (also TF, p. 280) and Rescher and Urquhart, *Temporal Logic*, chap. 7.

33. See the semantics of my "Tensed Modalities," *Journal of Philosophical Logic* 2 (1973): 406 f., and footnote 13 of "Leibniz's Principle of Pre-Determinate History."

34. L.501, 533, 534, 535 (G.iv.508, ii.258,263, 264). Leibniz had to make it clear to de Volder that this doesn't mean that a substance is unchanging. One can always be following the same script even though it lays down different things for different times. An action packed play is not a collage of different plays.

35. See also L.269, 458, 576 (C.521, G.iv.485, 557-58). Sellars ('Meditations Leibniziennes,' p. 6) observes that "to say that the statement 'S$_1$ *will be* ϕ_3 in 1959' is true because S$_1$ *now* plans to be ϕ_3 in 1959 is to . . . embark on an uncharted course." But *given* that S$_1$'s plans are never abandoned or frustrated, charts are hardly needed.

36. See also L.269, 455, 457-58, 460, Lt.219-20, Lg.233, LG.44, PM. 79, 80 (C.521, G.iv.480, 484, 498-99, vi.607-8, v.208, iv.451, vii.312, 313).

37. See K. C. Clatterbaugh, *Leibniz's Doctrine of Individual Accidents* (*Studia Leibnitiana*, Sonderheft 4, Weisbaden, 1973). pp. 20, 57-58; and L.329 note 30, 461 note 9.

38. Cf. Broad, *Leibniz*, pp. 47-48.

39. Leibniz does allow that there is "one case of substance acting immediately upon another: the action, namely of infinite substance upon finite substances" (L.535:G.ii.264).

40. See also L.441, 458, Lt.219, M.161, 170 (GM.vi.242, G.iv.485, vi.607, ii.126, 135).

41. Passages that suggest that even if it were not impossible transient causation would anyway be superfluous provide an overrich mixture of both views (L.269, 613, M.84, 87 [C.521, G.ii.503, 69, 71]).

42. See also L.576, LG.23-24, M.64, 84, 87, PM.79 (G.iv.557-58, 439-40, ii.57, 69, 71, vii.312). R. L. Saw, "Leibniz," *A Critical History of Western Philosophy*, ed. D. J. O'Connor (London, 1964), p. 226a, appears to have the matter completely reversed in saying "real beings cannot interact and consequently their history is enfolded."

43. See also L.195, 502, 505, 534, 555, 559, 594, 663, M.167 (PA.II.i.393, G.iv.508-9, 513, ii.262-63, vi.531, 536-37, D.ii.225, G.iii.575, ii.133).

44. See Broad, *Leibniz*, pp. 92-93; Parkinson, *Logic and Reality in Leibniz's Metaphysics*, pp. 138 ff.; R. L. Saw, *Leibniz* (Harmondsworth, 1954). p. 66.

45. See, for example, M. A. Arbib, *The Metaphorical Brain*, etc. (New York, 1972); P. Calow, *Biological Machines*, etc. (London, 1976); C. P. Raven, *Oogenesis* (Oxford, 1961). E. Mayr, "Teleological and Teleonomic, a new analysis," *Boston Studies in the Philosophy of Science* 14 (1974), makes a start on analyzing the metaphors,

46. "Leibniz's Principle of Pre-Determinate History."

47. *De Divinatione per Somnum* 463 b 29. Trans. J. I. Beare in *The Works of Aristotle*, etc. vol. iii, ed. W. D. Ross (Oxford, 1931); see also *De Generatione et Corruptione* 337 b 4-6. For a good discussion of the future in these terms see P. T. Geach, *Providence and Evil* (Cambridge, 1977), pp. 44 ff.

Some Difficulties in Leibniz's Definition of Perception

Mark Kulstad

There can be little question about the importance of perception in Leibniz's ontological scheme. For Leibniz claims that the only real beings are simple substances and that in them there is nothing to be found except perceptions and their changes.[1]

Given the importance of perception in Leibniz's system, an interpreter of Leibniz would no doubt want to provide a full and accurate account of the philosopher's conception of perception. Unfortunately this is not an easy task. For on a natural interpretation of Leibniz's standard definition of perception, there are serious inconsistencies between the definition and important segments of Leibniz's philosophical system. The interpreter would seem to be faced with a dilemma: either one must accept that Leibniz's system is inconsistent at a crucial point or one must formulate an alternative interpretation of Leibniz's conception of perception that avoids the inconsistency while yet remaining faithful to the Leibnizian text.

The purpose of this paper is to examine significant features of the dilemma. In the first section of the paper, I shall present what I have called Leibniz's standard definition of perception[2] and shall argue for a certain plausible interpretation of two of its key terms. In the second I shall argue that, given this interpretation, the definition is inconsistent with several important Leibnizian doctrines. In the third I shall discuss some alternative interpretations of Leibniz's definition, ones which may save him from the difficulty just mentioned.

I

A preliminary step in clarifying Leibniz's standard definition of perception is to note that the term 'perception' has a much broader sense for Leibniz than it has for us. For Leibniz, the term does *not* refer solely to sense perception. Rather, it

65

refers to the entire range of mental or quasi-mental activities, including such higher mental activities as thought and "intellection."[3] It is this fact that makes it possible for Leibniz to say,

> this is the only thing—namely, perceptions and their changes—that can be found in simple substance. It is in this alone that the *internal actions* of simple substances can consist.[4]

We may now turn directly to Leibniz's standard definition of perception. A representative formulation is the following:

(A)   perception is nothing other than the expression of many things in one.[5]

This is a bit compressed. I shall attempt a partial clarification by focusing on the terms 'many things' and 'one.'[6]

With respect to the term 'one,' the point is fairly straightforward: Leibniz uses the term to refer to a *simple substance*. He makes this clear when, in a revision of "A New Method of Learning and Teaching Jurisprudence," he defines perception as "the expression of many things in one, *or in simple substance*."[7] Consequently, we may expand (A) as follows:

(B) x is a perception of y = df. x is an expression of y in a simple substance and y is "many things."

In addition to capturing the point that the "one" of the original definition is a simple substance, this definition is cast in a form that will be useful in what follows. It might be well to note also that the phrase "in a simple substance" indicates merely that the entity in which the expression is found, i.e., the perceiver, is a simple substance.[8]

The next question is, what does the term 'many things' refer to? On this point Leibniz is not perfectly explicit. Nevertheless, there is good reason to believe that he uses the term to refer to *simple substances*.

To argue for this view, I shall consider three passages, the first of which is a formulation of Leibniz's standard definition of perception and the second and third of which will help clarify the first. The passages are these:

(1)   perceptions [are] the representations of *the compound* . . . in the simple.[9]

(2)   Simple substance is that which has no parts. Compound substance is a collection of simple substances, or monads. . . . Compounds, or bodies, are pluralities, and simple substances are unities.[10]

(3)   A body is an aggregate of substances.[11]

In (1), that is, in the definition of perception, we do not find the term 'many things.' Nevertheless, (1) is sufficiently similar to (A) to make it reasonable to suppose, first, that Leibniz would view them as two versions of the same definition, and, second, that determining what the term 'the compound' refers to will give us a good idea of what the 'many things' of (A) are.

What then does the term 'the compound' refer to? If we consider (1) alone, there is no easy answer to this question. But if we look back only a few lines in the work from which it comes, the *Principles of Nature and of Grace*, we find passage (2), which indicates quite clearly that for Leibniz a compound is a collection of simple substances.

Passage (2) yields this answer in two mutually supporting ways. First, if we take the term 'compound' to be a shortened version of the term 'compound substance,' we can determine immediately from the second sentence of (2) that a compound is a collection of simple substances. Second, if we note that Leibniz uses the term 'compounds' and 'bodies' interchangeably in the third sentence of (2), and note further that he often uses the term 'body' to refer to an aggregate of substances (see (3)), we can reasonably conclude that Leibniz uses the term 'compound' in the third sentence of (2) to refer to an aggregate of substances. Given these two points, there is good reason to believe that Leibniz uses the term 'compound' in the first section of the *Principles of Nature and of Grace* to refer to an aggregate of simple substances. Accordingly, we can believe that he so uses the term in the definition of the second section of the *Principles of Nature and of Grace*, and hence that he there defines perception as the representation of *an aggregate of simple substances* in the simple.

If what I have said thus far is correct, then the following is a natural interpretation of (A):

(C) x is a perception of y = df. (i) x is an expression of y in a simple substance and (ii) y is an aggregate of simple substances.[12]

II

We are now in a position to consider the inconsistencies that arise from Leibniz's definition of perception if the interpretation given in (C) (for the sake of brevity I shall call this interpretation (C)) is correct. To put this another way, we are in a position to show what doctrines Leibniz must give up if he wants to retain both consistency and his standard definition of perception.[13]

We begin with some consequences of Leibniz's standard definition of perception (as interpreted in (C)). The first is

(4)   If something is not an aggregate of simple substances, then there can be no perception of it.

This follows from (C) since any purported perception of what is not an aggregate of simple substances would fail to satisfy the second clause of the *definiens* of (C). The second consequence is

(5)   There can be no perception of a simple substance.

This follows from (4) since a simple substance is not an aggregate of simple substances.[14]

This second consequence is extremely important. If Leibniz retains his standard definition of perception, and consequently (5), he must give up some of his most important views. In the first place, he must give up his view that one simple substance can perceive another.[15] This flatly contradicts (5). In the second place, Leibniz must give up his view that there can be perception of God.[16] For God is a simple substance,[17] and according to (5), there can be no perception of a simple substance. Finally, Leibniz must give up his view that a rational simple substance can perceive itself.[18]

It should not be thought that Leibniz could give up these views and yet do no serious damage to his philosophical system. For example, consider the consequences if Leibniz were to give up the view that simple substances can have perception of God. According to Leibniz, each person is most correctly identified with one simple substance,[19] the dominating monad of a particular corporeal substance. If such a simple substance, or person, can have no perception of God, then it cannot know God, think of God, or believe in God, for knowledge, thought, and belief are all forms of perception.[20] In face of this, it is not at all clear how Leibniz could consistently propose a theological system. Such a proposal would presumably involve thought about and belief in God.

Consider next the consequences if Leibniz were to give up the view that certain simple substances, namely, rational souls, have perceptions of themselves. This view plays an important role in Leibniz's ethics and in his theory of rationality. As for ethics, Leibniz believes that it is a simple substance's perception of itself that "renders it capable of punishment and reward."[21] If his definition of perception makes such perception impossible, the result is an ethical system in serious trouble. With respect to his theory of rationality a similar point can be made. Leibniz regularly links the rationality of a substance with the substance's ability to perceive itself.[22] At one point, he even suggests that without such perception a substance could not reason.[23] If this suggestion gives his actual position on the matter, then it would follow from (C) that no simple substance — including Leibniz himself — could reason.

In short, Leibniz's standard definition of perception appears to be in serious conflict with his theories of theology, ethics, and rationality. This would be problem enough for anyone's theory of perception. But in Leibniz's case, the problem appears to run even deeper. What I shall argue in the next few paragraphs is that Leibniz's standard definition of perception, in conjunction with two of his other views about perception, entails (i) that there are no perceptions and (ii) that there are no simple substances.

The first of the two views is this:

(6)   Every existing simple substance has some perception.[24]

The second is derived from the following passage:

when there is perception of a whole, there are at the same time perceptions of the actual parts . . . ; and there is perception at the same time not only of each modification but also of each part.[25]

For our purposes, the key point here — the second view — is

(7)   If there is perception of something, there is perception of each part of the thing.[26]

Given these principles, and the definition of perception as interpreted in (C), we can construct a *reductio*. Suppose (contrary to (i)) that there *is* a perception. I assume that this perception is of something,[27] and that (by the definition of perception) this something is an aggregate of simple substances. Now according to (7), if there is perception of an aggregate of simple substances, there must be perception of each part of the aggregate, i.e., there must be perception of each simple substance.[28] But, by (5), there can be no perception of a simple substance. Thus, we have a contradiction. By the rule of reductio, we can conclude that there is no perception. And given (6), we can proceed to the conclusion that there are no simple substances.

To sum up this section: I have presented arguments to the effect that (i) Leibniz's standard definition of perception (as interpreted in (C)) is inconsistent with his views about a simple substance's perception of God, self, and any other simple substance; (ii) this inconsistency sets up serious conflicts between Leibniz's account of perception and his theories of theology, ethics, and rationality; and (iii) that Leibniz's standard definition of perception, taken in conjunction two of his principles concerning perception, leads to the untoward conclusion that there are no simple substances.[29]

III

In the preceding two sections, I have presented an interpretation of Leibniz's standard definition of perception (formulated in (C)), and have argued that, given this interpretation, we can conclude that Leibniz's standard definition is at the root of serious inconsistencies in his philosophical system. The alleged consequences are of such gravity that many are likely to think that the inconsistencies arise, not from Leibniz's doctrines, but from the foregoing *interpretation* of Leibniz's doctrines. In light of this, I shall devote the present section to a discussion of three alternative interpretations of Leibniz's theory of perception, each of which can be viewed as saving Leibniz from the putative inconsistencies noted above.

A. There are passages that suggest that my interpretation of the term 'many things' is not quite right. Consider, for instance, the following passage: "Perception is never directed toward an object in which there is not some variety or multitude."[30] Here the suggestion is not so much that the object of each perception *is* a multitude or an aggregate (let alone a multitude or aggregate of simple substances), but rather that *in* the object of each perception there is a multitude (or variety). This suggests the following revision of (C):

(D) x is a perception of y = df. x is an expression of y in a simple substance, and y has some multitude or variety in it.

If this interpretation were correct, the inconsistencies of the preceding section might not arise. For one could argue that since at each moment a multitude (of affections) exists in any simple substance,[31] then, contrary to (5), there *could* be perception of a simple substance. If this point were granted, the inconsistencies claimed in the preceding section would disappear, for every one of them involves (5), which would now be rejected. In short, (D) would save us from the difficulties associated with interpretation (C).

There is a certain plausibility to this interpretation; nonetheless, it is open to a serious objection. The passage does not provide definitive evidence that the plurality of affections present in a simple substance counts as the multitude or variety that must be present in every object of a Leibnizian perception. It merely leaves this open as a possible interpretation. But it also leaves open as a possible interpretation the view that an object of perception has in it a multitude or variety only if it has parts. This, of course, would lead us back to (5) and its associated difficulties. In the face of the imprecision of the passage in question, it is not at all clear that we can use it to provide a definitive answer to the question what the term 'many things' refers to. And even if it did provide a definitive answer taken by itself, there would remain the problem of reconciling it with the seemingly definitive answer provided in section II. What seems to be needed before the proposal above can be accepted as the solution to the difficulties noted in section II is a clearer quotation and some explanation of the initial plausibility of the earlier interpretation of 'many things.'[32]

B. Without further ado, let's proceed to another interpretation of Leibniz's standard definition of perception.

(E) x is a *sense* perception of y = df. (i) x is an expression of y in a simple substance, and (ii) y is a body.

This interpretation is rather radical. It carries with it the claim that Leibniz's standard definition is not, as we have supposed all along, a definition of perception in general, but only a definition of sense perception.

There are two main reasons for proposing this interpretation. The first is Leibniz's continual reference to body in his formulations of the standard definition. If one reflects on passages (1) through (3) above, it will be seen that we could easily have written (E)—*without* the word 'sense' in place of (C). Now it would follow from this that every perception is a perception of a body. This latter claim would be plausible if we viewed the definition as a definition of *sense* perception,[33] but not if we viewed it as a definition of perception in the broad sense sketched out in the first paragraph of section I. (In accordance with this point, I have inserted the term 'sense' in (E) and substituted the term 'body' for 'aggregate of simple substances.')

In the second place, (E) makes good sense of a passage that is quite puzzling given (C). To see this, we must first point out a consequence of (E), one that is analogous to but distinct from (5):

(8)   There can be no *sense* perception of a simple substance.

Notice that it is not stated in (8) that there is no perception at all of a simple substance, but only that there is no sense perception of a simple substance. Notice also that the reason for saying that (8) is a consequence of (E) is that a simple substance is not a body. Since it is a characteristic of a body that it has parts,[34] one could also say that (8) is a consequence of (E) because a simple substance lacks parts. (The reason for this addition will become clear shortly.)

Consider now the passage (from the correspondence with Bierling), which is fairly intelligible given that Leibniz's standard definition of perception is interpreted as a definition of sense perception (as in (E)), but rather puzzling if it is interpreted as a definition of perception in general (as in (C)):

> Spirits, souls, and simple substances or monads in general cannot be comprehended by the senses and the imagination, because they lack parts.[35]

This passage has three main features that fit perfectly the interpretation of Leibniz's standard definition of perception as stated in (E): (i) According to the passage there is no *sense* perception of a simple substance[36] (this is exactly the conclusion, *viz.*, (8), that we derived from (E)); (ii) according to the passage there may or may not be perception other than sense perception of a simple substance—this point is left indeterminate (exactly the same can be said given (E)); and (iii) according to the passage the reason that there is no sense perception of a simple substance is that a simple substance lacks parts (again, exactly the same can be said given (E)). In short, viewed from the vantage point of interpretation (E), this passage says just what we would expect Leibniz to say. The same, however, cannot be said with respect to interpretation (C). Any use of (C) to account for there being no *sense* perception of a simple substance would seem to lead immediately to the conclusion that there can be no perception at all of a simple substance.[37] Thus, given (C), it would be hard to say why Leibniz restricts the passage above to the perception of a simple substance *by means of the senses and the imagination.*

Unfortunately, there is a strong reason for rejecting interpretation (E). In both the *Monadology* and the *Principles of Nature and of Grace*, Leibniz gives every reason to believe that his standard definition of perception is intended to cover *every* case of perception that can be found in a simple substance, not just cases of sense perception. For he proceeds almost immediately from his definition to a statement (roughly) that the only internal activities in a simple substance are perceptions and their changes.[38] Unless Leibniz is being exceedingly careless, he must mean the term 'perception' here in the sense that he has just given it in his definition. Thus, he must be saying that perceptions, of the sort defined in the standard definition, are (along with their changes) the *only* internal activities of a simple substance. This implies that *every* perception in a simple substance is of the sort defined in the standard definition.[39] But it is fairly clear that, on Leibniz's view, there are kinds of perception other than sense perception.[40] Thus, there is good reason to think that Leibniz's standard definition of perception does not apply only to sense perception. Since such limited application is essential to the solution of this subsection, that solution is not without its difficulties.[41]

C. We come now the the final interpretation of Leibniz's standard definition of perception. Although it has problems of its own, it is perhaps the most interesting of the interpretations raised in opposition to (C). I shall sketch it briefly (and rather boldly) in the next paragraph and shall then turn to details.

The interpretation, and the argument associated with it, can be sketched as follows. Leibniz's formulations of his standard definition of perception may be taken in two very different ways, for the term 'perception' may refer to either an individual perception or a perceptual state. (The key terms here will be discussed below; for the moment, it may suffice to say that a perceptual state is the aggregate of all the individual perceptions a substance has at a given moment.) Now in sections I and II, I tacitly assumed that the term 'perception' refers to an individual perception.[42] But this assumption was mistaken. Evidence indicates that Leibniz's standard definition of perception is a definition of a perceptual *state,* not an individual perception. Once this is seen, Leibniz's theory of perception can be saved from the alleged difficulties of Section II.

So much for the sketch. The obvious place to start in considering details is with the claimed distinction between individual perceptions and perceptual states. Leibniz believes that perceptions, in at least one sense, are to be identified with the modifications or affections of a simple substance.[43] He claims further that each substance has several (in fact, infinitely many) perceptions at each moment.[44] Let each of these perceptions, rather, each of the modifications of a simple substance, be an *individual perception* of the simple substance. Consider now perceptual states. On Leibniz's view, "a state is an aggregate of changeable . . . contemporaneous predicates."[45] Since individual perceptions are changeable[46] predicates,[47] it seems reasonable to define the *perceptual state* of a monad at a moment as the aggregate of all the individual perceptions (modifications) that the monad has at that moment.[48]

There is no question that Leibniz often uses the term 'perception' to refer to individual modifications of a simple substance. This much is clear from the passages cited above. What has not yet been supported is that Leibniz sometimes uses the term 'perception' to refer to what we have called a perceptual state. In this regard, consider the following passages: "The passing *state* that enfolds and represents a multitude in unity, or in the simple substance, is merely what is called perception,"[49] and "perception, which is the inner *state* of the monad representing external things."[50] These passages assert that perception is a state. And since (i) a state is an aggregate of changeable, contemporaneous predicates,[51] and (ii) the changeable predicates of a simple substance appear to be individual perceptions, it is not implausible to claim that these passages reveal Leibniz's use of the term 'perception' to refer to a *perceptual state.*

Now the two passages above are definitions of perceptions (though the second may not be a formulation of Leibniz's standard definition). Thus, what they suggest is not merely that Leibniz sometimes uses the term 'perception' to refer to a perceptual state, but, more important, that he sometimes uses the term in this manner in his *definitions* of perception. This is a key point for the present interpretation.

Given the distinction between individual perceptions and perceptual states, we can state the third alternative interpretation of Leibniz's standard definition of perception as follows:

(F)   A perception = df. a perceptual state (of a simple substance) that is an expression or representation of a collection of simple substances.

A few comments are in order. First, despite the presence of the word 'perceptual state' in the definiens, the definition is not circular: as can be seen from the above, this word can ultimately be defined in terms of the modifications of an individual substance, without any reference to perceptions. Second, one might want to know what it is for a perceptual state to be an expression or representation of a collection of simple substances. Though I am not altogether happy with this, I shall say that a perceptual state is an expression or representation of a collection of simple substances if and only if the objects (taken together) of the individual perceptions making up the perceptual state constitute a collection of simple substances. Notice that this account leaves open the possibility that some individual perception has as its object a single simple substance.[52]

We must now consider how the present interpretation might save Leibniz's theory of perception from the difficulties of section II. If interpretation (F) is correct, then there need be no inconsistency in Leibniz's defining perception as the expression of *many* substances in one while yet claiming that there can be perception of a *single* substance; for the term 'perception' need not have the same sense in the definition and the claim. In the definition it might refer to a perceptual state (as indeed it does, given (F)); in the claim (that there can be perception of a single simple substance) it might refer to an individual perception. Thus, it would be perfectly consistent with (F) to assert that there can be perception of a simple substance.

The importance of this may be obvious. The difficulties of section II arose only because of (5), the claim that there can be no perception of a simple substance. And we were forced to (5) only because of interpretation (C) of Leibniz's standard definition of perception. Since interpretation (F) does not force us to (5) (that is, since it is consistent with the claim that there *can* be perception—individual perception—of a simple substance), it avoids the difficulties of section II.

Interpretation (F) and the proposal associated with it make for an attractive escape from the problems we earlier linked to Leibniz's theory of perception. But certain questions must be raised concerning the interpretation and the proposal. In the first place, as far as I know, Leibniz nowhere explicitly draws the distinction between individual perceptions and perceptual states. Indeed, the suggestion of his writings is that he did not have the distinction clearly in mind in thinking about his definition of perception. Consider, for instance, the following exchange from the correspondence with Des Bosses (we begin with Des Bosses's statement):

> Against your profound definition of perception, "the expression of many things in one," it occurs to me . . . that some perceptions seem to be directed toward one object only; how, then, will they be perceptions of many things?[53]

If the interpretation and proposal set out above were correct, Leibniz would very likely have given something like the following answer: "It is true that some perceptions (for example, the perceptions that a substance has of itself) are directed toward one object only; but such perceptions are individual perceptions, not perceptual states; since my definition is of a perceptual state, not an individual perception, the case you suggest in no way opposes my definition."

But Leibniz does not even hint at such an answer. His response consists of the simple assertion that "perception is never directed toward an object in which there is not variety or multitude."[54] Now if he had clearly in mind the distinction between perceptual states and individual perceptions and wanted to allow for the possibility that an individual perception might be "directed toward one object only" rather than "many things," he almost certainly would have stated his answer more fully.

There is a second problem with the present interpretation and the associated proposal. In some of Leibniz's formulations of the standard definition of perception, it is fairly clear that what is represented in perception is *outside of* the simple substance. For instance, in the second section of the *Principles of Nature and of Grace*, Leibniz proposes the following definition: "perceptions—that is to say, the representations of the compound, *or of that which is without,* in the simple."[55] Since a substance is not outside itself, it would seem to follow that no simple substance can have a perception of itself. This is a problematic conclusion, as we saw in section II. It does not seem that there is anything in the interpretation presently under discussion that would allow us to avoid it.[56]

IV

The discussion thus far indicates that a natural interpretation of Leibniz's standard definition of perception leads to devastating consequences and that three alternative interpretations face difficulties of their own. What is wanted, no doubt, is an interpretation of Leibniz's standard definition that avoids such difficulties. At the very least, some relief from this flurry of competing views seems desirable. Unfortunately, I have no such relief to offer. My hope is that I have presented considerations of sufficient importance and arguments of sufficient clarity so that they might be of use as stepping stones to an adequate account of Leibniz's theory of perception.

Notes

1. L. 538 (G., II, 271) and L. 644 (G., VI, 609). In this paper I shall use the following abbreviations: A. = G. W. Leibniz: *Sämtliche Schriften und Briefe*, Reihe 6, Band 6 (*Nouveaux Essais*), ed. the Leibniz-Forschungsstelle der Universität Münster (Berlin, 1962); C. = *Opuscules et fragments inédits de Leibniz*, ed. L. Couturat (Paris, 1903); G. = *Die philosophischen Schriften von Gottfried Wilhelm Leibniz*, ed. C. I. Gerhardt, 7 vols. (Berlin, 1875-1890); L. = *Gottfried Wilhelm Leibniz: Philosophical Papers and Letters*, ed. and trans. L. E. Loemker, 2nd ed. (Dordrecht, Holland, 1969); and Ln. = *New Essays Concerning Human Understanding by Gottfried Wilhelm Leibniz*, trans., with notes, A. G. Langley, 3rd ed. (La Salle, Illinois, 1949). Unless otherwise indicated, translations from C. and G. are my own. In general an effort has been made to cite both English and original language texts.

2. Leibniz does not always give the same account of perception. But numerous formulations, occurring repeatedly throughout the years of Leibniz's philosophical muturity, seem clearly to be variants of the same basic idea about perception. This basic idea I call his standard definition of perception. For versions of it see G., II, 112 and 121 (both from 1687). L., p. 91, n. 16 (from 1697-1700), G., VII, 566 (from 1706); L., p. 644 (from 1714—v. G., VI, 608), and G., III, 581 (from 1715).

3. See Ln., pp. 218 and 178 (A. pp. 210 and 173).

4. L., p. 644 (G., VI, 609).

5. G., II, 311.

6. Of course, Leibniz does not always use exactly these terms in his formulations. What I am trying to get at is the idea behind these terms and similar ones.

7. L., p. 91, n. 16; my italics. Confirmation of this point can be found at G., II, 112 and VI, 608.

8. See G., II, 317.

9. L. p. 636 (G., VI, 598); italics mine. Two points deserve comment here. First, notice that there is a shift from 'expression' in (A) to 'representations' in (1). This is not an accident of translation. In Leibniz's writings we sometimes find '*exprimere*' ('*exprimer*') in such contexts and sometimes '*repraesentare*' ('*représenter*'). Though this can be confusing, it need not detain us. As I have argued in Appendix *A* of "Leibniz's Expression Thesis" (Ph.D. dissertation, University of Michigan, 1975), there is good reason to believe that Leibniz uses the terms interchangeably. Second, it may seem as if I have omitted an important phrase, namely, "or of that which is without." But if I am right, that is, if the term 'the compound' refers to a collection of simple substances, then the phrase will be redundant. For the collection would hardly be within the simple substance.

10. L., p. 636 (G., VI, 598).

11. L., p. 360 (G., II, 135— see also G., III, 622— though it should be noted that Leibniz did not seem to be fully satisfied with the text from which this comes).

12. Some might be suspicious of the shifts between the term 'simple substances' and terms such as 'an aggregate of simple substances.' If we take the latter to mean 'a *set* of simple substances,' then someone might claim that the aggregate (set) of simple substances has some reality over and above the reality of the members of the set. It is clear, however, that Leibniz would not concur in this claim; for he says,

> whatever things are aggregates of several things are not one except in the mind, and they have no reality other than borrowed, that is, other than the reality of the things from which they are compounded. (G., II, 261)

Hence, I shall use terms like 'an aggregate of simple substances' and the term 'simple substances' pretty much interchangeably.

13. In this sentence and in the rest of this section, I speak as if there definitely are inconsistencies. This is not quite right, since I want to commit myself only to the existence of

prima facie difficulties in Leibniz's discussion of perception, that is, to the existence of difficulties *given* that interpretation (C) is correct. However, in the interest of simple exposition, I shall state the argument rather categorically in this section, saving reservations for later. In particular, I shall often talk as if Leibniz's standard definition of perception just is (C) without noting the provisional nature of this identification.

14. Some may feel that I am taking Leibniz's words too literally, that he cannot mean that it is impossible ever to have a perception of some one single thing, something that is not a collection or aggregate. As it turns out, Leibniz and Des Bosses address this question rather directly (in a passage I shall consider later: G., II, 316-17). Though their discussion is not perfectly conclusive, it suggests strongly that Leibniz really did mean to be taken strictly.

15. L., p. 711 (G., VII, 411)

16. In section thirty of the *Monadology*, Leibniz claims that rational souls or spirits can "think . . . of God himself" (G., VI, 612). Recall that thought is a kind of perception.

17. G., VI, 614.

18. See G., VI, 612 and Ln., p. 24 (A., p. 14— *'s'appercevant'* is used).

19. G., VII, p. 523.

20. For "in the simple substances themselves we know nothing besides perceptions or the reasons for them" (L., p. 539 – G., II, 282).

21. G., IV, 460.

22. See, for instance, G., VI, 612.

23. G., IV, 458.

24. Leibniz says, "It does not follow that during this state [a swoon] the simple substance is without any perception. For the reasons already given, that is not even possible, for it cannot perish and it cannot subsist without some affection, which is nothing but its perception" (L., p. 645 – G., VI, 610).

25. G., VI, 628.

26. In this formulation, I shift from Leibniz's term 'whole' to the vaguer term 'thing.' Although this shift does not seem to do any particular violence to Leibniz's meaning in the passage above, it may weaken my argument somewhat.

27. This assumption, while plausible, again weakens the argument a bit.

28. As evidence that Leibniz views these simple substances as parts of the aggregate of simple substances, see L., p. 350, n. 26 (admittedly a barred passage).

29. I shall not attempt to answer whether this conclusion applies to the primitive simple substance, viz., God.

30. G., II, 317.

31. See L., p. 645, (G., VI, 610), which indicates that the affections of a substance are its perceptions, and Ln., p. 47 (A., p. 53), which indicates that each simple substance has, at each moment, infinitely many perceptions. The conclusion above follows from these two.

32. Interpretation (D) may turn out to have problems analogous to some of those of interpretation (C). Assume that interpretation (D) is correct and one simple substance has a perception of another simple substance. According to a passage quoted in section II (G., VI, 628), the first will also perceive every modification or affection of the second. Given interpretation (D), each such modification or affection must have some multitude or variety in it. But if the second simple substance has at least some *simple* modifications or affections (and it seems likely that Leibniz would accept this – v. L. p. 160 for an early view), it is not clear that this will be the case.

33. I am taking the term 'sense perception' quite broadly here, so that it covers not only what is usually referred to by the term, but also imagination and memory that involve images. (Admittedly this is a bit vague, but for brevity's sake, I shall not go deeper.)

34. See L., p. 513.

35. G., VII, 501.

36. It might be thought that I am fudging here, and that what Leibniz is really saying is that there is no sense perception of simple substances. I contend, however, that my interpre-

tation is clearly superior to the interpretation just proposed since the last four words of the passage make sense on my interpretation, but not on the other.

37. Of course, it is possible that Leibniz wrote the passage above without intending any appeal to his standard definition of perception. But if he did have the standard definition in mind, then it seems quite likely that he had it in mind as interpreted in (E), not as in (C).

38. See L., pp. 636 and 644 (G., VI, 598 and 609).

39. In saying this I assume that any kind of perception would count as an internal activity of a simple substance.

40. See, for instance, L., p. 549 (G., VI, 501-2).

41. The solution may face yet another difficulty. The key question concerns a passage discussed earlier (G., VI, 628). If a key part of it ("when there is perception of a whole, there are at the same time perceptions of the actual parts") is interpreted in such a way as to entail that when there is a sense perception of a body, there are at the same time sense perceptions of each of the actual parts (the shift to "each" is supported by the text in question), and if simple substances are actual parts of bodies (v. L. p. 350, n. 26—a barred passage), then it follows that there are *sense* perceptions of simple substances. As we have seen, Leibniz explicitly rejects this view.

42. For simplicity of exposition, I hereby stipulate that (C) involves the claim that Leibniz's standard definition of perception is about individual perceptions rather than perceptual states.

43. See G., VI, 610 and 628. See also Kenneth C. Clatterbaugh, *Leibniz's Doctrine of Individual Accidents* (Wiesbaden, 1973), p. 9.

44. Ln., p. 47 (A., p. 53).

45. C., p. 473.

46. L., p. 644 (G. VI, 608-609).

47. That individual perceptions are predicates, at least in one sense, arises from the fact that they can be ascribed to a substance (on this point and for useful distinctions concerning the term 'predicate,' see G. H. R. Parkinson, *Logic and Reality in Leibniz's Metaphysics* [Oxford, 1965], p. 8).

48. The word 'aggregate' is vague enough to leave questions about the distinction between individual perceptions and perceptual states. Let me offer the suggestion that 'aggregate' be taken to mean what Nelson Goodman's term 'sum-individual' means (see *Problems and Projects* [Indianapolis and New York, 1972], pp. 156-60). We would say then that a perceptual state of a monad at a moment is the sum-individual having as its parts all the individual perceptions present in the monad at that moment.

Now an important question is whether a perceptual state is itself an individual perception. One might answer negatively on the grounds that it is implausible to think of individual perceptions (modifications) as having parts. But the following passage gives reason to believe that Leibniz does think this way: "the perceptions of ideas simple in appearance are composed of perceptions of the parts of which these ideas are composed" (Ln. p. 121 — A., p. 120). (There is no good reason to think that the first use of 'perceptions' refers to perceptual states only, for two examples of "ideas simple in appearance" are greenness and coldness, and we seem able to have distinct but concomitant perceptions of these. One cannot have distinct and concomitant perceptual states.)

What is suggested here is that at least some aggregates or sum-individuals of individual perceptions are themselves individual perceptions. If we allow the stronger principle that *every* aggregate or sum-individual of the individual perceptions that a monad has at a moment is itself an individual perception, it follows that each perceptual state is an individual perception. (The converse, of course, is false—assuming that there is a perceptual state having two or more individual perceptions as parts.) Now I am not at all sure that Leibniz would accept the stronger principle Nonetheless, I want to make it clear that I am interpreting 'aggregate' in such a way that nothing in the definition of 'perceptual state' rules out the possibility of a perceptual state being an individual perception.

49. L., p. 644; my italics (G., VI, 608).

50. L., p. 637; my italics (G., VI, 600).

51. I am appealing again to C., p. 473. There is, of course, the possibility that the term 'state' does not have the same sense there and in the two passages just quoted. If this were so, then the present argument would involve an equivocation. But I do not know of any strong reason to suppose that two senses are involved.

52. G. H. R. Parkinson has suggested that on Leibniz's view we do finally reach a point at which there are perceptions that have single simple substances as objects (v. Parkinson, *Logic and Reality in Leibniz's Metaphysics*, p. 181 — some of his remarks here were helpful in my early thinking about the material in section II).

53. G., II, 316.

54. G., II, 317. This was considered earlier in connection with interpretation (D). As we saw then, the passage suggests an interpretation different from (F). I shall not repeat the details here.

55. L., P. 636; my italics (G., VI, 598).

56. It might be noted that on the interpretation proposed in subsection *B*, there is a perfectly simple explanation of this apparent difficulty. It might also be noted that any interpretation that takes the passage just quoted to be a formulation of a perfectly general definition of perception would seem to be faced with the same difficulty.

"As Though Only God and It Existed in the World"

Robert McRae

Anti-Cartesianism in this century has generally had two main targets, dualism and the problematic idealism, egocentricity, or solipsism associated with Descartes and regarded as the principal influences he has had on the subsequent course of philosophy. By solipsism is meant here the view that all knowledge of existence is that of one's own self and of one's own states, and that the existence of anything else is problematic. In the earlier part of this century—dualism apart—anti-Cartesianism mainly took one form or another of a realism concerned with showing the unproblematic character of the existence of material objects. Since then anti-Cartesianism has been more concerned with the knowledge of other persons and their states of mind—this, however, though Descartes himself gave almost no attention to it, and in the following hundred years, few others who shared in his egocentricity did so either.[1] This anti-Cartesianism inevitably has had a great deal to do with stereotyping Descartes and those who followed him. For that reason I wish to look especially at Leibniz insofar as he may certainly be thought to share in the prevailing solipsism, and to look with particular attention to what he has to say about the existence and knowledge of other selves or persons.

Armed with the right selection of passages from Leibniz's writings there can be no difficulty in showing him to be a solipsist, certain only of the existence of himself and his own states. This is particularly manifest in his account of what constitutes primitive knowledge of fact. "The immediate apperception of our existence and our thoughts furnishes us with the first truths *a posteriori*, or of fact, that is to say the first *experiences*."[2] "Internal experiences are the foundation of all truths of fact."[3] But what other truths of fact can be raised on such foundations? It would appear that, the existence of God excepted, there can be none at all, for Leibniz says,

> I judge without proof, from a simple perception of experience, that those
> things exist of which I am conscious within me. There are, first, *myself*

79

who am thinking of a variety of things and, then, the varied *phenomena* or appearances which exist in my mind. Since both of these, namely, are perceived immediately by the mind without the intervention of anything else, they can be accepted without question, and it is exactly as certain that there exists in my mind the appearance of a golden mountain or of a centaur when I dream of these, as it is that I who am dreaming exist, for both are included in the one fact that it is certain that a centaur appears to me.[4]

How can I tell, then, that the whole of life is not one long dream? Leibniz's answer is that there is no way of telling.

By no argument can it be demonstrated absolutely that bodies exist, nor is there anything to prevent certain well-ordered dreams from being the objects of our mind, which we judge to be true and which, because of their accord with each other are equivalent to truth so far as practice is concerned.[5]

This epistemological solipsism is reinforced by the metaphysical solipsism based on Leibniz's conception of substances as monads. These, because of their simplicity, are incapable of being acted on by other monads. They "have no windows through which anything could enter or depart."[6] Hence all change in the monad arises from an internal principle, so that, as he says to Arnauld, "its succeeding state is a sequel . . . of its preceding state, as though only God and it existed in the world."[7] Nor is this possibility affected by the fact "that every individual substance is an expression of the entire universe,"[8] for the expression of something does not entail the actual existence of the thing expressed; for example, what is represented in a diagram or perspectival drawing need have no existence other than that of being represented. God is under no necessity to make the expressions of a world in one substance agree with the expressions in other substances, or even to create these other substances. Thus he says to des Bosses,

There would be no deception of rational creatures even if everything outside of them did not correspond exactly to their experiences, or indeed if nothing did, just as if there were only one mind; because everything would happen just as if all other things existed, and this mind, acting with reason, would not charge itself with any fault. For this is not to err. That the probable judgment which this mind formed of the existence of other creatures should be true, however, would no more be necessary than it was necessary that the earth should stand still because, with few exceptions, the whole human race once held this to be right.[9]

These passages taken together seem to be uncompromisingly solipsistic. But there is another Leibniz. For this other Leibniz I will look first at one of his statements about the *cogito*, insofar as the concept of the *I* contained in it involves other selves. Then I wish to look at his account of personal identity insofar as the criteria for my identity necessarily involve other persons. Finally I wish to look at Leibniz's argument that if I exist, others necessarily exist.

THE COGITO

Generally Leibniz is concerned with the *cogito* as a primitive truth of fact. In one case, however, in the letter entitled, "On what is Independent of Sense and of Matter," he is concerned with how the concept of the *I* in *I think* becomes the source of all the concepts of metaphysics. What makes it possible for the *cogito* to do this, according to Leibniz, is that I cannot have the thought of the *I* without at the same time having the thought of others capable like me of saying "I." Thus he says,

> This thought of *myself,* who perceives sensible objects, and of my own action which results from it, adds something to the objects of sense. . . . And since I conceive that there are other beings who also have the right to say "I," or for whom this can be said, it is by this that I conceive what is called *substance* in general . . . [and] other concepts in metaphysics.[10]

I shall suppose that what Leibniz calls "the thought of myself" does not differ in principle from the thought of individuals of any kind, whether these be persons or things. His position here is made clearest when he opposes himself to Locke on the knowledge of individuals. Locke in discussing the nature of general terms began by noting that all *things* that exist are particulars, whereas most *words* are general. He believed that it would be impossible to give every particular thing its own name, and in any case this would be useless either for communication or for the advance of knowledge. For these purposes, general words are needed. General words stand for general ideas, and general ideas are formed by abstraction from particular ideas of particular things. Locke illustrates his thesis by means of a child's initial acquaintance with persons.

> There is nothing more evident than that the *ideas* of the persons children converse with . . . are, like the persons themselves, only particular. The *ideas* of the nurse and the mother are well framed in their minds and, like pictures of them there, represent only individuals. The names they first give to them are confined to these individuals, and the names of *nurse* and *mama* the child uses determine themselves to those persons. Afterwards, when time and a larger acquaintance have made them observe that there are a great many other things in the world that, in some common agreements of shape and several other qualities, resemble their father and mother and those persons they have been used to, they frame an *idea* which they find those many particulars to partake in, and to that they give, with others, the name *man*, for example. And *thus they come to have a general name*, and a general *idea*.

Leibniz would agree with Locke that only particulars exist. He would deny, however, that we have particular *ideas*—though we may have particular *images.* Moreover, a general idea is involved in the awareness, recognition, or identification of any particular person or thing. It follows, then, that such ideas cannot be got by abstraction from particulars. All abstraction is from species to genera, never from individuals to species.

> It is impossible for us to have knowledge of individuals and to discover the means of *determining* exactly the individuality of anything except by keeping it under surveillance; for all circumstances may reappear; the slightest differences are unobservable to us; place or time, far from determining of themselves, need themselves to be determined by the things which they contain. What is the more notable in this is that *individuality* contains the infinite, and only he who is capable of mentally embracing the infinite can know the principle of individuation of this or that thing.[12]

As for the priority Locke attributes to proper names, Leibniz points out that, historically speaking, before ever there were proper names, there were common names, and the first proper names originated in the use of common names as descriptions.[13]

There were for Leibniz two kinds of concepts applicable to individuals, (a) complete concepts and (b) incomplete and abstract concepts. The complete concept of an individual, which exhaustively individuates him as, say, Alexander or Caesar, "embraces the infinite" and is thus possessed only by God. Incomplete and abstract concepts are those alone we can have of any individual. Thus we can never be certain that our concept of any individual, however detailed, may not apply to some other individual who would fit the description. That I am confronted by an individual is made evident to me by the senses, but to recognize or identify that individual is to see him as answering to an incomplete and abstract concept. No perception is possible to us of the individual as uniquely this individual, but always only as a bearer of resemblance to other possible individuals. And this would be the case when I conceive of *myself*—"I conceive that other beings *can also have* the right to say I."[14]

Leibniz and Descartes differ significantly in the way they conceive the relation of the *I* in the *cogito* to other thinking subjects. Descartes after establishing that he is a thinking thing goes on to consider his ideas of other things, among which are to be found the ideas of men similar to himself. It is only as a result of having the idea "which represents me to myself" that he is able "to form" ideas representing "men similar to myself."[15] But for Leibniz the idea of myself is at the same time the idea of other selves. The *I* is necessarily conceived as being one among many who can say "I."

Having separated Leibniz's from Descarte's solipsistic *cogito* it is only just, before continuing with Leibniz, to draw attention to an equally unsolipsistic Descartes. When Descartes raised the question, "What am I?" he took as his starting point his former belief that he was a man. In subjecting the former belief to doubt he found that he could reject all attributes of his mind that involved the body, but not the attribute of thought. He concluded that he was a thinking thing. This conclusion soon turned out to be highly ambiguous. On the one hand it could be, and was, taken to mean that he was a mind—"I am not more than a thing which thinks, that is to say, a mind, or a soul, or an understanding, or a reason."[16] On the other hand it could mean, and was taken to mean, that *he had* a mind, though uncertain that *he had* a body. This alternative makes its appearance in the *Second Meditation* every time Descartes refers to "my mind" to "my own mind." *His* mind is that part of *himself* which, unlike his body, is immune to doubt. The himself that has the mind is a man, as the title of the *Meditation* clearly indicates: "Of the Nature of the *Human* Mind, and that it is more easily known than the body" (my italics). In the *Principles* this is rendered: "How we may know *our* mind better than *our* body" (my italics).[17] The "we" are men, for it is men who have minds and bodies. It is the attribution of human identity to the I of the *cogito* that explains and justifies Descartes' copious use of "we" and "us" in the second half of the *Meditation*. It is his identity as human and not as a mind that places him in a public world discoursing with others about the nature of their mind—the human mind.[18]

PERSONAL IDENTITY

In the *Nouveaux Essais* the following dialogue occurs:

> *Philalethes* [representing Locke]. "The word *person* implies a thinking and intelligent being, capable of reason and reflection, who can consider himself as the *same*, as one and the same thing, which thinks at different times and places. This it does solely by the consciousness (*sentiment*) it has of its own actions. . . . We do not consider here whether the same self is continued in the same substance or in several substances; for since consciousness . . . always accompanies thought and is that whereby each is what he calls *himself* and distinguishes himself from all other thinking things, it is also in it alone that personal identity consists. . . . " *Theophilus* [representing Leibniz]. "I too am of this opinion that consciousness or the feeling (*sentiment*) of the *self* proves a moral or personal identity. . . . In the case of man it is conformable to the rules of divine providence, that the soul still retains its moral and apparent identity in order to constitute the same person. . . . It would seem that you maintain, Sir, that this apparent identity can be preserved when there is no real identity. I believe that this is possible by the absolute power of God, but according to the order of things the identity apparent to the person himself who feels himself the same supposes real identity."[19]

In spite of the appearance of agreement with Locke, Leibniz modifies Locke's theory significantly. Where Locke distinguishes the identity of a substance and the identity of a person as belonging to entirely different spheres of meaning or discourse, Leibniz makes his distinction an ontological one between real identity and apparent identity; he then equates personal identity with apparent identity. Thus, he continues,

In the case of the *self*, it is well to distinguish it from the *appearance of the self* and consciousness. The *self* constitutes real and physical identity, and the *appearance of the self*, when conjoined with truth, adds to it personal identity. . . . Both real and personal identity are in fact proved with the greatest certainty possible by present and immediate reflection; it is sufficiently proved for ordinary purposes by our memory through an interval of time or by the concurring testimony of others: but if God by some extraordinary act altered the real identity, the personal would remain, provided the man retained the appearances of identity, as much the internal ones (that is to say of consciousness) as the external, like those which consist in what appears to others. Thus consciousness is not the only means of constituting personal identity, and the witness of some one else or other indications can supply it.[20]

Leibniz's concept of personal identity creates many problems, and these are deserving of a separate study in itself.[21] One obvious question that arises is, to which self, the real or the apparent, does the apparent self appear? To say that it is to the real self that it appears, is to deny that God can separate the two selves, and to say that it is to the apparent self that it appears is to embark on an infinite regress. When Leibniz speaks of "the identity apparent to the person himself" he is implying that it appears to the apparent self. What is important for the present inquiry, however, is that the apparent identity that constitutes the identity of the person is apparent to both inner and outer sense. So far as the determination of identity is concerned, no privileged status is attributed by Leibniz to my appearances to my inner sense over my appearances to the external senses of others. Because no individual remains continuously conscious and any individual cán suffer lapses of memory, the testimony of others is necessary for determining that any individual is the same individual.

If an illness had caused an interruption in the continuity of the bond of consciousness, so that I did not know how I came into the present state, although I remembered things more remote, the testimony of others would fill the void in my memory. I could even be punished upon this testimony, if I had just done something evil with deliberate intention during an interval, which I had forgotten shortly afterwards because of this illness. And if I had just forgotten all things past and were obliged to let myself be taught anew, even my own name and even how to read and to write, I could always learn from others about my past life in my previous state. . . . All this suffices to maintain the moral identity which makes the same person.[22]

Although it may indeed be self-consciousness that makes a self a person, that is, one who knows what he is doing and is therefore a moral and responsible agent, there remains the question, What makes the person the same person at different times and places, or what is it that persists through time? This cannot be a function of consciousness, for consciousness does not persist uninterruptedly. In introducing the criteria provided by the external senses of others, Leibniz is anticipating an argument later used by Kant. Kant says, "For consciousness itself has always a degree, which always allows of diminution, and the same must hold also of the faculty of being conscious of the self, and likewise of all the other faculties. Thus the permanence of the soul, regarded merely as an object of inner sense, remains undemonstrated, and indeed indemonstrable. Its permanence during life is, of course, evident *per se*, since the thinking being (as man) is itself likewise an object of the outer senses."[23]

There is another qualification of Locke's theory of personal identity by Leibniz that may be noted, and it is implied in the quotation just taken from Kant. Locke distinguished between the identity of a person and the identity of a man. *Person* for Locke was a forensic concept; *man* was a biological one. To be the same person did not entail being the same man. The criteria for determining the identity of the person were provided by consciousness, those for the identity of the man were provided by the external senses, for that identity consists, as in the case of other animals, in the same continued organization of changing parts of matter. Leibniz, in making both the internal and the external senses essential for determining the identity of the same person, in effect rejected Locke's distinction between person and man. They are the same. In spite of Leibniz's dubious concession to Locke over the possibility of separating consciousness and substance, a concession that was to lead him to identify the person with the appearance of a self, Leibniz by means of that same concession was led also to substitute the public person or man for that private self that constituted Locke's person.

IF I EXIST OTHERS NECESSARILY EXIST

In the solipsistic passages cited from the letters to Arnauld and des Bosses, Leibniz maintained that it was logically possible that apart from God I should be the only existing mind. Elsewhere, nevertheless, he was prepared to show that it is impossible that other selves not exist if I exist. This change occurred when Leibniz turned to consider the testimony of others as among the criteria for distinguishing the real from the imaginary or illusory. Among the general criteria for making this distinction, the most powerful was "success in predicting future phenomena from past and present ones." Hardly less important, however, was the coherence of any given phenomenon with the rest of life, "especially if many others affirm the same thing to be coherent with their phenomena also." We have noted already that for Leibniz there are no criteria that will determine absolutely that bodies exist. Phenomena taken in their totality may satisfy all the criteria for distinguishing the real from the illusory and yet be illusory. But what, then, about the existence of others, those whose testimony counts among the criteria for distinguishing the real from the illusory? Is it not possible that all those who testify to me are illusory also? To this question Leibniz has two answers, yes and no. In the *Nouveaux Essais*, the others providing testimony are counted merely as phenomena among other phenomena. Thus Leibniz says,

> I think that the true criterion in the case of sensible objects is the connection of phenomena, that is to say, the connection of what occurs in different places and times, and in the experiences of different men, *who are themselves very important phenomena in this regard* [my italics].[24]

Here the value of the testimony of others lies simply in the greater comprehensiveness of the phenomena brought under the requirement of coherence in *my* world. But where the same subject is treated in *On the Method of Distinguishing Real from Imaginary Phenomena*, Leibniz finds the strength of the testimony of others to lie, not in greater comprehensiveness, but in that it is certain that others exist

> especially if many others affirm the same thing . . . for it is not only probable but certain, as I shall show directly, that other substances exist which are similar to us.[25]

Here the criterion for the real applies to phenomena as public objects in an intersubjective world. This demonstration Leibniz promises to give for the existence of other minds is stated in the following way:

> That all existing things have . . . intercourse with one another can be proved . . . both from the fact that otherwise no one could say whether anything is taking place in existence or not, so that there would be no truth or falsehood for such a proposition, which is absurd; and because there are no extrinsic denominations, and no one becomes a widower in India by the death of his wife in Europe unless a real change occurs in him. For every predicate is contained in the nature of a subject. . . . Hence it is at once clear that there exist many minds besides ours.[26]

This is not the only occasion on which Leibniz used this peculiar type of argument, i.e., the argument that "otherwise there would be no truth or falsehood." He used it for the principle of identity, as, for example, when he says that without it "there would be no difference between truth and falsehood,"[27] or again, that without it "all belief, affirmation or negation would be in vain."[28] In the present case he is saying that the same would follow for existential propositions about individuals that assert their relations with other individuals, for in all propositions whatever, including those about existing individuals, the predicate is contained in the subject. It is the denial of *this* general principle, *predicatum inest subjecto* that is the denial that there would be any truth or falsehood. Indeed, to Arnauld he makes this principle the very definition of truth—*"predicatum inest subjecto*—otherwise I do not know what truth is."[29] The principle of sufficient reason, in that one of its forms in which it means that every true proposition has an a priori proof, asserts simply that every truth is analytic, i.e., that in every true proposition the predicate is contained in the subject. The two principles, that of identity (or contradiction) and that of sufficient reason, are usually given by Leibniz as together constituting the basis of all reasoning. They are both defended in the same way, namely that without them there would be nothing true or false, or nothing could be affirmed or denied. Granted, then, the second of these principles, it is certain that if I exist other minds exist.

But if Leibniz uses this type of argument to establish with certainty the existence of other minds, surely, it will be said, the same argument will establish with equal certainty the existence of the whole physical universe, for the relation of everything in that universe to me is contained in my concept. The relational predicates of the widower in India include not only his wife in Europe but equally all the lands and seas between them. The latter must, then—it might be said—in all consistency, be real phenomena, not illusory or dream phenomena. By real phenomena I understand Leibniz to mean well-founded phenomena. It is entelechies or bare monads that well-found them. Entelechies are no less monads than are minds. So, must it not be that any argument for the existence of minds will be valid for entelechies, thereby establishing the reality of the whole world of coherent phenomena? Such a conclusion would follow, but on one condition, that the relational predicates of the widower include not only other minds and physical phenomena but also the entelechies well-founding these phenomena. This condition cannot, I think, be met. There is sufficient evidence for believing that Leibniz did not regard the relational predicates of individuals as including those entelechies that are the foundation of physical phenomena. To begin with, he did not regard the entelechies as contained in or as parts of phenomena. He says

Accurately speaking, matter is *not composed* of these constitutive unities [monads] but *results* from them, since mass is nothing but a phenomenon grounded in things, like the rainbow, or the mock-sun, and all reality belongs only to unities. Phenomena can therefore always be divided into lesser phenomena which could be observed by other more subtle animals, and we can never arrive at smallest phenomena. Substantial unities are *not parts* but foundations of phenomena.[30]

A reference to phenomena is not, then, a reference to the foundations of phenomena, that is, not a reference to these unities or entelechies. No scientific discourse on physical phenomena so much as mentions them or has any need to. A predicate relating a physical phenomenon to the life history of an individual does not in doing so relate the well-founding entelechies. these belong to no one's life history, except as possible subjects for them to talk about if they happen to be philosophers. There is a second point to consider. Leibniz speaks of active and passive forces insofar as they are attributed to physical phenomena as *abstractions* from the primitive forces or monads of which they are the changing modifications. As abstractions they are deprived of, or cut off from, their connections with monads, so that once again it must be said that the predication to an individual of any relations he may have to phenomena, including their dynamic properties, will exclude reference to the monads. The subjects of these dynamical properties are, within the context of experience, phenomena, not monads. Accordingly when relations to phenomena are predicated of the individual, monads are not included in those predications.[31] It will be useless therefore to appeal to the principle *predicatum inest subjecto* to establish that the whole physical world is not just a dream world.

If I exist, it is then certain that other minds exist; it is not certain that there are entelechies. If, however, the physical world, as opposed to the community of minds, is only a dream, or a grand illusion, it is nevertheless an intersubjective illusion, within which all minds are able to testify to the shared and interlocking coherence of their sensible experiences.

Notes

1. Apart from Leibniz the most prominent exception is Berkeley in the *Alciphron*: "At first methought a particular structure, shape, or motion was the most certain proof of a thinking reasonable soul. But a little attention satisfied me that these things have no necessary connexion with reason, knowledge, and wisdom. . . . Upon second thoughts, therefore, and a minute examination of this point, I have found that nothing so much convinces me of the existence of another person as his speaking to me. It is my hearing you talk that, in strict and philosophical truth, is to me the best argument for your being." *The Works of George Berkeley*, Vol. III, ed. T. E. Jessop (Edinburgh, 1950), p. 148.

2. *Nouveaux essais sur l'entendement humain* IV, ix, 2 (abbreviated as *NE*).

3. *Die philosophischen Schriften von Gottfried Wilhelm Leibniz*, ed. C. I. Gerhardt, 7 vols. (Berlin, 1875-1890), Vol. 4 p. 327 (abbreviated as G).

4. *On the method of Distinguishing Real from Imaginary Phenomena*, G VII, p. 319; also cited in *Gottfried Wilhelm Leibniz: Philosophical Papers and Letters*, ed. and trans. L. E. Loemker, 1st ed. (Chicago, 1956), p. 603 (abbreviated as L).

5. *Ibid*,. G VII, 320-21; L, 604-5.

6. *Monadology*, § 7.

7. G II, 57; L, 518.

8. *Ibid*.

9. G II, 496; L, 995.

10. G VI, 502; L, 891.

11. *An Essay Concerning Human Understanding*, III, iii, 7.

12. *NE*, III, iii, 6.

13. Leibniz provides numerous examples, *NE* III, iii, 5.

14. Cf. Margaret Wilson, "Leibniz: Self-Consciousness and Immortality in the Paris Notes and After," in *Archiv für Geschichte der Philosophie*, Band 58 (1976), p. 344. A propos the complete concept theory of the individual, Wilson quotes from a letter of Leibniz to Arnauld: "It is not enough in order to understand what this *I* is, that I feel myself to be a substance that thinks, it would be necessary to conceive distinctly that which distinguishes me from all other possible minds; but I have only a confused experience of this" (G II, 53). She comments on this, "It seems, then, that the most I can be aware of through self-consciousness is myself as *a* substance which thinks, *not* as some specific substance in distinction from others."

15. *Meditation III, Oeuvres philosophiques de Descartes*, ed. F. Alquié (Paris, 1963-1973), Vol. II, p. 441 (abbreviated as Alquié): *The Philosophical Works of Descartes*, ed. and trans. E. S. Haldane and G. R. T. Ross (Cambridge, 1931), Vol. I, 164 (abbreviated as HR).

16. *Meditation II*, Alquié, Vol. II, 419; HR, Vol. I, 152.

17. *Principles of Philosophy*, Part I, xi.

18. This second Descartes found in *Meditation II* must be reckoned among the "anti-Cartesians." P. F. Strawson, in describing a "central error in Cartesian dualism," writes, "The difference between the Cartesian and his opponent is a difference of view about the *relation* between the concept of a person on the one hand and the concept of a person's mind on the other. The anti-Cartesian holds that the concept of a person's mind has a secondary or dependent status. The fundamental concept, for him, is that of a human being, a man, a type of thing to which *all* those various classes I distinguished earlier can be ascribed . . . the anti-Cartesian holds that the concept of a mind or consciousness is dependent on the concept of a living person." "Self, Mind and Body," *Freedom and Resentment and Other Essays* (London, 1974), p. 171.

19. *NE*, II, xxvii, 9.

20. *Ibid.*

21. Margaret Wilson, "Leibniz," has considered this concept within the context of the problem of immortality. She finds that Leibniz's statements do not form a coherent position: "The difficulty arises from trying to conjoin the following propositions, as this chapter of the *New Essays* seems to require: (1) I *am* a particular immaterial substance; (2) it is metaphysically possible that I continue as an identical self-consciousness and identical self, independently of this particular substance" (p. 346).

Further difficulties are considered by Samuel Scheffler in "Leibniz on Personal Identity and Moral Responsibility," *Studia Leibnitiana*, Band VIII, 1976, pp. 219-40.

22. *NE*, II, xxvii, 9.

23. *Critique of Pure Reason*, trans. N. K. Smith (London, 1933), B 415. I cite Leibniz's position as anticipating Kant's because of the very great importance attached by P. F. Strawson to the latter. In commenting on Kant's statement he says, "A man is something perceptibly (if only relatively) permanent, a persistent and identifiable object of intuition, a possible subject of a biography or autobiography. Instead of talking, dubiously, of an experiential route through the world, of one series of experiences constituting such a route, we may talk confidently, of an undeniably persistent object, a man, who traces a physical, spatio-temporal route through the world and to whom a series of experiences may be described with no fear that there is nothing persistent to which they are being ascribed" *The Bounds of Sense* [London, 1966], p. 164).

24. *NE*, IV, ii, 14.

25. G VII, 320; L, 604.

26. G VII, 321-22; L, 606.

27. G V, 14-15.

28. *NE*, IV, xviii, 9.

29. G II, 56; L, 517.

30. G II, 26; L, 873.

31. See particularly the letters to De Volder 20 June 1703, 30 June 1703, G II, 248 ff, 268 ff; L, 859 ff, 873 ff.

Leibniz on Hypothetical Truths

Hidé Ishiguro

Throughout his life, Leibniz was interested in what he called "hypothetical truths" or truths that were expressed by conditional propositions. As his concern did not seem to be shared by his philosophical contemporaries, (nor for that matter by philosophers who wrote after him), he did not work out his thoughts as thoroughly as in areas where he was able to make long critical studies of the views of other philosophers (as for example on essence, on definitions, on innate ideas, on the mind-body problem), or where he entered into philosophical exchanges and debates with other important thinkers (as on matter, force, space and time, freedom and necessity). Nevertheless some of his thoughts on conditional propositions embody insights that were only rediscovered and articulated by twentieth-century thinkers such as Frank Ramsey[1] and Von Wright.[2]

Truths whose realizations depend on the obtaining of specific premises were among the topics that exercised Leibniz's thoughts since very early on. His interest in this subject was first aroused when he was a young law student. Many rights that people have under law are not absolute rights but conditional rights. For example, a person has a right to the family estate if his father dies; a person has a right to change his name so long as it does not lead to misappropriation. A man's liabilities may be conditional also. An insurer may be liable to pay a certain amount if a building burns down. This liability is something objective, not a subjective belief. If anyone buys his business, it is worth that much less.

When Leibniz was 19, he wrote a baccalaureate dissertation called *De*

This is based on a paper, given in French, to the conference of the 200th Anniversary of Leibniz in Paris, at Chantilly in November, 1976, organized by the Leibniz Gesellschaft. In writing that paper I profited from comments by Jonathan Bennett, Hugh Mellor, and Bas Van Fraassen, although I believe they would disagree with some of the views I hold. In writing this version I profited from discussions with Hans Kamp and David Wiggins.

Conditionibus (On Conditions). Leibniz explains that his aim is to clarify what is asserted by hypothetical propositions in law. He wrote two papers on the subject. He incorporated these into a more substantial paper *Specimina Juris* (Samples of Law), which he finished in 1669 when he was 23.[3] In these papers, as we shall see later in more detail, his algorithmic talents are used to work out a numerical computation of the likelihood of the truth of the consequent of conditional propositions given in the form: "If one of the ships returns from Asia, I shall give you 100 (thalers)."

Because Leibniz was prompted to his investigation of the logic of conditionals by his interest in conditional rights, he was able to treat the subject in a fresh way. The Stoic and the medieval logicians who discussed conditionals, such as Abelard and Peter of Spain, understood conditional statements as assertions of necessary connection between propositions.[4] Peter of Spain had written that all conditional truths were necessary. The necessity was assumed to come from the nature of the antecedent and consequent. In law, on the other hand, hardly ever does any logical or necessary relation of meaning exist between conditions and the rights they qualify. If we think of Leibniz's example given above, no one would be tempted to think that there is any logical relation, or meaning relation between the propositions "One of the Ships returns from Asia" and "I give you 100 thalers." Thus Leibniz was able to see that what was in question was a particular kind of link between the truth of one proposition and the truth of another. He was also able to see the assertion of a conditional not as the assertion of the existence of the link, but as a conditional assertion of the consequent. The assertion *indicates* but does not itself assert the link.

Three years later Leibniz went to Paris where he was to remain for 4 years. (He wrote that he hardly knew mathematics when he arrived, and had read Euclid as one would read history. But he invented the differential calculus during his stay.) He was exposed to the theories of games of chance that were then being developed by Pascal, Huygens, and Bernouilli, and he became interested in determining the degree of probablity of a conjecture relative to given data.[5] The problem was to estimate the degree of objective likelihood or probability of a conjecture, relative to a set of evidence and a body of beliefs. It is easy to see that this is a natural development of his attempt to work out the logic of hypothetical truths in law.

Leibniz also began to link his interest in hypothetical truths with his philosophical interest in the nature of things, and in essences. This is revealed most clearly in his letter to Foucher written in 1675, some passages of which we will examine later. In fact Leibniz's early interest in conditionals ties in with the central areas of his philosophical interest—the nature of things, essence, and modality, as well as with probability.

The view Leibniz expressed in his very early papers on conditionals were original and still seem so. The idea that the assertion of a conditional proposition is an expression of a conditional truth, or a conditional asserting of the consequent, is not only different from the view that the conditional expresses a special kind of link between two asserted propositions; it also diverges from what Frege claimed at the end of the nineteenth century, that when one asserts a conditional proposition, one is affirming *neither* the antecedent *nor* the consequent. For Frege, the status of the antecedent and the consequent of a conditional is the same so far as their illocutionary force is concerned.[6] Neither proposition occurs assertively.

Leibniz too believed that the antecedent and consequent have force only as constituents of the whole conditional. Each is a "propositio partialis" (non-independent proposition). For Leibniz however, the illocutionary status of the antecedent and consequent are quite different. The antecedent, which he calls the condition (*conditio*), is not affirmed—it is dangling (*in modo non indicativo sed conjunctivo*)—whereas the consequent, which he calls the conditioned (*conditionatum*), is asserted (*in modo directo seu indicativo*). What is Leibniz's point here? Suppose I assert "If the child will have no brothers, she will inherit the throne." Surely I am not asserting that the child will inherit the throne. So what is gained by saying that the proposition "The child will inherit the throne" is given in a direct or assertive mode? Although I am not making an unqualified assertion of this fact, Leibniz holds that I am making a conditional assertion of it. I am asserting that the child will inherit the throne on the condition that she will have no brothers. This is a qualified assertion of the consequent. The role that the antecedent is playing is quite different. I am not asserting in any manner whatsoever, qualified or unqualified, that the child will have no brothers. This is even clearer when I assert "If I can find absolutely no one else with any competence, I will employ you." Not only am I not asserting that I will not be able to find anyone with any competence, I insert this antecedent because I think it so likely that the opposite is true.

Just as a judge giving a suspended sentence can be described as giving a sentence in a certain qualified manner (i.e., on the condition of the accused's failing to behave in a certain manner during a specific period of time), so I can say of my previous assertion that I was asserting in a certain qualified manner that the child will inherit the throne. (I have been told by Professor Stig Kanger and Professor Ingmar Pörn that in Swedish and Finnish the word for suspended sentence means the same as conditional sentence.) Leibniz also refers to the consequent as "the principal" (*Principale*) and to the antecedent as "the accessory" (*Accessorium*).

A conditional proposition is not considered by Leibniz primarily as a complex proposition or a complex of propositions as contrasted with a simple proposition. He contrasted a conditional proposition with a pure proposition. In other words, it is a conditional assertion of the consequent, as opposed to a pure unqualified assertion of the consequent. We might say that we are committing ourselves to the consequent only if the antecedent obtains. As Leibniz writes to Foucher, "All hypothetical propositions assert what will be or will not be, given that some fact or its contrary holds."

Leibniz realizes that in making a conditional assertion of the consequent one is also indicating a certain specific connection between the truth of the antecedent and the consequent. Leibniz calls this a conditionality (*conditionalitas*). It is a link (*junctura*), which is as it were the form of the inference we make. The antecedent and consequent can be considered as the truths that are linked.

This link can be expressed either as an inference (*illatio*), which is the move from the truth of the antecedent to the truth of the consequent, or as a suspension (*suspensio*). Suspension (contrary to our philosophical expectation, as well as to the literary meaning), is not any suspending at all, but the move from the falsity of the consequent to the falsity of the antecedent. In fact it is *modus tollens*. (I had originally expected it to mean a move from the falsity of the antecedent to the suspension of the consequent. We will soon see that Leibniz's logic of conditionals does include such a rule, but what he says about *suspensio* cannot be read in this way.)

Leibniz somewhat misleadingly says at one point that the relationship of conditionality between antecedent and consequent is that of a necessary connection. It is clear from his examples that he is talking about the connection of their truth-values. That is to say, given the facts about the world and about our legal institutions, a necessary connection exists between the truth-value of the antecedent and of the consequent.

Three questions now arise about Leibniz's views on conditionals.

(1)   What happens when the antecedent is false (and when we do not know whether the consequent is false)?

(2)   If the chief point of treating an assertion of a conditional proposition as a conditional assertion of the consequent was to enable one to estimate the likelihood or the probability of the truth of the consequent, can one still talk of the truth of the conditional proposition itself?

(3)   If conditional propositions can be said to be true or false, where do their truth-values come from? Are there objective grounds for their truth-values?

Let us begin with (1). In considering what happens when the antecedent is false, we must examine (a) what happens in this case to the acceptability of the conditional itself, and (b) what happens to the truth of the consequent. (a) The falsity of an antecedent is, in general, compatible with the acceptability of the conditional. The conditional link does not depend on the obtaining in the world of the state of affairs expressed by the antecedent. The fourth theorem of Leibniz's *Specimina* is "An antecedent does not posit anything." The fact that a proposition occurs as an antecedent of a conditional does not entail its truth, or the truth of anything else, including that of the consequent. Thus the falsity of the antecedent does not by itself undermine the conditional link. Nor by itself does it render acceptable the conditional, as a false antecedent of a material implication would. The hypothetical truth "If the fleet returns from Asia, Titius will have 100 thalers" will not become false just because the fleet does not return. Neither will the conditional link be confirmed by the nonreturn of the ships. Thus the contingent falsity of an antecedent will never affect the truth or falsity of the hypothetical truth, or the acceptability or unacceptability of the conditional link. When the antecedent is an impossibility, or a contradictory proposition, the condition never obtains, and the conditional assertion of a truth becomes empty. Similarly the assertion of a right, conditional on the obtaining of an impossible situation does not amount to any assertion of a right. In this case we can ignore the whole conditional. As Leibniz writes "An impossible condition has no effect on rights." Nor need the antecedent be logically impossible but merely physically so. Thus if I say, "If your mother remarries I will give you the house," when your mother is already dead, it is as if I have made no undertaking of any kind. If the antecedent is a logical impossibility, no state of affairs corresponds to it in any possible world (to use the formulation of his later years). So there could be no link between the proposition and any other proposition. In other words, if 'p' corresponds to a logical impossibility, a conditional of the form "If p then q" does not say anything that could obtain. This relates to another seemingly controversial view that Leibniz expressed later when he wrote, "A non-being has no properties." He meant that all propositions of the form, "If anything is f then it is g" are false if f is an impossibility (a *non-ens*). Suppose that in "If *a* is f, then *a* is g," f is an impossible property. Then the antecedent of this hypothetical is a logically impossible proposition that can have no link with any other proposition. In other words, it could not be the case that "*a* is g" is true only on the condition that "*a* is f" is true, if the latter is impossible. As Leibniz equates 'false' with 'not true,' this means it is false that "If *a* is f, then *a* is g."

b) How is the truth-value of the consequent affected when the antecedent is false? As we have seen, if the antecedent is a logical impossibility, it is as if no conditional assertion has been made at all. So we need not even consider the consequent. If the antecedent is contingently false, that by itself does not affect the truth-value of the consequent. Suppose, for example, that the conditional truth "If the metal in the box is gold it is malleable" is true, and that the conditional link holds. Even if it is also true that the metal in the box is not gold, and that the antecedent is therefore false, the consequent may still be true or false. The metal may be malleable tin, or it may be cast-iron.

When the antecedent is a logical impossibility, Leibniz assigns the numerical value 0 to the conditional. When the antecedent is a necessary truth, then it is as if one asserted the consequent unconditionally. So Leibniz gives the numerical value 1 to the conditional. (These numbers correspond to the degree of likelihood of the antecedent, which conditions the consequent, and are used to "weigh" the conditional.) When the antecedent is neither a logical impossibility nor a necessary truth, but a contingent proposition of which it is prima facie equiprobable that it be true or false, then the right expressed by the consequent is properly conditional, and Leibniz initially gives ½ as the value attached to the conditional right. We can often do better than that, however. The estimation of conditional rights comes from a complex assessment of the right expressed by the consequent and of the degree of probability of the realization of the antecedent, which leads to an assignment of a more complex logical structure to the conditional itself. In assessing the first two items, we often find that the consequent or the antecedent (or both) can be seen to be a disjunction or conjunction of further constituent propositions. This enables us to make a further logical analysis of the original conditional proposition. We often find that it is a disjunction or conjunction of conditionals, each having as antecedent or consequent one of the constituent propositions into which the antecedent and consequent of the original conditional was analyzed. Then the numerical value attached to the original conditional right may no longer be ½. It is calculated on the basis of the numerical value attached to the conditional right expressed by the constituent disjuncts or conjuncts. (The value we find is derived with the help of a kind of Boolean algebra, whose elements are n-tuples of 0 and 1 for some appropriate n. It would be the nth direct power of the two-element Boolean algebra. The simplest example would be when the condition or the antecedent p of the conditional "If p then q" can be analyzed into a disjunction p_1 v p_2 . . . v p_n. Then the original conditional will be a conjunction of conditionals "'If p_1 then q' and 'If p_2 then q' . . . 'If p_n then q'." Some of the conjuncts may be given the numerical value 0, in which case the whole conjunction will be given 0, but if not, then since the others may be given the value of 1 or ½, the numerical value of the conjunction as a whole can be calculated accordingly.) Thus Leibniz writes that the numerical value attached to the conditional right can turn out to be any rational number between 0 and 1.

Leibniz's calculus of the degree of conditionality of the consequent carried out in this early work is both too abstract and inadequate. We can nevertheless gauge his intentions.

We come now to the second question (2). We see that when Leibniz gives a numerical value to a conditional right, the value that is derived from the measure of likelihood of the condition is meant to correspond to the degree in which the right expressed by the consequent is conditional. Similarly, when Leibniz talks of hypothetical truths, he is interested in establishing how the obtaining of the truths expressed by the consequent is dependent not only on the antecedents explicitly given but on other data or indications we have. Here we do not analyze the antecedent but weigh it in conjunction with other conditions. (He writes that reasons or indications should not be counted but weighed.[7]) The aim then is to assess the status of the consequent. Is this compatible with Leibniz's occasional talk of "the truths of hypothetical propositions?" It seems that for Leibniz the truth of a hypothetical proposition corresponds to the acceptability of the move from the truth of the antecedent to the truth of the consequent, or from the falsity of the consequent to the falsity of the antecedent; it is the truth of the consequent, given the antecedent. Thus when the conditional assertion of the consequent is justified, one can talk of the truth of the hypothetical proposition.

We are led to the third question. (3) What are the grounds of the conditional truths, of the acceptability of these inferences? Leibniz writes that hypothetical truths depend on something objective, even if neither antecedent nor consequent is realized. (That is to say that whether the consequent is true on the supposition that the antecedent is true depends on things that are independent of us.) Often the acceptability of the inference depends on a promise or contract that people have made, as in the case of conditional rights, which we examined before. In many other cases, the acceptability of the inference, that is, the truth of conditionals does not depend on contracts nor man-made laws. It is an objective fact or something to be discovered.

A hypothetical truth does not correspond to an arbitrary fantasy. Nor do we make hypothetical truths by just defining the meaning of words. We cannot arbitrarily define 'gold' to *mean* "metal that dissolves only in aqua regia," and thus make analytically true the following hypothetical: "If this is made of gold, it will dissolve only in acqua regia." Leibniz says that these truths in no way depend on us. We do not make the truth up, we discover it. And as he points out to Foucher, the possibility, impossibility, or necessity of these matters "is not a chimera that we create, since all that we do consists in recognizing it, in spite of ourselves and in a constant manner."[8] Why is this so? I think we can understand Leibniz's view in the following way. We do not assess hypothetical truths in isolation. To assess a hypothetical truth of the form "if p then q" is to assess whether q is true on the supposition that p is true. We have a body of knowledge and a set of beliefs and assumptions. The antecedent p together with all of these, will lead us to discover whether we are justified in asserting the consequent q. (There are, as we know, difficulties about counterfactual suppositions that Leibniz does not discuss here.)

On what then do the truths of hypothetical assertions depend? According to Leibniz, they depend on what is necessary, and what is possible or impossible in reality. "Necessity, possibility and impossibility make up (compose) what are called essences or the nature of things, as well as these truths which are usually called eternal truths."[9]

Two points of clarification must be made here.

First, it is clear that the modalities in question in this passage are not epistemic ones, but as Leibniz says, have to do with the nature of things. For example, when Leibniz writes in a later work about the possibility of a one-legged man (to point out the weakness of the definition of man as a featherless biped), he is not merely saying that he doesn't know whether there are one-legged men or not.[10] We do of course use the word "possible" for such epistemic purposes, as when I say, "It is possible that she will come wearing a red hat." But he was saying that, when a man loses his leg, he doesn't lose whatever it is that makes him human. Thus we can understand the possibility of a one-legged man whether we encounter one or not. The modality here has to do with whatever nature it is that men have that distinguishes them from other living things.

Second, although the modalities in question all have to do with the nature of things, Leibniz is not talking about one kind of necessity, possibility, impossibility. There are hypothetical propositions about logical and mathematical truths, about physical phenomena, or even about institutional or social arrangements. Correspondingly, the necessity or possibility on which the truth-value of these propositions depends may be logical or mathematical necessity, physical necessity, or even the connection that is consequential upon acceptance of certain institutions or arrangements that are based on natural possibilities. Lebiniz mentions the nature of things involved in "arithmetic, geometry, propositions of metaphysics, or physics, and of morals."[11] It is interesting to note that Leibniz here says that the necessities, possibilities, and impossibilities make up what are called essences or natures on the one hand *and* also what are called eternal truths on the other. The nature of physical things is what *we express* in our attempts to formulate laws of nature. We formulate them as general hypothetical propositions, and commit ourselves to the truth of each of their instantiations. Here we might be reminded of what Ramsey suggested 250 years later when he wrote that "variable hypotheticals are not judgments but rules of judging."[12] For Leibniz, no laws of nature existed apart from things and their properties. He thought that the foundation of the laws of nature was the conservation of energy, the property that all material things shared.[13]

The traditional dispute between realists and nominalists has been translated in recent times into a new idiom. There has been a lively realist-nominalist controversy concerning modalities. And sometimes the debate has been taken to turn on the question whether *de dicto necessity* depends on *de re necessity* or vice versa; this is to ask whether all notions of de re necessity derive *ex vi terminorum* or not. In the case of Leibniz, however, there is no room for so simple an opposition. He believes that things have natures or constitutional properties that make them behave in the way they do. But he also believes that we know these constitutional properties by acknowledging certain hypothetical truths. To grasp the nature of things *is*, for Leibniz, to acknowledge our commitment to these general hypothetical truths. In view of recent controversies, it is perhaps important to notice that there is nothing in Leibniz's letter to Foucher or elsewhere that implies that necessity or possibility is attached to a predicate. The claim he makes is only that the modality of hypothetical propositions are determined by and express *either* the nature of things *or* logical truths, *or* both. He proposes no property of necessarily being hot or necessarily being trilateral, as distinct from being hot or being trilateral. This is not of course to deny that it may be necessary that if something is a fire, then by the very nature of fire it is hot, or that it may be necessary that if something is a triangle, then by its very nature it is trilateral. It is rather the hypothetical proposition of the form "If a is f, then a is g" (rather than just any hypothetical of the form "If p then q") that is necessary, given how things are. As I have said, the necessity of such particular hypotheticals may be derived from a general hypothetical truth whose necessity is assumed. But again this necessity is the necessity of the truth of any instantiation of a propositional schema of the form "if fx then gx" and not of a predicate. In general, Leibniz uses 'necessity' only as a qualifier of truth or connection of ideas. Indeed, for Leibniz, propositions are made up of ideas, which he calls 'terms.' So necessity for Leibniz does derive ex vi terminorum (he considered himself a nominalist). However, just as a truth may be ascribed to a proposition, but is nevertheless a truth concerning the objects the proposition is about, so the necessity that is ascribed to a hypothetical proposition may concern the things the hypothetical proposition is about. It is de re, or about the nature of things.

Again it is important to remind ourselves that by the necessity of a proposition, Leibniz does not understand the analyticity of the sentence that expresse it. For Leibniz, a proposition "S is f" says that the instantiation of the concept S is an instantiation of concept f. (This is true if and only if the concept f is contained in the concept S. What is meant by "contained in" and *inesse* I have argued elsewhere.[14] I will not go into detail here. Very simply, the concept S contains the concept f just in case S is f.)

To say that the proposition that S is f is necessary is to say that its truth does not depend on the free decree of God, and his creation.[15] In other words, in all possible worlds an instantiation of the concept S also instantiates the concept f. Its contrary implies a contradiction. So its truth does not depend on facts about this world. This is not to say that the meaning of the expression 'f' is part of the meaning of the expression 'S,' or that the two meanings are identical. "Triangle" does not mean "trilateral," and the meaning of the latter is not part of the meaning of the former. Thus, "A triangle is trilateral" is not true in virtue of a synonymy, but because the nature of a triangle is such that in all possible worlds it will have three sides.

Similarly, to say that the proposition "S is f" is necessary, given the nature of things, is to say that in all possible worlds in which things are created, S is f. To assert the necessity of the proposition "If the cup is gold it will dissolve in aqua regia" is not to assert that a part of the meaning of "is gold" is "dissolves in aqua regia." The proposition will be true in all possible worlds in which the laws of nature are the same. (i.e., where things of same structures interact in the same way), if dissolving in aqua regia follows from the very structural properties of the stuff we call 'gold' and 'aqua regia.'[16] But this does not mean that people have to know the structure of gold to be able to use the general word 'gold.' It need not be a part of the meaning of the word 'gold' that the stuff it designates dissolves in aqua regia. So the hypothetical sentence used above is not an analytic one. It is the hypothetical propositions then that can be necessary or contingently true. In other words, that which justifies the move from the truth of the antecedent to the truth of the consequent may be necessary or contingent. But the necessity comes from the nature of the things that the hypothetical propositions are about.

If the truth-value of hypothetical propositions does not depend on us, how do we discover it? The truth of hypotheticals that depend on the physical nature of things cannot be discovered in the same way as hypotheticals that depend only on logical and mathematical truths. As Leibniz says, if all of us think carefully, we all come to the same conclusion about the nature of circles. Whereas, the power of reasoning by itself never gets us all the way to truths that depend on the nature of gold. These truths depend on how things in this world interact with other things in this world, i.e., on regularities of nature or the preestablished harmony, regularities that we must observe to come to any knowledge about the nature of things.[17]

Later in the *New Essays* Leibniz disagreed with Locke, who had claimed in the *Essay* that the real essence or nature of things was unknowable. According to Leibniz, the conjectures we base on observation may often be mistaken, and we may come to realize this by making further observations; but there is no *a priori* reason why we should not come to know the structural property of a thing that makes it the kind of thing it is.[18]

It is true that in the letter to Foucher quoted earlier, Leibniz does not work out the distinction between hypothetical truths that depend on logic and mathematics and those that depend on physics, or on morals. (His later works show much more reflection on these matters.) But it is interesting that Leibniz does not, as is often said, assimilate hypotheticals about empirical matters to logical truths. If anything, the direction of assimilation is the other way around. Leibniz here says of *all* necessities that "although they are first in the order of nature, they are not the first in the order of our knowledge." That is to say that even hypothetical truths concerning mathematics, such as "if *a* is a triangle, its angles add up to $180°$," are often discovered through the observation of particular drawings of triangles. By understanding that what we discover follows from the geometrical nature of lines and angles, we can see that they are necessary truths. To identify an object as a triangle is to identify an object whose angles add up to $180°$ in any possible world.

Now Leibniz thinks that we can discover necessary hypothetical truths of physics in the same way. We can observe that these truths seem to be constant and independent of us (this will be the case even if we take a phenomenalist view about the external world, as Foucher does), and we can then understand the nature of the objects that the propositions are about and give these hypothetical propositions determinate modalities. What we observe, Leibniz insists, is only concomitance or regularities. We can, however, grasp the necessity of the concomitance, by relating it to the nature of things and the laws of nature they embody Leibniz therefore agrees with Foucher that we only observe regularities; and yet he tries to develop a theory that will escape Foucher's phenomenalism. The first step is to notice that although a hypothetical proposition "does not assert the existence of anything in the external world," its truth is "something independent of us and does not depend upon us."[19]

We can elucidate Leibniz's thought with an example from the *Nouveaux Essais*. Think of propositions like

"If it is gold it resists nitric acid."
"If it is gold it is denser than any other body."

Both these hypotheticals were thought to be true in Leibniz's time. But Leibniz insists they are conjectures that we make on the basis of observation and induction, and could turn out to be false (as indeed one of them did). If a conjecture of this sort is true, it is true because of the structural property of gold (which Leibniz agreed with Locke that their contemporaries did not yet know).[20] That is to say that the structural property of gold, plus the relevant physical laws, would, if one knew it, enable us to demonstrate why gold has these other properties as well. For example, let a structural property of gold be that its atomic number is 79. If the number of electrons in the outermost shell determines the chemical reactions of atoms, we would see why gold, having this structural property, resists nitric acid and dissolves in aqua regia. Such structural properties are what Leibniz calls essence in the case of physical bodies that are aggregates.

It is important to realize that there may be hypothetical judgments, which we may be justified in asserting at a given time, given the evidence that we then have, but which are nevertheless false (as in the case of the hypothetical judgment that if something is gold it is denser than other metals). We may come to realize that it is false by acquiring further evidence. Thus the truth of hypothetical propositions does not depend on the *actual* state of knowledge of an individual, or even of the human community that has a store of common knowledge. Similarly in the case of conditional rights, the right a man has is dependent on constraints and conditions that actually exist and not merely on those that are believed to obtain. One can think analogously in the case of other hypothetical propositions. The truth of "if p then q" is the truth of q on the condition that p, and *not* on the condition that we believe that p or that we know that p.

It is of course *we* with our interests who assert conditional propositions. And it is only against the background of our knowledge of regularities in nature and of logical truths, that we can work out the truth-value of these conditionals that we assert. The assumptions and background knowledge presupposed depend on the context in which the hypothetical propositions are asserted. But hypothetical truths depend on the nature of things and not on our ideas or habits. Thus the truths may depend on facts about which we are still ignorant, or about which we are mistaken.

Let me summarize what I think is interesting in Leibniz's treatment of hypothetical truths:
(1) By treating the assertion of conditional propositions as the conditional assertion of the consequent, Leibniz was not tempted to look for a logical relation or a meaning relation between the antecedent and consequent in isolation. He was able to see that what is in question is the truth-value of the consequent conditionally upon the truth of the antecedent *and* the existing body of our knowledge, true beliefs, and institutional agreements. (2) He was able to treat conditionals with impossible antecedents in such a way as to be able to ignore them and thus avoid the paradox of strict implications. (3) He attempted, though in a not too successful way, to evolve a method of calculating the measure of condi-

tionality of the consequent.[21] (4) Leibniz believed that there were objective grounds for the truth of conditionals, even in cases where as a matter of fact the antecedent does not obtain; he realized also that these truth grounds do not depend simply on how we choose to define the meaning of words. Some conditional truths are necessary, and this necessity also comes from the things outside us. Leibniz therefore committed himself to the view that necessary hypothetical truths were based either on eternal truths of reason or on the nature or essence of things, and that this was the explanation of why conditional statements could represent real discoveries or errors.

Notes

1. Frank Ramsey, "Truth and Probability," in *Foundations of Mathematics* (London: Routledge & Kegan Paul, 1926).

2. G. H. Von Wright, "On Conditionals," in *Logical Studies* (London: Routledge & Kegan Paul, 1959).

3. G. W. Leibniz, *Sämtliche Schriften und Briefe*, Reihe 6, Band 1, ed. Deutschen Akademie der Wissenschaften zu Berlin (Darmstadt, 1923 –, Leipzig, 1938 –, Berlin, 1950 –), p. 367.

4. See W. E. M. Kneale, *The Development of Logic* (Oxford: Oxford University Press, 1962), pp. 137. 235.

5. See Ian Hacking, "The Leibniz-Carnap Program for Inductive Logic." *Journal of Philosophy* 68 (1971): 597-610.

6. I am using the expression "illocutionary force" in the sense of John Austin. See *How to do Things with Words* (Oxford: Oxford University Press, 1962).

7. Letter to Gabriel Wagner 1696, "Rationes non esse numerandas sed ponderandas, man müss die Anzeigungen nicht zählen sondern wägen," in *Die philosophischen Schriften von Gottfried Wilhelm Leibniz*, ed. C. I. Gerhardt, 7 vols (Berlin, 1875-1890) repr. Georg Olms (Hildesheim, 1965), Vol. 7, p. 521; *Gottfried Wilhelm Leibniz: Philosophical Papers and Letters, A Selection*, ed and trans. L. E. Loemker (Dordrecht Holland: Reidel, 1969), p. 467.

8. Letter to Foucher 1675, *Philosophischen Schriften*, Vol. 2, p. 369; Loemker, p. 152.

9. Loemker, p. 152.

10. *Nouveaux Essais*, Book 3, Chapter 10, Section 18, *Philosophischen Schriften*, Vol. 5., p. 326.

11. Letter to Foucher, 1675.

12. Ramsey, p. 241.

13. See, e.g., *"De Ipsa Natura,"* *Philosophischen Schriften*, Vol. 4, p. 505; Loemker, p. 499.

14. See my "Contingent Truths and Possible Worlds," in *Studies in Metaphysics*, Midwest Studies in Philosophy, Vol. IV (Minneapolis: University of Minnesota Press, 1979), pp. 359-60.

15. *Discourse on Metaphysics*, Section 13, 1686, *Philosophischen Schriften*, Vol. 4, p. 441.

16. See *Nouveaux Essais*, Book 3, Chapter 3, Section 18, and Book 4, Chapter 6, Section 8, *Philosophischen Schriften*, Vol. 5, pp. 273 and 385.

17. "For not all truths pertaining to the physical world can be obtained from merely arithmetical and geometrical axioms, but we must introduce other axioms about cause and effect, activity and passivity, and take account of the order of things" (*Specimen Dynamicum*, 1697, G. W. Leibniz: *Die Mathematischen Schriften*, ed. C. I. Gerhardt, 7 vols. [Berlin

1849-1863] , Vol. 6, pp. 234-45; *Leibniz: Selections*, ed. P. P. Wiener, [New York: Scribner, 1951] , p. 130).

18. *Nouveaux Essais*, Book 3, Chapter 3, Section 17, *Philosophischen Schriften*, Vol. 4.

19. Letter to Foucher, 1675, *Philosophischen Schriften*, Vol. 2, p. 369; Loemker, p. 152.

20. *Nouveaux Essais*, Book 3, Chapter 6, Section 14, and Book 3, Chapter 11 Section 24, *Philosophischen Schriften*, Vol. 4, pp. 289 and 335.

21. See also Heinrich Schepers, "Leibniz' Disputationen 'De Conditionibus': Ansätze zu einer juristischen Aussagenlogik," *Studia Leibniziana Sonderdruck; Acten des II Internationalen Leibniz-Kongresses* Band IV (Weisbaden: Franz Steiner, 1975.) It can be said that I disagree with several of Professor Scheper's interpretations of the formal calculi.

Superessentialism, Counterparts, and Freedom

David Blumenfeld

Leibniz held a view that can be called superessentialism: every property that an individual has (save existence) is an essential part of his nature.[1,2] Leibniz purported to deduce the truth of this doctrine from his Predicate-in-Notion Principle, which states that in every true affirmative proposition the concept of the predicate is contained in that of the subject. If all properties (other than existence) are part of the concept of an individual, he reasoned, then anyone with any other properties would be a different individual.[3]

Superessentialism leads to some rather serious problems about freedom since, for one thing, it seems to imply that *de re* modal predications to the effect that an individual could have behaved differently are always false. And yet Leibniz was firmly committed to a belief in both human and divine liberty.[4] In this paper I want to consider a way of understanding his views, based on counterpart theory, which appears to provide a way out of the difficulties. Later I shall state more precisely what I plan to do, but it is first necessary to formulate some of the problems with greater care.

The arguments I wish to introduce can best be appreciated against the background of a confusion that Leibniz often cautions his readers to avoid. One might suppose that superessentialism implies that all truths are necessary and that freedom—which presupposes contingency—is ruled out thereby. But Leibniz claims that this conflates absolute with merely hypothetical necessity.[5] For example, let us suppose that Adam actually existed and that he sinned by

The research for this paper was supported by a fellowship from the National Endowment for the Humanities. For comments on an earlier draft I wish to thank Bernard D. Katz, C. Anthony Anderson, and Laurence BonJour. I also wish to express my gratitude to the members of the philosophy department at Arizona State University where a version of this paper was read at a conference on the Rationalists. Many of the participants there made instructive comments, and I owe special thanks to Gregory Fitch for an objection that he raised.

accepting the apple offered by Eve. We may then infer that it is an essential property of Adam that he commit this sin. Still, it does not follow, Leibniz claims, that it is a necessary truth that Adam sins. All that follows is the truth of the hypothetical: "N(If Adam exists, Adam sins)." To derive the damaging "N(Adam sins)" we should need "N(Adam exists)" and the latter is false, since Adam's nonexistence is possible. Sinning is part of Adam's concept, but existence is not.

Now, considering Leibniz's system as a whole, it is curious that he should have thought that these considerations got at the heart of the matter. To begin with, if we take into account certain of his theological views, a rather strong argument can be given to show that all truths are (absolutely) necessary. Second, even if we put aside these considerations and grant the distinction between hypothetical and absolutely necessary truths, we can still generate a powerful argument against human freedom. Let us consider the more general argument first.

Leibniz holds that God is a perfectly good being who, in consequence of his goodness, wills whatever is best, viz., the actualization of the best possible world.[6] (Hereafter: 'the best possible world' = 'BPW'). If so, however, this goodness—this choice of the best—is an essential property of God. In other words it is necessary that God wills what is best, if he exists at all. But God's existence itself is necessary, and this, together with what has preceded, implies that BPW exists necessarily. If a certain possible world (BPW) exists necessarily, however, then *all* events are necessary, since everything that occurs is contained in the concept of the world to which it belongs. But, if all events are necessary, no one ever acts freely. One way of reconstructing this reasoning is:

Argument N

(1)   N(God exists).
(2)   N(If God exists, God wills what is best).
(3)   N(If God wills what is best, God actualizes BPW).
(4)   N(If God actualizes BPW, BPW actually exists).
(5)   Hence, N(BPW actually exists). (From (1)-(4)).
(6)   If (5) is true, then everything that occurs, occurs necessarily.
(7)   Thus, everything that occurs, occurs necessarily. (From (5) and (6)).
(8)   If everything that occurs, occurs necessarily, then no one ever acts freely.
(9)   Therefore, no one ever acts freely. (From (7) and (8)).

One thing that should be mentioned about this argument is that Leibniz apparently wanted to deny the truth of its second premise. He holds that it was possbile for God to have chosen something other than what is best,[7] from which it seems to follow: -N(If God exists, God wills what is best). Nevertheless, it is difficult to see how this stance is consistent with Leibniz's superessentialism: if God *is* good, then his goodness is among his essential properties.

An argument that rules out human freedom can be constructed, however, even if we allow that God could have actualized a different world. Let us assume that Adam's nonexistence is possible. Still, the fact that sinning is among Adam's essential properties seems to imply that it is not possible that he should *refrain* from sinning. (Anyone who refrained from sinning would not have been the very same individual as Adam.) But as Leibniz himself occasionally notes, a person acts freely only if it is possible that he refrain from acting as he does.[8] Thus, we may formulate the following argument against human freedom, based on the fact that is is hypothetically necessary that Adam sins.

Argument E

(1)   Adam acted freely only if Adam could have refused the apple.

(2)   But, it is hypothetically necessary that Adam accept the apple. (Adam's concept contains the concept of apple-acceptance and so it is necessary that Adam accept if he exists at all, i.e., it is not possible that Adam exist and fail to accept).

(3)   Therefore, it is not the case that Adam could have refused the apple. (From (2)).

(4)   Hence, it is not the case that Adam acted freely in accepting the apple. (From (1) and (3)).

One of the interesting things about this argument is that—unlike Argument N— it appears that Leibniz accepted all of its premises.

Leibniz had a large number of things to say that bear on these arguments and I cannot even begin to survey them here.[9] Instead, I shall restrict myself to discussing the relevance of some ideas expressed in the *Theodicy* and in the correspondence with Arnauld, which parallel the views of David Lewis in his recent essay on counterpart theory.[10] A number of writers have already noted this relationship and some have extracted from the passages in question a novel Leibnizian account of contingency in which counterfactuals and de re modal predictions are interpreted in terms of counterparts.[11] Although none of these writers has dealt specifically with the free will issue, there is an obvious connection to this problem that deserves to be explored. For example, if one can give a Leibnizian reading of statements like "Mr. so-and-so could have done otherwise" on which the latter sometimes comes out true, then there would appear to be an escape from Arguments N and E. In this paper I am going to examine this idea, arguing that, for all its intrinsic interest, the new way of looking at Leibniz does little to combat the old problems about freedom. I shall first try to show that the counterparts approach is of no help with Argument N, since—contrary to appearances—the counterparts idea cannot sensibly be applied to statements about God within a Leibnizian framework. I shall then argue that although the approach *can* be applied to the relevant statements about finite individuals such as Adam, the answer to Argument E that results from it depends on some extremely implausible assumptions. Finally, I shall show that even if these assumptions were granted, and Argument E were disposed of, this still would not solve the problem of human freedom. For at the end of this essay I shall introduce a third argument against freedom that resists even a tolerant attitude toward the questionable assumptions. It is to be noted, however, that the third argument turns on Leibniz's use of the Principle of Sufficient Reason, not on his super-essentialism per se.

I

Two important passages can be cited that suggest that Leibniz employed the notion of a counterpart. Although Leibniz stresses that Adam's *complete* concept forms a part of exactly one possible world, in writing to Arnauld he tells us that there is an infinity of possible persons who are very similar to Adam:

> by the individual concept of Adam I mean, to be sure, a perfect representation of a particular Adam who has particular individual conditions and who is thereby distinguished from an infinity of other possible persons who are very similar yet different from him.[12]

Leibniz calls these unactualized persons "possible Adams"—though he cautions us that in so referring to them he is speaking somewhat loosely.[13] The same sort of situation is described in the *Theodicy*, where the example is Sextus rather than Adam.

> I will show you [possible worlds] wherein shall be found, not absolutely the same Sextus as you have seen (that is not possible, he carries with him always that which he shall be) but several Sextuses resembling him, possessing all that you know already of the true Sextus, but not all that is already in him imperceptibly, nor in consequence all that shall yet happen to him. You will find in one world a very happy and noble Sextus, in another a Sextus content with a mediocre state, a Sextus, indeed, of every kind and endless diversity of forms.[14]

With these passages in mind, one can appreciate the distinctively Leibnizian character of the notion of a counterpart as it is introduced by Lewis.

> Where some would say that you are in several worlds, in which you have somewhat different properties and somewhat different things happen to you, I prefer to say that you are in the actual world and no other, but you have counterparts in several other worlds. Your counterparts resemble you closely in content and context in important respects. They resemble you more closely than do the other things in their worlds. But they are not really you. For each of them is in his own world. . . . The counterpart relation is a relation of similarity.[15]

On Lewis's account an individual A_2 in a world W_2 is a counterpart of an individual A_1 in world W_1 just in case A_2 closely resembles A_1 and no other individual in W_2 resembles A_1 more closely than does A_2. Although strictly speaking there is no identity of individuals across worlds, nevertheless:

> we might say, speaking causally, that your counterparts are you in other worlds, that they and you are the same; but this sameness is no more a

literal identity than the sameness between you today and you tomorrow. It would be better to say that your counterparts are men you *would have been* had the world been otherwise.[16]

If we use Lewis's concept it would appear that the "Adams" and Sextuses" to whom Leibniz refers are among the counterparts of "our" Adam and "our" Sextus, respectively.

Lewis wishes to use his counterpart scheme to give an account of counterfactuals and of de re modal predications, and there are indications that Leibniz may have had similar intentions. In the letter to Arnauld quoted above, Leibniz was responding to the latter's charge that, once God actualizes Adam, everything that will happen to the human race "is obliged to happen through a more than fatal necessity."[17] Leibniz's reply suggests that he thinks an account of what Adam could have done can be given by reference to the many other "possible Adams." Much the same is true of the *Theodicy* passage in which Leibniz is, in part, trying to rebut the claim that Sextus could not have behaved otherwise than he did. In the dialogue with which the *Theodicy* closes Leibniz has the character, Sextus, proclaim that he is condemned to be wicked and unhappy. The God, Jupiter, answers,

If you will renounce Rome, the Parcae shall spin for you different fates, you shall become wise, you shall become happy.[18]

Since the possibility of Sextus's renouncing Rome is explained vis-à-vis the various "possible Sextuses," it appears that Leibniz is trying to provide a legitimate sense, or reading, of counterfactuals in terms of counterparts.[19]

To come to closer grips with the issues involved here, we first need to set out the Leibnizian notion of a counterpart with greater care and in particular to see how it differs from Lewis's treatment of this idea. Fortunately, much of the work has already been done for us. In an exceptionally fine paper on the topic of Leibniz's essentialism, Fabrizio Mondadori calls attention to the similarities between Lewis's and Leibniz's views that I have mentioned so far.[20] But he argues that, despite the likenesses, there are several important dissimilarities. First, Lewis allows for the possibility of there being a world in which two individuals, A_1 and A_2, are both counterparts of, for example, "our" Sextus,[21] whereas Mondadori believes that Leibniz rejected this idea. It was Leibniz's view, he argues, that no individual of the actual world can have more than one counterpart in any of the worlds in which he has any counterparts at all. Mondadori calls this the "uniqueness requirement."[22]

We can see to it that the uniqueness requirement is satisfied, he claims, if we take it that Leibniz would have departed from Lewis's scheme in other ways too. For Lewis the counterpart relation is a relation between individuals,[23] but for Leibniz it would best be regarded as a relation between complete concepts.[24] As Lewis presents it, the counterpart relation is reflexive, but it is neither transitive nor symmetric.[25] Mondadori supposes that Leibniz would have regarded it as having all three of these properties.[26] In particular he believes that

Leibniz would have treated the notion of a counterpart as an equivalence relation on the set S_c of exemplified and nonexemplified complete concepts. If we make these assumptions and, following Mates,[27] identify each possible world (other than the actual world) with a maximal set of compossible complete concepts then,

> we easily see that such a relation partitions the set S_c into mutually exclusive equivalence classes of concepts. Each such class can be informally characterized by saying (1) that it has a "distinguished" member, to wit, the complete concept which is exemplified in the actual world, (2) that it has exactly one "distinguished" member, and (3) that no two members thereof can belong to the same possible world. (3) clearly implies that each exemplified complete concept has at most one counterpart in each world. (This was our uniqueness requirement).[28]

Treating the counterpart relation in this way we can regard each unactualized "Sextus" (or "Adam") as a complete concept that is a counterpart in its own world of the concept exemplified by "our" Sextus (or Adam) in the actual world. The equivalence class of concepts whose "distinguished" member is the concept exemplified by "our" Sextus is referred to by Mondadori as C_{Sextus}.[29]

On this basis Mondadori constructs a Leibnizian reading of counterfactuals and de re modal predications that is consistent with superessentialism. We know that according to Leibniz "our" Sextus could not have had a different history from the one he did have: it is hypothetically necessary that exactly these events befall him. Anyone who underwent other events would not have been the same individual denoted by the name "Sextus" in "our" world. So strictly speaking, the only modal property possessed by Sextus is that of *possibly not having existed*. In view of this Mondadori notes that we are not in a position to give a true, *literal* reading to any counterfactuals or de re modal predications whose antecedents contain a proper name. For example, consider the case where the counterfactual is: (1) If Sextus had not raped Lucretia, he would have led a happy life. If we wish to give a Leibnizian reading of (1) on which it comes out true, we may not interpret it to mean that Sextus has the counterfactual property expressed by the following formula: (2) If x had not raped Lucretia, x would have led a happy life. To claim that Sextus satisfied (2) would be to say that it is possible that Sextus himself ("our" Sextus) should have had a different history. But there is an alternative way of reading (1) on which it does come out true. We may take (1) to attribute to Sextus,

> the property of having a complete concept one of whose counterparts is such that (a) it does not entail the property of *raping Lucretia*, and (b), as a consequence of this, the property of *leading a happy life* follows from it. Alternatively, and equivalently, we could say that (1) is true just in case the property of *leading a happy life* follows from $c_i \epsilon C_{Sextus}$ which does not entail the property of *raping Lucretia*, and which otherwise differs minimally from the concept exemplified by Sextus in the actual world.[30]

When Leibniz asserts that (1) is true, this may tend to give rise to a paradox because it *seems* that he is attributing to Sextus the property expressed by (2). But *really* he is not doing this at all.

Likewise, when Leibniz asserts that Sextus might have ϕ'd, although he *appears* to be attributing to Sextus the property of *possibly having* ϕ'*d*, he really should be taken to be attributing to him the property of *having a complete concept one of whose counterparts entails the property of* ϕ'*ing*. He should be understood to be speaking, *via Sextus himself*, of the concept in another world that is the counterpart of the concept exemplified by "our" Sextus in the actual world. Specifically,

> a de re modal predication such as "*a* might have ϕ'd" will be true just in case there is a complete concept c_a from which the property of ϕ'ing follows, and which otherwise differs minimally from the concept exemplified by *a* in the actual world.[31]

"Sextus might have lived a happy life" (taken nonliterally) says that "our" Sextus has a complete concept one of the counterparts of which contains the property of *leading a happy life*. Had that counterpart been actualized, the name "Sextus" would have denoted this other individual and, consequently, "Sextus leads a happy life" would have been true.

This interpretation involves a treatment of proper names that Mondadori calls "deferred naming."[32] Deferred naming includes three separate stages. The "starting point" is an actual individual, the "middle point" is a nonexemplified complete concept, and the "end point" is whoever would have exemplified the concept in question had the world to which this concept belongs been actualized. We start from Sextus and his complete concept, where "Sextus" in, for example, (1), names "our" Sextus. Then, by altering Sextus's complete concept in the ways required by the relevant counterfactual or de re modal predication, we arrive at a "new" concept. The alterations we have made take us from Sextus and his complete concept to another complete concept. Thus, whereas (1) is *directly* about "our" Sextus, it is *indirectly* about whoever would have exemplified the "new" concept if the world of which the latter is a member had been actualized.

By stressing that there is a nonliteral reading to be given to counterfactuals and de re modal predications, we obtain an interpretation of the latter that is compatible with Leibnizian essentialism. With the exception of existence, all of Sextus's properties are essential. Among these, however, is the property of having such-and-such counterparts in such-and-such worlds. But since, for example, a de re modal predication to the effect that Sextus might have ϕ'd says only that Sextus has a concept with a particular counterpart, Leibniz's view of essential properties does not rule out that Sextus might have ϕ'd. On the contrary, it implies that if Sextus's concept has the appropriate counterpart, then it is essential to Sextus that he might have ϕ'd. Contingencies of this type are built into an individual's complete concept.[33]

II

The question we must now ask to whether this interpretation can be of help to Leibniz in dealing with the free will issue. Mondadori does not deal with this matter[34] and so we shall have to approach the problem on our own. The first thing I want to show is that the counterparts approach is inappropriate for analyzing and reconstructing Leibniz's claims about God, and consequently of no value against Argument N. *Prima facie*, this might not seem to be true. For initially it may appear that we can give a satisfactory rendering in terms of counterpart theory to the Leibnizian claim that God exists necessarily, but is only contingently good. To express the idea that God exists necessarily we should say merely that every possible world contains a distinct counterpart of "our" God, and that each of these counterparts entails the property of *being omniscient* and *being omnipotent.* To express the idea that God is contingently good, we should say that whereas "our" God exemplifies the property of *being perfectly good*, he has a complete concept certain of whose counterparts do *not* involve the property of *being perfectly good*. This would appear to provide a powerful explanation of how Leibniz could deny premise (2) of Argument N without violating his doctrine of superessentialism. If "our" God is perfectly good, this goodness is an essential part of his concept; but then so is the fact that his concept has counterparts that do not involve the property of *being perfectly good.*

Unfortunately, there is a fundamental difficulty in proceeding in this way. An important difference between Lewis and Leibniz that we have not yet discussed lies in their very divergent attitudes toward actuality. It is this that blocks a Leibnizian application of the idea of counterparts to the analysis of statements about God. Lewis analyzes "actual" and its cognates

> as *indexical* terms: terms whose reference varies, depending on relevant features of the context of utterance. The relevant feature of context, for the term "actual," is the world at which a given utterance occurs. According to the indexical analysis I propose, "actual" (in its primary sense) refers at any world w to the world w. "Actual" is analogous to "present," an indexical term whose reference varies depending on a different feature of the context: "present" refers at any time t to the time t. "Actual" is analogous also to "here," "I," "you," "this," and "aforementioned" — indexical terms depending for their reference respectively on the place, the speaker, the intended audience, the speaker's acts of pointing and the aforegoing discourse.[35]

According to Lewis, there are many possible worlds and "'This is the actual world' is true whenever uttered in any possible world."[36] Consequently,

> if we take an *a priori* point of view and ignore our own location in time, the big difference between the actual world and others should vanish. That is not because we regard all worlds as equally actual but rather because if we ignore our own location among the worlds we cannot use indexical terms like "actual."[37]

Lewis claims that a person

> who says that his world is special because his world alone is the actual
> world is as foolish as a man who boasts that he has the special fortune to
> be alive at a unique moment in history: the present. The actual world is
> not special in itself, but only in the special relation it bears to [the speak-
> er].[38]

Leibniz's view is utterly different. For him there is an absolute metaphysical distinction between the actual world and the other possible worlds. The latter have no reality outside God's mind. Their existence is "objective" in the Scholastic sense of that term. Ontologically speaking, they are nothing more than eternal thoughts in the divine understanding, and according to Leibniz, if they did not have this status they would be reduced to sheer fancies or figments of our imagination.[39] Thus none of them *really* exists (i.e., exists formally, or extra-mentally) until God decides to make one of them actual. When he does so, the world he has selected enjoys both objective and formal existence. It is *the* actual world—absolutely speaking and quite apart from any specified context. It is "special in itself" and not "only in the special relation it bears to the speaker." Where Lewis would be inclined to use a locution such as "There is a world in which . . . ," Leibniz would say, "It is logically possible that God should have actualized a world in which. . . ."[40] Thus it is through God's understanding that the various worlds are possible and through his will that one of them has the privileged status of being actual.

Leibniz's view that mere possibles have only an objective existence in the mind of God conflicts with the idea that there are a series of God-counterparts, each actual at its own world. On the contrary, it implies that a single divinity exists who is real in an absolute sense, and whose thoughts form the only basis of the existence of unactualized possibilities. As we have seen, Leibniz treats actuality as a unique status. It is possessed *tout court*, if it is possessed at all; and it is something conferred *by God* on the basis of perfection. But this means that the God who actually exists (and who exists of necessity) would himself have existed *whatever* world had been actual. After all, the one absolutely real God is the world-actualizer. So, naturally *he* would have existed at any world that he actualized. This again conflicts with the counterparts picture, which would express the fact that God necessarily exists in terms of an infinity of different Gods, each real at his own world.

Of course, to a certain extent the counterparts idea can be "detached" from the indexical theory of actuality and made to do partial service for Leibniz. If we treat actuality as a special status conferred by God, we are still free to regard the unactualized "possible Adams" as ideas in God's mind. In this case it remains open to us to treat these ideas or concepts as the counterparts of the concept of the "real" Adam, i.e., the one on whom God has bestowed formal existence. We can then analyze a de re modal predication to the effect that Adam might have done otherwise as: it is logically possible that God should have actualized a world that did not contain Adam himself, but an individual who would have been like him in crucial respects. An analogous treatment of a similar predication about God would run as follows: it is logically possible that God should have actualized a world that did not contain God himself, but a different individual who would have been like him in crucial respects. This, I take it, is nonsense. God can actualize a different Adam, but it is not possible that he should actualize a different God. To be sure, if Leibniz is right, God could have made another choice among worlds. But this is a completely different matter. For had he done so, it would have been a choice *he* made, and through which *he* would have continued to exist.

III

Let us now turn to Argument E. Since there is nothing in Leibniz's theory of actuality to prevent one from analyzing statements about finite individuals in terms of counterparts, it is possible to reply to this argument by invoking the distinction between the literal and the nonliteral readings of de re modal predications. One could argue that Leibniz would have granted the truth of (1) if it were asserted nonliterally, but denied it if it were taken in its literal sense. When Leibniz says that Adam's freedom requires that he be able to do otherwise, he is not suggesting that this requires a possible world that is such that, had God actualized it, *Adam himself* (our very Adam) would have refused the apple. This is something that Leibniz would have denied. What he is suggesting is that Adam's freedom requires that there be a possible world that contains a counterpart of Adam's concept and that this counterpart contains the property of *refusing the apple*. If we make this assumption about Leibniz's views, we will find that there is no interpretation of Argument E that both makes it valid and whose premises he would have been inclined to accept.

This point can be brought out in the simplest way by observing that four combinations of readings of the premises of E are possible:

  E1. Both premises are read literally.
  E2. Both premises are read nonliterally.
  E3. Premise (1) is read literally, (2) nonliterally.
  E4. Premise (1) is read nonliterally, (2) literally.

Of these readings, Leibniz would have claimed that only E4 gives us premises that are both true. For he accepts (1) when it is read nonliterally and rejects it when it is taken literally, while his attitude toward (2) is the reverse: it is true when read literally, and false otherwise. This can be shown as follows. Read non-literally, (1) says that Adam acts freely only if he has a complete concept one of the counterparts of which contains the property of *refusing the apple*. On the present interpretation, this is something to which Leibniz would have assented. Taken literally, however, (1) says that Adam acts freely only if there is a possible world at which he himself refuses the apple. And, it is essential to the present interpretation to suppose that Leibniz meant to deny that this is true. Considering premise (2), if this is read literally it merely asserts that there is no possible world at which "our" Adam refuses the apple. It is thus perfectly acceptable to Leibniz. If interpreted nonliterally, however, (2) asserts something that Leibniz surely would have denied, that is, that every counterpart of Adam's complete concept contains the property of *refusing the apple.*

The question that remains is whether the argument, construed along the lines of E4, is valid. Its structure is this. The conclusion (4) is derived by using the subconclusion, (3), to perform a modus tollens operation on (1). (3) itself is supposed to be a direct consequence of (2). It will be useful, in assessing the question of the validity of the argument, to ask first whether (3) does indeed follow from (2). Since (3) is an instance of a de re modal predication, it is subject to variant readings and consequently we have two separate cases to consider. Suppose, first, that (3) is taken in its nonliteral sense. In that case, it does not follow from (2). On the nonliteral reading, (3) says that the concept of Adam does not have any counterparts that entail the property of *refusing the apple.* And, clearly, this does not follow from the fact that there is no possible world at which *Adam himself* refuses the apple. Suppose, on the other hand, that (3) is read literally. In that case it *does* follow from (2); indeed, when so taken, (2) is equivalent to (3). Both say that there is no possible world at which Adam himself ("our" Adam) refuses the apple. But then the argument as a whole is invalid for a different reason: (3) fails to contradict the consequent of (1). On reading E4, the consequent of (1) is asserted nonliterally and cannot be denied by a *literal* assertion of (3). Consequently, all the various readings of Argument E make it either invalid or such that Leibniz would have been inclined to deny at least one of its premises.

One of the virtues of this interpretation is that it helps to explain why a proponent of Argument E should mistakenly think he has produced a valid argument whose premises Leibniz grants. The proponent of E fails to appreciate the possibility of a nonliteral reading of de re modal predications. So, when he finds Leibniz making statements like (1) he naturally assumes that these are to be taken literally. But if Leibniz had agreed to (1) in this sense, then he would have been committed to the conclusion of Argument E. For he does agree to (2) and (3) in the literal sense, and when all of the steps of E are read literally, the argument is valid. But on the present interpretation, the mistake is that Leibniz would in fact only have agreed to (1) in its nonliteral sense. He would have rejected this (valid) version of E by denying its first premise.

Another virtue of this interpretation is that it explains Leibniz's apparently contradictory statements about the role of counterfactuals in his theory of freedom. Leibniz was a soft determinist who emphasized that a person does not act freely unless it is true that he would have done otherwise if he had willed to do so. And, at many places, Leibniz expressed the belief that this condition is satisfied when an agent acts voluntarily.[41] Yet at other places he says, quite firmly, that such counterfactual statements are defective: any supposition of different predicates yields the concept of a different individual.[42] We are now in a position to explain away the appearance of inconsistency. Taken literally, the counterfactuals are defective; taken nonliterally, they are perfectly coherent. When Leibniz says that a person's freedom requires that he would have acted differently if he had willed to do so, he must be understood to be asserting this in its nonliteral sense only.

Now it may be that this is the sort of response that Leibniz would have given to Argument E. But if it is, it seems to me to be unsatisfactory. The heart of the critique is that premise (1) is true if it is read nonliterally, but false otherwise. This means that Adam's freedom does not require that there be possible circumstances under which *he himself* (i.e., the same individual) refuses the apple. What is required to satisfy the necessary condition of freedom expressed in (1) is only that there be a possible person who is very much like "our" Adam, but who is such that he would have refused an apple in circumstances similar to those of the Garden of Eden. But how plausible is this idea? Surely if I act freely there must be possible circumstances under which *I* would have done otherwise. What has the fact that there might have been an individual *like* me who did otherwise to do with *my* freedom? It is extremely counterintuitive to suppose that my freedom can be explicated in terms of what *somebody else* might have done.[43] When we make claims like (1), it is the literal reading that we have in mind, not the nonliteral one.

Some may be inclined to reject this response by reasoning as follows. Facts about what someone else might have done are relevant to your freedom—provided that person is very much like you in important respects. Suppose that you have committed some grievous act and you plead that you could not have done otherwise. Would it not be relevant to your claim—in fact, extremely damaging to it—if it were discovered that there was someone very much like you in important respects who found himself in circumstances virtually identical to yours, but who followed a different path? If this is relevant, however, then so is the fact that there might have been such a person. Whether the world does in fact contain such a person is beside the point.

What is said here is correct as far as it goes, but it has no tendency to establish the counterparts rebuttal to E. We do normally take the fact that relevantly similar people have behaved differently from a given individual to support the claim that the latter person could have done otherwise. But isn't this because we normally take such data to be evidence that *this person himself* could have done otherwise? We believe, that is, that data of the type described above support the hypothesis that the world might have been such that the very individual we are judging behaved differently. If we did not take the data to have this import, it seems to me that we would not find it relevant to the person's freedom. Suppose that after being presented with the data we were assured by a reliable authority that although a large number of persons have been like our man in important ways, and have behaved more decently, nevertheless, there are no possible circumstances under which our man himself would have done otherwise. It is, we are told, logically impossible that the world should have been such that our man himself behaved more laudably than he in fact did. If we were assured of this, I think we would discount the other data, and hold that the man had not acted freely.

It might seem tempting to reply that we would dismiss the data only if we found that the individuals in the sample were not *similar enough.* to our man. Suppose, for example, we learned that somewhere in the far reaches of space there had been a person who was qualitatively *identical* to our man up to the time of his unfortunate act, but different from that time on. Even though these are distinct individuals, it might be maintained that the distant "twin's" more decent behavior shows that our man acted freely. If so, it would show this regardless of whether the world might have been such that our man himself behaved differently.

Now it is not at all clear to me that the situation described in the preceeding paragraph is coherent. Fortunately, however, it is not necessary to try to decide this issue. The case of the distant "twin" is not one to which Leibniz can appeal in behalf of his rebuttal to E. In his system it is impossible that there should be two individuals in a given world who are qualitatively *identical* up to a certain point in their history, but different thereafter. On his view, each individual already contains within him "marks" or "traces" of what will happen to him.[44] Each individual, as he puts it, is "great with the future."[45] Thus, if individual A were qualitatively identical to individual B up to a certain point in time, A and B would have to be identical thereafter. But this entails, for Leibniz, that A would be numerically the same individual as B. The same rule applies to possible individuals. Speaking somewhat loosely, we can say that, for Leibniz, there are no two individuals at different worlds who have the very same history up to a given point.[46] Each individual contains in the concept of his earlier states, traces of his later states as well.

IV

In the previous dispute there was one point of agreement: it is a necessary condition of Adam's freedom that "Adam refuses the apple" express a possible truth. I argued that the counterparts theorist went wrong in supposing that this condition is satisfied if there is a possible world containing an apple-refusing Adam-counterpart. Nevertheless, I now propose to grant this contention for the sake of argument. For I believe it can be shown that Leibniz cannot account for human freedom even if this concession is made.

Let us suppose, then, that (in the sense required for freedom) "Adam refuses the apple" expresses a possible truth provided there is an apple-refusing Adam-counterpart whom God could have actualized. Since we may also grant that there is such a counterpart, this amounts to allowing—contra Argument E— that the following condition of freedom is actually satisfied: it could have been the case that Adam refused the apple.[47] But whereas the latter is a necessary condition of Adam's freedom, it certainly is not sufficient.[48] In general, that

"Person P does such-and-such" could have been true does not show that person P had it within his power to perform whatever sort of act is in question. Suppose that I am expected to attend a meeting at 9 A.M. on a certain day. A few minutes before I am to leave, someone who thinks it best that I not attend the meeting sees to it that I cannot do so. Let us imagine, for example, that he abducts me and chains me to a post. Now it seems that it *could have* been the case that I attended the meeting. Had my assailant changed his mind about capturing me, had he overslept, or for any other reason bungled the abduction, it would have been true that I attended the meeting. For I would have *made* it true. Still, I quite obviously did not act freely since, under the circumstances, it was not within my power to make it the case that I attended the meeting.

What this shows is that to settle the question whether Adam acted freely, we still need to know whether it was within his power to bring it about that Adam refused the apple. If it should turn out that it could have been the case that Adam refused, but that it was not within his power to make this the case, then he was not free to refuse. And indeed this is exactly the situation Adam is in. For what are the circumstances under which it would have been true that Adam refused the apple? Making the concessions that I have, we can say that it would have been the case that Adam refused the apple if and only if God had actualized a possible world that contained an apple-refusing Adam-counterpart. In fact, in Leibniz's system it is a *logically necessary* condition of its being true that Adam refuses the apple that God performs a world-actualizing act of this type. But God did not perform an act of this type; instead he actualized a world containing "our" Adam, one of whose properties is *accepting the apple offered by Eve*. Thus we may grant that it could have been true that Adam refused the apple: had God performed the appropriate act, it *would* have been true. But we must deny that Adam had it within his power to refuse, since God has decided not to perform this act, and there is nothing Adam can do to alter this.

Of course, if it were within Adam's power to cause God to actualize a world containing an apple-refusing Adam-counterpart, then Adam would be free to refuse the apple. For then it would be within his power to make it the case that Adam refuses the apple. But clearly it is not within Adam's power to do any such thing; Adam has no powers at all until he exists. And his existence (i.e., the existence of "our" Adam) entails that God has already made the decision that is logically incompatible with its being the case that Adam refuses. It is therefore absurd to suppose that Adam has the power to cause God to actualize a different world. *God* had the power to actualize a different world. *He* could have made it the case that Adam refused the apple—by actualizing a "different Adam." But God did not do this. Since Adam had no power to cause him to do so, Adam was not free to refuse the forbidden fruit.

It is important to observe that this argument does not rest on the principle that a person is exempt from responsibility merely because a logically necessary condition of his behaving otherwise fails to obtain. That principle is specious. It is a logically necessary condition of Adam's refusing the apple that he refuse the apple. Yet his not refusing the apple does not show that it was not within his power to do so. The argument I have given rests on an entirely different thesis, which has no such implication:

Principle F

If the occurrence of an event of type E is a logically necessary condition of its being true that person P performs an act of type T, and if an event of type E does not occur, and if person P never had it in his power to cause an event of type E, then person P was not free to perform an act of type T.

It is of some significance that Principle F is neutral between the three major positions on the free will problem. The issues separating the three positions revolve around the notion of causation. Determinists and libertarians disagree on the question whether all events are caused by prior events. Clearly, F says nothing in this regard. The question separating soft determinists from both hard determinists and libertarians, on the other hand, is whether causation is compatible with freedom. But F is also silent on this crucial issue. Note that if the phrase "logically necessary" in F were changed to read "causally necessary," this would make F stronger and hence more contentious. But as it stands, F does not have any implications for the question whether causation is compatible with freedom, and so there is no reason to think a soft determinist would reject it.

More importantly, however, Principle F is true. If a logically necessary condition of my doing such-and-such fails to obtain and if it is also the case that it was never within my power to make this condition obtain, then surely I am not free to perform the sort of act in question. Although I suspect that this principle will be immediately evident, it may still be helpful to consider a few examples that illustrate its force. Imagine that I am asked to snap a picture of a stellar explosion on a certain evening. But no stellar explosion occurs. Now it cannot be said that I was free to snap such a picture—unless perchance I had it within my power to cause a stellar explosion on that very evening. Or, suppose that I am assigned by my political party to attend a meeting and to publicly embarrass you by squelching your remarks. You, however, decide not to make any remarks. Suppose further that there is nothing I can do to cause you to make any remarks. I cannot in any way get you to utter a word. Then surely I was not free to perform an act of remark-squelching. Under the circumstances that was not within my power.

With Principle F in mind we can now formulate the latest argument against freedom more carefully. Because it is a Leibnizian version of the problem of predestination, I refer to it as Argument P.

Argument P

(1)   If (a) God's willing to actualize a different world from "our" world is a logically necessary condition of its being true that Adam refuses the apple, and (b) God does not will to actualize a different world from "our" world, and (c) Adam never had it in his power to cause God to

will to actualize a different world from "our" world, then Adam was not free to refuse the apple.

(2) (a) God's willing to actualize a different world from "our" world is a logically necessary condition of its being true that Adam refuses the apple, and (b) God does not will to actualize a different world from "our" world, and (c) Adam never had it in his power to cause God to will to actualize a different world from "our" world.

(3) Therefore, Adam was not free to refuse the apple.

Several things are worth pointing out about this argument. First, it is to be noted that Argument P (unlike Argument E) does not turn on the idea that Adam is unfree because there is no possible world at which he himself refuses the apple. Fundamentally the same argument could be given even if Leibniz had allowed for cross world identity and, in particular, for a world at which Adam himself refuses the apple. For even if there are possible circumstances under which Adam himself would have refused, he is not responsible for failing to refuse unless it is within his power to cause God to actualize a world at which he (Adam) *does* refuse. But God's choice of a world is logically prior to the existence of Adam, and so the latter has no such power.

The brunt of Argument P is that it is God who selects which possible world is to be actualized, and this act of selection itself logically guarantees the occurrence of every event. In selecting "our" world, then, God has predestined all of our sins, and the possibility of any other events occurring depends entirely on the possibility of *his* choosing a different order of things. Since we human beings have no power to cause God to choose a different order of things, we have no way of seeing to it that our sins do not occur. So, even if the world could have been such that Adam himself refused the apple, Adam would have had no way of bringing this possibility about. The power to have made things different is God's, not ours.

None of this is to say, of course, that God *did wrong* in refusing to make things different. As Leibniz points out, in actualizing Adam-who-accepts-the-apple rather than Adam-who-refuses, God did the very best thing he could have done. The concept of Adam-who-accepts-the-apple is part of the concept of BPW and so, on the whole, the selection of any other world would have been worse than the selection of this one. Thus nothing in Argument P implies that we can justifiably blame God for predestining this particular sequence of events. But then it is no part of the purpose of Argument P to provide grounds for blaming God for acting as he did. Its entire point is to call into question whether Adam acted freely.

Since Argument P is pretty obviously valid, we must ask which of its premises Leibniz would be inclined to deny. Let us begin with premise (2), which consists of three conjuncts. Leibniz is clearly not in a position to reject conjunct (a). This says that God's willing to actualize a different world from "our" world is a logically necessary condition of its being true that Adam refuses the apple, that is, N (Adam refuses the apple $\rightarrow$ $-$God wills to actualize "our"

world). But this proposition is directly entailed by the thesis that it is hypothetically necessary that Adam accept the apple, that is, N (God wills to actualize
"our" world → Adam accepts the apple). So it is evident that Leibniz cannot
consistently deny (a). Furthermore, the suggestion of the present counterparts
approach is that it will be the case that Adam refuses the apple only if God
actualizes a world containing the exemplification of an apple-refusing Adam-
counterpart. On this account too, then, God's choice of a different world is
logically required for it to be true that Adam refuses. Leibniz certainly has no
quarrel with conjunct (b), which says only that God has not willed to actualize
a different world from "our" world. It also seems unlikely that Leibniz would
have wished to deny conjunct (c) of premise (2). To deny this is to endorse the
evident absurdity that Adam had the power to bring it about that he ("our"
Adam) never existed, and there is no reason to think that Leibniz believed anything like this.

If this much is correct, then to escape from Argument P Leibniz would
have to deny its first premise. Indeed it seems that he is committed to denying
premise (1). For he believes both that Adam acted freely and that all of the conjuncts of the antecedent of (1) are true.

But there is a very serious problem with this. Premise (1) is merely a particular instance of Principle F, and so the denial of the former entails the denial
of the latter. Yet there is no reason at all to suppose that F is false. It is a highly
intuitive principle, which has all the earmarks of a necessary truth. I know of
nowhere that Leibniz offers any direct considerations against this principle, nor
am I aware of any good arguments from other sources that *can* be offered
against it. And this seems to me to be an extremely strong argument in favor of
(1) and against Leibniz's position on freedom.

Before concluding, I think it may be worth asking which of Leibniz's doctrines place him in the unenviable position of having to deny Principle F. The
answer, I think, lies in his commitment both to a belief that we human beings
act freely and to an extremely strong form of the Principle of Sufficient Reason.
It is the conjunction of these two views that entails that F is false. To see this,
one must appreciate just how strong a version of the Principle of Sufficient
Reason Leibniz endorsed. For example, on his understanding, this principle
implies much more than that every event has a cause. It implies that the casual
series as a whole has a sufficient reason in the will of God, and also that God's
will hypothetically necessitates exactly which events occur. So understood, the
Principle of Sufficient Reason has the consequence that God predestines all
contingent events: for any other events to have occurred it is logically necessary
(and sufficient) that God should have willed something other than he in fact did.
If God's will is to be the sufficient reason for the order of contingent things,
however, then no being within that order can have the power to see to it that
God acted differently. But God's acting differently is *logically necessary* for it to
be true that Adam refused the apple. Consequently, if one is to maintain that
Adam acted freely, one must say that Adam's freedom does *not* require that he
have the power to bring about a state of affairs which is logically necessary for

the truth of "Adam refuses the apple." That is, one must hold that Principle F is false.

To summarize, we may say that the following three propositions form an inconsistent triad: (A) Adam acted freely, (B) The Principle of Sufficient Reason is true, (C) Principle F is true. Since Leibniz doggedly adhered to (A) and (B), he was implicitly committed to the denial of (C). But although this may explain why Leibniz was committed to rejecting Principle F, it does nothing at all to make his position plausible. There is, I think, a much more reasonable stand to take, namely, that since Principle F is true, one cannot consistently maintain both that Adam acted freely and that the strong version of the Principle of Sufficient Reason is correct. Stated in other worlds: one who maintains the full-blown Leibnizian version of the Principle of Sufficient Reason must accept Argument P, and deny that there is any such thing as human freedom.

Notes

1. The abbreviations I use are as follows. CA = *The Leibniz-Arnauld Correspondence*, ed. and trans. H. T. Mason (Manchester, 1976); G = *Die philosophischen Schriften von Gottfried Wilhelm Leibniz*, ed. C. I. Gerhardt, 7 vols. (Berlin, 1875-1890); Grua = *G. W. Leibniz: Textes inédits*, ed. G. Grua (Paris, 1948). Ish = Hidé Ishiguro, *Leibniz's Philosophy of Logic and Language* (London, 1972). Lewis I = David Lewis, "Counterpart Theory and Quantified Modal Logic," *The Journal of Philosophy* 65, No. 5 (March 7, 1968): 113-26; Lewis II = David Lewis, "Anselm and Actuality," *Noûs* 4, No. 2, (May 1970): 175-88. L = *Leibniz: Philosophical Papers and Letters*, ed L. E. Loemker, 2nd ed. (Dordrecht, Holland 1969); Mates I = Benson Mates, "Leibniz on Possible Worlds," in *Logic, Methodology, and Philosophy of Science III*, ed. B. van Rootselaar and J. F. Staal (Amsterdam, 1968), also reprinted in *Leibniz: A Collection of Critical Essays*, ed. Harry G. Frankfurt (New York, 1972). Mates II = "Individuals and Modality in the Philosophy of Leibniz," *Studia Leibnitiana*, Band IV, Heft II (1972): 81-118; Mond. = Fabrizio Mondadori, "Reference, Essentialism, and Modality in Leibniz's Metaphysics," *Studia Leibnitiana*, Band V, Heft 1 (1973):74-101; Sch. = *Leibniz: Monadology and Other Philosophical Essays*, trans. Paul Schrecker and Anne Martin Schrecker (New York, 1965); T = *G. W. Leibniz: Theodicy*, trans. E. M. Huggard, (London, 1952).

In referring to Leibniz's works in the footnotes I first cite a standard edition of the original text and then an English translation. Quotations are from the English translation cited.

2. The term "superessentialism" is borrowed from Mond., which can be consulted for a detailed discussion of this doctrine. For another very important paper bearing on this topic see Mates II. A few places at which Leibniz expresses his superessentialism are: G II, 42, 53, 56, and G IV, 455; CA, 46, 59-60, 63, and L, 322.

3. For example, G II, 56; CA, 63.

4. For example, G IV, 436-39 and 454-56; L. 310-11 and 321-23.

5. *Ibid.*

6. For example, G IV, 427; L, 303-4.

7. For example, G VI, 254-57 and 284-85, G IV, 436-38; T, 270-71 and 284-85, L, 310-11. But it should be noted that Leibniz is not of one mind on this topic. At other places he seems to commit himself to the view that God's goodness is necessary (e.g., at Grua, 493). For an outstanding discussion of Leibniz's uncertainty and vacillation on this topic see Robert M. Adams, "Leibniz's Theories of Contingency," in *Essays on the Philosophy of Leibniz*, ed. Mark Kulstad, *Rice University Studies* 63 (Fall 1977): 1-41.

8. G VI, 453; Sch. 135. According to Leibniz's most frequent definition, a free act is one that is spontaneous, deliberate, and contingent. See for example G VI, 441; Sch. 117.

9. Leibniz's other responses to these arguments are considered in a work of mind still in progress.

10. Lewis I.

11. The parallel with Lewis's views was, to the best of my knowledge, first discussed in detail in Mates II, and shortly thereafter in Mond. But it is to be noted that whereas Mondadori bases an account of contingency and an interpretation of counterfactuals and de re modal predications on the counterparts conception, Mates does not. Mates uses the counterparts idea to try to explain why Leibniz thought no individual could have had different attributes, or in other words to illuminate why Leibniz was a superessentialist. See Mates II, 110-16. For another attempt to base an interpretation of contingency on counterparts, see Gregory Fitch's recent important paper, "Analyticity and Necessity in Leibniz," *The Journal of the History of Philosophy* 57, No. 1 (Jan. 1979): 29-42.

12. G II, 20; CA, 15.

13. G II, 41-42 and 54; CA, 45 and 60-61.

14. G VI, 368; T, 371.

15. Lewis I, 114.

16. *Ibid.*

17. G II, 9-15; CA, 15-21.

18. G VI, 361; T, 370.

19. In other contexts Leibniz suggests that, contrary to fact, conditionals such as the one under consideration here are defective (inepta) since they assert what would have been the case if a certain individual had not been that very individual. See for example Grua 358 (Mates II, 105) where Leibniz makes this remark about the question, "What would have happened if Peter had not denied Christ?" But it is of interest that Leibniz here allows that the name "Peter" *can* be taken to indicate only what is involved in the attributes of Peter from which his denial of Christ does not follow (and minus, so to speak, those aspects of the universe from which the denial does follow). If we proceed in this way, Leibniz suggests that the answer to a question about what would have happened under counterfactual conditions sometimes will be determined solely by the nature of the remaining things posited in the universe. In other cases, there will be no fixed answer unless we also assume a new divine decree based on considerations of perfection. But the point is that he does seem to be allowing for a reading of counterfactuals involving proper names on which they may come out true.

20. Cf. Mates II, 110-11.

21. Lewis I, 116.

22. Mond., 95. At the end of the *Theodicy* and in the correspondence with Arnauld, Leibniz does seem to hold the view that each possible world contains at most one counterpart of Adam or of Sextus. This assumption about Leibniz's view is also further justified by the role that the uniqueness requirement plays in the interpretation of counterfactuals and de re modal predications that Mondadori offers, and with the account of proper names (to be discussed shortly) associated with it. On the other hand, the argument Mondadori gives for the uniqueness requirement immediately on introducing it does not seem to me to be conclusive (Mond. 95, cf. Mates II, 111). Mondadori notes Lewis's remark that your counterparts can be characterized as "men you would have been had the world been otherwise" and infers from this that Leibniz would have rejected the idea that any individuals of the actual world can have more than one counterpart in another world. For, Mondadori reasons, suppose that Sextus had two counterparts, x_{i_1} and x_{i_2}, in a given world. Then each of these two counterparts could be characterized as men Sextus would have been had the world been otherwise. Yet on Leibniz's account of identity "there are no conditions such that, had they obtained, Sextus would have been x_{i_1} and he would have been x_{i_2}, but x_{i_1} would have been different from x_{i_2}" (Mond. 95). Leibniz's view is that for any two, distinct individuals

at most one of them is Sextus. But though these assumptions about Leibniz's view of identity are certainly correct, it can be replied that the counterpart relation is *not* a relation of identity. Your counterparts are men you would have been, only "speaking casually." Strictly speaking, none of your counterparts in a different world is really you, for "things in different worlds are *never* identical" (Lewis I, 114). Thus, if a world did exist at which there were two Sextus counterparts, it would not follow that, if God had actualized that world, there would have been two distinct individuals both of whom were Sextus.

23. Lewis I, 114.

24. Mond., 95.

25. Lewis I, 114-16.

26. Mond., 19. But Mondadori notes that he has assumed that the counterpart relation is an equivalence relation "for purely pedagogical purposes."

27. Mates I.

28. Mond., 96.

29. *Ibid.*

30. *Ibid.*, 98. For further discussion of the conditions of membership in C_{Sextus} and of the "minimally differs" clause see Mond. especially 87-88 and 96-98.

31. *Ibid.*, 99-100.

32. *Ibid.*, 100.

33. As Mondadori is clearly aware, the interpretation put forth here is in conflict with some of the things Leibniz says. This is probably to be expected since Leibniz is not always consistent and frequently offers a variety of solutions to problems in his system. Limitations of space prevent me from discussing the textual (and related philosophical) difficulties in detail, but the following points deserve at least to be mentioned here. First, as Mondadori notes, the notion of deferred naming is at odds with another account of proper names that can be associated with Leibniz's metaphysics. Very briefly, according to this other account Leibniz treats proper names as having complete individual concepts as their senses. Since each complete individual concept forms part of exactly one possible world in God's mind, it follows on this theory of names that, had a different world been actual, no proper name that denotes in "our" world, would have had a referent. (For the development of this account of names see Mond. Or see also Mates I.) But Mondadori thinks that in the Theodicy passage and in the correspondence with Arnauld, Leibniz does commit himself to a position involving the idea of deferred naming, and so we are entitled to "revise" Leibniz's other view of names to bring it into harmony with the conception of deferred reference. (The suggested revisions are set out at Mond. 100-101.)

Another difficulty that Mondadori notes is that the Principle of Continuity conflicts with the possibility of there being any concept that "differs minimally" from the concept of an individual in the actual world. But he points out that Leibniz does seem to commit himself (at G VI 363; T 731) to the view that such a concept exists. Mondadori suggests that the basic view of counterfactuals and de re modal predications that he argues for would be preserved if the Principle of Continuity were put in abeyance. He also indicates that the "minimally differs" clause is independent of the "uniqueness requirement" and that the former could be abandoned without abandoning the latter.

Some other interesting questions also arise here. See for example the important issue raised at Mates II, 113-15. But a discussion of these questions must be reserved for another occasion.

34. Since he does not, none of my comments about the counterparts approach in the following sections should be taken as being directed against him.

35. Lewis II, 184-85.

36. *Ibid.*, 186.

37. *Ibid.*, 187.

38. *Ibid.*

39. G VII, 304-5; L, 488.

40. Mond. 99. Mondadori does not discuss the question whether Leibniz's account of actuality prevents one from interpreting statements about God in terms of counterparts.

41. For example, G VI, 380; T, 381.

42. Grua, 358; Mates II, 105. For a comment on Grua 358 see footnote 19 above.

43. Cf. Alvin Plantinga, *The Nature of Necessity* (Oxford: Oxford at Clarendon Press, 1974), 116 ff.

44. G IV, 433; L, 308.

45. G VI, 610; L, 645.

46. G VI, 363; T, 371. In this passage Leibniz allows that there could have been an individual who was *to all appearances* exactly like "our" Sextus up to a certain point in the latter's career, and different thereafter. But Leibniz denies that an individual could have existed who was in truth altogether like "our" Sextus up to a certain point yet different thereafter. This point is made, astutely, by Margaret D. Wilson in her review of Ish. (*Archiv Für Geschichte Der Philosophie* 57, Band 1975, Heft 1, 86).

47. It should be remembered that the counterparts approach considered here explicates the de re predication "Adam could have refused the apple" in terms of the fact that it could have been the case that Adam refused. In this way the de re gets "cashed in" in terms of the *de dicto*.

48. Nor indeed does Leibniz think it is sufficient. See note 8.

Leibniz and Plato's *Phaedo* Theory of Relations and Predication

Hector-Neri Castañeda

INTRODUCTION

Leibniz's view of relations and relational facts is one of the most fundamental pieces of his metaphysics of monads and psychophysical preestablished harmony. Yet it is one of the most obscure pieces of that metaphysics. His extremely brief discussions of relations have provoked the most diverse interpretations and the harshest criticisms. Since the topic is intrinsically important, there is more than a purely historical interest in understanding Leibniz's view of relations. Thus, seeing no alternative but to turn to those brief texts and subject them to careful exegesis, that was precisely what I did in the fall of 1973. I was immediately struck by the similarity between those texts and Plato's *Phaedo* 102b3-103a2, which I had exegisized before. That led me to the experience of seeing the structure of Leibniz's metaphysics in a new way: as a masterful development of the ontology that Plato propounded in the *Phaedo*. Here, in Parts II and III, respectively, I subject both Plato's and Leibniz's texts on relations to severe scrutiny, squeezing them tight so that they can deliver most of their philosophical content: an *exégèse au fond*.

To what extent Plato influenced Leibniz is, as are all questions of ideological influence, extremely difficult to settle. In our present case, however, we have much more than the stunning similarities of the two philosophers' views. We have also documents that show how impressed Leibniz was both by the *Phaedo*

This study was written in May, 1977. I am pleased to acknowledge helpful criticisms by Massimo Mugnai, of the University of Florence, who kindly provided me with the continuation of the text, until now unpublished, of the famous Paris-Helen passage published by Couturat, p. 287. Mugnai's commentary is consistent with my interpretation. I hope that Professor Mugnai publishes his text and his commentary soon.

Unless otherwise indicated, the translations of both Leibniz's and Plato's texts are mine.

124

and by the puzzles about relations that Plato discussed in the *Theaetetus*. We will examine this historical connection in Part I below.

The standard view about Plato is that he confused relative with nonrelative terms.[1] Thus, the ontological insight of his discussion in *Phaedo* 102b2-103a2 has not been generally appreciated by Plato scholars. Likewise, Leibniz scholars have not generally appreciated Leibniz's development of the ontological theory of relations adumbrated by Plato. In large part, the reason for both phenomena lies in the fact that both Plato and Leibniz are concerned, rather than with the logic of relations, with the ontology of relations and the ontological structure of relational facts. Hence it is important both to separate the logic from the ontology of relations and to establish how logically viable that Platonic-Leibnizian ontology of relations is. These two operations provide a logico-ontological framework within which we can assess the power of Plato's adumbrations and of Leibniz's developments. In general, only when one completes the construction of a theory adumbrated by a certain thinker can one really appreciate the strength and the range of the thinker's adumbrations. Only the construction of the absent fragment of a theory can delineate the magnitude of the present fragment.[2] This I accomplish in Part IV.

I. THE HISTORICAL CONNECTION

Leibniz acquired his view of relations and relational states of affairs rather early. If that view was not suggested to him by Plato, he certainly developed it more fully after his abridgment in Latin of Plato's *Phaedo* and *Theaetetus*. He himself placed a marginal note in his abridgment of the *Phaedo* indicating that he did it in March 1676. It is easily assumed that his abridgment of the *Theaetetus* is later. This abridgment is hurried and incomplete; it also has more notes in which Leibniz puts down some of his reflections on Plato's arguments or views. If the abridgment of the *Theaetetus* is later than that of the *Phaedo*, it was most likely done also in March. For one thing, Leibniz wrote forty-five printed pages of very compact notes of intense reflections on different philosophical topics between April 1 and the end of April 1676.[3] Furthermore, an entry in late April does seem to have been written with a crucial passage of the *Theaetetus* in mind.

In *Theaetetus* 155a-b Plato formulates, first, several principles about change and relations. Then he puts forward the puzzle of Socrates, who without undergoing (relevant) changes himself does change from being taller than Theaetetus to being shorter than he, when Theaetetus grows. Leibniz summarizes the discussion well. He adds a note, as follows:

> This is a remarkable difficulty, and of great importance for other matters. But I do not understand how the ensuing response by Plato, namely, that everything flows [changes] relates to the difficulty.[4]

At that juncture Leibniz does not give any hint whatsoever about the "other matters" for which he thinks Plato's paradox of relations is very important. But presumably just a few weeks later, in April 1676, in the midst of a very compact entry about diversity of the world and about forms, in very much of Plato's sense of properties in abstract, Leibniz refers to some of them in this passage:

> When the mind perceives something in matter, it cannot be denied, since it perceives different and diverse things, that there is change in it. When somebody becomes taller than I, by growing up, certainly some change occurs in me too, since a denomination of mine is changed. And in this way everything is in a certain way contained in everything.[5]

This entry is clearly a commentary on Plato's *Theaetetus* paradox of relations. But it is much more than that: it includes a solution to that paradox. This solution is a step in the direction of Plato's Heraclitean view that everything not in the realm of Forms changes. Yet instead of going all the way with Plato, Leibniz veers toward a Parmenidean or static Anaxagorean view that is the germ of his monadology, namely, that everything is (statically) included in everything. This is a pregnant passage and we will subject it to obstetric exegesis later on.

At this stage I want to say only that Leibniz's Anaxagorean conclusion hinges on two central views that Plato formulated in the *Phaedo*: (1) Plato's view that relational predication is reducible to monadic predication; and (2) Plato's internalist views of the participation in Forms by ordinary individuals, like horses or men; that is, such predication is analyzable as the composition of such individuals by pure instances of Forms—pure in that each instance is a particular instantiating just one Form.

Plato illustrates (1) by 'taller-than' in *Phaedo* 102b3-c8, and most explicitly introduces (2) at 102c11-103a2. Leibniz summarizes the whole section as follows:

> Isn't it the case that Simmias is taller than Socrates and shorter than Phaedo, by tallness and shortness, respectively, and that the tall itself or tallness can never become short? Thus, the subject itself can admit contraries, but the contraries themselves do not admit each other. *There are*, however, *subjects that do not admit but a certain form*, which are destroyed when the form is removed.[6] [My italics]

This abridgment has two remarkable features. First, Leibniz's first sentence, which summarizes 102b3-c8, about the relational facts *Simmias is taller than Socrates* and *Simmias is shorter than Phaedo*, is much inferior to Plato's original discussion. As we shall see in Part II, Plato spent proportionally a long time clarifying the structure of those facts. My conjecture is that at the time of his abridgment of the *Phaedo* Leibniz did not understand fully what Plato was doing at *Phaedo* 102b3-c8. Indeed, it was later that Leibniz, probably of his own, without this *Phaedo* passage in mind, came to formulate some, yet not all, of Plato's insights in that passage. I am now referring to Plato's view of the ultimately irreducible relational core in relational facts, which he expressed by means of the preposition 'toward' ($\pi\rho\grave{o}\varsigma$). This is the element that Leibniz later on categorized as a being of reason (*ens rationis*). The second remarkable feature of the above abridgment pertains to the second and third sentences. They summarize 102d7-103a7. Leibniz's pithy summary reveals that he understood perfectly well what Plato was doing in his contrast, at 102c11-d9, between the tall itself and the tall in us. Leibniz's formula "subjects that do not admit but a certain form" (*subjecta quae etiam non nisi certam patiuntur forman*) is a splendid general description, not found in Plato, of what Plato's examples are supposed to illustrate. In fact, the only general, technical term Plato uses in the formulation of his views is εἶδος (Form).

In short, then, Leibniz studies seriously Plato's *Phaedo* and *Theaetetus* in March 1676. He worries about relations through March and April. In his philosophical meditations in April, he is thinking within the context of Platonic problems and uses Platonic terminology.[7] In April, the Platonic views of the *Phaedo* sink in, and then they develop into the Leibnizian metaphysics. (To be sure, that development was possible only because of Leibniz's antecedent views or half-views on connected topics.) What are those pregnant Platonic views? To this question we turn now.

II. *PLATO'S* PHAEDO *ONTOLOGY*

1. *Plato's Crucial Text: Phaedo 102b3-c4*

I have just claimed that Leibniz did not capture in his abridgment of *Phaedo* 102b3-c8 the whole power of Plato's view on the structure of the relational fact *Simmias is taller than Socrates*. As I also said, he caught on to Plato, and actually surpasses him in one respect. In any case, it is incumbent upon me to provide an exegesis of this passage to show both how much Leibniz captured and how much he left behind. This is especially so, since I am apparently the only scholar who thinks that Plato adumbrates an important theory of relations.[8] The passage, in a literal, but deliberately nonliterary translation, reads as follows:

102b3   "don't you, [D] whenever you say that Simmias is taller than Socrates and shorter than Phaedo, declare then that [P] there is in Simmias both tallness and shortness?"

b8   "But then," said Socrates, "do you agree [on the following] :

8   [(1)] that 'Simmias overtops Socrates' does not have as thus said in those words frankness[9] [ἀληθὲς] ;

c1   [(2)] for surely it is not the case that Simmias naturally overtops because of *this*: that he is Simmias, but because of the tallness he happens to have;

c2   [(3)] nor, further, [Simmias] overtops Socrates [naturally] because Socrates is Socrates, but because Socrates has

c4   shortness toward [πρὸς] his [Simmias'] tallness;

c6-8   [(4)] nor, indeed, further, [Simmias] is overtopped by Phaedo because Phaedo is Phaedo, but because Phaedo has tallness towards [πρὸς] Simmias' shortness?"

The structure of the passage is clear: (D) is a datum; (P) is a puzzle about relations; (1)-(4) constitute the solution to that puzzle.[10]

2. *The structure of the Text and Its Context*

Plato discusses examples, but he means them to be taken as paradigms of general cases. Thus, his datum (D) amounts to taking as data, not only the paradigm pair *Simmias is taller than Socrates* and *Simmias is shorter than Phaedo*, but also at least all facts involving two objects or persons related by a dyadic relation. I am not sure that we must take Plato, in that episode of philosophical analysis, to be thinking implicitly of relational facts of greater polyadicity than two.

Plato's puzzle (P) is interesting. He speaks of there being both tallness and shortness *in* Phaedo. This is the first time that in the *Phaedo* Plato suggests firmly that there is something *in* objects that accounts for their having properties. Thus, Plato is suggesting that the way in which ordinary objects participate in Forms is by *having in themselves* replicas of the Forms. This view of the *internality of ordinary predication* is the view that will emerge later on at 102d6. Up to 102b3 the Forms alone have been mentioned as involved in objects having properties. In fact, just a little earlier, at 100d5-6, Plato was noncommittal about how the Forms enter into facts: "by presence, or communion, or whatever way" the Forms themselves are involved. Yet the internality of predication is not crucial for the *Phaedo* puzzle about relations. Whatever the nature of ordinary predication may be, the puzzle about how Simmias can *be* both taller and shorter, can *have* both tallness and shortness, or can be *related* to both Forms Tallness and Shortness, remains. Plato has been fully aware of this puzzle for quite some time. He confronted it, but did not solve it, in his earlier *Euthydemus*. This dialogue displays part of the background behind Plato's discussion of puzzle (P) in the *Phaedo*. Now, in the *Phaedo*, he solves the puzzle for once and for all.

Plato develops his solution to puzzle (P) very carefully, deploying one piece of his machinery at a time, unhurriedly, in an impressive crescendo of logical power;

1. At 100b3-10, Plato introduces the Forms, thus beginning the formulation of his ontology;

2. At 100c3-7, he introduces his first principle of predication: things have properties by participation in the Forms;

3. At 100e5-6, he explains that tall and taller things are so by [participating in] Tallness, and short and shorter things are so by [participating in] Shortness;

4. At 100e8-101b2, he considers taller things and shorter things together

in the case of *one relational fact*, that of a man taller than another by his whole head;

5. At 102b3-8, he considers *two overlapping relational facts*, thus coming to grips with puzzle (P).

6. At 102c1-8, he expands his solution to that puzzle in what is really a brilliant ontological theory;

7. At 102c10-d2, he extends his theory of relations and of predication so as to include the relational facts about "the subjects that do not admit but a certain Form" (in Leibniz's phrase);

8. After 102d5, he formulates governing instantiational connections between Forms.

3. *Plato's macro-analysis of dyadic relational facts*

The core of Plato's relational puzzle (P) lies in the statements I have called (2) and (3) above, at 102c1-c4. In (2) Plato expands the point about Tallness being involved in the 'tallerness' of taller things, which he has been developing at steps *3* and *4* above. The expansion amounts to making the same point in the context of the two *datum* facts *Simmias is taller than Socrates* and *Simmias is shorter than Phaedo*. Plato is analyzing

(iTo) Simmias is taller than Socrates.

At 102bc1-2, in (2), Plato takes one part of fact (iTo), and analyzes it as follows:

First analysandum fragment: Simmias is taller . . .
First analysans fragment: Simmias has tallness . . .

It is important to keep in mind that here Plato is giving an analysis of just one *fragment*, and that neither the analysandum fragment nor the analysans fragment has an independent status. This is a point often neglected by commentators of the *Phaedo*, even though it is of the utmost importance.

At 102c2-4, in (3), Plato takes up the whole of the analysans (iTo) to provide the remaining fragment of the analysis in its proper context:

Analysandum: (iTo): Simmias is taller than Socrates.
Analysans of (iTo): Simmias has tallness *toward* ($\pi\rho\grave{o}\varsigma$) Socrates' short-
                                  ness.

[By (3) at 102c2-4.]

The tremendous importance Plato attaches to the prepositional factor (so to speak) *toward* in his analysis of relational facts can be appreciated better by comparing, as he undoubtedly wants us to do, his analysis of (iTo) with his analysis of the other datum fact mentioned in (D) at 1-2b3-4. The analysis is as follows:

Analysandum: (iSe): Simmias is shorter than Phaedo.
Analysans of (iSe): Phaedo has tallness *toward* Simmias' shortness.

[By (4) at 102c6-8.]

Of course, by parity of reasoning with the development of the analysis of (iTo) in (3), we must pair:

> *Analysans* of (iSe): Phaedo has tallness *toward* Simmias' shortness

> with

> *Analysandum* (eTi): Phaedo is taller than Simmias.

Hence, *the fact (iSe) is exactly the same as the fact (eTi)*. Furthermore, there is no ontological difference between the use of a complete sentence with the expression 'taller than' and one with the expression 'shorter than.' Note, moreover, the particularizing role of the factor *toward*. Let us keep these crucial results firmly in mind for the ensuing discussion.

The analyses Plato has so far offered of the facts *Simmias is taller than Socrates* and *Simmias is shorter than Phaedo* have a peculiar ambiguity. It is *not* harmful. Yet it is a minor blemish in what is otherwise, as I have underscored in my list of steps *1-7*, a magnificent piecemeal development.

Plato formulates his analysis of (iTo) in (3) as follows:

(5) Simmias has tallness *toward* Socrates's shortness.

Obviously, the scope of the preposition 'toward' is not clear. We can interpret (5) in either of two ways:

(5.a) Simmias has tallness, (which having is) toward Socrates' shortness.
(5.b) Simmias has (the following:) tallness-toward-Socrates' shortness.

In (5.a) the prepositional phrase 'toward Socrates' shortness' is adverbial, modifying the verb 'has.' In (5.b) that phrase is adjectival, modifying the noun 'tallness.'

Now, which one, (5.a) or (5.b), did Plato mean in (3), at 102c2-4? There is no way of answering this question conclusively. Moreover, things are even more complicated. There is a third interpretation, although it is one that distorts somewhat the Greek text, namely:

(5.c) Simmias has tallness, (which having is) toward Socrates' *having* shortness (toward Simmias' having tallness).

The distortion (5.c) makes to the Greek text is not, first appearances to the contrary, the introduction of a second parenthetical phrase. The comparison between Plato's analysis of "Simmias is taller than Socrates" and his analysis of "Simmias is shorter than Phaedo" clearly reveals that he means a reciprocal relationship between the elements linked by *toward* ($\pi\rho\delta\varsigma$). The distortion lies in the introduction of the underlined "*having*" in the prepositional phrase. We must, therefore, reflect further on what the text 102c1-8 as a *unitary* whole contains. Let us look at the text again. Let us focus our attention on the fact just noted: Plato wants the relationship denoted by the preposition $\pi\rho\delta\varsigma$ ('toward.') to be symmetrical! Well, then! The introduction of the verb $\xi\chi\epsilon\iota\nu$ ('having') in the prepositional phrase as the term of the preposition *is* perfectly all right. I submit, therefore, that the primary interpretation of (5) in Plato's (3) at 102c2-c4 is precisely (5.c). Thus, the analysis of (iTo) can be put even more perspicuously as follows:

> *Analysandum*: (iTo): Simmias is taller than Socrates.
> *Macro-analysans* of (iTo): (Simmias has tallness) *toward* (Socrates has shortness).

Of course, if we want to produce a readable sentence in English we can write the macro-analysans of (iTo) as follows: "Simmias has tallness toward Socrates' having shortness," or, better, "Simmias has tallness and Socrates has shortness toward one another." But there is no point in pursuing this. The ontological paraphrasing Plato was concerned with was *not* meant by him to constitute a revision of the grammar of ordinary Greek.[11] He is not doing ordinary-language analysis.

4. *Plato's micro-analysis of dyadic relational facts*

I have, abruptly, called the previous analysantia *macro-analysantia*. The reason is that in them we have the prepositional factor *toward* connecting the participation of the ordinary individuals Simmias, Socrates, and Phaedo in the relevant Forms. These macro-analyses are perfectly satisfactory for a general theory of relational facts. Yet Plato went further. As noted above, in data (D), at 102b5-6, Plato hints that the participation of an ordinary individual in a Form is analyzable in terms of the individual being composed of, having in it, a subject that can admit just of a certain Form (to use Leibniz's phrase again). Plato proceeds at 102c10-d2 to endorse explicitly what he has hinted at. Hence:

> (P*) Plato is committed to the analysis of macro-predication, i.e. the participation of ordinary individuals in Forms, in terms of both:
> (i) the analysis of ordinary individuals as bundles of micro-individuals, (ii) micro-predication, i.e., the participation of micro-individuals in just one Form; and in the case of relational facts, (iii) a primary micro-prepositional tie *toward*p.

Now, given (P*) Plato has simply to pursue his macro-analysis of relational facts into the requisite micro-analysis. This is precisely what he seems to be doing in the text immediately following (4), quoted at the beginning of this Part. The additional text reads as follows:

> 102c10 Thus, then: Simmias is said to be both 'short and tall,' being in between the two, the one to whose *tallness* he submits his shortness to surpass, and the other to whom
> d2 he supplies *tallness that overtops his (the other's) shortness.* [My italics]

The main development of this passage is precisely the introduction of the *micro-relational* facts:

(6)   [The tallness such that (Phaedo has it and Simmias has shortness toward each other) is tall] *toward* [The shortness such that (Simmias has it and Phaedo has tallness toward each other) is short] .

(7)   [The tallness such that (Simmias has it and Socrates has shortness toward each other) is tall] *toward* [The shortness such that (Socrates has it and Simmias has tallness toward each other) is short] .

This formulation is hard, although it is not entirely satisfactory. Part of the problem lies in that we cannot perceive, or think of, those subjects that admit exactly one Form in isolation. We can refer to them only through references to the ordinary individuals composed of them. Yet Plato's intention is rather clear:

(P*.1)   The micro-individuals are uniquely characterized by one Form and enter as components of just one fact (or state of affairs). They are also peculiar to the macro-individuals they compose. The only exceptions (wholly incoherent) that Plato makes to this principle are souls.[12] (See Section 8.)

Clearly, according to Plato's view, there is *in* Phaedo a large number of tallnesses, say, $tallness_1$ (toward Socrates' $shortness_a$), $tallness_2$ (toward Simmias' $shortness_b$), etc. These tallnesses in Phaedo are all wholly different from the tallnesses in other persons or objects. The crucial thing is that:

(P*.2)   If a micro-individual participates in a Form, like Tallness, which belongs with another Form, like Shortness, then that micro-individual exists as long as a correlated micro-individual participates in the correlated Form. Thus, every $tallness_j$ goes with some particular $shortness_j$, and vice versa.

Let us return to (5), (5.a), and (5.b). We have already seen that (5), as a statement of Plato's macro-analysis of "Simmias is taller than Socrates," must be understood as (5.c). Now, literally understood, in isolation from the context of the analysis and its implication of symmetry, as we noted in (5.c), both (5.a) and (5.b) are wrong. They appear to have the connection *toward* linking a macro-instantiation to a micro-instantiation. Nevertheless, we can consider (5) as a hybrid formulation, literally incorrect, but suggestive of the move Plato is planning, all through 102b3-c8, from the macro- to the micro-analysis. This hybrid, unstable formulation is precisely what I claim to be the only blemish in Plato's exposition of his analysis of relational facts.

5. *Platonic ontograms of ordinary individuals*

Laws (P*)-(P*.2) need some further clarification. By them Plato is commited to the view that ordinary individuals are bundles of micro-individuals. Plato is rather silent on whether or not at the bottom of such bundles there is an indeterminate, qualityless substrate. But what he says about the soul suggests that he was in the *Phaedo* rejecting substrates as the cores of ordinary individuals. Obviously, each self, with its memories throughout all its experiences, seems to remain one and the same in spite of all the changes of its corresponding body. Thus, identifying one's self with one's soul, one would seem to have at hand an entity that can be a self-identical substrate regardless of its properties, which are at bottom its experiences. Perhaps this idea is too advanced for the author of the *Phaedo*, that is, at the time of that authorship.[13] At any rate, throughout *Phaedo* 105c9-107a1 Plato takes the mind or the soul to be a micro-individual, i.e., just one of those subjects that admit of but one Form (again, in Leibniz's phrase), that Form being the Form of Aliveness. Patently, Plato was bound to drop such a limited view of the mind. It is already in conflict with earlier statements in the *Phaedo* itself.

Without a substrate, an ordinary individual is simply a structure of micro-individuals. Some micro-individuals are *singles*: they instantiate nonrelational Forms. Other micro-individuals are, so to speak, *married* to other micro-individuals, either in the same or in another ordinary individual.

We can represent the structure of ordinary individuals and the internality of ordinary predication in certain formulas that we call *ontograms*: they are diagrams of ontological constituents. Let A: $[A^1, A^2]$ be a dyadic relation such that Simmias is A to himself, and let $a_i^1, a_i^2, \ldots$ be the A micro-individuals; similarly, let Phaedo be B to himself and let $b_j^1, b_j^2, \ldots$ be the B micro-individuals. In the case of related micro-individuals we must use the same subscript. Thus, we have the following partial ontograms:

Simmias = $[\ldots, a_i^1, a_i^1,$ Greekness$_n$, tallness$_h$, $\ldots$ shortness$_k$, poorness$_t \ldots]$

Phaedo = $[\ldots, b_w^1, b_w^2,$ Greekness$_m$, tallness$_k$, tallness$_j$, $\ldots$ richness$_t$, richness$_s \ldots]$

Socrates = $[\ldots,$ wisdom$_{2000}$, Greekness$_r$, shortness$_j$, shortness$_h$, $\ldots$ poorness$_s$, $\ldots]$

The preceding ontograms clearly represent the following:

(A) *Micro-facts*:
  (11) (tallness$_h$ is tall) *toward*$_p$ (shortness$_h$ is short);
  (12) (tallness$_j$ is tall) *toward*$_p$ (shortness$_j$ is short);
  (13) (tallness$_k$ is tall) *toward*$_p$ (shortness$_k$ is short); etc.
  (14) (wisdom$_{2000}$) is wise.

(B) *Macro-facts*:
  (21) (Simmias has tallness) *toward*$_D$ (Socrates has shortness);
  (22) (Phaedo has tallness) *toward*$_D$ (Socrates has shortness);
  (23) (Phaedo has tallness) *toward*$_D$ (Simmias has shortness); etc.
  (24) Socrates has wisdom. (See footnote 8.)

The subscripted word *toward*$_D$ indicates the derivative nature of the factor *toward* present in the macro-relational facts. The ontograms also show that (21) is grounded on (11), (22) on (12), (23) on (13), and (24) on (14).

The general point is this:

(G*) Given the internality of ordinary macro-prediction on Plato's view, and given his reduction of dyadic relations to pairs of (monadic) Forms, whenever an ordinary object a is related by R to an object b, then: (i) the relation R is a pair of Forms $[R^1, R^2]$, (ii) there is in the object a a micro-individual that both is nothing but R^1 and is connected with a micro-individual in b, which is nothing but R^2.

Plato did not do much with this commitment of his views. But Leibniz did pursue the consequences of this commitment all the way—up to the principle that every monad mirrors the whole universe—even to the super Anaxogorean principle that at each time each monad represents the whole history of the universe.

6. Plato's ontological inventory.

Let us review our preceding exegesis of Plato's analysis of the relational fact (iTo), "Simmias is taller than Socrates." Clearly, the final micro-analysis of (iTo) involves the following distinct elements:

A. *Ordinary individuals:*
    (a) Simmias;   (b) Socrates.
B. *Forms:*
    (c) Tallness;   (d) Shortness.
C. *Macro- or ordinary Form-participation components, which have no independent reality, because of F below:*
    (e) Simmias having tallness;
    (f) Socrates having shortness:
D. *The corresponding micro-individuals, which are particular subjects that admit just a certain Form:*
    (g) the particular tallness involved in (e):
    (h) the particular shortness involved in (f).
E. The dependent micro-ontological Form-instantiations, which consist of each of the unique particular subjects that admit just a certain Form participating, in the primary sense of participation, in the Form in question:
    (i) Simmias' *tallness* toward Socrates' shortness being *tall* toward Socrates' shortness (it being nothing else at all);
    (j) Socrates' *shortness* toward Simmias' tallness being *short* toward Simmias' tallness (it being nothing else at all).
F. *The prepositional factors, which contain the strictly irreducible relational core of all relational states of affairs:*
    (k) *toward*$_D$, which: (α) links the Form-participation components (e) and (f); (β) is not a Form, but (γ) is a universal aspect of reality in that it is the same in all relational facts; and (δ) is as syncategorematic as the copula involved in the way a particular subject that admits just a certain Form admits the Form in question.
    (l) *toward*$_P$, which links (i) and (j); (β)-(δ) apply.

The above is an impressive array of factors. And all those factors are there in the text! How could Leibniz fail to be impressed by them? Obviously, because he had not yet *felt* Plato's *Phaedo* puzzle of relations. But the seed of the puzzle undoubtedly fell on fertile ground, as we shall see, and was fertilized by the *Theaetus* puzzles.

7. *Some principles of Plato's ontology*

We have not exhausted the riches in Plato's *Phaedo* 102b3-e8. We have so far gone through the list of factors involved in Plato's full analysis of relational facts. But to stop there would not do justice to a most impressive *Gestalt* feature of his analysis. Plato does *not* consider relations in themselves, in isolation from the facts in which they enter. His analysis of relations is implicit, deeply buried in his analysis of relational facts. Note how the seven stages *1-7*, distinguished above in Section 2, of the development of his analysis, show the analysis to be oriented toward the analysis of the unitary pattern of relational facts. We have seen already some principles in operation. Yet a summary of the principles underlying the structure of relational facts may be helpful.

The following important principles governing Plato's analysis of the facts *Simmias is taller than Socrates and Simmias is shorter than Phaedo* cannot be overstressed:

(I)   Singular sentences of the form "*x* is taller than *y*" express exactly the same fact, or better, state of affairs, as the corresponding sentences of the form "*y* is shorter than *x*."

(II)   There are *no* converse relational facts (or states of affairs). The fact *Simmias is taller than Socrates* is exactly the same as the fact *Socrates is shorter than Simmias*.

(III)   The prepositional factors denoted by "toward" connect, not individuals, whether ordinary or micro-ontological, but Form-instantiations components. There is, thus, the macro-ontological *toward*$_D$, which links to each other Form-instantiations of ordinary individuals; and there is also the micro-ontological *toward*$_P$, which links to each other Form-instantiations of micro-individuals. The latter is the primary one.

(IV)   The micro-individuals are governed by laws (P*), (P*.1), (P*.2), and (G*).

(V)   There are *no* converse relations.

(VI)   There are *no* converse Form-instantiations, whether macro- or micro-ontological.

(VII)   There *are* converse Forms composing dyadic relations, as Tallness and Shortness compose the relation *taller-than* (= the relation *shorter-than*).

(VIII) A dyadic relation is thus a pair of Forms, like Tallness and Shortness, such that: (i) they are governed by the *Law of Instantiation Enchainment*, which is law (P*.2); and (ii) their instantiations do not themselves constitute facts (or states of affairs): an atomic

8. *Change in the* Phaedo

We need a brief elaboration of principle (P*.1) above. Part of this principle is expounded at 102d5-e2, where Plato explains that the "tall in us" will either perish or withdraw when smallness approaches it. That is, when a thing changes from taller than to not taller than something else, the micro-individual that is the thing's tallness either withdraws from that thing or stops existing. Minds or souls seem to be, in 105-107, the only exceptions to the principle that micro-particulars simply perish when macro-objects change properties.

Plato's *Phaedo* theory of change is, at the beginning, the view that for an ordinary, macro-object to change, it must have first one property and then drop that property and acquire an opposite property. Properties are organized into opposites, and within families of opposites. This Plato discusses in detail in 102d-107. In this discussion, however, Plato develops that early view into the official theory according to which:

(i)   the exchange of opposites characteristic of an ordinary thing's change is an exchange of micro-particulars;

(ii)   each of a pair of micro-particulars involved in a change just instantiates each of a pair of two opposite Forms;

(iii) the Forms composing a (dyadic) relation are opposite to each other;

(iv)   normal micro-particulars (taking minds as utterly abnormal ones) cannot exist by themselves, outside an ordinary macro-object, and perish in their exchanges with their opposites.

To anticipate, Leibniz's view of accidents is precisely Plato's view of what we have called micro-individuals, governed by (i)-(iv).

9. *Plato's own view of relations*

The ontological inventory of Plato's and the ontological principles formulated above have a very strong textual support—as we have carefully seen. Undoubtedly, the preceding formulation of both goes beyond Plato's actual articulation of them. Thus, though it is obvious that he adumbrates the general theory that inventory and those principles lead to, he certainly was not clearly aware of them, or of the general theory, as we have formulated them. The degree of awareness he reached is a matter of opinion—but that he adumbrated that inventory and those principles is (or should be) beyond question. On the other hand, the general theory embedding that inventory and those principles must go beyond Plato's views in several respects: (i) it has to generalize from dyadic relational facts to n-adic facts for any value of n; (ii) it has to be general in the sense of providing general statements, rather than paradigms meant to be generalizable; (iii) it has to be more precise.

I have held[14] that Plato's view on the ontological structure of relational facts is exciting and logically viable. To understand this, it is essential to appreciate that the *ontological structure* of a fact, or a state of affairs, is the internal composition of the aspects, features, or factors entering in the fact in question. The ontological structure in a canonical language, whether formalized or not, is represented by the concatenation of primitive signs of the language in a well-formed formula or sentence, in accordance with the rules for sentence-formation of that canonical lnaguage. The ontological structure is presupposed by the logic of the fact in question. The logic of a fact, or a state of affairs, is the network of implication relationships of the fact (or state of affairs). In a cononical language, they are represented by the rules of implication, or of transformation (as Carnap used to call them). It is crucial to fasten to the principle that the ontological structure of a fact, or its logical form, if you wish, is not identical with the network of implications of the fact in question. For one thing, two different facts can be logically equivalent, and thus, have exactly the same implications.[15]

Plato's view of relational facts, and Leibniz's too, is an ontological view, *not* a logical one. Yet as we shall see in Part IV, that view is logically adequate in this sense: on the ontological (or logical) structure of relational facts propounded by Plato (and Leibniz), one can mount appropriate principles of implication, which yield a set of relational logical truths that is isomorphic to the set of relational logical truths mounted on the standard conception of relational facts (or of states of affairs).

Let us now proceed to Leibniz's developments under the influence of the *Phaedo* and the *Theaetetus.*

III. LEIBNIZ'S ONTOLOGICAL VIEWS ON RELATIONS AND PREDICATION

1. *Leibniz, the* Theaetetus, *and the* Phaedo

I have noted above in passing how the young Leibniz failed to be properly impressed either by the *Phaedo* puzzle about relations, or by the *Phaedo*'s rich ontology. Yet the *Theaetetus* puzzles of relational change did impress him. Those puzzles are fully discussed by Plato; it is easy, therefore, to be impressed by them. The *Theaetetus* does not, however, have a clear ontology. It must be read in connection with the *Phaedo.* I am sure that the fact that Leibniz studied them consecutively was instrumental in the influence Plato's views on relations, predication, micro-individuals, and change had on Leibniz. The *Phaedo* provided the framework for Leibniz's development; the *Theaetetus*, with its puzzles about relations, furnished the impetus for that development.

2. *Leibniz's crucial text on relations of April 1676*

The following briefest entry in Leibniz's metaphysical journal while he was in Paris is one of the most remarkable and significant of his discussions of relational facts:

[1]   When the mind perceives something in matter, it cannot be denied, since it perceives different and diverse things, that there is change in it.

[2]   When somebody becomes taller than I, by growing up, certainly some change occurs in me too, since a denomination is changed.

[3]   And in this way everything is in a certain way contained in everything. (See footnote 5; my labeling.)

Recall from Part I how serious Leibniz found the *Theaetetus* about Socrates not changing yet becoming samller than Theaetetus, when the latter grows up. That puzzle, Leibniz says, has great repercussions in other matters. Undoubtedly, through March and April of 1676, he thinks intensely about that puzzle. At the end of April, he finds a solution. He puts it down rather casually, even cryptically. Here is a case in which the knowledge of the immediately preceding intellectual history of a writer helps understand a piece of writing. In summary, my exegesis of the passage [1]-[3] is as follows:

(i)   sentence [1] formulates a theoretical decision of Leibniz;

(ii)   it is a decision important in itself, but in the present context its importance lies in its heuristic role: it paves the way for Leibniz's further theoretical decision in [2];

(iii)   Leibniz's theoretical decision in [2] illuminates the linguistic data mentioned in [2];

(iv)   this theoretical decision solves the *Theaetetus* puzzle about Theaetetus becoming taller than Socrates; it is a decision through which Leibniz adopts Plato's view of change in the *Theaetetus*;

(v)   Leibniz generalizes his decisions about perceiving and becoming taller to all relational facts—endorsing what I call the principle of the dynamical homogeniety of all relata in the same relational fact, or rather the same relational state of affairs, whether existing or not;

(vi)   Leibniz does not bother to state the general principle: he simply assumes it as a premise in his derivation of [3];

(vii)   the Anaxagorean-type conclusion formulated in [3] is pregnant with Leibniz's complete concepts of individual substances, which he developed into the monads;

(viii) that general principle behind [3] includes both Plato's internalist theory of ordinary predication and Plato's analysis of dyadic relational facts—both, as we saw in part II, fully expounded in the *Phaedo*;

(ix)   in [1]-[3] Leibniz does not reach the depth and richness of *Phaedo* 1-2b3-103a2.

I am not claiming that Leibniz reread the *Phaedo,* or thought of it, when he moved from [2] to [3]. Nor am I denying that either. Most likely, during his reflections during his abridgment of Plato's dialogues and the writing of [1]-[3],

Leibniz came to internalize, to make his, the *Phaedo* ontology. As noted in (iv)-(ix), Leibniz proceeds in the reverse order of Plato's: from the *Theaetetus* puzzle to the *Phaedo* ontology.

3. Commentary on sentence [1]

It is natural to think that the mind is passive, unchanging, when it simply perceives. In perception it is natural to think of the mind as the unaltered stage where things change. Thus, it takes a change of view of the mind to consider it as changing with its perceptions. Undoubtedly, if one is a phenomenalist and views physical objects as systems of perceived contents, one must consider the perceptual contents as internal to the mind. This internality of perceptual contents can easily lead to view each perception as identical with the occurrence of that content. Then, a change of content is a change of perception, and a change of mind. Now, Leibniz had in April of 1676 several times, but more fully on April 16, engaged in phenomenalist and reductionist reflections of that sort.[16] Also, even earlier, he had regarded the mind as active. In any case, in [1], Leibniz moves from general aspects of perception and the mind to a specific one. He sees perceiving as a relation between a mind and a perceptual content. He comes to believe that a change in a perceptual content is of and by itself a change in the perceiving mind. He is thus accepting a very special case of the following:

(L*) *Principle of the dynamical homogeneity of all the relata of a relational fact (or state of affairs):*
If relation R relates the members of an ordered n-tuple of ordinary individuals $[a_1, \ldots a_n]$ at a certain time t, then when at a later time t' R stops relating the members of $[a_1, \ldots a_n]$, each and all of the individuals $a_1, \ldots a_n$ undergo a change at t'.

I have stated (L*) in full generality. Yet is is not clear that Leibniz at this time is considering other than dyadic relationships.

The adoption of the instance of (L*) for the case of the relationship of perceiving liberated Leibniz from any prejudices he may have had against the instance of (L*) for the case of Theaetetus' becoming taller than Socrates by growing up.

4. Exegesis of sentence [2]

"When somebody becomes taller than I, by growing up, certainly some change occurs in me too, since a denomination of mine is changed."

To begin with, the contrast between growing up and becoming taller is very much like the contrast Plato discusses at length in *Phaedo* between a man being taller than another and being so by his whole head, or between being a pair of objects and being a pair of objects as a result of a partitioning of a larger whole. Plato in the *Phaedo* is concerned with the ontological analysis of facts in terms of the entities involved in them; his concern with the procedures that bring about those facts is not within his focus of interest. Likewise, Leibniz in [2] is not concerned with the procedure of growing, but with the ontological analysis of a relational change.

To fix our ideas, let us consider the two facts:

(4) At time t Socrates is taller than Theaetetus;
(5) At time t' Socrates becomes shorter than Theaetetus.

Stimulated by the change of the perceiving mind when its perceptions change, Leibniz proposes to consider the change (4)-(5) as also involving changes in Socrates and Theaetetus both. This decision is not yet the decision to adopt (L*) in its full generality. Leibniz's theoretical decision in [2] is grounded on especially appropriate data: in the change from (4) to (5) *both* Socrates and Theaetetus change denominations. What are these denominations? Obviously, the denominations 'shorter' and 'taller.' Thus, unpacking (4) and (5) so as to reveal those denominations that label the items involved in the changes, we have:

(4L)   At time t Socrates is taller (than Theaetetus) *given that* Theaetetus is shorter (than Socrates).

(5L)   At time t' Socrates is shorter (than Theaetetus) *given that* Theaetetus is taller (than Socrates).

I have added the parenthetical expressions not only for grammatical reasons, but for ontological perspicuity; clearly, at time t Socrates is taller than other people and also Theaetetus is shorter than many other persons or things. I have also added the connective *"given that"* to indicate that each of (4L) and of (5L) is a unitary whole. To be sure, this connective in (4L) and (5L) merely locates and labels a problem.

Now, Leibniz's formulations seem to express that each individual has a property with the other individual as a component! This, however, must be wrong, given that in [3] he says "everything is contained in everything *in a certain way*"—that is, *not* bodily or in person, but by containing an appropriate *representation*. This suggests that the proper names "Socrates" and "Theaetetus" in the parenthetical phrases, thus modifying the modifications 'tall' and 'short,' which change, when Theaetetus grows taller than Socrates, must have a different sense from the one they have when they are subjects of the verbs. Let us indicate this difference in sense by italicizing. Hence, we can rephrase (4L) and (5L) more perspicuously as:

(4L')   At time t: Socrates is taller-than-*Theaetetus given that* Theaetetus is shorter-than Socrates.

(5L')   At time t': Socrates is shorter-than-*Theaetetus given that* Theaetetus is taller-than-*Socrates*.

What can the sense of the italicized proper names be? Evidently, each of these names must signal that the property denominated with a predicate containing the name is connected with the corresponding property denominated with a predicate containing the other name. But then any other pair of correlated signs will serve the same purpose. We can use, e.g., the same subscript. Furthermore, once we see that the italicized names are signals of correlation, there is no point in using the comparatives 'shorter' and 'taller' rather than the simpler 'short' and 'tall.' Thus, we can rephrase (4L) and (5L) as:

(4L″)   At time t: (Socrates is tall$_j$) *given that* (Theaetetus is short$_j$)

(5L″)   At time t': (Socrates is short$_k$) *given that* (Theaetetus is tall$_k$).

Now we must raise a question: What sort of entities are *Socrates is tall$_j$* and *Theaetetus is short$_j$*? There are two views answering this question:

(A)   Relational instantiations, like
       Socrates is tall$_j$ and *Theaetetus is short$_j$*, are themselves facts, or
       states of affairs (or propositions)—they are independent, ontological-
       ly fully rounded complexes that exist, or occur, or are realized (or
       are true) or not;

(B)   Relational instantiations, like
       Socrates is tall$_j$ and *Theaetetus is short$_j$*, are incomplete entities,
       which can exist only as components of the atomic fact (state of
       affairs, proposition) (4L″).

It is not immediately obvious which of the two views Leibniz is adopting. We must stress, however, that he is *not* endorsing view (A). In fact, there are, within [1] - [3] , some hidden pressures towards view (B).

The issue about the ontological status of the predication components in (4L″) and (5L″) can be put in linguistic terms as follows: Which of the two rules, (a) or (b) below, govern the use of the expression *given that*?

(a)   Sentences like (4L″) and (5L″) are true, just in case the subscripts
       are the same.

(b)   Sentences like (4L″) and (5L″) are meaningless if the subscripts are
       different.

In the case of rule (a), we are treating the clauses flanking *given that* as detachable expressions, as fully meaningful in isolation. This is fine if each of them expresses a state of affairs, or a proposition, that is, something that is true or false, or exists or not, as the case may be. Then *given that* is, if governed by rule (a), a connective that has to be governed by other rules of implication, and it can link disparate elements like:

(6)   At time t: (Socrates is tall$_h$) *given that* (Plato is fat$_k$);

(7)   At time t: (Socrates is tall$_r$) *given that* (Socrates is tall$_g$).

Rule (a) then goes well with view (A).

On the other hand, if rule (b) governs sentences formed with the expression *given that*, then sentences (6) and (7) are meaningless. Included in rule (b) is the requirement that *given that* be flanked by predicates, like '(. . . tall)' and

'(. . . short), which together denote one relation, in this case the relation *taller-shorter-than*. We can thus simplify (4L″) and (5L″) to:

(4.L)   At time t: (Socrates is tall) *given that* (Theaetetus is short);
(5.L)   At time t': (Socrates is short) *given that* (Theaetetus is tall).

Once we drop the subscripts we are no longer allowing the expressions "(Socrates is tall)" and "(Theaetetus is short)" to have an independent meaning in (4L). To be sure, we can assign the independent meanings, but these must be *different* from the syncategorematic meanings they have in (4L). Thus, rule (b) is suitable for view (B). We shall interpret (4L) and (5L) as expressing view (B).

Patently, (4L) and (5L) are reminiscent of Plato's macro-analysis of dyadic relational facts. In the case of examples (4) and (5), we can put Plato's macro-analysis in semicanonical notation as follows:

(4P)   At time t: (Socrates is tall) *toward* (Theaetetus is short);
(5P)   At time t': (Socrates is short) *toward* (Theaetetus is tall).

The similarity between (4L)-(5L) and (4P)-(5P) is most striking. Doubtless, Leibniz is now committed to a type of Platonic view of relations. But he has not just taken the view from the *Pheado*. With the *Phaedo* in the back of his mind, he comes to such a view from a different route. On the one hand, in the *Phaedo*, Plato is concerned with the threat of contradiction in a man being both tall(er) and short(er). He proceeds very carefully to offer an account that extirpates any threat of contradiction. But Plato is not then concerned with relational change. Note that the time parameters in (4P) and (5P) never appeared in the *Phaedo*. On the other hand, Leibniz starts with the *Theaetetus* puzzle about change. By adopting a special instance of (L*) and by seizing the linguistic fact that denominations change for every term of a relational change, Leibniz approaches Plato's macro-analysis of relational facts. At this stage, however, Leibniz's view is less developed than Plato's. For one thing, there is the obscurity of whether Leibniz adopts view (A) or view (B); Plato adopts view (B). Later on Leibniz will adopt (B). For another thing, Plato analyzes, further, predication in terms of participation in Forms. Thus, as we saw in Part II, had Plato applied his *Phaedo* macro-analysis to the *Theaetetus* puzzle, he would have analyzed (4P) and (5P) as follows:

(4P*)   At time t: (Socrates has tallness) *toward* (Theaetetus has short-
        ness).
(5P*)   At time t': (Socrates has shortness) *toward* (Theaetetus has tall-
        ness).

In sentence [2] Leibniz speaks of a change occurring "*in* me, too." The preceding discussion has concentrated on the force of this "too." Let us focus on "in." This indicates that Leibniz is, like Plato, adopting an internalist account of ordinary predication. But it is not clear from [2] alone how that internality must be taken. For this we must go on to scrutinize Leibniz's conclusion [3].

5. *Exegesis of sentence [3]*

"And in this way everything is in a certain way contained in everything."

We have already commented that the adverbial phrase "in a certain way" reveals that no ordinary individual contains, literally, another to which it is related, by virtue of the relationship in question. The containment has to consist in that a relatum contains literally an item that is connected with the other relatum, or, better, an item that is connected with an item literally contained in the other relatum. Consider (4) again:

(4)   At time *t*: Socrates is taller than Theaetetus.

Leibniz is implying in [2] - [3] that (5) *involves all of the following:*

(i)   Socrates has in him *what* the denomination 'taller than Theaetetus' denotes; call it *tall*$_h$

(ii)   *tall*$_h$ in a certain way represents Theaetetus:

(iii)   by containing *tall*$_h$ at time *t* Socrates contains Theaetetus;

(iv)   Theaetetus has in him *what* the denomination 'shorter than Socrates' denotes; call it *short*$_h$;

(v)   *short*$_h$ in a certain way represents Socrates;

(vi)   by containing *short*$_h$ at time *t* Theaetetus contains Socrates.

Evidently, in (i)-(vi) *tall*$_h$ and *short*$_h$ function as very special particular individuals. They are very much like what we have called Plato's micro-individuals. Clearly, the relational fact *at time* t *Socrates is taller than Theaetetus* consists precisely in Socrates having at time *t* *tall*$_h$ and Theaetetus having *short*$_h$, and in these being governed by (i)-(vi).

Between writing sentence [2] and putting down sentence [3] Leibniz has undergone an important development: he has moved explicitly in the direction of Plato's micro-analysis of relational facts. He has also generalized his view from special cases of principle (L*) to at least the full general dyadic interpretation of (L*). Furthermore, he derives a sweeping ontological conclusion, which will turn out to be central to his whole metaphysics.

In sentences [2] - [3] Leibniz is adopting a general analysis of dyadic relational facts. Consider an ordinary dyadic fact formulated in everyday language with a sentence of the form:

(g)   A is R to B.

Leibniz is conceiving of the relation R as a pair of monadic properties, say [R^1, R^2] such that a pair of micro-relata, say, r_b^1 and r_a^2, instantiate R^1 and R^2, respectively, as the superscripted *r*s indicate. These individuals are contained in A and B, respectively, and each represents in its container the other ordinary individual. Hence, Leibniz is adumbrating the analysis of (g) as:

(g.L*)   (A has r_b^1) *given that* (B has r_a^2).

Clearly, (g.L*) is very much like the general Platonic schema, merely adumbrated by Plato in the *Phaedo,* for the micro-analysis of dyadic facts. (In conceptualization of generality, Leibniz is far above Plato). But is $(g.L^*)$ the same as, or tantamount to, Plato's adumbrated schema? More specifically, are the Leibnizian r_b^1 and r_a^2 Platonic micro-individuals? Undoubtedly, the Leibnizian micro-relata have some of the properties of the Platonic micro-individuals: (i) they are all individuals; (ii) they are contained, literally, in ordinary individuals; (iii) they bear ultimately the relationship of relational facts; (iv) they are necessarily (analytically, some philosophers would say) characterized by the monadic properties composing a relation. But two features remain unclear:

(Q.1)   Are Leibnizian micro-relata subjects *that admit of just one Form* (to use Leibniz's own words to describe the Platonic micro-individuals)?

(Q.2)   Are Leibnizian micro-relata dependent on ordinary individuals, having no separate existence, and perishing when the ordinary individuals undergo changes involving them?

An affirmative answer to each of these questions is correct, if and only if Leibnizian micro-relata are Platonic micro-individuals.

Let us consider (Q.1). At first sight, it seems that it cannot be answered on the sole basis of Leibniz's entry [1]-[3]. On a second look, however, [2] provides a mechanism for a partial answer. In [2] Leibniz adopts the criterion that a change occurs in an object when two stages of the object cannot correctly be described without changing a *denomination* of the object. Let objects A and B be related by two relations R and S, which are not logically equivalent. Clearly the change from it being the case that, to it not being the case that $(A$ has $R_b^1)$ *given that* $(B$ has $r_a^2)$ involves a change of denominations pertaining to relation R, but not a change of denominations pertaining to a different relation S, and vice versa. Hence, the micro-relata r_b^1, r_a^2, s_b^1, and s_a^2 are all pairwise distinct. What about logically equivalent relations? This certainly goes much beyond what Leibniz has in mind in [1]-[3]. There are reasons for insisting that logical equivalence of properties is not the same as identity. Among such reasons is that for numbers $m \neq n$ some n-adic properties are logically equivalent to some m-adic properties.[17] Yet, it is not incompatible with Leibniz's ontology of relations to require that the same micro-relata instantiate logically equivalent relations of the same adicity. In fact, Plato's view as deployed in the *Phaedo* does not say anything about logical equivalence of Forms.[18] It can be slightly revised so as to have the same micro-individuals bring in to ordinary individuals a whole package of logically equivalent Forms. I say "revised" because Plato's intentions seem to me to be precisely what Leibniz thought them to be, namely, to introduce in his ontology subjects that admit of just one Form.

Let us take up question (Q.2). Evidently, in [1]-[3] Leibniz is saying absolutely nothing about the perishibility of micro-relata. Later on, however, the Leibnizian micro-relata turn out to be species of *accidents,* and accidents are nothing but Platonic micro-individuals. (See, e.g., the quotation from Leibniz in Section 8 below.)

To conclude our examination of [3] let us turn to Leibniz's Anaxagorean-type conclusion that everything is in a certain way contained in everything. This conclusion anticipates his later

Mirror Principle: Each substance represents the totality of every other (finite) substance.[19]

Yet it is not quite this principle. In [3] each ordinary individual contains a representation of every other ordinary individual. For this is sufficient that the following assumption behind [3] be true:

Assumption: Between any two ordinary individuals there is at least one relation.

Several crucial principles are required to move from [3] to the Mirror Principle. All of them are assumptions about the nature of relations and relational facts. Among them are comprehension principles to the effect that on the basis of a relation between A and B (as by the above *assumption*), for any property of B there is another relation between A and B. From these principles and the above assumption behind [3], every ordinary individual will have a representation of each property of another individual. We cannot here discuss those other assumptions: We simply note that the Platonic view of relations and predication behind [3] is the core that, with those other principles about relations, led Leibniz to his Mirror Principle. That view is also behind Leibniz's other central theses—in particular, the windowlessness of the monads, the preestablished harmony, and monadism.

To sum up our discussion of [1]-[3], this passage contains implicitly almost the whole Platonic ontology of *Phaedo* 102b3-103a2. Hence, the ontological inventory of entities and principles offered in Part II, Sections 6 and 7 are not only Platonic but Leibnizian. The Platonic ontograms of Part II, Section 5 can be used to diagram Leibniz's analysis of ordinary individuals.

6. Leibniz's analysis of "Paris loves Helen"

Sometime before 1686, and probably around 1678, Leibniz wrote the following widely commented-on text:

[4] The genitive is the addition of a substantive to a substantive. . . . This will be the best way of explaining "Paris is the lover of Helen," that is, "Paris loves, *and by that very fact* [*eo ipso*] Helen is loved." Here, therefore, two propositions have been brought together and abbreviated into one.[20]

We have then, the example:

(11) Paris loves Helen

analyzed as

(11.L) (Paris loves) *eo ipso* (Helen is loved).

This is very much the macro-analysis of dyadic relational facts Plato and Leibniz gave before. The novelty is that before, in the passage [1]-[3] of April 1676, we had to supply the expression *given that*. Now Leibniz himself offers the expression *eo ipso*.

Leibniz's passage [1]-[3] contains notes of a metaphysical meditation. Passage [4], on the other hand, contains a reflection on grammar. It is undoubtedly true that if (11.L) is the grammatical analysis of (11), then two sentences have been abbreviated into one. Hence the initial question is this: Does Leibniz mean by 'proposition' (*propositio*) the same as what we mean by 'sentence'? If so, then passage [4] is of no philosophical value. Of course, it is still important for the theory of grammar to know that the surface grammatical structure of (11) has to be understood in terms of the structure of (11.L).

Now, three paragraphs before [4] Leibniz writes:

[5]   A noun expresses a certain idea, but no truth, i.e. [*seu*] proposition.[21]

Apparently, then, Leibniz does not mean by 'proposition' in [4] a mere sentence, but something that is true-or-false, and something that compares with ideas, which are expressed by nouns. Yet he speaks of the two propositions abbreviated (*compendiose collectae*) into one. He seems to be committing a confusion of use of sentences with their mention.

Philosophically speaking, we can treat [4] as saying that the fact (state of affairs, proposition) reported in sentence (11) is ontologically macro-analyzable as having the structure revealed more perspicuously by sentence (11.L). Furthermore, that *eo ipso* is a connection between the two propositions *Paris loves* and *Helen is loved*. Since by [5] a proposition is true, then there are the facts *Paris loves* and *Helen is loved*. Hence, *eo ipso* connects complexes that have an independent status of their own. Thus, Leibniz is in [4]-[5] adopting what we called view (A) in Section 4 above. Thus, there are, according to this interpretation of [4], facts like (6) and (7) of that section—where *eo ipso* substitutes *given that*.

If the above interpretation of [4]-[5] is correct, then when he wrote them Leibniz had diverged from Plato in a very important respect. Furthermore if *eo ipso* is a connection between two propositions (or facts), then Leibniz is proposing both a reduction of relations to sets of monadic properties (Forms) and a reduction of relational propositions (or facts) to nonrelational ones. Plato proposes just the former. On Plato's view the prepositional aspect *toward* is an internal factor that structures Form-instantiations into *atomic* relational facts. Logistically speaking, Plato's reduction of relations to monadic Forms occurs at the level of the *rules of formation* for well-formed atomic sentences. On the other hand, on the above interpretation of [4]-[5], Leibniz would be proposing a reduction of relations and relational propositions at the level of the *rules of transformation* or implication. These matters will become clearer in Part IV.

It is not clear, nevertheless, that in [4] Leibniz meant to endorse view (A) of Section 4 above. He may have been somewhat confused about sentences and propositions and meant to offer only a grammatical account—which account is what he is offering anyway in the essay to which [4] and [5] belong.

7. Leibniz's analysis of "David is the father of Solomon"

Another well-known discussion of relations by Leibniz occurs in a letter to Des Bosses written in 1714. It is:

> For since [6] no modification can subsist by itself but essentially entails a substantial subject, . . .
>
> [7] I do not believe that you will admit an accident that is in two subjects. My judgment about relations is that [8] paternity in David is one thing, sonship in Solomon another, but that [9] the relation common to both is a merely mental thing [*rem mere mentalem*] whose basis is the modifications of the individuals.[22]

From [6] and [7] we see that Leibniz calls 'accidents' the modifications of substance. They are, clearly, like the Platonic micro-individuals we discussed in Part II. He is now endorsing their dependence on one substance. This interpretation leaves it open that they may transfer from one substance to another.

In [8]-[9] we find something like the familiar Platonic macro-analysis of

(12) David is the father of Solomon.

The analysans of (12) is:

(12.L) (David has paternity) *r* (Solomon has sonship).

I have written "*r*" in between the two property-instantiations to represent that 'common relation,' which is "a merely mental thing." This *r* is the old *eo ipso* of four decades earlier. We must ask the same question we raised about *eo ipso*: Is it a propositional connective, or is it some deeper syncategorematic factor that belongs to the very formation of an *atomic* relational proposition (or fact)? That is, is view (A) or is view (B), both discussed above in Section 4, the one that Leibniz holds?

In contradistinction with the Paris-Helen passage, in [6]-[9] we have no words like 'proposition' that can tip the scales in one rather than the other direction. The words 'one thing' and 'another' in [8] translate the Latin *aliud*. Since this is a very general word, there is no textual support for ascribing to Leibniz view (A), namely, that the instantiation components *David has paternity* and *Solomon has sonship* in (12.L) are facts or propositions. May we take advantage of the generality of Leibniz's *aliud*s and interpret him as endorsing view (B), namely, that those instantiation components are not facts (or propositions, or true-or-false items) in themselves, but only elements in an atomic, irreducible truth? Perhaps.

Leibniz's use of the abstract nouns 'paternity' and 'sonship' makes (12.L) identical with Plato's macro-analysans of (12). It is clear from [9] that under-

lying that macro-analysis is a micro-analysis in terms of the accidents or modifi-
cations in David and Solomon. These are the micro-relata whose presence in
David and Solomon, respectively, constitutes their having paternity and sonship.
Hence the more informative formulation of (12) is:

(12.M)   (David has p_j) *given that* (David has s_j).

Leibniz in [8]-[9] goes beyond his 1676 Paris text [1]-[3] in one important respect. He now discusses the pure relation, that is, the irreducible core in
all relational facts (and propositions). That core is what underlies what *eo ipso*,
given that, and *r* express. He seems to be talking about that prepositional factor
toward$_D$ that appears in Plato's macro-analysis. (See Part II, Section 4-6.) This is
what Leibniz calls "a purely mental thing." It is of the utmost importance to
avoid misinterpreting Leibniz as meaning that pure relations are imaginary entities, that they do not have a role to play in the structure of reality. Just the
opposite: they are precisely what keeps the monads or individual substances as
members of one and the same world. (For contrast see the quotation from Russell in the next section.)

In raising the issue of the ontological status of pure relations, Leibniz
reaches a higher philosophical awareness than Plato does. Nevertheless, Leibniz
did not match Plato's awareness that, once you introduce micro-individuals, you
have to have them instantiate Forms and stand in relations. Clearly, underlying
the pure relation "common" to David and Solomon, there must be a deeper pure
relation "common" to both David's paternity of Solomon and Solomon's son-
ship. This deeper pure relation is the Platonic *toward*$_P$ ($\pi\rho\dot{o}\varsigma$), discussed in Part
II, Sections 4-6. Undoubtedly, this too, is "a merely mental thing" (*rem mere
mentalem*).

8. *Leibniz's three ways of conceiving rational facts*

Besides the crucial text [1]-[3] of April 1676, the most important text by
Leibniz on relational facts is the following classic, a fragment of his fifth letter
to Dr. Clarke:

[10]   I shall allege another example to show how the mind uses, upon
        occasion of accidents which are *in* subjects, *to fancy [se former] to
        itself some thing [quelque chose]* answerable to those accidents,
        [my comma] out of subjects. [11] The ratio or proportion be-
        tween two lines L and M may be conceived three several ways: [*a*]
        as a ratio of the greater L to the lesser M, [*b*] as a ratio of the
        lesser M to the greater L, and, lastly, [*c*] as something *abstracted*
        from both, that is, the ratio between L and M without considering
        which is the antecedent or which is the consequent, which the
        subject and which the object. [12] And thus it is that proportions
        are considered in music. [13] In the first way of considering them,
        L the greater, in the second, M the lesser, is the subject of that ac-

cident which philosophers call "relation." [14] But which of them will be the subject in the third way of considering them? It cannot be said both of them, L and M together, are the subject of such an accident; for, [15] if so, *we should have an accident in two subjects*, with one leg in one and the other in the other, which is contrary to the notion of accidents. Therefore, [16] we must say that this relation, in the third way of considering it, is indeed out of the subjects; but [17] being neither substance nor accident, it must be a *mere ideal thing*, the consideration of which is nevertheless useful.[23] [My labeling and my italics]

This passage belongs to an important context in which Leibniz discusses spatial relations.

The above passage seems remarkably clear. The phrase "three ways of conceiving" appears on a second reading to be troublesome. This phrase is particularly naughty in the light of the first sentence, namely, [10]. Leibniz is objecting to the reification (*de se former quelque chose*) of certain entities. This can easily give the impression that one (the third) way of conceiving relations is erroneous. That impression would, however, be erroneous. A look at sentence [12] and at the final clause in [17] should dispel that error. In fact, as my underlining of 'reification' was meant to convey, the error Leibniz is trying to exorcise is the error of reifying relations as conceived in the third way. Nothing is wrong with any of the three ways of conceiving relations. Each has its place in the pursuit of knowledge, and each gets hold of an important entity. In brief, the three ways of conceiving relations are three ways of apprehending *three different entities*. Leibniz also points out at [13] that in the first and the second ways of conceiving relations we are dealing with entities of exactly the same type: accidents. In the third way of conceiving relations we deal with an entity of an altogether different type: one that is neither substance nor accident, Leibniz says at [17]. Since accidents are internal to substances, the external relations of the third way of conceiving belong to *another category*. This category Leibniz calls in this fragment 'mere ideal things,' and in the David-Solomon fragment he called 'mere mental things,' and at other places he has called 'beings of reason' (*entia rationis*). The first of these three expressions is by far the best. They are all meant to convey Leibniz's view that the primary existents are substances, the secondary existents are accidents, and everything else does not truly exist, its reality being parasitic in the connections between accidents and substances. Of course, they have also a status as thought of by God.

Nothing, then, can be further from the mark than the following commentary by Bertrand Russell:

After he [Leibniz] has seemed, for a moment, to realize that *relation* is something distinct from and *independent* [sic] of subjects and accidents, he thrusts aside the awkward discovery, by *condemning* [sic] the third of the above meanings as 'a mere ideal thing.' If he were pushed to this 'ideal thing,' I am afraid he would declare it to be an *accident* [sic] of the mind, which contemplates the ratio [or proportion].[24] [My italics]

Concerning the ontological structures of relational facts in [10]-[17], the familiar distinctions that were implicit in [1]-[3] seem to become explicit. The first two ways of conceiving relations seem to deliver the properties of the macro-relata. If so, those properties are the macro-relata's accidents. Since the accidents are internal to the macro-relata, they contain a representation of the other correlated relata. The novelty of the passage seems to be the casual identification of the properties in things with accidents, that is, with the micro-relata. These accidents are, then, Platonic micro-individuals. In fact, the peculiarity of each accident to just one substance is one of Leibniz's major premises, earlier in the same letter to Clarke, for the claim that neither space nor places are properties. When objects exchange place, as we say, they just change their own relationships to all other objects. We speak of the same place because the networks of relationships have certain patterns of similarity. But space is not "a strange property or affection, which passes from one subject to another . . . subjects would leave off their accidents like clothes, that other subjects may put them on" (Loemker, p. 702).

On a third reading, the above passage [10]-[17] is perplexing. Leibniz's talk of three ways of conceiving relations suggests that we are confronting three *alternatives* equally good, provided we do not confuse the categories of the entities we are discussing. But are they really alternatives to each other? Let us see. The example is:

(13)   M is greater than L.

On the first way of conceiving (13), we find:

(13.a)   L is greater-than-M:
(13.a')   L has the-ratio-from-L-to-M.

On the second way we find:

(13.b)   M is lesser-than-L:
(13.b')   M has the-ratio-from-M-to-L.

On the third way we have:

(13.c)   (L is great) r (M is less):
(13.c')   the ratio M/L.

Doubtless, the sentences (13.a) and (13.b) are linguistic alternatives to each other; and so are (13.a') and (13.b'). They all contrast with the expression (13.c'), which is not a sentence. Yet Leibniz was not talking about sentences. He was talking about facts out there in the world. Thus, the only way in which we have genuine alternatives is this: each of the alternatives is an *analysis* of one and the same fact. We would have, then (13.a), (13.b), and (13.c) as different parsings or conceivings of the same fact (13). If this is so, however, (13.a) and

(13.b) are equivalent to (13.c) and to (13). But then neither is (13.a) the relational instantiation component (*L is great*) that appears in (13.c), nor is (13.b) the component *M is less* of (13.c). Then, is it not clear that the accidents *greater-than-M* and *lesser-than-L* are the micro-relata we found in Leibniz's crucial passage [1]-[3] of April 1676? This is very perplexing. What has happened?

The only hypothesis I can think of that sheds some light on Leibniz's classic text [10]-[17] is this: Leibniz has implicitly endorsed view (A), introduced in Section 4 above. That is the view that the instantiation components connected by the irreducible prepositional core *eo ipso*, or *r* [as in (13.c)], or *given that*, or *toward*, are themselves facts (or states of affairs, or propositions). From that view it is quite easy to regard those instantiations as somehow self-sufficient—after all they somehow represent the other relation. Now we can take those instantiations as equivalent to each other, and hence, as equal alternatives for consideration.

If the preceding is an accurate account of the moves implicit in Leibniz's classic passage [10]-[17], then Leibniz is there rejecting a most important thesis in Plato's theory of relations and relational facts. That departure, naturally, creates problems. For one thing, an account is needed of those peculiar relational accidents, like *greater-than-M* and *lesser-than-L,* which seem to include a whole substance in them. For another thing, if the reduction of relations to monadic properties (or Forms) is to go through the implicational route, then we must have those reductive principles of implication.

There is no point in raising more problems. Perhaps Leibniz's mistake in [10]-[17] is just a verbal one. Perhaps he spoke of "ways of conceiving" carelessly. Perhaps he meant to say that in all relational facts there are those three relational entities, besides the ordinary individuals—the two monadic relational properties, and the pure relation that ties instantiations, *not* individuals—and that this is in part what makes it an ideal, syncategorematic entity; further, that the instantiations of the monadic relational properties, whether by substances or by accidents, are *not* themselves facts (or truths). If Leibniz's error in [1]-[17] is just a verbal one, then Leibniz's view in that passage is the one advocated by Plato in *Phaedo* 102b3-103a2.

9. *Leibniz's orderings*

In the preceding sections we have discussed Leibniz's passages about the relational facts about ordinary individuals, like persons, trees, and rocks. In all of them we have seen a Platonic theory of relations at work. Other types of facts, however, can be said to be relational; yet they do not fit the Platonic pattern. Relational propositions about numbers seem to be relevant examples. The orderings of facts involved in spatial relations may also be of that sort. Relations of implication between universals or propositions are other examples. In all of these cases, we have relations between, or among, abstract entities. Perhaps the fundamental division of the two types of relations runs along the line separating the concrete, or existing in the primary sense, and the abstract. Leibniz's introduction of order as a way of distinguishing dreams from waking experience need not be an exception. This order is *not* just a set of relations between, or among, items of experience, which are concrete; it must be an ordering of states of affairs or facts.

But we cannot spend time on this topic.[25] The fact is that Leibniz never dealt with this most important issue. (See Part IV.)

10. *Final comment*

We have subjected both Plato's and Leibniz's discussions of the ontological structure of relational facts to careful scrutiny. They both seem to have pretty much the same view. Plato's meticulousness is awesome. He was discovering the problems himself for the most part; he did not have at his disposal any logical, even grammatical, tool; yet he developed his view piecemeal, relentlessly taking up question after question, from the mere postulation of the Forms, to the macro-analysis of relational facts, to the micro-analysis of relational facts. His formulations are seldom abstract, being for the most part careful discussions of paradigmatic examples meant to illustrate general principles. That is precisely the juncture where Leibniz surpassed Plato's discussions. Leibniz put to himself the questions in general terms; and he formulated general answers. Yet on the ontology of relations, Leibniz's discussions never reached the level of systematic meticulousness that characterized Plato's development in *Phaedo* 100-105. On the other hand, precisely because of the highly abstract level of his thinking, Leibniz was able to see, in flashes, encompassing metaphysical consequences or applications of his Platonic view of relational facts and of predication.

One final remark is pertinent. Leibniz was a logician who made important advances in the theory of implication. He conceived all propositions to be of the subject-predicate form, and he made some attempts at reducing propositions ostensibly of different forms to the subject-predicate form. He had some success. But that success was modest indeed. Furthermore, his modest success was partly due to his reduction of subject-predicate propositions to a type of equational proposition.[26] But Leibniz *never* let the successes of his logical work, or of his hopes about his logical reductions, influence his philosophical views. The fact is that he was not better off than Plato concerning the *logic* of relations. Yet his Platonic view of the ontological structure of relational facts (or propositions) is, as we shall show in Part IV, a perfectly viable view, logically speaking.

IV. THE LOGICAL VIABILITY OF THE PLATONIC-LEIBNIZIAN ONTOLOGY OF RELATIONAL STATES OF AFFAIRS

1. *The standard and the Platonic-Leibnizian macro-views of relations compared.*

We must cut orthogonally to the issue about the ultimate ontological status of universals. On the Realist position, there are such abstract entities as universals.

This position compares with the Platonic-Leibnizian view in a straightforward way. However, what we are concerned with here has a counterpart within the Nominalist camp. If there are no entities as universals, then we have the basis or ground for the use of a general term, even if that ground is some system or structure of individuals. Again, our issue about relations is perpendicular to the issue of whether or not we want to quantify over predicates. Further, whether universals are individuated as required by nominal quantifiers, or are quantified by adjectival quantifiers, the issue we are interested in here has a counterpart within each camp. Thus, for convenience we shall adopt the Realist context, assuming that the reader can produce the appropriate transformation of the issue into his/her favorite view of universals.

On the standard view, there are simple, or atomic relations, and they differ from qualities and other monadic properites in that they are, so to speak, instantiated by ordered n-tuples. Thus,

(1)   Simmias gives Socrates the copy of Evenus' poem

is conceived to have the ontological (or logical) form exhibited in

(1.a) *Gives* (Simmias, the copy of Evenus' poem, Socrates).

Clearly, this state of affairs is entirely different from

(2) *Gives* (Socrates, the copy of Evenus' poem, Simmias).

The relation *Gives* or Givenship is the same in both (1) and (2), but the ordered triple that instantiates it is different in each case.

There are powerful arguments that seem to establish that relational states of affairs are not reducible to nonrelational ones. That is, we cannot break the state of affairs (1), or (1.a), into a complex state of affairs having as components states of affairs composed of one of the three elements of the triple ⟨Simmias, the copy of Evenus' poem, Socrates⟩ instantiating simply a monadic property.[27] I will not rehearse them here. For our present purposes we may accept that such irreducibility of relational to nonrelational *states of affairs* (facts, propositions, sentences) has been established. But we must demur at the conclusion some philosophers have derived from that irreducibility, that *relations* are not reducible to sets or sequences of monadic properties. The latter reduction is the one Plato accomplished in *Phaedo* 1 2b3-c4, and he accomplished it in the context of *irreducible* relational facts (or states of affairs). It is also the kind of reduction Leibniz was committed to when he adopted what we called view (B) in Part III, Section 4.

On the standard view of relations, then the relation *Gives*, or some other relation (in case the example is not adequate), is a simple entity with no internal complexity. It has an external complexity in that it cannot be instantiated by any other entity than a triple of individuals in a certain order, say, as suggested in (1.a). Those are precisely the respects in which the Platonic-Leibnizian view differs from the standard one. On the Platonic-Leibnizian view: (i) the relation *Gives* is not simple, but complex; (ii) it is a set of three monadic properties

(Forms); (iii) no instantiations of these Forms is itself a state of affairs; and (iv) a minimal or atomic state of affairs composed of those instantiations is a complex composed of instantiations of each of the three Forms. The three Forms composing the relation *Gives* can be named: Givership (or *Giver*), Giveeship (or *Givee*), and Givenship (or *Given*). These Forms (or monadic, but dependent properties) can be called *conditions*. This, (iii)-(iv), which is what we called in Part II, Section 7 the Law of Enchainment, is the requirement that the instantiation of a relational condition *not* be something true or false by itself, but *be* only a component of something true or false, namely, the whole complex of instantiations of the three conditions. Hence, on the Platonic-Leibnizian view (when Leibniz adopts view (B)), example (1) above is more perspicuously put as follows:

(1.P-L)   *Giver*(Simmias)*Given*(the copy of Evenus' poem)*Givee*(Socrates)

Clearly, (1.P-L) is, in the terminology of Part II, Section 3, a macro-analysis of (1). Because of (iii)-(iv), this macro-analysis provides a reduction of the relation *Gives*, but does not furnish a reduction of the relational state of affairs (1) to nonrelational states of affairs.

On the Platonic-Leibnizian view, conditions, as just illustrated, are Forms, and they are simple entities. The relation *Gives* is just the set of conditions ⟨Giver, Given, Givee⟩, which is governed by (iii)-(iv), or the Law of Instantiation Truth-value Enchainment. The order of an ordered n-tuple that instantiates a relation is simply the specification of the conditions instantiated by the members of the n-tuple in question. The order is, thus, incorporated in the Forms, and does not belong to the individuals per se. On the other hand, on the standard view, the relation *Gives* is (or may be) a simple entity. Our Platonic conditions have a complex counterpart in the standard view, namely, each condition corresponds to an abstract pair of a relation and a position within an instantiating ordered n-tuple. Thus, the condition *Giver* has as the standard counterpart the pair ⟨*Gives*, position 1⟩, and the condition *Givee* has as the standard counterpart the pair ⟨*Gives*, position 3⟩.

The standard view and the Platonic-Leibnizian view are ontological alternatives insofar as we are dealing with the structure of atomic relational states of affairs. Are they genuine alternatives with respect to the implications of relational states of affairs (or propositions)? Specifically, can we build on them logical systems that deliver isomorphic sets of logical truths? An affirmative answer to this question establishes that the two views are genuine ontological alternatives. Establishing such an affirmative answer is what we call establishing the logical viability of the Platonic-Leibnizian ontological view of relations and relational facts. Naturally, if the two ontological views are logically viable, we must choose between them in the light of comprehensive and subtle data. Here we cannot engage in gathering such data. But we can establish the logical viability of the Platonic-Leibnizian view.

2. *The logical viability of the Platonic-Leibnizian view*

We shall limit ourselves to defending the viability of the Platonic-Leibnizian macro-analysis of relational states of affairs. Since the micro-analysis of relational states of affairs goes much beyond the conceptual repertoire of the standard functional calculus, it must, of course, introduce new logical truths. On the other hand, if the macro-analysis is logically defective, so is the micro-analysis. Hence the establishment of the logical viability of the Platonic-Leibnizian macro-analysis of relations is a necessary condition for the micro-analysis to be a genuine ontological alternative.[28]

3. *A formal Platonic-Leibnizian language*

A Platonic-Leibnizian formal language P-L is a language for the standard first-order predicate calculus in which all the primitive predicates are of degree 1. For convenience, let us suppose that all the predicates are expressions with three indices: $A^{i,n,j}$, where $i,n,j > 0$, j is a number assigned to the predicate in question by an enumeration of all the predicates, n indicates the degree of the relation that n predicates express together, and i indicates that the predicate in question is the ith member of the relation $[A^{1,n,j}, \ldots, A^{n,n,j}]$, where $1 \leqslant i \leqslant n$. The only new rule of formation of P-L is the following:

(R.1)   Sequences of primitive signs of P-L* of the following form are wffs:
$$A^{b_1,n,j}(x_1)A^{b_2,n,j}(x_2) \ldots A^{b_n,n,j}(x_n),$$
where: (a) $b_s \neq b_t$, if $s \neq t$; (b) $b_1 + b_2 + \ldots + b_n = n(n+1)/2$; and (c) each of $x_1, x_2, \ldots$, and x_n is an individual sign.

4. *The Platonic-Leibnizian calculus P-L**

As we noted in Part II Section 3, Plato is committed to the view that the sentences of the forms "Simmias is taller than Socrates" and "Socrates is shorter than Simmias" say the very same thing. Hence, a minimal axiom of the Platonic-Leibnizian relational calculus P-L* is an axiom postulating the logical equivalence of the well-formed formulas introduced by rule (R.1), when they differ merely in the order of their n components of the form $A^{s,t,j}(x_s)$, for $s = h_1, \ldots, h_n$. The remaining axioms are the same as the axioms of the standard predicate calculus.

5. *Standard and Platonic-Leibnizian set-theoretical semantics*

We cannot take for granted that the standard meta-theorems of the first-order functional calculus hold. For one thing, any proof of consistency, or of completeness, will have to reckon with the fact that each predicate $A^{i,n,j}$ is assigned a set of individuals in its domain of interpretation. We need semantical models suitable to the Platonic-Leibnizian first-order predicate calculus.

As it will be recalled, for the standard quantificational calculus,

A *standard model* is an ordered pair $\langle S, D \rangle$, where,

1. $S \neq \phi$
2. $D \neq \phi$
3. Every member of D is a set of sets D_n of ordered n-tuples $\langle r_1, \ldots r_n \rangle$ such that: (i) $n > 0$; (ii) each r_i is a member of S.

A *standard interpretation* I over a standard model is a function that assigns to each individual sign of the calculus a member of S and to each predicate $A^{n,j}$ of degree n a member of $D_n \in D$.

A *standard valuation* V determined by a (standard) interpretation I over a (standard) model m is a function that assigns *truth* or *falsity* to each closed wff. The fundamental clause for atomic formulas is that:

VI. $V(A^{n,j}(x_1, \ldots, x_n)$ I, $m)$ is true, if and only if $\langle I(x_1, m), \ldots, I(x_n, m) \rangle$ is a member of $I(A^{n,j}, m)$.

Now, a *Platonic-Leibnizian relational structure* is an ordered pair $\langle S, F \rangle$, where:

1. $S \neq \phi$.
2. $F \neq \phi$.
3. Every member f_n of F is a set ordered n-tuples $\langle r_1, \ldots, r_n \rangle$, such that: (i) $n > 0$; (ii) $r_i \neq 0$, for $i = 1, \ldots, n$; (iii) each r_i is a sequence of members of S, perhaps with repetitions.

Let $m = \langle S, F \rangle$ be a Platonic-Leibnizian relational structure. Then an *interpretation* I over m of an individual sign x and a predicate symbol A of the Platonic calculus is a function satisfying these conditions:

I1. $I(x, m)$ is a member of S.

I2. $I(A^{i,n,j}, m)$ is the ith member of a member f_n of F.

Each interpretation yields a valuation of the wffs of the calculus in the standard way, except for the case of atomic relational wffs, namely:

V1. $V(A^{b1}(x_1) \ldots A^b n(x_n)$, I, $m)$ is true, if and only if there is an ordinal k such that the kth member of $I(A^{bi}, m) = I(x_i, m)$, for $i = b_1, \ldots, b_n$.

As is customary, a set β of wffs of the Platonic-Leibnizian calculus is *satisfiable* if and only if there is a Platonic-Leibnizian relational structure m and there are functions I and V such that for each member p of β, $V(p, I, m)$ is true.

It is a routine affair to construct both a consistency proof and a Henkin-type proof of the completeness of calculus P-L* with respect to Platonic-Leibnizian relational structures.

First let us define the following syntactical function c that maps wffs f and g of P-L* onto standard wffs,

1. $c[A^{b1,n,j}(x_1) \ldots A^b n^j(x_n)] = A^{n,j}(x_1, \ldots, x_n)$
2. $c[\sim f] = \sim c[f]$
3. $c[f \text{ k } g] = c[f] \text{ k } c[g]$, where k is any dyadic connective.
4. $c[Qf] = Qc[f]$, where Q is any quantifier.

Metatheorem. A Platonic wff f is satisfied by a Platonic structure, if and only if the corresponding standard formula $c[f]$ is satisfied by some standard model.

Proof of the case of atomic wffs: Patently, given an atomic wff f and a model $m = \langle S, F \rangle$ that satisfies f, we can construct a standard model $m' = \langle S, D \rangle$ that satisfies $c[f]$, and vice versa.

Let f be $A^{b_1, n, j}(x_1) \ldots A^{b}n, {}^{n,j}(x_n)$,

and let the model that satisfies f be $m = \langle S, F \rangle$ and let I be the interpretation involved. Then there is an ordinal d such that dth member of each $I(A^{i,n,j}, m)$ is $I(x_{i,m})$. Consider the standard interpretation I' and model m' such that $I'(x, m')$ $= I(x, m)$ and $I'(A^{n,j}, m')$ is the set of all ordered n-tuples $\langle r_1, \ldots, r_n \rangle$ such that for some ordinal e the eth member of $I(A^{i,n,j}, m)$ is r_i. Let $m' = \langle S, D \rangle$, where D is the set of all such $I'(A^{n,j}, m')$ for all n and j. Clearly, $\langle I'(x_1, m'), \ldots, I'(x_n, m') \rangle$ is a member of $I'(A^{n,j}, m')$. Hence, $c[f]$ is satisfied by m'.

Now, if $c[f]$ is satisfied by a standard model $m' = \langle S, D \rangle$, by the well-ordering theorem (that is, the axiom of choice), each member of D can be well-ordered into a set D_n of ordered n-tuples $\langle r_1, \ldots, r_n \rangle$. Let $p^{i,n}$ be the ordered set whose eth member is the element r_i of the eth n-tuple of D_n. Let p^n be the ordered n-tuple $\langle p^{1,n}, \ldots, p^{n,n} \rangle$ for each n. Let P be the set of all such p^ns. Then the structure $m = \langle S, P \rangle$ is a Platonic-Leibnizian model that satisfies f.

Notes

1. See the appendix to Hector-Neri Castañeda, "Plato's *Phaedo* of Relations," *Journal of Philosophical Logic* 1 (1972): 467-480, where there are brief discussions of R. C. Cross, A. D. Woozley, Julius Moravcsik, G. E. L. Owen, R. Hackforth, R. S. Bluck, *et al.*

2. That is, "the contrast between the finished whole and the missing part illuminates the furnished fragment," as said in H-N. Castañeda, "Leibniz's Syllogistico-Propositional Calculus," *Notre Dame Journal of Formal Logic* 17 (1976): 481-500. This essay shows how close Leibniz was to the axiomatization of a complete propositional calculus based on biconditional, as the primary propositional connective, and conjunction and negation, as term connectives. It is a great pity that L. Euler could not read the papers by Leibniz examined in my study.

3. See *Elementa philosophiae de summa rerum*, ed. I. Jagodinski (Kasan, 1913). I am very grateful to Professor Leroy E. Loemker for having very kindly lent me his copy of this inaccessible book. I am indebted to Ms. Barbara Halporn, the Indiana University Humanities Librarian, for having searched for a copy of this book and finally contacting Professor Loemker on my behalf.

4. Leibniz's own words are: "*Notabilis est haec difficultas et magni etiam ad alia quaedam momenti. Responsio autem quae in Platone sequitur, quod scilicet omnia fluant, non intelligo quomodo satis ad difficultatem referatur.*" From *Nouvelles lettres et opuscules inédits de Leibniz* ed. A. Foucher de Careil (Paris: Auguste Durand, 1857, with a long introduction and selective translations into French by Careil himself), p. 108.

5. "*Cum Mens aliquid percepit in Materia, negari non potest, dum alia atque alia percipit, etiam in ipsa esse mutationem. Dum alius fit me major, crescendo, utique in me quoque aliqua accidit mutatio, cum mutata sit denominatio de me. Et hoc modo omnia in omnibus quodammodo continentur.*" From Jagodinski, p. 122. This passage is not translated in *Gottfried Wilhelm Leibniz: Philosophical Papers and Letters*, ed. L. E. Loemker, 2nd ed. (Dordrecht, Holland: Reidel, 1969).

6. "*Nonne Simmias Socrate major, Phaedone minor, magnitudine utique et parvitate ac ipsum per se magnum sive magnitudine nunquam parvum esse potest? Idem ergo subjectum contraria potest pati, contraria ipsa se non patiuntur. Sunt tamen et subjecta quae etiam non nisi certam patiuntur formam, qua ablata destruuntur. . . .*" From Foucher de Careil, p. 84.

7. During that period Leibniz also studies Descartes' writings and Spinoza's. In the spring of 1676 his philosophical reflections have the effect of internalizing both Cartesian epistemological views and Platonic metaphysical doctrines. An excellent example of that blending appears in the marvelous passage examined in great detail in H-N. Castañeda, "Leibniz's Meditation on April 15, 1676, about Existence, Dreams, and Space," written for the Conference *Leibniz à Paris,* Chantilly, France, November 14-17, 1976. See *Studia Leibnitiana, Supplements La Philosophie de Leibniz* (Wiesbaden: Franz Steiner Verlag, 1981), vol. 2: 91-130.

8. See Note 1 and David Gallop, "Relations in the *Phaedo,*" in *New Essays on Plato and the Pre-Socratics,* ed. Roger A. Shiner and John King-Farlow (Guelph, Ontario: Canadian Association for Publishing in Philosophy, 1977). This paper defends the traditional view of *Phaedo* 102 and attacks my interpretation of it in the essay mentioned in Note 1. My rejoinder to Gallop's attack is contained in H-N. Castañeda, "Plato's Relations, *not* Essences or Accidents, at *Phaedo* 102b2-d2," *Canadian Journal of Philosophy* 8 (1978): 39-53. That paper contains the detailed grammatical analyses of Plato's Greek text that ground the exegesis contained in Part II of the present paper. The two complement each other. A highlight of that paper is this: if the translation by Gallop of *Phaedo* 102c2-4 is correct, then my exegesis is sound. Gallop's translation is in fact correct. In 1980 Mark McPherran adopted my interpretation of *Phaedo* 102-103 and used it to advantage in interpreting the "worst difficulty" argument at *Parmenides* 133-135. See his "Plato's *Parmenides* Theory of Relations," *Canadian Journal of Philosophy* (forthcoming in 1982).

9. Here I am taking advantage of a suggestion made by a former student, Joseph Chester, who, against a well entrenched tradition pointed out to me that 'frank' is in the context of *Phaedo* 102b8-c1 the only correct translation of τὸ ἀληθὲς. This word is always translated as 'true.' Yet it is clear that Plato is *not* claiming that the ordinary relational sentences of Greek (or English) are not true. They are indeed true, but not ontologically perspicuous, or frank.

10. The fact that Leibniz both passed very quickly over this relational puzzle and did not dwell upon Plato's exciting solution suggests that Leibniz abridged the *Phaedo* before he abridged the *Theaetetus.*

11. See Note 9 above.

12. Naturally, Leibniz did not accept Plato's final argument for immortality of the soul. He succinctly remarks that a demonstration that what participates in Life (i.e., the Form Aliveness) is indestructible is required. In his own words: "*Sed hoc, mea sententia, demonstrandum restabat, quicquid vitae sit particips, non posse extingui*" (Foucher de Careil, p. 86).

13. By the time Leibniz came around, things had changed. He found the self to be the very best candidate for a substrate. This is one strand of his mentalism, i.e., his view that the ultimate realities are mental substances.

14. See the papers mentioned in Note 8.

15. See, e.g., H-N. Castañeda, "Ontology and Grammar: I. Russell's Paradox and the Basic Theory of Properties," *Theoria* 42 (1976): 44-92, especially Part I Sections 8 and 9 and the Appendix.

16. See materials mentioned in Note 7.

17. See Castañeda, "Ontology and Grammar: I."

18. Doubtless, analyses of concepts, like the ones Plato had Socrates search for in his early dialogues, are at least logical equivalences. This seems to create a conflict with his view that all Forms are both monadic and simple. For a discussion of this see H-N. Castañeda, *La*

teoria de Platón sobre las Formas, las relaciones, y los particulares en el Fedón (Mexico: University of Mexico Press, 1976, translation from English by Margarita Valdes).

19. For this principle and other principles of Leibniz's metaphysics see, among other texts, his *Discourse on Metaphysics*, "First Truths," *The Monadology*, and "The Principles of Nature and of Grace, Based on Reason," all of which can be found in the Loemker anthology.

20. *"Genitivus est adjectio substantivi ad substantivum . . . Optime sic explicabitur, ut Paris est amator Helenae; id est: Paris amat et eo ipso Helena amatur. Sunt ergo duae propositiones in unam conpendiose collectae."* From *Opuscules et fragments inédits de Leibniz,* ed. L. Couturat (Paris, 1903), p. 287. The translation quoted above is from *Leibniz: Logical Papers,* ed. and trans. G. H. R. Parkinson (Oxford: Clarendon Press, 1966), p. 14.

This text continues, as has been discovered by Prof. Massimo Mugnai (University of Florence), and the continuation supports my interpretation. I do not publish here that text so that Prof. Mugnai can publish it first, thus, not acting on his permission to use it. But I do publish with his permission the following passage from his letter of November 4, 1977:

Como può vedere Leibniz, nel caso di Evandro, stablisce una correlazione stretta fra *patitur-agit* e *subditus-dominus* attribuendo a ciascuno dei due soggetti (Evander, ensis) una delle due proprietà correlative *(patitur, agit, ecc.).* Può darsi che cio rafforzi la Sua interpretazione: in ogni caso le dò amplia facolta di interpretare e decifrare il brano citato.

21. *"Nomen ideam quandam exprimit, nullam autem veritatem seu propositionem."* From Couturat p. 286; Parkinson, p. 13.

22. *"Cum enim nulla modificatio per se subsistere possit. . . . Neque enim admittes credo accidens, quod simul sit in duobus subjectis. Ita de Relationibus censeo, aliud esse paternitatem in Davide, aliud filiationem in Solomone, sed relationem communem utrique esse rem mere mentalem, cujus fundamentum sint modificationes singulorum."* From *Die philosophischen Schriften von Gottfried Wilhelm Leibniz* ed. C. I. Gerhardt, 7 vols. (Berlin; Weidmannsche Buchhandlung, 1879), Vol. 7, p. 486.

23. This is Dr. Clarke's own translation, except for my putting 'some thing' instead of something,' adding a comma and italics as noted. The whole correspondence between Leibniz and Clarke appears in the Loemker anthology, pp. 675-717; the quoted passage appears on p. 704.

24. Bertrand Russell, *The Philosophy of Leibniz,* 2nd ed., (London, 1937), p. 13.

25. See Castañeda, "Leibniz's Meditation." (Note 7 above.)

26. See Castañeda, "Leibniz's Syllogistico-Propositional Calculus." (Note 2 above.)

27. Some arguments are presented by Bertrand Russell in his *The Principles of Mathematics* 2nd ed. (New York: W. W. Norton, 1938) in Chapter 26. See Milton Fisk, "Relatedness without Relations," Nous 6 (1972): 139-51. Fisk's very interesting proposal reduces relations among objects to relations of propositions. It has however, a problem with asymmetric relations among individuals.

28. For a full discussion of the logical viability of the total theory of relations, including both the macro- and micro-analyses adumbrated by Plato in the *Phaedo,* see the monograph mentioned in Note 18 above. The last three sections that follow are based on my 1972 paper mentioned in Note 1 above.

Motion and Metaphysics in the Young Leibniz

Daniel Garber

In 1714 Leibniz, then 68 years old, looked back on his philosophical development and made the following remarks:[1]

> After finishing the Trivial Schools [that is, having completed the trivium], I fell upon the moderns, and I recall walking in a grove on the outskirts of Leipzig called the Rosental at the age of fifteen, and deliberating whether to preserve substantial forms or not. Mechanism finally prevailed and led me to apply myself to mathematics. . . . But when I looked for the ultimate reasons (*dernières raisons*) of mechanism . . . I was greatly surprised to see that they could not be found in mathematics but that I should have to return to metaphysics. This led me back to entelechies and from the material to the formal, and at last brought me to understand . . . that monads or simple substances are the only true substances.[2]

By 'mechanism' in this passage, Leibniz means what others of his contemporaries called the *mechanical philosophy*. The mechanical philosophy was a complex of theses and attitudes that dominated scientific thought in the seventeenth century — an ambitious program for explaining a variety of things, from complicated physical phenomena like magnetism to chemical and biological phenomena like digestion, in terms of the quantitative and geometrical properties of bodies in motion. In the passage quoted above, Leibniz suggests that it was his own coming to terms with this program that ultimately led him to the metaphysics characteristic of his later years.

It would be an interesting project, one that has not received much attention from recent Leibniz scholars, to trace out the development of Leibniz's

I would like to thank Roger Ariew, Barbara Horan, and Lesley Cohen Spear for comments on an earlier version; an earlier draft of this paper was presented at the University of Colorado at Boulder.

mature metaphysics from the writings of the young mechanical philosopher.[3] In this paper I shall begin such a project by presenting a critical examination of Leibniz's early writings and attempting to show just how it happened in that period that the mechanical philosophy, in particular, questions about the metaphysical status of motion in the mechanical philosophy, led Leibniz to metaphysics.

I shall be concerned largely with the work that Leibniz did from 1668 to 1672, when he left for Paris. A number of considerations motivate the choice of this period. Before 1668, relatively few of Leibniz's writings that survive deal with the mechanical philosophy. In the period that begins in 1668, on the other hand, Leibniz's writings on mechanism are sufficient in number for us to be able to piece together a coherent picture. The concluding year 1672 is appropriate because this is the date of Leibniz's important trip to Paris, where he met with a number of the main figures of European scientific and intellectual life, and where he began the evolution of his earlier views into his more mature later views. Thus, the years from 1668 to 1672 contain the earliest coherent version of Leibniz's mechanism and the related metaphysics that can be documented and studied. But there is another, more important, reason for choosing this period for careful study. As I shall attempt to show, it is in the period 1668-1672 that we observe the first clear emergence of what will later become Leibniz's mature metaphysics.

I shall not attempt a general characterization of the mechanical philosophy, or attempt any systematic evaluation of the extent to which Leibniz corresponds to or deviates from any particular school of mechanist thought.[4] However, from time to time it will be helpful to compare what Leibniz says with the doctrines of one mechanical philosopher in particular, Descartes. Such a comparison will, I think, help to put Leibniz's thought into historical perspective. But more important, it will help to point up certain otherwise easily missed but crucial features of Leibniz's early thought to which I would like to call special attention. In making use of Descartes in this way, though, I do not intend to imply that Leibniz's thought derives from Descartes or from a reaction against Descartes. It has been well established that if Leibniz had a philosophical master at this time, it must have been the Hobbes of *De Corpore*.[5] Furthermore, whereas Leibniz mentions Descartes often and seems generally acquainted with his thought, Leibniz claims not to have read him seriously in his youth.[6] All I claim is that certain aspects of Leibniz's early work are seen most clearly against the backdrop of Descartes's thinking, whatever Leibniz may have known of it.

My discussion is divided into two main parts. In the first of these I shall consider Leibniz's earlier writings, from 1668-1670, outlining his mechanism and related issues in metaphysical and theological writings. There I shall point out some important relations between Leibniz's early thought and Descartes's. In the second part, I shall consider the important changes in Leibniz's thinking in the years 1670-1672. I shall show both how they grow out of the earlier and more Cartesian writings, and how they relate to his own later thought.

I. THE CARTESIAN PERIOD: 1668-1670

Leibniz's early espousal of the mechanical philosophy is most evident in his adherence to that most fundamental of the mechanist's claims, the explicability of all of the properties of bodies in terms of their primary qualities. For example, Leibniz wrote to his mentor Jakob Thomasius in 1669 in a letter that he published largely unaltered in the following year:

> I maintain the rule which is common to all these renovators of philosophy that only magnitude, figure, and motion are to be used in explaining the properties of bodies.[7]

So sure is Leibniz of this principle that he argues in this letter and a preceding one to Thomasius from 1668[8] that all of the basic features of the Aristotelian theory of matter—form, substance, change, etc.—*can* and *must* be reinterpreted in mechanical terms. Thus, Leibniz claims, the writings of Aristotle are fully consistent with the teachings of the mechanical philosophy. To be sure, this mechanization of the Aristotelian metaphysics of nature is not a position that Leibniz will maintain for very long. Neither is it a position that is original to Leibniz. Leibniz himself cites a number of other philosophers in this connection.[9] The reconciliation of the Aristotelian and the mechanical philosophy, or better, the reduction of the former to the latter, is also one of the themes of Robert Boyle's *Origin of Forms and Qualities*, a basic text in the mechanical philosophy published in 1666, before the two letters in question, but apparently unknown to Leibniz until sometime after the letter of 1669.[10] Nevertheless, Leibniz's passionate defense of this point suggests the depths of his conviction to the principle in question.

Not unrelated to the claims about the explicability of the properties of bodies in mechanical terms is Leibniz's discussion of the nature of body. Like other mechanists, Leibniz claims that all body has the same nature: "All bodies are of the same kind (*homogenea*), or do not differ [from one another] except through magnitude, fugure, and motion."[11] However, Leibniz is not entirely clear about what this nature is. Sometimes he defines body as "that which is in space."[12] Since Leibniz also writes in this period that "to be extended . . . is nothing other than to be in space,"[13] this suggests that bodies are essentially extended and nothing else. However, elsewhere Leibniz explicitly denies this and argues that the nature of body consists in both extension and another quality which he calls antitypy, resistance, impenetrability, or solidity.[14]

These two positions place Leibniz squarely among the mechanists. Like every mechanist, he argues for the elimination of secondary qualities in favor of primary. And though he sometimes seems inclined to deny the Cartesian claim that the whole nature of body is extension, this is nothing unusual. Boyle and, later, Locke, for example, good mechanists both, take the same position Leibniz does with respect to the nature of body.[15] But what is especially interesting in Leibniz's thought during this period is not what he has in common with most other mechanists, but where he seems to differ.

One thing of particular importance to Leibniz the young mechanical philosopher is the metaphysical foundations of that doctrine, the "ultimate reasons of mechanism" that he is to mention much later. These questions are evident in remarks too numerous to cite about God and his role in the physical world found throughout Leibniz's writings during this period. One essay, though, is particularly important in this respect, the *Confessio Naturae Contra Atheistas* of 1668-1669. In that essay Leibniz explicitly argues that the mechanical philosophy, truly considered, leads us not away from God but toward a true understanding of his importance in the physical world.[16] But although Leibniz's position is clear, the argument that he offers is somewhat less than satisfactory. Leibniz considers three main questions: (1) Why do bodies have the particular magnitudes and figures they do? (2) Why do bodies have the motion they do? and (3) Why do bodies have the firmness (*cohaerentia*) they do? In each case, Leibniz argues that no purely mechanical answer is possible. Without any further argument, though, he concludes that *God* must be called upon to explain magnitude, motion, and firmness, giving no indication of precisely *how* the appeal to God solves the problems at hand. He says simply that:

> Through the ultimate analysis of bodies (*in extreme corporum resolutione*),
> it becomes clear that nature cannot dispense with the help of God.[17]

Given Leibniz's interests in the not too distant future, it would be worth looking at one of these three claims more closely. In the *Confesio*, Leibniz argues that there can be no purely mechanical account of motion because motion does not follow from the nature of body:

> Considering the matter more accurately, however, it becomes clear that
> mobility arises from the nature of a body but that motion itself does
> not. . . . Therefore no reason for motion can be found in bodies left to
> themselves.[18]

This question is taken up again in the letters to Thomasius. There, unlike in the *Confesio*, where motion is in this respect on a par with figure and magnitude, motion is identified as the *only* one of the mechanical qualities that does not follow from the nature of body.[19] But in those letters Leibniz is much clearer about how this leads us to God. In the letter of 1668 Leibniz argues:

> Since body is nothing but matter and figure, and since a cause of motion
> cannot be understood from either matter or figure, it is necessary that the
> cause of motion be outside of body. And since outside of body nothing is
> conceivable except a thinking thing or mind, the cause of motion will be
> mind. Moreover, the ruling mind of the world is God.[20]

Similarly, Leibniz argues in the letter of 1669:

> Physics deals with the matter of things and the unique affection resulting
> from the combination of matter with the other causes, that is to say, with
> motion. For mind supplies motion to matter in order to achieve a good

and pleasing figure and state of things for itself. *Matter in itself is devoid of motion. Mind is the principle of all motion*, as Aristotle rightly saw. . . . Aristotle regards it as certain that no body has a principle of motion within itself alone, and it is by this argument that he ascends to the prime mover.[21]

What Leibniz has in mind, at least in part, in these passages is a conception of God as the prime mover. Without a mind to *put* bodies *into* motion, bodies would have no reason to move; they would remain at rest. But something else, something deeper is going on in this argument. In the 1668 letter to Thomasius, Leibniz continues the passage earlier quoted as follows:

Indeed, unless we admit some incorporeal and as it were spiritual substantial forms or other in bodies by means of which a body would be able to move, by means of which a stone could tend downward and fire upward, . . . we close off from ourselves the most apt way of proving the existence of God, and destroy that admirable theorem of Aristotle's that whatever is moved has a cause of motion outside of itself.[22]

Here an incorporeal principle of motion seems required for something more than to put matter into motion. Just what this something more is becomes clearer in the Thomasius letter of 1669:

The nature of body . . . is constituted by extension and antitypy, and since there is nothing in things without a cause, nothing ought to be posited in bodies whose cause cannot be discovered in their first or constitutive principles. . . . Therefore, we can assume nothing in bodies which does not follow from the definition of extension and antitypy. But from these concepts are derived only magnitude, figure, situation, number, mobility, etc. Motion itself is not derived from them. Hence, *there is no motion as a real thing (ens reale) in bodies.*[23]

To say that motion does not follow from the nature of body means that we need not only an external *reason* for motion, but an external *subject* as well. Motion requires a mind external to body in which it is an *ens reale*. The mind that Leibniz proposes for this purpose is the mind of God, in whom motion seems to be the successive recreation of body at different points in space:

I have demonstrated . . . that whatever moves is continuously created and that bodies are something at any instant in assignable motion, but that they are nothing at any time midway between the instants in motion—a view that has never been heard of until now but which is clearly necessary and will silence the atheists.[24]

The significance of this analysis of motion for Leibniz can be seen in the outline for the *Catholic Demonstrations* that Leibniz was planning in this period. There, the claim that "motion could not happen without a continuous creation" is the basis both of a proof for the existence of God (there clearly distinguished from a first mover argument), and a proof for the possibility of creation.[25]

This position on motion is intimately related to Leibniz's views on metaphysics in this period, most particularly his account of *substance*. It is clear from his early writings that Leibniz considered a number of different conceptions of the notion of substance. In the *Dissertatio de Arte Combinatoria* of 1666 substance is defined as "whatever moves or is moved."[26] This is reflected in a later attempt at defining substance (1672) as "anything which is active or passive, or better, what is thought of absolutely or completely."[27] In the important letter to Thomasius of 1669 he says that "space is a substance and figure something substantial (*quiddam substantiale*) because all science deals with substance and it cannot be denied that geometry is a science."[28] But there is another account of substance that seems to dominate Leibniz's thinking in this period and beyond. On this conception, which arises in a note on transubstantiation from 1668, "a substance is a being that subsists in itself, that is, which has a *principle of action within itself.*"[29]

This definition of substance, together with the account of body and motion given above, has some interesting consequences. Leibniz argues both in his theological writings on transubstantiation and in his physical writings that every action of body is motion.[30] But, of course, no body contains within itself a principle of motion. So, we must conclude, no body taken by *itself* could be a substance.[31] Since the principle of motion for body is *mind*, corporeal substances *must* be the union of body with mind:

> No body separated from a concurrent mind (*praecisa mente concurrente*) has a principle of motion within itself. . . . Therefore no body separated from a concurrent mind is to be taken as substance. . . . Something is substance when taken together with a concurrent mind; something separated from a concurrent mind is accident.[32]

Since, as was argued, the principle of motion for bodies is God, who is the first cause of motion and in whom motion exists as the continual recreation of body, it must be the union with God that makes (nonrational) bodies substances:

> Substance is union with mind (*unio cum mente*). Thus the substance of the human body is union with the human mind, and the substance of bodies which lack reason is union with the universal mind, or God.[33]

This position is not without its difficulties. Leibniz must take care to distinguish the sense in which God is united to all bodies in motion from the sense in which minds are united to their bodies, and God is united with some minds.[34] Leibniz also must take care to distinguish his position from a pantheistic position, according to which God is the world soul, the single substantial form of all matter. He meets this difficulty by proposing that bodies are joined not to the mind of God itself, but to the ideas in God's mind.[35] But this position and the difficulties it generates seem inevitable given Leibniz's account of the real nature of motion and his definition of substance.

These, then, are the "ultimate reasons" of mechanism in the period 1668-1670. The world is made up of extended, antitypic things, at least some of which are in motion. But the existence of motion requires a noncorporeal principle of motion, God, who must serve two functions. God is, first of all, the prime mover, the agent who sets the world into motion. But also, God is the true subject in which motion exists as an ens reale, as the successive creation of moving bodies at different places. From this and an account according to which activity is the defining characteristic of substance, it follows that the bodies of the mechanical philosophy are not themselves substances.

Although this account of the metaphysical foundations of mechanism may look like a radical departure from mechanist thinking, it is not. In fact, in a number of respects it bears a striking resemblance to Descartes's thought, whether or not the young Leibniz was aware of that fact. For Descartes as well, all features of the physical world are explicable in terms of bodies in motion.[36] More important, Descartes sees God as playing something of the same role with respect to motion that we have seen in Leibniz's writings. Like Leibniz, Descartes sees God as the first cause of motion:

> As far as the general cause [of motion] is concerned, it seems obvious to me that this is none other than God Himself, who, being omnipotent, in the beginning created matter with both motion and rest.[37]

This by itself is hardly significant, though. A great many philosophers have seen God as the first mover. But as in Leibniz, Descartes's God is not merely the first mover, the mind who, having set matter into motion, leaves the world to develop on its own. As in Leibniz, Descartes's God is continually involved in the moment by moment re-creation of the world:

> Actually it is quite clear and evident to all who will consider attentively the nature of time that a substance, to be conserved at every moment that it endures, needs the same power and same action which would be necessary to produce it and create it anew if it did not yet exist. Thus the light of nature makes us see clearly that conservation and creation differ only in regard to our manner of thinking.[38]

And as in Leibniz, the theory of continual re-creation plays a major role in the account of the phenomenon of motion. It is because God "now maintains as much motion and rest as he placed in it [at the beginning]" that quantity of motion is conserved.[39] It is because God maintains things in the same state as they are, from moment to moment, that bodies contain *force*, the force to resist the acquisition of new motion or the diminution of old.[40] Even Descartes's famous principle of inertia is a consequence of the theory of continual re-creation, in conjunction with God's immutability and the claim that at every instant a body in motion has a tendency in one particular direction.[41] What Descartes says explicitly about the law of inertia holds in general for his theory of motion: virtually every law "rests on the fact that God preserves each thing through continual activity, and consequently, that he does not preserve it as it may have been some time previously, but as it is precisely at the very instant in which he preserves it."[42] Descartes's physical world, like Leibniz's, then, is a world of mechanical bodies in motion through the continual acitivty of an external mind, God.

But whereas there are striking similarities with Descartes, there are important differences as well. An obvious difference relates to the notion of substance. For Leibniz, the defining characteristic of substance seems to be *activity*: substances must contain the sources of their own activity. As a consequence, the true substances are not the bodies of physics, but those bodies united with a concurrent mind, God. For Descartes, on the other hand, substance is defined either as the subject of any property, quality, or attribute, or as that which requires nothing else (except God) for its existence.[43] Consequently, for Descartes the bodies of physics *themselves* constitute substances and do not require the "concurrent minds" that Leibniz's corporeal substances require.[44]

But a less obvious though no less important difference must be pointed out as well. Although both Descartes and Leibniz ground their accounts of motion in God's continual re-creation of the world, the activity of God has very different functions in the two systems. In Leibniz, the theory of continual re-creation is advanced primarily to deal with a metaphysical problem about the very existence and intelligibility of motion. Since motion cannot be an ens reale in a body, Leibniz must find something in which it can really exist. Descartes, on the other hand, is not at all motivated by this concern. Whereas God is the first and continuing cause of motion, Descartes argues that motion itself is a mode *in* bodies.[45] For Descartes, the important consequences of the theory of continual creation are physical and not purely metaphysical. Because bodies in motion are being continually re-created by God, one can appeal to the nature of God, in particular his immutability, to derive facts about the laws motion obeys in the physical world. Most important, it is God who adds *force* to the bare extended bodies in the physical world, the force that is manifest in the tendency that bodies have to persist in their states of motion or rest, and that underlies the entire physics of motion Descartes presents. Leibniz, though, draws no physical consequences from the metaphysical theory of continual re-creation. Once God is introduced to make motion metaphysically intelligible, Leibniz's God seems to have performed his function. Put succinctly, the difference comes to this: in Descartes, the theory of continual re-creation is metaphysics in the service of physical theory; in Leibniz, it is pure metaphysics.

Despite these differences, it certainly seems fair to consider Leibniz's early account of the ultimate reasons of mechanism as being fundamentally Cartesian in inspiration, even if it lacks the full complexity of Descartes's thinking. However, in the following few years this will change. Out of Leibniz's perhaps unconsciously Cartesian beginnings will emerge an account of the metaphysical foundations of physics and the theory of motion that is distinctly non-Cartesian, and that constitutes a recognizable ancestor of the later monadology.

II. THE MENTALIZATION OF BODY: 1670-1672

The metaphysical picture of 1668-1670 did not survive for long. Already, in the writings of 1670-1672, we see a new account of the ultimate reasons of mechanism emerging, an account significantly different from the earlier, more Cartesian one. This new picture is intimately connected with Leibniz's technical work in two essays, the *Theoria Motus Abstracti*, a work on motion and the laws of impact, and the *Theoria Motus Concreti*, also known as the *Hypothesis Physica Nova*, a physical hypothesis meant to supplement the more abstract laws of motion given in its companion piece, both published in 1671.[46] Although for the most part I shall not be concerned with the technical details of Leibniz's elaborate theory of motion, it will be helpful to have at hand a brief summary of this work, Leibniz's first attempt at serious physics.

The *Theoria Motus Abstracti* (TMA hereafter) presents what Leibniz intends to be a purely geometrical theory of motion, "the true laws of motion, demonstrated in the geometrical method from the definitions of terms alone," as he promises Oldenburg.[47] Underlying this account of motion is an analysis of continuous magnitude. According to Leibniz:

> There are *actually* parts in a continuum . . . and these are *actually* infinite. . . . There are indivisibles or unextended beings, for otherwise we could conceive neither the beginning nor the end of motion or body.[48]

In claiming that all continuous magnitudes are divided into an *actual* infinity of parts, Leibniz is consciously breaking with Descartes, for whom continuous magnitudes, like extension, are divisible *indefinitely*, but not into an *actual* infinity of parts.[49] This analysis of continuous magnitude goes back at least as far as the *Dissertatio de Arte Combinatoria* of 1666.[50] But what is important in the TMA is the particular use to which the analysis is put. Of special interest to Leibniz in the TMA are the indivisible parts of motion, what he calls 'conatus.' In the TMA conatus is defined by way of a mathematical analogy:

> The ratio of rest to motion is not that of a point to space but that of nothing to one. . . . Conatus is to motion as a point to space or as one to infinity.[51]

Elsewhere, though, Leibniz defines conatus in a somewhat more explicit fashion: "Conatus is motion through a point in an instant."[52] Consequently, in the TMA Leibniz draws the following conclusion: "No conatus last longer than a moment without motion. . . . For what is conatus in a moment is the motion of a body in time."[53] Bodies in motion, then, are analyzed as bodies that, at every instant, have some conatus. This effectively reduces the laws of motion to laws of persistence of conatus.[54]

The laws of impact are more complicated, though. Consistent with his intention to present a purely geometrical theory of motion, Leibniz treats bodies as if they were purely geometrical objects, objects that *themselves* offer no resistance to motion. Consequently, the laws of impact are formulated as independent of the *size* of the bodies in question:

It makes no difference what the length of the contiguous body is. . . . In a coherent or continuous body it also makes no difference what its width is. . . . Indeed, one coherent body, however long and however wide can be set in motion through an excess in motion from another body however short and however narrow *just as if it were as much smaller as you like.*[55]

The laws of impact, thus, are formulated purely in terms of the combination of velocities (conatus) of the two colliding bodies. Although Leibniz does not give the full demonstration of the laws of impact "in the geometrical method from the definitions of the terms alone" that he had promised Oldenburg, the laws are straightforward enough. At the moment of impact, each body transfers to the other a conatus equal to its own without thereby losing any of its own original conatus. Thus, at the moment of impact, each body has more than one conatus.[56] These multiple conatus last only for an instant insofar as they are at the next instant resolved into one resultant conatus. If the two conatus are unequal, the resultant conatus will retain the *direction* of the greater conatus, and have for its *magnitude* the *difference* between the two original conatus. When the two original conatus are equal, the magnitude of the new conatus equals the magnitude of the original two, and the direction is determined by bisecting the angle of collision, unless the collision is direct, in which case both conatus are annihilated and rest results.[57]

An extremely interesting feature of the physics of the TMA is the status given to bodies at rest. An obvious consequence of the laws of impact is that a body in motion in collision with a body at rest continues in the same direction at the same speed. Thus, from the point of view of *impact*, a body at rest is indistinguishable from empty space. Similarly, bodies at rest have a peculiar status with respect to cohesion. Leibniz argues that cohesion *must* be explained in terms of two moving bodies in impact:

At the *time* of impulsion, impact, or *collision,* the boundaries or points of two bodies either penetrate each other or *are in the same point of space.* . . . Therefore *bodies which push* or impel *each other* are in a state of cohesion.[58]

From this Leibniz concludes that "there is no cohesion in resting things."[59] So, resting bodies are *also* indistinguishable from space with respect to *cohesion.* Leibniz's conclusion, then, is that the essence of body does not consist in extension and antitypy, but in *motion*:

I have demonstrated some propositions of great importance about motion. . . . First, there is no cohesion or consistency in bodies at rest, contrary to what Descartes thought, and furthermore, whatever is at rest can be impelled and divided by motion, however small. This proposition I later extended still further, discovering that there is no body at rest, for such a thing would not differ from empty space. . . . From [this] it follows that the essence of body consists . . . in motion.[60]

That is, motion is the *essential property* of body. And since motion is to be analyzed in terms of conatus, we can equally well say that *conatus* is the essential property of body.[61]

The laws of impact of the TMA, though, are quite obviously in conflict with what is observed in real bodies in the real world. Thus the TMA must be supplemented with the *Theoria Motus Concreti*—an elaborate physical hypothesis about the origin and present makeup of the physical world that, together with the TMA, will yield the laws of motion and impact for bodies in the phenomenal world.[62] Consequently, the observed laws of motion follow from the purely *geometrical* laws given in the TMA, operating in a particular physical situation. Thus Leibniz criticizes some of his contemporaries in the very first letter he wrote to Henry Oldenburg:

> For I have established certain elements of the true laws of motion, demonstrated in the geometrical method from the definitions of terms alone, . . . and this has also shown that those rules of motion, which the incomparable Huygens and Wren have established, are not primary, not absolute, not clear, but, no less than gravity, follow from a certain state of the terrestrial globe, not demonstrable by axiom or theorem, but from experience, phenomena, and observation, however fertile and admirable . . . they may be.[63]

This, in brief, is the version of the mechanical philosophy that Leibniz presented in his publications of 1671. The physics Leibniz offers in this period is radically different from the version Descartes offered. Consider, for example, the laws of impact. In Descartes, a fundamental determinant of the basic laws of impact is the force a body has to persist in a given state of motion *or rest,* a force deriving from both its *size* and its speed. This force, a metaphysically basic part of the Cartesian world, grounded in God's activity, is almost entirely missing from the basic laws of the TMA.[64] In Leibniz's self-proclaimed geometry of motion, the only thing that resists motion (conatus) is *another* motion (conatus). In Leibniz's geometrical physics, a body at rest offers no resistance to the acquisition of motion, regardless of its size, and in the impact of two bodies it is *only* the conatus of each that determines the outcome. But in this period, Leibniz and Descartes differ not only in their accounts of the laws of nature. Associated with the physical writings of 1670-1672 is a substantially new account of the ultimate reasons of mechanism, an account that, unlike the earlier metaphysical writings, is distinctly non-Cartesian. The extent of Leibniz's departure from his earlier metaphysics of motion is most evident in the new account of the role of mind in the physical world that emerges.

One way that mind enters is closely linked to a serious technical problem in the TMA. Although the concrete theory of motion is able to remedy some of the seeming defects of the abstract theory, one remains uncorrected by the physical hypothesis of the *Theoria Motus Concreti.* An unfortunate and undeniable consequence of the laws of impact proposed in the TMA is that in *every collision* (except a *nondirect* collision between two bodies with the *same speed*) *motion is lost.* So, Leibniz argues: "If bodies are devoid of mind it is impossible for motion ever to be eternal."[65] Leibniz, however, is never clear just how it is that mind is supposed to supply the motion that the physical world seems to lose, and prevent the world from grinding to a halt. Although a reconstruction may be possible, Leibniz himself gave few hints as to how it might proceed.[66]

But there is a second way in which mind enters the world of the TMA. In the TMA Leibniz abruptly presents the claim that *"every body is a momentary mind."*[67] Or, as he puts it in a letter to Oldenburg:

> Every body is a momentary mind and consequently without conscious-
> ness, sense, memory. If in a single body, two contrary conatus could simul-
> taneously persevere beyond the moment, every body would be true mind.
> Anywhere this happens, true minds are produced.[68]

How are we to understand this claim and its grounds?

Although Leibniz himself offers no argument and little explanation, one cannot help but recall the worries about the ontological status of motion in the letters to Thomasius only a little earlier. There Leibniz argued that motion requires nor only a mental *cause* but a mental *seat* as well. Such an argument should hold valid for the infinitesimal parts of motion as well: if motion requires a mind, then, so should conatus. This reasoning, of course, led Leibniz to present the theory of motion in terms of God's continual re-creation, enabling him to say that motion is an ens reale in God's mind. This doctrine, it would seem, *could* have been extended to the new analysis of motion. In that hypothetical extension, conatus could have been interpreted in terms of God's intention to create the body in a different place in the following (or, at least, in a following) instant. But, interestingly enough, this is not the path that Leibniz seems to choose. By the time that the TMA appeared, references to continual re-creation in connection with the metaphysics of motion *seem* to disappear.[69] Most signifi-cant is a comparison between the letter that Leibniz sent to Thomasius in 1669 and its published version in 1670 as part of a preface to an edition of *De veris principiis* of Marius Nizolius. Although there are very few significant differences between the two versions of the letter, one seems striking: *both* references he makes to the doctrine of continual re-creation are deleted.[70] However, the argument leading up to the doctrine of motion as continual re-creation is still present, suggesting that Leibniz still thought that motion cannot be an ens reale in bare extended (and antitypic) things, and requires a metaphysical foun-dation in mind.

This allows us to make some sense of Leibniz's statement that bodies are momentary minds. As we have seen, the physics of the TMA seems to entail that motion or conatus is the essential property of body; all bodies, as such, must have some conatus or other. Now, if Leibniz still held that motion (conatus) requires a metaphysical foundation in mind, then the metaphysical foundation for the motion (conatus) that every body must have must itself be in mind. But if the mind in question is not *God*, then what is it? My suggestion is this: *Leibniz,*

I claim, *has put motion, now conatus, into the bodies themselves.* But since mere extended things cannot properly speaking have conatus or motion, and since the essential property of body *is* motion, then bodies must not be mere extended things: *they must be minds of a sort.* That they are only *momentary* minds follows, in a sense, from the physics of the TMA. According to the TMA, "there can . . . be many contary conatus in the same body at the same time."[71] For example, at the instant of impact between two moving bodies, each body will have both its own original conatus, and the conatus given it by the other body. However, the two conatus will be, at that moment, resolved into a single resultant conatus, which conatus will *alone* persist. Thus "every body is a *momentary* mind, or one lacking recollection, because it does not retain its own conatus and the other contrary one together for longer than a moment."[72]

In saying that all bodies are momentary minds, Leibniz is not intending to obliterate the distinction between mind and body altogether. Quite the contrary. Leibniz argues, in fact, that the account of bodies as momentary minds "opens the door to the *true* distinction between body and mind."[73] To understand what Leibniz has in mind here, we should consider the science of mind that Leibniz was working out in this period. The science of mind that occupied Leibniz grows directly out of his studies in physics. As he wrote to Arnauld:

> I saw that geometry, or the philosophy of position, is a step toward the philosophy of motion and body, and that the philosophy of motion is a step toward the science of mind.[74]

Although Leibniz never presents his account of mind in full, remarks he makes in letters and in other surviving documents suggest that one insight that the theory of motion led him to is the realization that "thought is conatus, or a minimal motion."[75] Or, as he explains it to Arnauld, after noting that the essence of body is motion, "thought consists in conatus as body in motion."[76] This claim is not easy to understand. If true, it would certainly serve to link the worlds of mental and physical events, but in what sense can a thought be understood as a conatus? To appreciate (if not fully understand) Leibniz's remark we must remember that although conatus is a technical term in the theory of motion, it also has a less technical meaning, something like effort, tendency, or inclination. Descartes, in fact, when he uses this word in his own physics, feels that he must warn the reader explicitly against interpreting conatus mentalistically and supposing (as Leibniz later seems to) that there is "some act of thought (*cogitatio*) from which this conatus proceeds."[77] But once the thought of minds and the motion of bodies have been reduced to this common concept of conatus, how can body differ from mind? The key to the true distinction is *memory.* Unlike bodies, which are only *momentary* minds and retain conflicting conatus only at the moment of impact, *true* minds *retain* conatus. As he says in a note from the period:

> In mind all conatus persist. . . . The retention of all conatus, indeed of all comparisons among them, that is, of all of their states: this constitutes mind.[78]

The lack of memory in bodies and its presence in true minds is highly significant for Leibniz. Like Hobbes, Leibniz believes that recollection and comparison are essential for all *true* thought.[79] So, in lacking memory, bodies lack true sensation, perception, and genuine thought. Leibniz in fact seems to think that memory is the *only* thing that distinguishes minds from bodies. As noted somewhat earlier,

> If in a single body, two contrary conatus could simultaneously persevere beyond the moment, every body would be a true mind. Anywhere this happens, true minds are produced.[80]

So, whereas minds are distinct from bodies, it is undeniable that for Leibniz at this time bodies have become mental things of a sort: imperfect and rudimentary minds, but minds nevertheless.

However, puzzles remain. Although Leibniz's new way of distinguishing minds from bodies is reasonably clear, it seems puzzling that he never mentions the old one. In fact, when he discusses the new distinction between mind and body, the fact that body is extended never seems to come up. Furthermore, in other writings of the same period, Leibniz talks about the relation between body and substance in a way that seems inconsistent with his claims that bodies are momentary minds, and thus, on his definition, substances. For example, he tells Duke Johann Friedrich that he wants to show

> with the influence of the principles of the corrected philosophy that it is necessary that there be an intimate incorporeal principle in all bodies, substantially distinct from mass [i.e., extension and antitypy], what the ancients and scholastics called substance.[81]

Similarly Leibniz writes to Arnauld:

> The substance or nature of body (*substantia corporis*) . . . is the principle of motion . . . and the principle of motion or substance of body lacks extension.[82]

If bodies are minds, containing their own principle of motion, and are thus substances, then how can the substance of body lack extension? Why does Leibniz say, as he does, that the substance of body is distinct from mass and *incorporeal*?

Leibniz never addresses these questions directly. But the texts suggest that there is something more to Leibniz's conception of bodies as momentary minds than we have seen so far, something that goes a long way toward accounting for these oddities and seeming inconsistencies in his thought in this period.

As pointed out earlier, Leibniz goes beyond Descartes in dividing continuous magnitudes into an *actual infinity* of indivisible and nonextended parts. It might be thought that this division holds only in the ideal world of the geometrical.[83] But Leibniz was quite explicit about applying this idea not only to abstract geometrical quantities, but to *bodies* as well. For example, his argument in the TMA for the existence of such indivisibles begins as follows: "There are indivisibles or nonextended things, for otherwise we could conceive neither the beginning nor the end of motion *or body*."[84] Even more clearly, Leibniz writes in a fragment dated from the same period: "Matter (*materia*) is actually divided into [an] infinite [number of] parts. There are [an] infinite [number of] creatures in any given body whatsoever."[85] So, we can conclude, bodies seem to be composed of an infinity of nonextended parts, presumably one corresponding to each point in body.[86] Consider, now, a body in motion. Properly described, one would say that at every moment the body as a whole has some conatus. But if the body contains (or even, perhaps, is *composed of*) an infinity of nonextended parts, each of these parts must *also* have its *own* conatus. Here we go beyond the texts, but not by far. Although the laws of conatus, their persistence and combination, seem to be given for conatus in gross and extended bodies, Leibniz sometimes suggests that they hold as well for conatus in the nonextended points of body. For example, in the TMA he says: "*One point of a moving body* during the time of a conatus, or in a time less than any assignable time, is in many places or points of space."[87] Or even more explicitly, Leibniz writes to Oldengurg in a passage that we have already seen in part:

> Every body is a momentary mind and consequently without consciousness, sense, memory. If in a single body, two contrary conatus could simultaneously persevere beyond a moment, every body would be a true mind. Anywhere this happens, true minds are produced, and they are naturally indestructible, since, as I shall demonstrate in its proper place, two contrary conatus capable of enduring together simultaneously beyond a moment *in the same point of body* can never be removed by any effort of other bodies, or by any force.[88]

Leibniz's reasoning is not clear, but it is apparent that he at least allows conatus to exist in the nonextended *points* of body.

If, as I have suggested, each infinitesimal part of body has its own conatus, then it is plausible to suppose that Leibniz thought that it is these infinitesimal parts of body that constitute the *true subjects* of conatus, the true bodies about which it is correct to say that they are momentary minds. This interpretation is supported by some of the statements Leibniz makes about minds. For Leibniz, the new doctrine of mind is closely tied to his position on the infinitesimal parts of bodies. He wrote the Duke Johann Friedrich that

> I shall demonstrate that mind consists in a point . . . from which it follows that mind can no more be destroyed than a point. For since a point is indivisible, it cannot be destroyed.[89]

Similarly, he tells Arnauld:

> I demonstrated that the true locus of our mind is a certain point or center, and from this I deduced some remarkable conclusions about the imperishable nature of the mind.[90]

Now, if mind is located at a point, and if every momentary mind (body) becomes a true mind simply with the addition of memory, then the sorts of momentary minds that Leibniz is speaking of must be *points* as well. That is, when he says that bodies are momentary minds, the bodies must be not gross extended bodies, but the *infinitesimal points* of body.

If this is what Leibniz had in mind, then it would help to resolve some of the problems I noted earlier. If the *true* subjects of conatus, the *true* momentary minds are the indivisible *parts* of body, then, indeed, extension is *not* at all relevant to the true distinction between mind and body. Memory is *indeed* the only thing that distinguishes true minds from bodily minds. This interpretation also would explain the remarks that Leibniz makes to the Duke Johann Friedrich and Arnauld. If the true bodily substances are those located at each point of body, then they are nonextended and substantially distinct from extension and antitypy. Whereas each is a *corporeal* substance insofar as it is located at a point of body and constitutes an infinitesimal part of body, each is *incorporeal* from the point of view of the classical mechanical philosophy, because each is mental and lacks extension.

If my reconstruction is right, even in part, the new picture of the world that emerges in these writings relating to motion in the period 1670-1672 bears a striking resemblance to the metaphysics that emerges more fully later in the 1680s. In this early as in the later metaphysics, bodies *must* contain something over and above extension, something *mental*:

> I believe that anyone who will meditate about the nature of substance
> . . . will find that the entire nature of the body does not consist merely
> in extension . . . , but that there must necessarily be recognized in it
> something related to souls.[91]

In the early as in the later metaphysics, this bodily mind is something imperfect:

> The souls and the substantial forms of the other bodies are very different
> from intelligent souls, who alone know their actions and . . . preserve
> always the fundamental knowledge of what they are.[92]

Furthermore, if I am right in seeing Leibniz's early view as the claim that bodies contain an infinity of minds, each localized at some point of body, this too is a doctrine that finds its reflection in the later metaphysics:

> I believe . . . that everything is filled with animated bodies. And in my
> opinion there are incomparably more souls than there are atoms according
> to Mr. Cordemoi, who makes their number finite while I hold the number
> of souls . . . infinite. And since matter is infinitely divisible, no portion
> can be designated so small that it does not contain animated bodies, or at
> least bodies endowed with a primitive entelechy or . . . , with a vital
> principle; in short, corporeal substances.[93]

This, of course, is not to suggest that Leibniz's *complete* metaphysical picture can be traced back to this period. Many of the most characteristic features of Leibniz's later metaphysics are conspicuously missing. Nowhere, for example, do we have even a suggestion of the theses of mirroring or noncommunication, or of the ideality of space and time. Furthermore, the account of the nature of the physical world seems utterly unconnected with the doctrines of contingency, necessity, and creation that make up such an important part of his later philosophy and even his later physics.[94] But despite these differences, in the writings of 1670-1672 we see the first clear steps toward the mentalization of the physical world, and its grounding in an infinity of nonextended things—in short, *the first clear steps toward the monadology.*

These relations between the mature metaphysics and its first real beginnings should be obvious to anyone acquainted with Leibniz's later writing. But there are other more subtle and less obvious relations between the early and later metaphysics, particularly in connection with its functions in grounding the physics. Leibniz is certainly correct in seeing his later metaphysics as growing out of a search into the ultimate reasons of the mechanical philosophy, as he suggests in the quote at the beginning of this paper. And as Leibniz matures, his metaphysics maintains a close relation to his work in physics, ultimately grounding the new science of dynamics he presents in the writings of the late 1680s and 1690s. But in arguing for the necessity of grounding dynamics in metaphysics in his *Specimen Dynamicum* of 1695, Leibniz makes some curious remarks about his early writings, remarks that seem to clash with what we have found them to contain:

> When I was still a youth and followed Democritus, and Gassendi and Descartes . . . in holding that the nature of body consists in inert mass [i.e., extension and antitypy] alone, I brought out a small book entitled *A Physical Hypothesis* in which I expounded a theory of both abstract and concrete motion. . . . I showed that if the body is understood in mathematical terms only—magnitude, figure, position, and their change— . . . then it must follow that the conatus of even the smallest colliding body must be transmitted to even the largest receiving body, and thus that the largest body at rest will be carried away by a colliding body, no matter how small, without any retardation of its motion. . . . Later, however, after I had examined everything more thoroughly, I saw wherein the systematic explanation of things consists and discovered that my earlier hypothesis about the definition of body was incomplete. In this very fact along with other arguments I found a proof that something more than magnitude and impenetrability must be assumed in body, from which an interpretation of forces may arise. . . . I concluded therefore that besides purely mathematical principles . . . there must be admitted certain metaphysical principles . . . and that a higher and so to speak formal principle must be added to that of material mass, since all the truths about corporeal things cannot be derived from logical axioms alone.[95]

Read literally, as an account of his early thought, this later summary is surely mistaken. As we have seen, the bodies of the TMA and related writings are *not* the extended bodies that Leibniz refers to in this later recollection, but the momentary minds located, it seems, at every point of body. But Leibniz's mistake is highly revealing: it allows us to see an essential deficiency in his earlier system and an important difference between his earlier and his later thought. Though the bodies of the TMA are not purely geometrical, they may as well be, from the point of view of the physics. The physics of the TMA is intended to be the pure *geometry* of motion, the laws supposedly derived from the geometrical analysis of motion. The *metaphysics* of motion that results in the account of the bodies as momentary minds bears no particular relation to the *physics* of bodies in motion. This, of course, is of a piece with Leibniz's earlier Cartesian metaphysics of motion. There, the function of God is merely to *contain* motion, unlike in Descartes, where the metaphysics of God's continual re-creation determines its *laws*. In the TMA, the metaphysics of motion is similarly unrelated to the physics: though the seat of motion is now *internal* to body, it no more influences the laws of motion than God, the external seat, did earlier. A crucial step in Leibniz's development will occur when he, like Descartes before him, learns to ground the *physics* of bodies in motion in *metaphysics*, when not only the *nature* of motion, but also the very *laws* that it obeys require "ultimate reasons" in metaphysics. When he does so, then the monads, whose early ancestors are the momentary minds of the TMA, will become the ground of the *forces* and the seat of the *general metaphysical principles* necessary for understanding, not how bodies can *have* motion, but why motion in this world satisfies the *laws* that it does. In this final position, the metaphysics and physics will finally be united, and the *nature* of body will at least in part determine the physics of body, the *laws* body must obey.[96] However different this later position is, the path is obviously prepared by the earlier writings. From one point of view, we might see the dynamical arguments for forms in the later writings as exactly parallel to the earlier argument that leads to momentary minds. In the later writings, Leibniz will put forms into bodies to account for the *laws* they satisfy, just as he earlier put minds in bodies to account for motion itself. Or, put another way, the later metaphysics will arise when the indivisible minds of the TMA become the metaphysical foundation of the forces and metaphysical principles that determine the laws of motion, rather than the mere seat of bare motion. The earlier metaphysics prepares for the later by providing a place into which Leibniz can later put the principles that his later physics demands.

I have argued that the first step toward the mature metaphysics begins with a simple transformation of Leibniz's idiosyncratic version of the Cartesian world, taking motion from God and putting it into bodies, making them minds. What, though, is to account for this first step? One consideration that may have lead Leibniz toward making this step derives from his physics. As I noted earlier, the physics of the TMA demanded that bodies always be in motion, and that a body that lacks motion is undifferentiated from empty space. From this Leibniz concluded that the essence of body is motion. But if *this* is so, then motion must follow from the nature of body, and since only *mind* can constitute a principle of motion, body must be mental in nature.[97] But another motivation is possible for the later metaphysics, one that derives more from metaphysical considerations than from physical. As I pointed out earlier, the arguments of 1668-1670 push Leibniz to the view that bodies themselves are not substances, but only bodies in conjunction with God. This is a position that Leibniz might well have been dissatisfied with. Though Leibniz thought he had an answer to this worry, it certainly comes uncomfortably close to pantheism, making God a world soul.[98] Also, one might suspect, Leibniz was probably inclined to believe that the bodies of physics and common experience are *themsleves* genuine substances, or at least *made up* of genuine substances. But if bodies are to be substances, they must contain their own principles of motion. That is, they must *themselves* be somehow mental.[99]

If my account of Leibniz's early writings is correct, Leibniz's later metaphysics does indeed grow out of his reflections on the mechanical philosophy, as he wrote much later. This conclusion should have some bearing on recent debates about the sources of Leibniz's mature metaphysics. It has been a popular thesis since the turn of the century that Leibniz's metaphysics derives from his logic. This thesis seems clearly false, at least when taken as a historical claim.[100] Logical considerations seem to have no important role to play in the first steps to the monadology that I have been sketching. But if my account of these early texts fails to support a logicist thesis, it equally well fails to support a traditional contrary thesis, that the metaphysics is derived from the physics. Physics is a factor, of course, since the concept of motion on which Leibniz's reasonings are centered is the fundamental concept of the mechanical philosophy. But as I have argued, Leibniz's *metaphysical* worries about motion, those that lead him to the metaphysics of momentary minds, are curiously distant from the *physics* of motion. Motion drives Leibniz to his early metaphysics, but it is a purely metaphysical problem relating to its *nature*, not to its *laws*. Furthermore, the nature of motion presents a problem not in and of itself, but only in the context of related metaphysical worries about extension, substance, and activity, and theological worries about the role of God in the world. Although the immediate problem at hand is the ultimate reasons of mechanism, what directs Leibniz to the path that leads him to his final metaphysics is a rich mixture of approaches that in their diversity characterize Leibniz's thought from its beginnings to its end.

Notes

1. The works most often cited will be referred to as follows:

   AG *Descartes: Philosophical Writings* ed. and trans. G. E. M. Anscombe and P. T. Geach (London, 1954).

   AT *Oeuvres de Descartes* ed. C. Adam and P. Tannery (Paris, 1964-1974).

   E   *Descartes: Selections* ed. and trans. R. M. Eaton (New York, 1927).

   GM *G. W. Leibniz: Mathematische Schriften* ed. C. I. Gerhardt, 7 vols. (Berlin and Halle, 1849-1855).

GP   *G. W. Leibniz: Philosophischen Schriften* ed. C. I. Gerhardt, 7 vols. (Berlin, 1875-1890).

HR   *Philosophical Works of Descartes* ed. and trans. E. S. Haldane and G. R. T. Ross (Cambridge, 1911).

L   *Gottfried Wilhelm Leibniz: Philosophical Papers and Letters*, ed. and trans. L. E. Loemker 2nd ed. (Dordrecht, 1969).

PA   *G. W. Leibniz: Sämtliche Schriften und Briefe* ed. the Preussische Akademie der Wissenschaften, (Darmstadt and Leipzig, 1923-).

W   *Leibniz: Selections* ed. and trans. P. Wiener (New York, 1951).

In the citations, the original language source is always cited. When a translation is available, the translation is cited in parentheses following. When no translation is cited for a quotation, then the translation used is my own.

2. GP III, p. 606 (L 655). Leibniz's recollection is not entirely accurate. He was probably closer to seventeen when he made the conversion to mechanism. See Willy Kabitz, *Die Philosophie des jungen Leibniz* (Heidelberg, 1909), pp. 49-51.

3. There are few secondary sources in which this period is treated in any detail. In addition to Kabitz, *Die Philosophie*, there is Arthur Hannequin's careful and influential monograph, "La Première Philosophie de Leibnitz," originally his Latin thesis, published in French in volume II of his *Études d'histoire des sciences et d'histoire de la philosophie* (Paris, 1908), pp. 17-224. Shorter presentations of Leibniz's early philosophy derived from Hannequin's work are presented in chapter II of M. Guerault, *Dynamique et metaphysique Leibniziennes* (Paris, 1934, and 1967), and in P. Costabel, *Leibniz and Dynamics* (Ithaca, 1973), pp. 16-21. Although all scholars working on this material owe an enormous debt to Hannequin, I shall point out a number of significant differences I have with his readings. Another discussion of these texts is given in M. Čapec's paper, "Leibniz on Matter and Memory," in *The Philosophy of Leibniz and the Modern World*, ed. I. Leclerc (Nashville, 1973).

4. For general accounts of the mechanical philosophy and its history, see, e.g., Marie Boas, "The Establishment of the Mechanical Philosophy," *Osiris* 10 (1952): 412-541, or E. J. Dijksterhuis, *The Mechanization of the World Picture* (Oxford, 1961), esp. part IV chapter III.

5. See, e.g., Hannequin, "La Première Philosophie," pp. 22, 94-102, 133-35, 172-74, 204-6, 222; F. Tönnies, "Leibnitz und Hobbes," *Philosophische Monatshefte* 23 (1887): 557-73; Howard Bernstein, "*Conatus*, Hobbes, and the Young Leibniz," *Studies in History and Philosophy of Science* 11 (1980): 25-37; and J. W. N. Watkins, *Hobbes's System of Ideas* (London, 1973), pp. 87-94.

6. See Leibniz's remarks on this to Simon Foucher in 1675, PA II, i, 247. For a discussion of Leibniz's early acquaintance with Descartes's thought and the text of what appears to be his notes on first reading Descartes's *Principia* in 1675, see Y. Belaval, "Premières animadversions de Leibniz sur les *Principes* de Descartes," in *Mélanges Alexandre Koyré t. II: l'aventure de l'esprit* (Paris, 1964), pp. 29-56.

7. PA II, i, 15 (L94). See also, e.g., PA II, i, 24 (L102); PA VI, i, 489-90 (L110).

8. PA II, i, 10-11.

9. See PA II, i, 10 and PA II, i, 19 (L 97-98). The main work in question seems to be Jean de Raey's *Clavis philosophiae naturalis seu introductia ad naturae contemplationem Aristotelico-Cartesianam* (Amsterdam, 1654), though in the letter of 1669 Leibniz also cites Scaliger, Digby, White, Weigel, and Trew.

10. See Robert Boyle, *The Works of the Honorable Robert Boyle*, ed. T. Birch, 2nd ed. (London, 1772), Vol. III, pp. 28-29, 36, 39, 47, 114. On Leibniz's relation to Boyle see L. E. Loemker, "Boyle and Leibniz" in I. Leclerc, *The Philosophy of Leibniz*, pp. 248-75, esp. 249-51, where Leibniz's earliest acquaintance with Boyle's work is discussed.

11. PA VI, ii, 161.

12. PA VI, ii, 167. See also PA VI, i, 490 (L 110). Note that Leibniz here (and throughout these early writings) presupposes the reality of space, in radical contradistinction to his later writings.

13. PA II, i, 23 (L 101).

14. See PA II, i, 16, 21-22, 23 (L 95, 100, 101).

15. See Boyle, *Works*, Vol. III, 15, and John Locke, *Essay Concerning Human Understanding*, II iv, II viii 9, II xiii 11-27.

16. See PA VI, i, 489 (L 109-10).

17. PA VI, i, 492 (L 112).

18. PA VI, i, 491 (L 111).

19. See PA II, i, 23 (L 101-2) and PA VI, ii, 167-68.

20. PA II, i, 11.

21. PA VI, ii, 440 (L99). I follow Loemker in substituting for the original version of the last sentence quoted the slightly expanded version given in the 1670 publication of the letter. See PA II, i, 20. Leibniz's assertion that mind is the *principle of motion* is given in a number of different ways. Sometimes he says that mind provides an external *cause* or *reason* for motion, as he does in the passages from the *Confesio* and the 1668 Thomasius letter quoted above. But in this period Leibniz claims that motions constitute the only actions of bodies. See PA VI, i, 493 (L 113); PA VI, i, 508 (L 115); PA VI, ii, 168. So, instead of talking about mind as the principle of *motion* of bodies, he sometimes talks of it as the principle of *action* of bodies. See PA VI, i, 508 (L 115).

22. PA II, i, 11.

23. PA II, i, 23 (L 101-2). Emphasis added. I have altered Loemker's translation.

24. PA II, i, 23-24 (L 101-2).

25. See PA VI, i, 494, 496. The theory of continual re-creation is also discussed in a fragment of the period concerning incarnation. See PA VI, i, 532-35.

26. PA VI, i, 169 (L 73).

27. PA VI, ii, 488.

28. PA II, i, 19 (L 98).

29. PA VI, i, 508 (L 115). Emphasis added.

30. See passages cited in this connection in note 21.

31. See PA VI, i, 508-9, (L 116).

32. *Ibid*.

33. PA VI, i, 509 (L 116).

34. See PA VI, i, 532-35.

35. See PA VI, i, 511-12 (L 118).

36. On the mechanical explicability of the qualities of bodies, see *Principia Philosophiae* (hereafter *Pr*) II 64: AT VIIIA 78-79 (AG 221). On the nature of body see *Pr* II 4: AT VIIIA 42 (HRI 255-56).

37. *Pr* II 36: AT VIIIA 61 (AG 215). See also AT XI 37 (E 322).

38. *Meditationes* III: AT VII 49 (HRI 168). See also *Pr* I 21: AT VIIIA 13 (HRI 227).

39. *Pr* II 36: AT VIIIA 61 (AG 215). See also AT XI 37-38, 43 (E 322, 326-27).

40. See *Pr* II 43: AT VIIIA 66-67 (AG 219).

41. See *Pr* II 39: AT VIIIA 63-65 (AG 217-18) and AT XI 43-47 (E 327-28).

42. AT XI 44 (E 327-28). Especially good on the roles played by God and the theory of continual recreation in Descartes's theory of motion are Jean Wahl, *Du rôle de l'idée de l'instant dans la philosophie de Descartes* (Paris, 1920), esp. 10-11, 18-19, 25-43, and M. Gueroult, "Métaphysique et physique de la force chez Descartes et chez Malebranche," *Revue de métaphysique et de morale* 59 (1954): 1-37 and 113-34, esp. 1-37. These questions are also discussed in T. L. Prendergast, "Motion, Action, and Tendency in Descartes' Physics," *Journal of the History of Philosophy* 13 (1975): 453-62 and Gary Hatfield, "Force (God) in Descartes' Physics," *Studies in History and Philosophy of Science* 10 (1979): 113- 40.

43. The former account is given in AT VII 161 (HR II 53), and the latter in *Pr* I 51-52: AT VIIIA 24-25 (HRI 239-40).

44. See, e.g., *Pr* I 52: AT VIIIA 24-5 (HRI 240) and *Pr* II 55: AT VIIIA 71. Although

Descartes does sometimes refer to individual material bodies as substances, the whole question of the individuation of bodies in Descartes is a very tricky one. On this question, see Geneviève (Rodis-) Lewis, *L'individualité selon Descartes* (Paris, 1950), esp. pp. 39-60.

45. See *Pr* II 25: AT VIIIA 53-54 (HRI 266) and AT V 403-4 (A. Kenny, *Descartes: Philosophical Letters* [Oxford, 1970], p. 257).

46. Although these two works appeared first in 1671, Leibniz may have begun to work out the abstract laws of motion as early as August or September of 1669, within a few months after the important letter of 1669 to Thomasius. See PA VI, ii, 157-65. I shall not attempt to trace out the development of Leibniz's thought on the laws of motion between that earlier effort and the first publications.

47. PA II, i, 59.

48. PA VI, ii, 264 (L 139). §§ 1, 2, 4. Leibniz's position on the continuum in this period is confusing and complex. Leibniz wants to maintain both that the continuum is made up of an actual infinity of nonextended points, and that each point itself has magnitude and parts. Leibniz's solution is to recognize in continuous magnitudes indivisible and nonextended parts, and to argue that each such nonextended part itself has parts that are *indistant* from one another: "a point is not something without parts, or whose parts are not considered, but something *without extension*, or whose parts are indistant" (PA VI, ii, 264, § 5). Thus, even though the infinitesimal parts of continuous magnitudes may be *unextended*, different points may be of different magnitudes, presumably by virtue of containing different numbers of parts. See PA VI, ii, 265-66, §§ 13, 18. Although Leibniz's reasoning is not clear here, he seemed to think that the problem that was to vex him later, that if a continuous magnitude were infinitely divisible, it would contain as many parts in the whole as in each of its parts, is solved by giving each indivisible part of the continuous magnitude its own parts. See PA VI, ii, 264, § 3. For a relatively lucid treatment of this, see Hannequin, "La Première Philosophie," pp. 75-79. It should be noted that the translation of the relevant passages of the TMA given in L 139-40 is seriously flawed.

49. See *Pr* I 26-27: AT VIIIA 14-15 (HRI 229-30). A possible exception to this is time, which, as we have seen, Descartes seems to divide into instants.

50. See PA VI, i, 169 (L 74).

51. PA VI, ii, 265 (L 140), §§ 6, 10. The debt to Hobbes is clear here and throughout the theory of motion. See the references cited in Note 5.

52. PA II, i, 102.

53. PA VI, ii, 266 (L 141), § 17. I have altered Loemker's translation.

54. See PA VI, ii, 265 (L 140), § 9.

55. PA VI, ii, 270, §§ 23-24.

56. PA VI, ii, 265, 268 (L 140, 142), §§ 11, 12, 20.

57. The basic principles underlying the rules of impact are given in PA VI, ii, 268 (L 142), §§ 20-23, followed by 24 *"theoremata"* where the laws are worked out for special cases. Although the rules are supposed to be geometrical, no derivation is given. In fact, the only justification given is the principle of sufficient reason: "there is nothing without a reason," something Leibniz was later to consider a metaphysical principle.

58. PA VI, ii, 266 (L 141) §§ 15-16. Emphasis in original.

59. PA VI, ii, 270, § 20. See also PA II, i, 63, 102, for example. For a full account of Leibniz's theory of cohesion see Hannequin, "La Première Philosophie," pp. 96-103.

60. PA II, i, 172 (L 148). See also PA II, i, 167, 175. This, of course, makes it *possible* for there to be a vacuum.

61. This conclusion, while it appears to be radically anti-Cartesian, has its roots in Descartes. Though Descartes does explain cohesion in terms of the mutual *rest* of corpuscles (*Pr* II 55: AT VIIIA 71), and though bodies at rest do have force, as I shall later note, it is still motion that for Descartes *individuates* bodies. See *Pr* II 25: AT VIIIA 53-54 (HR I 226). Thus, in a *sense*, even for Descartes, the essence of an individual body *might* be thought of as motion. This account of individuation is reflected in Leibniz's 1669 letter to

Thomasius, See PA II, i, 17 (L 96). On the complexities of Descartes's position on the individuation of body, see G. (Rodis-) Lewis, *L'individualité.*

62. On the necessity for appealing to a physical hypothesis, see PA VI, ii, 229-30. An important problem addressed in the concrete theory is accounting for the fact that in the phenomenal world, the size a body has enters into the laws of impact. When dealing with *discontinuous* bodies, those made up of smaller coherent and differentiated parts, Leibniz's abstract laws allow him to include considerations of size. So, for example, if A moving with v_1 directly collides with the discontinuous B (say, a row of parts, oriented on the line of impact) moving with v_2, then B can "resist" the motion of A in proportion to the number of parts it contains, since when A collides with *each* particle making up B, it will lose a speed of v_2 according to the abstract laws. And after n successive collisions, the resulting speed of A will be $v_1 - nv_2$. Thus, discontinuous bodies will appear to resist the acquisition of new motion in proportion to the number of parts they contain. See PA VI, ii, 164 (§33), 270 (§22), and 271, (§ 11), and Hannequin, "La Première Philosophy," pp. 103-7. Consequently, the central problem of the *Theoria Motus Concreti* is to frame a hypothesis about the initial state of the plenum that, together with the abstract laws of motion, will result in the production of discontinuous bodies on earth. For a detailed summary of the physical hypotheses Leibniz proposed and the consequences he drew, see Hannequin, pp. 107-30.

63. PA II, i, 59. Huygens's laws of motion are discussed in detail in the very earliest of the notes we have for Leibniz's theory of motion, thought to date from August or September of 1669. See PA VI, ii, 157-65. This suggests that it may have been the acquaintance with Huygens's writings that started Leibniz on the path to his own account of motion. For later discussions of the Huygens-Wren laws, see PA VI, ii, 228 (§20), 231 (§23), 271 (§11). In another fragment of this period, thought to date from sometime between the summer of 1669 and the early part of 1670, Leibniz makes the general argument that experience is incapable of revealing to us the true laws of motion, and that we must depend upon reason for their discovery. See PA VI, ii, 165-66. Leibniz's general attitude toward his fellow scientists here is somewhat reminiscent of Descartes's attitude toward Galileo. See, e.g., AT II 380.

64. Strictly speaking, it is not entirely missing from Leibniz's early physics, since these considerations reenter in the concrete theory of motion. But considerations of size and force have a radically different status in Leibniz's early physical world, where they are not basic determinants of the laws of motion, but only secondary considerations derived from the hypothesized accidental properties of the physical world. It is the lack of any considerations of force and size in the early laws of motion that Leibniz particularly emphasizes in his later discussions of the early work. See, for example, GM VI 240-41 (L 440-41). These later discussions are not completely accurate, as I shall later note.

65. PA VI, ii, 280 (W 91). Here, and in other similar passages, mind is linked with curvilinear motion. See, e.g., PA VI, ii, 163.

66. For one possible reconstruction, see Hannequin, 160-64.

67. PA VI, ii, 266 (L 141). § 17.

68. PA II, i, 90. See also PA II, i, 102 and PA II, i, 173 (L 149).

69. This is not to say that Leibniz rejects the theory of continual re-creation. He does not. What I claim is that starting in 1670, the theory of continual re-creation is no longer appealed to in order to ground the theory of motion, either in the way Descartes did, or in the way that Leibniz earlier used that theory. For an account of Leibniz's later remarks on the theory of continual re-creation, see Jacques Jalabert, *La théorie Leibnizienne de la substance* (Paris, 1947), pp. 167-78.

70. Compare PA II, i, 23-24 (L 102) with PA VI, ii, 443.

71. PA VI, ii, 265 (L 140) § 11.

72. PA VI, ii, 266 (L 141) § 17. Hannequin's reading of this passage is very different from mine. Hannequin pays little attention to the theory of continual re-creation and the metaphysical role played by God in the account of motion given in the Thomasius letters

(see Hannequin, pp. 43-44), and does not notice the important rejection of this account at the time that the theory of momentary minds is introduced. His account of momentary minds emphasizes the distinction between bodies and minds, and seems to deny the mentality that Leibniz clearly attributes to bodies at this time. See Hannequin, pp. 156-64. Though Hannequin does not put it in this way, he seems to be reading Leibniz as a Hobbesian materialist.

73. PA VI, ii, 266 (L 141) § 17.

74. PA II, i, 172 (L 148).

75. PA II, i, 113, § 11.

76. PA II, i, 173 (L 149). For Hannequin's somewhat different reading of these passages, see pp. 157-59. It is because thought and conatus are identified that body can be both a momentary mind *and* a thing whose essence is motion.

77. *Pr* III 56: AT VIIIA 108 (AG 226). See also AT XI 84 (E 341). Hannequin's reading of the momentary minds forces him to deny that Leibniz made this move. See pp. 81-82, 154-55.

78. PA VI, ii, 283, 285. See also PA II, i, 90; PA II, i, 113, § 11, and PA II, i, 173, (L 149). Leibniz seems unsure in these passages what precisely is retained in mind that is not retained in body.

79. See PA VI, ii, 266 (L 141) § 17; PA VI, ii, 282-83; and PA II, i, 113 § 11. Cf. Sir William Molesworth, ed., *The English Works of Thomas Hobbes* (London, 1839), Vol. I, pp. 393-94. Although Leibniz follows Hobbes on this question in the philosophy of mind, one difference between the two should be emphasized. Whereas the identification of conatus and thought drives Hobbes to materialism, Leibniz seems to tend in the opposite direction, toward the mentalization of the material world. Thus, with some justice, Watkins claims that Leibniz's account of the world is "at bottom, an inverted version of Hobbes's materialist theory of mind." See J. W. N. Watkins, *Hobbes's System*, p. 87.

80. PA II, i, 90.

81. PA II, i, 163. I presume that Leibniz means here by mass (*moles*) what he meant earlier in the 1669 letter to Thomasius by mass (*massa*). See PA II, i, 16 (L 95).

82. PA II, i, 175.

83. This is what Hannequin seems to argue. See pp. 144, 166-68.

84. PA VI, ii, 264 (L 139), § 4.

85. PA VI, ii, 280 (W 91).

86. The *exact* relationship between the extended body and the nonextended points into which it can be divided is unclear. However, Leibniz's discussion of the continuum in the TMA (see note 48) strongly suggests the account I give, that the extended body is *composed of* nonextended things, which are present at every point of a coherent body. The relative position of these points can be fixed with relation to the background space, whose reality Leibniz has not yet denied. Also, as I noted earlier, Leibniz thinks that he can solve the problem that bodies so analyzed would contain as many points in a part as in the whole by stipulating that whereas the points that make up bodies are nonextended, they nevertheless contain parts. Later, of course, Leibniz gives up both the reality of space and the early account of the continuum, and the simple formula relating extended bodies to their nonextended "parts," later monads, breaks down in Leibniz's mature writings. For a good discussion of the relations between individual substances and extended bodies in Leibniz's later writings, see R. M. Adams, "Leibniz's Phenomenalism," an as yet unpublished manuscript. I would like to thank John Earman for several helpful discussions on this question.

87. PA VI, ii, 265 (L 140), § 13.

88. PA II, i, 90. Emphasis added.

89. PA II, i, 113, § 11.

90. PA II, i, 173 (L 149).

91. GP IV 436 (L 309). Note the deleted passage from an earlier draft that Loemker cites in note 15, p. 328. Cf. *Monadology* §§ 17-19: GP VI 609-10 (L 644).

92. GP IV 436 (L 310). Cf. *Monadology* § 20: GP VI 610 (L 645).

93. GP II 118 (L 343). Cf. *Monadology* §§ 1-3: GP VI 607 (L 643). Note the caveats in note 86.

94. On the important role played by contingency in Leibniz's later physics, see Margaret Wilson, "Leibniz's Dynamics and Contingency in Nature," in *Motion and Time, Space and Matter*, ed. P. Machamer and R. Turnbull (Columbus, Ohio, 1976), pp. 264-89.

95. GM VI 240-41 (L 440-41).

96. Leibniz's later position on the relationship between the nature of body and the laws it obeys is complex and interesting, and deserves more attention than I can give it in the context of this paper. In essence, Leibniz argues as follows. Since the TMA fails, the laws of motion are not purely geometrical. Rather, they involve the notion of *force*, and are governed by (contingent) metaphysical principles. Thus, some nonextended source for force and for these metaphysical principles must exist, since extended stuff, left on its own, would obey the incorrect geometrical laws of the TMA. Whereas God *could* be *directly* responsible for force and for bodies' satisfying the appropriate metaphysical laws, as he is in Descartes's physics, Leibniz argues that it is more perfect for God to have put the force and the metaphysical principles into bodies themselves. Thus, Leibniz concludes, bodies contain *forms*, which serve as the source of force and metaphysical determinants of the laws of motion. In outline, this argument is sketched in the long passage from the *Specimen Dynamicum* quoted above. That forms account for force in bodies is argued in GM III 552 (L 512) and GP II 171 (L 517). How forms account for the fact that the laws of motion are governed by metaphysical principles is somewhat unclear. Sometimes Leibniz seems to argue that the metaphysical principles are *imprinted* in the forms when God creates them. See, e.g., GP IV 507 (L 500-501). Elsewhere, Leibniz seems to argue that it is simply by virtue of *containing* force that bodies satisfy the metaphysical principles presupposed by the laws of motion. See, e.g., GP IV 465-66 (W 101-2) and GM VI 241 (L 440-41). For Leibniz's arguments as to why the form must be in bodies and different from God, see GP IV 507-9 (L 500-502); GP IV 568 (L 583); and GM VI 102-3.

97. This reasoning is suggested in PA II, i, 175. If the bodies in question are the infinitesimal points of body, then without motion they are undifferentiated from space not because they lack coherence, but because they would have no properties (like resistance to motion) that would distinguish them from the points of empty space. For what appear to be later versions of the same argument, now directed at establishing the necessity of forms, see GM VI 235 (L 436) and GP IV 512-13 (L 505).

98. Leibniz's answer is found in PA VI, i, 511-12 (L 118). Whether or not the threat of pantheism is worrying Leibniz at this point, it is something that he later cites as an argument against occasionalism and for putting force *in* bodies. See GP IV 508-9 (L 502); GP IV 568 (L 583). This is a problem that seemed to worry Descartes as well, motivating him to put motion *in* bodies. See AT V 403-4 (A. Kenny, *Letters*, 257).

99. This argument is suggested in the opening passage of *Specimen Dynamicum*. See GM VI 235 (L 435).

100. For a similar judgment based on a study of the writings of 1675-1676, see Albert Rivaud's review article "Textes inédits de Leibniz publiés par M. Ivan Jagodinsky," *Revue de Métaphysique et de Morale* 22 (1914): 94-120, esp. 119.

A Leibnizian
Theory of Truth

Ian Hacking

"In every true proposition, necessary or contingent, universal or particular, the concept of the predicate is in a sense included in that of the subject, *praedicato inest subjecto*, or I know not what truth is."[1] Every truth has an a priori proof, and the proof is an analysis that shows how the predicate is contained in the subject. Necessary propositions have finite proofs but the analysis of contingent propositions is infinite.

By 1686, when he corresponded with Arnauld, Leibniz had repeatedly stated versions of this doctrine. Whether his statements of it are found in private jottings, public essays, or serious correspondence, he is crisp and incisive. We may not understand him but our task is not to uncover beneath the words what Leibniz meant. He meant just what he said. There are questions of interpretation aplenty, but our immediate task is to state a coherent theory of truth that fits Leibniz's words: not because the theory will be exactly what Leibniz intended but because if we do not have some model for his words we shall not be able to think about these matters at all.

PROPOSITIONS

Terminology is a problem not because Leibniz uses strange words but because he uses familiar ones that have since been burdened with three more centuries of philosophizing. "Proposition" is one such word. We have come to expect a theory about truth to give truth conditions for "what we say." Modern philosophy discusses sentences, statements, and, grudgingly, propositions as the bearers of truth. For those who do use the word, a proposition is what is expressed by a declarative sentence. It is the meaning of intertranslatable sentences; propositions are also held to be objects of belief. Because a proposition is an abstract entity over and above what is said, it is rejected by nominalists, of whom the most successful has been W. v. O. Quine. But the real difficulty with

185

propositions is not their abstractness but that they skim too near the surface of what is said to have power in explaining language. Propositions are supposed to be what I understand by sentences, what I mean when I speak. But do I not understand what is said? Do I not mean what I say? A theory about communication, it appears, need only consider just what is said. Proposition-theorists who meekly insist that there are no propositions outside of what can be expressed in language have given up any reason for talking of propositions.

The same accusation cannot be leveled at Leibniz, who was not, in his theory of truth, aiming at a theory of communication at all. His propositions do not skim over words but may, as it were, be infinitely far away from them. My words may signify a proposition, but I may be no more acquainted with the proposition signified by "Peter denies" than I am acquainted with the person whom we call St. Peter. Leibniz's propositions have more in common with Platonic ideas than anything else that we have known in modern philosophy.

A proposition, for Leibniz, is a complex term. "By term I understand not a name but a concept, that is to say, what is signified by a name; you could also call it notion or idea."[2] The Latin words are *significatur, conceptum, notionum,* and *ideam.* Leibniz used the last three fairly interchangeably at the time he was devising his theory of truth. Translators commonly render *notio* as 'concept,' but like C. D. Broad[3] I use 'notion,' not because it is a better translation but because it has no role in modern philosophy. Leibniz's own practice in French was to use 'notion.' For example, in his celebrated discussions of the "complete individual concept" he actually wrote *notion de l'individual* or *notion complète.*[4]

A notion is signified by a name. Names include both proper names like 'Peter' and common names such as 'circle.' One would expect sentences to name propositions. Propositions may be made up out of a subject and a predicate, which are notions also signified by names. It is better to write "Peter is a denier" than "Peter denies," for the former shows a predicate signified by the common name, 'denier.'

Now what exactly are these notions that are signified by names? Sometimes Leibniz gives a subjective cast to notions, as in a well-known attack on Arnauld and Malebranche published in 1684.[5] He says that I have an obscure notion of a flower when I recall it but cannot recognize it again. "Any proposition that contains such a notion is also obscure." The notion is clear when I am able to recognize the flower. I have a distinct notion when I can enumerate the criteria for differentiation, as when an assayer tests for gold. I have adequate knowledge when I have distinct notions of all the ingredients of a distinct notion, "that is, when the analysis is carried to the end."

Leibniz's classification is both a classification of knowledge and of notions, but it seems to ride better with the former. Let us take his example seriously. Shortly after coming to California I recall being shown a blue flowering shrub and knew enough to conjecture "*Cenothus,* or false lilac, is resistant to drought." Yet I cannot confidently distinguish this shrub from others. So my notion is obscure. Hence the proposition in question must also be obscure. Hence, it cannot be the same proposition as that signified by the botanist, using the same words, but knowing the criteria for distinguishing *Cenothus* from other shrubs.

Leibniz certainly does invite this subjective account of propositions and notions in which the proposition signified must differ according to how well I understand the subject. But that cannot be his considered view. My ignorant and obscure notion of *Cenothus* does not include resistance to drought, but my guess is correct all the same. The truth of the proposition results from the fact that the predicate, "resisting drought," is contained in the subject. But it is certainly not contained in my obscure notion of *Cenothus*. For the theory of truth to work, both the botanist and I must signify the same thing with the name *Cenothus* — and that conclusion is surely correct. My obscure notion of *Cenothus* is perhaps like what Frege calls the 'associated idea,' my own thoughts about the false lilac, and distinguished from both the sense and the reference of the word *Cenothus*.

For Leibniz's theory of truth even to get started, one must abandon the "subjective" indications given in the 1684 paper, and instead have an "objective" view of signification. When I say that *Cenothus* is drought resistant, the name *Cenothus* must signify an adequate notion of the false lilac, even though I have no such notion, and probably could never have such an adequate notion. Nothing is intrinsically absurd about this formulation, although a decent theory demands an account of how such signification can work. I shall give a model of this as part of my Leibnizian theory of truth.

NAMES, THINGS, AND NOTIONS

"Peter denies," I say, and use the name 'Peter' to refer to the disciple who denied Christ thrice before cockcrow, the man to whom Christ gave the name 'Peter' because he was the rock upon which He would found His church. The relation between the name and the person is what J. S. Mill called denotation and Saul Kripke calls designation. There is a historical tradition linking the name 'Peter' with the very person for whom Christ chose that designation. If the gospels delude us, and do not after all lead us back to one historical personage, then I fail to refer to anyone when I use the name 'Peter' in this context.

Leibniz notoriously held that for every individual there is a complete individual notion that includes every aspect of the individual. Thus if the name 'Peter' does, in my context, denote a saint, it is thereby associated with a complete individual notion, namely, the notion of St. Peter. This is the relation that Leibniz calls signification. I shall say that the name 'Peter' denotes the man, and is a sign of, or signifies, the complete individual notion of that man.

This account is entirely nonpsychological. I do not need to know anything about the complete notion of Peter to use the name to signify that notion. Paralleling what Kripke says about designation, *my* subjective notion of Peter might be so obscure as to contain nothing true about Peter. But if a historical line carries the name back to a real person, then my use of the name denotes that person. It thereby also picks out a complete individual notion, even though, in extreme cases, I need not know what the notion is.

Since the time of Frege it has been customary to distinguish what an expression refers to, on the one hand, and an abstract entity, the sense of that expression, on the other. The sense is what we know when we know how to use an expression, and is clearly an entirely different sort of entity from Leibniz's notion. A notion is a more abstract entity than anything we know about in the modern theory of meaning.

There is, regrettably, less to say about the predicate 'denier,' than the name 'Peter.' There must exist a notion of denial with which, one supposes, I am to some extent acquainted when I make sensible use of the verb 'to deny.' The proposition signified when I say "Peter is a denier" is just the proposition according to which the one notion is contained in the other. Note that although we make no use of the theory of descriptions here, there is a curious resemblance to Russell's account of language. Like Russell, our Leibnizian theory takes great pains to say how names for particulars work, but says deplorably little about how names signify universals.

TRUTH CONDITIONS

I shall now give a two-level theory of truth. At the top level are propositions, and at the second level is what is said. The truth of what is said is defined in terms of the truth of propositions. In this paper it is the lower level that I am concerned with. When I say that "Peter denies," what I say is true if and only if a true proposition is signified. That is, if and only if (i) 'Peter' denotes an individual and (ii) the predicate 'denier' is included in the individual notion of that person. There are two distinct circumstances in which what I say may fail to be true. The name I use may fail to denote one individual, or the predicate of denial may fail to be included in the notion of the individual denoted. It does not matter much whether, when 'Peter' does not denote, we say the statement is false or lacks a truth value, although Leibniz would have taken the former alternative.

Following the recent terminology of P. T. Geach and P. F. Strawson, it is natural to call this a presupposition theory. When I say that Peter denies I do not assert that there is a person denoted by 'Peter;' rather, this is presupposed. It is far from anachronistic to use this in a Leibnizian model, for the Aristotelian theory of the universal proposition employs an element of presupposition. "All brakeless trains are dangerous" is true only if brakeless trains exist. The formalism for this and for a presupposition theory of names and descriptions are exceedingly similar.[6]

The presupposition account holds for elementary sentences and can be extended to define truth conditions for complex sentences. Indeed the devices of Tarski's theory of truth will do this fine. It is one of the virtues of Tarski's theory that it is rather neutral among traditional philosophies. It is to be applied only at the lower level, at the level of what is said, and at that level Tarski's criterion of adequacy is satisfied. "Peter denies" is true if and only if Peter denies.

POSSIBLE SAINTS PETER

Many individual notions of possible saints are not instantiated by anyone. Leibniz permits talk of possible saints peter. There cannot be a name for one definite possible, but not actual, saint.[7] No one can ever point to a nonactual saint, so the name cannot be introduced by ostensive definition. Nor can a picture or description introduce the name, for every finite definite description will omit differentia—the lengths of the various hairs on the beard, and so forth. I can signify the complete individual notion of the actual St. Peter because I have a name that latches on to Peter. But I cannot signify the notion of a merely possible saint.

There will still be complete notions of a multitude of possible saints, and it will be useful to have a system for pretending to refer to such things. Let us adopt the following heuristic convention. 'Peter,' I shall assume, denotes a real historical personage, St. Peter. The inscription "[Peter denies]" shall be the name of the proposition signified by my words, "Peter denies." Then the inscription "[Peter* is loyal]" shall serve as if it were the name of a proposition about one specific possible Peter—a possible saint whose complete notion includes absolute fidelity to Christ.

Since loyalty is contained in the subject, the proposition [Peter* is loyal] is just as true as the proposition [Peter denies]. This has no consequences at all for the truth conditions of anything that I can say. When I say that Peter denies, what I say is true if and only if the proposition [Peter denies] is true. But I cannot say that Peter* is loyal, and infer that too is true because the proposition [Peter* is loyal] is true. This is because 'Peter*' is not a name of anyone and there simply is no statement to make to the effect that Peter* is loyal.

CONTINGENT TRUTH

"A necessary proposition is one that is true in all possible worlds." That is a doctrine commonly attributed to Leibniz but I think he never said it. It certainly does not define necessity. A necessary truth is one with a finite proof; contingent truths require infinite proof. Recent developments in the foundations of constructive mathematics show that there is some coherent idea of infinite proof.[8] But until we have an adequate model of infinite analysis we shall never understand Leibniz on these matters. We grope in the dark.

As I understand it, both the propositions [Peter denies] and [Peter* is loyal] are true and contingent. This certainly sounds strange, for contingency, we suppose, has to do with the way the world actually is. But the truth of [Peter denies] is not, in my model, contingent upon anything! E. M. Curley, in his judicious survey of these matters, holds that the proposition [Peter* is loyal] does involve infinite analysis but says that Leibniz "would not wish to claim that the proposition in question is contingent."[9] I disagree, but when we have to debate what a philosopher "would have wanted to say" we are in a weak position indeed.

To understand Leibniz's doctrine about contingency we have to reflect on human freedom. Infinite analysis is what allows for contingency, and then freedom is defined in a trite way, as spontaneity, intelligence, and contingency.

Now the concept of St. Peter is a concept of someone who freely denies. We are inclined to expostulate, "but that very Peter could not, on Leibniz's theory, possibly help denying." But nonetheless that is what Leibniz means by free. Sometimes it is suggested that Peter's freedom consists in there being a counterpart to Peter (a handy term of David Lewis's).[10] A counterpart is a possible individual such as [Peter*], much like Peter, but loyal. Now indeed if Peter's denial is a free act, such a counterpart will exist, simply because there is no contradiction in deleting denial from Peter's notion, and replacing it by loyalty. But the counterpart is not what constitutes Peter's freedom: it is a mere corollary of it. To say that Peter freely denied is to say that Peter's denial is an action of his own (spontaneity), that he understood (intelligence), and it is such that no contradiction can be derived, in a finite number of steps, from the supposition that Peter did not deny (contingency).

Now what of [Peter*]? This too, in my view, is a notion of an individual who freely chooses to follow Christ and is, of his own free will, ever loyal. Thus I urge that the loyalty inherent in this individual notion is just as free as the denial contained in the individual notion of St. Peter. Thus Leibniz "would have wanted to say" that the proposition [Peter* is loyal] is contingent. In this I dissent not only from Curley but also from Russell. "As Russell pointed out in 1903 truths about unactualized possible individuals, *qua* possible, involve an infinite analysis just as much as do truths about actual individuals. Yet the former are necessary, the latter contingent. So involving an infinite analysis does not appear to be a sufficient condition of contingency. How Leibniz could have thought it was remains a mystery."[11] The mystery quite disappears on my view, for I reject Curley's premise, that truths about unactualized possibles are necessary. Leibniz's conviction that infinite analysis is a sufficient condition of contingency is vindicated. Which is not to say that we understand the condition!

INFINITY AND CONTINGENCY

Curley thought that infinite analysis is not a sufficient condition for contingency. A second worry has been put to me by R. M. Adams: might not some contingent propositions be finitely provable, so that infinite analysis is not a necessary condition of contingency? Even though no finite analysis could generate all aspects of Peter, might not some features of Peter appear in finitely many steps? Nicholas Rescher has compared an individual notion to a computer program. That makes Adams's worry even more pressing. Press the button and the computer starts printing out bits of information. Why should not Peter's denial be the trillionth bit?

Here it may be useful to resort to an entirely speculative model. We should seriously scrutinize the idea of a computer program. Kolmogorov, Martin-Lof, and others have recently formulated a theory on the complexity of sequences and of programs.[12] One considers the length of a computer program necessary to generate a sequence. If, as probably sometimes happens, a sequence can be generated only by a program already as long as the sequence itself, then the sequence is said to be random. There are also infinite random sequences that cannot with certainty be generated by any designated finite program.

So let us think of an individual notion as an infinite computer program that cannot be simulated by any finite program. For an infinite analysis one would first have to write the whole program to have any output at all. Such a program is not open to Adams's worry. For although "Peter denies" might come out in finitely many steps, once the program had been set up, infinitely many steps of analysis must precede the very setting up of the program. Interestingly, there is a viable theory on the asymptotic approximation to such programs that seems to fit many of the hints Leibniz himself gives us, as to what an infinite analysis would be like.

THE PROBLEM OF EXISTENCE

"What is to be said about the propositions 'A is an existent,' or 'A exists'?"[13] Every logicist commentator since Russell and Couturat has been vexed by this question. The truth is, I think, that Leibniz never obtained a clear view of the connection between his theories of truth and of creation. The badness of fit comes out, for the logician, when one tries to analyze existential propositions about individuals. Once again Curley has an excellent survey of the various passages, which confirm precisely the conclusion that there is no established Leibnizian doctrine on existence. I shall not argue about what Leibniz wanted, but shall simply state the position of existential propositions in my Leibnizian theory of truth.

1) The truth conditions for my statement, "Peter denies," are (*i*) 'Peter' denotes an individual and (*ii*) the complete notion of that individual includes the notion of denial. My statement does not covertly assert that Peter exists, but presupposes it. However, see (3) below.

2) The proposition [Peter denies] does not presuppose or imply that Peter exists. It does imply that if the concept of Peter is instantiated—if Peter exists—then he denies.

3) I can assert significantly that Peter exists, and may even use the words "Peter denies" intending to convey "Peter denying is an existent."[14] Understood literally, however, my assertion that Peter exists is almost vacuous, for it is true if 'Peter' denotes at all.

4) There is, however, something of real content that I can express with the

words "Peter exists." Now existence cannot be defined in such a way that we get a clearer notion of it.[15] But we can do something else, giving a real definition that assigns the cause or reason for existence. This cause or reason is not part of logic but is part of the theory of creation, as follows:

5) "An existent entity is that which is compatible with most things."[16] Leibniz continues by saying that what this comes to, is that "existent" means pleasing to something intelligent and powerful, and he tries to frame this so as not to illicitly involve a presupposition of existence in the definition. When we say that Peter exists we may properly mean that Peter belongs to a maximum compossibility class, that is, a class maximizing the variety of phenomena and the simplicity of laws of nature, and which, being most perfect, is created by God out of his goodness and wisdom. Thus the truth conditions for "Peter exists," used in this way, may be (i) 'Peter' denotes, and (ii) the individual notion of the denoted individual belongs to a maximum compossibility class. Note that (ii) does not entail that God creates Peter, although it is God's reason for creation.

6) The proposition signified by "Peter exists" appears to be different in logical form from "Peter denies." The former is [Peter ϵ maximal class], whereas the latter is [denial ϵ Peter]. The analysis of the latter may bring in every aspect of our world, especially if there is an implicit reference to time. But the analysis of the former must bring in every possible world to check out that our world is best.

COMPOSSIBILITY

God, it is conjectured as part of the theory of creation, chooses to create substances in a maximal compossibility class. Leibniz has very little to say about compossibility, even less than about existence. Early in his career he confessed ignorance:

> It is yet unknown to men what is the reason of the incompossibility of different things, or how it is that different essences can be opposed to each other, seeing that all positive terms seem to be compatible.[17]

Hide Ishiguro notes that in the *New Essays* Leibniz suggests that there may be privative concepts, so that not all positive terms would have to be compossible after all.[18] But this does not seem to be worked out into a theory of compossibility.

Benson Mates and Nicholas Rescher offer a simple definition of compossibility. Two entities are compossible if their individual notions are logically consistent, or if the assumption that both concepts are instantiated entails no contradiction. Rescher goes on to observe that substances defined by monadic predicates cannot, on this definition, fail to be compossible, so that Leibniz's system, as a whole, is inconsistent.[19]

Now if Rescher and Mates are right about compossibility, my model of truth must be abandoned. Peter and Peter* cannot be compossible, for only St. Peter exists. Yet there is no contradiction to be derived from the pair of them, as is shown by the fact, that on my theory, [Peter denies] and [Peter* is loyal] are both true. Rescher and Mates cannot be right about compossibility. Leibniz never says what they would like him to say. He regularly explains possibility as freedom from contradiction, but never goes on to give the same explanation for compossibility. Moreover, we should examine how Leibniz does use the concept of compossibility.

> The immortality of the mind must be taken to be proved at once by my method, because it is possible within itself and compossible with all other things, that is to say (sive) it does not impede the course of things. For minds have no volume.[20]

To say that things are compossible when they do not impede each other is very different from saying that they are logically consistent. Compossibility is a more demanding relation than mere consistency. For one thing to impede another is more a matter of laws of nature than of logic. Compossibility must be something like consistency under general laws of nature. As Russell puts it:

> Without the need for some general laws, any two possibles would be compossible, since they cannot contradict one another. Possibles cease to be compossible when there is no general law to which both conform.[21]

Russell is providing an account that is not precisely backed up by text. But it certainly squares with Leibniz's occasional remarks about compossibility far better than the merely logical definition of compossibility offered by Rescher and Mates. Unless someone points to further Leibnizian texts, one should leave it at that. But one may also recall the long scholastic tradition surrounding the idea of compossibility and creation. Throughout this tradition, familiar to Leibniz, God chose to create a world of compossible things, compossible under the realm of law.[22]

COMPOSSIBILITY AND LAW

The idea of compossibility under law is so obscure as to make the Rescher-Mates reading a temptation after all. Some possible worlds must have laws of nature different from others. With respect to what laws are [Peter] and [Peter*] supposed to be incompossible? Does Peter come with one set of laws contained in his individual notion, while the notion [Peter*] has different laws? That will not do. If the laws are contained in individual notions, they must ultimately be expressed in monadic simples and the notions [Peter] and [Peter*] would be compossible after all. Leibniz did not give an adequate lead on this question so I shall introduce a speculative model that I have developed in detail elsewhere.[23]

Space and time are "well founded phenomena." I explain that in the following way. For any class of substances, there may be a large number of different possible spatiotemporal arrangements consistent with the internal properties of the substances. But the laws of nature that may be introduced to describe the activities of these substances will, of course, vary according to the spatiotemporal relations assigned to the substances. So we should think of a set of trios (Space, Time, Law) compatible with the internal description of various substances. Not all laws will be equally simple. My Leibnizian postulate is that among all (S, T, L) trios, there will be a simplest law L^*. The associated S^* and T^* are the well-founded space-time of that set of substances. On this postulate, then, various sets of substances will have their own designated (space*-time*-law*). The world that God chooses to create is the one that maximizes the variety of phenomena while minimizing the complexity of the simplest set of laws that can be used to describe that world.

This model applies to compossibility in the following way. In the correspondence at the end of his life, Leibniz discussed a novel called *Astrea*.[24] He suggests that it is internally consistent, but implies that the substances and events related in this story are not compossible with the existing universe. If they were compossible, then in fact *Astrea* would be true of something past, present, or future. Now let us suppose that *Astrea* is pure fiction, and contains no identifying reference to anything historical. How then could *Astrea* fail to be compossible with the existing universe? I answer that substances and events answering to the descriptions given in *Astrea* may form a class that is logically consistent with the substances and events of the actual universe. It is not logical inconsistency that prevents compossibility. Compossibility may fail for one of two reasons: (i) there is no spatiotemporal arrangement of the universe plus the substances and events of *Astrea* that has a set of lawlike regularities; or (ii) there is such an arrangement, but the simplest law for such an arrangement is more complex than the simplest law of nature for our universe, a loss of simplicity not compensated for by a gain in variety of phenomena. In alternative (i), *Astrea* is strictly not compossible with the rest of the universe. In alternative (ii), it is strictly compossible but that compossible set of substances is not created because the laws that govern it are too messy. This second alternative is not something that Leibniz admits, but it is part of a coherent model of what he actually does say.

Notes

Abbreviations

C *Opuscules et fragments inédits de Leibniz*, ed. L. Couturat (Paris, 1903 and Hildesheim, 1966).

G *Die philosophischen Schriften von Gottfried Wilhelm Leibniz*, ed. C. I. Gerhardt, 7 vols. (Berlin, 1885-1890 and Hildesheim, 1965).

L *Gottfried Wilhelm Leibniz: Philosophical Papers and Letters*, ed. and trans. E. Loemker, 2nd ed. (Dordrecht, Holland, 1969).

P *Leibniz: Logical Papers*, ed. and trans. G. H. R. Parkinson (Oxford, 1966).

1. To Arnauld, 4/14 July 1686. G II, 56; L,377.

2. A specimen of the universal calculus (1679-1686?), C, 243, P, 39. See Hidé Ishiguro, *Leibniz's Philosophy of Logic and Language* (London, 1972). Chapter 2.

3. C. D. Broad, *Leibniz, an Introduction* (Cambridge, 1975).

4. For example G II, 38, 54.

5. *Meditations on knowledge, truth and ideas* 1684. G IV, 422-26; L, 291-95. For an earlier, more subjective cast given to *Idea*, see *Quid sit Idea* G VII, 263. Subsequent to the period examined in this paper, Leibniz may have been led to ideas as "capacities" for using words. Cf. Ishiguro.

6. T. J. Smiley, "Sense without denotation," *Analysis* 78 (1960-1961): 125-35.

7. To Arnauld, 4/14 July 1686, G, 54, L, 336.

8. Ian Hacking, "Infinite Analysis," *Studia Leibnitiana* 6 (1974): 126-30.

9. E. M. Curley, "The Root of Contingency," in *Leibniz*, ed. Harry G. Frankfurt (New York, 1972), p. 94.

10. David Lewis, "Counterpart theory and quantified modal logic," *The Journal of Philosophy* 65 (1968): 113-26.

11. Curley, "The Root," p. 92.

12. See Terence Fine, *Theories of Probability* (New York and London, 1973), Chapter 5.

13. *General Inquiries* (1686), C, 375; P, 65.

14. *Ibid.*

15. G. Grua, *G. W. Leibniz, Textes inédits* (Paris, 1948), I, 325.

16. *General Inquiries.*

17. (About 1677?) G VII, 195.

18. Ishiguro, *Leibniz's Philosophy*, p. 47.

19. Benson Mates, "Leibniz on possible worlds," in *Leibniz*, ed. Harry G. Frankfurt, pp. 335-64. Nicholas Rescher, *The Philosophy of Leibniz* (New Jersey, 1967). p. 16.

20. 2 December 1676. C, 530; L, 169.

21. Bertrand Russell, *A Critical Exposition of the Philosophy of Leibniz* (Cambridge, 1900), p. 67.

22. I am indebted to discussions with Professor Eileen Serene for advice on this point.

23. Ian Hacking, "A Leibnizian Space," *Dialogue* 14 (1975): 89-100

24. To Bovrguet, December 1714. G III, 572; L, 661.

Leibniz and Locke on Essences

Nicholas Jolley

Classification is one of the liveliest topics of debate between Leibniz and Locke. It is also one of the most elusive. Leibniz himself often seems uncertain about the precise nature of his dispute with Locke, and a note of exasperation disturbs the surface of the *Nouveaux Essais*. Leibniz's impatience is understandable, for it is not always easy to know what question Locke is trying to answer at any point in Book III of his *Essay*. But there can be little doubt that the opposition between the two philosophers is a substantive one. Leibniz's own distinctive version of essentialism is in direct conflict with Locke's insistence that classification is the "workmanship of the understanding," and indeed the dispute here foreshadows the debates of modern philosophers on essences and natural kinds. Obvious points of resemblance exist between some of Leibniz's arguments and views put forward in recent times by Kripke, Putnam, and others. Yet, though Leibniz advances arguments that have modern parallels, the motivation of his critique is highly traditional. For Leibniz, the really disturbing element in Locke's theory of nominal essences is what he takes to be its degrading consequences for the definition of 'man.' We shall also see that Leibniz objects to Locke's denial that the individual has an essence, because it conflicts with his own metaphysical doctrine of substance.

That it is not always easy to know what question Locke is answering should not surprise us, for there are at least two important questions that might be asked in connection with the problem of classification. One might ask whether things are naturally classified independently of any human needs or interests: to put the matter another way, does it make sense to ask what a particular substance really is? Alternatively, one might be interested in the way in which our actual classifications are made: this issue might be called the question of the de

I am grateful to Professor J. F. Bennett, Dr. D. H. Mellor, and Dr. W. von Leyden for their comments on previous drafts of this paper.

facto basis of classification. Now Locke's primary concern may seem to be to argue that no natural kinds exist independently of our classification. This certainly seems to be the question at issue when Locke attacks what he takes to be the traditional doctrine that there is "a certain number of Forms or Moulds wherein all natural Things, that exist, are cast, and do equally partake."[1] Yet into this context Locke introduces his doctrine of real essences, and this complicates the issue. For although Locke presents this doctrine as an alternative to the traditional view of essences that he rejects, they do not seem to be answers to the same sort of question. Locke's theory of real essences states that all the observable properties of substances are causally dependent on a structure of insensible particles. As Woodhouse observes, such a view of essences is not so much concerned with issues concerning classification as with the correct form of scientific explanation.[2]

Although Locke's theory of real essences seems to involve other issues, in one major way it is relevant to the problem of classification. The theory of real essences duplicates the world by postulating a realm of micro-objects that stand beneath the sensible properties and explain them. Yet it is also a major part of Locke's theory that these essences are unknown. Taken in conjunction, these elements in the theory seem to have important consequences for Locke's argument against the essentialist view that there really are natural kinds. For even if Locke can argue that the observable properties of bodies furnish no evidence for such a belief, it is still an open question whether things are not naturally classified at the submicroscopic level. The essentialist view that Locke attacks may hold for the real essences even if it does not fit the observable facts: perhaps there are natural kinds at the micro-level that cut across our actual classifications.

As Locke characterizes it, then, the notion of real essence raises special problems for his antiessentialist program, and his way of coping with these difficulties is not altogether consistent. At points Locke argues that since the real essence explains the observable properties, any two substances that differ in their macroscopic properties must differ in respect of their real essences as well. Indeed Locke even implies that this is a logically necessary truth, and this argument is consistent with the very strong claim he sometimes makes that if we knew the microstructure of bodies, their observable properties could be inferred a priori. Locke offers a clear statement of this position when he introduces his own concept of the real essence as a rival to the traditional view of essences that he rejects:

> The frequent Productions of Monsters, in all the Species of Animals, and of Changelings, and other strange Issues of humane Birth, carry with them difficulties, not possible to consists with this *Hypothesis* [i.e., the traditional view of essence]: Since it is as impossible, that two Things partaking exactly of the same real Essence, should have different Properties, as that two Figures partaking in the same real *Essence* of a Circle, should have different Properties.[3]

Locke here rests his antiessentialist case on the evidence of anomalies at the observational level, combined with the deductive model of explanation: a monster and a human being could not possibly depend on the same internal constitution. This line of thinking leads Locke to claim that even the real essence relates to sorts:

> Essence, even in this sense, *relates to a Sort*, and supposes a *Species*: For being that real Constitution, on which the Properties depend, it necessarily supposes a sort of Things, Properties belonging only to *Species*, and not to Individuals.[4]

Thus having apparently dragged the notion of real essence away from the sort at its introduction, Locke here reestablishes the connection. This may seem curious in view of his antiessentialist program; for he now says that our actual classifications are paralleled at the level of internal constitutions. In this form Locke's relativism amounts to no more than the assertion of borderline cases and monsters; but, as we shall see, the existence of such cases is not sufficient to show that essentialism is false.

In its ontological aspect, then, Locke's antiessentialist thesis is that substances are not cast in a certain number of molds and that this is true even at the corpuscularian level. Yet Locke also states his antiessentialist thesis in an epistemological form. He argues that since their real essences are unknown, we cannot know whether substances are distinguished into sorts at this level, and he combines this view with an answer to what we have termed the de facto problem of classification: our actual classifications are based not on the unknown real essences of substances but on their observable properties. Locke is not always careful to distinguish these theses, and it is easy to see how one could slide from one to the other; for the statement: "Substances are not distinguished into sorts according to their real essences" is ambiguous as between both claims.[5] It could be taken to mean either that substances are not so distinguished in nature, or that this is not the basis of our actual classifications. In some passages it is necessary to assume that Locke has the second claim in mind in order to make sense of what he says:

> But if Things were distinguished into *Species*, according to their real Essences, it would be as impossible to find different Properties in any two individual Substances of the same *Species*, as it is to find different Properties in two Circles, or two equilateral Triangles.[6]

Locke is here concerned with the fact that two individual substances possessing the same nominal essence may nonetheless fail to have all their properties in common: two bits of sulfur may differ in respect of some of their qualities not contained in the nominal essence. Now if Locke were answering the question of whether things were naturally classified, his claim could not stand; for one could reply that, in the posited case, there was no reason to suppose that they were of the same kind. In this way the problem Locke raises would simply be dissolved;

as it is, it only arises because he is inquiring into our actual basis of classification. At times, however, Locke seems uncertain about the relationship between the two issues. In the following passage in particular he appears unclear about how much he is seeking to claim:

> But the sorting of Things by us, or the making of determinate *Species*, being in order to naming and comprehending them under general terms, I cannot see how it can be properly said that Nature sets the Boundaries of the *Species* of Things: Or if it be so, our Boundaries of *Species*, are not exactly conformable to those in Nature.[7]

Perhaps Locke allows somewhat hesitantly at the end here that essentialism may be true, even though the divisions in nature are not the basis of our actual classification.

Thus we have distinguished two forms of an antiessentialist thesis in Locke, though we have suggested that he does not always succeed in keeping them apart. On the one hand, Locke makes the strong claim (a) that there are no natural kinds independently of our own minds; on the other hand, he advances the weaker claim (b) that in practice we classify things on the basis not of their real essences but of their observable properties. The relationship between these two theses appears to be at most one of one-way entailment, for though (a) may entail (b), the converse is clearly not true: it is quite consistent to maintain (b) while denying (a), in other words, while holding that nature does divide things up into kinds. Locke's tendency to confuse these issues may obscure the point, but the possibility of holding (b) while denying (a) is implicit in Leibniz's challenge to Locke: "You ought then to prove, Sir, that there is no common specific interior when the whole exterior is not common."[8] According to Leibniz, there is a presumption in favor of natural kinds that would not be undermined even if (b) were true. But, as we shall see, Leibniz also wishes to deny that (b) is in fact true, and this is the issue that has the most vital consequences for the debate.

Leibniz aims to show that Locke conflates issues that need to be distinguished. He also exposes the invalidity of some of Locke's arguments against natural kinds where no confusion arises. It is not difficult to feel some sympathy with the impatience Leibniz sometimes manifests. When Locke claims that essences are the "workmanship of the understanding" because different people mean different things by the same general term, Leibniz's puzzlement is well-founded:

> I confess, Sir, that there are few places where I have less understood the force of your reasonings than here, and that causes me distress. If people differ with regard to the name, does that change things or their resemblances? If one person applies the name 'avarice' to one resemblance, and some one else to another, there will be two different species designated by the same name.[9]

Leibniz is surely right to accuse Locke of a gross non sequitur here. That some people may mean different things when they talk of gold has no tendency to show that gold is not a natural kind. Perhaps there are those who simply do not have the concept of this substance, just as there are those who do not have the concept of an enzyme. Even if essentialism is true, such people may still be found. Leibniz has equally little trouble in disposing of some of Locke's other bad arguments against essentialism. Thus Locke thinks that the existence of monsters and borderline cases is evidence that nature does not divide things up into natural kinds. Yet as Leibniz points out, it is a concealed premise of Locke's argument that if a natural kind exists it must have many instances, but there seems no a priori objection to the idea of a species with just one member.[10] Moreover, Locke assumes that the transition from one species to another must be abrupt, but, as Leibniz points out, "the passage from species to species may be insensible."[11]

But if Leibniz concedes the existence of monsters, and claims they do not refute essentialism, he also adopts a different strategy. According to Leibniz, before one considers the bearing of borderline cases on the issue of natural kinds, it is necessary to resolve the logically prior issue of what is involved in saying that a given individual is or is not of a certain species. Leibniz believes that Locke's theory of our actual basis of classification is fundamentally mistaken. In opposition to Locke, he holds that our general words do involve a reference to the inner constitutions of bodies. The implications of Leibniz's critique here extend beyond the philosophy of science, for he devotes considerable space to criticizing Locke's application of his theory to the concept of man, and it is theologically important to settle the extension of this term.

The debate between Leibniz and Locke over the nature of our basis of classification has some strikingly modern features, and in the case of Locke, the contemporary aspect of his views has not gone unnoticed. Mackie has recently claimed that Locke advances a theory similar to Kripke's position in "Naming and Necessity."[12] Yet the title of Mackie's original paper—"Locke's Anticipation of Kripke"—is somewhat misleading. As Mackie makes clear in his paper, Locke puts forward a thesis that anticipates Kripke, only to reject that thesis. On the contrary, it is Leibniz, not Locke, who is tempted to agree with Kripke and who might more properly be credited with anticipating him. As we have seen, Locke denies that we have any knowledge of the real essence of bodies; he holds that our natural kind terms like 'gold' stand for certain combinations of observable properties that are regularly co-instantiated. Locke's position must not be oversimplified. His theory does not state that the only candidates for inclusion in the nominal essence are a substance's manifest properties: Locke is prepared to allow that passive powers, like malleability and solubility in aqua regia, form a large part of the concept of gold. Such dispositional properties are clearly founded in the internal constitutions of bodies, but Locke denies that our general words involve any reference to the real essence. Indeed he thinks that it is an abuse of language to set our general words in place of the internal constitutions of substances. In Locke's view this practice is objectionable because it represents an attempt to make our words signs of something we do not know.[13] As Mackie points out, Locke's view implies that if, counterfactually, a substance were discovered that had the structure of gold but lacked one or more of its nominally essential properties (for example, malleability), then such a substance would not be gold; conversely, if, counterfactually, a substance were discovered that possessed all the nominally essential properties of gold but lacked its real essence, then such a substance would nonetheless be gold.[14]

Leibniz quite clearly rejects the Lockean view that general terms stand only for the nominal essences and involve no reference to the internal constitution, and he is skillful in bringing out the objectionable consequences of Locke's view. Leibniz's position is well represented by a passage that calls to mind Putnam's contention that our linguistic community can be regarded as a factory in which there is a division of labor. "In this 'factory' some people have the 'job' of *wearing gold wedding rings*; other people have the 'job' of *selling gold wedding rings*; still other people have the job of *telling whether or not something is really gold*."[15]

> You see then, Sir, that the name 'gold,' for example, signifies not only what he who pronounces it knows about it, for example, something very heavy and yellow, but also what he does not know, and that another can know about it, that is to say, a body endowed with a certain internal constitution from which color and weight flow, and from which still other properties arise that he admits are better known by experts.[16]

A little earlier in Book III, Leibniz answers Locke's complaint against those who abuse language by trying to make their words stand for the internal constitutions of substances:

> And I would think rather that it is clear that one is wrong to blame this common usage, since it is very true that it is part of the complex idea of gold that it is a thing which has a real essence, the constitution of which is not otherwise known to us in detail than by the fact that qualities such as malleability depend on it.[17]

A page later Leibniz remarks that "one has no cause to blame this relation to the internal essence."[18] Leibniz is not claiming that the internal constitution of gold is known to us in detail: on the contrary, he explicitly states that the real essence is known only through observable properties such as malleability. But, for Leibniz, the lack of detailed knowledge of the internal constitution does not mean that our general terms stand only for the so-called nominal essence. Leibniz's view implies, however, that it may not always be possible for us to say whether a particular substance belongs to a certain kind; unlike Locke, he is not committed to saying that this must be an easy matter. In this respect, Leibniz's position may seem decidedly superior to Locke's, for the only reason Locke has for saying that it must be possible to know to what species an individual belongs is his view that species are abstract ideas. But this is question-begging.

Leibniz elaborates his anti-Lockean view that sortal words are annexed to the internal constitutions by saying that our definitions of such terms are essentially provisional.[19] We may define 'gold' in part as the heaviest of substances, but if we discover a substance heavier than gold lacking in some property like fixedness that forms part of our definition, then we must abandon our definition. Leibniz seems to envisage that our definitions, which are at present provisional, should approximate to the internal structure, even if this remains an ideal. Like Kripke, Leibniz would hold that once we discover, say, that gold has atomic number 79, then gold is necessarily identical with a body having that structure.[20] It is a consequence of this view that if we discovered a body that displayed all the nominally essential properties of gold but lacked its internal constitution, then we should not say that such a body was gold. Leibniz seems to draw this conclusion quite happily. In a revealing passage, he points up the unsatisfactory nature of the Lockean theory by speculating about the case of counterfeit gold:

> For example, one could find the means of counterfeiting gold, so that it satisfied all the tests that we have of it up till now, but one could also then discover a new manner of assaying, which would furnish the means of distinguishing natural gold from *that made artificially*.[21]

For Leibniz, then, to say that something is gold is to say that it has a certain inner constitution, and not merely (or even necessarily) to say that it satisfies the nominally essential criteria of gold, for these are by nature provisional. Such a position may call to mind Kripke's speculation that gold might turn out not to be yellow, that hitherto everyone had been the victim of an optical illusion.[22] Leibniz seems to be at one with Kripke that such a speculation involves no absurdity.

Thus Leibniz rejects the Lockean theory of nominal essences and insists that whether a particular substance belongs to a certain kind depends on whether it has a certain internal constitution. But Leibniz does not limit the scope of his thesis to topics like the criteria for identifying gold: on the contrary, he offers an analogous treatment of the criteria for saying that an individual is a man; and it is this issue that really engages his attention, for Locke's handling of this topic in terms of his theory of nominal essences seems to him to have unfortunate consequences for the way 'man' is defined. To resolve this issue, Leibniz subtly adapts his theory to the purpose of rescuing the traditional definition of 'man' as 'rational animal.'

Locke's overall theory of classification requires him to say that whether a given individual is a man depends on whether it displays the requisite nominal essence. However, Locke is by no means consistent in maintaining this position. As we have seen, he often takes his theory of nominal essences to imply that discovering the species membership of an individual is a simple matter of comparing it with the nominal essence in question. Yet in one place Locke makes a statement that suggests a quite different view of the matter:

So uncertain are the Boundaries of *Species* of Animals to us, who have no other Measures, than the complex *Ideas* of our own collecting: And so far are we from certainly knowing what a *Man* is; though, perhaps, it will be judged great Ignorance to make any doubt about it.[23]

Here it is difficult to interpret Locke's remarks except as an expression of the very thesis he is meant to be attacking. If our knowledge of man is imperfect and could be improved, then the nominal essence is not an adequate standard for resolving puzzles about classification. What, then, would certainty about the nature of man involve if not knowledge of the real essence of the species? Thus for Locke, it is because people have only nominal essences to go by that they sometimes have difficulty deciding, say, whether an individual is a man or a monster. What seems to lead Locke in this direction is his belief that nominal essences are unstable: they vary from person to person. At other times this consideration prompts Locke to draw quite different conclusions; he suggests that the question whether or not a monster is a man is really improper because definitions depend on arbitrary human decision.[24] So Locke implies at points that one definition is as good as another, that Plato's 'wingless biped' is as good as, though no better than, 'rational animal,' and that no criterion exists for deciding between them.

Despite some statements of a contrary tendency, Locke often claims that whether a particular individual is a man is a matter of arbitrary human decision. Yet although he insists that nominal essences are unstable, he thinks that in practice people do tend to identify the essence of man with a certain physical shape. How far Locke is justified in either claim seems highly questionable. As Woolhouse observes,[25] Locke's theory of nominal essences does not require him to suggest that it is an arbitrary matter which definition of a species we adopt. Leibniz disputes both these claims of Locke's, and though the theory of nominal essences is not to blame, his strategy is to invoke the rival theory that general terms refer to the real essence. The question at issue in deciding whether a changeling is a man or a monster is whether it has the requisite internal constitution, and in the case of man, Leibniz identifies the internal constitution with reason.

Leibniz makes this point repeatedly, but one may well wonder whether what he says is free from ambiguities.[26] Reason is clearly not internal to man in the sense that having atomic number 79 is internal to gold. If Leibniz intends to imply as much, he is simply punning on the word 'internal.' In the sense in which the atomic structure is internal to gold, presumably what is internal to man is simply his atomic structure; at least man's internal constitution must be specified in physical terms of some kind if the analogy with gold is to hold. Today, especially, when reason is likely to be construed on behavioristic lines, to say that reason is internal to man may be held to conjure up a misleading picture of thoughts locked away in the breast—Ryle's "ghost in the machine." But perhaps the analogy may be rescued by invoking Leibniz's distinctive metaphysical doctrines. Ultimately, for Leibniz, even the atomic structure of gold is merely phenomenal and in a certain sense external and superficial: what is real about gold is its monadic structure, and at this deep metaphysical level there is a continuity with reason in man. For Leibniz, the difference between gold and man is of course vast, but it is one of degree—in the clarity and distinctness of the perceptions. In this sense, of course, the microstructure of gold is not anything to which one could point.

Perhaps it is possible to gloss Leibniz's talk of reason as internal to man in a respectable way that preserves the analogy with gold. But in any case it furnishes a powerful argument against Locke. For it is because Leibniz holds that our general terms refer to the real essence (in the Lockean sense) that he does not think the task of deciding whether an individual should be admitted to a certain species is necessarily a simple matter of comparing it with a general idea. Thus Leibniz is not embarrassed that theologians sometimes have difficulty in deciding whether a monstrous-looking individual is a man or not. Though we know the real essence of man, reason, in a way we do not know the real essence of gold, this does not mean we can always detect its presence. Uncertainty about how to classify individuals is compatible with knowing what the essence of the species is. Thus, for Leibniz, that people have recourse to external characteristics when judging whether a monster is a man does not mean that they identify the essence of man with a certain physical shape. Rather, as Leibniz says quite explicitly, the physical shape serves as an index:

> If we distinguish man from beast by the faculty of reasoning, there is no middle possibility, the animal in question must either possess it or not possess it: but as this faculty sometimes does not appear, one judges about it by indices, which are not truly demonstrative, until this reason shows itself.[27]

It is true that Leibniz sometimes allows that human shape may be a necessary condition of being a man, but he never says that it is also sufficient. Leibniz's most usual position is that ancestry and shape are simply good criteria that have served us well until now:

> Up till now no rational animal has been found with an external shape very different from our own, that is why when it was a question of baptizing a child, breed and shape have never been considered as other than indices for judging whether it was a rational animal or not. Thus theologians and lawyers have had no need to renounce their sacred definition on that count.[28]

A definition based on shape and 'rational animal' have the same extension, but the latter is to be preferred; it is in virtue of possessing the faculty of reason that some individuals are baptized. In the above passage the theological implications of the issue are clear. Theological issues are also involved in Leibniz's reaction to Locke's theory that the individual has no essence. This is one of the points at which Locke's philosophy comes into open conflict with Leibniz's deep metaphysics.

Locke's denial that the individual has an essence has attracted considerable attention in recent years, and much of it has been critical. It has been argued that Locke's theory falsely implies that one could identify and reidentify an individual without reference to the sort: there is no "being the same" without "being the same such and such."[29] I cannot just pick out an individual and then say that it belongs to a certain sort, for any question as to what I am identifying or picking out can be answered only by using a general term. Commentators have tended to consider this issue in relation to such questions as whether one could pick out some substance in the world without identifying it as, say, a man or a scarecrow. Locke does, it is true, discuss cases like whether it is essential to this particular white piece of paper to have black letters on it; but significantly, when he introduces this topic, the initial example he gives is in the first person. Locke seems primarily interested in the question: Is anything essential to me? and only secondarily does he go on to ask whether anything is essential to other people or to individual bits of paper. In a fascinating passage Locke explains:

> 'Tis necessary for me to be as I am; GOD and Nature has made me so: But there is nothing I have, is essential to me. An Accident, or Disease, may very much alter my Colour, or Shape; a Fever, or Fall, may take away my Reason, or Memory, or both; and an Apoplexy leave neither Sense, nor Understanding, no nor Life. Other Creatures of my shape, may be made with more, and better, or fewer, and worse Faculties than I have: and others may have Reason, and Sense, in a shape and body very different from mine. None of these are essential to the one, or the other, or to any Individual whatsoever, till the Mind refers it to some Sort or *Species* of things; . . . So that if it be asked, whether it be *essential* to me, or any other particular corporeal Being to have Reason? I say no; no more than it is *essential* to this white thing I write on, to have words in it.[30]

As Locke expounds his view here, a marked element of anti-Cartesian polemic is apparent, for the statement that neither sense nor understanding nor even life is essential to me is in clear opposition to the Cartesian thesis that what I essentially am is a *res cogitans*.

Locke's theory that the individual has no essence is of course diametrically opposed to Leibniz's metaphysics, for it is one of Leibniz's most famous doctrines that every individual substance has a concept so complete that one can deduce from it everything that is ever true of it. In other words, Leibniz holds that every property that can ever be correctly predicated of a substance is essential to it. As Benson Mates has observed, Leibniz is no essentialist in the sense of believing in, as it were, partial essences.[31] It is because of his doctrine of complete individual concepts that Leibniz rejects the Lockean assumption, so strongly criticized by Professors Geach and Anscombe, that one could have the concept of an individual without assigning it to any kind. For though Leibniz holds that every individual substance has a complete concept or essence, he does not believe that this concept is available to finite minds: "Otherwise," as Leibniz says in correspondence with Arnauld, "it would be as easy for us to be prophets as geometers."[32] On the contrary, Leibniz thinks that every individual substance involves the infinite, inasmuch as it expresses the whole universe according to its point of view. This is the reason that Leibniz gives at III.VI of the *Nouveaux Essais* for our inability to have knowledge of the individual, and thus for holding that the sort is logically prior to the individual:

> it is impossible for us to have knowledge of individuals and to find the means of determining exactly the individuality of anything. . . . What is most worth noticing in this is that *individuality* envelops the infinite, and only that person is capable of understanding it who could have knowledge of the principle of individuation of such or such a thing.[33]

Thus Leibniz is in full agreement with Anscombe and Geach that the sort is logically prior to the individual, and hence that individuals necessarily have essences, but he goes far beyond them in his theory of complete individual concepts. He has been correctly described as a super-essentialist.[34] In the *Nouveaux Essais*, however, the theory of complete individual concepts makes only a shadowy appearance in such phrases (like the one quoted above) as "the individual envelops the infinite," which he does little to explain in terms of his logical doctrines. In reply to Locke's denial that individuals have essences, Leibniz does state that more is essential to individuals than one thinks; nonetheless he expounds a version of the doctrine of partial essences that we know is not an adequate representation of his more esoteric views:

> I believe that there is something essential to individuals, and more than one thinks. It is essential to substances to act, to created substances to suffer, to minds to think, to bodies to have extension and movement.[35]

Leibniz now proceeds to draw a distinction between those properties that are essential to a substance (like life, organs, and perception), and those that are merely accidental: the examples given are health, beauty, and wisdom.[36] Although somewhat misleadingly expressed, this distinction is not formally incompatible with Leibniz's deeper theories, for there is room in his philosophy for a distinction between those properties that are absolutely essential to a substance and those that are essential to it only in a nontemporal sense: properties of this latter type are ones an individual can acquire and cease to have. In Dummett's terminology, such properties are absolutely accidental.[37]

Thus, "not having been to Paris" is an absolutely accidental property of Leibniz, for it is a property that was presently accidental up to 1672, and yet, according to Leibniz, it is also essential: it is impossible that Leibniz (that very individual *Leibniz*) should have lacked the property of not having been to Paris before 1672. But in the *Nouveaux Essais* Leibniz does not state his view that if it is true of a substance a that there is some time t at which a property P is correctly ascribed to it, then P is essential to a. In this more limited sense, being an essential property is compatible with being an accidental property, though Leibniz does not point this out.

To Locke's denial that individuals have essences, Leibniz quite clearly replies with a restricted version of the essentialist thesis, which, if not actually inconsistent with his deeper views, at least gives the appearance of being so. (In this respect there is an analogy with Leibniz's treatment of innate ideas in the *Nouveaux Essais*, for there he gives only a partial account of his esoteric views.) The reason for this is, I think, clear, and is connected with the general nature of his case against Locke. Leibniz understandably is not particularly anxious to insist that every property that I will come to possess is essential to me, for this doctrine seems to smack of logical necessitarianism, as we know it did to Arnauld; but he does wish to emphasize those properties essential to me in that they belong to me as a member of the species 'man.' What Leibniz really finds objectionable in Locke's doctrine is the idea that it is not essential to me to have sense, understanding, and even life; for this leaves open the possibility that someone could point to Locke's lifeless corpse and say: "That individual is John Locke." In reply Leibniz insists that substances can never be without action, and that minds can never be without thought. For Leibniz, clearly, Locke's denial that individuals have essences is of a piece with his polemic against the idea that the soul always thinks. Leibniz himself draws attention to this connection. In the very passage in which he opposes Locke's theory he expressly notes that he is going over familiar ground:

> Thus one can cease to be healthy, handsome, learned, and even visible and palpable, but one does not cease to have life and organs, and perception. I have said above sufficiently why it appears to men that life and thought cease sometimes, although they still continue and produce effects.[38]

Unlike Descartes, Leibniz has no wish to identify a person with his mind, but he is quite as insistent as Descartes that thinking is an essential property of a person, and that its subject is an immaterial and hence immortal substance. Earlier in this paper, I suggested that Leibniz objected to Locke's theory of nominal essences chiefly on the ground that it subverted the traditional definition of 'man' as a rational animal. We can now see that Leibniz's reply to Locke's denial that individuals have essences is similarly motivated by a desire to defend traditional orthodoxy. Leibniz's obsession with the subversive character of Locke's philosophy turns up in places where one might least expect it.

Notes

1. *John Locke: An Essay Concerning Human Understanding*, ed. P. H. Nidditch, (Oxford: Clarendon, 1975), III iii 17. Subsequent references are to this edition.

2. R. S. Woolhouse, *Locke's Philosophy of Science and Knowledge* (Oxford: Blackwell, 1971), p. 98.

3. *Essay*, III iii 17.

4. *Ibid.*, III vi 6.

5. Cf. Woolhouse, p.115.

6. *Essay*, III vi 8.

7. *Ibid.*, III vi 30.

8. *Nouveaux Essais sur l'Entendement, G. W. Leibniz: Sämtliche Schriften und Briefe,* ed. German Academy of Sciences (Darmstadt, 1923-), Series VI, Vol. VI, p. 311. Subsequent references are to this edition. Translations are my own.

9. *Ibid.,* p. 292.

10. *Ibid.,* p. 311.

11. *Ibid.,* p. 321.

12. S. Kripke, "Naming and Necessity," in *Semantics of Natural Language,* ed. D. Davidson and G. Harman (Dordrecht, Holland: Reidel, 1972), pp. 319 ff.

13. *Essay,* III x 17-18

14. J. L. Mackie, "Locke's Anticipation of Kripke," *Analysis* 34 (June, 1974): 177-80; now incorporated in *Problems from Locke* (Oxford: Clarendon; 1976). pp. 93-100. Cf. J. Troyer, "Locke on the Names of Substances," *The Locke Newsletter* 6, (Summer, 1975): 27-39.

15. H. Putnam, "Meaning and Reference," *Journal of Philosophy* 70 (1973): 704.

16. *Nouveaux Essais,* p. 354.

17. *Ibid.,* p. 345.

18. *Ibid.,* p. 346.

19. See for instance *Ibid.,* pp. 311-12.

20. Kripke, pp. 315-16.

21. *Nouveaux Essais,* p. 312.

22. Kripke, pp. 315-16.

23. *Essay,* III vi 27.

24. *Ibid.,* III x 17.

25. Woolhouse, pp. 104-5

26. *Nouveaux Essais,* p. 326.

27. *Ibid.,* pp. 394-95.

28. *Ibid.,* p. 319.

29. P. Geach, *Mental Acts* (London: Routledge, 1957), pp. 68-69; E. Anscombe, "Aristotle," in E. Anscombe and P. Geach, *Three Philosophers* (Oxford: Blackwell, 1961). p. 8.

30. *Essay,* III vi 4.

31. B. Mates, "Leibniz on Possible Worlds," in *Leibniz: A Collection of Critical Essays,* ed. H. G. Frankfurt (New York: Doubleday, 1972), p. 338.

32. Leibniz to Arnauld, n. d., *Die Philosophischen Schriften von Gottfried Wilhelm Leibniz,* ed. C. I. Gerhardt, 7 vols. (Berlin, 1875-1890), Vol. II, p. 45.

33. *Nouveaux Essais,* pp. 289-90.

34. In what follows I am indebted to the discussion in F. Mondadori, "Leibniz and the Doctrine of Inter-World Identity," *Studia Leibnitiana* 7, I (1975): 48-49.

35. *Nouveaux Essais,* p. 305.

36. *Ibid.*

37. M. Dummett, *Frege: Philosophy of Language* (London: Duckworth, 1973): 130-31.

38. *Nouveaux Essais,* p. 305.

Truth and Sufficient Reason in the Philosophy of Leibniz

Robert Sleigh

Leibniz's account of truth occupies a central role in his philosophical scheme. He was well aware of its importance to his system; witness, for example, his pleasure at Arnauld's apparent acceptance of his account of truth (G/2/73-74 (M 91), C10 (MP135)).[1] In paragraph eight of the *Discourse on Metaphysics* Leibniz set out to motivate his complete concept account of an individual substance in terms of his account of truth. In correspondence with Arnauld concerning the complete concept account of individual substance, Leibniz said: "If you could find time to look again one day at what we had finally decided about the concept of an individual substance, you would perhaps find that in conceding me

Early versions of various parts of this paper were read on three occasions at the Institute for Advanced Study at Princeton. Some of the research was done at the Institute. I thank the Institute and the members of the Seventeenth Century Study Group who met there and discussed topics with me. I am especially grateful to Martha Bolton, Vere Chappell, Willis Doney, Michael Hooker, Ruth Mattern, Fabrizio Mondadori, and Margaret Wilson. A version of this paper was my contribution to a symposium on Leibniz conducted at meetings of the Western Division of the American Philosophical Association in April, 1979. Nicholas Rescher commented on the paper. I have profited from his comments and his many important publications on the philosophy of Leibniz. I wish to thank Robert Adams for helpful comments concerning the dating of some of Leibniz's papers. I also wish to thank Carol Gabriel, Gareth Matthews, and Wendy Wegener for help with translations. Special thanks to Carol Gabriel for help in understanding the April 1679 Logic Series. Special thanks, also, to Blake Barley, who caught a serious error in an earlier version.

I am grateful to Dennis Fried, Leon Galis, Michael Roth, and John Tienson, all of the Philosophy Department of Franklin and Marshall, for penetrating criticisms offered after a careful scrutiny of the paper. Some alterations have been made to meet their objections; no doubt more are required. On the whole, I have avoided references to the secondary literature. I found the following books extremely useful: C. D. Broad, *Leibniz — An Introduction* (Cambridge, 1975); Nicholas Rescher, *Leibniz An Introduction to his Philosophy* (Totowa, NJ, 1979); Bertrand Russell, *A Critical Exposition of the Philosophy of Leibniz* (London, 1937), and, most of all, Louis Couturat, *La Logique de Leibniz* (Paris, 1901); and G. H. R. Parkinson, *Logic and Reality in Leibniz's Metaphysics* (Oxford, 1965).

these beginnings one is obliged subsequently to grant me all the rest" (G/2/127 (M162)). The beginning of the beginnings is the notion of truth. Bearing in mind the magnificent metaphysical structure that constitutes "all the rest," it behooves us to try to understand Leibniz's conception of truth and his reasons, or motivation, for accepting it. This essay is no more than a prolusion to that understanding.

The scope of this paper is limited in a number of dimensions. In the first place attention is restricted to a limited time period. In December of 1676 Leibniz arrived in Hannover to take up his duties as librarian to the Court of Hannover. In June of 1690 Leibniz returned to Hannover after a journey of approximately two and one-half years. This paper focuses almost entirely on work I take to have been produced (at least in its original version) during this period—roughly, 1677-1690. This is partly because of the importance of the work Leibniz produced on truth during this span, but it is also because I have not studied Leibniz's work in other time periods with the requisite care. Second, the paper raises many more problems than it solves. For the most part I resist the temptation to fill in with a constructive account where there seem to be gaps in Leibniz's account. Some of these gaps provide the scaffolding for intriguing exercises in formal construction. These exercises are left to others. Third, although the major aims of the paper are historical as much as philosophical, the account presented is idealized to a degree some may find disconcerting.

The basic structure of the paper is this: Section I outlines various characterizations of truth to be found in Leibniz's writings from the period 1677-1690. Section III relates the principle of sufficient reason to these characterizations of truth. Section II concerns Leibniz's reaction to various problems he encountered in connection with these characterizations of truth. The most pressing is simply described; the characterizations seem to have as a consequence that a proposition is true just in case it is necessarily true. The leading element in Leibniz's proposed solution is not so easily described but it has to do with the dreaded distinction between finite and infinite analysis. It is a question of considerable importance to Leibniz scholarship when the idea of infinite analysis came to Leibniz—surely during our period, 1677-1690. But I do not have the skills that would be required to settle on an exact date, if indeed that can be settled; 1686 sounds good to me. If the idea of infinite analysis came to Leibniz before 1682 then the discussion in sections I and II describes distinct logical moments of Leibniz's thought that were not temporally consecutive. For those with a scholarly bent, here is the most troublesome case: the essay "Necessary and Contingent Truths" (C16-24 (MP96-105)) contains the infinite analysis idea full-blown. Schepers suggests 1678 as the date for "Necessary and Contingent Truths" (Heinrich Schepers, "Zum Problem der Kontingenz Bei Leibniz," in *Collegium Philosophicum* (Basel and Stuttgart, 1965)). Parkinson suggests 1686 as the date for "Necessary and Contingent Truths." I hope Parkinson is right in this case.[2]

I. THE INITIAL STATE

In the writings of 1677-1690 we find the following accounts of truth:

Let p, q, r, etc., range over propositions that are categorical, affirmative, and either universal or singular.[3]

(1)   p is true if and only if the predicate of p is in the subject of p.
(C51 (P19), C69, C85, G/7/300 (L349/226), G/7/44, C401-2
(MP93), G/4/433 (DM12), G/2/56 (M63), C518-19 (MP87);
G/7/309 (MP75), C388 (P77), C16 (MP 96), C1, Grua 303, FC179
(MP107)).[4]

(2)   p is true if and only if the concept of the predicate of p is contained in the concept of the subject of p.
(C51 (P19), C85, G/7/300 (L349/226), G/7/44, C402 (MP93-94),
G/4/433 (DM12-13), G/2/46 (M50), G/2/56 (M63); C388 (P77),
C16 (MP96), G/7/199-200 (Schrecker 13), Grua 304, FC179 (MP107)).

(3)   p is true if and only if p is reducible to an identical proposition.[5]
(C68, G/7/300 (L348/226), G/7/44, C513 (MP7), G/7/295 (MP14),
C402 (MP94), C518 (MP87)).[6]

(4)   p is true if and only if there is an a priori proof of p.
(G/7/300-1 (L348-49/226), G/7/44, C513 (MP7), Grua 287,
G/7/295 (MP14), C402 (MP94), Le Roy 47 (DM18-19), G/4/438
(DM22), G/2/62 (M71), C518 (MP87)).[7,8]

The accounts of truth characterized in (1) through (4) are intimately related to another fundamental component of Leibniz's system—the principle of sufficient reason. We may restrict our attention to formulations of that principle that concern the conditions under which a proposition is true.

Consider these assertions, which Leibniz regarded as formulations of the principle of sufficient reason and which are to be found in texts from our period:

(7)   p is true only if there is a sufficient reason why p is true.
(G/7/301 (L349/227), C513 (MP7-8), Grua 287, G/7/295-96
(MP15), C402 (MP93), G/4/438 (DM22), G/2/62 (M71), C519
(MP88); G/7/309 (MP75), G/7/199 (Schrecker 13), C1, Grua 325,
Grua 303, FC182 (MP109)).

(8)   p is true only if there is an a priori proof of p. (See the citations under (4).)

Even a casual acquaintance with Leibniz will suggest that various reductions are possible. Moreover, one would certainly hope for some reductions since all the equivalences have the same left-hand member. It is plausible to attribute the following doctrines to Leibniz; they yield the reductions one would expect.

(a)   The predicate of p is in the subject of p if and only if the concept of the predicate of p is contained in the concept of the subject of p.

(C51, C85, G/7/300 (L348-49/226), C401-2 (MP93-94), G/4/433
(DM12-13), G/2/43 (M47), G/2/56 (M63); C388 (P77), C16 (MP96),
C1, Grua 303, FC179 (MP107))

(b)   p is reducible to an identical proposition if and only if there is an a
priori proof of p.
(G/7/300 (L348/226), G/7/44, C513 (MP7), G/7/295 (MP14), C402
(MP94), C518 (MP87); C369 (P59), C17 (MP96-97), C1, Grua 303,
FC181 (MP108))[9]

(c)   There is sufficient reason why p is true if and only if there is an a priori
proof of p.
(G/7/301 (L349/226), C513-14 (MP7-8), Grua 287, G/7/295-96
(MP15), C519 (MP88), C402 (MP93), G/4/438 (DM22), G/2/62 (M71))

(d)   The concept of the predicate of p is contained in the concept of the
subject of p if and only if there is an a priori proof of p.
(G/7/300 (L348-49/226), G/7/43-44, C513 (MP7), Grua 287, C401
(MP93), G/2/62 (M71), C518-19 (MP87-88))[10]

Acceptance of (1) through (4), (7) and (8), and (a) through (d) characterizes what I shall call the initial state. I believe that in the early stages of our
time period Leibniz was in the initial state. That is, where p is any proposition
that is categorical, affirmative, universal or singular, he then took the following
to come to the same thing:

The predicate of p is in the subject of p,
The concept of the predicate of p is contained in the concept of the subject
    of p,
p is reducible to an identical proposition,
There is an a priori proof of p,
There is a sufficient reason why p is true.

And what he took them to come to is—p is true. By my lights matters had
altered considerably by 1690. Leibniz had by then abandoned the initial state
rejecting (3), (4), (8), (c) and (d). It is no easy matter to discern exactly what
views he then held, but that's the topic of section II. Let's probe the initial state
in more detail by focusing on the various notions employed in the propositions
whose acceptance constitutes the initial state.

It is necessary to say something about propositions, subjects, predicates,
the concept of the subject, the concept of the predicate, terms, etc. There is
a lack of uniformity in Leibniz's use of the relevant terminology.[11] I am not at
all confident that his views on these topics remained fixed even over the period
that concerns us. Still I think the following sketch is a fair account of a view that
dominated his thinking during our time period.

Propositions are to be distinguished from sentences that may express them
(G/7/191) just as concepts are to be distinguished from nouns that may signify
them (C351, 432, 497). Every categorical proposition has as constituents a subject concept and a predicate concept (C49 (P17), C77 (P25), C85). Since we are

restricting attention to propositions that are categorical, affirmative, and either universal or singular, it will do no harm to equate a proposition p with an ordered pair [α, β] where α is the subject concept of p and β is the predicate concept of p. This relation of constituency that holds between concepts and propositions must be distinguished from a relation of containment (or involvement or inclusion) that may hold between a concept and other concepts that, in some sense, compose it.[12] No doubt sometimes when Leibniz talked about the subject and the predicate of a proposition he intended to talk about the subject-concept and the predicate-concept of the proposition (perhaps C51 (P18-19) and C16 (MP96) are examples). With the relevant terminology so construed (a) is a triviality. But there is another approach to be found in Leibniz's writings and I will use terminology in accord with it. In this mode, by the subject of a proposition Leibniz meant that of which the proposition predicates something and by the predicate he meant that which is predicated of the subject. (See, for example, G/4/438 (DM21) and G/2/58 (M58).) With 'subject' and 'predicate' so construed (and p restricted as stipulated) (1) does not seem wayward or particularly daring. Thus where p is some singular proposition, what (1) says is that p is true just in case the individual that is the subject of p has the property that is the predicate of p. By contrast, (2) and (a) may seem daring and wayward. Many of the passages cited as textual evidence in connection with (a) suggest that Leibniz took the right-hand side of that equivalence to provide an analysis of the left-hand side (see, for example, C401-2 (MP93-94), G/2/43 (M47) and G/2/56 (M63-64)). (2), then, appears to be more significant than (1).

Consider this passage from the Leibniz-Arnauld correspondence:

> There must always be some foundation of the connection of the terms of a proposition which must be in their notions. This is my main principle on which I believe all philosophers should be agreed. (G/2/56 (M63-64)[13]

Broad calls this "main principle" *The Principle of Grounded Connexion* and sees (a) as "specifying the nature of the foundation," i.e., as giving it content.[14]

The content of (a) (and, hence, of Leibniz's "main principle") depends on how Leibniz construed 'the concept of.' There are two avenues of investigation worth pursuing here. We might focus attention on how Leibniz implicitly defined 'the concept of' by studying how he related the relevant notion to important metaphysical and epistemological notions that he used, for example, nature, essence, essential property, a priori knowledge, and a priori proof. This study certainly merits doing but it will not be undertaken in a systematic way in this paper except with respect to the notion of an a priori proof. Obviously an alternative avenue is to look for some direct explanation of the notion of a concept that Leibniz may have offered. Let's try the direct approach first.

We are primarily concerned with the concepts that enter into ordered pairs that are propositions. We have restricted attention to propositions that are categorical, affirmative, and either universal or singular. One more restriction. Let's consider only propositions about individuals; that is, propositions whose subject-concepts, if exemplified at all, are exemplified by individuals.[15] Such propositions will be called first-order hereafter. Here's a simplification I will utilize where it proves useful: although Leibniz thought of a concept as being composed of concepts, for many purposes it is harmless to think of a concept as a set of properties.

The most detailed direct explanations of "the concept of" to be found in writings from our period are those of the *Discourse on Metaphysics* and the Leibniz-Arnauld correspondence. The first point to note is that in the Discourse and throughout the correspondence with Arnauld, Leibniz assumed an association between entity and concept that made it legitimate to talk of *the* concept of x, for any entity x. Apparently Arnauld made the same assumption. (See, for example, G/2/30 (M30).) Arnauld formulated a rule for determining the contents of the concept of a species. It comes to this:

where S is some species,

(i)   For any property f, f is in the concept of S if and only if, for any x, were x of lack f, then x would not be an S. (G/2/32-33 (M32-33))

Arnauld extended this rule to individuals in this manner:

where x is an individual,

(ii)   For any property f, f is in the concept of x if and only if were x to lack f then x would not be x. (G/2/30-31 (M30), G/2/33 (M32-33))

It is reasonably clear that Arnauld took (ii) to be equivalent to:

(iii) For any property f, f is in the concept of x if and only if it is necessarily true that if x exists then x has f.

That is, according to Arnauld, the concept of an individual contains all and only its essential properties. It also seems likely (though not clear) that according to Arnauld the concept of an individual distinguishes that individual from all other individuals (G/2/30 (M30)). So it is likely that Arnauld would have accepted this condition:

(iv)   For any individual x, if C is the concept of x then there is no individual y such that y is distinct from x and y has every property in C.

Perhaps Arnauld was prepared to go further and accept this condition:

(v)   For any individual x, if C is the concept of x, then it is not possible that there is an individual y such that y is distinct from x and y has every property in C.

So much for Arnauld. It is not quite so easy to find something that could be called "Leibniz's rule" in the correspondence. We know of course that the notorious Leibnizian complete individual concept is the outcome of whatever rule it is that Leibniz applied. It is also clear that when pressed in the correspondence, Leibniz defended the thesis that the concept of an individual is nothing shy of its complete individual concept by deriving that result from the application of the concept-containment account of truth (i.e., (2)) to singular propositions about individuals.[16] (See G/4/433 (DM12-13) and G/2/46 (M50), G/2/52 (M58), G/2/56 (M63), Schmidt 476.) But I believe that it will prove worthwhile to seek for some basic intuition concerning concepts that underlies this derivation. A leading contender would be whatever intuition we would extract from the following passage in the correspondence:

> Furthermore, if one thinks at all about what I am saying, one will find that it is evident ex terminis. For by the individual concept of Adam I mean . . . a perfect representation of a particular Adam who has particular conditions and is thereby distinguished from an infinite number of other possible persons. (G/2/20 (M15)

The phrase 'perfect representation' ('parfaite representation') may indicate that the concept in question must be complete in the sense of containing all (and only) the properties Adam had. But it may indicate no more than that the concept in question is a haecceity, i.e., a concept that distinguishes its bearer from all other possible individuals. Leibniz was certainly prepared to talk about possible objects and their properties. Let us say that a set of properties A is a haecceity set just in case A is a consistent set of properties (i.e., some possible object has them all) and for any possible objects x and y, if x has all the members of A in some world and y has all the members of A in some world, *then* x is identical to y.[17] Leibniz held the following doctrine:

(vi)   For any individual x, C is the concept of x only if C is a haecceity set for x.[18]
       (In addition to G/2/20 (M15) see also (G/2/45 (M49) and G/2/52-53 (M59).)

What about the converse of (vi)? Consider:

(vii) For any individual x, if C is a haecceity set for x then C is the concept of x.

Did Leibniz accept (vii)? Surely the answer ought to be no, if Leibniz thought that there might be distinct sets that were haecceity sets for the same object. It is important at this point to note that Leibniz used both a strict and a nonstrict notion of a concept. Consider this passage from the correspondence (G/2/44 (M48)):

> For all the predicates of Adam depend or do not depend upon other predicates of this same Adam. Setting aside, therefore, those which do depend on others, one has only to consider together all the primitive predicates in order to form the complete concept of Adam adequate to deduce from it everything that is ever to happen to him.

This passage deserves some attention. A bit of machinery will help. Where A is some set of properties and f a property, let's say:

(viii) A entails f if and only if it is not possible that something has every property in A and yet lacks f.

Two sets of properties A and B are *equivalent* if A entails every member of B and B returns A the favor.

Let's say that a set of properties is *strict* if all its members are primitive; *nonstrict*, otherwise. The distinction between primitive versus derived properties (often concepts) played an important role in Leibniz's thinking during our time period. For some comments on it see p. 217, below.

Where A and B are sets of properties let's say that B *corresponds* to A just in case A is strict and B is equivalent to A. I shall assume that Leibniz assumed that each consistent set of properties corresponds to exactly one set, equivalent sets to the same set, and nonequivalent sets to distinct sets.[19]

Sometimes Leibniz meant by the complete concept C of x the set that has as members all and only the properties of x; but in our passage quoted above he meant the strict set C' to which C corresponds. Similarly, we should distinguish a strict haecceity set S from various flabby haecceity sets that correspond to S. Obviously then, (vii) should be rejected. But the really interesting question here concerns Leibniz's attitude toward this doctrine:

(ix)   For some individual x, there are nonequivalent haecceity sets for x.

If Leibniz accepted (ix) then he would be obliged to reject:

(x)   For any individual x, C is the strict concept of x if and only if C is the strict haecceity set for x.

At G/2/54 (M60-61) we seem to get a clear identification of haecceity sets with complete concepts. Leibniz said there that "whatever finite number of predicates that one may take incapable of determining all the rest" there will be "several [possible] individuals whom all that would fit" (cf. Grua 31). Apparently, then, Leibniz rejected (ix) and accepted (x) because he accepted:

(xi)   For any individual x, C is a haecceity set for x if and only if C is equivalent to the strict complete concept of x.

We seem to be coming out exactly where one would expect. However, we should take note of some passages in the correspondence that might suggest to some that Leibniz *rejected* (xi). At G/2/42 (M45), G/2/46 (M51), G/2/52 (M58), and G/2/54 (M60-61) Leibniz made use of the idea of conceiving something *sub ratione generalitatis*. We may focus on G/2/42 (M45) and G/2/54 (M60-61). The first of these contains remarks Leibniz drew up while preparing a reply to Arnauld; the second is from Leibniz's edited copy of the letter sent to Arnauld. Both say that if we conceive of Adam as having the properties of being the first man, being placed in a garden of pleasure, being such that God draws forth a woman from his rib, etc., then we conceive Adam sub ratione generalitatis. Both say that to so conceive him is to conceive him under a description that may individuate him from all actual men but that does not individuate him from all possible men. This surely suggests that to conceive x as having a set of properties C is to conceive x sub ratione generalitatis just in case C is *not* a haecceity set for x. Couple this with an admonition to be found in the preparatory remarks

(G/2/42 (M45)) and we have a problem. The admonition is that we must not mention Eve, Eden, "and other circumstances which complete individuality"; otherwise, we will not be conceiving Adam sub ratione generalitatis.[20] But then singleton of the property of being married to Eve would be a haecceity set. But it does not appear to be equivalent to any complete concept of Adam. This presents us with a problem: No doubt Leibniz did accept (xi). So the above reasoning needs to be explained away. We need to say something about why Leibniz accepted (xi), particularly the inference from left to right.

Consider singleton of the property of being identical with Adam. Isn't that a haecceity set for Adam? Isn't it obvious that it is not equivalent to any complete concept of Adam? What follows is speculation about how Leibniz would answer these questions. The topics broached deserve detailed consideration; that detail is not offered here.

Leibniz would claim that singleton of the property of being identical with Adam *is* a haecceity set for Adam and *is* equivalent to a (every) complete concept of Adam. He would first ask us to distinguish the property of being identical with Adam from something Eve might have referred to by saying 'the property of being identical with *him*,' while pointing to Adam. The haecceity set for Adam is a concept God contemplates prior (so to speak) to creation when there is no Adam and, indeed, no possible Adam distinct from the relevant concept (G/2/54 (M61)). It must be composed of properties that can be identified without reference to individuals; it must be composed of properties that were ingredients in the process of creation as Leibniz envisaged it.

In the *Specimen inventorum de admirandis naturae Generalis arcanis* Leibniz said:

> Since the full reason of a thing is the aggregate of all its primitive requisites (which do not require other requisites) it is evident that the causes of all things are reduced to the attributes of God. (G/7/310 (MP77))

An idea involved here is that the positive primitive properties of created things are various limited versions of attributes of God (G/6/615 (MP186)).

According to Leibniz, God's attributes are perfections, i.e., simple properties that are "positive and absolute, i.e., express whatever they express without any limits" (G/7/261 (L259/167)). Leibniz believed that the perfections are all compatible among themselves (G/7/261 (L259/167), Schmidt 480). Mates notes: "When he [Leibniz] speaks of the 'compatibility' of positive attributes, he evidently has in mind something more like their independence" (Benson Mates, "Leibniz on Possible Worlds," in *Leibniz, A Collection of Critical Essays*, ed. Harry G. Frankfurt (New York, 1972) p. 339). Suppose that the feature of logical independence carries over to the limited versions that are the positive primitive properties of created things. Indeed, suppose it carries over to each basic pair composed of a positive primitive property and its complement, so that an element of a basic pair is independent of every element of every other basic pair. It is plausible to suppose that a set of those purely qualitative, independent primitive properties will fail to individuate its bearer from all other possible objects unless it is complete. Hence, it is plausible to suppose that a strict set with no member from some basic pair is not a haecceity set. A strict concept is complete just in case it has a member from each basic pair. Hence, every strict haecceity set is a strict complete concept. According to Leibniz every genuine property is equivalent to a conjunction of elements from basic pairs. Hence, every haecceity set is a complete concept. (For references to textual evidence supporting some of this speculation see pages 224-225, below.)

We have been speculating as to why Leibniz accepted (xi). This problem is intimately connected with the question why Leibniz accepted a concept-containment account of truth. Given Leibniz's commitment to (vi), if we could explain one, we could explain the other. Thus, given (vi) and (xi), the concept-containment account of truth (at least applied to singular propositions) seems a straightforward consequence. Given (vi) and the concept-containment account of truth, (xi) seems a straightforward consequence. Something is said about Leibniz's motivation for accepting the concept-containment account of truth later in this paper (see page 234).

For our present purposes it is not important to distinguish the strict complete concept of a thing from various flabby concepts corresponding to it. Let's, then, work with that than which there is none more flabby, i.e.,

> where x is an individual:

(xii)   For any property f, f is in the concept of x
       if and only if x has f.

Compare (ii), which gives Arnauld's rule for associating concept and individual, with (xii). Did Leibniz believe that his rule, i.e., (xii), and Arnauld's rule produced the same association of concept and individual? I think we can derive an affirmative answer from some statements of Leibniz and a negative answer from some (other) of his statements. First, the affirmative: At G/4/455 (DM50, G/2/42 (M46), G/2/45 (M52), and G/2/53 (M59-60) we find that Leibniz asserted that:

(xiii) For any individual x and property f, x has f if and only if were x to
       lack f then x would not be x.

Obviously, in the presence of (xiii), (xii) and (ii) are equivalent. So much for the derivation of an affirmative answer.

At G/4/437-38 (DM20-21), G/2/38 (M40), G/2/40 (M43), G/2/46 (M50-51), Grua 309 and 311, we find that Leibniz *denied* the following doctrine:

(xiv)   For any individual x and property f, x has f if and only if it is neces-
       sarily true that if x exists then x has f.

Consider, now:

(xv)   For any individual x and property f, it is necessarily true that if x
       exists then x has f if and only if were x to lack f then x would not be
       x.

From (xv) and Leibniz's denial of (xiv), we reach the conclusion that for some individual x and property f, f is in the concept of x according to (xii), but it is not according to (ii). Thus, a negative answer.

This derivation of a negative answer may seem less satisfying than the derivation of a positive answer. Perhaps Leibniz would have rejected (xv) on which it is based. Perhaps there are plausible ways of construing the passages cited above so that they do not support the contention that Leibniz denied (xiv). (I am aware that many think so; I think they are wrong.)

To conclude our account of Leibniz's direct approach to those concepts that are constituents of propositions that are categorical, affirmative, universal or singular, and first-order, it is necessary to say something about concepts other than those of individuals. Paragraph 8 of the Discourse suggests that Leibniz held one pattern of association between concept and object in the case of individuals, and a distinct pattern for what he called abstractions, e.g., genera, species, and properties of individuals.

Where x is an abstraction from individuals, we have:

(xvi) For any property f, f is contained in the concept of x if and only if,
       for any y, if y were x (or were an instance of x) then y would be f.

The concept of an abstraction will not contain properties of the abstraction but rather properties of those things from which it is abstracted.[21]

My suggestion is that (xiii) and (xvi) result from Leibniz's intuition that the concept of an entity must be a haecceity set for that entity, coupled with some unorthodox metaphysical theses about haecceity sets, e.g., (xi). *Given* (xii) and (xvi), (2) and (a) are no more surprising than (*1*). Some of Leibniz's remarks suggest that the doctrines involved here were standard fare in the seventeenth century. See, for example, G/4/433 (DM12), G/2/56-57 (M63-64) and the following from G/2/43 (M47):

> In saying that the individual notion of Adam contains everything that will ever happen to him I do not mean anything other than what all philosophers mean when they say that the predicate is in the subject of a true proposition. It is true that the consequences of so evident a doctrine are paradoxes, but that is the fault of philosophers who do not follow far enough the clearest notions.

The deductions of these paradoxes (in fact, the main metaphysical theses of Leibniz's philosophy) use various principles connecting the notion referred to by 'the concept of' with such notions as nature, essence, essential property, necessary property, a priori knowledge, and a priori proof.[22] We may usefully pursue the indirect approach to understanding Leibniz's concept of a concept by concentrating on the notion of an a priori proof. Let's focus on (b) and (d).[23]

Here are samples from citations in support of (b). In the "Introduction to a Secret Encyclopedia" we find a proposition is true which is either identical or reducible to identicals, that is, which can be demonstrated apriori. (C513 (MP7))

In the important essay "On Freedom" we find this:

Demonstration consists simply in this: by the analysis of the terms of a proposition, and by substituting for a defined term a definition or part of a definition, one shows a certain equation or coincidence of predicate with subject in a reciprocal proposition, or in other cases at least the inclusion of the predicate in the subject. (FC181 (MP108))

We may safely assume that, according to Leibniz, providing an a priori proof of the proposition consists in demonstrating that proposition, which is the same as reducing it to an identical proposition. Our quotations also shed some light on how this reductive process is to proceed. We start with our original proposition. Substitutions are made on the basis of definitions. This process generates a series whose first term is the original proposition or some proxy (for example, a sentence expressing it) and whose last term is an identical proposition (or some proxy). One item y follows another item x in the series, provided some relationship based on a definition holds between some component of x and a corresponding component of y. An affirmative identical proposition is one of the general form AB is B (which includes as special cases AA is A and A is A). (see C369 (P58), C367 (P57).) Luckily we do not need to bother with negative identicals and, in particular, the dreaded disparates.[24] Are these items that occur in demonstrations linguistic entities or conceptual entities or entities that are neither conceptual nor linguistic? The texts lead in various directions. This topic is without question one of the most difficult one faces in trying to fathom Leibniz's philosophy. I will make a proposal that is close to many of the relevant texts and no more complicated than our present purposes require. This proposal raises at least as many questions as it resolves; I leave them for another occasion.

I begin with some background material that requires elucidation, Leibniz's conception of an analysis of concepts. Probably the truth is that Leibniz had various conceptions of an analysis of concepts even during our period and, certainly, during his lifetime. The notion of analysis that I fix on is surely the most austere of the candidates for consideration. Analysis will be treated here, not as a human activity, but as a relation among concepts that human beings may or may not (be able to) uncover by various means, one of which might be called 'analysis' in a sense other than the austere one employed here.

In the important paper "Concerning Universal Synthesis and Analysis or the Art of Discovery and of Judgment" (G/7/292-98 (MP10-17)), which is usually dated after 1680 and before 1684, Leibniz outlined "the art of handling distinct concepts."[25] It is the relationships underlying this art to which I refer when I talk of analysis in the austere sense. Analysis in this sense concerns the decomposition of concepts into simpler component concepts. It is based on the account of concept composition that Leibniz outlined in *The Art of Combinations* published in 1666 (A/6/1/163-230). The idea is this: There is a set of absolutely primitive concepts; all other concepts are formed from these by concept conjunction.[26] Composite concepts result from the conjunction of primitive concepts. These composite concepts may in turn be conjoined to form yet other composite concepts. Thus from the concept 'rational' and the concept 'animal,' the concept 'rational animal' arises by conjunction. Complete (or perfect) analysis would decompose a composite concept down to primitive concepts. Thus with any composite concept we may associate its ultimate decomposition set that contains all and only the primitive concepts composing it.

In *The Art of Combinations*, compound concepts are ranged into classes depending on the number of primitive concepts conjoined to form the given compound concept. A concept c is said to contain another c' just in case the ultimate decomposition set of c' is a subset of the ultimate decomposition set of c. My view is that this account, coupled with some theses about analysis to be explained below, constituted Leibniz's primary account of concept formation and concept containment during the early years of our period. As texts I would cite G/7/186, C277, C42-92 (the April 1679 Logic Series) and, of course, "Concerning Universal Synthesis and Analysis or the Art of Discovery and Judgment."

Let's look at the April 1679 Logic Series (C42-92, C245-47). Leibniz's intent in these papers was to construct a set of rules governing the assignment of numbers to concepts that would be adequate to decide validity for all three-term categorical syllogisms. In this series Leibniz developed a number of distinct systems. I concentrate on the last system developed in the series (C77-92). Here is a somewhat simplified version of it:

Preliminaries

(-2)   The following rules apply to categorical propositions, i.e., those ready for entry into syllogisms. Hence each proposition has two *terms*; one subject (concept), one predicate (concept). Each proposition is either universal or particular, affirmative or negative.

(-1)   Each term in a proposition is associated with a pair of integers x and y with these provisos:
(a)   x is positive if and only if y is negative
(b)   There is no integer z ($|z| \neq 1$) such that z is a factor of both x and y.

(0)   By an *assignment* to a proposition p we mean any association of integers with the terms (concepts) of p that is in accord with (-1).
Let '+s,' '-s,' '+p,' '-p,' stand respectively for the positive integer (+s) and the negative integer (-s) associated with the subject (concept) of a proposition under some assignment; similarly for the predicate concept.

Conditions on holding

(1)   If p is a universal affirmative propositon and α is an assignment to p then p holds under α if and only if

      (a) $+p$ is a factor of $+s$

and (b) $-p$ is a factor of $-s$

(2)   If p is a particular affirmative proposition and α is an assignment to p then p holds under α if and only if

for any integer z ($|z| \neq 1$)

      (a) z is not a factor of both $+p$ and $-s$

and (b) z is not a factor of both $-p$ and $+s$.

(3)   If p is a universal negative proposition and α an assignment to p then p holds under α if and only if the corresponding particular affirmative does not hold under α.

(4)   If p is a particular negative proposition and α is an assignment to p then p holds under α if and only if the corresponding universal affirmative does not hold under α.

Extension to sets of propositions

Let λ be a finite set of categorical propositions. By an assignment to λ we mean an assignment of numbers to terms in members of λ that satisfies (0) and is uniform, i.e., same term, same assignment; distinct term, distinct assignment.[27]

Leibniz's Theses

(A)   Let $\lambda = \{p,q\}$ where p and q are categorical propositions: p logically implies q if and only if there is no assignment α to λ such that p holds under α but q does not. (This is intended to generate the square of opposition.)

(B)   Let $\lambda = \{p,q,r\}$ where $\begin{matrix} p \\ q \\ \hline \therefore r \end{matrix}$ is a syllogism in three terms, i.e., p,q,r are categorical, universal, or particular, the predicate of r occurs in p or q (but not both); same for the subject of r; some term (the middle term) occurs in both p and q but not in r, etc. Then $\begin{matrix} p \\ q \\ \hline \therefore r \end{matrix}$ is syllogistically valid if and only if there is no assignment α to λ such that p and q hold under α but r does not.[28]

That's the system (or a simplified version thereof). It works. That is, Leibniz's theses (A) and (B) turn out to be true. Thus, provided 'syllogistically valid' is understood in the sense of classical Aristotelian logic, Leibniz's system gives the right results.[29] Couturat, Kauppi, and Parkinson speculate on why Leibniz moved on to alternative systems for determining syllogistic validity.[30] Both Couturat and Parkinson refer to a passage from C246. Leibniz there considered this argument:

Every pious person is happy
Some pious person is not wealthy
Some wealthy person is not happy

He made these assignments: pious, $+70$, -33; happy, $+5$, -1; wealthy, $+8$, -11, and then said of the argument that it "is not valid because" and there the text breaks off. Couturat (*Ibid.*, p. 334) concludes that Leibniz saw that his system failed because the argument is invalid, but the assignments cited render both the premises and the conclusion true. My hypothesis is this: Leibniz broke off his remark because he saw that the assignments chosen do not show that the argument in question is invalid. He was well aware that an assignment in virtue of which premises and conclusion are true does not settle the question whether the argument is valid. Indeed, on C247 we find this:

> All modes and figures can be derived from this calculus through rules of numbers alone. If we wish to know whether some figure is valid in virtue of its form we see whether the contradictory of the conclusion is compatible with the premises, i.e., whether numbers can be discovered simultaneously satisfying the premises and the contradictory of the conclusion; but if none can be found that demonstrates the argument in virtue of its form.

Try these assignments: pious, $+20$, -7; happy, $+5$, -1; wealthy, $+10$, -3; they show the argument invalid.

So why did Leibniz move on to alternative systems? Maybe he just liked inventing such systems. Maybe minor irritants such as the problem of infinite terms (see fn. 28) loomed large after a time. My view is this: Leibniz thought that an adequate conception of truth ought to have as a by-product an adequate conception of necessary truth, and, as a consequence, an adequate conception of formal validity.[31] Whenever his conception of truth changed he looked for an adequate account of validity based on the new notion of truth. To this hypothesis it may be objected that after the April 1679 Logic Series was completed, he did shortly commence to construct an alternative account of validity. But his conception of truth remained the same, i.e., a proposition is true just in case the concept of the predicate is contained in the concept of the subject. My reply is this: that slogan is retained; but when we move to the notion of an infinite analysis, the notion of containment is so radically altered that we might as well say we have a new conception of truth. More on this in Section II.

Subject to the restrictions detailed in the rules just stated, assignments of numbers to concepts in this system are arbitrary because it is formal (syllogistic) validity that concerned Leibniz at this point, not truth. Still, it is clear that it was his conception of truth and concept compositions that led him to this characterization of syllogistic validity. Thus at C85-86 Leibniz made clear that the arbitrary assignments used in his systems are surrogates for the "true characteristic numbers" (C85) that would be utilized if only we were capable of analyzing concepts into their primitive components.

What is stated in C85-86 suggests a certain method of constructing "true characteristic numbers." The system developed is one of those that assumes primitive concepts that are affirmative and primitive concepts that are negations.

Each primitive concept (simples, hereafter) is associated with a prime number. Let C be some composite (i.e., nonprimitive) concept. Then z is the right positive number to assign to C if the product of all the primes associated with affirmative simples that compose C is z; and $-|v|$ is the right negative number to assign to C if v is the product of all the primes associated with simples composing C that are negations (C86-87).

Leibniz used the following example at C86-87: Suppose the characteristic numbers for the concept animal are $+13$ and -5; let those for rational be $+8$ and -7. Then, since the concept human results from the conjunction of the concepts animal and rational, its characteristic numbers will be $+104$ and -35. Leibniz, of course, was well aware that every integer is uniquely factorable into primes and was utilizing that fact. I think (here I am speculating) that bearing in mind some obvious facts about prime factorization may shed light on some otherwise obscure aspects of Leibniz's pronouncements concerning analysis. For example we can make some sense out of the idea that an analysis is a definite series governed by some well-defined rule. Suppose C is a composite concept whose true characteristic number is 6006.[32] Suppose that at each step in an analysis we move from a concept to a pair of concepts that yield the replaced concept when conjoined. We might analyze C into D and E, where 42 is the true characteristic number of D, and 143, that of E. Obviously there are alternatives: We might have analyzed C into F and G, where 33 is the true characteristic number of F, and 182, that of G. Alternative routes (to the same ultimate destination, i.e., primitive concepts with the true characteristic numbers 2, 3, 7, 11, and 13) will present themselves at each step. Still, the idea of a well-behaved series may be extracted from these considerations and I think that is important.

Most of Leibniz's remarks suggest that he viewed concepts as containing concepts as components. As noted previously, we may treat concepts as sets of properties for our present purposes. Where C is the concept rational, for example, let C° be the property of being rational; I propose to identify (confuse may be more like it) C with $\{C^{\circ}\}$. Where C is the concept 'rational animal' we may let C = $\{$the property of being a rational animal$\}$.

With 'A,' 'B,' 'C,' 'α,' 'β,' 'γ,' 'δ,' referring to sets of properties, let's try the following:

Def 1/

Set A $\dashv$ Set B (read: Set A directly yields Set B by definitional replacement) = df. There are distinct properties f, g_1, . . . , g_n such that:

i) $f \in A$

and ii) g_1, . . . , $g_n \in B$

and iii) $\triangle (f \equiv g_1 \wedge . . . \wedge g_n)$

and iv) $A - \{f\} = B - \{g_1, . . . , g_n\}$.

What is this '$\triangle$' in iii)? It indicates that f may be defined in terms of the conjunction of g_1 through g_n. This is where the discussion of *The Art of Combinations* and the April 1679 Logic Series proves helpful. We know that the product of the characteristic numbers of the g_is must be the characteristic number of f.[33] We know that we have reached bedrock when every characteristic number of a member of a set is a prime. But obviously there's more to be said. I will introduce some other notions based on Def 1/ and then return to '$\triangle$.'

Def 2/

χ is an analysis of concept C = df.

χ is a sequence of sets (of properties) such that:

i) C° is the first term of χ

and ii) (x) ((x $\neq$ C° $\wedge$ x is a term of χ) $\rightarrow$

($\exists$ y) (y ϵ χ $\wedge$ y is the immediate predecessor of x in χ and y $\dashv$ x).

Def 3/

$\langle \alpha, \beta \rangle \Rightarrow \langle \gamma, \delta \rangle$ (read: proposition p = $\langle \alpha, \beta \rangle$ yields proposition q = $\langle \gamma, \delta \rangle$ by definitional replacement) = df

either: $\alpha \dashv \gamma$ and $\beta \dashv \delta$

or: $\alpha \dashv \gamma$ and $\beta = \delta$

or: $\beta \dashv \delta$ and $\alpha = \gamma$

or: $\alpha = \gamma$ and $\beta = \delta$.[34]

Def 4/

ψ is an analysis of proposition p (p = $\langle \alpha, \beta \rangle$ = df.

ψ is a sequence such that:

i) p is the first term in ψ

and ii) (x) (x $\neq$ p $\wedge$ x is a term in ψ $\rightarrow$ ($\exists$ y) (y ϵ ψ $\wedge$ y is the immediate predecessor of x in ψ $\wedge$ y $\Rightarrow$ x).

Def 5/

Proposition p is reducible to proposition q = df. There is an analysis of p of which q is a term.

Def 6/

ψ is an a priori proof of proposition p = df.

ψ is an analysis of p and there is an identical proposition q such that q is a term in ψ.[35]

The ideas taken from *The Art of Combinations* and the April 1679 Logic Series tell us something about how '$\triangle$ (f $\equiv$ g_1 $\wedge$ . . . $\wedge$ g_n)' is to be understood, but more detail is required. To simplify matters, take the case where n = 2. Texts taken from our period suggest that 'g_1 $\wedge$ g_2' may be used to define 'f' provided the following conditions all obtain:

i) The conjunction of g_1 and g_2 is a *reciprocal property* of whatever has the property f, i.e., (x) (fx $\equiv$ g_1x$\wedge g_2$x) (A/2/1/413 (L297-98/ 194), G/4/450 (DM24), C258, C406, C50 (P18), C55 (P22), G/7 293 (MP11), G/7/83 (W78))

and ii) g_1 and g_2 are *requisites* of whatever has f, i.e., (x) ($\sim g_1$x $\rightarrow$ $\sim$ fx) $\wedge$ (x) ($\sim g_2$x $\rightarrow$ $\sim$ fx) (Grua 267, C258, C50 (P18), G/7/293 (MP11)).

None of this is surprising. Obviously ii), although stated separately by Leibniz, is a consequence of i). Unfortunately a careful analysis of the texts cited fails to reveal Leibniz's position on the crucial question whether '$\triangle$ (f $\equiv g_1$ $\wedge g_2$)' entails '$\square$ (f $\equiv g_1 \wedge g_2$).' In particular it is unclear whether '$\triangle$ (f $\equiv g_1 \wedge g_2$)' requires the following analogs of i) and ii) above:

i) $\square$ (x) (fx $\equiv g_1$ x $\wedge g_2$ x)
and ii) $\square$ (x) ($\sim g_1$ x $\rightarrow \sim$ fx) $\wedge \square$ (x) ($\sim g_2$ x $\rightarrow \sim$ fx)

The papers from our period that do not use the infinite analysis idea have little direct discussion of this question. Nonetheless, there is discussion of something that appears to be a consequence of maintaining that '$\triangle$ (f $\equiv g_1 \wedge \ldots$ $\wedge g_n$)' entails '$\square$ (f $\equiv g_1 \wedge \cdots \wedge g_n$).' If this supposition is conjoined with (4) (i.e., that p is true if and only if there is an a priori proof of p) and the fact that every identical proposition is necessarily true, we seem to have as a consequence that every true proposition is necessarily true. In the papers mentioned in note 2 Leibniz explicitly denied that every true proposition is necessarily true. Clearly, Leibniz wanted an explanation of the nature of contingency that was not primarily epistemological;[36] indeed, the fundamental motivation for the infinite analysis idea was to secure such an explanation. But, in the papers cited in note 2 that do not contain the infinite analysis idea, Leibniz came close to explaining contingency in terms of our (relative) ignorance. He came close to asserting these theses:

(9) p is necessarily true if and only if human beings can provide an a priori proof that p.

(10) p is contingently true if and only if there is an a priori proof that p but human beings cannot provide an a priori proof that p. (G/7/44, C514 (MP8), G/7/296 (MP15))

"Providing an a priori proof" means showing in some fashion that an a priori proof exists in our austere sense. Some of the pre-infinite analysis papers suggest that the contrast between contingent and necessary truth captured in (9) and (10) can be given a deeper explanation. The paper, "The Nature of Truth," is a good example. There we find:

(In true propositions) . . . the predicate can be proved from the subject . . . the connection is necessary in the case of propositions of eternal truth, which follow from ideas alone or from definitions of universal ideas. But if a proposition is contingent there is no necessary connection, but it varies in time and depends on an assumed divine decree and on free will. In such a case a reason can always be given (at any rate by one who knows all) from the nature of the thing, or from the notion of the terms. . . . But this reason only inclines and does not impose necessity. (C402 (MP94))

The suggestion seems to be that '$\triangle$ (f $\equiv g_1 \wedge \ldots \wedge g_n$)' may hold either because of a purely definitional connection involving universal ideas, between f and the conjunction of the g_is, or because of certain free decrees of God (or other free agent). The idea seems to be that '$\triangle$ (f $\equiv$ g$_1$ Λ . . . Λ g$_n$)' entails '$\square$ (f $\equiv$ g$_1$ Λ . . . Λ g$_n$)' in the former case but not in the latter (Cf. G/7/300-1 (L349/226-27), G/4/436-37 (DM19-21)). The most thorough elaboration of these ideas is to be found in the *Discourse on Metaphysics*. In paragraph 13 Leibniz considered the objection that his account of truth has the unacceptable consequence that all truths are necessary. He noted: "But (it will be said) if a conclusion can be deduced infallibly from a definition or notion, it will be necessary" (G/4/437 (DM19)). This is followed by a discussion of the distinction noted above—which amounts to a distinction between what depends on God's understanding versus what depends on God's will.

My view is that Leibniz came to regard this as inadequate if taken as the ultimate explanation of the distinction between contingent and necessary truths. In 1695 (or thereabouts), while making reading notes on *Scientia Media*, Leibniz noted: "According to Scotus the root of contingency is in the will of God insofar as it is free." To this Leibniz objected, "But this is circular" (Grua 348). The ultimate explanation that Leibniz found satisfactory is based on the infinite analysis idea.[37] Let's turn to that idea.

II. INFINITE ANALYSIS

My claim is that in the early part of our period Leibniz accepted *(1)-(4)*, *(7)*, and *(8)*, (a)-(d). He had no explanation that he ultimately regarded as adequate of the distinction between necessary and contingent truths. In the latter part of our period, he achieved an explanation of this distinction that he regarded as adquate for the rest of his life. This explanation required the rejection of *(3)*, *(4)*, *(8)*, (c), and (d). The basis of the explanation is the infinite analysis idea. By the infinite analysis idea, I mean two theses, the first of which is this:

(e) There are concepts whose analyses are infinite.[38]

An examination of the relevant texts suggests to me that even after formulating the infinite analysis idea, Leibniz retained crucial elements of the view of concept formation outlined on p. 221; in particular, that there are absolutely primitive concepts, that with each concept we may associate its ultimate decomposition set, and that concept c contains concept c' just in case the ultimate decomposition set of c' is a subset of the ultimate decomposition set of c. What is altered is his notion of analysis, which is an integral part of his conception of containment.

Once the notion of an infinite analysis is introduced, we can no longer think of the ultimate decomposition set of a concept as the set of primitive concepts that analysis of the concept ultimately yields. We might say that one set A is the ultimate decomposition set of concept c just in case all the members of A are primitive properties and $\{C^\circ\}$ and A are equivalent (i.e., in the language of p. 216, $\{C^\circ\}$ corresponds to A).

Thesis (e) requires that there are infinitely many primitive concepts and that some composite concepts are such that their ultimate decomposition sets are infinite. These assumptions play havoc with the prime factorization model—the very model employed to explain the idea of a Leibnizian analysis as a well-defined sequence of terms. I do not know whether Leibniz filled in the gap here. I will simply suppose that even where an infinite analysis is involved, some well-behaved sequence is specified.

The second thesis involved in the infinite analysis idea requires some slight preparation. Let's call a proposition of the form 'AB is non-B' a contradiction in form. Let's say that an analysis ψ of a proposition p has a terminus at a proposition q just in case q is a term in ψ that is either an identical proposition or a contradiction in form. The second thesis is this:

(f)   There are propositions none of whose analyses has a terminus.[39]

      To explain what I will call the doctrine of infinite analysis, the following are introduced. (For the sake of ease of reference I repeat Def 6/).

Def 6/

    ψ is an *a priori proof* of proposition p = df.

    ψ is an analysis of p and there is an identical proposition q such that q is a term in ψ.

Def 7/

    χ is a *proof-sequence* for p = df.

    χ is an analysis of p and there is an identical proposition q such that either:

   i) q is a term in χ

or ii) χ converges on q.

Obviously the notion of convergence involved here needs explanation. I will try to say something helpful about it shortly.

Def 8/

    λ is a *meta-proof* of p = df.

    There is a sequence χ such that:

   i) χ is a proof-sequence for p

and ii) λ is a finite proof, restricted to a priori information about the terms in χ, that χ is a proof-sequence for p.[40]

Consider the following theses, which constitute the doctrine of infinite analysis (with the usual restriction to categorical, affirmative propositions that are either universal or singular):

(11)   p is true if and only if there is a proof-sequence for p.

(12)   p is necessarily true if and only if there is an a priori proof of p.

(13)   p is contingently true if and only if there is a proof sequence for p but there is no a priori proof of p.

That's it. It will be useful to state two consequences of (13) and one of (11) separately:

(*14*)· If p is contingently true, then there is no a priori proof of p.

(*15*) If p is contingently true, then there is a proof-sequence for p.

(*16*) If there is a proof-sequence for p, then p is true.

Textual references raise some problems. Let's begin with the (relatively) straightforward cases; namely, (*12*) and (*14*).

For (*12*) I would cite: G/7/309 (MP75), C371 (P61), C387 (P77), C17 (MP96), G/7/200 (Schrecker 13), C270, C1, Grua 305, FC181 (MP108).

For (*14*) I would cite: C387 (P77), C17 (MP97), C19 (MP99), G/7/200 (Schrecker 13), C272, C2, Grua 304, FC182 (MP109), FC184 (MP110).[41]

Obviously we need not consider separate citations for (*11*), (*13*), (*15*), and (*16*); citations for (*15*) and (*16*) would do the trick, since (*15*) and (*16*), conjoined with (*14*) and (*12*), yield (*13*), while (*13*) and (*12*) yield (*11*). Still, there are problems. Many of the passages cited in support of (*14*) clearly suggest something stronger. Consider a typical example— FC182 (MP109):

in the case of contingent truths, even though the predicate is in the subject, nevertheless this can never be demonstrated of it, nor can the proposition ever be reduced to . . . an identity. Instead, the analysis proceeds to infinity.

Similar remarks can be found in all of the texts cited in connection with (*14*). These remarks suggest that Leibniz did extend the infinite analysis idea to propositions, i.e., that he accepted (f). But they do not provide direct confirmation for (*15*) or (*16*). Direct confirmation for (*15*) and (*16*) can be found in *Generales Inquisitiones* and *Origio Veritatum Contigentium ex Processu in Infinitum*. *Generales Inquisitiones* provides the most detail. I think that all those passages in which Leibniz claimed that necessary truths differ from contingent truths, in the manner in which commensurable numbers differ from incommensurable numbers, provide indirect confirmation for attributing (*15*) and (*16*) to Leibniz. (Passages that mention this comparison are to be found in the following works from our time period: G/7/309 (MP75), C388 (P77), C17-18 (MP97), G/7/200 (Schrecker 13), C272, C1-3, Grua 303-4, FC183-84 (MP110)).

Let's go directly to those passages in the *Generales Inquisitiones* that bear on (*15*) and (*16*) and hence may help explain the notion of convergence as it occurs in Def 7/.

Consider this passage:

A true contingent proposition cannot be reduced to identical propositions, but is proved by showing that if the analysis is continued further and further, it constantly approaches identical propositions, but never reaches them. Therefore it is God alone, who grasps the entire infinite in his mind, who knows all contingent truths with certainty. (C388 (P77))

This passage is followed immediately by the following:

So the distinction between necessary and contingent truths is the same as that between lines that meet and asymptotes, or between commensurable and incommensurable numbers.[42] (C388 (P77))

To the best of my knowledge there are no published texts that include more detail concerning the nature of convergent analyses than the *Generales Inquisitiones*. Here is one of those gaps that call for exercises in formal construction mentioned in the introduction. I leave the details for others. But we may say something relevant here. Suppose $p(= \langle \alpha, \beta \rangle)$ is a contingent truth. Suppose that the ultimate decomposition sets for α and β are infinite. Let $\cup\alpha$ and $\cup\beta$ be, respectively, the ultimate decomposition sets for α and β. Consider, then, the proposition $q = \langle \cup\alpha, \cup\beta \rangle$. Obviously if $\cup\beta \subseteq \cup\alpha$ then q is an identical proposition. Perhaps this is an identical propositon to which an analysis of p converges.

Here's a sample of the kind of construction that might be tried in order to explain convergence. We start with a contingent proposition p with subject concept C_s and predicate concept C_p. Then $p = \langle \alpha, \beta \rangle$, where $\alpha = \left\{ C_s^\circ \right\}$ and $\beta = \left\{ C_p^\circ \right\}$. We characterize a certain analysis of C_s thusly: $\alpha_0 = \alpha$ and α_{n+1} is any set such that $\alpha_n \dashv \alpha_{n+1}$. Analogously, for C_p. The sequence $\langle \alpha_0, \beta_0 \rangle$, . . . $\langle \alpha_n, \beta_n \rangle$ . . . constitutes an analysis of p in the sense of Def 4/. Let's try saying that such an analysis converges after its kth term provided that after its kth term the proportion of elements in β_{k+i}, but not in α_{k+i}, steadily decreases and approaches zero as its limit.[43] Such a sequence constitutes a proof-sequence for p. Leibniz's mature view seems to be this: if p is necessarily true, then eventually a sequence constructed along these lines will contain an identical proposition; if p is necessarily false, a contradiction in form. If p is a contingent proposition, no sequence so constructed will contain either an identical proposition or a contradiction in form. But if p is contingently true then for some sequence so constructed, convergence will occur, whereas if p is contingently false, for no sequence so constructed will convergence occur.

The concept of a Meta-proof is introduced on a number of occasions in the *Generales Inquisitiones* (C371 (P60-61), C374 (P63-64), C388 (P77)). The notion is not very important in the case of an a priori proof. In this case a Meta-proof might be a sequence of words exactly reflecting the sequence of sets of properties making up the a priori proof. But a Meta-proof must be of finite length; hence, it cannot bear this one-to-one relationship to a proof-sequence that is not an a priori proof.

Here is a sample passage:

But if, when the analysis of the predicate and of the subject has been continued, a coincidence can never be proved, but it does at least appear from the continued analysis (and the progression and its rule which arise from it) that a contradiction will never arise, then the proposition is possible. But if, in analyzing it, it appears from the rule of progression that the reduction has reached a point at which the difference between what should coincide is less than any given difference, then it will have been proved that the proposition is true.[44] C374 (P63).

I take it that the "progression" mentioned in the last sentence is our proof-sequence and the "proof" that would be available, were certain information concerning convergence to appear, is our Meta-proof. Note that this passage raises the hope that Meta-proofs of contingent propositions are possible. To the best of my knowledge, in all those texts other than the *Generales Inquisitiones* in which Leibniz explicitly raised the question whether Meta-proofs of contingent propositions are possible, he answered it in the negative (see C18 (MP97) and C272-73). The *Generales Inquisitiones* contains Leibniz's most extended discussion of these matters. Consider his last word (in that work) on the question whether Meta-proofs of contingent truths are possible: Having noted that necessary truths are related to contingent truths in the way commensurable numbers are related to incommensurable numbers Leibniz said:

> But a difficulty stands before us. We are able to demonstrate that some line, namely, an asymptote, constantly approaches some other line . . . by showing what will be the case if the progression is continued as far as one pleases. Therefore human beings will be able to comprehend contingent truths with certainty. But it must be replied that there is indeed a likeness, but there is not complete agreement. There can be relations which, however far an analysis is continued, will never reveal themselves sufficiently for certainty, and are seen perfectly only by him whose intellect is infinite. It is true that as with asymptotes and incommensurables, so with contingent things we can see many things with certainty, from the very principle that every truth must be capable of proof. . . . But we can no more give the full reason for contingent things than we can constantly follow asymptotes and run through infinite progressions of numbers. (C388-389 (P77-78))

This passage is preceded by one in which Leibniz asserted a connection between contingent truth and infinite analysis. He concluded:

> Therefore it is God alone, who grasps the entire infinite in his mind, who knows contingent truths with certainty.

At a later date Leibniz added an 'omnium' to the last clause so that it read: 'who knows all contingent truths with certainty" (C388 (P77)).

I think it is reasonably clear that 'with certainty' here means 'a priori'.[45] Obviously inserting an 'all' does not indicate that Leibniz then thought that a difference between us and God is that God knows *all* contingent truths a priori whereas we only know *some* a priori; but it surely suggests a hesitation on this point on Leibniz's part. Why is Leibniz vacillating here? Is there anything fundamental at stake? I think there is. Consider these doctrines, all of which Leibniz accepted:

(2) p is true if and only if the concept of the predicate of p is contained in the concept of the subject of p.

(17) The distinction between necessary truths and contingent truths is metaphysical and not simply epistemic.

(*18*) For any finite mind S, S knows p a priori only if p is a necessary truth.

(G/7/44, C18 (MP98), G/7/200 (Schrecker 13), FC181 (MP108))

The glory of the doctrine of infinite analysis is that it permitted Leibniz to hold (2) and (*17*) simultaneously.[46] The doctrine of infinite analysis provided an account of concept containment that permitted him to hold fast to his basic slogan concerning truth, i.e., (2), while making room for a metaphysical distinction between necessary truth and contingent truth. The possibility of Meta-proofs concerning proof-sequences for contingent truths, although posing no threat to the joint tenability of (2) and (*17*), does generate problems for the trio that results from adding (*18*) to the two doctrines just mentioned. The basic problem is whether it is at all plausible to maintain both (*18*) and

(*13*) p is contingently true if and only if there is a proof sequence for p but there is no a priori proof that p.

A Meta-proof of a proposition p provides a priori knowledge of p to anyone in possession of such a proof. Hence, if Meta-proofs of contingent propositions are available to us, then (*18*) must be rejected. But a casual reading of (*13*) would suggest that Meta-proofs of contingent propositions are at least possible.

A close study of those texts in which Leibniz claimed that knowledge of convergence in some infinite mathematical series is available to us whereas Meta-proofs of contingent truths are not, coupled with a close study of those texts in which he claimed that we lack a priori knowledge of contingent truths, makes one thing clear: his main appeal is to the infinite complexity of those complete concepts that he took to be components of contingent propositions[47] (C367 (P66), C18-19 (MP98-99), Grua 325, Grua 303, FC184-85 (MP110-11). Consider this from C376 (P66): "the concept of Peter is complete, and so involves infinite things." Roughly, the idea is this: an analysis of the complete concept of Peter will yield infinitely many distinct and logically independent propositions of the form 'Peter is f'; the same cannot be said of the concept of an abstraction such as a number. Suppose this is so far so good; the question remains why Leibniz thought this alleged difference between abstractions and individual substances to be relevant to the impossibility of Meta-proofs of contingent truths. I believe a careful investigation of this question is bound to shed light on the very foundations of Leibniz's system, particularly on his conception of analysis. I leave it for another occasion.

III

Recall:

(7) p is true only if there is a sufficient reason why p is true;

(8) p is true only if there is an a priori proof of p;

and (c) there is a sufficient reason why p is true if and only if there is an a
priori proof of p.[48]

Some of the citations noted for (c) suggest that Leibniz took the right-hand side of that equivalence as providing an analysis—a deep form—of the left-hand side, i.e., the principle of sufficient reason as applied to truths.[49] My claim is that (8) and (c) are doctrines that Leibniz rejected after he formulated the infinite analysis idea. Here are some points relevant to that claim.

(i) It is worth noting that in papers from our period that contain the infinite analysis idea and that contain an account of the principle of sufficient reason what we are offered is not (c) but rather:

(g) There is sufficient reason why p is true if and only if the concept of
the predicate of p is contained in the concept of the subject of p.
(G/7/199 (Schrecker 13), FC182 (MP109))

(ii) Nevertheless, in texts written after formulation of the infinite analysis idea, Leibniz claimed that there is a sufficient reason for a proposition just in case the connection between the predicate and the subject can be revealed through an analysis of concepts. (See for example, C11 (MP172) usually dated around 1712.) My inclination in such cases is to suppose that the doctrine defended is this:

(h) There is a sufficient reason why p is true if and only if there is a proof-
sequence for p.[50]

The principle of sufficient reason has been used in an interesting and provocative way to explain what surely is the most pressing question that remains once Leibniz's conception of truth has been clarified; namely, what on earth prompted him to accept it—to accept (2), for example? Some of Leibniz's remarks concerning the principle of sufficient reason suggest that it is a basic axiom in his system, bedrock, so to speak. (See, for example G/2/62 (M71) and G/6/612 (MP184).) So, if acceptance of it accounts for acceptance of the concept-containment account of truth, we might have reached as full an explanation as we can reasonably hope for. This is Couturat's view.[51] His reasoning seems to go this way (using my terminology).

Consider:

(8′) p is true only if there is a proof-sequence for p.

(8′) is Leibniz's precise formulation of the common axiom (7). The notion of a proof-sequence, in turn, is Leibniz's way of making precise the idea of concept-containment. Hence, Leibniz was committed to:

(d″) The concept of the predicate of p is contained in the concept of the
subject of p if and only if there is a proof-sequence for p.

But from (8′) and (d″) we may derive the "hard-half" of the concept-containment account of truth, i.e.,

(2′)   If p is true then the concept of the predicate of p is contained in the concept of the subject of p.

Therefore Leibniz accepted (2′) (and hence (2)) because he accepted (7), i.e., the principle of sufficient reason.

I'm not convinced. It seems to me that Leibniz had no reason to offer (8′) as an explication of the common axiom (7), i.e., no reason to accept (h), other than a commitment to (2), i.e., the concept-containment account of truth. I think a close examination of the texts supports my view here. To the best of my knowledge there are no texts in which Leibniz asserted the equivalence of (7) and (8′) that predate his acceptance of (2′). I suggest then that acceptance of (2′) (more exactly, the concept-containment account of truth of which (2′) is the hard-half) provided him with (some of) the tools to formulate what he regarded as a deep analysis of the principle of sufficient reason.[52]

Various commentators have suggested that the concept-containment account of truth was in the air in the seventeenth century and that Leibniz simply adopted the then standard account of truth and drew the consequences with a more discerning eye than his predecessors and contemporaries.[53] We have previously noted (see p. 219) that Leibniz himself sometimes talked this way. Indeed, the concept-containment account of truth appears to be the official account of truth Descartes offered in the "Reasons Proving the Existence of God and the distinction of the Soul from the Body" appended to the replies to the second set of objections. There the Latin (original) version has:

> When we say that something is contained in the nature or concept of something, it is the same as if we had said that it is true of that thing or can be affirmed of it.[54]

Perhaps commentators have failed to note this possible source because the subsequent French version contains something different:

> When we say that some *attribute* is contained in the nature or in the concept of a thing, that is just as if we said that this *attribute* is true of this thing and that it can be affirmed that it is in it.[55] (italics mine)

However, as Jarrett has noted, Descartes only used this definition at one place in the "Reasons Proving the Existence of God. . . . " and all that is required there is the "easy half" of (2), i.e., the doctrine that if the concept of the predicate of p is contained in the concept of the subject of p then p is true.[56]

In any case we should look for a systematic explanation of Leibniz's commitment to (2) along with a historical explanation. Consider the following account, variations of which occur in the secondary literature.

If we concentrate attention on singular propositions, then Leibniz's notes for a reply to Arnauld, taken in conjunction with the first of two letters to Arnauld dated July 14, 1686, provide illuminating texts. In the letter Leibniz stated his "main principle" that "there must always be some foundation of the connection of the terms of a proposition which must be in their notions"

(G/2/56 (M63-64)). Why not in the things themselves, rather than in their notions? The beginnings of an answer can be found in the same texts. True propositions about possible but nonactual entities play a significant role in Leibniz's doctrine of creation. These propositions must be true of something (G/2/45 (M49), Grua 310-11. Leibniz held: "As to the reality of purely possible substances, . . . they have no other reality than that which they have in the divine understanding" (G/2/54 (M61)). According to Leibniz, what exists in the divine understanding are various concepts. Hence, it appears that he held that propositions about purely possible substances are reducible to propositions about concepts. So far, so good; still, we need an explanation of why he thought that true propositions about *actual* substances are true in virtue of certain connections among concepts. Consider the following propositions:

(i)   Existent Adam is f.
(j)   Possible Adam is f.

(i) is equivalent to the conjunction of:

(k)   Adam exists;
and (l)   Adam is f.

Suppose, for the sake of discussion, that Leibniz had an account of (k), formulated in purely conceptual terms—having to do with Adam's individual concept being a member of the best world, where worlds and their relative merits are explained in conceptual terms.

Consider, next, Leibniz's admonition to Arnauld:

All actuality can be conceived as possible, and if the actual Adam has . . .
a particular posterity, one cannot deny this same predicate to this Adam
conceived of as possible. (G/2/55 (M62))

This suggests that Leibniz took (l) and (j) to be equivalent—perhaps, the same proposition. But since, for Leibniz, (j) holds in virtue of relations among concepts, so must (l). Since (i) is equivalent to the conjunction of (k) and (l), it must hold in virtue of relations among concepts. Some would say that we have here at least the structure of as complete an explanation as we can reasonably hope for (at least with respect to singular propositions.)

There are problems. On the face of it, (j) appears incomplete; it seems to lack a reference to a specific possible world in which possible Adam is f—to be contrasted with worlds where Adam exists but is not f. The reply is this: as noted above, talk of possible substances is reducible to talk about concepts, according to Leibniz; to say that possible Adam exists in exactly one world is to say that the individual concept of Adam is a member of exactly one set of concepts constituting a world. But each consistent individual concept exists in exactly one such set, i.e., one world. Therefore, there is no need to make reference to a specific world to provide content to (j).

Now we need an explanation of why Leibniz held that consistent individual concepts exist in exactly one world. The usual explanation is this: according to Leibniz, each individual (possible or actual) will be represented in all propositions about it by a unique concept; each such concept must be a complete individual concept. A complete individual concept is a member of at most one world. But why must the unique concept that represents an individual (possible or actual) in all propositions about it be complete? Beware the reply: because the concept-containment account of truth requires it; that reply is blatantly circular in the present context. The usual (noncircular) answer to our question is this: the unique concept in question must individuate the relevant individual from all other possible individuals — only a complete concept will do the trick. Now we must ask why only a complete concept will do the trick. One would naturally suppose that any haecceity set for the relevant individual would serve; moreover, one would naturally suppose that haecceity sets that are incomplete might exist in more than one world. So we need an explanation of why Leibniz thought that only complete concepts will serve as haecceity sets for individuals. Pp. 217 and 218 contain speculation on that topic.

Variations on the theme discussed above deserve further elaboration. The theme is this: to show that Leibniz's effort to explain possible individuals, possible worlds, and creation in terms of God and his concepts lead him to the concept-containment account of truth. Further elaborations will be explored on another occasion.

Notes

1. All of the passages taken from Leibniz are given in English and are followed by a reference to a source containing the quoted passage in the original language and by a reference (in parentheses) to a source containing a translation of the passage into English in those cases where I know of a published English translation. In some cases the words in a passage quoted in this paper will not be exactly the same as those in the English translation cited. Citations to unquoted material follow the same format, i.e., reference to a source containing the relevant material in the original language followed by a reference (in parentheses) to an English translation when I know of one.

The following abbreviations are used in referring to texts:

A/k/l/m = *Gottfried Wilhelm Leibniz: Sämtliche Schriften und Briefe*, Academy Edition (Darmstadt and Berlin, 1923-), series k, volume l, page m.

C = *Opuscules et fragments inédits de Leibniz*, ed. L. Couturat (Paris, 1903).

DM = Leibniz—*Discourse on Metaphysics*, trans. Peter Lucas and Leslie Grint (Manchester, 1953).

FC = *Nouvelles Lettres et Opuscules inédits de Leibniz*, ed. Foucher de Careil (Paris, 1857).

G/m/n = *Die Philosophischen Schriften von Gottfried Wilhelm Leibniz*, ed. C. I. Gerhardt (Berlin, 1875-1890), volume m, page n.

GM/m/n = *Die Mathematische Schriften von G. W. Leibniz*, ed. C. I. Gerhardt (Berlin, 1849-1863), volume m, page n.

Grua = *Leibniz, Textes inédits*, ed. G. Grua (Paris, 1948).

Huggard = *Theodicy*, trans. E. M. Huggard (New Haven, 1952).

Lm/n = *Gottfried Wilhelm Leibniz: Philosophical Papers and Letters*, ed. and trans. E. Loemker (1st edition-Chicago, 1956; 2nd edition-Dordrecht, Holland, 1969), page m of the 1st edition and page n of the 2nd edition.

Le Roy = *Leibniz—Discourse de Metaphysique et Correspondance avec Arnauld*, ed. Georges Le Roy (Paris, 1970).

M   = *The Leibniz-Arnauld Correspondence*, trans. H. T. Mason (Manchester, 1967).

MP   = *Leibniz—Philosophical Writings*, ed. G. H. R. Parkinson, trans. Mary Morris and G. H. R. Parkinson (London, 1973).

NE   = *New Essays Concerning Human Understanding by Gottfried Wilhelm Leibniz*, trans. Alfred Langley (La Salle, Illinois, 1949).

P   = *Leibniz—Logical Papers*, ed. and trans. G. H. R. Parkinson (Oxford, 1966).

Schmidt = *Gottfried Wilhelm Leibniz—Fragmente Zur Logik*, ed. and trans. Franz Schmidt (Berlin, 1960).

Schrecker = *Leibniz—Monadology and other Philosophical Essays*, trans. Paul Schrecker and Anne Martin Schrecker (New York, 1965).

W   = *Leibniz—Selections*, ed Philip P. Wiener (New York, 1951).

2. Here is a listing of the main writings of Leibniz discussed in Section I and II. They are listed in what I take to be chronological order. The titles are either those bestowed by Leibniz or his editors or the first few words of a piece not otherwise titled or my own title. Items preceded by an asterisk contain the infinite analysis idea explicitly.

> *1679*
> On the General Characteristic (G/7/184f (L339f/221f))
> Cum animadvertem (G/7/299f (L346f/225f))
> April 1679 Logic Series (C42f)
> Praecognita ad Encyclopaediam (G/7/43f)
> Introductio ad Encyclopaediam Arcanam (C511f (MP5f))
> *1680-1684*
> De Libertate (Grua 287f)
> De Synthesi et Analysi Universali (G/7/292f (MP10f))
> Meditationes de Cognitione, Veritate et Ideis (G/4/422f (L448f/291f))
> *1685-1686*
> The Nature of Truth (C401f (MP93f))
> Discourse on Metaphysics (G/4/427f (DM))
> Leibniz-Arnauld Correspondence (G/2/11f (M))
> First Truths (C518f (MP87))
> *Specimen Inventorum (G/7/309f (MP75f))
> *Generales Inquisitiones (C356f (P47f))
> *Necessary and Contingent Truths (C16f (MP96f))
> *On the Universal Science (G/7/198f (Schrecker 11f))
> *Universalia ut aggregata (C270f)
> *Origio Veritatum Contingentium ex Processu in Infinitum (C1f)
> *1687-1690*
> *Origio Veritatum Contingentium (Grua 325f)
> *De Contingentia (Grua 302f)
> *On Freedom (FC178f (MP106f))

3. As is well known, propositions that are negations and propositions that are particulars caused Leibniz significant problems. I intend to discuss them on another occasion.

4. In items (*1*) through (*8*) textual citations preceding the semicolon refer to what I take to be pre-infinite analysis texts; citations after the semicolon refer to texts using the infinite analysis idea.

5. The texts cited actually support this doctrine: p is true if and only if p is or is reducible to an identical proposition. Similarly, the texts cited in connection with (*4*) actually support this formulation: p is true if and only if either p is an identical proposition or there is an a priori proof of p. A slight extension of Leibniz's notions of reduction and a priori proof will save some ink.

6. Note that there are no citations from sources utilizing the infinite analysis idea. A passage at C369 (P59) of the *Generales Inquisitiones* supports (*3*). However, the *Generales Inquisitiones* is a working draft where ideas are put forward, subjected to criticism, and

modified. My view is that support for (3) is explicitly withdrawn in the *Generales Inquisitiones* at C388 (P77).

7. Again, note that there are no citations from sources utilizing the infinite analysis idea. The passage at C369 (P59), mentioned in footnote 7, also appears to support (4) and appears to be repudiated at C388 (P77). G/7/309 (MP75) may also appear to be troublesome; see footnote 11 for comments on it.

8. Two other accounts of truth are found in texts from our period that should be mentioned. Consider:

(5) p is true if and only if it is false that p is reducible to a contradiction, i.e., to a proposition of the form B and non-B. (C370-71 (P60))

Let A be the subject concept of p and let B be the predicate concept of p with both A and B consistent concepts then:

(6) p is true if and only if A coincides with AB. (C407-8)

I think we may safely set (5) and (6) aside. (5) seems to imply that if a proposition does not imply a contradiction then it is true. But since a proposition that is possibly true does not imply a contradiction, (5) is equivalent to the unacceptable—p is true if and only if p is possibly true. (6) also looks peculiar. Leibniz reasoned from (6) thusly:

> (From (6)) . . . it follows, if A is B is a true proposition then A non-B implies a contradiction, for by substituting the equivalent AB for A it becomes AB non-B which is manifestly a contradiction. (C407-8)

The conclusion Leibniz drew from (6) sounds like "p is true if and only if the negation of p implies a contradiction," which yields the unacceptable "p is true if and only if p is necessarily true." Of course (5) is equivalent to the same unacceptable principle but then (2), (3), and (4) appear to be equivalent to it also. And we must say the same about (1), if it is taken to be equivalent to (2). What is interesting in the case of (5) and (6) is that each is repudiated (or at least modified) in the very text where it is to be found. Thus, I would claim that in C371-74 (P63-64) we find Leibniz repudiating (5) just because it has as a consequence that p is true if and only if p is possibly true. And a marginal note appended by Leibniz to the passage from which (6) is taken draws our attention to the distinction between finite and infinite analysis and employs that distinction to deny the implication previously drawn from (6). Perhaps 'coincides' was understood by Leibniz in one manner prior to formulating the distinction between finite and infinite analysis and in a different manner thereafter. Perhaps some such strategy would allow a resuscitation of (6). But since both (5) and (6) are repudiated (or modified) in the very texts where they are to be found, I will ignore them hereafter.

9. The citations of C17, C1, Grua 303, and FC181 presuppose that a demonstration and an a priori proof are the same thing for Leibniz. Here's some evidence: At C518 (MP87) an a priori proof is defined as a reduction to identicals via the analysis of notions; almost eaxctly the same definition of a demonstration is to be found at FC181 (MP108). At C519 (MP87) and C513 (MP7) the same definiens is given and the definiendum is called 'a priori demonstration.' It is important to realize in this connection that Leibniz distinguished between having a priori knowledge that p and having a priori proof (or demonstration) that p (see, for example, FC182 (MP109)).

10. Some of the passages cited for (d) actually support the following:

(d') The predicate of p is in the subject of p if and only if there is an a priori proof of p.

But (a) is an equivalence Leibniz never repudiated; hence, no harm in running (d) and (d') together.

Note that there are no citations from sources utilizing the infinite analysis idea in support of either (c) or (d). There are some troubling passages, however. Consider C388 (P77):

> Every true proposition can be proved; for since (as Aristotle says) the predicate is in

the subject, or, the concept of the predicate is involved in the concept of the subject
. . . , then it must be possible for a truth to be shown by the analysis of terms.

This passage may seem straightforward; it isn't. I shall argue in section II that the notion of proof mentioned in it is distinct from a priori proof.

G/7/309 (MP75) is an infinite analysis text that appears to support (4) and (8) as well as (c) and (d). It is a curious text: although it affirms (4) (and, hence, (8)) it explicitly rejects (3); yet (b), which connects (3) and (4), is a doctrine with strong textual support throughout our time period. I draw the conclusion you would expect: G/7/309 (MP75) is not only an anomaly; it's an aberration.

11. For an informative, scholarly discussion of these and related matters see chapter 1, "The Nature of the Proposition," in G. H. R. Parkinson, *Logic and Reality in Leibniz's Metaphysics* (Oxford, 1965).

12. On this topic see Hector-Neri Castañeda, "Leibniz's Concepts and their Coincidence Salva Veritate," *Nous* 8, Number 4 (1974): 381-398.

13. The French and Latin words that would naturally be translated by the English word 'term' were used in various senses by Leibniz. I assume that here a term is either a subject or predicate in the sense explained above.

14. C. D. Broad, *Leibniz — An Introduction* (Cambridge, 1975), p. 11.

15. I am inclined to think that Leibniz thought that every proposition is equivalent to some proposition that either satisfies this condition or is compounded from propositions that do. This deserves separate treatment. Something relevant is said in my paper "Leibniz on the Simplicity of Substance," in *Essays on the Philosophy of Leibniz*, ed. Mark Kulstad, Rice University Studies 63, No. 4 (Fall 1977): 107-21; see especially pp. 111-12.

16. For a discussion of the question why Leibniz did not apply the same mode of reasoning to concepts of species, see *ibid*.

17. Arnauld's basic intuition about the concept of an individual x is that it contains all (and only) the essential properties of x. What is not so clear is whether he thought that if a set C contains all and only the essential properties of x then C is a haecceity set.

18. Let's say that A is a haecceity set for x just in case A is a haecceity set and x has every property in A.

19. The basic assumption here is that primitive properties are independent.

20. There is no such admonition at G/2/54 (M60-61), which is based on Leibniz's *edited* copy of a letter he sent to Arnauld. However, the letter received by Arnauld contains the following sentence deleted by Leibniz from his own copy:

For one must not mention Eve, nor Paradise taking them to be determined individuals, otherwise this would no longer be sub ratione generalitatis. (Le Roy 119)

21. *Ibid*., pp. 110-14. The treatment there is somewhat more accurate than that outlined here.

22. In a helpful essay, "The Root of contingency," in *Leibniz — A Collection of Critical Essays*, ed. Harry Frankfurt (Garden City, NY, 1972), E. M. Curley argues persuasively against Russell's idea that Leibniz had two systems of philosophy; the public version, which is "fantastic and shallow," and the private version, which is "profound and . . . logical." In virtue of this alleged behavior Russell had said of Leibniz "as a human being he was not admirable." (Quotations are from Bertrand Russell, *A History of Western Philosophy* [New York, 1945].) Still, a close study of the Discourse and the Leibniz-Arnauld correspondence suggest (to me anyway) that Leibniz was a bit slippery. The concept-containment account of truth is defended as a mere triviality but it seems magically to acquire an enormous amount of content just when Leibniz set out to derive the paradoxes. Another example of slipperiness: the evidence is that Arnauld never received *The Discourse* but only summaries of the various paragraphs (see Le Roy 16). The Leibniz-Arnauld correspondence begins with Arnauld's suggestion that the thesis propounded in the summary of paragraph

13, "That the individual concept of each person contains . . . everything that will ever happen to him" leads to "a more than fatal necessity" (Le Roy 83 (M9)). Leibniz replied with considerable disdain, "As if concepts . . . made things necessary" (G/2/17 (M12)). Yet paragraph 13 itself (i.e., the part never sent to Arnauld) constitutes a sustained and somewhat tortured effort to meet exactly this objection.

23. I have not found what Leibniz said about natures, essences, and essential properties during our time period very helpful. Paragraph 8 of the Discourse identifies the complete concept of an individual with its haecceity (presumably, its essence) (Le Roy 43 (DM13)). Paragraph 13 initially identifies the nature of an individual with its complete individual concept (Le Roy 47 (DM19)) but then, more cautiously, states that the nature or form of an individual must *correspond* to its complete individual concept (Le Roy 48 (DM20)). Paragraph 16 identifies the essence of an individual with its complete individual concept and distinguishes both from its nature (Le Roy 16 (DM27-28)). Midway in the Leibniz-Arnauld correspondence we find the complete individual concept of an individual identified with its essence or nature (G/2/68 (M84)). All of this is mildly confusing but probably can be made coherent by some scholarly efforts. However, there's G/2/52 (M58) to contend with. Using a particular individual substance (himself) as an example, Leibniz began to make an important point with this clause:

There is nothing in me of all that can be conceived in general terms, i.e., in terms of essence, or of a specific or incomplete concept.

This passage suggests that the essence of an individual is (or, better, corresponds to) an incomplete concept that is a subset of the complete concept of that individual. Fabrizio Mondadori has convinced me that a dose of scholarly effort might save the day. Grua 309 contains an attempt by Leibniz to set these matters straight. It is worth an essay in its own right.

24. "Heat is not the same thing as color" is an example of a proposition that Leibniz regarded as a disparate, and, hence, a negative identical (A/G/6/362 (Langley 405)). For an informative discussion of the problems the disparates pose for Leibniz's account of necessary truth, see Margaret D. Wilson, "On Leibniz's Explication of 'Necessary Truth'" first published in *Akten des Internationalen Leibniz-Kongresses* and reprinted in *Leibniz—A Collection of Critical Essays*, ed. Harry Frankfurt.

25. For more detail on this see C50 (P18).

26. Some texts suggest that Leibniz also allowed something we might call concept complementation; others suggest that he admitted primitive concepts other than positive ones and restricted operations on concepts to conjunction. The question of whether Leibniz had in mind the possibility of infinite conjunction turns out to be of some importance in connection with the topics discussed in section II.

27. For more on this uniform assignment provision see C77, C83-84 (P31-32), C89, and C247.

28. The system is restricted to syllogisms in three terms and to simple inferences that do not introduce a new term as, for example, contraposition does. Leibniz noted that contraposition of "Every wise man is pious" introduces what he called infinite terms such as 'not-pious.' He said: "The properties of this sort of infinite term . . . should and can be proved by our calculus separately . . . they have many peculiarities." C83 (P31).

29. See J. Lukasiewicz, *Aristotle's Syllogistic* (Oxford, 1951), pp. 126-29.

30. See L. Couturat, *La Logique de Leibniz* (Paris, 1901), pp. 326-35; Raili Kauppi, *Uber Die Leibnizsche Logik* (Helsinki, 1960), pp. 145-53; P xx-xxiii.

31. An example: "I considered what would be a clear notion of truth for I hoped, not unreasonably, to derive from this some light on the problem of how necessary truths can be distinguished from contingent truths" FC179 (MP107).

32. Here I am simplifying by supposing a single characteristic number per concept.

33. See C49-50 (P17). Here I am pretending that properties have characteristic numbers in Leibniz's scheme. Not true, but no harm.

34. This trivial condition is written with Def 6/ in mind. It permits a quick a priori proof of an identical proposition. See footnote 5.

35. Definitions 5 and 6 are constructed so that (b) is confirmed. That is, definitions 5 and 6 yield that p is reducible to an identical proposition if and only if there is an a priori proof of p. Notice that in definitions 3 through 6 a proposition is treated as an ordered pair whose terms are sets of properties. On this construal, an identical proposition is an ordered pair whose second term is a subset of its first term. With this in mind, we may say that there is an a priori proof of p (p = $\langle \alpha, \beta \rangle$) just in case there is an analysis χ of α and an analysis ψ of β such that, for some γ in χ and some δ in ψ, $\delta \subseteq \gamma$.

36. For a superb discussion of this and related matters, see Robert Adams, "Leibniz's Theories of Contingency," pp. 243-83, this volume, especially pp. 259-61.

37. It is worth noting that the idea of reasons that incline but do not necessitate, which plays an important role in the early efforts to account for the distinction between necessary and contingent truths, was finally explicated by Leibniz, using the infinite analysis idea. See Grua 479.

38. This thesis is contained explicitly or implicitly in every starred item in note 2. See, in particular, C373 (P63).

39. See footnote 38.

40. The notion of proof mentioned in ii) is the usual informal notion with which we are all familiar. It contrasts with the austere notion employed in the definitions of a priori proof and proof-sequence. I do not claim that a clear-cut distinction between the informal notion and the austere one is to be found in Leibniz. It seems to me that the distinctions involved allow us to formulate in a reasonably clear way various doctrines to which he was committed. Leibniz used the notion of the a priori in a bewildering variety of ways. The intention here is that a Meta-proof yields a priori knowledge where a priori knowledge is knowledge based entirely on conceptual information.

41. It is assumed here that for Leibniz a demonstration is the same as an a priori proof. See note 9.

42. As noted above, I take the 'Hinc' ('so') in this passage to be of considerable significance. It suggests that, wherever we find Leibniz noting that the difference between necessary and contingent truths is like the difference between commensurable and incommensurable numbers, the idea of convergence and, hence, of a proof-sequence is lurking in the background.

43. This is rough and crude. Here is an area of Leibniz's thought that yields material for formal construction. Even in this rough form, numerous difficulties will strike the reader; but many of them seem inherent in the route Leibniz took.

44. It must be noted that at a date subsequent to the date of the first draft of this passage Leibniz appended the following note:

If, on the other hand, it appears from the progression that nothing of this sort will ever arise, then it has been proved to be false. C374 (P63-64)

And at a yet later date he appended this remark: "That is to say, in the case of necessary propositions" C374 (P64). I think this last is a slip of the Leibnizian pen—surely (?) he meant "in the case of contingent propositions."

45. The texts cited in support of (18) (below) provide indirect support for this claim.

46. See Adams, loc cit.

47. It may seem clear enough that each singular proposition contains a complete concept as a component but Leibniz recognized that not all contingent propositions are singular. (For example, at C19 (MP99) we find: "Nevertheless it ought not to be thought that only

singular propositions are contingent.") He claimed that some of what he called subordinate laws of nature are true but contingent (C19 (MP99)). Consider then:

(i) All gold is malleable.

(i) may express either an essential or an existential proposition (see, for example, C391 (P80)). The essential proposition expressed by (i) is about all possible instances of gold and is either necessarily true or necessarily false. The contingent proposition (i) may express comes to this:

(ii) All existing instances of gold are malleable.

I believe that Leibniz so construed (ii) that, for each (actual) instance of gold, its complete concept is a component of the proposition expressed by (ii) (or, a component of some proposition entailed by it).

48. See pages 211 and 212 for citations.

49. See, for example, G/7/301 (L349/226).

50. See note 10 for comments on the troublesome G/7/309 (MP75).

51. See L. Couturat, *La Logique de Leibniz* (Paris, 1901), pp. 208-18.

52. Suppose we start with (2') and conjoin it with (d''). We can then derive (8'). (8') surely supports (7). So the principle of sufficient reason is a consequence of (2') (assuming (d'')) and, hence, of the concept-containment account of truth. Noting these facts (but using different terminology) Fabrizio Mondadori concludes: "We might then say that while, on the one hand, the definition of truth as containment "vindicates" the principle of sufficient reason (for the latter . . . follows from the former in an obvious way), on the other hand Leibniz's definition of truth as containment is ultimately motivated by Leibniz's adherence to the principle of sufficient reason." (See Fabrizio Mondadori, "Reference, Essentialism, and Modality in Leibniz's Metaphysics," *Studia Leibnitiana*, Band V, Heft 1 [1973]: 90.) The reader should study Mondadori's subtle, imaginative and textually informed article. I have a reservation. Perhaps there is no likely definition of truth that will yield (7) via (8') other than (2). But, as noted previously, there seems little reason to suppose (7) and (8') equivalent other than prior acceptance of (2). If we consider (7) without supposing it equivalent to (8') then there seem to be accounts of truth other than the concept-containment account that will support (7).

53. See, for example, Loemker (L549-550/60) and Lewis White Beck, *Early German Philosophy* (Cambridge, 1969), pp. 207-8. For interesting and enlightening critical discussions of these claims see, Baruch Brody, "Leibniz's Metaphysical Logic," in *Essays on the Philosophy of Leibniz* Rice University Studies 63: 45-55; and Charles E. Jarrett, "Leibniz on Truth and Contingency," *New Essays on Rationalism and Empiricism*, ed. Jarrett, King-Farlow, and Pelletier, Canadian Journal of Philosophy, Supplementary Volume IV (1978): 83-100.

54. Adam and Tannery, eds., *Oeuvres de Descartes*, Vol. VII, p. 162.

55. *Ibid.*, Vol. IX, p. 195.

56. Jarrett, pp. 88-89.

Leibniz's
Theories of Contingency

Robert Merrihew Adams

INTRODUCTION

There is a familiar conception of Leibniz's views about the nature of necessity and contingency that portrays him as a sort of grandfather of possible worlds semantics for modal logic. According to this conception, Leibniz envisages an infinity of possible worlds, of which God (who exists necessarily) chooses and actualizes one (the best). Necessary truths are propositions that are true in all possible world belongs necessarily to the world that has it. The root of all world but false in at least one other possible world. What worlds are possible, what would happen in them, and how they are related to one anther as similar or dissimilar, better or worse, do not change from one world to another, and therefore all truths about what is possible are necessary. (This Leibniz is, to be precise, a grandfather of possible worlds semantics for S5, the strongest of the usual systems of modal logic.) For this reason also the property of being the best possible worlds belongs necessarily to the world that has it. The root of all contingency is that it is not necessary but only contingent that God chooses to actualize the best. All and only those truths are contingent whose truth depends on God's free choice of the best.

We meet this Leibniz in Chapter III of Bertrand Russell's *Critical Exposition of the Philosophy of Leibniz.* An important part of Russell's interpretation is the famous exception he makes in Leibniz's principle that in every true proposition the concept of the predicate is contained in the concept of the subject. "The assertion of existence, alone among predicates, is synthetic," Russell says, "and therefore, in Leibniz's view, contingent."[1] All other predicates are contained in the concepts of subjects that have them; but existence is not, except in the case of God. Therefore truths about what any possible indi-

---

vidual or possible world is like, or would be like if it existed or were actual, are all necessary; but it is contingent which possible world is actual, and therefore which possible individuals exist.

Russell gave up these views after reading Couturat. But according to E. M. Curley, "Recent discussions . . . have tended in some measure to go back to Russell's original view (before Couturat) that, apart from the proposition that God exists, existential truths are not analytic."[2] I think that the tendency described by Curley does indeed exist, and is quite broadly favorable to the picture of Leibniz held by Russell before Couturat. But it seems to me to be leading us backward, not only in time, but also in our understanding of Leibniz. For the familiar Leibniz described above is in large part a creature of misunderstanding, though not exactly of fiction.

A variety of conceptions of the problem of contingency, and solutions to it, can be found in Leibniz's writings. There was development in his thought on it, and he held more than one solution at once. There are two main solutions, to be set out in sections 1.0-1.5 and 2.0-2.6, respectively, of the present paper. An accurate account of Leibniz's theories of contingency will therefore be rather complex. We will come toward the end of it, rather than at the beginning, to the question whether he regarded existence as a predicate contained in the concepts of things that exist.

1.0 LEIBNIZ'S FIRST MAIN SOLUTION

Leibniz tells us that even before he thought of the problem of contingency in terms of his analytic theory of truth, he had "found [himself] very close to the opinion of those who hold everything to be absolutely necessary," but "was pulled back from this precipice by considering those possible things which neither are nor will be nor have been" (FC 178/L 263).[3] Just how close he was to the cliff, we shall see in section 1.1; and in sections 1.2-1.5 we shall consider the way in which he says he was rescued from it.

1.1 THE LETTER TO WEDDERKOPF

In May 1671 Leibniz wrote a letter to Magnus Wedderkopf, a legal scholar in Kiel, about "the necessity of events" (A II,i,117f./L 146f.).[4] He begins by arguing that everything that happens is determined by God's decree, and admitting that this is a "hard" conclusion. He then begins to trace the cause of Pilate's damnation, from his lack of faith to his failure to pay attention, to his failure to understand the utility of paying attention, to a lack of causes of such understanding.

> For it is necessary to analyze everything into some reason, and not to stop until we arrive at a first reason — or else it must be admitted that something can exist without a sufficient reason for its existence, and this admission destroys the demonstration of the existence of God and of many Philo-

sophical theorems. What then is the ultimate reason of the divine will? The divine intellect. For God wills those things that He understands to be best and most harmonious, and selects them, as it were, from an infinite number of all possibles.

Leibniz goes on to state that the ultimate reason of things is found in the essences, possibilities, or ideas of things, which "coincide with God Himself," are understood by Him, and have no reason outside themselves. Leibniz draws a strongly necessitarian conclusion:

> Since God is the most perfect mind, however, it is impossible for Him not to be affected by the most perfect harmony, and thus to be necessitated to the best by the very ideality of things. . . . Hence it follows that whatever has happened, is happening, or will happen is best and therefore necessary, but . . . with a necessity that takes nothing away from freedom because it takes nothing from the will and the use of reason.

Three points deserve comment here.

1) Leibniz has already slipped over the edge of the precipice in this letter. He states flatly and without qualification that everything that ever happens is necessary. This is his simplest solution of the problem of contingency. If there is no contingency, there is no need to account for it or explain its nature.

But Leibniz did not remain content with this position. On his own copy of the letter to Wedderkopf he later wrote, "I have since corrected this; for it is one thing for sins to be infallibly going to happen, and another thing for them to be going to happen necessarily." He continued to ascribe necessity to all things, but only with some qualification. "What is actual is *in some way* necessary" (GR 536; emphasis mine). Even in free actions there is allowed to be "hypothetical" and "moral" necessity, but not "absolute" or "metaphysical" necessity (G VI,37/Preface to the *Theodicy*).

2) Leibniz was a compatibilist, maintaining to the end of his life (to Clarke, V,3) that every event is determined but some acts are nonetheless free. According to the formula of his maturity, freedom consists in intelligence (understanding the object of deliberation), spontaneity (insofar as the source of the action is within the agent), and contingency (which excludes absolute, logical, or metaphysical necessity, but not hypothetical or moral necessity) (T 288-290, 302). In the letter to Wedderkopf, however, we meet a more extreme compatibilism, which does not make contingency a necessary condition of freedom. In this early work voluntariness and intelligence seem to suffice for freedom: necessity "takes nothing away from freedom because it takes nothing from the will and the use of reason." The later addition of contingency as a condition of freedom is surely related to the change in Leibniz's willingness to admit without qualification the necessity of all events, but the latter development in his thought comes sooner than the former. In a work of 1673, in which he argues vigorously against the claim that sins are (unqualifiedly) necessary (Conf 54ff.), he still says, "To preserve the privilege of free will, it is enough that

we have been so placed at a fork in the road of life, that we do only what we will, and will only what we believe to be good" (Conf 82). Later, however, Leibniz distinguished a sense in which freedom is opposed to necessity and a sense in which it is opposed only to compulsion (B 121); and in several texts from the years 1681-1685 (Gr 299, 308, 229; cf. G VII, 108-11) and later (Gr 421, G III,58f.) he ascribes *both* kinds of freedom to human agents.

3) In the letter to Wedderkopf the argument for the necessity of all events is not based (at least not explicitly) on the analytic theory of truth, but rather on the nature of God and the principle of sufficient reason. This latter, more theological argument against contingency is by far the one most often addressed by Leibniz in his writings; and we shall be concerned with it in most of the present essay.

The letter to Wedderkopf is an exceptional text. It is hard to regard as merely tentative a view that Leibniz communicated to an eminent person with whom he was by no means intimate. But he may not have held the extreme necessitarian position for any length of time. It seems not to have been held in a fragment on free will written just a few months before or after the letter (A VI,i,540f.).[5]

1.2 THINGS POSSIBLE IN THEIR OWN NATURE

The necessaritarian position was soon replaced by a theory that Leibniz repeated incessantly, publicly and privately, to the end of his career, and that must be regarded as his principal (and most confident) solution to the problem of contingency. The basic idea of this solution is very clearly stated in a paper on freedom written about 1681.

> But we must say that God wills the best by His own nature. Therefore He wills necessarily, you will say. I shall say with St. Augustine that that necessity is happy. But surely it follows from this that things exist necessarily. Why? Because a contradiction is implied by the non-existence of that which God wills to exist? I deny that that proposition is absolutely true. Otherwise those things which God does not will would not be possible. For they remain possible, even if they are not chosen by God. It is possible indeed that even that should exist which God does not will to exist, because it would be able to exist of its own nature if God willed that it exist. But God cannot will that it exist. I agree; yet it remains possible in its own nature, even if it is not possible in respect to the divine will. For we have defined possible in its own nature as that which does not imply a contradiction in itself[6] even if its coexistence with God can be said in some way to imply a contradiction. . . .
>
> Therefore I say: that is possible, of which there is some essence or reality, or which can be distinctly understood. . . . If God had decreed that no real line must be found which should be incommensurable with other real lines (I call real a line that actually bounds some body), it would

not therefore follow that the existence of an incommensurable line implies a contradiction, even if God, from the principle of perfection, could not fail to ordain in this way. (Gr 289f.)

On this view the actual world, and things that exist in it, are not necessary but contingent, because other worlds are possible in which those things would not exist. And the possibility of those other worlds does not depend on the possibility of God's choosing them. It is enough, for the contingency of the actual world, if the other possible worlds are "possible in their own nature" or "do not imply a contradiction in themselves," considered apart from God's choice.

Leibniz still takes this position in the *Theodicy*. He reports that Abelard agreed "that it can well be said that that man [who in fact will be damned] can be saved, in respect to the possibility of human nature, which is capable of salvation, but that it cannot be said that God can save him, in respect to God Himself, because it is impossible for God to do that which He ought not to do." And he comments that Abelard therefore need not have held, as he did, that "God cannot do anything but that which He does." For "the others . . . do not mean anything else when they say that God can save that man, and that He can do that which He does not do" (T 171). The possibility of the alternatives among which God chooses is internal to them; and this internal possibility of the alternatives is enough to make God's choice free.

In a word, when one speaks of the *possibility* of a thing it is not a question of the causes that can bring about or prevent its actual existence: otherwise one would change the nature of the terms and render useless the distinction between the possible and the actual. . . . That is why, when one asks if a thing is possible or necessary, and brings in the consideration of what God wills or chooses, one alters the issue. For God chooses among the possibles, and for that very reason He chooses freely, and is not compelled; there would be neither choice nor freedom if there were but one course possible. (T 235; cf.T 44, 45, 228, 230-232, 234, 367)

The first problem about this theory is to understand what is meant by "possible in its own nature." If a certain world is inferior and so cannot be chosen by God, is that not by virtue of its own nature? Why, then, should we not say that it is impossible in its own nature? Here we must think of the nature or concept of a possible world as built up by stages. We start with the notion of a group of monads, of the different degrees of distinctness with which each perceives the others, and of the geometrical configurations and motions that are expressed by their perceptions and have thus a phenomenal reality. If there are spirits among the created monads of the world in question, we include their thoughts, actions, speeches, and cultural productions. Thus is built up what we may call the *basic concept* of a possible world. It is to include everything that happens in that world, but not everything that is true about its relation to God's will. By analogy with the complete concept of an individual, we can also speak of the *complete concept* of a possible world, which is to be fuller than the basic concept and contain everything that is true about the possible world, including whether it is the best, or nearly the best, or far from the best, of all possible worlds, and whether God therefore chooses or rejects it.[7] We may take it to be Leibniz's position that a world is possible in its own nature if its *basic* concept contains no internal contradiction, and nothing that is incompatible with its actuality so long as certain determinants of God's choice are kept out of the picture; its *complete* concept may contain God's rejecting it, but that does not keep it from being possible in its own nature.

Interesting questions arise about just what is to be included in a world's basic concept. (1) Are any concepts of other possible worlds included? It might seem natural to exclude them, since we are trying to capture the idea of a possibility that is internal to one possible world. And by excluding them we can be certain of not including enough information to imply God's rejection of the world to which the basic concept belongs. On the other hand, the solution of the problem of contingency does not strictly require the exclusion of this information if the right information about God is excluded.

2) Are any facts about God included in basic concepts of worlds? Leibniz refers to the world as "the Aggregate of finite things" (G VII,302/L 486).[8] which presumably excludes God. On the other hand, he speaks of the possible things that are the objects of God's choice as containing in their concepts certain decisions of God, considered as possible, so that God chooses among certain possible actions of his own, as well as among possible creatures (C 23f.; G II, 49-51/L-A 55-57; cf. G I,360). This causes no problem, provided that the divine decisions that are included in the objects of God's choice are noncomparative decisions concerned only with the laws or order of the world to which they belong. What is important for Leibniz's treatment of contingency is that the basic concepts of possible worlds do not contain God's choice *among* possible worlds. If in addition they do not include the fact that God is perfectly good, they can contain concepts of other possible worlds, without damage to the theory of contingency.

1.3 HYPOTHETICAL NECESSITY

Even if a satisfactory explanation can be given of what it is for a world (or more generally, a state of affairs or thing) to be possible in its own nature, there remains an important objection to Leibniz's use of this notion in accounting for contingency. His claim is that the actuality of this world is contingent because other worlds remain possible in their own natures even if they are not possible in relation to God's will. But in presenting this theory of contingency, Leibniz at least sometimes seems to admit that it is necessary that God chooses this world (Gr 289f., Conf 64f.). And if it is necessary that God chooses this world, and it follows necessarily from that that this world is actual, must not the actuality of this world be necessary and not contingent? As Curley puts it,

It is an uncontroversial truth of modal logic that if p is necessary and p entails q, then q is necessary. So if it is (absolutely) necessary that God choose the best, and if the existence of the best world is (hypothetically) necessary in relation to his choice, then it is (absolutely) necessary that the best world exist.[9]

Leibniz makes much use of the term "hypothetically necessary," which Curley rightly brings in here. Leibniz says repeatedly that contingent truths are *hypothetically* but not *absolutely* necessary (e.g., in §13 of the *Discourse on Metaphysics*). "Hypothetical necessity" is normally, as he recognized (G III, 400/W481), a synonym of "necessity of the consequence." So he seems to be using the traditional distinction between necessity of the consequence and necessity of the consequent: "If p then necessarily q"[10] can mean either that "If p then q" is necessary (necessity of the consequence), or that if "p" is true then "q" is necessary (necessity of the consequent). But then necessity of the consequence (hypothetical necessity) combined with necessity of the antecedent implies necessity of the consequent. If "p" and "If p then q" are both necessary, then "q" is necessary.

Leibniz raised this very objection against himself in his "first Theodicy," written in dialogue form in 1673 as *The Philosopher's Confession*, and given to Arnauld and others.[11]

> God's existence is necessary. From it follow the sins that are contained in [this actual] series of things. What follows from the necessary is necessary. Therefore the sins are necessary. (Conf 64)

The answer that Leibniz first wrote was:

> I reply that it is false that whatever follows from what is necessary is necessary. From truths, to be sure, nothing follows that is not true. Yet since a particular [conclusion] can follow from purely universal [premises], as in [the syllogistic figures] Darapti and Felapton, why not something contingent from something necessary? (Conf 64)[12]

Thus baldly stated, Leibniz's answer seems simply to ignore the modal axiom appealed to by Curley. Leibniz acknowledged the axiom, however, at least by 1675, when he wrote, "Whatever is incompatible with something necessary is impossible." He therefore distinguished two types of necessity and impossibility. "The concept of the impossible is twofold: that which has no essence; and that which has no existence or which neither was nor is nor will be, and which is incompatible with God or with existence or with the reason which makes things to be rather than not."[13] Leibniz accordingly corrected his answer in the manuscript of *The Philosopher's Confession* (probably sometime between 1673 and 1677), to incorporate such a distinction:

> I reply that it is false that whatever follows from what is necessary *through itself,* is necessary *through itself.* From truths, to be sure, nothing follows

that is not true. Yet since a particular [conclusion] can follow from purely universal [premises], as in [the syllogistic figures] Darapti and Felapton, why may not something that is contingent, or *necessary on the hypothesis of something else*, follow from something that is necessary *through itself*? (Conf 64)[14]

He also added,

In this place we call *necessary* only that which is necessary *through itself* — that is, which has the reason of its existence and truth within itself. Such are the Geometrical truths, and of existing things only GOD. The others, which follow from the supposition of this series of things — that is, from the harmony of things — or from the Existence of GOD, are *contingent through themselves* and only hypothetically necessary. (Conf. 66)[15]

Here it is clear that in spite of the traditional terminology of hypothetical necessity, the absolute or *per se* necessity that Leibniz denies in affirming contingency is something more than the traditional necessity of the consequent. In his conception of hypothetical necessity the absolute necessity or contingency of the antecedent is no more important than the externality of the antecedent to the consequent. What follows necessarily from what is necessary through itself is certainly necessary by necessity of the consequent, in the traditional sense. It is not necessary through itself, however, but only hypothetically necessary, and contingent, in Leibniz's sense, if the antecedent from which it follows is external to it, and not contained in its own nature. The phrase Leibniz uses here, "necessary *ex alterius hypothesi*" ("necessary on the hypothesis of *something else*") expresses his meaning better than the more usual "necessary *ex hypothesi*."

This conception of hypothetical necessity is expressed only slightly less clearly in another early passage. On November 27, 1677, Leibniz recorded his side of a conversation with Bishop Nicholas Steno (Niels Stensen), who read *The Philosopher's Confession* and commented on it.[16] In this memorandum Leibniz says that "there is an *absolute necessity* when a thing cannot even be understood, but implies a contradiction in terms," and "there is a *hypothetical necessity* when a thing's being *some other way* can indeed be understood through itself, but it is necessarily *this way*, nonessentially [*per accidens*], on account of other things outside itself already presupposed" (Gr 270f.).

In his later writings Leibniz is usually less explicit about his interpretation of hypothetical necessity, and indeed does not remain consistent on the point. The conception we have found in his early work occurs in a paper dating from 1692 or later (according to Schepers; Grua dated it 1677):

All things therefore have a reason, either in themselves and from their terms [*in se et ex terminis*], as things that are necessary through themselves [*per se*]; or from elsewhere, as things that are free and contingent or, so to speak, non-essentially or hypothetically [*per accidens sive ex hypothesi*] necessary. (Gr 273; cf. Gr 297f. [1681], T 53 [1710])

The evidence that Leibniz's adherence to this position was not consistent and unwavering has to do with the question whether effects that are contingent in the sense of being only hypothetically necessary must have contingent causes. There are a paper from about 1683 (Gr 310f.) and a reading note from about 1695 (Gr 353) that hint at, but do not unambiguously imply, an affirmative answer to this question. And writing to Arnauld in 1686, Leibniz says that "the possibilities of individuals or of contingent truths contain in their concept the possibility of their causes, namely of the free decisions of God" (G II, 51/L-A 56). Similarly, Leibniz seems to think that the possibility of an effect requires the possibility, though not the actuality, of some cause of it, when he says, in a letter of 1714 to Louis Bourguet, "Generally speaking, in order for a being to be possible, it suffices that its efficient cause be possible; I except the supreme efficient cause, which must exist in fact" (G III, 572/L 661).[17] In neither of these passages is it explicit that the possibility of the cause is required for a thing to be possible *in itself*, nor how far up the explanatory chain the possibility of the cause must extend. Perhaps it is enough if particular divine decrees or decisions to establish such and such laws of nature are possible in themselves, or included in consistent basic concepts of worlds; perhaps they need not be possible in relation to God's perfect goodness. But it is natural to read these passages as incompatible with the view that contingency is definable in terms of the internal possibility of basic (but incomplete) concepts of alternative worlds.

On the other hand, Leibniz does say in the *Theodicy* that considerations about what God chooses, and in general about the causes of a thing, are not relevant to the question of the thing's possibility (T 235, quoted in section 1.2 above). And it would not be plausible to interpret Leibniz there as meaning only that the actuality of the causes is irrelevant, while tacitly assuming that the possibility of the causes is relevant; for he is explicitly attacking Abelard, whom he reads (T 171) as arguing, not merely from the nonactuality, but from the alleged impossibility of God's having chosen otherwise than He did.

Perhaps Leibniz in his later work found it easier to vacillate on the question whether a contingent effect can follow by hypothetical necessity from an absolutely necessary cause, because the question had lost some of its importance for him. For, as we shall see, he had come to believe that God's choice of this world to actualize is contingent, and therefore that contingent existences do have a contingent cause in God. Nevertheless the idea that it is enough for contingency that there are a plurality of alternatives for God's choice that are possible in themselves is more clearly and emphatically presented in the *Theodicy* than any other well articulated solution to the problem of contingency.

1.4 THE REALITY OF CHOICE

We may be tempted to object that the conception of the contingent as that which has some alternative that is possible *in itself* (if not in relation to God) does not really show how there can be any contingency in the Leibnizian universe, nor how God's choice among possible worlds can be free. For what is contingent in this Leibnizian sense may still be necessary by necessity of the consequent—that is, absolutely necessary—in the traditional (and twentieth century) sense. And God's choice of this world to actualize may be necessitated by His nature as perfectly good, even if other worlds remain possible in themselves. If this is all that Leibniz has to offer in defense of contingency, his system may be thought as necessitarian as Spinoza's.

Most of what is said in this objection is right, in a way; but it overlooks the nature of Leibniz's interest in free will and contingency, and his stated view of the difference between his determinism and Spinoza's. His interest in contingency is rooted in his interest in divine and human free will—with respect to which he is, after all, a compatibilist. We must let him define for himself what kind of compatibilist he is. At one time, as we have seen, he regarded unqualified necessity as compatible with freedom. Later his principal reason for insisting on some sort of contingency in connection with free action seems to have been to insure the reality of choice—to insure that what happens is really influenced by final causes and judgments of value.

This is the point that Leibniz most often insists on in distinguishing his views about necessity from Spinoza's. Spinoza held that there are no final causes in nature, that God does not act for an end, and that things are called good or bad with regard only to how they affect us, being quite indifferent to God (*Ethics,* I, Appendix). He said that actual intellect and will must be referred to God-as-an-effect (*natura naturata*) and not to God-as-a-cause (*natura naturans*) (*Ethics*, I, prop. 31), and denied that a divine intellect or will could resemble ours in anything more than name alone (*Ethics,* I, prop. 17, schol.). Indeed there is no room in Spinoza's system for God to choose, for there is nothing to be excluded by His choice. By the necessity of the divine nature, since it is infinite in Spinoza's sense, absolutely everything possible must be actual (*Ethics,* I, prop. 16).

On all of these points Leibniz disagreed with Spinoza. Even on the most extremely necessitarian interpretation of his system, God's choice has a real and important role to play. For even if God's choice of this world is necessary, other worlds are possible in their own nature, and are not excluded without God's choice but only through (the necessity of) His choosing this one. God's choice is an indispensable link in the chain of explanation for the actuality of this world. "The nature of things, taken without intelligence and without choice, has nothing sufficiently determining" (T 350). The comparative value of the different worlds also has a crucial explanatory role, in which Leibniz employs a notion of final cause.[18]

Leibniz emphasizes this disagreement in his discussions of Spinoza, early and late. In the period 1676-1678, near the time of Spinoza's death, Leibniz commented, "But it is not at all to be thought that all things follow from God's nature without any intervention of the will" (G I,124; cf. Gr 279), and "Even if it is true that not everything happens for the sake of men, it still does not follow that [God] acts without will or understanding of the good" (G I,150/L 205). In the *Theodicy* he wrote,

> Spinoza . . . appears to have explicitly taught a blind necessity, having denied to the author of things understanding and will, and imagining that good and perfection relate only to us and not to Him. It is true that Spinoza's opinion on this subject is somewhat obscure. . . . Nevertheless, as far as one can understand him, he acknowledges no goodness in God, properly speaking, and he teaches that all things exist by the necessity of the Divine nature, without God making any choice. We will not amuse our-selves here in refuting an opinion so bad, and indeed so inexplicable. Our own is founded on the nature of the possibles — that is to say, of the things that do not imply any contradiction. (T 173; cf. T 174, 371-374).

If we will allow Leibniz to disagree with Spinoza in his own way, rather than in some way that we might impose on him, this should be enough to show that his determinism is not properly called Spinozistic.

1.5 MORAL NECESSITY

When Leibniz says that he opposes a "brute" or "blind" necessity (T 174, 349), he means (sometimes with explicit reference to Spinoza) a necessity that denies to God intelligence and choice (T 371-372). Similarly, in the *Theodicy*[19] he admits a "moral" but not a "metaphysical" necessity of God's choosing the best. Leibniz usually gives little or no explanation of this distinction; and one might be tempted to take it as a promissory note for a less strongly necessitarian theory that he was unable to provide in detail. But in fact "morally necessary" had a precise meaning. The morally necessary is what one morally ought to do. In his early jurisprudential writings (1671-1678) Leibniz enunciated a system of moral modalities (a very rudimentary deontic logic) in terms of what is possible, impossible, necessary, or contingent (i.e., omissible or not necessary) "to be done by a good man" (A VI,i,465ff.). "I call *morally impossible* that which it is not possible to do without committing a sin" (A IV,i,471). "*Obligation* . . . is a moral necessity — that is, a necessity imposed on him who wants to keep the name of 'a good man'" (Gr 608). Similarly, "*duty* is whatever is necessary in the perfectly just" (C 517). Accordingly, when Leibniz says that God's choice of the best is morally necessary, we must take him to mean that it is necessary that if God did not choose the best, He would not be perfectly good. It is noteworthy that Clarke, his contemporary, did take this to be Leibniz's meaning. Clarke's examples of moral necessity are "that a *good Being*, continuing to be *Good*, cannot do *Evil*; or a *wise* Being, continuing to be *Wise*, cannot act *unwisely*; or a *veracious* Person, continuing to be *veracious*, cannot tell a Lie" (G VII,423). (Clarke also thought this a "figurative" and philosophically uninteresting sense of "necessity.")

It is in keeping with this conception that the *Theodicy* speaks of being "necessitated morally by wisdom" (T 237), identifies moral necessity with "the choice of the wise, worthy of his wisdom" (Preliminary Discourse, §2), and says that "it is a moral necessity that the wisest is obliged to choose the best" (T 230). And in some of his discussions of moral necessity Leibniz's concern for the reality of choice comes together pretty explicitly with his idea of the contingent as that which receives necessity only from outside itself and has alternatives that are possible in themselves. He distinguishes between "metaphysical necessity, which leaves no place for any choice, presenting only one possible object, and moral necessity, which obliges the wisest to choose the best" (T 367), and says,

> But that sort of necessity which does not destroy the possibility of the contrary has that name only by analogy. It becomes effective, not by the essence of things alone, but by that which is outside them and above them, namely by the will of God. This necessity is called moral, because with the wise, what is necessary and what ought to be are equivalent things. (Abridgment, VIII [G VI,386])

2.0 LEIBNIZ'S SECOND MAIN SOLUTION

We have now explored the set of ideas that constitute the innermost and surest bastion of Leibniz's defenses against the denial of contingency. Even if everything actual is necessarily actualized by God, on account of His goodness, the things that God chooses are not necessary through themselves, but only on the hypothesis of something external to them, and they have alternatives that are possible in themselves. They are therefore in a certain sense contingent, and only hypothetically necessary. Leibniz finds contingency in this sense of worth defending, because it preserves the reality of God's choice, distinguishing the "moral" necessity that he ascribes to God's action from the "brute" or "blind" necessity that he thinks belongs to it in Spinoza's system. Leibniz adhered to these views from 1673 to the end of his life.

But we have yet to examine the outer walls of his castle of contingency. In the end Leibniz denied, not only that this world, which in fact is actual, is necessary through itself, but also that it is necessarily actualized by God. In several papers from the 1680s we see him struggling to justify this denial and fit it into his philosophy. But by 1690 he had made much progress in understanding the problem, and had attained a solution that seems to have satisfied him fairly well.

2.1 THE CONTINGENCY OF WHICH WORLD IS BEST

According to Leibniz, this world, rather than any other possible world, is actual because God chooses to actualize whatever is best, and this is the best of all possible worlds. Therefore, if it is contingent that this world is actual, it must either be contingent that God chooses whatever is best, or else contingent that this is the best. Which is it that is contingent? Leibniz explicitly raised this question in several papers written between 1689 and 1706; he tended to favor the answer that it is contingent that this world is the best.

In one note from about 1695 he raises the question without answering it:

> The formal cause [of the knowability of future contingents] is the coherence of terms, or the fact that the predicate inheres in the subject, even if the cause why it inheres depends on two things, the universal bestness and God's decision to choose the best. Or is God's general decision necessary.[20] Or is it not that "This is the best" is true, but not necessary: it is true but not demonstrable a priori. Is it therefore contingent? (Gr 351)

Although the question is not answered here, Leibniz's inclination is clear.

It is explicit in other texts, including the important paper "On Contingency," from 1689 or 1690, the earliest work known to me in which Leibniz defined the alternatives:[21]

> We must see whether if we suppose that this proposition is necessary: *the proposition which has the greater reason for existing exists*, it follows that the proposition which has the greater reason for existing is necessary. But the inference is rightly rejected. For if the definition of a necessary proposition is, that its truth can be demonstrated with geometrical rigor, then it can indeed happen that this proposition can be demonstrated: *every truth, and only a truth, has the greater reason*, or this one: *God always acts most wisely*. But it will not therefore be possible to demonstrate this proposition: *contingent proposition A has the greater reason*, or *contingent proposition A is conformed to the divine wisdom*. And therefore also it does not follow that contingent proposition A is necessary. And therefore even if it were conceded that it is necessary that God chooses the best, or that the best is necessary, still it does not follow that that which is chosen is necessary, since no demonstration that it is the best is given. (Gr 305f.)

Here Leinbiz is rather careful not to assert that it is necessary that God chooses the best. but he does commit himself to the view that it is not necessary that this (which God has chosen) is the best, although it is in fact the best. Of the two ways in which the necessity of that which God has chosen could be denied, Leibniz is readier here to deny the necessity of "This is the best" than the necessity of "God chooses the best."

His stance is the same in a note written in the early 1690s:

> Or does this follow: "This proposition is necessary: God does the best. Therefore that which God does is necessary"? The inference is not valid. For the conclusion follows the weaker part. But it is not demonstrable that a certain thing is the best, nor, therefore, [can it be demonstrated] what must be done. Or shall we rather say that this proposition too, "God does the best," is not necessary but only certain? The previous opinion appears to be best, since this proposition: A is the best, is certain, but is not necessary since it cannot be demonstrated. (Gr 336)

We do not have to deny the necessity of "God does the best," since that which is the best is not necessarily the best.

In another text, the latest and most important of the series, Leibniz begins by stating again that "This is the best" is not necessary even if "That which is the best is chosen" is necessary. He says that he does not know whether God's not choosing the best implies a contradiction. But he asserts flatly that "This is the best," though true, "is not demonstrable by a demonstration that shows that the contrary implies a contradiction." Then he seems to change his mind, how-ever, and shifts to a less cautious position on the necessity of God's choosing the best:

> It is the same argument: God wills necessarily the work that is most worthy of His wisdom. I say that He wills it, but not necessarily, because although this work is the most worthy, that is not a necessary truth.[22] It is true that this proposition: God wills the work that is most worthy of Him, is necessary. But it is not true that He wills it necessarily. For this proposi-tion: This work is the most worthy, is not a necessary truth; it is indemon-strable, contingent, a truth of fact. (Gr 493)

The argument here turns on an ambiguity of "necessarily." Leibniz saw it as an ambiguity of scope. He accepts the "necessarily" as "applied to the cop-ula" (that is, to the whole proposition), but not as applied to "what is contained in the copula" (that is, as internal to the predicate). He will affirm that "God is necessarily the one who wills the best. But not the one who necessarily wills the best" (Gr 494). It is misleading, however, for Leibniz to make an issue of which verb "necessarily" modifies. The crucial point in the ambiguity is whether the necessity applies de re to the object that God in fact wills. This point could be brought out by distinguishing wide from narrow scope of the definite descrip-tion operator in "God necessarily wills the work that is most worthy of His wisdom." If it has wide scope, the necessity applies de re to the work, and the sense of the proposition is, "The work that is most worthy of God's wisdom is such that it is necessary that God wills *it*" — which Leibniz denies. But if the definite description operator has narrow scope, the sense is rather, "It is neces-sary that God wills whatever work is most worthy of His wisdom" — which Leib-niz here accepts. Of course it would be anachronistic to expect Leibniz to have made the point in that way.

The date of this text deserves comment. It cannot possibly have been written before 1706, because it is a note made in reading the third volume of Bayle's *Réponses aux questions d'un provincial*, which was published at the end of the previous year.[23] This refutes Rescher's suggestion that it was only "until the year 1686, when his mature philosophy took form" that Leibniz preferred denying the necessity of "This is the best" to denying the necessity of "God chooses the best."[24]

It should also be noted that the proposition, "God wills necessarily the work that is most worthy of His wisdom," which is quoted from Bayle, is discussed again (with the same reference to Bayle) in the *Theodicy*, where it is denied (T 237). Leibniz does not make there the distinctions that he had made in the note from 1706, but only appeals to the difference between metaphysical and moral necessity. What he is denying in the *Theodicy*, however, should probably be understood in the light of the earlier note.

2.2 NECESSITY, DEMONSTRABILITY, AND INFINITE ANALYSIS

The thesis that the property of being the best of all possible worlds belongs only contingently to the world that has it has seemed so evidently false to some recent philosophers that they have been unwilling to regard it as a part of Leibniz's mature philosophy. "That this world is the best possible world is presumably a necessary fact," according to Curley;[25] and Rescher says, "it is difficult to see how what is best could avoid being determined with necessitation when the substances are conceived *sub ratione possibilitatis*."[26] That this world is the best does not depend on which world exists, or is actual, or chosen by God. Leibniz insists that the values of possible things are completely independent of God's will.[27] The bestness of this world is rather the ground of its being chosen by God and hence actual and existent.

Nevertheless, Leibniz did in several of his later writings assert that the bestness of that which is best is contingent, as we have seen. And I do not know of any text from the mature period of his philosophy in which he asserts or implies the opposite. How can he have thought what he appears to have thought? The explanation is to be sought in the idea, which occurs in all of the crucial passages, that it cannot be *demonstrated* what is best. Leibniz brings in here, implicitly, his very formal ideal of demonstration by analysis in a finite number of steps. For of all his solutions to the theological version of the problem of contingency, that which proceeds by denying the necessity of facts about which things are best is the most clearly connected with his conception of contingency in terms of infinite analysis.

This conception is indeed rather fully stated in the earliest of the papers in which we have found Leibniz saying that it is contingent what is the best.

> And here[28] is uncovered the inner distinction between necessary and contingent truths, which no one will easily understand unless he has some tincture of Mathematics—namely, that in necessary propositions one arrives, by an analysis continued to some point, at an identical equation (and this very thing is to demonstrate a truth in geometrical rigor); but in contingent propositions the analysis proceeds to infinity by reasons of reasons, so that indeed one never has a full demonstration, although there is always, underneath, a reason for the truth, even if[29] it is perfectly understood only by God, who alone goes through an infinite series in one act of the mind. (Gr 303)

This is Leibniz's solution to the version of the problem of contingency that has fascinated his twentieth century readers, the version that asks, "if the concept of having the predicate at a given time inheres in the concept of the subject, how can the subject then lack the predicate without contradiction and[30] impossibility, and without loss of its concept?" (FC 179/L 264). The solution is that a predicate can be contained in the concept of a subject without this containment being provable by analysis in a finite number of steps. Leibniz will say that in such a case the subject's lacking the predicate does not "imply a contradiction," and that its having the predicate cannot be "demonstrated" and is contingent (FC 181/L 264; similarly at C 17/SG 346f.; cf. C 376f., 387/P 66, 76f.).

An example may help us to understand how such cases may arise. It may be that there is a property, ϕ, such that for every natural number n, it can be proved that n has ϕ, but the universal generalization that every natural number has ϕ cannot be proved except by proving first that 7 has ϕ, then that 4 has ϕ, and so on until every natural number has been accounted for—a task that can never be completed. In this case it is a purely mathematical truth that every natural number has ϕ, but it cannot be demonstrated. And it is a purely mathematical falsehood that some natural number lacks ϕ, but no contradiction can be derived from it in a finite number of steps. Tarski decided to say that a system of which these conditions hold, but in which "Some natural number lacks ϕ" can be proved, is *consistent*, but not *ω-consistent*.[31] He thus reserved the use of "consistent" and "inconsistent," without qualification, to express proof-theoretical notions rather than notions of mathematical possibility and mathematical falsity. Similarly, Leibniz reserves "implies a contradiction" to express a proof-theoretical notion rather than the notion of conceptual falsity or being false purely by virtue of the relations of concepts. He thinks, of course, that the latter notion is expressed simply by "false."

It is not difficult to see how it would follow, from this conception of contingency, that it is contingent which possible world is the best. For one would presumably have to consider infinitely many aspects of a world to assign a value to it as a whole. And then one would have to compare infinitely many worlds to determine which is best. It could not be determined by any finite analysis; hence it is contingent. Several commentators have explained Leibniz's reasoning along these lines,[32] and Leibniz himself did so. In a paper on "Necessary and Contingent Truths" (Couturat's title), which may contain the earliest surviving statement of his infinite analysis conception of contingency, he points out that the universe has infinitely many aspects, and adds,

> Indeed, even if one could know the whole series of the universe, one still could not give the reason for it, unless one had set up a comparison of it with all the other possible [series]. From this it is clear why no demonstration of any contingent proposition can be found, no matter how far the analysis of concepts is continued. (C 19/SG 349 [dated 1678 by Schepers]; cf. Gr 343 [from the early 1690s])

There remain difficult questions, never resolved by Leibniz or his commentators, about just how analysis is supposed to work in the relevant cases. Analysis, for Leibniz and the seventeenth century, was a method of proof beginning with the conclusion to be proved and working back to the axioms from which it follows—though in an infinite analysis the axioms are never reached. The method that begins with the axioms was called synthesis.[33] In conformity with this distinction, Leibniz described finite and infinite analyses as proceeding from the proposition to be proved, by substituting definitions, or parts of definitions, for its terms (FC 181f./L 264f.). But the process of determining which is the best of all possible worlds by comparing the values of all the worlds seems likely to be a synthesis, rather than an analysis, in this sense. Indeed Leibniz gives us no idea how one would even begin an analysis, finite or infinite, to determine which world is the best possible, although it is clear that he thought the infinite number of worlds to be compared is one ground of the contingency of God's choice of this world. Perhaps something like the following form of analysis is intended. Let "W*" be a proper name of the world that happens to be actual. An analysis of "W* = the best of all possible worlds" will require the replacement of one or both sides of the equation by an analysans. But to reduce the equation to identities by such replacement we would need on the right-hand side an analysans including a statement of the complete (or at least the basic) concepts of all possible worlds; and that is not finitely statable.

Another difficulty is that while it does seem that it could not be proved in a finite number of steps that a certain world is the best possible, there might perhaps be a finite proof that a certain world, or any world of a certain sort, is not the best possible. Leibniz himself seems to have thought it could be demonstrated that no world in which God damns the innocent is the best.

> The damnation of the innocent is indeed possible in itself, or something
> that does not imply a contradiction; but it is not possible for God. . . .
> For we do not need to examine the whole harmony of things in order to
> know whether God is going to damn someone innocent eternally. (Gr 300)

Here Leibniz seems to be confronted with a truth, "No one innocent will be damned eternally," which satisfies one of his criteria for contingency (its contrary is possible in itself), but not the other (it would not require an infinite analysis to prove it). Leibniz does not tell us how to resolve this conflict; indeed I doubt that he realized its existence.

We may also be tempted to object that the infinite analysis conception of contingency represents contingency as illusory, or at best merely relative to our intellectual incapacity (as Spinoza had regarded it: *Ethics*, I, prop. 33, schol. 1). It is natural to conclude that for Leibniz, as Lovejoy has put it, "though we are unable to attain an intuitive apprehension of the necessity [of a judgment which appears to us as contingent], . . . we can nevertheless be sure that the necessity is there, and is recognized by the mind of God."[34] Russell took a similar view in 1903, when he wrote, "Where an infinite analysis, which only God can perform, is required to exhibit the contradiction, the opposite will *seem* to be not contradictory"; he did not think the alternative suggestion, "that the denial of an analytic truth might be not self-contradictory," would commend itself to Leibniz.[35]

This objection rests on a fundamental misunderstanding of Leibniz's conception of necessity and contingency. The distinction between them "is drawn on logical grounds alone," as Rescher rightly points out.[36] It is not an epistemological distinction, and is not based on a relation in which contingent propositions stand to us but not to God. It is based on a difference in the logical form of the reasons by virtue of which propositions of the two sorts are true. Contingent truths are just as contingent for God as they are for us, and He can no more *demonstrate* them than we can; for not even He can "see . . . the end of the analysis, since there is no end" (FC 182, 184/L 265f.).[37] Leibniz does say that God can know contingent truths *a priori* (that is through their reasons), and that we cannot. But these epistemological relations are not constitutive of contingency; they are only consequences of the logical property that is constitutive of contingency.

Two initially plausible principles about (logical) necessity are that whatever is true purely by virtue of the relations of concepts is necessary, and that whatever is necessary must be logically demonstrable. Leibniz seems at first to have assumed both of these principles. The light that was kindled for him by the knowledge of the analysis of infinites (C 18/SG 348) was the realization that the two assumptions are incompatible because some propositions that are true solely by virtue of the relations of concepts are nonetheless not provable by anything that he would count as a demonstration. Leibniz held consistently to the second principle. His usual definition of the logically necessary is that it is that whose contrary implies a contradiction (e.g., Premliminary Discourse to the *Theodicy*, §2). And we have seen that Leibniz treats "implies a contradiction" as expressing a proof-theoretical property that does not belong to propositions whose falsity can be discovered a priori only through an infinite analysis (FC 181/L 264; cf. C 17/SG 346f.). The realization of the incompatibility of the two principles therefore enabled Leibniz with a clear conscience to give up the first principle, which had made his theory of truth seem to leave no room for contingency.

When Russell charged that the infinite analysis conception of contingency would at most yield truths that only seem to be contingent, he was explicitly and mistakenly assuming that whatever is false purely by virtue of the relations of concepts must be self-contradictory for Leibniz. Similarly Curley seems to be assuming a conception of necessity in terms of conceptual truth, rather than in terms of demonstrability, when he says that the bestness of this world "is not rendered any the less necessary by the number of other possible worlds being infinite rather than finite."[38] For our own use, of course, we may well prefer a conceptual truth conception of necessity to a demonstrability conception. If so, we will rightly conclude that Leibniz's infinite analysis theory does not give us real contingency. But that presents no internal objection to Leibniz's system.

The contingency we are demanding, he can only regard as a brute fact and a violation of the principle of sufficient reason, which he has no intention of admitting in his mature philosophy.

It is just as clear in the essay "On the Radical Origination of Things" (G VII,302-308/L 486-491 [November 23, 1697]) as in the letter to Wedderkopf (A II,i,117f./L 146f. [May 1671]) that Leibniz thinks of everything in the world as determined ultimately by the divine nature, and particularly by the relations of concepts in God's intellect. From this point of view the problem of contingency is to find a difference between *ways* in which facts are determined by relations of concepts—a difference that is both important and plausibly related to the preanalytic notions of logical necessity and contingency. The difference between truths that are and that are not demonstrable in a finite number of steps fills this role admirably.

2.3 CONTINGENT CONNECTIONS AMONG POSSIBLES AS SUCH

As a consequence of his infinite analysis theory of contingency Leibniz accepted another thesis that some commentators have been most reluctant to admit as part of his philosophy. Russell noted in 1903 that "the view that infinite complexity is the defining property of the contingent has the curious consequence that truths about possible substances are contingent."[39] Both Broad and Curley have claimed that Leibniz did not accept this consequence,[40] but their claim is untenable. That you exist in the best possible world is a fact about you conceived as a possible substance; but its contingency follows from what Leibniz wrote in several places about the contingency of which world is best.

Indeed the idea that there are contingent connections among things considered as possible becomes quite important to Leibniz in the *Discourse on Metaphysics* and correspondence with Arnauld. This is to be expected, in view of Leibniz's insistence that all of the acts of any individual follow from the concept of that individual considered as possible. If it is important to our freedom that we be contingently connected with our actions, this following of our actions from our concepts must somehow be a contingent connection between them and us considered as possible. Accordingly Leibniz says in §13 of the *Discourse* that there are two sorts of connection, one absolutely necessary but the other contingent, by which different events follow from the complete concept of a created person.

Arnauld was perhaps the first to find this strange. He argued that on Leibniz's view, the connection between Adam and everything "that has happened and will happen to him and his posterity" must be necessary, "because," as Leibniz put it, "I consider the individual concept of Adam as possible," and "possible concepts in themselves do not depend on the free decisions of God" (G II, 28-30, 40/L-A28f., 42f.). There are two main points in Leibniz's reply to this objection.

a) "The possibles are possible before all the actual decisions of God, but not without presupposing sometimes the same decisions taken as possible" (G II,51/L-A 56). This is because the complete concept of any possible thing involves (as possible) some decisions that God would make (for instance, in establishing laws of nature) if He actualized the world to which that thing belongs. Here Leibniz clings to the idea that truths involving God's decisions are contingent. But now it seems they need not depend on what He actually decides; it is enough if they involve divine decisions considered as possible. Why the merely possible divine decisions should be thought to have this relevance is obscure to me.

b) The connection between a person, considered as possible, and the events of his possible world is "intrinsic" (G II,51/L-A 56) and "certain" but not "necessary," although the failure of the connection would destroy the individual concept of the person (G II,52/L-A 58; cf. G II,41/L-A 44). Here Leibniz seems to be quite clear that his position involves contingent connections within possible worlds, and hence contingent truths that do not depend on God's actual decisions, nor on which world is actual.[41]

The same view is expressed by Leibniz in other texts.

> It is of the nature of an individual substance that its concept be perfect and complete, and contain all its individual circumstances, even contingent ones, down to the least detail. . . . Yet these individual [circumstances] are not therefore necessary, and do not depend on the divine intellect alone, but also on decisions of the divine will, insofar as the decisions themselves are considered as possible by the divine intellect. (Gr 311 [1683])

About 1695, in a reading note, he stated flatly, "There are some indemonstrable truths even in possible things—namely about contingent things regarded as possible" (Gr 353). And probably a little later he wrote that "God decided to create a creature whose full concept involves such a series of graces and free actions, although not necessarily but by such a connection as the nature of the thing involves" (Gr 383 [1697]).

How can the connection between an individual substance and some of the properties or events involved in its concept be contingent? Leibniz offers hints of some answers to this question, but they are by no means so clear as his best-worked-out answers to the question how the existence of those creatures that are actual can be contingent. Three answers may be distinguished.

1) In §13 of the *Discourse* Leibniz says that the predicate of deciding to cross the Rubicon and winning the battle of Pharsalus is contained in the concept of Julius Caesar, but that it is not "necessary in itself" that those things happen to him. This suggests that Leibniz thought of Caesar's deciding not to cross the Rubicon, or his losing at Pharsalus, as things that are possible in themselves, in the same way that nonactual possible worlds are possible in themselves, although they are impossible on the hypothesis of something else. But it is hard

to make sense of this suggestion, if the source of the threatening necessity is in Caesar's own complete concept. That would seem to constitute a necessity internal to Caesar's deciding and winning.

In the case of possible worlds, I suggested[42] a distinction between the complete concept of a world and a fragment of it, the world's "basic" concept; only what is contained in its basic concept determines whether a world is possible in itself. Leibniz had the similar idea that properties and events that are contingently contained in the complete concept of an individual substance are distinguished by not following from any incomplete and general fragment of it. Thus in explaining to Arnauld how "the connection of events, though it is certain, is not necessary," and how he is free in taking a journey that is contained in his complete concept, Leibniz says,

> And there is nothing in me, of all that can be conceived as general, or as essence or specific or incomplete concept, from which one can infer that I shall take it necessarily; whereas from the fact that I am a man one can conclude that I am able to think. (G II,52/L-A 58)

Similarly Leibniz writes that the complete concept of Peter as possible contains "not only essential or necessary [matters], which derive, that is, from incomplete or specific concepts, . . . but also . . . existential (so to speak) or contingent [matters]" (Gr 311 [1683]). The use of "essence" and "essential" here is significant. In the *Discourse on Metaphysics* Leibniz identified the "essence" with the "individual concept" of a substance (DM 16), but in a later paper he distinguished them, using "essence" to refer to a fragment of the individual concept to which he attributed particular importance for modality:

> Of the essence of a thing is what belongs to it necessarily and perpetually; of the concept of a singular things, however, is also what belongs to it contingently or by accident, or what God sees in it when He has perfectly understood it. (Gr 383 [1697])

But whereas the basic concept of a possible world suffices to distinguish it from all other possible worlds, an essence or specific concept of Caesar that left out his decision to cross the Rubicon would not suffice to distinguish him from all other possible individuals, for "a concept that is still indeterminate even in the slightest circumstances . . . could be common to two different individuals" (Gr 311). It seems strange to say that *Caesar's* deciding not to cross the Rubicon is possible *in itself* on the ground that his decision to cross is not contained in a concept that he shares with one or more other possible individuals.

2) A more plausible idea can be read into the statement, in §13 of the *Discourse,* that if someone did the opposite of something that is involved in his complete concept, "he would do nothing impossible in itself, although it is impossible (*ex hypothesi*) for that to happen." Maybe just as God chooses freely because He chooses among a plurality of possible worlds, each of which is possible in itself even if it is impossible in relation to God's choice, so a creature

can act freely because he chooses among a plurality of actions, each of which is possible in its own nature even if it is impossible in relation to the complete concept of the choosing creature. If this is to work, the alternatives for choice must be regarded as somewhat general, rather than as completely individual actions. Caesar's alternatives on the bank of the Rubicon, for example, must be crossing and not crossing, rather than Caesar's crossing and Caesar's not crossing. Individual concepts must be kept out of the objects of choice. This line of thought, therefore, does not show us a way in which *Caesar's* deciding to cross the Rubicon can be *contingent.* But it does show us a way in which Leibniz should say that the *reality* of Caesar's choice is preserved. I am not sure that Leibniz really had in mind this treatment of the freedom of created spirits, but it would have been worth developing.

3) Contingent connections between possibles can be explained in terms of the infinite analysis theory of contingency. Leibniz gives such an explanation of the contingency of "Peter denies": "The concept of Peter is complete, and so involves infinite things; therefore one never arrives at a perfect demonstration" (C 376/P 66). Leibniz does not say here whether Peter is considered as actual or merely as possible. But the argument evidently works just as well as if the subject is considered only as a possible person—as Russell perceived with dismay.

There are even more difficult problems, however, about how infinite analysis is supposed to work in this case than in the case of bestness among possible worlds. Leibniz mostly ignores these difficulties, and I cannot do much more here than point them out. The first is the problem of the Lucky Proof.[43] Even if infinitely many properties and events are contained in the complete concept of Peter, at least one of them will be proved in the first step of any analysis. Why couldn't it be Peter's denial? Why couldn't we begin to analyze Peter's concept by saying, "Peter is a denier of Jesus and . . . "? Presumably such a Lucky Proof must be ruled out by some sort of restriction on what counts as a step in an analysis of an individual concept, but so far as I know, Leibniz does not explain how this is to be done. On the other hand, we may wonder how we can even begin an analysis of the individual concept of any person, as Leibniz implies we can. For such a concept, being complete, is not our concept but God's, and we do not seem to have a definition with which to begin to replace it.[44]

2.4 REASONS THAT INCLINE WITHOUT NECESSITATING

One of the things Leibniz never tired of saying about free choices is that their causes, motives, or reasons "incline" but do not "necessitate." Lovejoy called this "misleading if edifying phraseology," and a "verbal distinction, absolutely meaningless in the light of [Leibniz's] other doctrines."[45] One is tempted to agree with this harsh judgment, for Leibniz does not give much explanation of the difference between inclining and necessitating. But I think the distinction has a place in the interpretation of Leibniz we have been developing.

Leibniz presents the idea of reasons that incline without necessitating, sometimes in connection with the notion of a choice among alternatives that are possible *in themselves* (T 45, 230; to Clarke, V,8-9), and sometimes in connection with the infinite analysis theory of contingency. In the latter connection, which seems to me the more illuminating of the two, Leibniz says, "There is the same proportion between necessity and inclination that there is in the Mathematicians' Analysis between exact Equation and limits that give an approximation" (Gr 479; cf. Gr 303 and G VI,414 [Remarks on King, §14]).

The preceding statement was written about 1702 in a memorandum that also makes clear how infinity is supposed to enter into the influence of reasons on the will. The word "incline" suggests the image of a balance that is tipped or inclined to one side or the other by the preponderance of weights; and "balance" (noun and verb) occurs, at least figuratively, several times in the memorandum. Leibniz liked mechanical analogies for volition (T 22, G VII,304/L 488), and in particular that of the balance (cf. NE II,xxi,40). He later wrote to Clarke (V,3) that "reasons in the mind of a wise being, and motives in any mind whatsoever, do that which answers to the effect produced by weights in a balance." Though not necessitating, the balance of motives determines as certainly as the balance of weights. "We always follow the direction toward which there is more inclination or disposition" (Gr 479); we never fail to do so (T 43).

The motives that play the role of weights in the scales of volition include all our perceptions, subconscious as well as conscious, according to Leibniz.

> Several perceptions and inclinations contribute to the complete volition, which is the result of their conflict. Some of them are separately imperceptible; the mass of these makes an uneasiness which pushes us without the subject of it being seen (NE II,xxi,39; cf. Gr 480).

Here the infinite makes its appearance. For in Leibniz's system the mass of subconscious perceptions in a finite spirit is a confused perception of the whole universe, in all its infinite complexity. Every fact about the world is perceived, and our perception of it has some influence on our will; those perceptions of which we are not conscious are nonetheless weighed in the balance *en masse,* by virtue of their contribution to our feelings. Our minds, being finite, cannot completely understand the motives of our choices, because they are infinitely complex. On the same ground the connection between a free decision and its ultimate reasons or motives will be contingent, and cannot be demonstrated, in the senses laid down in the infinite analysis theory of contingency. Much of this, including some connection between contingency and the infinity of influences, is explicit in the memorandum quoted above. Leibniz speaks there of our ignorance "of an infinity of little influences on us of which we are not conscious," which sometimes lets us have the illusion that the factors moving our will are equally balanced. And he immediately adds,

> That shows that it is indeed always true that our *freedom,* and that of all other intelligent substances right up to God Himself, is accompanied by a

certain degree of indifference or contingency, which has been defined in such a way that we and those substances are never necessitated, since the contrary of that which happens always remains possible or implies no contradiction. (Gr 480f.)

The reference to God should not be taken as suggesting that God has sub-conscious motives; for Leibniz's God perceives everything distinctly. But Leibniz did say that "God had infinite reasons competing with each other, which He considered when He judged this possible universe worthy to be chosen"; he offered it as an explanation of why the truth of "This series of the universe is the best" cannot be known *a priori* by us (Gr 343). God's reasons, like ours, incline but do not necessitate, because they are involved in a conflict of such infinite complexity that the resulting volition cannot be demonstrated (in the strict sense) from them.[46]

2.5 IS "GOD CHOOSES WHAT IS BEST" CONTINGENT?

The contingency of "God chooses this world" could be explained and defended by holding either that "God chooses what is best" is contingent or that "This world is the best" is contingent. We have seen that Leibniz prefers the latter alternative; but he explicitly rejects the other in only one of the texts we examined. More often he leaves open the possibility of holding that both are contingent. There seems to have been more vacillation and uncertainty in Leibniz's mind about whether it is necessary or contingent that God chooses what is best than about any other main issue in the problem of contingency. I shall argue, however, that the view that it is necessary is required by other features of Leibniz's philosophy.

Many passages in which Leibniz appears to address this issue yield no solid evidence on it, in view of some of the subtleties that we have already seen in his position. When he says, for example, "God's decisions about contingents certainly are not necessary" (Gr 385), the claim can be taken *de re* with respect to the contingents: for any contingent, what God decides about *it* is not necessary (because it takes an infinite analysis to determine what is best). It may not be implied, therefore, that it is not necessary that God decides to order contingent things as well as possible. Similarly, when Leibniz says that "God was infallibly led by His wisdom and goodness . . . to give [the world] the best form possible; but He was not led to it necessarily" (G VI,414 [Remarks on King §14]), the expression "to it" (in French "*y*") does not make clear whether the denial of necessity applies de re to that form which is the best possible for the world, or whether it applies *de dicto* to God's giving the world *whatever* form is best. We have to bear in mind Leibniz's saying that "it is a necessary proposition" that God wills the best, but He does not will it "necessarily," because what is best is not necessarily so (Gr 493f.).

On the other hand, our present question remains equally unanswered when Leibniz says, as he often does, such things as "God cannot fail to choose the best" (see T Abridgement, VIII). For Leibniz has distinguished several sorts of inability and necessity. He may mean only a moral necessity (as he says, *ibid.* [G VI,386]); whereas we are interested in logical or metaphysical necessity.

And when Leibniz says that "God wills the best by His own nature" (Gr 289), or that the reason for His eternal free action is "the divine nature or perfection itself" (C 405), he says nothing more than is implied by his analytic theory of truth. What we want to know is whether God's voluntary optimizing is *demonstrable*—that is, whether it follows by a finite or only by an infinite analysis from the divine nature. In fact, in both the texts I have just quoted on this point, it is stated or suggested that it is not demonstrable (Gr 288, C 405).

First of all, therefore, we must seek texts in which necessity is asserted or denied, de dicto, of some such propositions as "God chooses what is best," and in which the necessity is explicitly or contextually indicated as logical or meta-physical, or is stated or explained in terms of demonstrability. There are several such texts, and they speak on both sides of the question.

The most explicit texts for the contingency of the crucial propositions date from about 1681, when Leibniz was actively engaged in formative work on a variety of solutions to the problem of contingency. He had already written, in "Necessary and Contingent Truths," that "in a certain way it is of physical necessity [which he had distinguished there from metaphysical necessity] that God does all things as well as He can" (C 21/SG 351). But about 1681 he denied flatly that the proposition, "that God chooses the best," or "God wills to choose the best," can be demonstrated (Gr 301).[47] A contrast is introduced in a similar denial in another paper from about the same time:[48] "Thus, that God loves Himself is necessary, for it is demonstrable from the definition of God. But that God does what is most perfect, cannot be demonstrated, for the contrary does not imply a contradiction" (Gr 288).

The contrast recurs in some later texts. In the early 1690s Leibniz noted with approval Thomas Aquinas's opinion "that God's attitude toward Himself is necessary and natural, but His attitude toward other things is not necessary, nor forced, but voluntary" (Gr 333).[49] And in the *Theodicy,* he says, "The love that God has for Himself is essential to Him; but the love of His glory, or the will to obtain it, is not essential to Him at all" (T 233; cf. T 175, 230). (Here God's glory is conceived as an external attribute, "the reflection of the divine perfec-tion in created beings."[50])

The contingency of "God chooses what is best" seems more favored in the *Theodicy* than in the private papers Leibniz wrote while preparing the book. In addition to this passage about God's love of His glory, there is a list of things said to be necessary "in a certain sense," but not "logically, geometrically, or metaphysically"; among them is "that God Himself chooses the best" (T 282; it would not be plausible to read this denial of logical necessity as de re with re-spect to the best). If the *Theodicy* were our only source for Leibniz's opinions, I think we would find nothing incompatible with the impression that Leibniz thinks it contingent, de dicto, that God chooses what is best. And the general tenor of the book would leave us with that impression, although most passages in it can be interpreted otherwise in the light of his other works.

Section 13 of the *Discourse on Metaphysics* gives a similar impression. Probably the most important utterance bearing on the issue there is the mention of "the first free decision of God, the import of which is to do always that which is most perfect." For if this decision is free and freedom implies contingency, it will follow that "God decided to do what is best" is contingent.

The strongest texts on the other side are those already discussed in section 2.1 above, in which Leibniz pointedly refrains from denying, and in 1706 affirms, that "God chooses the best" is logically necessary. Those texts date from about 1689 to 1706; but there is an earlier note, from about 1681, in which Leibniz says, "From God's essence or supreme perfection it follows, certainly and, so to speak, by a necessary implication, that God chooses the best" (Gr 297). He goes on to explain God's freedom in terms of the plurality of alternatives possible in their own nature. The phrase "by a necessary implication" is important here. When Leibniz wrote in 1698 that "if follows from the nature of God that He prefers the most perfect" (Gr 393), he left some ambiguity. For he also said that *all* truths, even contingent ones, follow from God, who is the highest truth (Gr 347). Might God's preference for perfection follow from His nature by an infinite rather than a finite analysis, and therefore contingently? But what follows from God's essence "by a necessary implication" must be necessary— though the qualification "so to speak" or "if you will" ("*si ita loqui placet*") still leaves a little uncertainty.

In reading notes from the 1690s Leibniz held that "the inability to do evils can be demonstrated in God" (Gr 333) and "rigorously, it can be said that the good Angels can sin, and that does not imply a contradiction, but in God it does imply one" (Gr 360). Leibniz held more consitently to this thesis than to the more general claim that it is demonstrable that God chooses the best. Even in one of the papers from about 1681 in which he states flatly that "God chooses the best" is not demonstrable, Leibniz says that damning the innocent eternally is not possible for God and is therefore one of those things "whose . . . existence implies a contradiction" (Gr 300).

The only text against this of which I am aware is in the *Theodicy*: "However it does not imply a contradiction for God to will (directly or permissively) a thing that does not imply a contradiction" (T 234). Nothing is said here explicitly about whether it is contingent, de dicto, that God does no evil or that God chooses the best. For the possibility that is asserted is pretty clearly de re with respect to the objects of God's choice: it is claimed about everything, that if it is possible in itself, considered without regard to its relation to God's will, then it is also possible for God to will to actualize it. But since Leibniz thought the eternal damnation of the innocent is possible in itself (Gr 300), it does follow that it is possible for God to damn the innocent eternally—which is not far removed from the conclusion that it is possible for God to do evil.

In general, however, Leibniz seems inclined to the view that it is demonstrable that God does no evil, whether or not it is demonstrable that He chooses the best. Indeed, even his 1706 reading note on Bayle in which he says that "God wills the work that is most worthy of Him" is a necessary proposition ends with a hint that God "cannot do or will moral evil" in some sense stronger than that in which He cannot fail to create the best possible world (Gr 494).

But if Leibniz holds that it is demonstrable that God does no evil, how can he avoid the conclusion that it is demonstrable that God does not prefer the less perfect? "For as a lesser evil is a kind of good, by the same token a lesser good is a kind of evil, if it forms an obstacle to a greater good" (T 8). And in maintaining the axiom, "*Minus bonum habet rationem mali*" ("A lesser good has the character of an evil") (T 194, DM 3, G III,33), Leibniz does not suggest that it is contingent. So it seems that preferring the less perfect would necessarily be doing something evil.

God is more than sinless. That "God is an absolutely perfect being," morally as well as metaphysically, is virtually a definition for Leibniz (DM 1); and so far as I know he never suggests that it is contingent. If it is not true by definition, or at least demonstrable, how is he so confident that it is true at all? Surely he does not know it by experience. And he denies that it is known only by faith (T Preliminary Discourse 44). Both Rescher and Curley seem to me to err in saying that Leibniz would solve the problem of contingency by holding that God's goodness is contingent.[51]

But that is not the only way in which he could deny that it is necessary that God does what is best. For the belief that God does what is best is based on two premises: that God is "a most perfect Being," and that "the operation of a most perfect Being is most perfect" (Gr 16). And Leibniz did once say that the second of these is contingent: "God's choosing a less perfect from among many perfect things does not imply an imperfection in God" (Gr 300 [about 1681]). I agree with this statement,[52] but find it astonishingly un-Leibnizian and do not think it fits in his philosophical system.

One objection to including it in the system is inconclusive. Leibniz says it is morally necessary for God to choose the best. And this means that it is necessary that a perfectly good agent in God's position would choose the best (see section 1.5 above). It follows that it is necessary that if God chooses the less perfect, He is imperfect (cf. G III,33). But the crucial question here is whether this is a *logical* necessity. Is the morally necessary only what it is *demonstrable* that a perfectly good agent would do? Or is it enough for moral necessity if the action is contained in the concept of a perfectly good agent, even though an infinite analysis would be needed to show the reason of the containment? The weaker requirement seems to me to be the one assumed in Leibniz's mature writings. For he appears to regard God's choice of this world as morally necessary (cf. T Preliminary Discourse 2); but it is not demonstrable that a perfectly good agent would choose this world, since it is not demonstrable that this world is the best.

There are other arguments, however, which show that Leibniz cannot consistently hold that it is contingent that a supremely perfect being would choose the more perfect. For suppose that is contingent. Then it must either be contingent that a supremely perfect being is perfectly good, wise, and just; or else contingent that a perfectly good, wise, and just being would choose the more perfect. Neither of these is contingent for Leibniz.

For he regards justice as "an essential attribute of God" (Dutens IV,iii, 280; this is not asserted but contextually implied there). And since God's justice, for Leibniz, "depends on wisdom and goodness" (Dutens IV,iii,261; cf. G III, 34), the latter perfections must presumably he regarded as essential to God too.

Leibniz would also have to admit that it can be demonstrated, from acceptable definitions of these perfections, that they imply a preference for the best. For he says,

> The end of goodness is the greatest good, but in order to recognize it, wisdom is needed, which is nothing other than knowledge of the good, as goodness is nothing other than the inclination to do good to all, and to prevent evil unless it is necessary for a greater good or to prevent a greater evil.[53]

Thus Leibniz seems unable to escape the conclusion that it is demonstrable, and hence logically necessary, that God, as an absolutely perfect being, does what is best.

The conflict in Leibniz's thought is reflected in divergent pronouncements about "the root of contingency." About 1683 he set out, somewhat tentatively, the idea that in dealing with problems of contingency we must "have recourse to that one thing which is not essential in God, but free—namely, the decision of the will, from which alone a source of contingency in things can be sought" (Gr 311). This is not unambiguous, but seems to agree with Rescher's judgment that for Leibniz "the ultimate source of contingent truth is clearly" in God's choosing "to act in the most perfect way," rather than in the bestness of that which is chosen.[54] But elsewhere Leibniz locates the root of contingency, not in the divine will, but in the objects among which God chooses. About 1681 he wrote, "The root of freedom in God is the possibility or contingency of things"—by which he means the plurality of alternatives possible in themselves, as the context shows (Gr 298). About 1695, likewise, he wrote notes on the views, ascribed to Scotus and Aquinas respectively, that the root of contingency is in the will of God as free, and that it is in the will of God as efficacious. Leibniz commented on the former view that it was circular, and on the latter that "contingency is in the nature itself of truth, or of the object, as of possibility, as of existence" (Gr 348; cf. Gr 353). Here perhaps what he has in mind is that contingent truths cannot be proved by a finite analysis.

The circle with which Leibniz charged Scotus has to do, presumably, with seeking the ultimate reason for all contingent facts in a divine decision that is itself one of the contingent facts to be explained. Often Leibniz sees an infinite regress in place of this circle, and almost always he condemns it as vicious. There is one text, however, in which he accepts the infinite regress; and this acceptance assumes great importance for the interpretations of Rescher and Curley.

The first principle about Existences is this proposition: *God wills to choose the most perfect.* This proposition cannot be demonstrated; it is the first of all propositions of fact, or the origin of every contingent existence. . . . For if anyone asks me why God decided to create Adam, I say; because He decided to do what is most perfect. If you ask me now why He decided to do what is most perfect, . . . I answer that He willed it freely, or because He willed to. Therefore He willed because He willed to will, and so on to infinity. (Gr 301f.)

Curley says that this text presents "the only one of the various ways in which Leibniz invokes infinite processes which seems . . . to have any bearing on the problem of contingency."[55] Rescher does not cite this passage, but proposes, as Leibniz's main solution of the problem of contingency, that "God's moral perfection follows from His metaphysical perfection, but the deduction would require an infinity of steps."[56] Something of this sort is required, of course, if the supposed contingency of "God chooses what is best" is to be reconciled with Leibniz's analytic theory of truth and infinite analysis theory of contingency.

Rescher's formulation deftly avoids the obvious objection that the infinite regress of reasons violates the principle of sufficient reason. Leibniz's use of the principle in proving the existence of God requires him to refuse to accept an infinite regress of reasons as itself constituting a sufficient reason. Furthermore Leibniz had said "it is absurd. [to suppose] that a free will is an ultimate reason, since the free will itself has its necessary conditions [*requisita*], for it is not an independent Being [*Ens a se*]" (Conf 46 [a marginal comment, probably from late 1677 or early 1678]). A sufficient reason must be found in something of metaphysical necessity; the ultimate reason for the existence of all things is to be found in the divine essence and intellect. Rescher recognizes and accepts this. On his interpretation the ultimate sufficient reason is found in God's metaphysical perfection; if there is an infinite regress of volitions, it has a reason outside itself in God's nature. But in conformity with the infinite analysis theory of contingency, this reason cannot be proved by a finite analysis.

In the paper in which he accepts the regress, however, Leibniz was not so deft as Rescher. For he refused there to ground the infinite regress of volitions in God's essence. "No other reason can be given why God chooses the most perfect than because He wills to. . . . And certainly He wills freely, because outside His will no other reason can be given than the will." He goes on to claim that "nothing is therefore given without a reason, but that reason is intrinsic to the will" (Gr 301). But the infinite regress of volitions he describes certainly does not satisfy his principle of sufficient reason.

It is noteworthy, moreover, that this rather early paper contains no explicit appeal to the infinite analysis theory of contingency. I know of no work in which Leibniz develops the infinite regress of volitions into the sort of solution that Rescher proposes for him.

For this text, as Grua says (Gr 259), is exceptional. It is the same short paper in which Leibniz denied that choosing the less perfect would imply an imperfection in God. And the infinite regress of volitions, and the whole idea of willing to will, were explicitly rejected by Leibniz, at about the same time as well as both earlier and later. About 1681 he wrote, "indeed God cannot will voluntarily; otherwise there would be a will to will [and so on] to infinity" (Grua 289). In the letter to Wedderkopf and in *The Philosopher's Confession* he had denied, with explicit reference to God, that anyone wills what to will (A II,i,117/L 147) or wills because he wills (Conf 54). In the *New Essays* Leibniz says, "We do not will to will, but we will to do; and if we willed to will, we would will to will to will, and that would go to infinity" (NE II,xxi,22-23). Here nothing is said explicitly about God. But there is explicit reference to God in the *Theodicy* where Leibniz says, "It is, in a sense, an abuse of terms to say here: one can will, one wills to will; power is related here to the actions that one wills" (T 234).

There are, it must be granted, two texts that support the idea that divine decisions, considered as possible, are part of the object of other divine decisions (C 24), or more vaguely, that "God executes all reflex acts at once and once for all" (Gr 345). And indeed Leibniz thought of possible divine decisions as involved in the concepts of possible creatures among which God chooses. But in these texts it is not stated or suggested that God's general decision to do what is best is the object of a prior decision, nor that the regress of decisions provides the *reason* for the decision to act.

At any rate the infinite regress of volitions is clearly not a keystone of Leibniz's position on contingency. On this as well as other grounds that we have reviewed, it is fair to say that the view that "God chooses what is best" is contingent must not be regarded as a thesis of Leibniz's philosophy, much less as a basis of one of his principal solutions to the problem of contingency.

2.6 AN EXCEPTION FOR EXISTENCE?

We are now in a position to deal with the question whether Leibniz meant to solve the problem of contingency by making existence an exception to the rule that the predicate of a true proposition must be contained in the concept of the subject. There are several compelling arguments for a negative answer.

1) Leibniz says something that looks very much like an explicit negative answer, in the *New Essays*:

> But when one says that a thing exists, or that it has real existence, this existence itself is the predicate—that is to say, it has a concept linked with the idea that is in question, and there is a connection between these two concepts (NE IV,i,3-7).[57]

2) In many formulations of his analytic theory of truth Leibniz says explicitly that the concept of the predicate is contained in the concept of the

subject in contingent as well as necessary truths (FC 179/L263f.; G II,56/L-A 63; C 16/SG 346; C 519/L 267f.; C 272; G VII,199f.; Gr 303). In view of these statements, it seems perverse to suppose that Leibniz meant to explain the possibility of contingency by making an exception to the theory for those propositions that he regarded as contingent.

3) Leibniz made a number of attempts to explain how existence is contained in the concepts of those things that exist. These attempts typically involve some or all of the following claims. The predicate of existence is in some way equivalent to "entering into the most perfect series of things" (C 9; cf. Gr 325, B 119f., C405, C360, 376/P 51, 65f.), or to pleasing God (C 405; cf. C 376/P 65f.). The analysis of concepts would have to be carried to infinity, however, to prove the existence of any contingent thing (C 376/P 66; cf. Gr 304f.). The underlying idea, of course, is that existence is contained in the concept of existing things, not directly but by virture of the factors that determine God to create those things.

4) As Couturat pointed out, "existential propositions are not the only contingent propositions" for Leibniz.[58] Couturat chose an unfortunate example: laws of nature, which are indeed contingent, but are also existential according to Leibniz, as Curley has pointed out.[59] But in sections 2.1 and 2.3 above we have seen better examples of contingent propositions whose truth, according to Leibniz, does not depend on what exists—namely, the propositions asserting the bestness of this possible world and the contingent connections within possible worlds.

5) The version of the problem of contingency that troubled Leibniz most persistently throughout his life does not depend on his conception of the nature of truth, and cannot be solved by making the predicate of existence an exception to that conception. For the problem is that the existence of all actual things seems to follow, not just from their own concepts, but from the concept of God, whose existence Leibniz always regarded as necessary.

There are some texts, however, that seem to speak on the other side of the question. Foremost among them is a passage near the end of the early paper "Necessary and Contingent Truths." The paper seems somewhat confused on the point that concerns us. For although it contains a statement that the concept of the predicate is contained in the concept of the subject even in contingent truths (C 16), and an effort to explain how the existences of contingent things are involved in their concepts, it also contains the statement, "For the possibility or Concept of a created mind does not involve existence" (C 23). The most favorable interpretation that we can put on this statement is that Leibniz is groping after the distinction that he later articulated between the complete concept of a thing and its essence (Gr 383). The essence or specific concept of any created substance would not contain the existence of that substance, although the complete concept would. As was noted in section 2.3 above, this distinction does not seem to me to serve the purpose of rendering propositions contingent in themselves.

It is a distinction that is needed, however, to bring into any sort of tolerable harmony with the rest of Leibniz's system the fairly numerous texts in which he treats "essential" and "existential" as equivalent, respectively, to "necessary" and "contingent." In some of these texts, indeed, he explains "essential" in terms of things that "flow from incomplete and specific concepts" (Gr 311; cf. Gr 383). In other texts he leaves the sense of "essential" unexplained (Gr 354, 373); and he never manifests any concern about reconciling his use of "existential" with the fact that he holds, and his system implies, that some contingent truths do not depend on which finite things actually exist. It is difficult to shake off the impression that Leibniz was subject to some persistent confusion on this point.

3. LEIBNIZ AND POSSIBLE WORLDS SEMANTICS

It has been discovered that by beginning with the idea that the possible is what is true in some possible world and the necessary is what is true in all possible worlds, and varying our assumptions about the relations of possible worlds to each other, we can obtain models that validate different systems of modal logic. This discovery has given birth to possible worlds semantics—the interpretation of modal notions in terms of truth and falsity in (or at) possible worlds. It has shed so much light on modal logic, and has so affected our interest in the notion of possible worlds, that it is especially natural for us to assume that Leibniz too conceived of necessity as truth in all possible worlds and contingency as truth in some but not all possible worlds. But it is not at all clear that he did.

Probably the closest he comes to expressing this conception is in the early paper on "Necessary and Contingent Truths," where he says that necessary truths, which can be demonstrated by analysis of terms, "not only will obtain while the World stands, but also would have obtained if GOD had created the World on a different plan" (C 18/SG 348). This is suggestive but not conclusive; for on any reasonable interpretation of Leibniz, he regards no world as possible in which something demonstrable is false (if we overlook the problem about the damnation of the innocent that was discussed in section 2.2 above). What we want to know is whether he thought that all the truths that do not depend on which world God created are necessary. He almost says that they are. He says that contingent truths, which cannot be demonstrated by analysis, "do not express only what pertains to the possibility of things, but also what actually exists, or would be going to exist if certain conditions were satisfied" (C 18/SG 348). In this statement it is not clear whether the counterfactual conditional is supposed to rest on causal laws, in which case its truth depends on which world is actual, or whether it just means "would exist in some possible world." But the initial parts of "Necessary and Contingent Truths" seem to me in general to reflect the assumption that contingent truths depend on which world is actual.

On the other hand, Leibniz regarded as contingent some truths that he would hardly have regarded as depending on which world God actualized. The most obvious example in this category is the proposition that this world is the best possible.

The first step in dealing with this problem is to distinguish two things Leibniz may mean by "possible world." He may mean a world whose concept is not *demonstrably* inconsistent, or he may mean a world whose *basic* concept does not involve (demonstrably or otherwise) a contradiction or conceptual falsehood.

The first of these interpretations fits with Leibniz's usual conception of necessity in terms of demonstrability, and indeed yields a possible worlds semantics for it. Because it is plausible to suppose that not all conceptual truths are demonstrable, the conceptual truth and demonstrability conceptions of necessity demand different modal logics. The strong system S5 seems to be the right modal logic for the conceptual truth conception of necessity.[60] But the characteristic axiom of S5, "$\sim Np \supset N \sim Np$" (if not necessarily p, then necessarily not necessarily p), is not valid on the demonstrability conception of necessity. For a proposition may be indemonstrable without being demonstrably indemonstrable. (In rejecting this axiom, it should be noted, one rejects the assumption that all truths about the possible as such are necessary.) The weaker system S4 seems to be the right system for the demonstrability conception of necessity. Its characteristic axiom, "$Np \supset NNp$" (if necessarily p, then necessarily necessarily p), will be valid under that conception; for what can be demonstrated can thereby be demonstrated to be demonstrable.

By the same token, if we assume that a world w_2 is possible in a world w_1 if and only if nothing is true in w_2 whose falsity can be demonstrated in w_1, we obtain the result that the relation among possible worlds expressed by "possible in" is reflexive and transitive but not symmetrical. It is reflexive, if we restrict consideration to worlds that are possible (that is, possible in the actual world); for Leibniz will surely hold that "Something is true which is demonstrably false" is (in the actual world) demonstrably false, but it must be true in any world that is not possible in itself. The transitivity of the "possible in" relation is proved as follows. Suppose there is a world w_2 that is possible in world w_1, and a world w_3 that is possible in w_2 but not in w_1. There must be some proposition p that is true in w_3 but whose falsity can be demonstrated in w_1, though not in w_2. But then there is a proposition (that p is not demonstrably false) that is true in w_2 but demonstrably false in w_1; its falsity is demonstrated in w_1 by demonstrating the falsity of p. So w_2 is not possible in w_1, contrary to the hypothesis; and the "possible in" relation must be transitive after all. It is not symmetrical, however. For there is, as Leibniz supposes, at least one proposition p that is possible, and actually true, but not demonstrably possible. A world in which it is true that p is demonstrably false will therefore be possible in the actual world, but the actual world will not be possible in such a world.

It is known that a "possible in" relation that is reflexive and transitive but not symmetrical is the principal feature that a system of possible worlds should have if it is to provide a semantics for S4 but not for S5.[61] Thus the possible worlds semantics based on the demonstrability conception of possible worlds seems to fit the modal logic suggested by the demonstrability conception of necessity.

But does Leibniz hold this conception of possible worlds? Certainly he does not work out an S4 semantics; he does not even raise the question of a "possible in" relation among possible worlds. The crucial question is whether he understands "possible" in "possible world" in terms of demonstrability and indemonstrability.

He says something that implies that he does:

> There are as many possible worlds as there are series of things that can be thought up which do not imply a contradiction. This thesis is identical with me, for I call possible that which does not imply a contradiction, and so in this sense it cannot be refuted. (Gr 390 [March, 1698])

I assume that "does not imply a contradiction" expresses a proof-theoretical notion here, as it usually does in Leibniz. On this interpretation Leibniz here lets a consistent, univocal use of modal terms carry the proof-theoretical or demonstrability conception of possibility into his conception of possible worlds.

On the other hand, the demonstrability conception of possible worlds has some strikingly un-Leibnizian consequences. (1) A possible individual will in general exist in more than one possible world. Leibniz holds that many of the properties contained in an individual's complete concept cannot be demonstrated from the concept. Worlds in which the individual lacks various of those properties will therefore not be demonstrably inconsistent. (2) Each actual individual will be compossible with individuals of almost every possible sort, in the sense of coexisting in some possible world with an individual of that sort. For the coexistence of a certain actual individual with any possible sort of individual will rarely if ever be demonstrably inconsistent.

3) There will be possible worlds in which different worlds will be the best possible; for the bestness of this world is not demonstrable. (4) There will be possible worlds that have (with one exception) all the perfections that the actual world (considered as possible) has, and more. There will be, for example, a world as good as the actual world in other respects, from which the horrors of the Thirty Years war are absent. Leibniz surely did not think it could be demonstrated that the world would be less perfect without the Thirty Years War. The exception, the perfection that the actual world has but those worlds lack, is *conceptual consistency,* as we may call the property of not involving, not even indemonstrably, a contradiction.

Leibniz never accepts these consequences. Indeed he explicitly rejects the idea of an individual existing in more than one possible world (DM 30, T 414). And for certain crucial purposes in his theory of creation he *needs* modalities quite different from those that are generated by the demonstrability conception of necessity. His explanation of why God did not create Judas (precisely and individually Judas) without his treason is that even God *couldn't* do that.

Similarly he must claim that God couldn't have created a world as good as the actual world in other respects but lacking the horrors of the Thirty Years War. These "couldn't"'s cannot be explained in terms of demonstrability. And Leibniz certainly does not mean that God was prevented by His *goodness* from choosing these worlds, having judged that Judas's treason and the horrors of the Thirty Years War are better than conceptual inconsistency. Rather it is not within God's *power* to create such worlds, because they are not possible in their own nature.

The claim that two possible substances are *compossible,* likewise, is surely not just the claim that they are not *demonstrably* incompatible, in spite of that fact that Leibniz defined "compossible" as "that which with another does not imply a contradiction" (Gr 325). For it is lack of compossibility that keeps additional excellent substances from existing in the actual world (G III,572f., C 534). But the addition of such substances is surely not demonstrably inconsistent with the concept of actual things.

One may be tempted to accuse Leibniz of cheating in his theodicy by using modal terms equivocally. There is a sense in which God couldn't have created a better world than He did (it is conceptually false that there is such a world). But in that sense He also couldn't have done anything different at all (it is conceptually false that He does anything different). There is also a sense in which He could have done something different (it is not demonstrable that He does not, say, omit to create giraffes). But in that sense He could also have made something better than this world (it is not demonstrable that no possible alternative is better).

There is yet another sense of "could" and "couldn't" available to Leibniz, however, in which he can say, without equivocation, both of the things he wants to say. God could have done something different, in the sense that only His goodness keeps Him from doing so. But He couldn't have created a better world than this, in the sense that it is not only His goodness that keeps a better alternative from being possible. We could systematize these modalities (although Leibniz did not) by using "It is possible that p" to mean roughly that if it were not a conceptual truth that God is perfectly good, it would not be a conceptual falsehood that p.[62]

Leibniz's chief use of the imagery of possible worlds is at those points in his theory of creation that require this last sort of modality. "There are several possible Universes, each collection of compossibles making one of them" (G III, 573). The possible worlds are the alternative among which God chooses, and among which only His goodness keeps Him from choosing otherwise than He does. There must not be among them a world in which Judas exists but is not a traitor, or which is as good in other ways as the actual world but lacks the horrors of the Thirty Years War. The conception of a possible world that is implied by this use of the imagery, and which must therefore be reckoned Leibniz's principal conception, is not that of a world that is not demonstrably inconsistent. It is rather that of a world whose basic concept does not involve (demonstrably or otherwise) a contradiction or conceptual falsehood, a world whose basic concept is conceptually consistent.[63]

If we admit to the basic concepts of worlds information about everything except God's goodness and His choice among worlds (see section 1.2 above), this conception of possible worlds probably yields a satisfactory semantics for "It is possible that p" interpreted as meaning that if it were not a conceptual truth that God is perfectly good, it would not be a conceptual falsehood that p. But although it would be helpful in explaining his theory of creation, Leibniz does not really develop this interpretation, and does not usually use "it is possible that" in this sense. His main conception of possibility is the proof-theoretical one that can be analyzed in terms of indemonstrability of falsehood. Thus Leibniz's main conception of possible worlds does not provide a possible worlds semantics for his main conception of possibility. If we put the two main conceptions together, we get the result that there are propositions that are possible but are not true in any possible world. "Judas exists without betraying Jesus" is such a proposition.

I do not mean to suggest that Leibniz was fully aware of the diversity of sorts of modality at work in his philosophy. Had he been conscious of it he would presumably have articulated the relevant distinctions more clearly, and avoided some apparent inconsistencies. He might also have explored the relations between the different sorts of modality and the notion of a possible world. But he did not, and it is quite misleading to think of him as a grandfather of possible worlds semantics, given the bad fit between his principal conception of possible worlds and his principal modal concepts.

4. EPILOGUE: ON LEIBNIZ'S SINCERITY

On no point has more suspicion of a cleavage between a public and a private Leibnizian philosophy arisen than on the problem of contingency. Leibniz's sincerity in the *Theodicy* has often been impugned, and often defended. It is partly but not entirely vindicated by the results of the present investigation.

It is emphatically clear in the *Theodicy*, as in the rest of his work, that Leibniz is a compatibilist and a determinist. The solution of the problem of contingency that is most clearly developed in the *Theodicy*, that nonactual things are possible in themselves even if they are not possible in relation to God's will, is one that Leibniz also held, and never abandoned, in his private papers from 1673 on. It is a solution that imposes a minimum of qualification on the necessity of all things.

The infinite analysis theory of contingency is partly stated in the *Theodicy*, in §14 of the Remarks on King:

For one may say in a way that these two principles [of contradiction and sufficient reason] are contained in the definition of True and False. Nevertheless, when in making the analysis of the truth that has been proposed one sees it depending on truths whose contrary implies a contradiction, one may say that it is absolutely necessary. But when in pushing the analysis as far as one pleases one is never able to arrive at such elements of given truth, one must say that it is contingent. (G VI,414)

Here, as in a letter to Louis Bourguet in 1715 (G III,582), Leibniz says that necessary truths receive a finite analysis and contingent truths do not, but without stating that this is what contingency consists in, or that the concept of the predicate is contained in the concept of the subject even in contingent truths.

We have seen that the view that "God chooses what is best" is contingent, about which Leibniz was very hesitant in his private papers, seems to occur in one or two passages of the *Theodicy*. This might be due to some development in his thought, but no such explanation is plausible for the *Theodicy's* striking omission of any mention of the view that it is contingent that this world is the best. The latter view was well worked out, affirmed, and never rejected in Leibniz's private papers; and it is plausibly inferred from his infinite analysis theory of contingency, which he clearly continued to believe when he wrote the *Theodicy*.

Moreover, the frequent and unelucidated use that the book makes of the terms "moral necessity," "hypothetical necessity," and "incline without necessitating" leaves the reader with a less necessitarian impression of Leibniz's thought than these terms would leave if they were accompanied by the explanations of their meaning that are presented or suggested by his less public writings. One is not reassured about Leibniz's sincerity when one reads, in a letter from Leibniz to Des Bosses discussing the use of "moral necessity" in the *Theodicy*, the comment, "And in general I should prefer the words to be interpreted in such a way that nothing bad-sounding follows" (G II,419).

The lack of candor in the *Theodicy* is evident; the motives for it, whether pedagogical or self-protective, are not. It is interesting that Leibniz had written once, probably during the years 1675-1677,

Metaphysics should be written with accurate definitions and demonstrations, but nothing should be demonstrated in it that conflicts too much with received opinions. Thus this metaphysics will be able to be received. If it is once approved, then afterwards, if any examine it more profoundly, they will deduce that the consequences are necessary.[64]

One of the difficulties in the *Theodicy*, however, is that so many of Leibniz's "accurate definitions" are omitted that one must turn to other works to find the material necessary for a profounder examination.[65]

Notes

1. Bertrand Russell, *A Critical Exposition of the Philosophy of Leibniz*, 2nd ed. (London: George Allen & Unwin, 1937), p. 27. The views discussed here belong to the first edition, however, and were retracted in the Preface to the second edition.

2. E. M. Curley, "Recent Work on 17th Century Continental Philosophy," *American Philosophical Quarterly 11* (1974): 242.

3. The works of Leibniz are cited by the following abbreviations: A = Leibniz, *Sämtliche Schriften und Briefe*, Academy edition (Darmstadt and Berlin, 1923–), cited by series, volume, and page. B = *Die Leibniz-Handschriften der Königlichen Öffentlichen Bibliothek zu Hannover*, ed. Eduard Bodeman (Hannover and Leipzig, 1895). C = *Opuscules et fragments inédits de Leibniz*, ed. Louis Couturat (Paris, 1903). Conf = Leibniz, *Confessio Philosophi*, ed. and trans. (into German), with commentary, Otto Saame (Frankfurt, 1967). DM = *Discourse on Metaphysics*, cited by section number. Dutens = Leibniz, *Opera omnia*, ed. L. Dutens (Geneva, 1768), cited by volume, part, and page, FC = *Nouvelles lettres et opuscules inédits de Leibniz*, ed Foucher de Careil (Paris, 1857). G = *Die philosophischen Schriften von Gottfried Wilhelm Leibniz*, ed, C. I. Gerhardt (Berlin, 1875-1890), cited by volume and page. Gr = Leibniz, *Textes inédits*, ed. Gaston Grua (Paris, 1948). L = Leibniz, *Philosophical Papers and Letters*, trans. and ed. Leroy E. Loemker, 2nd ed. (Dordrecht and Boston, 1969). L-A = *The Leibniz-Arnauld Correspondence*, ed. and trans. H. T. Mason (Manchester, 1967). NE = *New Essays Concerning Human Understanding*, cited by book, chapter, and section. P = *Leibniz: Logical Papers*, trans. and ed G. H. R. Parkinson (Oxford: Clarendon Press, 1966). SG = *From Descartes to Kant*, ed. T. V. Smith and Marjorie Grene (Chicago, 1940). T = *Theodicy*, cited by the main series of section numbers, unless otherwise noted. To Clarke = Leibniz's side of the Leibniz-Clarke correspondence, cited by letter and paragraph number. W = *Leibniz Selections*, ed. Philip P. Wiener (New York, 1951).

All works are cited by page number unless otherwise noted above. Entries separated by a slash refer to the original and an English translation of the same passage. I take responsibility for the translation of all quotations, although I have made some use of existing English versions.

For the dating of Leibniz's works I follow, where available, the estimates given by Heinrich Schepers, "Zum Problem der Kontingenz bei Leibniz," in *Collegium Philosophicum* (Basel and Stuttgart, 1965), pp. 326-50, on the basis of the then current thinking of the staff of the Academy edition. Otherwise the dates used here are those given in the editions.

4. All quotations in this section are from this letter, unless otherwise indicated.

5. Both dates are allowed, though perhaps the earlier is favored, in the Academy edition (A VI.i,537 and ii,579). But Willy Kabitz, the principal editor, seems to have assumed the later date in his previous work, *Die Philosophie des jungen Leibniz* (Heidelberg: Carl Winters Universitätsbuchhandlung, 1909), pp. 121-26.

6. Here Grua inadvertently omits the clause, "*etsi eius coexistentia cum Deo aliquo modo dici possit implicare contradictionem.*"

7. Leibniz does not spell out such a distinction as this. Does he mean the basic or the complete concept of a possible world when he says, "this universe has a certain principal or primitive concept, of which particular events are only consequences" (G II, 41/L-A 44)?

8. This suggests a conception of possible worlds as less complete than they are normally conceived to be today. A similarly restricted conception persisted in post-Leibnizian German philosophy. Thus "the world" is defined by Wolff as a connected "series of changeable things," and by Crusius as "the whole aggregate of all finite things" (Christian Wolff, *Vernünftige Gedanken von Gott, der Welt, und der Seele des Menschen*, 9te Auflage [Halle, 1743], §544; and Christian August Crusius, *Entwurf der nothwendigen Vernunft-Wahrheiten*, 2te vermehrte Auflage [Leipzig, 1753; reproduced Darmstadt: Wissenschaftliche Buchgesellschaft, 1963], §204).

9. E. M. Curley, "Recent Work on 17th Century Continental Philosophy," p. 243. Substantially the same objection was raised by a "Roman Catholic Theologian" whom Des Bosses consulted and quoted in a note to §201 in his Latin translation of the *Theodicy* (Dutens I,273).

10. I use ordinary quotation marks in place of corner quotes, since the latter are not universally understood.

11. I owe this information, and the phrase "first Theodicy," to Saame's introduction, Conf 14, 16, 22.

12. Here I translate Saame's text, minus Leibniz's later additions.

13. Leibniz, *Leibnitiana: Elementa philosophiae arcanae de summa rerum*, ed. I. Jagodinsky (Kazan, 1913). p. 8, quoted by Schepers, "Zum Problem der Kontingenz," p. 355, n. 24. The previous quotation is from the same page of Jagodinsky, quoted by Saame in Conf 167, n. 107. Both quotations are dated December 1675.

14. Here I translate Saame's full text, italicizing Leibniz's principal additions.

15. Here the emphasized words were underlined by Leibniz.

16. On Steno's dealings with Leibniz, see Saame, Conf 20-23.

17. The two passages quoted here were called to my attention by David Blumenfeld, who also pointed out to me the problem that they cause for my interpretation.

18. Since first writing this section I have discovered that Margaret Wilson has also remarked on this respect in which Leibniz's determinism is not Spinozistic, in her interesting paper, "Leibniz's Dynamics and Contingency in Nature," in Peter Machamer and Robert Turnbull, eds., *Motion and Time, Space and Matter* (Ohio State University Press, 1976). p. 285.

19. Leibniz used the concept of moral necessity much earlier, but had applied it to God's choice of the best only since 1707, according to Gaston Grua, *Jurisprudence universelle et théodicée selon Leibniz* (Paris: Presses Universitaires de France, 1953) (Cited as *Jurisprudence* hereafter), p. 235.

20. Leibniz first wrote "God's general decision is necessary"—then changed it, producing a sentence that is quite awkward in the original.

21. Schepers's date; Grua suggested 1686. The paper belongs to a period when Leibniz was in comfortable possession of the infinite analysis theory of contingency. Grua is responsible for the title, "On Contingency." In my translation I omit the many phrases crossed out by Leibniz.

22. "*Verité.*" Grua, by mistake, has "*suite.*" Grua has also inserted quotation marks in the text of this passage.

23. December 1705, dated 1706. See Elisabeth Labrousse, *Pierre Bayle*, Vol. 1 (The Hague: Martinus Nijhoff, 1963), p. 259, n. 88. Leibniz had seen the volume by February 1706 (G III,143).

24. Nicholas Rescher, *The Philosophy of Leibniz* (Englewood Cliffs: Prentice-Hall, 1967), pp. 69f.

25. E. M. Curley, "The Root of Contingency," in *Leibniz: A Collection of Critical Essays* ed., Harry Frankfurt (Garden City, N.Y.: Doubleday Anchor Books, 1972), p. 94.

26. Rescher, *Philosophy of Leibniz*, pp. 69f.

27. As Lovejoy points out in this connection (Arthur O. Lovejoy, *The Great Chain of Being* [Cambridge, Mass.: Harvard University Press, 1936], p. 173).

28. Grua has "*Et hoc arcano*" where he should have "*Et hic arcanum.*"

29. "*Etsi.*" Grua has "*et.*"

30. FC's "*ab*" is a misreading of "*atque.*"

31. Alfred Tarski, "Einige Betrachtunger über die Begriffe der ω-Widerspruchsfreiheit und der ω-Vollständigkeit," *Monatshefte für Mathematik und Physik* 40 (1933): 97-112.

32. Louis Couturat, "On Leibniz's Metaphysics," trans. in Frankfurt, ed., *Leibniz*, p. 31; Rescher, *Philosophy of Leibniz*, pp. 38f; William E. Abraham, "Complete Concepts and Leibniz's Distinction between Necessary and Contingent Propositions," *Studia Leibnitiana* I (1969): 278; C. D. Broad, *Leibniz: An Introduction* (Cambridge University Press, 1975). p. 35; cf. Curley, "The Root of Contingency," p. 94.

33. Cf. Ian Hacking, "Infinite Analysis," *Studia Leibnitiana* 4 (1974): 127f.

34. Lovejoy, *Great Chain of Being*, p. 175. Cf. Frederick Copleston, S. J., *A History of Philosophy*, Vol. IV (Garden City, N.Y.: Doubleday Image Books, 1963), p. 286.

35. Bertrand Russell, "Recent Work on the Philosophy of Leibniz," *Mind* 12 (1903), reprinted in Frankfurt, ed., *Leibniz*, p. 378, n. 8.

36. Rescher, *Philosophy of Leibniz*, p. 44, n. 24.

37. In DM 13 and §§131 and perhaps 74 of *Generales Inquisitiones* (C 388, 376f.),

Leibniz seems to speak of a "demonstration" of contingent truths that is beyond the powers of finite minds to accomplish. And in an early text (G VII,194) he speaks of all truths as "demonstrable." This may be due either to carelessness or to some variation in his terminology during a formative period of his thought. Usually (e.g., C lf.) he is careful not to say contingent truths have "demonstrations" though they have "proofs" *a priori* that are known to God.

38. Curley, "The Root of Contingency," p. 94.

39. Russell, "Recent Work on the Philosophy of Leibniz," p. 374, n. 5; cf. Russell, *A Critical Exposition of the Philosophy of Leibniz*, p. 26.

40. Broad, *Leibniz: An Introduction*, p. 36; Curley, "The Root of Contingency," pp. 92f.

41. Fabrizio Mondadori, in "Leibniz and the Doctrine of Inter-World Identity," *Studia Leibnitiana* 7 (1975): 32f., takes it that what is not necessary here is the actualization of the individual; but that does not adequately explain why Leibniz should call the *connection* contingent.

42. See p. 247f.

43. I am indebted to William Irvine for this name for it.

44. Cf. Broad, *Leibniz: An Introduction*, p. 27.

45. Lovejoy, *Great Chain of Being*, p. 174.

46. Leibniz seems strangely to overlook this point in a letter to Jaquelot of 1704, where he explicitly links the notion of inclining with things being too complex for us to understand them. For he says that "future things are contained in the soul even less than in God, because they are in the soul distinctly only in an inclining and confused way, and not explicitly and perfectly as in the Divine ideas" (G III,472). This linkage of themes is revealing, but Leibniz has the shoe on the wrong foot in this text. For he thinks that God too is only inclined, not necessitated by reasons (T 230), although His perceptions are in no way confused. It is not confusion, therefore, but the infinity of factors which in our finite minds gives rise to confusion, that is of the essence of inclination.

47. Leibniz muddied the waters a little by adding "or identical" to the claim that the first of these is "a first proposition"; but the context makes clear that what he really wanted to say is that it is *like* an identical proposition in being a truth but undemonstrable.

48. This paper (quoted in section 1.2 above) is also an important source for the view that nonactual things remain possible in their own natures even if they are not possible in respect to the divine will. It might be quibbled whether in the quoted passage demonstrability is denied only de re, with respect to that which is most perfect; but I think that would be an unnatural reading of the text.

49. The same set of notes, however, expresses the view that it is demonstrable that God cannot do evils, which I will discuss below. The reference to Aquinas is given as *Summa contra gentiles*, I,lxxxii ff.; it should have been given as I,lxxx ff.

50. Grua, *Jurisprudence*, p. 307.

51. Rescher, *Philosophy of Leibniz*, p. 45; Curley, "The Root of Contingency," p. 95.

52. Robert Merrihew Adams, "Must God Create the Best?" *The Philosophical Review* 81 (1972): 317-32.

53. Quoted by Grua, *Jurisprudence*, pp. 212f., from *Mittheilungen aus Leibnizens ungedruckten Schriften*, ed G. Mollat (Leipzig, 1883), p. 48. Grua says the text is from 1701-1705. On this subject see in general pp. 198-222 of Grua's *Jurisprudence*.

54. Rescher, *Philosophy of Leibniz*, p. 39.

55. Curley, "The Root of Contingency," p. 96.

56. Rescher, *Philosophy of Leibniz*, p. 45.

57. I owe this reference to Abraham, "Complete Concepts," p. 278.

58. Couturat, "On Leibniz's Metaphysics," p. 28.

59. Curley, "The Root of Contingency," p. 91.

60. See Robert Merrihew Adams, "The Logical Structure of Anselm's Arguments," *The Philosophical Review* 80 (1971): 45f., for a brief argument on this point.

61. Saul Kripke, "Semantical Analysis of Modal Logic 1: Normal Propositional Calculi," *Zeitschrift für mathematische Logik und Grundlagen der Mathematik* 9 (1963): 67-96.

62. I assume here that a counterfactual conditional with a conceptually false antecedent need not be vacuously true or vacuously false. I think this assumption could be justified within the framework of Leibniz's analytic theory of truth.

63. Cf. Schepers, "Zum Problem der Kontingenz," pp. 345f.

64. In a note published by Henri Lestienne in his critical edition of Leibniz's *Discours de Métaphysique*, 2nd ed. (Paris: Vrin, 1952), p. 14n.

65. My greatest debt in this essay is to the monumental scholarship of Gaston Grua's *Jurisprudence universelle et théodicée selon Leibniz*, whose copious textual references provide an indispensable guide for anyone exploring this subject in Leibniz. I am also indebted to those who have attended my classes on Leibniz at the University of Michigan and UCLA, and particularly to John Earman, for helpful discussion. When I presented the paper at the Leibniz conference at Rice University in 1977, I discovered that David Blumenfeld had arrived independently at some of the ideas I have expressed here. He does not entirely agree with me, and has persuaded me that I ought perhaps to have been more sharply critical of what I have called Leibniz's second main solution to the problem of contingency, as not really being relevant to issues about *freedom*, which is not a proof-theoretical concept even if contingency may be. I have found Blumenfeld's comments very helpful in revising the paper. Several improvements are due to Heinrich Schepers, who read and commented on a draft of the paper. I am particularly indebted to him and the other members of the staff of the Leibniz-Forschungsstelle of the University of Münster for advice and for access to transcriptions and microfilms of Leibniz manuscripts, which have enabled me to correct the texts of Grua and Foucher de Careil in a few places, which I have indicated in the notes. The responsibility, of course, for any textual error that may have been introduced or overlooked here is mine.

Space, Point, and Void
in Leibniz's Philosophy

Martial Gueroult

The difficulties with the Leibnizian doctrines of extension and space stem from their complexity and the various degrees of abstraction implied by it. Failure to distinguish these degrees and to perceive the various elements of the theory in accordance with rigorously Leibnizian perspectives has led some critics, Bertrand Russell, for example, to perceive insurmountable contradictions everywhere.

One ought to distinguish within the Leibnizian conception of extended space four moments that correspond with various degrees of abstraction:

1) The *extensum*, or the extended, a concrete being or *corpus physicum* that possesses its own extension and occupies a space.

2) The *qualitas extensa*, or first matter (*a quality abstracted* from extended bodies). It is, at the same time, an *abstract being* (separated from other properties) and a *concrete term* (like the hot and the large), its quality being captured in its concrete reality and not outside of its matter as a general concept.

3) The *extensio*, or geometric extension, a discursive concept and an *abstract term*. It is properly speaking the *corpus mathematicum* to which Descartes reduced the former two [degrees] according to Leibniz.

4) The *spatium*, or space, an innate idea expressing the intellectual order of possibles (coexistents).

We will examine the spatium here, and the two problems it poses specifically, that of the point and of the void.

The spatium differs radically from the discursive concept of abstract extension (extensio) that is acquired by abstraction from a perceived property.

Translated by Roger Ariew from Martial Gueroult, "L'Espace, le point, et le vide chez Leibniz," *Revue Philosophique de la France et de l'étranger* (1946), pp. 431-52. (I would like to thank Robert Ariew, Department of French, Pennsylvania State University, for his numerous suggestions concerning the translation).

It does not stem from an abstraction, but is perceived in the same manner as all the innate ideas, within ourselves, on the occasion of external perceptions. Although it does not stem from a process of abstraction, we can state nevertheless that it is still more abstract than the concept of extension in that abstraction of *all quality* is accomplished with it: the notion of extensive quality is abolished in the idea of space, which retains only the simple notion of necessary relation or order (which disappeared in the indeterminate nexus of extensio). Since what was confused and imaginary in this concept was precisely what it retained of the quality as *partes extra partes,* we can therefore state that, by means of this ultimate abstraction, the confusion subsisting in the general notion of extensive quality disappeared, and that thus the intellectual and logical element constituting the deep structure of the notion, and at the same time what it received of intrinsic truth, shed its imaginative envelope to appear in its own clarity. In this way the abstraction does not arise from the infirmity of our intellect, and if, on the one hand, we can conceive it as the extreme point of a process developed from the external perception of actual [things], we must conceive it, on the other hand, as possible only from the *internal and innate consciousness of the necessary relation.*

Here the junction of two different directions takes place. The one, which goes from the concrete of the external perception to the indefinite possibility of the discursive concept, is only some kind of empirical possibility that represents generality with respect to an instance of the determination. This indefinite possibility *supposes* the perception of concrete extension; it is posterior to the perception of the partes extra partes. The other goes from the internal intuition of a necessary and universal relation to the perception of the partes extra partes, which, instead of being presupposed by it, is on the contrary conceived as conditioned by this order. The possible here is no longer an indeterminate generality of a discursive nature, but a *condition of possibility* that precedes the actual and its perception, and that by virtue of this precedes any partes extra partes. In this way we understand that the innate idea of spatial and temporal relation is completely different from the discursive concept of abstract extension or duration, because, since it is the relation or the order that conditions the possibility of the partes extra partes, it is in itself prior to it (meaning to extendedness properly speaking), and consequently it can, and even must be, considered without it; on the other hand, extension as a discursive concept cannot consider relation without the intermediary of the partes extra partes, which it always supposes as its condition. The direction that goes from the external perception to the discursive concept of abstract extension represents the unfolding of the process of the acquisition of knowledge, the *ratio cognoscendi*; the one that goes from the intellectual knowledge of order to the discursive concept and to the actual perception of "extended [beings]" represents the process of real conditioning, the *ratio essendi.* Without the intellectual knowledge of the innate relation of space (and time), geometry and, in a general way, the exact sciences would only attain (as with the empiricists) an external and contingent coincidence with the real—that of the concrete and the abstract; because of it, on the other hand, it can express truth in a rigorous, perfectly necessary and a priori fashion. Therefore there is no conflict in Leibniz's philosophy between the two opposed conceptions of science and the possible, but, in conformity with his thesis of innate ideas, there exists a collaboration between knowledge through the senses (and the process of abstraction and discursive generality that it brings) and innate intellectual knowledge.

Finally, the notion of space (and that of time) manifests its characteristic of notion stemming from pure understanding by means of two irrefutable signs, namely:

1) *A priori universality*, which is, in fact, not the concept of an order between real existences, a concept stemming from an abstraction of the perception of things realized in experience, but is of an order between the possibles, a concept whose absolute universality infinitely surpasses any generality of empirical nature or origin.

2) *Absolute necessity*, which is, in any case, the other side of a priori universality (Kant will retain these two characteristics as criteria of the transcendental).

But this intellectual nature of space (and time) is also implied by its origin, since it results from logical relations of compatibility and incompatibility between the possibles. Space is the order of coexistent possibles and we say that two things coexist *"when they do not exclude each other reciprocally"* (at the same time) (cf. *Initia rerum mathematicarum metaphysica*, Gerhardt, *Mathematische Schriften* VII, p. 17). Time, as the order of inconsistent possibles having necessarily some connection, determines its order by the priority of what contains the reason or cause of the effect with respect to this effect (*Ibid.*). The pure concepts of space and time far surpass the sphere of real things since they are valid not only for our universe, but also for all possible nonrealized universes. By that we understand that space (and time) appears truly like a frame (that of possibility in God) within which relations of real coexistence between things extended (actually) are established, as if it were a form independent of its contents. And we could even conceive (for other universes that could have been called into existence) real extensions different from those we know to exist in our universe (geometries with more or less than three dimensions), as Leibniz seems to have conceived in some of his letters, space as the pure possibility of a relation of coexistence being in itself indifferent to the number of dimensions, meaning to the modalities of this relation of coexistence. The contained (the perceived extended existences in space) is possible for perception only by virtue of these preliminary possible relations of coexistence, relations prior to the things actually perceived as extended.

These characteristics of the spatium as being an innate intellectual notion, an expression of the possibility founded in God's understanding and a preliminary condition of the concrete order, allow two Leibnizian conceptions to be explained:

1) That space can be conceived as what allows the measurement of exten-

sion, and at the same time as what receives from extension its (actual) magnitude; it is thus that one may be able to resolve the problem of the point.

2) That the void can be affirmed.

Let us consider the first problem.

Being prior to the concrete [things], space (and time) constitutes a system of abstract relations that must be conceived independently from the things we measure with them when applying them: "Duration and extension are attributes of things, but time and space are taken as [things] outside of things and serve to measure them" (*Examination of Malebranche's Principles,* Gerhardt VI, p. 584). In fact, we cannot measure an extension except by its *relation of distance* between two points. The notion of relation of distance is precisely what is brought to us a priori by the idea of space. But a relation, whether it consists of a relation of distance, a relation of proportion, or a relation of cause and effect, is not only not divisible into parts, but is absolutely heterogenous to such a divisibility. Each relation, even if it is comparable to another relation, even if we can enumerate what results from this comparison, is some *sui generis* that constitutes an irrefutable intellectual unity. That is immediately perceivable for the relation of distance; this relation, in fact, is established between two points, but these points are in no way part of the relation, they are merely possible terms for these possible relations (temporal or spatial): "The instant is not a part of time" (Gerhardt III, p. 591); "neither is a point a part of space" (Gerhardt I, p. 416, II p. 279, IV, p. 482, Letter to Dangicourt, Erdmann [see reference, note 8], p. 746, etc). No relation of distance is therefore constituted by the addition of smaller relations, and consequently, none ought to be conceived as divisible into parts.

There exists therefore yet another difference between space and abstract extension, a difference Leibniz did not, in any case, entirely elaborate. Abstract extension, even when it is not divided, *remains divisible,* and consequently retains from the concrete from which it stems the idea of partes extra partes, these parts remaining indetermined, however, which is what makes the whole appear prior to the actually determined parts, and the partition be abandoned to the arbitrariness of the mind: "There are no divisions there, none that the mind does not make, and the part is posterior to the whole (to de Volder, Gerhardt II, p. 279).[1] Space does not include possible parts in itself; it does not arise from the abstraction of what has parts, but from a possible logical and a priori relation of nonextended things, with respect to their possible existence. For space there are only points, which are extremities and which cannot be conceived as discontinuous unities:

The extremities of the line and the unities of matter do not coincide. Three continuous points on a straight line cannot be conceived. Only two are conceived: the extremity of a straight line and the extremity of another, from which the same whole results. Similarly for time one can conceive only two instants, the instant of birth and the instant of death. (Gerhardt II, p. 279)

Similarly, position is nothing more than the *mode* of a thing like priority or posteriority (meaning a relation), and in the same way a mathematical point itself is nothing more than a mode, meaning an extremity. That is why when two bodies are conceived as touching and two mathematical points are joined, there does not result from them a new position or a whole larger than its part, for the conjunction of the two extremities is not greater than one of the two extremities, in the same way that two dark perfections are not darker by their union than when taken separately. To say that a point has a position is merely to be able to designate the position where the body ends. (To des Bosses, Gerhardt II, 347-48)

What can be divided, on the contrary (and because of this the idea of divisibility is born), is the concrete reality to which this relation applies, meaning the real extension that goes from one extremity of the distance to the other. Thus it is the thing that is divided into parts, or even divisible into parts, not the relation applied to it and by which it is measured. However, the relation, which is without parts, and the abstract extension, which is *divisible* into indetermined parts, have a common property that tightly binds them, that is, continuity. Russell is therefore right when he asserts that distances are not extensive qualities, but qualities that are somewhat extensive, since such qualities, while being irreducible to a number of elements, can nevertheless express variation by variations of magnitude (Bertrand Russell, *The Philosophy of Leibniz* [London, 1900], p. 126). That, in any case, is what Leibniz remarks: "Relative things have their quantity as well as absolute ones. For instance, ratios or proportions in mathematics have their quantities and are measured by logarithms, and yet they are relations" (To Clarke, Gerhardt VII, p. 404).

But if on the one hand the application to concrete extension of a priori relations of distance stemming from the innate notion of space allows one to measure concrete extension, on the other hand, seems to actualize and *determine* space. The latter becomes then a space of *some extension,* such that extension can be conceived as the magnitude of space (by measuring the extensions by relations of distance, we establish the differences of *magnitude* between these relations of distance): "Extension is the magnitude of space. When the magnitude of space lessens in a continuous fashion, it leads to a point from which no magnitude can return" (*Initia mathematicarum metaphysica,* Gerhardt, *Mathematische Schriften* VII, p. 18 sqq.). This text not only succeeds in marking the difference between concrete extension (matter) and space, but also between abstract extension and space properly speaking. In fact, it indicates that space is, in itself, foreign to magnitude, while magnitude is necessary to extension, extension not being able to exist without some extensio. One can therefore state that there could be no extension that is not spatial, but that there are spaces without extension, which is natural if space, as a possibility founded in God, is the condition for the world of real existences (extended [things]), which is always more restricted than space. Extension is a certain existential quality that space can measure, but space is in itself indifferent to extension. In this way one could illuminate the following obscure text from the *Examination of Malebranche's Principles:*

> I should always distinguish between the extended or extension, and the attribute to which extension, or diffusion (a relative notion), refers, that is, *situation or locality.* Thus the diffusion of place forms space, which would be like the πρῶτον δεχτιχόν, or the primary subject of extension and by which it would also apply to other things in space. Thus extension, when it is the *attribute* of space, is the diffusion or continuation of situation or locality, just as the extension of body is the diffusion of antitypy or materiality. For place is in a point as well as in space, and as a result place can be without extension or diffusion; but diffusion or simple length allows for a localized line to be endowed with extension. The same thing is true of matter; it is in a point as well as in a body, and its diffusion in simple length makes up a material line. Other continuations or diffusions in breadth and depth form the surface and the solid of geometry—in a word, space in relation to position, and body in relation to matter. (Gerhardt VI, p. 585)

By making use of the definitions of the *Initia rerum mathematicarum*, one could draw the following consequence: absolute space, which is the place of all places, would stem from the diffusion of point (mathematical point), which is the simplest of places, or the place of no other place (Gerhardt, *Mathematische Schriften* VII, p. 23).

However, if the preceding text is explained in part by what we have asserted insofar as extension appears as an attribute of space that it receives when it becomes concrete as a magnitude, the text remains obscure in that it conceives the genesis of space on the model of extension, and even concrete extension. Moreover, extension as a collection of places issued from the repetition of materiality must precisely oppose itself to space as a priori intellectual relation of logical nature between possibles; on one side we have an abstract quality and a discursive concept, and on the other an a priori intellectual relation and an innate idea.

The text is obscure also because it seems to generate space from the repetition of point and consequently to identify material unities, which are real, with points, which are ideal, contrary to Leibniz's repeated assertions: "The extremities of the line and the unities of matter do not coincide; three continuous points on a straight line cannot be conceived" (to de Volder, Gerhardt II, p. 279). And elsewhere:

> A point is not a definite part of matter, and even an infinity of points gathered into one will not make an extension. Let us join a multitude of triangles by means of their sides such that their apexes (*apices*) are common; clearly this infinity of apexes compounded together in this way make up only a common apex which will not have any more extension

than a single one. Extension arises from situation, but it adds continuity to the point. Points have a situation, but they neither have nor compose a continuity, nor can they subsist by themselves. Thus points can come into being or perish, coincide or be outside one another, without any increase or diminution of matter and extension, because they are not parts but extremities. (to des Bosses, Gerhardt II, p. 370)

This difficulty opens up the problem of the point and its relation with extension in general. Sometimes Leibniz pits the diffusion of substances with the fluxion of point; as he states to de Volder, "unities do not diffuse themselves in the sense in which *one commonly conceives the fluxion of a point,* nor do they constitute a homogeneous whole; in fact, the homogeneity of matter consists only in abstraction" (Gerhardt II, p. 277). But on the other hand he compares this diffusion with fluxion or a process of generation from infinitesimals; he writes in the same letter, "I understand by diffusion nothing more than the continuation by which the part is similar to the whole, in the same manner that we conceive whiteness diffused in milk, and the same direction diffused (repeated) in a straight line, or even the same curvature repeated in the circumference" (Gerhardt II, p. 277). To des Bosses he declares: "Extension is continuous simultaneous repetition, as when we say that a line is made by the fluxion of a point, since several positions are conjugated in this vestige of a point" (Gerhardt II, p. 339).

How should one take these apparent contradictions?

Here, as elsewhere, these difficulties arise from a lack of rigor with respect to terminology. We know that Leibniz distinguished three kinds of points: (i) the metaphysical point, which is unextended substance; it is exact and real; (ii) the mathematical point, which is the point of view from which each substance expresses the universe; it is exact, but unreal—it is a modality or an aspect of real terms; and (iii) the physical point, which is the restriction of the parts of corporeal substances such that they appear as a point—this latter [point] is not rigorously a point, but an infinitely small extension, an infinitesimal; it is real, but inexact (Gerhardt IV, p. 482).

However, the mathematical point is also conceived differently by Leibniz. It is sometimes conceived in the manner of an infinitesimal: "the point is an infinitely small or disappearing line" (Gerhardt, *Mathematische Schriften* V, p. 385). Such a point is not absolutely exact; it is not rigorously indivisible and smaller than any assignable or sensible magnitude (cf. To Arnauld, Gerhardt I, p. 72, *Theoria motus abstracti, Fundamentum,* Gerhardt, *Mathematische Schriften* VI, pp. 66-68). It is therefore not strictly a nothing. It has some continuity; it is a disappearing extension. It is an infinitely small movement of a point that cannot be distinguished from its rest, a fluxion of a point in which "several positions are conjugated" such that this plurality of positions can no longer be distinguished from a single position at the limit. Hence, one can conceive that a point thus defined can generate an extension by its fluxion or repetition, for it is homogeneous with extension because of its continuity, in the same way that the same infinitely small directions are homogeneous with the circumference. Under these conditions, it is easy to conceive the genesis of extension from point, and it is possible to compare with this fluxion the generation of extension by the repetition or diffusion of substances. But Leibniz soon adds that the repetition of substances is not immediately comparable to the fluxion of a point, because points, directions, or curvatures are homogeneous among themselves, whereas substances are heterogeneous among themselves; homogeneous extension would therefore never be able to stem from the repetition of substances, if abstraction did not intervene to conserve what is homogeneous for these repeated elements (meaning passivity) and homogeneous with the whole abstracted from the extension resulting from this repetition (Gerhardt II, p. 277).

The mathematical point is sometimes also conceived as absolutely exact, unextended, indivisible—rigorously a point. It is clear that this unextended point cannot, by repeating itself, engender anything extended. That is what Leibniz indicates to des Bosses (Gerhardt II, pp. 347-48; *New System of the Nature and the Communication of Substances*, sec. 3; Letter to Sophie, Gerhardt VII, p. 560). Points are nothing but *limits* and are by themselves noncontinuous. Even though they have a situation, they could not constitute the extension that arises out of the situation, but add continuity to a point. They do not exist by themselves, but are the extremities of bodies. To say that a point has a position is nothing other than to be able to designate where the body ends (Gerhardt II, p. 348).

But [mathematical] point, on the other hand, is equally conceived as place, locality, or *position,* and by position (of substance) one must understand something corresponding to what Leibniz called the *point of view* of the monad, for position, like point of view, results from the monad (which Leibniz called the metaphysical point). Hence it is evident that the point conceived as position or *point of view* is altogether different from the point conceived as limit or extremity. That is why we see Leibniz, in the letter to des Bosses that we have already cited, distinguish *position* from *point.* Position is a mode just like point, but if point has a position, it is only insofar as it is the limit of the position of two bodies. As Leibniz wrote to des Bosses, "simple substance, even if it does not have any extension, has, however, a position which is the foundation of extension" (Gerhardt II, p. 339). Further, he explains that extension stems from the repetition of position just as line stems from the fluxion of point. To des Bosses, who then asks him whether position is identical with the substance for which it is a position, or whether it is a *mode* and if, in the case where such a position is conferred to the mathematical point, could not an extension be constituted by a plurality of mathematical points, Leibniz replies that position is but a mode (like priority), that the mathematical point is also a mode—extremity—but that the addition of these extremities would never yield an extension (Gerhardt II, pp. 347-48).

Therefore, if we wish to utilize a rigorous terminology, we would distinguish place, situation, locality, position (these terms being synonymous) from point (even though Leibniz, in the *Initia mathematicarum,* for example, defines point as the *place of no other place*). This place is what corresponds to the point of view of the monad whose proper nature it expresses *extrinsically*; it must therefore be conceived in some way as the generic element of space, meaning as what space is prior to the diffusion (repetition of places) from which it arises as space. Place is therefore originally without space, without *diffusion* and that is how it can be compared with point, for point is without extension; but place is nevertheless prior to point itself, for properly speaking point supposes the space for which it is a limit—it supposes for its own position the position of two substances, meaning place. That is how we understand what Leibniz asserted in the *Examination of Malebranche's Principles*: "place is in point as well as in space, and as a result, place can be without extension or diffusion, . . . and the diffusion of place forms space" (Gerhardt VI, p. 585). As the generic element of space (from substances as the position of these substances), place is analogous to the infinitesimal point that is its image, for it sums up and virtually contains the properties of space, meaning both punctuality and extensivity, together with the continuity that characterizes the latter. That is why the summation of places yields continuous space, which the summation of points, which properly speaking are without continuity, cannot yield. Moreover, place, if it has to be conceived on the image of infinitesimal point, is not itself the infinitesimal point either, for point, serving the genesis of shapes in space, supposes space, whereas here we are concerned about an element that is at the source of space itself. Space being the possible in relation to the extended existent, the relation between concrete extension and space must be that of existence to possible essence. And existence remains present in essence under the form of a differential; thus position—as possibility of concrete extension, a possiblity that depends on possible relations of essences under the condition of their existence—must contain in itself potentially (that is, without realized extensivity) extensivity and its properties: that is, point, as well as extension, continuity and its limits, possible position and its possible limits (points).

One exposes oneself to inextricable confusions (as Russell did) when one does not distinguish point as extremity, and point as position, place, or locality that does not contain anything other than extrinsic [things], since it is reduced to the relation of exclusion from itself, which is characteristic of point in the sense of position of term ("place which excludes all other places"). Insofar as it is the position of a *possible* term, place is *unextended,* for there is no real extension without a real term. Thus it has the characteristic of point, which is without extension although it is spatial; but it is the possible principle of something extended, which point conceived as extremity could not be. As a place that excludes all other places, it expresses under the form of extrinsic relation the inalienable intrinsic quality proper to every possible monad. It is because each monad constitutes a different quality that could never be confused with any other (by virtue of the principle of indiscernibles) that it will have to occupy a different place from any other, if it is ever to exist, by excluding all others from itself, meaning from its place. Thus place (or position) is truly the external expression of an internal quality, an expression conceived as simply possible with respect to the possible existence of the monad. It is not a quality of the monad itself but a relation or order that results from it; neither is it something completed, existing outside the monads; it is therefore merely a simple *modality*, as Leibniz states.[2] Outside the real existence of the monad that realizes this order, space is only the pure concept (without the least reality) of a possible relation. Moreover, the multiplicity of monads implies the multiplication of the relations of exclusion, or multiplicity of locations. Thus pure possible space is also conceived as resulting from the diffusion or repetition of places, as real extended matter is conceived as resulting from the diffusion of antitypies, from which arises the possibility of having recourse to comparisons stemming from the fluxion of a point, locality also being wholly homogeneous with space as the geometric infinitesimal point is to extension. Thus position (or locality) is the *envelope* or *possible sphere* of the possible existence of the monad, a sphere implied in the very possibility of the position of the monad in existence. As a position, place, without being a space (and thus able to be characterized as a point) sums up in itself the essential characteristics of space, for the creation of place by the exclusion of everything else (by virtue of the principle of indiscernibles) that is the fact of position, implies that the same place (pointlike) cannot be occupied by different things at the same time, nor can different places be occupied by the same things at the same time—in brief, by the absolute *outside of one another* that is the essence of externality and the prerequisite of distance.[3] As for continuity, it also results directly from the extrinsic characteristic of relation that considered in itself, independently from its internal reason, implies the abstraction of all intrinsic difference, the foundation of discreteness.

Let us now go on to the problem of void.

The characteristic of spatium, being an innate intellectual notion, an expression of the possibility founded in God's understanding, a condition prior to the concrete order, allows one to explain the *conception of void.*

In fact, that is the characteristic that renders intelligible the concept Descartes rejected a priori for geometric reasons, while Leibniz admitted it (Gerhardt V, p. 140), and rejected only its *reality.*[4] The void outside the world and inside the world is conceived as the simple possible not realized by God; it is the concept of possible order as opposed to what exists actually: "In fact, time and space are only kinds of order, and in these orders the empty place (which in relation to space is called void), *if there were any,*[5] would mark the possibility of only what is lacking together with its relation to the actual" (*New Essays*, II, ch. iv, Erdmann p. 230a); "One can give limits to a body, but one cannot do it with regard to space. . . . It is as I just said that time and space indicate possibilities beyond the supposition of actuals. Time and space are of the nature of eternal truths which consider equally the possible and the actual. . . . This void which may be conceived in time, indicates, like that of space, that time and space extend to the possibles as well as the actuals" (*New Essays* II, ch. xiv, sec. 24-26, Erdmann, p. 242a,b).[6] Insofar as the immense understanding of God includes all possibles, the void, which marks the opposition between the possible and the actual, appears even to achieve a high degree of reality: it is what is filled more or less completely (but always incompletely) by existence, which depends on the will of God: "God is the source of possibilities as well as of existences, of the one by His essence, of the other by His will. Thus space, like time has its reality only from Him, and *He can fill up the void when it seems good to Him*" (*New Essays,* II, ch. xv, sec. 4, Erdmann, p. 242b, 243a). Because the laws of possibility are independent from existence, one would not be able to demonstrate a priori the nonexistence of the void, as Descartes attempted to do, by saying that, if one placed a void between the sides of a vessel, the two sides would touch (Descartes, *Principles of Philosophy* II, art. 18). It is true that Descartes understood by "void" not the absence of solid matter, but the absence of space or extension, material substance having been reduced to extension only. But Leibniz asserts that geometry demonstrates the contrary: "Although I do not admit the void, I distinguish matter from extension, and I admit that if there were a void in a sphere, the opposite poles in the hollow space would not touch on that account: But I believe that this is not a case which the divine perfection allows" (*New Essays* II, ch. xiii, sec. 22, Erdmann, p. 241a). "One can refute the one who would maintain that two bodies between which there is a void would touch because the two opposite poles of a hollow sphere would not touch: for geometry prohibits it" (*New Essays* II, ch. xv, Erdmann, p. 241a).[7] One could therefore go so far as to attribute the void in Leibniz's philosophy the worth of an idea of the understanding and of an eternal truth.

But one must refrain from excessive interpretation that would lead one to introduce into Leibnizian philosophy a Newtonian or Kantian absolute space, or something analogous to this. To suppose a void rigorously is to conceive a reality of space outside the reality of the bodies that may occupy it; to conceive space like an independent frame is to lend it a certain subsistence and a certain actuality. And space being but a possible relation between coexistents *for the case where these coexistents would be real or actual,* is absolutely not real or actual outside these coexistents. It is actual only insofar as the actual coexistents are effectively ordered according to the order where their existence is possible. One must therefore not distinguish two extensions in the universe: (i) the concrete extension of bodies, which is their solidity or impenetrability by which they may reorder themselves by leaving the places they occupy, and (ii) abstract space, which is like a frame existing by itself in which bodies determine their place or situation; this place is nothing more, in fact, than the relation of bodies between themselves, in the same way that a number is nothing more than the plurality of things numbered and *does not constitute by itself a different multitude from that of these things*:

> Although it may be true that in conceiving body one conceives something more than its number, that is the *res numeratas,* there are not two multitudes, the one abstract—that of number—and the other concrete— that of the things numbered. Likewise, one can say that one must not

imagine two extensions, the one, abstract, of space, and the other concrete, of body—the concrete existing as such only through the abstract.
And since bodies pass from one part of space to another—meaning that
they change order among themselves—things pass from one part of the
order or of a number to another, when for example the first becomes the
second, and the second becomes the third, etc. (*New Essays* II, ch. iv,
Erdmann, p. 230a)

Thus the void, like space in itself, is nothing real, but is only what *one conceives
would be missing and would be possible* with respect to the actual. Although we
represented the void as an idea in God's understanding, we would now say that it
is simply something *imaginary*: "We attribute extension only to matter which is
finite, and call the spaces beyond the universe *imaginary*" declares Philalèthe
who represents Locke, Leibniz's adversary in the *New Essays* (*New Essays* II, ch.
xv, sec. 4, Erdmann, p. 242b). Leibniz ratifies the term 'imaginary': "The same
reason which makes the space outside the world be imaginary proves that all
empty spaces are imaginary, for they differ only as greater and lesser" (Fourth
Letter to Clarke, sec. 7, Erdmann, p. 756). "Space, in fact, being nothing outside
the order of bodies between themselves, is nothing at all without the bodies, but
the possibility of placing them" (Third Letter to Clarke, Erdmann, p. 752a).
"Space marks, in terms of possibility, an order of things which exist at the same
time, considered as existing together" (Third Letter to Clarke, sec. 4, Erdmann,
p. 752a). It therefore has reality only insofar as there are actual [things], hence,
the fictive and imaginary aspects of the void soon disintegrate. But one must
note that when he refutes the void thus, Leibniz, although referring to the term
'space,' in fact refers to the notion of abstract extension, more than he does to
the idea of space, an eternal truth, such as it is described in the *New Essays,* for
example. In fact, extension (or space) being but the abstraction of what is
extended and the abstraction of the order of extended things, appears in itself
like an indefinite possibility that has no other reality than abstraction and no
other support than the concrete order from which it stems. Hence one can
fully affirm that there are not two extensions, any more than that there are two
multitudes, that of number and that of numbered things.[8]

But the question presents itself otherwise if we conceive of space as an
idea founded in God's understanding and an order of possibles that reside in
God's understanding. For these possibles, if they are without existential reality, have an essential reality; there is therefore a plurality of possibles distinct
from the plurality of existences, and, since the set of possible worlds is greater
than the existing world, this multitude of possibles is greater than the multitude
of existing [things], although one and the other are infinite and comparisons of
magnitude between kinds ought only be carried out provisionally and metaphorically. In this case, the void (meaning the concept of what can be missing with
respect to the actual) takes a more real signification; it is not only the lacuna
that we conceive with respect to an order that we ourselves perceive between
things realized, but it also represents a possible that has not passed to existence—

hence a true lacuna in the world of existences. Thus there would be basically two conceptions of the void, corresponding to the two concepts of abstract extension and space, properly speaking. To some extent, under the concept of space as idea of the understanding, the void would be conceived as preceding the contents, and the order of possibles as preceding and managing the order of actuals; to some extent, the order would be in the concrete, since it is first in the abstract: concrete extension *realizes* space—which is what manifests itself most in the passage already cited: "God is the source of possibilities as well as of existences . . . ; He can fill up the void when it seems good to Him"(*New Essays* II, ch. xv, sec. 4, Erdmann, p. 242b, 243a). In the other case, the void is, on the contrary, an imagination posterior to the perception of the concrete, and "one cannot say that [. . .] the concrete exists as such only through the abstract" (*New Essays* II, ch. iv, Erdmann, p. 230a): the extended concrete does not realize the abstract, but the abstract extension is drawn out of it.

Is that to say that a conflict exists between these two concepts, between which Leibniz's thought vacillates?

Two facts allow one to reconcile them. The relevant spatial order has meaning (in the conception of space as idea of the understanding) only with respect to the *existence* of these possibles. Taken in themselves, having abstracted the existence they can engender, the possibles, reduced to simple notions, are without relation; they are disparate—the relations they maintain appear only with respect to these existences that imply compatibilities and incompatibilities. Thus the relations *implied* by the possibles are absolutely stripped of reality and even of meaning outside the existential order, or at least outside the conception of this order. That is why Leibniz when defining space and time speaks of "the order between possibles, *as if they existed*" (*New Essays* II, ch. xiii, Erdmann, p. 240a). Without the existences, the relations implied by the possibles are not made explicit; without the concept of these possible existences, the implication of these relations cannot even be conceived. Because of this, the idea of an a priori frame subsisting by itself and in itself cannot be sustained.

Further—the second fact—in the same fashion that in this universe abstract extension does not precede the order of real coexistent things, in God's understanding space as idea could not be prior to the possibles or to the essences about which space only expresses the order flowing with respect to their existences (possibles); it becomes reduced, on the contrary, to the order and relation of these possibles and it begins to drift, being nothing outside them. What is ontologically prior to extended existences is not the empty frame of a space subsisting by itself as an absolute space, the *sensorium Dei* of Clarke and Newton, nor the a priori form of Kantian sensible intuition, but only the set of possibles or essences with the logical relations (of compatibility or incompatibility) they imply. If there are innate spatial relations that are in some way a priori with respect to our perception of concrete extension, it is only insofar as they are reducible to logical relations between the possible eternal [things] that predetermine the relations that, within a concrete extension and a duration, realized existences will have among them. Finally, one must note that the intellectual idea of space (and of time) is not known in the same way in God and in created [things]. In God, the possible relations of possibles are effectively conceived in virtue of the intrinsic compatibilities of these possibles or essences and, consequently, are entirely determined, and each of these possibles is something very positive. On the other hand, created [things] do not actually attain the internal mechanism by which the possible spatial and temporal relations result from essences brought together under the idea of possible creation; of course, they do capture these possible relations with their own necessity, but *in abstracto*, without perceiving them as derived from the essences previously posited, and they thus replace in some way the possible terms determined in God by possible indetermined terms. *"Possible"* then no longer represents a possible essence, which is a determined reason, but only any term *whatever*, something indeterminate. In this way the intellectual notion of space overlaps the notion of abstract extension, which, by virtue of the abstraction of actual terms, retains only relations between *indetermined terms.*[9] Thus, the innate intellectual idea of spatial (and temporal) relation, although entirely exact and necessary, and founded in the understanding, does not purely and simply rejoin the order of the possibles in God, which is its foundation. It is therefore false to speak of a rigorously metaphysical space: the order of possibles in God is not a spatial order; not only does it occur only with respect to things that are without parts, unextended and real at the same time, but it is also an order to exclusion or of logical tolerance that *engenders the situation*, without being conditioned by it. Thus, what one calls the *point of view* of the monad, the point of view from which it reflects the universe, is only the result, in the actual world, of this logical nature, and is conceivable only *with respect to this existence.* Originally, there is a simple intrinsic qualitative difference that is expressed externally by a representative difference, which itself is expressed, at a lower degree, by the comparisons of the "geometrical." If one now thinks that there are no points of view and no differences in points of view except between the monads, meaning between the finite beings, for God is the negation of any point of view, being all the points of view at the same time (the center is everywhere, the periphery is nowhere), then every "point of view" expresses, simultaneously with the proper activity of each monad, its finitude or its own passivity. And this passivity or passive primitive force (or prime matter) is precisely the principle of impenetrability. Thus impenetrability—meaning the impossibility of being where something else is—only expresses the original irreducible quality of each monad that is irreparably *other* than the original quality of another. But it expresses it under an abstract form—meaning an abstraction of this indestructible and inalienable individual specificity of the *quality* and the *point of view* that is the only real foundation of alteration. In this way only alteration without intrinsic difference is *retained*—meaning the numerical alteration of extension.

We understand that the innate idea of space in the understanding ought not lead us to conceive the imaginary space in God as a rigorous void that could be filled with existences; this would introduce in God the substitute for a partes extra partes and a true sensorium; there is in God but one idea, the idea of an order and a relation, the idea of a relation of qualitative alteration conceived as being able to express itself externally by a relation of spatial difference.[10]

Thus the theory of the ideality of space joins up with that of its objective validity, for the relations expressed by space are objectively valid and real outside our perception, *in a certain way* translating an order founded in God. One of the errors that contributed to Russell's confusion is the wish to consider at all cost that space ought also be as subjective as extension, and to have conceived that the ideality of space had necessarily to encompass its subjective characteristic. That is a bias of Kantian origin that ought not intervene in the interpretation of Leibnizian philosophy and that here as elsewhere rendered impossible the intelligibility of the doctrine.

At the base of Leibnizian philosophy, there is, in fact, no critique of knowledge, but the deepening of a scientific conception of the world, together with some speculations in logic.[11] It largely rests on a critique of Cartesian science, a critique that presupposes also the critique of Cartesian methodology and logic. And physics, as Leibniz conceives it, leads him to posit an infinite multiplicity of substances, and forces; it encompasses the realism of the monadology, the affirmation of the existence of external things. Descartes' starting point is, on the contrary, the assumption of the problem of knowledge, the doubting of the external world, a preliminary doubting that Leibniz had refused himself, contesting, from a logical and epistemic point of view, the criteria of evidence in the name of which Descartes believes he is able to justify his provisional doubt. Leibnizian idealism therefore remains objective. It reduces the external things to representative beings and not to the representations of a subject: absolute subjective idealism, transcendental idealism, or its substitutes are foreign to him. His notion of the ideality of space simply signifies that space is not an absolute being, but a being of reason, a relation posterior to things in themselves conceived as possible existences—relation not prior to these things, although prior to their real existence. Moreover, what there is in space that is properly extensional is not a property of the thing in itself. The Leibnizian negation of the reality of space does not therefore force us to admit that we know only the phenomena, meaning the things that appear to our minds, as Russell gratuitously affirms (p. 82). Doubtless, the things we know in extension and as extended are known to ourselves as phenomena, since they are basically unextended; but awareness of phenomena allows a necessary, objective, intelligible, and nonphenomenal order to appear: the spatial order whose basis is the logical relation of possible unextended things.

What occasioned this counter-indication is that the word "phenomenon" does not designate the same thing for Leibniz and Kant. A phenomenon, in the sense taken by Leibniz, whose common example is the rainbow or the mock-sun, corresponds with the Kantian *empirical appearance,* and at the end of the "Transcendental Aesthetics," Kant himself rightly denoted what separates the two notions: there is no radical solution of continuity between the appearance and the (phenomenal) thing; however, there is a radical discontinuity between the phenomenon and the thing (in itself). And Leibniz conceives the relation between the phenomenon and the intelligible thing in the manner that Kant conceives the relation between the appearance and the phenomenal thing.

To reduce the spatial order to a subjective creation, one must deny precisely the whole Leibnizian theory of space (as order of coexistents resting on logical compatibility) by making space into a property *entirely* issued from a single subject, and also by denying the theory of extension (as repetition of the passivity of substances).

The thesis of the objectivity and ideality of space is therefore implied by Leibnizian philosophy, instead of being in contradiction with it. Leibniz, said Russell,

> had two theories of space, the first subjective and Kantian, the second giving an objective counterpart, i.e., the various points of view of the monads. The difficulty is, that the objective counterpart cannot consist *merely* in the difference of points of view, unless the subjective space is *purely* subjective; but if it be purely subjective, the ground for different points of view has disappeared, since there is no reason to believe that the phenomena are *bene fundata.* (Russell, p. 136)

What is unfortunate is that this dilemma cannot be posited for Leibniz, and that Leibniz reverses the reasoning: precisely because, if space is *purely* subjective, the objective counterpart can consist only in the *simple* difference of points of view, then space is not purely subjective and the objective counterpart does not consist in the simple difference of points of view; the difference of points of view adequately *translates* the intrinsic differences of monads, differences that constitute the ultimate foundation of their effective reality in conformity with the principle of indiscernibles; further, these intrinsic differences serve at the same time as support for the possible a priori order, which is the order of space, and for the imaginary extension that each monad detaches for itself by abstraction from the content of its representations. It is true that Leibniz, according to Russell, ought to have denied the objective plurality of monads under the pretext that the proposition that affirms it is not reducible to an analytic proposition attributing a predicate to a subject (Russell, pp. 13, 129). But does not this affirmation of the plurality of monads come to attribute to God infinite predicates implied in His infinite reality, God's infinite reality implying the real *distinction* between the monads,[12] a numberless multitude, a real distinction that makes of them true *realities* in conformity with the principle of indiscernibles? What is ideal and subjective in space is consequently the *form* of the relation and not the *necessity* expressed in it. There is therefore nothing intrinsically contradictory there; on the contrary, everything in this reduction of synthetic judgment to analytic judgment (which remains an ideal for finite beings) links up. Doubtless one can contest the thesis itself, but that is something other than to accuse as absurd the demonstration given by the Leibnizian system.

Notes

1. Russell applies this reflection to space; the text appears to support him: Leibniz speaks of a spatium. But in the correspondence with de Volder, Leibniz does not distinguish space from extensio in a strict fashion. A few lines above, Leibniz speaks of the extensio (*non constat ex punctis*) by making use of the two terms indifferently. See also, in the correspondence with des Bosses: "For space, like time, is a certain order, indeed (in the case of space) [an order] of coexisting [things], which contains not only actuals but also possibles. It follows that [it is], a certain indefinite, as [are] all continuums whose parts are not actual, but able to be received by an observer equally as unitary part or fractions" (*Die philosophischen Schriften von Gottfried Wilhelm Leibniz*, ed. C. I. Gerhardt, 7 vols. [Berlin, 1875-1890], Vol II, p. 379).

2. That is the sense one has to give *mode* here, and not that of changing modification of a substance. Leibniz has refuted the conception of space or extension as mode of substance, extension being immutable, and mode being changeable (cf. to de Volder, Gerhardt II, p. 221). Modality is a relation between substances that leaves them intact in some way, themselves not being modifications or accidents.

3. This logicalization (externality brought to exclusion outside itself by virtue of the principle of indiscernibles) is also accomplished by H. Bergson when he makes of impenetrability a requirement of *logical thought* (Henri Louis Bergson, *Essai sur les données immédiates de la conscience* [Paris, 1889]).

4. He rejects it for physical reasons (propagation of movement) and metaphysical reasons (principle of reason, of the better, of continuity, of order, of indiscernibles).

5. God's wisdom (principle of the better) is opposed to there being any.

6. "There is no more void in numbers as in place, time, and all other orders, unless one supposes that the real universe is destroyed and that we keep only the possibles" (to de Volder, Gerhardt II, p. 234).

7. Therefore if there were a spatial void, one could determine its extent, for space has several dimensions and the empty space could be measured by the dimensions of the real bodies circumscribing it. If on the other hand, there were a temporal void, it would remain indeterminable, for time has only one dimension, "it is uniformly continuous and simple like a straight line" and can only be measured by the change in the duration that fills it up. And empty time is a duration without change; "one cannot therefore refute one who would maintain that two worlds, one of which succeeds the other, touch as to duration, such that one necessarily begins when the other ends, without there existing an interval. One could not refute him, I say, because this interval is indeterminable. If space were only a line, and if body were immovable, it would not be possible to determine the length of the vacuum between two bodies either" (*New Essays,* II, ch. xv, sec. 11). In fact, one could neither measure it by the intermediary of other dimensions—angles, etc.—nor directly, for this measurement supposes that the path is traveled by a point along a straight line, which is excluded by immobility. (Cf. *Initia rerum mathematicarum metaphysica, Mathematische Schriften,* ed. C. I. Gerhardt, 7 vols. [Halle, 1849-1850], Vol. VII, pp. 21-22, 26-27, sqq.)

8. This fusion of extensio and spatium for the benefit of extensio is found throughout the whole correspondence with Clarke, particularly when it concerns the refutation of the substantialization of space and time as absolute space and time. The error of the Newtonians is to convert into absolute reality what is only of a relative and ideal order. But the Newtonians differ from the Cartesians insofar as they continue to distinguish space, radically transmuted as absolute being, as *sensorium Dei*, from the matter that resides there, in contradiction with the Cartesians, who reduce the two to the unity of the same substance. They can therefore admit the infinite divisibility of space and the discreteness of matter (atomism), at the same time, and consequently, to escape the labyrinth of the continuum (2nd Kantian Antinomy), which rests on the identification of the ideal (abstract) with the actual (concrete). But they immediately fall into another labyrinth: that of the place of the world in space or of its first

beginning in time (1st Kantian Antinomy). In fact, Leibniz demonstrates that space being something absolutely uniform, one can distinguish nothing different in it without things having been placed in it. God therefore has no reason for placing bodies in space thus and not otherwise, and for everything being reversed by an exchange of east and west, for example. But if space is nothing more than the order of bodies, these two states (the one as it is, and the other, its reverse) would not differ from each other, for they would be discernible only with respect to an absolute space that differs from their order, a space that, by definition, does not exist. In this fashion is revealed a new demonstration refuting the thought of those who take space as a substance (Third Letter to Clarke, *God. Guil. Leibnitii opera philsophiae quae extant*, ed. J. E. Erdmann, 2 vols. [Berlin, 1840], p. 752a). It is evident that throughout this demonstration the possible order appears strictly as a simple abstraction, drawn from the order of real bodies and not as an essential order prior to the order of actuals.

9. One can assert, consequently, that in finite being, the idea of space does not yet entirely manifest its logical nature, as in God, where it expressly reduces itself to relations of compatibility and incompatibility between determined possibles. What guarantees the finite being its logical nature, in the absence of the internal awareness of compatibilities (for we merely conceive this nature of space, *without realizing an adequate knowledge of it*) is its universal and necessary characteristic. One must note that for Kant, this universal and necessary characteristic is that of the transcendental and a priori, but not that of the intellectual and the logical. This characteristic, in fact, guarantees for Kant, the *nonempirical* origin of the notions which possess it, but not their intellectual characteristic, for there exists an *a priori sensibility*. That is why the disciples of Leibniz who were opposed to Kant attempted expressly to deduce space and time from relations of compatibility and incompatibility, even though Leibniz had never conceived of such a deduction, being contented with *conceiving* this logical origin, which appears to him evident by virtue of the *necessity* of this notion.

10. The legitimacy of the imaginary term applied to space considered as outside matter, or as void, is thus explained; also explained is why Leibniz, in his correspondence with de Volder could not sometimes distinguish between the spatium and the extensio, since the spatium, in spite of its logical nature and its characteristic of eternal truth, is not in itself devoid of an imaginative element, and since, in addition, insofar as it is ideal, it could not be distinguished from the extensio (for example, when Leibniz denounces in the labyrinth of the continuum the confusion of the ideal and the actual).

11. There are, of course, also religious elements that we do not have to consider here.

12. Even if they are not originally taken in God *as* distinct.

Leibniz on Locke on Personal Identity

Edwin Curley

Much recent discussion of Leibniz's *Nouveaux essais* has focused on his defense of innate ideas against Locke's attack on them—understandably so, given the current resurgence of interest in innate ideas generated by the work of Chomsky.[1] My purpose in this paper is to develop a theme in Leibniz's work that has received much less attention, his critique of Locke's theory of personal identity. Given the intense interest philosophers have lately shown in Locke's theory,[2] the neglect of that part of the *Nouveaux essais* is puzzling. I hope to show that the confrontation of Locke and Leibniz on this topic will illuminate the thought of both philosophers. But because the interpretation of Locke on personal identity is difficult and controversial, I begin with a detailed look at Locke's *Essay.*

I

It is well known that Locke's chapter on identity (II, xxvii)[3] was not part of the first edition, but was added to the second edition. The story of how it came to be added is not as well known and is worth our attention. On 20 September, 1692, Locke, contemplating the revisions he might make in the second edition of the *Essay,* wrote to William Molyneux to solicit objections.[4] Molyneux responded with a number of objections, but urged Locke to let his *Essay* stand "as it does." Locke's next work

> should be of a Model wholly New, and that is by Way of Logick, something accomodated to the Usual Forms, together with the Consideration of Extension, Solidity, Mobility, Thinking, Existence, Duration, Number,

For their comments on earlier versions of this paper I am much indebted to Margaret Wilson, Nicholas Jolley, Robert Cummins, Talie Alexander, and Jonathan Bennett.

etc., and of the Mind of Man, and its Powers, as may make up a Compleat Body of what the Schools call Logicks and Metaphysicks. (Letter 1579, 22 December 1692)

What Molyneux wanted, evidently, was a work that would have stood to Locke's *Essay* as Descartes' *Principles of Philosophy* stood to his *Meditations*—a work more conventional in form, more comprehensive in treatment, aimed at the needs of the students put off by the stylistic peculiarities of the *Essay*.

Locke—wisely, I suspect—resisted this suggestion on the grounds that other more appealing projects, such as the treatise on morals that Molyneux had also urged on him, would leave him insufficient time for writing a logic. But he did ask Molyneux,

since you mention logick and metaphysicks in relation to my book, whether either of those sciences may suggest to you any new heads fit to be inserted into my *Essay* in a second edition. (Letter 1592, 20 January 1693)

Molyneux replied that he knew none,

unless you think it may not do well to insist more particularly and at large on Aeternae Veritates and the Principium Individuationis. (Letter 1609, 2 March 1693)

Molyneux acknowledged that Locke's first edition had "some touches" concerning both these topics. The implication, however, was that they deserved much fuller treatment.

Two things are interesting about this exchange. First, the task Molyneux sets Locke is not the one we might have expected. A reader of the first edition might well have found that edition unsatisfactory, in that it granted identity statements a prominent place among the objects of knowledge (IV, i, 3), that it rejected the notion that the idea of identity was innate (I, iv, 4), and yet that it nowhere undertook to account for the origin of that idea in experience. Surely this was an important gap in Locke's argument for the origin of all our ideas in experience. And although Locke's account of the idea's origin, as he presents it in II, xxvii, 1 of the second and later editions, is admittedly brief and perfunctory, it is natural to assume that the chapter was meant to fill that gap. The correspondence, however, shows Locke being pressed, not to make his case for concept empiricism more complete, but to deal with the traditional logico-metaphysical problem of individuation. This helps to explain why so little of what Locke says in this long chapter has any bearing on the origin of the idea of identity.

Second, Molyneux makes no explicit criticisms of anything Locke says about either individuation or identity. When he calls attention to two passages in which Locke has "some touches" on the problem of individuation, his references do not, as we might have expected, include one to III, vi, 4, where Locke contends that nothing is essential to an individual as such. Instead he refers us to

I, iv, 4-5 and II, i, 11-12. He does not say that Locke's theory of individuation in these passages is unsatisfactory; but he might well have done so. As we shall see, Locke's treatment of problems of identity and individuation in these two first edition passages is quite inconsistent.

In the first passage, Locke's primary target is the doctrine of innate principles. Attacking the view that the principle of identity is innate in us, he argues that it could not be unless the idea of identity were also innate in us (I, iv, 1-3). But if our idea of identity were innate, and hence, "settled and clear," we would not find ourselves so perplexed by puzzle cases as we are. Locke then (I, iv, 4) lists three identity questions that he regards as troublesome:

(1) Whether a Man, being a Creature consisting of Soul and Body, be the same Man, when his Body is changed?

(2) Whether Euphorbus and Pythagoras, having had the same Soul, were the same Man, though they lived several Ages asunder?

(3) Whether the Cock, too, which had the same Soul, were not the same with both of them?

A number of things need to be noted about these questions.

First, they all involve diachronic identity. They are questions about identity through time. Locke seems to have regarded synchronic identity statements as inherently unproblematic, as a paradigm of the knowable (cf. II, xxvii, i; IV, i, 4).

Second, the first question is prompted, apparently, by the recognition that the particles of matter composing the body are constantly being replaced by others (cf. II, i, 12 ad fin.). As such, the question would interest any philosopher tempted by the notion that some kind of bodily continuity is a necessary condition for a man's remaining the same man.[5]

In the second edition (II, xxvii, 3-6) Locke will deal with questions of human identity by contending that the identity conditions for living creatures are different from those for masses of matter. The former survive the replacement of their component particles and the addition or subtraction of parts, so long as we assume continuity of the organization of the parts into a coherent body, "partaking of the same life." A mass of matter, on the other hand, loses its identity if even one atom is taken away or added, and preserves it, if the components remain the same, no matter how they are organized.

In our present passage, Locke gives no hint of that solution. Instead, he shifts to quite different identity questions involving the doctrine of transmigration. The rationale for this shift in focus appears to be as follows. We do not, in fact, regard substantial bodily changes as sufficient to show that a man is not the same man he was. Should we infer that this is because continuity of the soul is sufficient to show identity? If so, how will we deal with the paradoxes of the doctrine of transmigration?

Locke is not consistent in the moral he derives from these puzzle cases. At the end of I, iv, 4 the suggestion is that we may be uncertain about how to answer his identity questions because not all of us have the same idea of identity:

> every one's *Idea* of *Identity,* will not be the same, that Pythagoras, and Thousands others of his Followers, have.

The implication would seem to be that the dispute over the correct answer to questions (2) and (3) is ultimately a verbal one, to be resolved by realizing that we mean by "identity" something different from what the Pythagoreans mean. But in the middle of I, iv, 4 and at the end of I, iv, 5 the suggestion is that we may be uncertain because "our *Idea of Sameness*" (the common idea we and the Pythagoreans share?) is just not clear enough for us to answer these identity questions with any certainty.

It is not Locke's contention that (as some more recent philosophers hold[6]) the puzzle questions have no answer. He wants no one to think "the Questions, I have here proposed about the *Identity* of Man, are bare, empty Speculations" (I, iv, 5). God must know their answers, to dispense divine justice on the day of judgment. It is just terribly difficult for men to discover the correct answers.

Again Locke does not make, in this passage, the distinction he will later make (*both* in our next first edition passage, II, i, 11-12, *and* much more fully in the second edition, II, xxvii, 7) between the identity of the man and the identity of the person. In I, iv, 5, he uses "man" and "person" interchangeably. And from the perspective of his later discussion, the second and third questions in I, iv, 4, desperately need reformulation. If a man is a creature consisting of both a soul and a body of a certain kind, or even if he is just a creature consisting of a certain kind of living body,[7] and if Euphorbus and Pythagoras, while having the same soul, have different bodies, then from Locke's later point of view we should say that they were clearly not the same man, though they might be the same person. When Locke formulates his third question, he does not explicitly say whether it is a question of human or personal identity; ignoring his own thesis that nothing is essential to an individual as such, he avoids the issue by omitting to complete "the same . . ." with a kind-term. But since the cock is not a man at all (if II, xxvii, 8 is correct), the question cannot be whether it is the same *man* as Euphorbus and Pythagoras. The question must be whether it is the same person.

So Locke's treatment of these puzzle cases in I, iv, 4-5 is both inconsistent in itself and inconsistent with the other first edition discussion of identity to which Molyneux called attention. But perhaps the most interesting thing we can derive from this first bout with problems of identity is a clue to the philosophical concerns his mature theory addressed. His choice of examples indicates a preoccupation with transmigration. I suggest that the need Locke will feel to distinguish between the man and the person comes, in considerable measure at least, from his sense that the hypothesis of transmigration raises an important question that cannot be dismissed by anything we might observe about bodily differences or discontinuities.

It may seem strange to give this much prominence to a doctrine we are apt to regard as one no modern Western thinker would take seriously. But any thoroughgoing mind-body dualism must allow the possibility of transmigration. If the mind is, in the Cartesian sense, really distinct from the body, i.e., able to exist apart from the body, there is no apparent reason why its capacity for separate existence should be realized only after its incarnation in this body. So far as I am aware, Descartes never considers the possibility of pre-existence. His concern is with establishing post-existence. But the Cambridge Platonists, naturally enough, were intensely interested in the doctrine of pre-existence and debated the issue vigorously, with More and Glanvill arguing for pre-existence and Cudworth arguing against it.[8] The subtitle of Glanvill's *Lux orientalis* makes it clear that this hypothesis was attractive not only because of its consonance with dualism:

> An enquiry into the opinion of the eastern sages concern the pre-existence of souls, being a key to unlock the grand mysteries of providence concerning man's sin and misery.

Glanvill and More found this doctrine appealing partly because they believed that it explained how a man who was the creature of an omnipotent and benevolent deity might nevertheless be born sinful and miserable. Locke, with his latitudinarian sympathies and his connections with the Cudworth family,[9] was surely familiar with this debate. The extent to which it concerned him is indicated not only by his choice of examples in I, iv, 4-5, but by the frequency of his allusions to it later in the *Essay* (cf. II, i, 12; and II, xxvii, 6, 14, 15, 19, 21, 26, and 27). *Why* this doctrine of transmigration so concerned him will emerge as we proceed.

I turn now to the second of the two first edition "touches" on the problem of individuation to which Molyneux drew attention, II, i, 11-12. The primary target here is the Cartesian doctrine that the soul always thinks. Against this Locke deploys the following argument: if the soul thinks even in dreamless sleep, it must at that time be conscious of its thoughts; that is a necessary condition for all thinking; but the man (the composite of body and soul) who sleeps without dreaming is not at any time conscious of the thoughts his soul has in dreamless sleep; while he is asleep, he is not conscious of anything; when he awakes, he has no recollection of any thoughts his soul may have had in dreamless sleep; so the soul that thinks in dreamless sleep and the man (or the waking man) are two distinct persons. Locke regards this conclusion as absurd enough to refute the hypothesis that the soul always thinks.

Note that, although this passage belongs to the first edition, it definitely anticipates the more extended treatment of identity in the second edition. Here Locke observes and emphasizes, without explaining it, his distinction between the man and the person; he makes it clear that the questions at issue are questions of personal identity; he has no doubt that *we* can answer them; and he presumes that in doing so we will regard continuity of consciousness as a necessary condition for personal identity.

Characteristically, Locke now proceeds to rerun the argument with a special twist by introducing transmigration:

Let us suppose the Soul of *Castor* separated, during his Sleep, from his Body, to think apart.

We are to suppose also that his body continues to live without the presence of his soul. This is, after all, a polemic against the Cartesians, who do not think the presence of a soul essential to life.

Let us suppose too, that it chooses for its Scene of Thinking, the Body of another Man, v.g. *Pollux,* who is sleeping without a Soul. . . . We have here then the Bodies of two men with only one Soul between them, which [men] we will suppose to sleep and wake by turns; and the Soul still thinking in the waking Man, whereof the sleeping Man is never conscious, has never the least Perception.

Locke asks whether Castor and Pollux are not, on this hypothesis, "two as distinct Persons, as *Castor* and *Hercules*; or, as *Socrates* and *Plato* were?" But now the question is rhetorical. It is not a puzzle case that is supposed to perplex us and show us something about our idea of identity (that it is confused, or not the same as someone else's). We are supposed to be clear that these are not the same persons. The Cartesians, allowing the soul to think what the man is not conscious of, make the man and his soul two persons. And this absurdity refutes their hypothesis.

Whether or not Molyneux was conscious of the inconsistencies we have been exploring, he was clearly right not to be satisfied with the first edition treatment of identity. From the point of view of the second passage, Locke should at least have rewritten the first passage. Probably he should have dropped altogether his use of identity-puzzles as an argument against the innateness of the idea of identity.

But he did not. Instead he retained the first passage without alteration and elaborated on the account presupposed by the second passage. Locke's central thesis is that we can avoid "the Difficulty about this Relation" of identity if we attend carefully to our notions of the things to which identity is attributed. The identity conditions for different kinds vary with the kinds, so that we may get quite a different answer depending on what question we ask:

"Is this the same body as that?"
"Is this the same living body as that?"
"Is this the same man as that?"
"Is this the same person as that?"

Locke's primary concern is with the latter two questions, and this preoccupation reflects the ethical and religious interests that led Locke to write the *Essay*.[10]

To answer identity questions of the form "Is x the same man as y?" we must, Locke thinks, be clear about the precise idea we associate with the term 'man.' Unfortunately Locke is not clear in his account of the nominal essence of this term. In the first edition, his view seems to be that the idea of a man is a complex of the ideas of "voluntary Motion, with Sense and Reason, join'd to a Body of a certain shape" (III, vi, 3). Though he acknowledges that different men annex different ideas to this term, some taking the shape to be the essential difference between men and other animals (III, vi, 26), he regards this as an unreasonable way of proceeding, dependent on the fiction that a certain limited number of species exist in nature (IV, iv, 13-16).

In the chapter on identity in the second edition, however, Locke seems sometimes to adopt the definition of man disparaged in the first edition:

And whatever is talked of other definitions, ingenuous observation puts it past doubt, that the *Idea* in our Minds, of which the Sound *Man* in our Mouths is the Sign, is nothing else but of an Animal of such a certain Form. (II, xxvii, 8; cf. II, xxvii, 6)

Locke's account here is based not so much on observation as on a hypothesis about what we would say if we encountered an animal of our own shape who gave no sign of rationality or a rational animal of a quite different shape. Denying manhood to a rational parrot is perfectly consistent with the first edition's definition of man. But Locke's confidence about what we would call an irrational creature of the right shape conveniently forgets the perplexities about changelings in the first edition.

By the end of II, xxvii, 8, however, Locke seems to have reverted to the essentials of his doctrine in the first edition:

'tis not the idea of a thinking or rational Being alone, that makes the *Idea* of a *Man* in most Peoples Sense; but of a body so and so shaped joined to it, and if that be the Idea of a Man, the same successive Body, not shifted all at once, must as well as the same immaterial Spirit go to the making of the same *Man*.

Later discussions of the idea of man (II, xxvii, 21, 29) are somewhat noncommittal, allowing the threefold possibility of a purely physical definition, a purely mental definition, and a complex definition combining mental and physical traits. But it is probably fairest to regard the third of these as Locke's dominant view.

So much for man. What, then, does Locke think are the defining characteristics of a person? It is, he says,

a thinking intelligent Being, that has reason and reflection, and can consider it self as it self, the same thinking thing in different times and places. (II, xxvii, 9)

So physical characteristics are not essential to a person. Mental ones of a fairly high order are essential. A person must be rational and it must have the capacity for conceiving of itself as an entity with a past and a future.

What is supposed to make possible the person's conception of itself as a being persisting through time is the fact that consciousness is inseparable from thinking, so that a thinking thing is necessarily aware of its thoughts. But of course the most Locke will claim is that this necessary awareness applies to present thoughts. He does not dream that a thinking thing is necessarily aware of, or able to recall, all, or even any, of its past thoughts. He acknowledges, and indeed, insists, that forgetfulness is common (II, xxvii, 10) and total amnesia possible (II, xxvii, 20).[11] His contention is that, however far back the identity of the thinking thing may extend, the identity of the person extends only so far as his consciousness can reach.

This account of personal identity is teeming with paradox. For example, if I cannot now remember any of the thoughts I had as a very young child, I am not the same person as that child. This has the further consequence that personal identity is nontransitive.[12] Suppose an aged general recalls his actions as a young lieutenant (and hence is identical with the young lieutenant). Suppose the young lieutenant recalls the events of his childhood (and hence is identical with the child). It is quite conceivable that the aged general will not recall the events of his childhood (and hence not be identical with the child).

Thirty years ago the tendency was to regard such objections as fatal to Locke's theory.[13] More recently the tendency has been to say, "Look, there is something right about this theory. Let's patch it up so that it won't be vulnerable to these obvious counter-examples."[14] But admirable as this constructive spirit may be, it should be emphasized that Locke would certainly have refused such aid. As Mackie has pointed out,[15] Locke does consider the objection:

> Suppose I wholly lose the memory of some parts of my life, beyond the possibility of retrieving them . . . yet am I not the same Person that did those Actions, had those Thoughts, that I was once conscious of, though I have now forgot them? (II, xxvii, 20)

Locke's answer to this apparently rhetorical question, as we shall see in more detail later, is "no." Locke is aware of the paradoxes and accepts them.

Why, in the face of what seem to us insuperable difficulties, is Locke so attached to this theory? It may help us to understand his position if we recall a curious irony of history. Nowadays Locke's view tends to be associated with Platonic or Cartesian dualism. Flew, for example, in an influential article, traced Locke's distinction between the man and the person to (*inter alia*)

> his Platonic-Cartesian conviction that people are essentially incorporeal spirits, and that human bodies are in fact controlled by internal shadow beings in ways similar to, but much less intelligible than, that in which ships are directed by their captains.[16]

One senses the influence of Ryle's *Concept of Mind* even in the style of this passage.

Similarly, Perry,[2] who notices that

Locke is very explicit in saying that identity of 'immaterial substance' is neither a necessary nor a sufficient condition for personal identity (Perry, p. 21; he cites no text, but cf. Locke II, xxvii, 10),

thinks Locke must not

jettison the notion of substance entirely; he thought that at every moment of a person's life, or at least at every conscious moment, he must be in 'vital union' with some immaterial substance or other . . . we must be in vital union with immaterial substances to think, just as we must be in vital union with material substances . . . to reach or walk or stand up.

But to say this is to miss the main point of the theory. Although Locke certainly does not jettison the notion of substance entirely, he is most anxious to develop a theory of personal identity that will make no essential use of that notion. What matters, at least as far as personal identity is concerned, is the relation between the states of a substance, not the continuity of the substance that is the subject of those states (II, xxvii, 10, 12-16). Each of the states entering into the relation that makes for personal identity will be a state of a substance, and a state of a thinking substance. But it does not follow that it will be a state of an immaterial substance. Locke thinks it only likely, not certain, that thinking substance is immaterial; he is anxious to leave open the possibility that it may be a material substance (notoriously in IV, iii, 6, but also in II, xxvii, 12, 16, 17, 25).[17] Much of the point of his theory is to locate the conditions for personal identity in something that will not require us to decide what kind of substance it is that thinks, or even whether it is numerically the same substance that thinks throughout the history of the person. If a Platonic or Cartesian dualism makes personal identity depend on the continued existence of the same immaterial substance, as Locke certainly thought it did,[18] then that dualism is the opposition theory, not Locke's.

    To see why Locke is anxious to locate the conditions for personal identity in a relation between states of substance, rather than in the substance itself, we must keep in mind his remark that "person" is

a Forensick Term appropriating Actions and their Merit; and so belongs only to intelligent Agents capable of a Law, and Happiness and Misery. This personality extends it *self* beyond present Existence to what is past, only by consciousness, whereby it becomes concerned and accountable, owns and imputes to it *self* past Actions, just upon the same ground, and for the same reason that it does the present. (II, xxvii, 26)

This last sentence seems to mean that, just as we cannot hold you responsible for what you are doing now, if you are not now aware of doing it, so we cannot hold you responsible for what you did in the past if you are not now aware of (i.e., able in fact to recall) having done it. We may doubt whether this equivalence holds. Your not knowing what you *are* doing now makes your present behavior involuntary; your not knowing now what you *did* then need not make your past behavior involuntary. But the essential point here is that a Lockean person is a subject of rights and responsibilities. So whatever is necessary and sufficient for constituting a subject of rights and responsibilities is necessary and sufficient for constituting a Lockean person.

Substantial theories of personal identity are, in Locke's view, pernicious because they locate the conditions of personal identity in the presence of something unverifiable:

> *self* is not determined by Identity or Diversity of substance, which it cannot be sure of, but only by Identity of consciousness. (II, xxvii, 23)

Identity of consciousness *is* something the self can be sure of. Locke insists on a principle of personal identity that the subject himself can be sure of, because he thinks it important that reward and punishment not only be just, but also be seen to be just by the subject who is rewarded or punished. If personal identity depended on continuity of substance, whether material or immaterial, the subject of reward and punishment could have no assurance that it was being properly distributed. If it depends on continuity of consciousness, he can have that assurance.

In spite of the term "forensic," Locke is primarily concerned with moral rights and responsibilities, not with legal ones. The judgment that matters is the Last Judgment. In the section quoted earlier Locke goes on to say:

> whatever past Actions [the self] cannot reconcile or appropriate to that present self by consciousness, it can no more be concerned in, than if they had never been done. And to receive Pleasure or Pain; i.e., Reward or Punishment, on the account of any such Action, is all one has to be made happy or miserable in its first being, without any demerit at all. For supposing a Man punish'd now, for what he had done in another Life, whereof he could be made to have no consciousness at all, what difference is there between that Punishment, and being created miserable? (II, xxvii, 26)

From the subject's point of view, there is no difference at all. Hence the Platonist solution to the mysteries of providence is no solution at all.

The importance of Locke's statement that "person" is a forensic term has often been noted, but not, I would argue, properly appreciated. Consider Mackie, who is careful to avoid so many major mistakes of interpretation, and who yet complains that what Locke gives us is

> hardly a theory of personal identity at all, but might better be described as a theory of action appropriation. Locke seems to be forgetting that 'person' is not only a "forensic term, appropriating actions and their merit,' but also the noun corresponding to all the personal pronouns. (Mackie, p. 183; cf. pp. 173, 191)

It is, I submit, a mistake to think that it is Locke's intention to give us a theory of personal identity if that requires giving an account of "the noun corresponding to all the personal pronouns."

First of all, Locke does not think that the correct use of personal pronouns settles questions of personal identity. This is evident from his response to the following objection:

> suppose I wholly lose the memory of some parts of my Life, beyond a possibility of retrieving them, so that perhaps I shall never be conscious of them again; yet am I not the same Person, that did those Actions, had those Thoughts, that I was once conscious of, though I have now forgotten them? To which I answer, that we must here take notice what the Word *I* is applied to, which in this case is the Man only. And the same Man being presumed to be the same Person, *I* is easily here supposed to stand for the same Person. (II, xxvii, 20)

The years of my early childhood *are* a part of *my* life, even though I have completely forgotten them. But this is only because I am the same *man* as I was then, not because I am the same *person* as the one who then used the first person pronoun to refer to himself. Locke's theory is not intended to be a theory of "personal identity," in the sense of providing a theory of the reference of personal pronouns. If Locke is to be consistent with his doctrine that identity is relative, that nothing is essential to the individual as such, he *cannot* offer a theory of personal identity in Mackie's sense. Nothing is essential to me as me, not even my memory (III, vi, 4).

Again, Locke's theory is not intended to be an exercise in the conceptual analysis of the term 'person' (cf. Mackie, 189ff.). Locke does not think his theory of personal identity is an analysis of what people ordinarily mean by the term 'person,' because he does not think people ordinarily distinguish between 'man' and 'person' in the way he does. Consider once more the tale of the Prince and the Cobbler:

> should the Soul of a Prince, carrying with it the consciousness of the Prince's life, enter and inform the Body of a Cobler as soon as deserted by his own Soul, *every one sees,* he would be the same Person with the Prince, accountable only for the Prince's actions: But *who would say* it was the same Man? The Body too goes to the making the Man, and would I guess, to every Body determine the Man in this case, wherein the Soul, with all its Princely Thoughts about it, would not make another Man: But he would be the same Cobler to every one besides himself. (II, xxvii, 15, my emphasis)

This means, I think, that everyone who knew about the transfer of the soul and its consciousness would agree that if we want to punish anyone for what the Prince did before the transfer, we should punish the person who has the body of the Cobbler. But no one would think that the Cobbler was the same man as the Prince, because everyone regards bodily continuity as necessary for human identity, and spiritual continuity as insufficient. (The last sentence is mysterious, since Locke gives us no identity conditions for "same Cobbler.")

In any case, so far it seems that the ordinary man is making a distinction between 'man' and 'person.' But Locke immediately proceeds to deny this:

> I know that in the ordinary way of speaking, the same Person, and the same Man, stand for one and the same thing.

Then we get a bit of linguistic libertarianism:

> And indeed everyone will always have a liberty to speak as he pleases, and to apply what articulate Sounds to what *Ideas* he thinks fit, and change them as often as he pleases.

Finally we get, as I read it, a plea for conceptual reform:

> But yet when we will enquire, what makes the same *Spirit, Man,* or *Person,* we must fix the *Ideas* of *Spirit, Man,* or *Person,* in our Minds; and having resolved with our selves what we mean by them, it will not be hard to determine, in either of them, or the like, when it is the *same,* and when not.

I take the point to be this. Ordinary language is confused. People use 'person' as a forensic term, whose identity conditions require continuity of consciousness; they use 'man' as a biological term whose identity conditions require bodily continuity; and they also use 'person' and 'man' interchangeably. But we have no guarantee that continuity of consciousness is properly correlated with bodily continuity. On the most likely hypothesis about what a thinking thing is (viz. the Cartesian or Platonistic theory that it is an immaterial substance), if there is a correlation, this will be a matter of luck or divine grace. So one prerequisite of clarity of thought in these matters is to distinguish between 'man' and 'person.'

Locke's theory of personal identity, then, to sum up what I have argued so far, is a theory about what constitutes a subject of rights and responsibilities, not about what constitutes the referent of personal pronouns, or the ordinary use of the term "person." It attempts to locate personal identity in a relation of co-consciousness between the states of a thinking substance because this avoids the disadvantages of the main alternative, Platonic-Cartesian dualism, which relies too heavily on the obscure notion of an immaterial substance. One major attraction of Locke's theory is that it can dispense with trying to prove that the soul is an immaterial substance:

> All the great Ends of Morality and Religion, are well enough secured, without philosophical Proofs of the Soul's immortality; since it is evident that he who made us at the first begin to subsist here, sensible intelligent Beings, and for several years continued us in such a state, can and will restore us to the like state of Sensibility in another World, and make us capable there to receive the Retribution he has designed to Men, according to their doings in this Life. (IV, iii, 6, Nidditch, 542; Fraser II, 195)

There can be no philosophical proof of the Soul's immortality. But to have a proper respect for the Last Judgment, we need no such proof. All we need is to believe that God has the capacity to bring it about that a thinking being appropriates past thoughts and actions to himself, thinks of them as his own. Whether the substance who has those thoughts is material or immaterial, whether or not those past thoughts and actions inhered in a substance continuous with it, none of this is of the slightest moment. The main function of Locke's theory is to reconcile our invincible ignorance on these metaphysical issues with our moral and religious conviction that we will be judged, and judged fairly.

II

Leibniz's criticisms of Locke's theory of personal identity in the *Nouveaux essais* need to be seen against the background of his own earlier thought on the same topic, before the stimulus from across the Channel. The general problem of individuation had, of course, interested Leibniz from the beginning. But I shall concentrate on the key metaphysical treatise of his mature period, the *Discourse on Metaphysics.*[19]

What is most striking about Leibniz's position in the *Discourse* is how very Lockean it is. In section xxxiv, discussing the difference between minds and other substances, Leibniz observes that the souls of beasts and the substantial forms of bodies

> cannot perish entirely, any more than [atoms or the ultimate parts of matter in the sentiment of other philosophers]; for no substance perishes, although it may become quite different.[20]

The doctrine that substances cannot perish, or at least cannot perish naturally, without an act of God, is good Cartesian doctrine,[21] though Descartes, of course, would deny that bodies have substantial forms, or that beasts have souls. For Leibniz, however, the main difference between minds and other substances will be, not that bodies and beasts lack a soul, but that they

> do not know what they are [nor what they do, and that, being consequently unable to reflect, they cannot discover [necessary and universal] truths. It is also for lack of reflection on themselves that they have no moral quality,] whence it comes that passing through a thousand transformations, almost like a caterpillar which turns into a butterfly, it is all one for morals or for practice if they are said to perish. (Lucas and Grint, 57-58)

The editor's annotation of this passage tells us that the phrase "that they have no moral quality" was a replacement for "that they do not make a person." Leibniz may well have made this change because the former phrase makes explicit the implications of being a person. For Leibniz, as for Locke, 'person' is a moral term, which entails being a subject of reward and punishment. That is why the special case of personal identity dominates both their discussions of individuation. Other questions of identity may be of merely academic interest, but determining whether or not *a* is the same person as *b* inevitably has practical consequences.

In contrast with the substantial forms of bodies and the souls of beasts

the intelligent soul, knowing what it is and being able to say this *I* which says so much, remains and subsists not merely Metaphysically . . . but it also remains the same morally and makes the same person. For it is the memory or knowledge of this *I* which makes it capable of punishment or reward.

So for Leibniz here, as for Locke in the *Essay,* what Locke would call 'identity of consciousness,' the self's appropriation to itself of its own past, and particularly its past actions, is essential to its remaining the same person.

The continuation of the passage makes it plain that eschatological concerns are as present to Leibniz's mind as they are to Locke's:

the immortality which is demanded [in morals and in religion] does not consist in this perpetual subsistence [alone], which belongs to all substances, for without the memory of what one had been it would not be in any way desirable. Let us suppose that some individual were to become King of China at one stroke, but on condition of forgetting what he had been, [as if he had just been born anew], is it not so much in practice, [or as regards the effects which one can perceive,] as if he were to be annihilated and a king of China to be created in his place at the same instant? which this individual has no reason to desire.

We are reminded of Locke's man, punished now for something he had done in a previous life, but something which he could not in any way recall (II, xxvii, 26). There would not, Locke thought, be any difference between having that happen and being created miserable.

But Leibniz's focus is different. Locke, preoccupied with the Platonic doctrine of pre-existence, looks to the past and queries the propriety of the punishment. Leibniz, thinking probably of the Spinozistic doctrine of an immortality without memory of this life (*Ethics* VP23S), looks to the future and queries the desirability of the supposed reward. The individual would have no reason to want to be King of China if that required complete ignorance of what he had been.[22]

Differences of perspective apart, there seems to be another, more important difference between the Leibniz of the *Discourse* and the Locke of the *Essay.* For Locke, continuity of consciousness is not only necessary for personal identity, it is also sufficient. If I can recall a past action and have the same sense of its being *my* action that I now have regarding my present actions, then it does not matter whether that action is the act of numerically the same substance; it will still be the act of the same person (II, xxvii, 10). This part of Locke's theory has been sharply criticized both by sympathetic and by unsympathetic interpreters.[23] For Locke does not seem able to stick consistently to it. In II, xxvii, 13 he insists that God, in his goodness, will not allow transfers of consciousness from one thinking substance to another. But if continuity of consciousness really were sufficient for personal identity, independently of the identity of the thinking substance, then there would be no injustice in such a transfer. There would be nothing repugnant to God's goodness in his allowing it to take place.

In the *Discourse* Leibniz gives us no reason to think that he would go so far. The passage we have been considering presumes that there will be continuity of substance and to be more concerned to argue that the continued existence of what is numerically the same substance is not enough:

> The immortality which is demanded [in morals and in religion] does not consist in this perpetual subsistence [alone], which belongs to all substances.

Leibniz's addition of "alone" serves to emphasize that the continued existence of numerically the same substance will be necessary, even though not sufficient for the continued existence of the same person. Perhaps the possibility of a transfer of consciousness from one substance to another does not occur to him as one requiring discussion, because he thinks it is strictly inconceivable. If Leibniz regards the perceptions of thinking substances as individual entities themselves, which logically could not exist in more than one subject, then the notion of the same consciousness being transferred from one substance to another might well seem to involve a contradiction.[24]

By the time Leibniz writes the *Nouveaux essais,* he is, I shall argue, considerably less Lockean about personal identity than he was in the *Discourse.* The key passage is Leibniz's long and difficult comment on II, xxvii, 9, which begins as follows:

> I, also, am of this opinion, that consciousness, or the sense of the self, proves a moral or personal identity. That is how I distinguish the uninterruptibility of an animal's soul from the immortality of a man's soul. Each retains real, physical identity. But in man the rules of divine providence require that the soul *also* retain moral identity, which is apparent to us, ourselves, in order to constitute the same person, capable, consequently, of feeling punishments and rewards [my emphasis].

So far this looks like the quasi-Lockean position of the *Discourse.* Personal identity is equated with being a proper subject of reward and punishment, and the sense of self, the subject's appropriation to himself of his past actions, is a necessary condition of his feeling punishment and reward *as* punishment and reward. By implication, his feeling punishment and reward *as* punishment and reward is a necessary condition of its being true punishment and reward. But though the sense of self is treated as a necessary condition for personal identity, there is no suggestion that it would be sufficient in the absence of continuity of substance. Indeed, one and the same substance ("real, physical identity") is assumed and treated as an additional necessary condition of personal identity. It is somewhat misleading of Leibniz to begin by saying that he and Locke share the same opinion.[25]

Leibniz is, quite generally, anxious to find as much common ground between himself and Locke as he can.[26] But reflection on Locke's position seems to have driven him further from Locke, not drawn him closer. This gradually becomes evident as our passage continues:

> It seems, Sir, that you hold that this apparent identity could be preserved when there was no real identity at all. I should think that perhaps that could happen, by the absolute power of God. But according to the order of things, the identity apparent to the person himself, who feels himself to be the same, implies real identity, accompanied at each proximate transition by reflection, or the sense of self.

Professor Wilson (p. 346) takes this passage as showing that for Leibniz there is no logical impossibility in the supposition that a person, i.e., a particular consciousness, might be dissociated from the substance in which it inhered, and yet remain the same person, but that God in his goodness would not allow this to occur. On this reading, Leibniz would adopt the position of Locke in his moments of backsliding (cf. Locke, II, xxvii, 13). But *what*, precisely, is it that Leibniz thinks God could, but wouldn't allow? That the same person might continue to exist without continuity of the same immaterial substance? That is what Wilson's reading requires. But when Leibniz explains why "the order of things" requires a coincidence between apparent and real identity, he says that "an intimate and immediate perception cannot deceive naturally." What is incompatible with God's goodness is that a person should be deceived in thinking himself identical with the person who did x a moment ago. This implies that the person *would* be deceived if he thought he had done x just then and x were not the act of numerically the same substance as the one who thought that. So continuity of substance is really essential to the continued identity of the person. Continuity of consciousness alone is not sufficient for personal identity.[27]

So far we have nothing that would be inconsistent with Leibniz's position in the *Discourse*. As he proceeds, however, it appears that continuity of consciousness, in Locke's sense, is no longer even a necessary condition of personal identity:

> I should not wish at all to say . . . that I am not the same self who was in the crib, on the pretext that I no longer remember anything I did then. It is sufficient to discover moral identity by oneself if there is an intermediate connection between one state and its neighbor, or even between two states a bit distant.

If an illness interrupted the continuity of consciousness and I could no longer remember how I had come to my present state, or what sins I had committed before the illness struck, the testimony of others could fill the gap. I could even be punished on the strength of this testimony.

This shift reflects Leibniz's training as a lawyer and the lawyer's characteristic insistence on a generalizable theory. Punishment and reward, rights and responsibilities, go together. If I lost all consciousness of my past life, I would not lose the rights I possessed before. It would not be necessary "to divide me in two persons and make me my own heir" to safeguard my rights. The same must hold of my responsibilities. No doubt something is lost if I genuinely cannot remember doing what I did wrongly and am now to be punished for. But do we seriously want to maintain that I could not properly be punished for those acts?

Locke, of course, had appealed to legal practice in support of his intuitions about punishment. Where continuity of consciousness breaks down, we would distinguish between the man and the person, holding that the same man is present, but not the same person. This is

> the Sense of Mankind in the solemnest Declaration of their Opinion, Humane Laws not punishing the *Mad Man* for the Sober Man's Actions, nor the *Sober Man* for what the *Mad Man* did, thereby making them two Persons. (II, xxvii, 20)

Locke seems to be thinking here of something like a Jekyll and Hyde case, but one in which neither party is conscious of the actions of the other.

Locke, however, recognizes that legal practice does not entirely square with his theory. So he imagines someone objecting as follows:

> is not a Man Drunk and Sober the same Person, why else is he punish'd for the Fact he commits when Drunk, though he be never afterwards conscious of it? Just as much the same Person as a Man that walks, and does other things in his sleep, is the same Person, and is answerable for any mischief he shall do in it. (II, xxvii, 22)

To which Locke replies that human laws justly punish both the drunk and the somnambulist because in these cases the laws

> cannot distinguish certainly what is real, what counterfeit . . . the ignorance in Drunkenness or Sleep is not admitted as a plea . . . because the Fact [deed] is proved against [the defendant] , but want of consciousness cannot be proved from him.

This is very curious. As far as sleepwalking is concerned, Locke is trying to explain away a legal practice that is apparently not a legal practice at all. Sleepwalking *is* generally accepted as an excuse in modern law, and apparently was in Locke's day.[28] As for drunkenness, it is not generally accepted as an excuse in modern law, and was even less widely accepted in Locke's day. But the reasons for this apparently have to do wih the fact that drunkenness is voluntarily contracted, rather than difficult to prove.[29]

Locke's contemporary critics recognized the weakness of his legal analysis. Molyneux seems uncertain that the law does not excuse somnambulists, and inclined to think that it should, but presses particularly the issue of drunkenness (Letter 1685, 23 December 1693). Leibniz attacks on both fronts:

> There is a great deal of difference between the actions of a drunk and
> those of a true and acknowledged somnambulist. We punish drunks be-
> cause they can avoid drunkenness, and can even have some memory of the
> punishment during their drunkenness. But it is not so much in the power
> of sleepwalkers to refrain from their nightly walk and from what they do
> in it. (II, xxvii, 22)

What is critical in the case of both drunkenness and sleepwalking is that at the
time of action the person is not fully conscious and hence lacks normal control
of his actions. If this lack of control is itself voluntarily induced, then it cannot
serve as an excuse. If it is involuntary, it can. Consciousness is relevant because it
is not fully present at the time of action, not because its continuity is subsequently interrupted. Though commentators sometimes allege that Locke capitu-
lated to Molyneux,[30] the correspondence seems rather to indicate that Locke
never did see this point.[31]

These moral and legal issues aside, there may be a deeper ground for
Leibniz's rejection of Locke's theory of personal identity. It is difficult to make
Locke's theory plausible, or even to state it coherently, without invoking his
doctrine that identity is relative to kinds, that nothing is essential to the individual as such. I am not the same person as the infant in the crib forty-three years
ago because I do not remember the thoughts I had then or anything I did. What
licenses my use of the term "I" to refer to that person? Locke will say: the fact
that I am the same man. An individual, x, may be the same F as y, and not the
same G as y.

Leibniz takes no notice of this distinction, nor indeed or any of Locke's
other applications of the relativity of identity (cf. II, xxvii, 3). The general
doctrine that nothing is essential to an individual as such, that things have
essential properties only insofar as they are related to some sort, has not been
announced yet. When it is (III, vi, 4), Leibniz will reject it, though not as sharply
as readers of the *Discourse on Metaphysics* might have expected:

> I think there is something essential to individuals, and more than one
> thinks. It is essential to substances to act, to created substances to be
> acted on, to minds to think, to bodies to have extension and movement.
> That is, there are sorts or species of which an individual cannot (naturally,
> at least) cease to be, when he has once been of that sort, whatever changes
> may happen in nature. But there are, I admit, sorts or species which are
> accidental to the individuals of those sorts . . . so, one can cease to be
> healthy, handsome, wise, and even to be visible or tangible, but one does
> not [cannot naturally?] cease to have life, and organs, and perception.

What is surprising here is Leibniz's apparent adoption of an essentialist, rather
than 'superessentialist' position.[32] He seems prepared to allow that some properties might be accidental to an individual, and not disposed to insist that all of an
individual's properties are essential to it.

Presumably Leibniz's moderate essentialism here is merely tactical. We may compare it with the position he takes on innate ideas in the *Nouveaux essais*. His own system requires *all* our thoughts to be innate, but against Locke he chooses to defend the more moderate and conventional position that *some* are, since it can be given an acceptable interpretation within his system. Similarly, his doctrine that the nature of an individual is to have a concept so complete that it includes all the individual's predicates (*Discourse on Metaphysics*, viii) entails that all of an individual's properties are essential to that individual as an individual. But there is no need here to defend so theologically sensitive a doctrine if the more conventional opinion can be given a defensible interpretation within his system.

This accommodating spirit is not characteristic only of 'popular' works like the *Nouveaux essais*. In their correspondence, Arnauld tries to refute Leibniz's doctrine of individual concepts by insisting that it obliterates the distinction between the essential and the accidental. Just as having all the points of its circumference equidistant from the center is essential to a sphere's being a sphere, whereas having a diameter of one foot is not, so, Arnauld argues, thinking is essential to my being me, but my taking a particular journey is not. On Leibniz's doctrine of individual concepts, this would not be true.[33]

Leibniz's reply insists that the distinction can be drawn:

the connection between events, although certain, is not necessary, and . . . I am free to take this journey or not, for although it is contained in my concept that I shall take it, it is also contained therein that I shall take it freely. And there is nothing in me of all that can be conceived in general terms, i.e., in terms of essence, or of a specific or incomplete concept, from which one can infer that I shall necessarily take it, whereas from the fact that I am a man one can conclude that I am capable of thought; and consequently, if I do not take this journey, that will not do violence to any eternal or necessary truth.[34]

The traditional essentialist distinction can be interpreted as a distinction between predicates that follow from a general or incomplete concept and predicates that follow only from a complete concept. That I [am able to] think follows from my being a man, but that I shall take this journey does not. It follows only from my complete concept.

This, though, misses the point. The question is not what follows from my being a man, but what follows from my being myself. And to that question Leibniz must, to be consistent, answer "everything":

if in the life of some person . . . , something were to proceed in a different way from what it does, . . . it would thus truly be another individual.[35]

It is only through confusing the issue that Leibniz can accommodate (moderate) essentialism.

Leibniz's commitment to essentialism of any kind, whether moderate or extravagant, would require him to deny Locke's doctrine that identity is relative to kinds and hence to deny that I might be the same man as the infant in the crib without being the same person. To that extent, it interferes with his acceptance of Lockean theory of personal identity. But the very extravagance of Leibniz's essentialism *ought*, it seems to lead Leibniz in the direction of a Lockean theory.

Suppose the infant in the crib has a particular sensation that it is conscious of, a cold, wet feeling, perhaps. If every predicate of an individual is essential to the individual's being that individual, then it would seem to follow that if Leibniz is no longer conscious of that sensation, he is not the same individual as that infant. Leibniz does not want to deny his identity with the infant, but neither does he want to deny that he remains the same individual through changes in his predicates. Part of the point of the theory of individual concepts is to explain how it is that an individual can remain the same through change. As Leibniz writes to Arnauld,

> there must of necessity be a reason for the true statement that we continue to exist, i.e., that I who was in Paris am now in Germany. For if there is no reason, one would be as justified in saying that it is another person . . . it is impossible to find another identity except that my attributes of the preceding time and state as well as those of the following time and state are predicates of one and the same subject, they are present in the same subject.

So far this is quite a conventional treatment of the problem of identity. Where Leibniz differs from the conventional substance philosopher is that he regards this last notion as needing explanation via the conceptual containment analysis of truth:

> What does it mean to say that the predicate is in the subject, except that the concept of the predicate is in some sense contained in the concept of the subject?

But if the subject changes, won't two contrary predicates both be contained in the same individual concept? And doesn't that make the individual concept self-contradictory?

A natural move, for a modern interpreter of Leibniz, is to suppose that Leibniz's predicates will be temporally indexed predicates holding timelessly of their subjects. What are contained in Leibniz's individual concept are predicates like " . . . is in Paris on 24 August 1676" or " . . . is in Hanover on 14 July 1686."[36] But generally Leibniz's own examples of the predicates contained in individual notions are not temporally indexed and are not expressed in the timeless present: " . . . would conquer Darius and Paris" (DM, viii), " . . . will become perpetual dictator and master of the repulic, etc." (DM, xiii), " . . . resolved to cross the Rubicon" (*Ibid.*), " . . . would have so many children" (to Arnauld, 12 April 1686).[37]

To the extent that Leibniz shows any awareness of this problem, he seems inclined to move in a different direction. When he introduces his conceptual containment account of truth in the *Discourse* (viii), he observes that God, seeing the individual concept of Alexander, sees "the foundation and reason of all the predicates that can be truly said of him." What *could* God see in the individual concept of Alexander that could be predicated of him essentially? Surely not anything true of Alexander only at one time and not at another. What then? Well, Leibniz does go on in the same passage to observe that

> when we consider well the connection of things, we can say that there are at all times in the soul of Alexander vestiges of all that has happened to him and the marks of all that will happen to him.

This seems to me an important clue to Leibniz's way of thinking.

Clearly, a thinking thing can contain its past 'by representation.' Not so clearly, but still, conceivably, a thinking thing might contain its future 'by representation.' People do generally remember much of their past, and there is no logical reason why they could not remember all of it. They do sometimes claim to have premonitions of their future, and there is no logical reason why they could not 'pre-cognize' all of it.[38] So a thinking thing could contain its entire past and future 'by representation.' If it did, and if containing 'by representation' is enough, then there would be a sense in which a spiritual substance would contain at all times what is true of it at any time. Perhaps these perceptions provide 'the foundation of all the predicates' that can truly be said of the individual.

In this connection it is interesting that in his first draft of this passage Leibniz had a significantly different example:

> The circular figure of the ring of Gyges/Polycrates does not include all that the notion of this individual ring comprises; whereas God, seeing the individual notion of this ring, as that it will be swallowed by a fish and nevertheless returned to its master, sees in it at the same time the foundation and reason of all the predicates that can be truly said of it . . . when we consider well the connection of things, we can say that there are at all times in this ring vestiges of all that has happened to it and the marks of all that will happen to it . . . *I speak here as if it were assured that this ring had a consciousness/is a substance.* (Lucas and Grint, 13; my emphasis)

I conjecture that Leibniz changed the example because he thought the conceptual containment account of truth would strictly hold only for genuine substances, i.e., for thinking things, which would be capable of containing their past and future by representation. From this standpoint Alexander's soul is a better example than Gyges' ring. If this hypothesis is correct, if only spiritual substances can be truly individual substances, because only they can contain at all times, by representation, a foundation for all the predicates they possess at any time, then that might explain why Leibniz thinks that only a spiritual being can possess a true unity (II, xxvii, 4).

By the time of the *Nouveaux essais,* the thinking thing's perceptions of its past and future do play a very important and explicit role in determining its individuality:

> An immaterial being, or a Spirit, cannot be stripped of all perception of its past existence. There remain in it impressions of whatever has formerly happened to it, and it even has presentiments of all that will happen to it. (II, xxvii, 14)

This is not Locke's continuity of consciousness, since

> these perceptions [sentiments] are usually too slight to be distinguishable and noticed, though they could perhaps be unfolded some day.

But this element of continuity, this "liaison of perceptions" of the past and the future, is what

> makes the same individual really. The apperceptions (i.e., the reflexive awarenesses of past perceptions) prove in addition a moral identity and make the real identity apparent.

In the end, Leibniz, like Locke, does not want to base the diachronic identity of persons on the continuity of a transcendental subject. Instead, like Locke, he makes it depend on a relationship of continuity among the states of the subject. But since he disagrees with Locke that the thinker is necessarily aware of his thoughts, persons do not, for Leibniz, exhaust the class of thinking things. He will extend his account of identity to all thinking things. And since, for Leibniz, all genuine individuals are thinking things, this account will hold for all individuals. In the end, Leibniz's initial tendency to agree with Locke's moral intuitions about identity has vanished. His grounds for adopting this extraordinary generalization of Locke's theory appear to be far more metaphysical than moral.

Notes

1. See, for example, *Innate Ideas,* ed. Stephen P. Stich (Berkeley: University of California Press, 1975).

2. See, for example, *Personal Identity,* ed. John Perry (Berkeley: University of California Press, 1975), and *The Identities of Persons,* ed. Amelie Rorty (Berkeley: University of California Press, 1976).

3. Generally it is possible, by using book, chapter, and section numbers, to give a fairly precise reference to passages both in Locke's *Essay* and in Leibniz's *Nouveaux essais* without referring to the pagination of any particular edition. Where necessary, page references are to John Locke, *An Essay Concerning Human Understanding,* ed. P. H. Nidditch (Oxford: Clarendon Press, 1975), and G. W. Leibniz, *Nouveaux essais sur l'entendement humain, Sämtliche Schriften und Briefe,* hrsg. von der Deutschen Akademie der Wissenschaften zu Berlin, Reihe 6, Band 6, 1962. One complication; Nidditch's edition follows the first five English editions of the *Essay* in numbering the first introductory chapter as Book I, chapter i; Leibniz (like Fraser) follows Coste's French version in separating the first chapter from Book I and treating Nidditch's Book i, chapter ii, as Book I, chapter i. So when I refer below to I, iv, 4-5, readers using the Fraser edition, or looking up the corresponding passage in Leibniz, should see I, iii, 4-5. By the time this chapter appears, English language readers will have available to them what promises to be an excellent new translation of the *New Essays,*

edited by Peter Remnant and Jonathan Bennett, and published by Cambridge University Press.

4. See Letter 1538, in *The Correspondence of John Locke*, ed. E. S. De Beer, Vol. IV (Oxford: Clarendon Press, 1979). Subsequent references to the correspondence will be by date and number in this edition.

5. E.g., Spinoza. His treatment of identity-questions makes for an interesting comparison with Locke's. His view is that *any* compound body (and not only living ones) can survive the replacement of its components, provided that the same proportion of motion and rest is maintained (cf. the definition in the physical excursus following E II P13S, Gebhardt II/99/26ff.). But for human beings he is inclined to count a really total amnesia as destructive of personal identity (cf. his discussion of the Spanish poet in E IV P39S). Presumably he would think this strictly correlated with the disruption of the body's proportion of motion and rest (cf. the long note to the Preface to Part II of the *Short Treatise*).

6. E.g., Derek Parfit, "Personal Identity," reprinted in Perry, *Personal Identity*.

7. As we shall see below, Locke vacillates on the issue of the nominal essence of man.

8. For More, see *The Immortality of the Soul* (London, 1659); for Glanvill, *Lux Orientalis* (London, 1661); for Cudworth, *The True Intellectual System of the Universe* (London, 1678). Glanvill was a fellow student of Locke's at Oxford in the 1650s and a fellow member of the Royal Society. Perhaps even more important, for our purposes, is Francis van Halmont, a friend of Locke's from his Rotterdam days, who visited England in 1693 (see Letters 779, 16 June 1684 and 1662, 2 October 1693. He defended transmigration in two treatises, *Two Hundred Queries . . . Concerning . . . the Revolution of Humane Souls* (London, 1684), and *The Paradoxical Discourses* (London, 1685). For a fascinating discussion of the broader content of the debate over pre-existence, see D. P. Walker, *The Decline of Hell, Seventeenth-Century Discussion of Eternal Torment* (Chicago: University of Chicago Press, 1964).

9. On which see Maurice Cranston's *John Locke* (London: Longmans Green, 1957); particularly pp. 124-28.

10. Cf. Fraser's edition of the *Essay* (Oxford: Clarendon Press, 1894). Vol. I, p. 9, n. 3.

11. That forgetfulness is common, and total amnesia possible, might seem too trite an observation to be of interest. But since so many critics of Locke have argued as if Locke were ignorant of these facts, it may be worth adding that they were facts of some importance to the defenders of pre-existence, who used them in responding to the objection that we have no recollection of our soul's previous existence. (The denial of recollection was a key point of difference between the seventeenth century Platonists and their ancient predecessors.) Cf. More, *Immortality* II, xiii. Locke would not be making this observation casually.

12. Cf. Perry, *Personal Identity*, p. 114. This form of the objection is often ascribed to Reid, but it would be more accurate to say that Reid thought Locke's view led to a contradiction, since he thought the nontransitivity of personal identity was not even to be considered.

13. Cf. A. G. N. Flew, in "Locke and the Problem of Personal Identity," *Philosophy* 26 (1951): 53-68. Reprinted in C. B. Martin and D. M. Armstrong, *Locke and Berkeley, A Collection of Critical Essays* (London: Macmillan).

14. For example, John Perry, Anthony Quinton, and H. P. Grice, in their contributions to Perry's *Personal Identity*. Similarly, David Lewis, John Perry, and David Wiggins in their contributions to Rorty's *The Identities of Persons*.

15. In *Problems From Locke* (Oxford: Clarendon Press, 1976), p. 181.

16. Cf. Martin and Armstrong, p. 169. Recently, however, Flew has recanted on the point at issue here. See "Locke and Personal Identity—Again," *Locke Newsletter* 10 (1979): 33-42.

17. As Jolley has argued ("Perception and Immateriality in the *Nouveaux Essais*," *Journal of the History of Philosophy* 16 (1978): 181-94, and "Leibniz on Locke and

Socinianism," *Journal of The History of Ideas* 39 (1978): 233-50), this is one of Leibniz's main objections to Locke's *Essay*.

18. Though Locke clearly has Descartes in mind as representative of the kind of theory he wants to attack, it is not clear that Descartes has *any* theory of personal identity. As Margaret Wilson has observed ("Leibniz: Self-Consciousness and Immortality in the Paris Notes and After," *Archiv für Geschichte der Philosophie* 58 (1976): 335-52), he seems never to have given any systematic consideration to problems of personal identity. Still, various remarks he makes on related issues suggest that, if he had considered the matter, he would have adopted a theory of the kind Locke attacks, i.e., a theory that would allow for my continued existence as me in spite of a complete change in the contents of my consciousness. Cf. Wilson, pp. 338-41. I conjecture that it was the elaboration of Cartesian dualism by the Cambridge Platonists that brought home to Locke the consequences of Descartes' position.

19. In the article cited above, Margaret Wilson deals with the development of Leibniz's mature doctrine of personal identity from his early reflections on the inadequacy of the Cartesian account of immortality.

20. Leibniz, *Discourse on Metaphysics,* trans. P. G. Lucas and L. Grint, 2nd ed., (Manchester: Manchester University Press 1961), p. 57. I use brackets for the punctuational devices Lucas and Grint use for additions to the first draft. Here the addition replaces "our own soul,"

21. Cf. the Synopsis of the *Meditations*, AT IX, 10.

22. The thought experiment is reminiscent of those in Bernard Williams, "The Self and the Future," reprinted in Perry's *Personal Identity*.

23. Cf. Mackie 184; Flew, 163-64.

24. Apparently Leibniz does conceive the perceptions of thinking substances in this way. Cf. Kenneth Clatterbaugh, *Leibniz's Doctrine of Individual Accidents* (Wiesbaden: Franz Steiner, 1978). (*Studia Leibnitiana*, Sonderheft 4). If I read II, xxvii, 13 aright, Locke too is tempted to regard consciousness as "annexed" to the particular substance whose consciousness it is. So the discussion of the possibility of transfers in that section is somewhat tentative. But by the end of the section he seems to have opted for the view that the same consciousness, unlike the same figure or motion, can exist in different substances.

25. Nicholas Jolley has an alternative reading of this passage in his "Perception and Immateriality in the *Nouveaux Essais*." See particularly pp. 192-93.

26. The remark that introduces his comment on II, xxvii, 6—"cela se peut entendre dans mon sens"—is characteristic. Cf. the treatment of innate ideas in the Preface (Akademie edition, pp. 51f.)

27. The passage discussed here is only one of three Wilson cites in support of her interpretation. In a second passage (from II, xxvii, 18) Leibniz allows the possibility of a divine transfer of consciousness from one soul to another. (Leibniz seems to be thinking of a quite general confusion about who has done what.) He remarks that it would be necessary to treat these consciousnesses "according to moral notions *as if* they were the same" (my emphasis). I take it that this means that after the transfers no person is the same as the one whose actions he 'remembers,' though other finite minds, not knowing this, would have to act as if this were not so.

Wilson's third passage is more difficult:

> But if God, by an extraordinary action, changed real identity, personal [identity] would remain, provided that the man preserved the appearances of identity, both internal (i.e. consciousness) and external (i.e. those which consist in what appears to others). (II, xxvii, 9)

I can see no way of interpreting this as consistent with the generally anti-Lockean tenor of Leibniz's remarks, or with the statement that almost immediately precedes it:

> The self [= soul = immaterial substance] makes real physical identity. The appear-

ance of self, *accompanied by truth*, unites personal identity to real identity. (my emphasis)

This last means, I think, that the subject's *true* belief that he is the same substance that performed a given action is sufficient to render him morally responsible, but that a mistaken belief would not be sufficient.

28. For the situation in modern law, see Sanford H. Kadish and Monrad G. Paulsen *Criminal Law and Its Processes*, (Boston: Little, Brown, 1975), pp. 76-77; *Criminal Law and Its Administration*, Jerome Michael and Hubert Wechsler (Chicago: Foundation Press, 1940), pp. 29-35; "Automatism," Glanville Williams, in *Essays in Criminal Science*, ed. Gerhard Mueller (London: Sweet and Maxwell), 1961. I have been unable to locate any authoritative statement of the legal situation in Locke's time, but the reactions of Molyneux and Leibniz (discussed in the text) and the vehemence with which Justice Stephen (cited in Kadish and Paulsen, 77) excuses somnambulists suggest that the modern position must go back a long way: "Can anyone doubt that a man who, though he might be perfectly sane, committed what would otherwise be a crime in a state of somnambuilism would be entitled to be acquitted?" The reason Stephen offers, however, would not accord with Locke's theory: "because he would not know what he was doing."

29. See, for example, Michael and Wechsler, pp. 903-20; W. S. Holdsworth *A History of English Law* (London: Methuen, 1925), vol. VIII, pp. 441-43; Sir William Blackstone, *Commentaries on the Laws of England*, ed. Thomas Cooley (Chicago: Callahan, 1884), IV, ii, 3. Blackstone does mention that drunkenness is easy to counterfeit, but his emphasis is on its character as a "voluntarily contracted madness."

30. See Allison, "Locke on Personal Identity," p. 47.

31. Cf. Letter 1744, 26 May 1694. To say, as Locke does, that "want of consciousness ought not to be presum'd in favour of the drunkard," is not, as Allison appears to think, to make a fatal concession to Molyneux. It is to reiterate Locke's original view that the issue is one of proof, not of the legitimacy of the excuse if we could be certain that the person really had been drunk. Paul Helm, in "Locke's Conditions For Person Identity," *Locke Newsletter* 10 (1979): 43-51, announces an article forthcoming in the *Journal of the History of Ideas*, "Did Locke Capitulate to Molyneux?" which presumably will take up these issues in more detail.

32. Cf. Benson Mates, "If essentialism is the doctrine that distinguishes 'some traits of an object as essential to it . . . and other traits as accidental,' then Leibniz is no essentialist. It seems that in effect he chooses the alternative of regarding *every* trait of an object as essential to it." From "Leibniz on Possible Worlds," in *Leibniz, A Collection of Critical Essays*, ed. H. G. Frankfurt (Garden City: Doubleday, 1972), p. 338.

33. *The Leibniz-Arnauld Correspondence*, ed. and trans. H. T. Mason (Manchester: Manchester University Press, 1967), pp. 32-33.

34. *Ibid.*, p. 58.

35. *Ibid.*, pp. 55-60.

36. Cf. C. D. Broad, "Leibniz's Predicate-in-Notion Principle," in Frankfurt's *Leibniz*, p. 8. Broad's reason for adopting this conception of predicates is quite different from that suggested in the text, but is connected with what seems to me a very un-Leibnizian conception of truth.

37. The only exception I know of (and a partial one at that) occurs in the *Theodicy*, xxxvi, where the doctrine of individual concepts is not explicit: "It was already true a hundred years ago that I would write today."

38. At least there is no logical reason, so long as we assume that the future is, in some sense, 'fixed' and hence knowable. Certainly Leibniz, believing in God's foreknowledge, does assume this.

Leibniz
and Duhemian Compatibilism

Michael Hooker and Mark Pastin

A number of Leibniz's metaphysical views have been held to be incompatible with human freedom. Among them are his theory of complete individual concepts, his view that God foreordains and foreknows everything that happens in the world, and his view that the physical universe is a deterministic system. The last-named doctrine should be distinguished from the former ones, which in one guise or another confront the problem of fatalism. We are concerned in this essay with determinism.

On many occasions, his correspondence with Arnauld being among them, Leibniz maintains that his metaphysics is compatible with human freedom. Unfortunately, he is unclear in those few passages where he attempts to reconcile freedom with his system. In this essay we will use several of Leibniz's metaphysical and epistemological concepts to argue that a special kind of compatibilism has plausibility. Although we make no claim to Leibnizean orthodoxy, we do take ourselves to be tracing out Leibniz's observation that whereas the material world is governed by the laws of force and mechanics, the world of spirits acts in accordance with a different set of laws, those of justice (Gerhart, Vol. II, p. 124).

If one accepts physical determinism and wishes to hold that there is free will, the standard strategy is to argue for the compatibility of free will, as ordinarily conceived, with physical determination of actions. Our view is that even if such an argument were to succeed for free will as *ordinarily conceived*, it would not yield a reflectively sound account of free will and determinism. Suppose that we discovered that the ordinary conception of free will is such that *no* problem obtains in holding that an agent's action, for which there was a sufficient cause thousands of years before his birth, is free. Unless we have an explanation of why such a cause does not conflict with my freedom in the way that a similar contemporaneous cause would, we have made no progress toward a

327

philosophical understanding of free will and determinism. It is not enough to maintain that "that just is the ordinary notion of free will." More important is that the ordinary concept or language type of compatibilism abdicates the central philosophical task of explicating what physical theory, presently, in the guise of physical determinism, says.

Pursuing this task leads to a variety of compatibilism that is distinct from ordinary concept/language compatibilism and from other compatibilisms. It is a version of compatibilism that uses distinctively Leibnizean metaphysical and epistemological themes. These include Leibniz's pluralism with respect to types of possibility, his phenomenalistic monism, and his conception of individuals as both complete and reflective of all individuals. We also make use of the idea that whereas individuals are in a sense inclusive of all individuals and facts, a particular mental grasping of an individual is necessarily limited, given the finiteness of our minds. The best way to explain how we use these themes is to proceed to use them.

Leibniz is most accurately regarded as *some sort* of phenomenalist. We begin by considering the content of physical determinism, i.e., what determinism says about particular physical situations, on one type of linguistic phenomenalism. Of course it is clear that Leibniz is *not* a linguistic phenomenalist—he holds nothing about the equivalence or nonequivalence of physical sentences and sentences about monads and their aspects.

Linguistic phenomenalism commonly is read as a thesis to the effect that sentences used to make statements about physical objects can be translated, preserving something, into sentences that do not refer to physical objects. This undoubtedly is an accurate reading of the views of some phenomenalists, for example, A. J. Ayer. It also is clear that this is not an accurate reading of the views of other phenomenalists, such as J. S. Mill, C. I. Lewis, and Roderick Firth.[1] These latter phenomenalists are properly understood to ask: What is the content of physical sentences, sentences whose terms apparently refer to physical objects? Somewhat better: What entities are denoted by the constituent terms of physical sentences? Although these questions require considerable definition, they are clearly distinct from the question of whether physical sentences can be translated into another vocabulary. Our concern is with the questions that do not directly concern translation.

The philosophical framework for these questions is that sentences, including sentences used to describe physical reality, do not come paired with a "natural" or "standard" interpretation. It is philosophically sound to ask what physical sentences describe or are about. The linguistic phenomenalist *may* respond that individual physical sentences, *as such and untranslated,* are about actual and possible experiences. Reasons for pursuing this sort of response generally have been epistemic—to show that what we can have evidence about bears interesting relations to what we talk about—but also have included considerations of ontological simplicity and economy.

We do not consider this version of linguistic phenomenalism by way of arguing for it. In fact, we shall embrace the strongest objection to this and many other types of phenomenalism. Our point is that this view raises an important issue about the relevance of physical determinism to free will.

Consider what a phenomenalist, such as Lewis or Firth, would take to be the content of the physical sentence (or a particular use of the sentence) "The door is open." The content of this sentence will be perspicuously represented by independent-of-factual sentences (presupposing neither truth nor falsity of the antecedent) or counter-factual sentences, whose antecedents refer to experiences and apparent undertakings and whose consequents refer to further experiences. Thus, for Lewis, *part of* the content of "The door is open" might be given by independent-of-factuals or counter-factuals such as "If one should have experiences of seeing a doorway and of seeming to reach before oneself, one would have the experience of seeing one's hand pass through the doorway" and "If one should have experiences of seeing a doorway and seeming to walk ahead, one would have experiences of proceeding unimpeded." It is likely to be objected that these sentences use physical terminology, in fact, terminology that is used in the original sentence. It is not germane to examine this objection here. These conditionals are intended not as translations but as more perspicuous (for certain philosophical purposes, some revealed below) representations of part of the content of the original sentence. And, whether it is possible to eliminate physical terminology, and whether it is important to do so, are questions internal to the debate about translational versions of phenomenalism. We have no interest in translational versions of phenomenalism.

We make two observations about nontranslational linguistic phenomenalism. First, if this approach is to be workable, independent-of-factuals connecting actual and possible experiences must be explainable in terms of "laws of experience." Our assumption is that counter-factuals and independent-of-factuals are evaluated against a background of relevant laws. And, translational claims aside, if there are no "laws of experience" (laws connecting experiences of certain types without reference to mediating physical objects), then there would be little plausibility to the claim that physical sentences ultimately are about experiences only. One of the main objections to phenomenalism, forcefully raised by Wilfrid Sellars,[2] is that no laws of experience exist. But if theoretical claims are evaluated in terms of lower level generalizations not employing the theoretical vocabulary, then it is hard to see why even the trenchant antiphenomenalist would deny that there are laws of experience. These laws might be supposed to be related to claims expressed in physical sentences, as generalizations about physical objects are related to higher-level theoretical claims.

The upshot of this for our purposes is that such laws of experience differentiate a type of possibility distinct from physical possibility. If "It is ϕ-ly possible that P" is approximately explicable as "P is compatible with the laws and assumptions of ϕ" ('physically possible' and 'physics' for example), then we might say that P is *experientially possible* given laws of experience. This comports with Leibniz's pluralism concerning types of possibility.

The second observation about this version of phenomenalism is that although "The door is open" expresses a specific, determinate physical fact, what it expresses is far from specific in terms of experience. It tells us what experiences to expect *if* we undertake or apparently undertake certain actions, *given* certain background experiences. But it does not tell us what actions will be undertaken or apparently undertaken. If the content of physical sentences is through and through to be represented by such experiential conditionals, then there is no reason to expect any conglomeration of physical sentences to say what experiences will occur.

To apply this to physical determinism: Even if physical determinism is true (every fact properly expressed by a physical sentence is "fixed" in-truth-value in any relevant sense), there are alternative, incompatible, and sometimes radically different courses of experience that might occur. Physical laws and a complete physical description of a situation are not sufficient for deduction of specific, nonconditional results about experiences. Also needed are experiential laws, a description of the experiential background, and, crucially, information about what actions will be undertaken.

A caveat. Allowing that *something* can be deduced about experience, given laws of experience and appropriate background information, does not entail determinism at the level of experience. There is no reason to regard experiential laws as complete (in the sense of giving a unique output for a certain input) or deterministic. One could argue independently for some sort of psychological determininism, but that is not our topic.[3]

These observations may seem uninteresting for understanding both Leibniz and free will. Linguistic phenomenalism is widely regarded as unacceptable. However, if we look at the *reasons* for which linguistic phenomenalism is regarded as unacceptable, we find that the gap widens between what is arguably physically determined and the world as we experience it, and we approach a view congenial to Leibnizian themes.

Two basic reasons may be given for regarding linguistic phenomenalism as unacceptable. The *first* reason, noted above as applying to *translational* linguistic phenomenalism, is that we can conceptualize and describe the experimental facts said to be expressed by physical sentences only in explicitly physical terms. This point does not apply to the view we develop. The *second* reason, driven home by Chisholm in his famous essay on phenomenalism,[4] is that the relation between physical sentences and experiences is "Duhemian." Let P be a physical sentence and E an experiential sentence *supposedly* entailed by P as part of the content of P. Chisholm points out that for any such P and E there is a physical sentence C, describing perceptual circumstances, such that P and C clearly can be true while E is false. The upshot is that if physical sentences have consequences for experience, they have such consequences not individually but collectively à la Duhem. We shall not repeat the numerous examples that reinforce this point.

Before continuing the main argument we note an interesting side issue. In Lewis's response to Chisholm he makes a suggestion that has proven difficult to interpret.[5] However, on one reading it leads to a result analogous to quantum indeterminism. Lewis seems to argue that the connection between antecedent and consequent of an experiential conditional is irreducibly probabilistic. In the example considered earlier, the appropriate form of a representative experiential conditional would be "If one should have such and such experiences and undertake such and so, then *in all probability* these further experiences would occur." The Duhemian line of objection can be extended to show that physical sentences do not entail even these probabilistically qualified conditionals. But if a relative of Lewis's position is correct, then physical reality is indeterministic *independent of the determinism or indeterminism of physics,* with whatever consequences this has for the issue of free will. (Hilary Putnam argues in an interesting unpublished essay that we really do not know how to conceptualize freedom of choice within an indeterministic framework. The usual assumption of macro-*randomness* is not an obvious consequence of such a framework.)

To return to the main argument: Although the Duhemian objection refutes sentence-by-sentence atomistic phenomenalism, it shows neither that physical sentences need no interpretation nor that physical sentences *taken collectively* are not to be understood in terms of actual experiences. Even if individual physical sentences do not entail experiential conditionals, it may be that sets of physical sentences entail that the required sort of connections among actual and possible experiences obtain. (For that matter, why suppose that interpretation in experiential terms requires *entailment* of such conditionals?) Would relations of epistemic support suffice?[6] How extensive is the set of physical sentences regarded as having experiential consequences depends on the details of different holistic views. Note that our earlier differentiation of a type of experiential possibility shows that appeal to possible experiences need not render a holistic phenomenalism circular.

Instead of taking the Duhemian objection to refute all phenomenalisms, we swallow the objection within a holistic phenomenalism, a phenomenalism that presupposes a Leibnizean plurality of types of possibility. Physical determinism has even fewer implications for the (nonconditional) course of experience on such a Leibnizean holistic phenomenalism than it does on traditional atomistic phenomenalisms of either translational or nontranslational species. On the holistic approach, that a certain physical sentence is true cannot, by itself, even tell us what experiences will occur *if the background experiences and apparent undertakings are given.* A physical sentence will tell us something about the course of experience only against the background of a set of further physical sentences with which it forms a significant unit of discourse (in the sense that the physical sentences collectively have consequences for experience).

The holistic phenomenalist view of the relation between particular physical sentences and experiences is best understood on the Leibnizean model of our thoughts about an individual and the full infinite individual. Roughly, on the Leibnizean model, to think about an individual is to think in terms of an individual concept, something we could express as 'the F,' which is a component of that individual. The full individual is an infinite structured collection of which we take a limited sample in thinking of the individual. To comprehend a full individual is to have each component of the individual, in its appropriate structure of relations to other components, "before the mind." Given the finiteness of our minds, this cannot happen. Another aspect of the Leibnizian model is that comprehending a full individual requires comprehending all other individuals and their structures of components. Comprehension of one full individual requires comprehension of all full individuals and, thereby, of all facts. This is a Duhemianism focused primarily at the level of individuals rather than sentences, propositions, or facts, and it is an extreme Duhemianism, settling for nothing less than all of the individuals and facts about them.

The Leibnizean model applied to holistic phenomenalism looks like this: Particular experiential conditionals are representatives that serve to bring the full content of a physical sentence "before the mind" (or "before the speaker or listener"). To comprehend the full content of a particular physical sentence is to grasp the complete set of interrelated experiential conditionals and categorical assertions associated with the significant unit of discourse (set of physical sentences) to which the particular physical sentence belongs. Depending on the features of different holistic views, this may require that one grasp the experiential content of a significant theory fragment, or whole theory, or a more comprehensive belief system.

One important question for this approach is the nature of the relations among the experiential conditionals and assertions associated with a significant chunk of physical discourse. We suggested above that interpretation of physical sentences may not require entailment of the interpreting sentences, and that epistemic relations between a sentence and its supposed interpreters might suffice for interpretation of the sentence (in a sense of 'interpretation' that, we believe, is philosophically sound, but not *defined* so as to require entailment). It seems too that the relations among the experiential conditionals and assertions associated with a physical sentence are epistemic— these experiential claims are clumped together under one physical sentence because they evidentially support one another, are likely to be true together, and have related experiential content. This approach would introduce epistemic possibility in addition to experiential possibility and so broaden our Leibnizean plurality of types of possibility.

Let us bring to bear on determinism considerations that have been developed so far. The *determined* physical setences (expressing individual physical facts), those entailed by a physical description of the world at a given time and the laws of physics, are associated with experiential claims. These experiential conditionals and assertions are not entailed by individual physical sentences. They are entailed (if they are entailed at all and if they need be to provide interpretation) only by sufficiently comprehensive chunks of discourse. Certain "designated" experiential conditionals (perhaps "designated" owing to closer epistemic relevance to a particular physical sentence, "designated" as more likely to indicate the truth of that physical sentence) represent the full set of interrelated experiential claims associated with the encompassing chunk of physical discourse. Earlier we noted that if physical sentences are interpreted mainly through experiential conditionals, then determination of a particular physical sentence determines what experiences will occur only conditionally – upon other experiencings and upon undertakings. If even some of the conditionals through which physical sentences are interpreted are probabilistically qualified, this further weakens the informativeness and content of physical sentences vis-à-vis experiences. What we have now added is that no *individual* physical sentence has even probabilistic and conditional consequences for experience. At best, the whole comprehensive-enough-to-be-significant set of sentences including a particular sentence has experiential consequences. *And it is far from obvious that such a set is the sort of thing that is determined even if it is conceded that physical determinism is true.* For instance, it may be necessary that the set include some physical laws and it is not clear that these are determined to be true or false even within a physical determinist view. In short, a Leibnizean phenomenalism *illustrates* that physical determinism may have little bearing on free will, at least in so far as one finds degrees of freedom in what we experience to be significant. We say 'illustrates' since many other interpretations of physical sentences (e.g., Russell's "neutral monism") support the same point.

A Leibnizean phenomenalism has resources not available to traditional phenomenalisms. We noted that one reason for finding linguistic phenomenalism unacceptable is that the experiential facts said to be expressed by physical sentences can be conceptualized and described only in explicitly physical terms. Leibniz is distinguished from other phenomenalists, either linguistic or ontological (Mill), in taking physical objects to have *conceptual* (not reducible to experiences) and experiential components. So the full individual *the present President of the United States* includes not only all of the actual and possible experiences of the present President. It also includes conceptual components such as the concept of the present President of the United States and the concept of the husband of Nancy Reagan. It is worth considering whether the holistic phenomenalism outlined here might be broadened along these lines. Although holistic phenomenalism does not make a translational claim, there is a question as to what role, if any, physical terminology can play in explicating the supposedly experiential content of physical sentences.

Developing such a broadened Leibnizean/holistic phenomenalism is too ambitious a task for this essay. We limit ourselves to a proposal based on Pastin's work in this area. The proposal is to take the content of physical sentences (in sufficiently comprehensive sets) to include not only clusters of epistemically connected experiential claims, but also further claims about physical reality that are *warranted by* the experiential claims. The structure of the view is that what is asserted by physical sentences is to be understood in terms of experiential claims, but what is warranted (or warrantedly asserted) by physical sentences is to be understood in terms of both experiential and other physical claims. Pastin has developed this approach and argued that it conflicts neither with the epistemological motivations for phenomenalist views nor the ontological features of a holistic phenomenalism of the sort outlined here.[7]

An important advantage of the compatibilism possible within our Leibnizean holistic phenomenalism is that it is consistent with either the *identity* or correlation of every mental fact, event, state, or whatever type of entity, with a physical entity of the same type. The reason is that the sentences expressing psycho-physical identities or correlations require interpretation just as other physical sentences do. And we can interpret them within the means of our view. Thus these identities or correlations, against the background of sufficiently rich encompassing information, will express relations between clusters of epistemically interrelated experiential claims and the correlated or identified mental entities.

We have emphasized several Leibnizean themes, including the need for a plurality of types of possibility, the interconnectedness of individuals, and the possibility of a conceptual and experiential monism, in sketching an account of the content of physical determinism and its implications for free will. The main contentions of our view are (1) that physical sentences tell us what experiences will occur only conditionally—given that certain background experiences occur and that certain actions are undertaken, (2) that *individual* physical sentences do not give us even this information, (3) that chunks of discourse of sufficient scope to give conditional information about what experiences will occur may not express facts that can be reasonably viewed as determined *within physical determinism,* and (4) that there is reason to doubt that units of physical discourse of sufficient scope to be informative about experiences are thus informative in virtue of *entailing* anything about experience. These claims give wide scope for "freedom," for nondetermined outcomes, within the domain of experience. We have not analyzed the notion of freedom to ascertain whether we have left room for a *kind* of freedom that is significant vis-à-vis various philosophical issues. But we have shown that physical determinism, as such, has few consequences for the issue of freedom. Is freedom in the domain of experience worth much? This is a profound question to which we can only claim to have hinted at a postive answer. But in moving in that direction, we have also gone a ways toward vindicating Leibniz's contention that his determined universe is compatible with human freedom.

Notes

1. See C. I. Lewis, *An Analysis of Knowledge and Valuation* (La Salle, Illinois, 1946) and Roderick Firth, "Radical Empiricism and Perceptual Relativity," *Philosophical Review* (1950), 164-83, 319-31.

2. See "Phenomenalism" in Wilfrid Sellars, *Science, Perception and Reality* (London, 1963).

3. Vicki Levine pointed out that an argument for psychological determinism not based on physical determinism might undermine our view.

4. "The Problem of Empiricism," in *Perceiving, Sensing and Knowing*, ed. Robert J. Swartz (Garden City, NY, 1965), pp. 347-54.

5. See Lewis, "Professor Chisholm and Empiricism," *Perceiving, Sensing and Knowing*, pp. 355-63 and Mark Pastin, "Meaning and Perception," *Journal of Philosophy* 73 (1976): 571-85.

6. See Pastin, "Meaning and Perception."

7. "Meaning and Perception," and "The Need for Epistemology: Problematic Realism Defended," in *Justification and Knowledge,* ed. George Pappas (Dordrecht, Holland, 1979), pp. 515-68.

Bibliography

A Leibniz Bibliography

Aarsleff, H., "The Eighteenth Century, Including Leibniz," in *Current trends in linguistics*, ed. Thomas A. Sebeok (The Hague), 1975, pp. 383-479.

——, "Leibniz on Locke and Language," *American Philosophical Quarterly* 1, 1964, pp. 165-88.

——, "Schulenburg's Leibniz als Sprachforscher, with Some Observations on Leibniz and the Study of Language," *Studia Leibnitiana* 7, 1975, pp. 122-34.

——, "The Study and Use of Etymology in Leibniz," *Studia Leibniziana Supplementa* III, 1969, pp. 173-89.

Abraham, W., "Complete Concepts and Leibniz's Distinction between Necessary and Contingent Propositions," *Studia Leibnitiana* 1, 1969, pp. 263-79.

——, "The Incompatibility of Individuals. First Symposium. Commentators: Rhoda Kotzin, Wilfrid Sellars," *Nous* 6, 1972, pp. 1-13.

——, "Predication," *Studia Leibnitiana* 7, 1975, pp. 1-20.

Adams, R. "Existence, Self-interest, and the Problem of Evil," *Nous* 13, 1979, pp. 53-65.

——, "The Locke-Leibniz Debate" in *Innate Ideas*, ed. Stephen P. Stich (Berkeley), 1975, pp. 37-67.

——, "Middle Knowledge," *The Journal of Philosophy* 70, 1973, pp. 552-54.

Agassi, J., "Leibniz's Place in the History of Physics," *Journal of the History of Ideas* 30, 1969, pp. 331-44.

Agostino, F., "Leibniz on Compossibility and Relational Predicates," *Philosophical Quarterly* 26, 1976, pp. 125-38.

Aiton, E., "The Celestial Mechanics of Leibniz," *Annals of Science* 16, 1960, pp. 65-82.

——, "The Celestial Mechanics of Leibniz in the Light of Newtonian Criticism," *Annals of Science* 18, 1962, pp. 31-41.

——, "The Celestial Mechanics of Leibniz: A New Interpretation," *Annals of Science* 20, 1964, pp. 111-23.

——, "Leibniz on Motion in a Resisting Medium. Communicated by I. B. Cohen," *Archive for History of Exact Sciences* 9, 1972, pp. 257-74.

——, *The Vortex Theory of Planetary Motions* (New York), 1972.

Alexander, H., ed. and trans., *Leibniz-Clarke Correspondence* Manchester), 1956.

Allaire, E., "Ontologically Speaking, Things are . . . ," *Theoria* 42, 1976, pp. 93-114.

Allison, H., "Kant's Refutation of Realism," *Dialectica* 30, 1976, pp. 223-53.

Altwicker, N., "Tendenzen der Spinoza-Rezeption und Kritik" in *Texte zur Geschichte des Spinozismus* (Darmstadt, 1971, pp. 1-58.

Angelelli, I., "On Identity and Interchangeability in Leibniz and Frege," *Notre Dame Journal of Formal Logic* 8, 1967, pp. 94-100.

——, "Leibniz's Misunderstanding of Nisolius' Notion of Multitudo," *Notre Dame Journal of Formal Logic* 6, 1965, pp. 319-322.

Arndt, H., "Die Entwicklungsstufen von Leibniz' Begriff einer 'lingua universalis,' in *Das Problem d. Sprache* (Heidelberg), 1966, pp. 71-79.

——, "Der Zusammenhang von Ars iudicandi und Ars inveniendi in der Logik von Leibniz," *Studia Leibnitiana* 3, 1971, pp. 205-13.

Auerbach, S., *Zur Entwicklungsgeschichte der Leibnizschen Entwicklungslehre* (Dessau), 1884.

Axelos, C., *Die ontologischen Grundlagen der Freiheitstheorie von Leibniz* VIII (New York), 1973.

Balestra, D., "The Centrality of Perception: a Phenomenological Perspective in Leibniz." *Dialogue* (Phi Sigma Tau), 19, 1976, pp. 20-26.

Ballard, K., "Leibniz's Theory of Space and Time," *Journal of the History of Ideas* 21, 1960, pp. 49-65.

Barber, W., *Leibniz in France, from Arnauld to Voltaire: A Study in French Reactions to Leibnizianism* (Oxford), 1955.

Barnes, J., "Mr. Locke's Darling Notion," *Philosophical Quarterly* 22, 1972, pp. 193-214.

Barnette, R., "Does Quantum Mechanics Disprove the Principle of the Identity of Indiscernibles?" *Philosophy of Science* 45, 1978, pp. 466-70.

Barrett, W., "Leibniz's Garden: Some Philosophical Observations on Boredom," *Social Research* 42, 1975, pp. 551-55.

Baruzi, J., *Leibniz* (Paris), 1909.

——, *Leibniz et l'organisation religieuse de la terre* (Paris), 1907.

——, "Letres de Leibniz a Henfling," *Revue Philosophique*, 1946.

——, "Trois dialogues mystiques inèdits de Leibniz," *Revue Metaphysique et Morale*, 1905.

Bayart, A., "Leibniz et les Antinomies en Droit," *Revue Internationale de Philosophie* 20, 1966, pp. 257-63.

Bearsley, P., "Another Look at the First Principles of Knowledge," *The Thomist* 36, 1972, pp. 566-98.

Becco, A., "Leibniz, Bergson et le langage," *Etudes bergsoniennes* 11, 1976, pp. 9-24.

——, "Aux Sources de la monade: paleographie et lexicographie leibniziennes," *Les Etudes Philosophiques* 3, 1975, pp. 279-94.

Beck, L., *Early German Philosophy: Kant and His Predecessors* (Cambridge), 1969.

——, "Kant's Strategy," *Journal of the History of Ideas* 28, 1967, pp. 224-36.

Belaval, Y., "Anti-Cartesianism in Bayle, Leibniz and Vico," in *Giambattista Vico Tricentennial Symposium Volume* (Baltimore), 1969.

——, "La Doctrine de l'essence chez Hegel et chez Leibniz," *Archives de Philosophie* 33, 1970, pp. 547-78.

——, "Une 'drole de pensee' de Leibniz," *Nouvelle Revue francaise*, 1958.

——, "L'Idee d'harmonie chez Leibniz," in *Hommage a M. Gueroult*, 1964.

——, *Leibniz critique de Descartes*, (Paris), 1960.

——, "Leibniz et la langue allemande," *Revue germanique*, 1947.

——, "Note sur la pluralite des espaces possibles d'après la philosophie de Leibniz," *Perspektiven der Philosophie* 4, 1978, pp. 9-19.

——, *Pour connaitre la pense de Leibniz* (Paris), 1952.

——, "Premieres animadversions de Leibniz sur les principles de Descartes," in *Melanges Alexandre Koyre*.

——, "Le Problem de l'erreur chez Leibniz," Zeitschrift fur Philosophische Forschung 20, 1966, pp. 381-95.

——, "Le Probleme de la perception chez Leibniz," *Dialogue* 8, 1969, pp. 385-416.

Bennett, J., *Kant's Dialect* (London), 1974.

Berczeller, E., "The Leibnizean Paradox," *Philosophical Forum* 23, 1965-66, pp. 3-11.

Bergenthal, F., "Monade und Gestalt. Interpretation der "Monadologie," *Wissenschaft und Weisheit* 33, 1970, pp. 122-31.

Bergman, G., "Russell's Examination of Leibniz Examined," *Philosophy of Science* 23, 1956, pp. 175-205.

Bernstein, H., "Leibniz and the Sensorium Dei," *Journal of the History of Philosophy* 15, 1977, pp. 171-82.

Biema, E. van, *L'Espace et le temps chez Leibniz et chez Kant* (Paris), 1908.

Bigelow, J., "Possible Worlds Foundations for Probability," *Journal of Philosophic Logic* 5, 1976, pp. 299-320.

Blondel, M., *Une Enigme historique: le "Vinculum substantiale" d'apres Leibniz, et l'ebauche d'un realisme superieur* (Paris), 1930.

——, *De vinculo substantiali et de substantia composita apud Leibnitium* (Alcan), 1843.

Blumenfeld, D., "Is the Best Possible World Possible?" *The Philosophical Review* 84, 1975, pp. 163-77.

——, "Leibniz's Modal Proof of the Possibility of God," *Studia Leibnitiana* 4, 1972, pp. 132-40.

——, "Leibniz's Proof of the Uniqueness of God," *Studia Leibnitiana* 6, 1974, pp. 262-71.

——, "Leibniz's Theory of the Striving Possibles," *Studia Leibnitiana* 5, 1973, pp. 163-77.

Boas Hall, M., "Leibniz and the Royal Society, 1670-76," in *Leibniz a Paris 1672-1676* (Chantilly), 1976, pp. 171-82.

Bodemann, E., *Der Briefwechsel des Gottfried Wilhelm Leibniz in Koniglichen offentlichen Bibliotek zu Hannover* (Hanover), 1889.

——, *Die Leibniz-Handschriften der Koniglichen offenlichen Bibliotek zu Hannover* (Hanover), 1895.

Boeder, H., "Leibniz und das Prinzip der neueren Philosophie," *Philosophisches Jahrbuch* 81, 1974, pp. 1-29.

Boehm, A., *Le "Vinculum Substantiale" chez Leibniz* (Paris), 1962.

Bohle, R., *Der Begriff des Individuums bei Leibniz* (Meisenheim am Glan), 1978.

——, "Notes sur l'histoire des 'Principes de la Nature et de la Grace' et de la 'Monadologie' de Leibniz," *Revue Philosophique de Louvain*, 1957.

Bolton, M., "Leibniz and Hobbes on Arbitrary Truth," *Philosophy Research Archives* 3, 1977.

Borowski, E., "Identity and Personal Identity," *Mind* 85, 1976, pp. 481-502.

Bos, H., "Differentials, Higher-order Differentials and the Derivative in the Leibnizian Calculus," *Archive for History of Exact Sciences* 14, 1974, pp. 1-90.

——, "The Influence of Huygens on the Formation of Leibniz' Ideas," in *Leibniz a Paris 1672-1676* (Chantilly), 1976, pp. 59-68.

Boutroux, E., *La Monadologie (Commentary)* (Paris), 1956.

——, *La Philosophie allemande au XVIIe siecle* (Paris), 1929.

Brekle, H., "Die Idee einer generativen Grammatik in Leibnizens Fragmenten zur Logik," *Studia Leibnitiana* 3, 1971, pp. 141-49.

Breytman, V., "Le Determinisme leibnizien," in *Archives internationale d'histoire des sciences* 26, 1976, pp. 254-63.

Broad, C., *Leibniz. An Introduction* (London), 1975.

——, *"Leibniz's 'Predicate in notion principle' and Some of its Alleged Consequences,"* *Theoria* 15, 1949.

Brody, B., "Leibniz's Metaphysical Logic," in *Essays on the Philosophy of Leibniz* ed. Mark Kulstad (Houston), 1977, pp. 43-55.

Brooks, R., *Voltaire and Leibniz* (Geneva), 1964.

Brown, C., "Leibniz and Aesthetic," *Philosophy and Phenomenological Research* 28, 1967, pp. 70-80.

Brun, V., "Leibniz' Formula for Pi Deduced by a Mapping of the Circular Disc," *Nordisk Matematisk Tidskrift* 18, 1970, pp. 73-81.

Brunet, L., "La Conception leibnizienne du lieu de l'espace," *Laval Theologique et Philosophique* 35, 1979, pp. 263-77.

Brunner, F., *Etudes sur la signification historique de la philosophie de Leibniz* (Paris), 1951.

Brunschvicg, L., *Les Etapes de la philosophie mathematique* (Paris), 1947.

——, *L'Experience humaine et la causalite physique* (Paris), 1922.

——, *Spinoza et ses contemporains* (Paris), 1951.

Brunswig, A., *Leibniz. Wien und Leibniz*, 1925.

Buchdal, G., *Metaphysics and the Philosophy of Science. The Classical Origins—Descartes to Kant* (Oxford), 1969.

Bugg, E., "Criticism of Leibniz's Theory of Consonance," *The Journal of Aesthetics and Art Criticism* 21, 1963, pp. 467-72.

Burch, R., "Plantinga and Leibniz's Lapse," *Analysis* 39, 1979, pp. 24-29.

Burgelin, P., *Commentaire du discours de metaphysique de Leibniz* (Paris), 1959.

Burkhardt, H., "Anmerkungen zur Logik, Ontologie und Semantik bei Leibniz," *Studia Leibnitiana* 6, 1974, pp. 49-68

Calinger, R., *Gottfried Wilhelm Leibniz. With an Essay by Leibniz on the German Language*. Transl. Caryn and Bernhard Wunderlich (New York), 1976.

Candlish, S., "The Inexplicability of Identity," *The Australasian Journal of Philosophy* 49, 1971, pp. 23-37.

Capek, M., "Leibniz's Thought Prior to the Year 1670, from Atomism to a Geometrical Kinetism," *Revue Internationale de Philosophie* 20, 1966, pp. 249-56.

Cariou, M., *L'Atomisme. 3 essais: Gassendi, Leibniz, Bergson et Lucrece* (Paris), 1978.

Carr, H., *Leibniz* (New York), 1960.

Carvin, W. "Leibniz on Motion and Creation," *Journal of the History of Ideas* 33, 1972, pp. 425-38.

Caspari, O., *Leibniz's Philosophie, beleuchtet vom Gesichtspunkt der physik* (Leipzig), 1870.

Cassirer, E., *Das Erkenntnisproblem in der Philosophie und Wissenschaft der neueren Zeit* (Berlin), 1922-23.

——, *Freiheit und Form: Studien zur deutschen Geistesgeschichte* (Berlin), 1918.

——, *Individuum und Cosmos in der Philosophie der Renaissance* (Berlin), 1927.

——, *Leibniz' System in seinen wissenschaftlichen Grundlagen* (Marburg), 1902.

——, "Newton and Leibniz," *The Philosophical Review* LII, pp. 366-91.

——, *The Philosophy of the Enlightenment*, trans. C. A. Koelin and J. P. Pettegrove (Princeton), 1951.

——, *The Platonic Renaissance in England* trans. J. P. Pettegrove (London), 1953.

——, *The Renaissance Philosophy of Man*, ed. P. Kristeller and J. Randall, Jr. (Chicago), 1948.

Castañeda, H., "Leibniz's Concepts and their Coincidence salva veritate," *Nous* 8, 1974, pp. 381-98.

——, "Leibniz's Meditation on April 15, 1676 about Existence, Dreams, and Space," in *Leibniz a Paris* (Chantilly), 1976, pp. 91-129.

——, "Leibniz's 1686 Views on Individual Substances, Existence, and Relation," *The Journal of Philosophy* 72, 1975, pp. 687-90.

——, "Leibniz's Syllogistico-propositional Calculus," *Notre Dame Journal of Formal Logic* 17, 1976, pp. 481-500.

Cavailles, J., *Remarques sur la formation de la theorie abstraite des ensembles. Etude historique et critique* (Paris), 1938.

Child, L., *The Early Mathematical Manuscripts of Leibniz* (Chicago), 1920.

Cichowicz, S., "Sur quelques demarches de Leibniz. Trad. du polonais par Hanna Rosnerowa," *Studia Leibnitiana* 3, 1971, pp. 150-57.

Clarke, S., *A Collection of Papers, which passed between the late learned Mr. Leibniz and Dr. Clarke in the years 1715-1716, relating to the Principles of Natural Philosophy and Religion* (London), 1717.

Clatterbaugh, K., *Leibniz's Doctrine of Individual Accidents* (Weisbaden), 1973.

——, "Leibniz's Principle of the Identity of Indiscernibles," *Studia Leibnitiana* 3, 1971, pp. 241-52.

Cohen, I., "Newton and Keplerian Inertia: An Echo of Newton's Controversy with Leibniz," in *Science, Medicine and Society in the Renaissance*, ed. Allen G. Debus (New York), 1972, pp. 199-211.

Cook, D., "Leibniz and Hegel on the Language of Philosophy," in *Akten des II. Internationalen Leibniz-Kongresses Hanover*, (Weisbaden), 1972, pp. 229-38.

Cooper, D., "Innateness: Old and New," *The Philosophical Review* 81, 1972, pp. 465-83.

Copleston, F., *A History of Philosophy* (New York), 1963.

Copp, D., Leibniz's Thesis that not all Possibles are Compossible," *Studia Leibnitiana* 5, 1973, pp. 26-42.

Corr, C., "Christian Wolff and Leibniz," *Journal of the History of Ideas* 36, 1975, pp. 241-62.

Cortes, A., "Leibniz's Principle of the Identity of Indiscernibles: a False Principle," *Philosophy of Science* 43, 1976, pp. 491-505.

Costabel, P., "Contributions à l'étude de l'offensive de Leibniz contre la philosophie Cartesienne en 1691-1692," *Revue Internationale Philosophique* 20, 1966.

——, *Leibniz et la dynamique* (Paris), 1960.

——, "Newton's and Leibniz's Dynamics," trans. J. M. Briggs, *Texas Quarterly* 10, 1967, pp. 119-26.

——, "En relisant 'Les Principes mathematiques de la philosophie naturelle,'" *Revue de Metaphisique et de Morale* 73, 1968, pp. 480-91.

Couturat, D., "Sur les rapports de la logique et de metaphysique de Leibniz," *Bulletin de la Societe Francaise de Philosophie* 27, fevrier 1902.

Couturat, L., *La Logique de Leibniz d'apres des documents inédits*, (Paris), 1901.

——, "Sur la metaphysique de Leibniz," *Revue de metaphysique et de morale*, Jan. 1902.

Couzin, R., "Leibniz, Freud and Kabbala," *Journal of the History of Behavioral Sciences* 6, 1970, pp. 335-48.

Cox, C., "The Defense of Leibniz's Special Relativism," *Studies in History and Philosophy of Science*, 1975, pp. 87-111.

Cresson, A., *Leibniz: sa vie, son oeuvre, avec un expose de sa philosophie*, (Paris), 1958.

Cresswell, M., "Identity and Intensional Objects'" *Philosophia Israel* 5, 1975, pp. 47-68.

Curley, E., "Did Leibniz state 'Leibniz' Law'? *"The Philosophical Review* 80, 1971, pp. 497-501.

Dascal, M., "About the Idea of a Generative Grammar in Leibniz," *Studia Leibnitiana* 3, 1971, pp. 272-90.

——, "Language and Money. A Simile and its Meaning in 17th Century Philosophy of Language," *Studia Leibnitiana* 8, 1976, pp. 187-218.

Daville, L., *Leibniz bistorien. Essai sur l'activite et les Methods historiques de Leibniz* (Paris), 1909.

——, "Le Sejour de Leibniz a Paris," *Archiv fur Geschichte der Philosophie* neue folge, 27, 1921, pp. 33-34.

Davis, J., "Berkeley, Newton, and Space," in *The methodological Heritage of Newton*, ed. Robert E. Butts and John W. Davis (Toronto), 1970, pp. 57-73.

——, "The Molyneux Problem," *Journal of the History of Ideas* 21, 1960, pp. 392-408.

Den Uyl, D., "The Aristocratic Principle in the Political Philosophy of Leibniz," *Journal of the History of Philosophy* 15, 1977, pp. 281-92.

——, "Science and Justice in Leibniz's Political Thought," *New Scholasticism* 52, 1978, pp. 317-42.

Dewey, J., *Leibniz's New Essays on Human Understanding*, 1888.

Diamond, S., "The Debt of Leibniz to Pardies," *Journal of the History of Behavioural Sciences* 8, 1972, pp. 109-14.

Dillman, E., *Eine neue Darstellung der Leibnizschen Monadenlehre* (Leipzig), 1891.

Dilthy, W., *Weltanschauung und Analyse des Menschens seit der Renaissance und Reformation* (Gottingen), 1970.

Drzewieniecki, W., "The Knowledge of China in XVII Century Poland as Reflected in the Correspondence between Leibniz and Kochanski," *Polish Review* 12, 1967, pp. 53-66.

Dubs, H., "The Misleading Nature of Leibniz's Monadology," *The Philosophical Review* 50, 1941, pp. 508-15.

Duchesneau, F., "Leibniz et la theorie physiologique," *Journal of the History of Philosophy* 14, 1976, pp. 281-300.

Dugas, R., *La mecanique au XVII siecle* (Neuchatel), 1950.

Dummett, M., "Review of Nicholas Rescher's 'Leibniz's Interpretation of his Logical Calculi," *Journal of Symbolic Logic* 21, 1956, pp. 197-99.

Durr, K., "Die mathematische Logik von Leibniz," in *Studia Philosophica* (Basel), 1947, pp. 87-102.

Earman, J., "Infinities, Infinitesimals, and Indivisibles: the Leibnizian Labyrinth," *Studia Leibnitiana* 7, 1975, pp. 236-51.

——, "Leibnizian Space-Times and Leibnizian Algebras," in *Historical and Philosophical Dimensions of Logic, Methodology and Philosophy of Science*, ed. Robert E. Butts and Jaakko Hintikka (Boston), 1977.

——, "Perceptions and Relations in the Monadology," *Studia Leibnitiana* 9, 1977, pp. 212-30.

——, "Was Leibniz a Relationist?" *Midwest Studies in Philosophy* 4, 1979, pp. 263-76.

——, "Who's Afraid of Absolute Space?" *The Australian Journal of Philosophy* 48, 1970, pp. 287-319.

Echelard-Dumas, M., "Der Begriff des Organismus bei Leibniz: 'biologische Tatache' und Fundierung," *Studia Leibnitiana* 8, 1976, pp. 160-86.

Erdmann, B., *Orientierende Bemerkungen uber die Quellen zur Leibnizschen Philosophie* (Berlin), 1917.

Erickson, S., "Leibniz on Essence, Existence and Creation," *Review of Metaphysics* 18, 1965, pp. 476-87.

Eslick, L., "Aristotle and the Identity of Indiscernibles," *Modern Schoolman* 36, 1959, pp. 279-87.

Feldman, F., "Leibniz and 'Leibniz' Law,'" *The Philosophical Review* 74, 1970, pp. 510-22.

——, "Leibniz's Commitment to Monism," *Idealistic Studies* 3, 1973, pp. 18-31.

Fellman, E., "Leibniz und Newtons Principia Mathematica," *Archives Internationales d'histoire des sciences* 22, 1969, p. 288.

Ferguson, J., *The Philosophy of Dr. Samuel Clarke and its Critics* (New York), 1974.

Fielchenfeld, W., *"Leibniz und Henry More"* Kanstudien 28, 1923, pp. 323-34.

Finkelstein, D., "The Leibniz Project," *Journal of Philosophic Logic* 6, 1977, pp. 425-39.

Fisch, M., "Pierce and Leibniz," *Journal of the History of Ideas* 33, 1972, pp. 485-96.

Fischer, K., *Geschichte der neueren Philosophie II. G. W. Leibniz und seine Schule* (Mannheim), 1855.

——, *Gottfried Wilhelm Leibniz: Leben, Werke und Lehre* (Heidelberg), 1920.

——, *G. W. von Leibniz*. ed. W. Kabitz (Heidelberg), 1930.

Fitsch, G., "Analyticity and Necessity in Leibniz," *Journal of the History of Philosophy* 17, 1979, pp. 29-42.

Fleckenstein, J., *G. W. Leibniz: Barock und Universalismus* (Munich), 1958.

Foucher de Careil, A., *Leibniz, Descartes et Spinoza, avec un rapport par M. V. Cousin* (Paris), 1863.

——, *Memoire sur la philosophie de Leibniz*, precede d'une preface de M. Alfred Fouillee (Paris), 1905.

Fox, M., "Leibniz's Metaphysics of Space and Time," *Studia Leibnitiana* 2, 1970, pp. 29-55.

Franke, O., "Leibniz und China," *Zeitschrift der Deutschen Morgenlandischen Gesellschaft* 7, 1928, pp. 155-78.

Frankfurt, H., ed., *Leibniz. A Collection of Critical Essays* (New York), 1972, p. 425.

Friedman, J., "On some Relations between Leibniz' Monadology and Transfinite Set Theory. (A Complement to the Russell Thesis.)," in Akten des II. Internationalen Leibniz-Kongresses Hanover (Weisbaden), 1972, pp. 335-56.

Friedmann, G., *Leibniz and Spinoza* (Paris), 1946.

Friedrich, C., "Philosophical Reflections of Leibniz on Law, Politics, and the State," in *Leibniz: A Collection of Critical Essays*, ed. Harry Frankfurt (New York), 1972, pp. 47-68.

Furth, M., "Monadology," *The Philosophical Review* 76, 1967, pp. 169-200.

Gabaude, J. "La Religion selon Leibniz," *Revue de l'enseignment philosophique* 24, 1973, pp. 1-11.

Gabbey, A., "Force and Inertia in Seventeenth-century Dynamics," *Studies in History and Philosophy of Science* 2, 1971, pp. 1-67.

Gale, G., "Did Leibniz Have a Practical Philosophy of Science? Or, Does "Least-Work" Work?" in *Akten des II. Internationalen Leibniz-Kongresses Hanover* (Weisbaden), 1972, pp. 151-60.

———, "Leibniz and Some Aspects of Field Dynamics," *Studia Leibnitiana* 6, 1974, pp. 28-48.

———, "Leibniz' Dynamical Metaphysics and the Origins of the Vis Viva Controversy," *Systematics* 11, 1973, pp. 184-207.

———, "The Physical Theory of Leibniz," *Studia Leibnitiana* 2, 1970, pp. 114-27.

———, "On What God Chose: Perfection and God's Freedom," *Studia Leibnitiana* 8, 1976, pp. 69-87.

Ganz, R., *Das Unbewusste bei Leibniz* (Zurich), 1917.

Gerhardt, C., *Briefwechsel zwischen Leibniz und Christian Wolff* (Hildesheim), 1963.

Gerland, E., "Leibnizens nachgelassene Schriften physikalischen, mechanischen und technischen Inhalts," in *Abhandlungen zur Geschichte der Mathematischen wissenschaften*, 1906.

Gertzberg, B., *Le Probleme de la limitation des creatures chez Leibniz* (Paris), 1937.

Geyer, C., "Zur Nahe Klassischer und moderner Theodizeeversiche zum mythischen Denken, Platon, Leibniz, Horkheimer," *Franziskanische Studien* 57, 1975, pp. 196-229.

Gorland, A., *Der Gottesbegriff bei Leibniz. Ein Vorwort zu seinen System*, 1907.

Gotterbarn, D., "Leibniz's Completion of Descartes's proof," *Studia Leibnitiana* 8, 1976, pp. 105-12.

Gregory, J., "Leibniz, the Identity of Indiscernibles, and Probability," *Philosophy and Phenomenological Research* 14, 1954, pp. 365-69.

Grell, H., "Philosophische Aspekte der Infinitesimalmethode und der Lehre vom Raum bei Leibniz und Newton und ihre Auswirkung in der Mathematik der Folgezeit," *Spektrum* 14, 1968, pp. 235-40.

Grene, M., and Ravetz, J., "Leibniz's Cosmic Equation: A Reconstruction," *The Journal of Philosophy* 59, 1962, pp. 141-46.

Grimm, R., "Individual Concepts and Contingent Truths," *Studia Leibnitiana* 2, 1970, pp. 200-23.

Grimm, T., "China und das Chinabild von Leibniz," *Studia Leibnitiana*, Special Edition, 1, 1969, pp. 38-61.

Grimsley, R., "Kierkegaard and Leibniz," *Journal of the History of Ideas* 26, 1965, pp. 383-96.

Grua, G., *Jurisprudence universelle et theoricee selon Leibniz* (Paris), 1953.

———, *La Justice humaine selon Leibniz* (Paris), 1956.

Gueroult, M., "La Constitution de la substance chez Leibniz," *Revue de Metaphysique et de Morale*, janvier 1947, pp. 55-78.

——, *Dynamique et Metaphysique Leibniziennes* (Paris), 1934.

——, "L'Espace, le point et le vide chez Leibniz," *Revue de la France et de l'Etranger*, janvier a juin 1946.

——, *Etudes sur Descartes, Spinoza, Malebranche et Leibniz* (New York), 1970.

——, "Raum, Zeit, Kontinuitat und Principium indiscernibilium," in *Systemprinzip und Veilheit der Wissenschaften* (Weisbaden), 1969. pp. 62-77.

——, "Substance and the Primitive Simple Notion in the Philosophy of Leibniz," *Philosophy and Phenomenological Research* 7, 1947, pp. 293-315.

Guhrauer, G., *Gottfried Wilhelm Freiherr von Leibniz: Eine Biographie* (Breslau), 1846.

Guitton, J., *Pascal et Leibniz. Etude sur deux types de penseurs* (Paris), 1951.

Gurwitsch, A., "Compossibility and Incompossibility in Leibniz," in *Phenomenological Perspectives. Historical and systematic essays in honor of Herbert Spiegelberg*, ed. Philip J. Bossert (The Hague), 1975.

——, *Leibniz. Philosophie des Panlogismus* (New York), 1974.

Hacking, I., "Equipossibility Theories of Probability," *British Journal for the Philosophy of Science* 22, 1971, pp. 339-55.

——, "The Identity of Indiscernibles'" *The Journal of Philosophy* 72, 1975, pp. 249-56.

——, *Individual Substance* (Frankfurt).

——, "Infinite Analysis," *Studia Leibnitiana* 6, 1974, pp. 126-30.

——, "The Leibniz-Carnap Program for Inductive Logic," *The Journal of Philosophy* 68, 1971, pp. 597-610.

——, "Leibniz and Descartes: Proof and Eternal Truths. Dawes Hicks Lecture on Philosophy, 1973," *Proceedings of the British Academy* 59, 1973, pp. 1-16.

——, "A Leibnizian Space," *Dialogue: Canadian Philosophical Review* 14, 1975, pp. 89-100.

Halbwachs, M., *Leibniz* (Paris), 1906.

Hall, R., "Leibniz and the British Mathematicians 1673-1676," in *Leibniz a Paris 1672-1676* (Chantilly), 1976.

Hamelin, "Ce que Leibniz doit a Aristotle," *Les Etudes philosophiques*, 1957.

Hammond, A., *Ideas about Substance* (Baltimore), 1969.

Hannequin, A., *Etudes d'histoire des sciences et d'histoire de la philosophie* (Paris), 1908.

——, "La Preuve ontologique cartesienne defendue contre la critique de Leibniz," *Revue de Metaphysique et de Morale*, 1896, pp. 433-58.

Harris, J., "Leibniz und Locke zum Thema der angeborenen Ideen," *Ratio* 16, 1974, pp. 210-26.

Hartmann, N., *Leibniz als Metaphysiker* (Berlin), 1946.

Hartshorne, C., "The Compound Individual," in *Philosophical Essays for Alfred North Whitehead* (New York), 1936. Reprinted (New York), 1967, pp. 203-10.

——, "Leibniz's Greatest Discovery," *Journal of the History of Ideas* 7, 1946, pp. 411-21.

——, "Psychicalism and the Leibnizian principle," *Studia Leibnitiana* 8, 1976, pp. 154-59.

Heimann, P., "'Geometry and Nature': Leibniz and Johann Bernoulli's Theory of Motion," *Centaurus* 21, 1977, pp. 1-26.

Heimoeth, H., "Leibniz's Weltanschauung als Ursprung seiner Gedankenwelt," *Kanstudien* 21, 1916, pp. 365-95.

——, *Die Methode der Erkenntnis bei Descartes und Leibniz* (Giessen), 1914.

Heinekamp, A., "Uber Leibniz's Logik und Metaphysik. Zu Martin Schneiders Analysis und Synthesis bei Leibniz," *Studia Leibnitiana* 8, 1976, pp. 265-87.

——, "Sprache und Wirklichkeit nach Leibniz," in *History of Linguistic Thought and Contemporary Linguistics*, ed. Herman Parret (New York), 1976, pp. 518-70.

——, "Ein ungedruckter Brief Descartes' an Roderich Dotzen," *Studia Leibnitiana* 2, 1970, pp. 1-12.

Heinemann, F., "Toland and Leibniz," *The Philosophical Review* 54, 1945, pp. 437-57.

Heintel, E., "Der Begriff der Erscheinung bei Leibniz," *Zeitschrift fur Philosophische Forschung* 20, 1966, pp. 397-442.

——, "Die beiden Labyrinthe der Philosophie nach Leibniz," *Philosophia Naturalis* 10, 1968, pp. 186-97.

Heinze, M., *Leibniz in seinem Verhaltnis zu Spinoza* (Leipzig), 1875.

Helffrich, A., *Spinoza und Leibniz* (Hamburg), 1846.

Heller, M., and Strauszkiewicz, A., "A Physicist's View on the Polemics between Leibniz and Clarke," *Organon*, 1975, pp. 205-13.

Herring, H., "Uber Weltbegriff bei Leibniz'" *Kant-Studien* 57, 1966, pp. 142-54.

Herzberger, H., "Dimensions of Truth," *Journal of Philosophic Logic* 2, 1973, pp. 535-56.

Heufelder, K., *Leibnizsche System* (Leipzig), 1939.

Hildebrandt, K., *Leibniz und das Reich der Gnade* (The Hague), 1953.

Hintikka, Y., "Leibniz on Plentitude, Relations and the Reign of Law," *Ajatus* 1969. Reprinted in Frankfurt, pp. 155-90.

Hlawka, E., "Leibniz als Mathematiker," *Philosophia Naturalis* 10, 1968, pp. 146-68.

Hochstetter, E., "Leibniz Interpretation," *Revue Internationale de Philosophie* 20, 1966, pp. 174-92.

——, *Leibniz zu seinem 300 Geburtstag 1646-1946* (Berlin), 1946-1952.

——, *Zu Leibniz' Gedachnis, eine Einleitung* (Berlin), 1948.

——, "von der Wahren Wirklichkeit bei Leibniz," *Zeitschrift fur Philosophische Forschung* 20, 1966, pp. 421-46.

Hofmann, J., *Die Differenzenrechnung bei Leibniz* (Berlin), 1931.

——, *Die Entwicklungsgeschichte der Leibniz'schen Mathematik* (Munich), 1949.

——, *Leibniz in Paris 1672-1676. His growth to mathematical maturity* (Cambridge), 1974.

——, "Leibniz und Wallis," *Studia Leibnitiana* 5, 1973, pp. 245-81.

——, *Leibniz' mathematische Studien in Paris* (Berlin), 1948.

——, "Neue Newtoniana," *Studia Leibnitiana* 2, 1970, pp. 140-45.

——, *Das Opus Geometricum des Gregorius a S. Vinventio und seine Einwirkung auf Leibniz* (Berlin), 1942.

——, *Studien zur Vorgeschichte des Priortatstreites zwischen Leibniz und Newton um die Entdeckung der hoheren Analysis* (Berlin), 1943.

——, "Uber fruhe mathematische Studien von G. W. Leibniz," *Studia Leibnitiana* 2, 1970, pp. 81-114.

——, *"Zusatzliche Bemerkungen uber den mathematischen Inhalt von Leibniz' Abhandlung uber die chinesische Philosophie."*

Hollinger, R., "A Defense of Essentialism," *The Personalist* 57, 1976, pp. 327-44.

Holz, H., *Herr und Knecht bei Leibniz und Hegel. Zur Intepretation d. Klassengemeinschaft* (Berlin), 1968.

——, *Leibniz* (Stuttgart), 1958.

Honigswald, R., *G. W. Leibniz. Ein Beitrag zur Frage seiner problemgeschichtlichen Stellung* (Tubingen), 1928.

Hooker, C., "Remarks on the Principle of the Identity of Indiscernibles," *Southwestern Journal of Philosophy* 6, 1975, pp. 129-53.

Hoppner, H., "Zur Datierung des Stuckes 'De Calculo Situum,'" *Studia Leibnitiana* 2, 1970, pp. 233-35.

Hostler, J., *Leibniz's Moral Philosophy* (London), 1975.

——, "Some Remarks on 'omne possible exigit existere,'" *Studia Leibnitiana* 5, 1973, pp. 281-85.

Howe, L., "Leibniz on Evil," *Sophia* 10, 1971, pp. 8-17.

Hubener, W., "Sinn und Grenzen des Leibnizschen Optimismus," *Studia Leibnitiana* 10, 1978, pp. 222-46.

Huber, K., *Leibniz* (Munich), 1951.

Hubner, W., "Monade und Welt. Ein Beitrag zur Interpretation der Monadologie," *Studia Leibnitiana* 7, 1975, pp. 105-21.

Hutin, S., "Leibniz a-t-il subi l'influence d'Henry More?" *Studia Leibnitiana* 2, 1970, pp. 59-62.

Iltis, C., "The Decline of Cartesianism in Mechanics: The Leibnizian-Cartesian Debates," *Isis* 64, 1973, pp. 356-73.
——, "Leibniz' Concept of Force: Physics and Metaphysics," in *Akten des II. Internationalen Leibniz-Kongresses Hanover* (Weisbaden), 1972, pp. 143-49.
——, "The Leibnizian-Newtonian Debates: Natural Philosophy and Social Psychology," *British Journal for the History of Science* 6, 1973, pp. 343-77.
Inwagen, P., "Ontological Arguments," *Nous* 11, 1977, pp. 375-95.
Ishiguro, H., "Leibniz and the Ideas of Sensible Qualities," in *Reason and Reality* (London), 1972, pp. 49-63.
——, "Leibniz's Denial of the Reality of Space and Time," *Annals of the Japan Association for the Philosophy of Science* 3, March 1967.
——, *Leibniz's Philosophy of Logic and Language* (London), 1972.
——, "Leibniz's Theory of the Ideality of Relations," in *Leibniz: A collection of critical essays*, ed. Harry Frankfurt (New York), pp. 191-213.
——, "Les Verites hypothetiques. Un Examen de al nature de Leibniz a Foucher de 1675," in *Leibniz a Paris 1672-1676* (Chantilly), 1976, pp. 33-42.
Iwanicki, J., *Leibniz et les demonstrations mathematiques de l'existence de Dieu* (Strasbourg), 1933.
Jager, R., "Analyticity and Necessity in Moore's Early Work," *Journal of the History of Philosophy* 7, 1969, pp. 441-58.
Jalabert, J., "Creation et harmonie preetablie selon Leibniz," *Studia Leibnitiana* 3, 1971, pp. 190-98.
——, *Le Dieu de Leibniz* (Paris), 1960.
——, "Etre et valeur," *Studia Leibnitiana* 10, 1978, pp. 87-91.
——, "Leibniz, Philosophe de l'unite," *Zeitschrift fur Philosophische Forschung* 20, 1966, pp. 447-56.
——, *La theorie leibnizienne de substance* (Paris), 1947.
Janke, W., "Theodizee oder Uber die Freiheit des Individuums und das Verhangnis der Welt," *Philosophische Perspektiven* 5, 1973, pp. 57-77.
——, "Die Zeitlichkeit der Reprasentation, zur Seinfrage bei Leibniz," in *Durchblicke. Festschrift fur Martin Heidegger zum 80. Geburtstag* (Frankfurt), 1970, pp. 255-83.
Jansen, B., *Leibniz als erkenntnistheoretischer Realist* (Berlin), 1920.
Jarrett, C., "Leibniz on Truth and Contengency," in *New Essays on Rationalism and Empiricism*, ed. Charles E. Jarrett, John King-Farlow, and F. J. Pelletier (Ontario), 1978, pp. 83-100.
Johnson, A., "Leibniz and Whitehead," *Philosophy and Phenomenological Research* 19, 1959, pp. 285-305.
——, "Leibniz's Method and the Basis of his Metaphysics," *Philosophy* 35, 1960, pp. 51-61.
Jolley, N., "Leibniz on Hobbes, Locke's Two Treatises and Sherlock's Case of Allegiance," *The Historical Journal* 18, 1975, pp. 21-35.
——, "Leibniz on Locke and Socinianism," *Journal of the History of Ideas* 39, 1978, pp. 233-50.
——, "Perception and Immateriality in the Nouveaux Essais," *Journal of the History of Philosophy* 16, 1978, pp. 181-94.
——, "An Unpublished Leibniz manuscript on Metaphysics," *Studia Leibnitiana* 7, 1975, pp. 161-89.
Jordan, G., *The Reunion of the Churches: A Study of G. W. Leibniz and his Great Attempt* (London), 1927.
Joseph, H., *Lectures on the Philosophy of Leibniz* (Oxford), 1949.
Jourdain, P., "The Logical Work of Leibniz," *The Monist* 26, 1916, pp. 504-23.
Kabitz, W., *Die Philosophie des jungen Leibniz* (Heidelberg), 1909.
Kangro, H., "Joachim Jungius und Gottfried Wilhelm Leibniz. Ein Beitr. zum geistigen Verhaltnis beider Gelehrten," *Studia Leibnitiana* 1, 1969, pp. 175-207.

Kanitz, H., *Das Ubergegensatzliche bei Leibniz* (Hamburg), 1951.

Kaulbach, F., "Der Begriff des Charakters in der Philosophie von Leibniz," *Kant-Studien* 57, 1966, pp. 126-41.

——, "Das Copernicanische Prinzip und die philosphische Sprache bei Leibniz. Zur 500. Wiederkehr des Geburtstages von Nicolaus Copernicus am 19. 2. 1973," *Zeitschrift fur Philosophische Forschung* 27, 1973, pp. 333-47.

——, "Gekurzte Fassung," in *Akten des II. Internationalen Leibniz-Kongresses Hanover*, 1972, pp. 95-103.

——, *Die Metaphysik de Raumes bei Leibniz und Kant* (Koln), 1960.

——, "Philosophie und einzelne wissenschaft bei Leibniz," *Philosophia Naturalis* 10, 1968, pp. 169-85.

——, "Subjektivtat, fundament der Erkenntnis und lebendiger Speigel bei Leibniz," *Zeitschrift fur Philosophische Forschung* 20 (1966), pp. 471-95.

Kauppi, R., "Einige Bemerkungen zum Principium Indentitatis Indiscernibilium bei Leibniz," *Zeitschrift fur Philosophische Forschung* 20, 1966, pp. 497-506.

——, "Die Idee der Logik in der Philosophie Leibnizens," in *Erkenntnislehre* (Weisbaden), 1969, pp. 80-91.

——, "Uber die Leibnizsche Logik, mit besondere Besuchsichtung der Intension und Extension," *Acta Philosophica Fennica*, 1960.

Kedrov, B., "Leibniz' Prinzip vom zureichenden Grund und die Entstehung der Chemie als Wissenschaft im 17. und 18. Jahrhundert," in *Akten des II. Internationalen Leibniz-Kongresses* Hanover (Weisbaden), 1972, pp. 269-91.

Khamara, E., "Eternity and Omniscience," *Philosophical Quarterly* 24, 1974, pp. 204-19.

Khatchadourain, H., "Individuals and the Identity of Indiscernibles," in *Erkenntnislehre* (Weisbaden), 1969, pp. 190-272.

Kiefel, F., *Leibniz* (Mainz), 1913.

Kluge, E., "Frege, Leibniz et alii," *Studia Leibnitiana* 9, 1977, pp. 266-74.

Knapp, H., "'Determining Reason' and Prognosis in Leibniz," *Ratio* 17, 1975, pp. 18-34.

——, "Notwendige und zufallige Wahrheiten. Die Summerierung unendlicher Reihen in Lichte der Leibnizschen Begriffslogik," *Studia Leibnitiana* 10, 1978, pp. 60-86.

——, "Some Logical Remarks on a Proof by Leibniz," *Ratio* 12, 1970, pp. 125-37.

Kneale, M., "Leibniz and Spinoza on Activity," in *Leibniz: A Collection of Critical Essays*, ed. Harry Frankfurt (New York), 1972, pp. 215-37.

Kneale, W., "Leibniz and the Picture Theory of Language," *Revue Internationale de Philosophie* 20, 1966, pp. 204-15.

Kneale, W., and M. Kneale, *The Development of Logic* (Oxford), 1962.

Knecht, H., "Leibniz et Euclide," *Studia Leibnitiana* 6, 1974, pp. 131-43.

Knobloch, E., "Die entscheidende Abhandlung von Leibniz zur Theorie linearer Gleichungssysteme," *Studia Leibnitiana* 4, 1972, pp. 163-80.

——, "Leibnizens Studien zur Theorie der symmetrischen Funktionene," *Centaurus* 17, 1973, pp. 280-94.

——, "The Mathematical Studies of G. W. Leibniz on Combinatorics," *Historia Mathematica* 1, 1974, pp. 409-30.

Koch, H., *Materie und Organismus bei Leibniz* (Halle), 1908.

Kohler, P., *Der Begriff der Represantation bei Leibniz* (Bern), 1913.

Korner, S., "Material Necessity," *Kant-Studien* 64, 1973, pp. 423-30.

——, "On Russell's Critique of Leibniz's Philosophy," in *Bertrand Russell Memorial Volume*, ed. George W. Roberts (London), 1979, pp. 171-81.

Korsmeyer, C., "Is Pangloss Leibniz?" *Philosophy and Literature* 1, 1977, pp. 201-8.

Koyre, A., "Leibniz and Newton," in *Leibniz: A Collection of Critical Essays*, ed. Harry Frankfurt (New York), 1972, pp. 239-80.

Krause, W., "Leibniz and Post-Newtonian Physics," *American Journal of Physics* 43, 1975, pp. 459-64.

——, "Nimmt Bezug auf Alfred Lande: Albert Einstein and the Quantum Riddle," *American Journal of Physics* 42, 1974, pp. 459-64.

Kreiling, F., "Leibniz," *Scientific American* 218, 1968, pp. 94-100.

——, "Leibniz and Information Theory," *Information* 4, 1972, pp. 177-79.

——, "Leibniz' Views on the History of Science," in *Actes du XII. Congres International d'Histoire des Sciences, Paris 1968*, (Paris), 1971, pp. 67-79.

Kretzman, N., "History of Semantics," in *Encyclopedia of Philosophy*, ed. P. Edwards, vol. 7, p. 365.

Krueger, L., *Rationalismus und Entwurf einer universalen Logik bei Leibniz* (Frankfurt), 1969.

Kulstad, M., *Essays on the Philosophy of Leibniz* (Houston), 1977.

——, "Leibniz's Conception of Expression," *Studia Leibnitiana* 9, 1977, pp. 55-76.

Lacey, H., "The Scientific Intelligibility of Absolute Space," *British Journal for the Philosophy of Science* 21, 1970, pp. 317-42.

Lach, F., "Leibniz and China," *Journal of the History of Ideas* 6, 1945, pp. 436-55.

Lamarra, A., "The Development of the Theme of the 'logica inventiva' during the Stay of Leibniz in Paris," in *Leibniz a Paris 1672-1676* (Chantilly), 1976, pp. 55-71.

Lasswitz, K., *Geschichte der Atomistik vom Mittelatler bis Newton* (Hamburg), 1890. Reprinted: (Darmstadt), 1963.

Leblanc, H., "Deux Reves de Leibniz. Reflexions sur une lecture de Skolem et de Godel," in *La Communication. Actes du 15. congres de l'Association des societes de philosophie de langue francaise, Universite de Montreal, 1971* (Montreal), 1973, pp. 134-39.

Le Chevalier, L., *La Morale de Leibniz* (Paris), 1933.

Leclerc, I., "Kant's Second Antinomy, Leibniz, and Whitehead," *Review of Metaphysics* 20, 1966, pp. 25-41.

——, "Leibniz and the Analysis of Matter and Motion," in *The Philosophy of Leibniz and the modern world*, ed. Ivor Leclerc (Nashville), 1973, pp. 114-32.

——, ed. *The Philosophy of Leibniz and the Modern World* (Nashville), 1973.

——, "The Problem of Physical Existent," *International Philosophical Quarterly* 9, 1969, pp. 40-62.

Lenders, W., "Kommunikation und Grammatik bei Leibniz," in *History of Linguistic Thought and Contemporary Linguistics*, ed. Herman Parret (New York), 1976, pp. 571-92.

Le Roy, G., *Discours de Metaphysique et Correspondance avec Arnauld* (Paris), 1957.

Leroy, M., "Les curiosites linguistiques de Leibniz," *Revue Internationale de Philosophie* 20, 1966, pp. 193-203.

Leslie, J., "Morality in a World Guaranteed Best Possible," *Studia Leibnitiana* 3, 1971, pp. 199-205.

Lewis, G., *Lettres de Leibniz a Arnauld* (Paris), 1952.

Leyden, W., *Seventeenth-century Metaphysics. An Examination of Some Main Concepts and Theories* (London), 1968.

Lloyd, G., "Leibniz on Possible Individuals and Possible Worlds," *The Australisian Journal of Philosophy* 56, 1978, pp. 126-42.

Loades, A., "Kant's Concern with Theodicy," *Journal of Theological Studies*. New Series, 26, 1975, pp. 361-76.

Loemker, L., "Boyle and Leibniz," *Journal of the History of Ideas* 16, 1955, pp. 22-43.

——, "Das ethische Anliegen des Leibnizschen Systems," *Studia Leibnitiana Supplementa* 4, (Wiesbaden), 1969, pp. 63-76.

——, "Leibniz and the Herborn Encyclopedists," *Journal of the History of Ideas* 22, 1961, pp. 323-38.

——, "Leibniz and the Limits of Empiricism," in *The Philosophy of Leibniz and the modern world*, ed. Ivor Leclerc (Nashville), 1973, pp. 158-75.

——, "Leibniz and Our Time," in *The Philosophy of Leibniz and the Modern World*, ed. Ivor Leclerc (Nashville), 1973, pp. 3-10.

——, "Leibniz's Conception of Philosophical Method," *Zeitschrift fur Philosophische Forschung* 20, 1966, pp. 507-24.

——, "Leibniz's Doctrine of Ideas," *The Philosophical Review* 55 1946, pp. 229-49.

——, "Leibniz's Judgments of Fact," *Journal of the History of Ideas* 7, 1946, pp. 397-410.

——, "The Metaphysical Status of Regulative Maxims in Leibniz and Kant," *Southern Journal of Philosophy* 11, 1973, pp. 141-47.

——, "A Note on the Origin and Problem of Leibniz's Discourse of 1686," *Journal of the History of Ideas* 8, 1947, pp. 449-66.

——, *Struggle for Synthesis. The 17th Century Background of Leibniz's Synthesis of Order and Freedom* (Cambridge), 1972.

——, "On Substance and Process in Leibniz," in *Process and Divinity. The Hartshorne Festschrift*, ed. Reese and Freedman (Lasalle), 1964, pp. 403-25.

Loewer, B., "Leibniz and the Ontological Argument," *Philosophical Studies* 34, 1978, pp. 105-9.

Lomasky, L., "Leibniz and the Modal Argument for God's Existence," *The Monist* 54, 1970, pp. 250-69.

Loux, M., "Kinds and the Dilemma of Individuation," *Review of Metaphysics* 27, 1973-74, pp. 773-84.

Lovejoy, A., "Plentitude and Sufficient Reason in Leibniz and Spinoza," in *Leibniz: A Collection of Critical Essays*, ed. Harry Frankfurt (New York), 1972, pp. 281-334.

Ludovici, C., *Ausfuehrlicher Entwurff einer vollstaendigen Historie der Leibnizischen* (Leipzig), 1737.

Lycan, W., "Materialism and Leibniz' Law," *The Monist* 56, 1972, pp. 276-87.

MacDonald, G., "Identity," in *Proceedings of the XVth World Congress of Philosophy. 17th to 22nd September 1973* (Sofia), 1975, pp. 561-64.

MacIntosh, J., "Leibniz and Berkeley," *Proceedings of the Aristotelian Society* 71, 1970-71, pp. 147-63.

——, "Primary and Secondary Qualities," *Studia Leibnitiana* 8, 1976, pp. 88-104.

Mackie, J., *Life of Godfrey William von Leibniz* (Boston), 1845.

Madigan, P., "Space in Leibniz and Whitehead," *Tulane Studies in Philosophy* 24, 1975, pp. 48-57.

Mahnke, D., "Leibniz als Begrunder der symbolischen Mathematik," *Isis* 9, 1927, pp. 279-83.

——, "Leibniz als Gegner der Gelehrten Einseitigkeit," in *Wissenschaftliche Beilage zu Jahresbericht des koniglichen Gymansiums zu Stade* (Stade), 1912.

——, "Leibnizens Synthese von Universal Mathematik und Individual Metaphysik," *Jahrbuch fur Philosophie und phanomenologische Forschung*, 7, pp. 305-611.

——, *Neue Einblicke in die Entdeckungsgeschichte der haheren Analysis* (Berlin), 1926.

——, *Unendliche Sphaere und Allmattelpunkt* (Halle), 1937.

Maizeaux, *Recueil de diverses pieces sur la Philosophie, la Religion naturelle, l'Histoire, les Mathematiques, etc., par Mrs. Leibniz, Clakre, Newton, et autres auteurs celebres* (Amsterdam), 1720.

Majorov, G., "Filosofija Lejbnica i ee novejsie zapadnye interpretacii (Die Philosophie von Leibniz und ihre neuesten westlichen Interpretationen, russ.), *Voprosy filosofii* 10, 1968, pp. 173-79.

Manier, E., "Leibniz: First Principles and Systematic Philosophy," *Modern Schoolman* 43, 1965, pp. 39-54.

——, "Matter and Individuation in Leibniz," in *The Concept of Matter*, ed. E. McMullin (Notre Dame), 1963, pp. 392-98.

Margolis, J., *Persona and Minds. The Prospects of Non-reductive Materialism* (Boston), 1978.

Marshall, D., "Lukasiewicz, Leibniz and the Arthmetization of the Syllogism," *Notre Dame Journal of Formal Logic* 18, 1977, pp. 235-42.

Martin, G., "Der Begriff der Realitat bei Leibniz," *Kant-Studien* 49, 1957-58, pp. 82-94.

——, "Existenz und Widerspruchsfreiheit in der Logik von Leibniz," *Kant-Studien* 48, 1956-57, pp. 202-16.

——, *Leibniz: Logic and Metaphysics*, trans. K. J. Northcott and P. G. Luca (New York), 1967.

——, "Leibniz, der Philosoph der Aufklarung," in *Der Internationale Leibniz-Kongress in Hanover* (Hanover), 1968, pp. 74-78.

——, "Thesaurus omnis Humanae Scientiae," *Archives de Philosophie* 30, 1967, pp. 388-97.

Mates, B., "Individuals and Modality in the Philosophy of Leibniz," *Studia Leibnitiana* 4, 1972, pp. 81-118.

——, "Leibniz and the Phaedo," in *Akten des II. Internationalen Leibniz-Kongresses Hanover* (Weisbaden), 1972, pp. 135-48.

——, "Leibniz on Possible Worlds," in *Logic, Methodology, and Philosophy of Science*, ed. Rootselaar and Staal (Amsterdam), 1968.

Matzat, H., *Untersuchungen uber die metaphysischen Grundlagen der Leibnizschen Zeichenkunst* (Berlin), 1938.

May, W., "The God of Leibniz," *New Scholasticism* 36, 1962, pp. 506-28.

McCullough, L., "Leibniz and the Ideality of Relations," *Southwestern Journal of Philosophy* 8, 1977, pp. 31-40.

——, "Leibniz and Traditional Philosophy," *Studia Leibnitiana* 10, 1978, pp. 254-70.

McGuire, J., "Atoms and the 'Analogy of Nature': Newton's Third Rule of Philosophizing," *Studies in History and Philosophy of Science* 1, 1970, pp. 3-58.

——, "Boyle's Conception of Nature," *Journal of the History of Ideas* 33, 1972, pp. 523-42.

McRae, R., *Leibniz: Perception, Apperception, and Thought* (Toronto), 1976.

——, "Time and the Monad," *Nature and System* 1, 1979, pp. 103-9.

McTighe, T., "Nicholas of Cusa and Leibniz's Principle of Indiscernibility," *Modern Schoolman* 42, 1965, pp. 33-46.

Meijering, T., "On Contingency in Leibniz's Philosophy," *Studia Leibnitiana* 10, 1978, pp. 22-59.

Merz, J., *Leibniz* (New York), 1948.

Meschkowski, H., "Leibniz und die chinesische Philosophie," *Humanismus und Technik* 19, 1975, pp. 71-82.

Metz, A., "Descartes et Leibniz," *Archives de Philosophie* 31, 1968, pp. 473-76.

Meurers, J., "Leibniz und das Problem des atomaren," *Philosophia Naturalis* 10, 1968, pp. 133-45.

Meyer, R., *Leibniz und die europaische Ordnungskreise* (Hamburg), 1948.

——, *Leibniz and the 17th Century Revolution* (Glasgow), 1956.

——, "Zum Problem der Wissenschaftstheorie bei Leibniz," *Verhandlungen d. Schweizerischen Naturforschenden Gesellschaft Aarau.*, 148, 1969, pp. 155-63.

Mijuskovic, B., "Locke and Leibniz on Personal Identity," *Southern Journal of Philosophy* 13, 1975, pp. 205-14.

Mitschke, A., *Staat und Politik bei Leibniz* (Marburg), 1941.

Mittelstrass, J., "Monada und Begriff. Leibnizens Rekonstruktion des klassischen Substanzbegriffs und der Perzeptionensatz der Monadentheorie," *Studia Leibnitiana* 2, 1970, pp. 171-200.

Mondadori, F., "Leibniz and the Doctrine of Inter-World Identity," *Studia Leibnitiana* 7, 1975, pp. 21-57.

——, "The Leibnizian 'Circle'," in *Essays on the Philosophy of Leibniz*, ed. Mark Kulstad (Houston), 1977, pp. 69-96.

——, "Reference, Essentialism, and Modality in Leibniz's Metaphysics," *Studia Leibnitiana* 5, 1973, pp. 54-101.

Moreau, J., "L'Espace et les verites eternelles chez Leibniz," *Archives de Philosophie*, 1966, pp. 483-506.

——, "Introduction a la metaphysique Leibnizienne," *Stuida Leibnitiana* 6, 1974, pp. 248-61.

——, "Mathematik und Metaphysik in der Naturphilosophie des XVII. und XVIII. Jahrhunderts," in *Akten des II. Internationalen Leibniz-Kongresses Hanover* (Wiesbaden), 1972, pp. 37-48.

——, "Nature et individuality chez Spinoza et Leibniz," *Revue Philosophique de Louvain* 76, 1978, pp. 447-56.

——, "Tradition et modernite dans la pensee de Leibniz," *Studia Leibnitiana* 4, 1972, pp. 48-60.

——, *L'Univers Leibnizien* (Paris), 1956.

Mueller, K., *Gottfried Wilhelm Leibniz und Nicolaus Witsen* (Berlin), 1955.

——, "Korrespondenten von G. W. Leibniz," *Studia Leibnitiana* 2, 1970, pp. 284-97.

Mueller, K., and Koernert, G., *Leben und Werk von G. W. Leibniz: Ein Chronik* (Frankfurt), 1969.

Mugani, M., "Bemerkungen zu Leibniz' Theorie der Relationen," *Studia Leibnitiana* 10, 1978, pp. 2-21.

Mulvaney, R., "Divine Justice in Leibniz's 'Discourse on Metaphysics'", in *Akten des II. Internationalen Leibniz-Kongresses* Hanover (Weisbaden), 1972, pp. 61-82.

——, "Leibniz's Early Idea of Justice," *Journal of the History of Ideas* 29, 1968, pp. 53-72.

Mungello, D., *Leibniz and Confucianism: The Search for Accord* (Honolulu), 1977.

——, "Leibniz's Interpretation of Neo-Confucianism," *Philosophy East and West* 21, 1971, pp. 3-22.

Naert, E., "Du Fondement de l'individualite selon Leibniz," *Les Etudes Philosophiques*, 1977, pp. 405-19.

——, *Leibniz et la querelle du pur amour* (Paris), 1959.

——, *Memoire et conscience de soi selon Leibniz* (Paris), 1961.

——, *Le Pensee politique de Leibniz* (Paris), 1964.

Nagel, G., "The Identity of Indiscernibles," *The Journal of Philosophy* 73, 1976, pp. 45-50.

Nason, J., "Leibniz and the Logical Argument for Individual Substances," *Mind* 51, 1942, pp. 201-22.

——, "Leibniz's Attack on the Cartesian Doctrine of Extension," *Journal of the History of Ideas* 7, 1946, pp. 447-83.

Nelson, J., "Logically Necessary and Sufficient Conditions for Identity through Time," *American Philosophical Quarterly* 9, 1972, pp. 177-85.

——, "Prior on Leibniz's Law," *Analysis* 30, 1970, pp. 92-94.

Nisbet, H., *Herder and the Philosophy and History of Science* (Cambridge), 1970.

Nobis, H., "Die Bedeutung der Leibniz Schrift de Ipsa Natura im lichte ihrer Begriffsgeschichtlichen Voraussetzungen," *Zeitschrift fur Philosophische Forschung* 20, 1966, pp. 525-38.

Northrop, F., "Leibniz's Theory of Space," *Journal of the History of Ideas* 7, 1946, pp. 422-46.

Norton, D., "Leibniz and Bayle: Manicheism and Dialectic," *Jouranl of the History of Philosophy* 2, 1964, pp. 23-36.

O'Briant, W., "Leibniz's Preference for an Intentional Logic," *Notre Dame Journal of Symbolic Logic* 8, 1967, pp. 254-56.

Odegard, D., "Locke, Leibniz and Identical Propositions," *Studia Leibnitiana* 1, 1969, pp. 241-53.

Pape, I., *Leibniz. Zugang und Deutung aus dem Wahrheitsproblem* (Stuttgart), 1941.

——, *Tradition und Transformation der Modalitat. Bd 1: Moglichkeit-Unmoglichkeit* (Hamburg), 1966.

Parkinson, G., "Bertrand Russell, 1872-1970," *Studia Leibnitiana* 2, 1970, pp. 161-70.

——, "Freedom and Foreknowledge," in *Philosophy in the Open* , ed. G. Vesey (Walton Hall), 1974.

——, *Leibniz on Human Freedom* (Wiesbaden), 1970.

——, "Leibniz's Paris Writings in Relation to Spinoza," in *Leibniz a Paris 1672-1676* (Chantilly), 1976, pp. 73-89.

——, *Logic and Reality in Leibniz's Metaphysics* (Oxford), 1965.

——, "Science and Metaphysics in the Leibniz-Newton Controversy," in *Mathematik-Natur-wissenschaften* (Weisbaden), 1969, pp. 79-112.

——, "Science and Metaphysics in Leibniz's 'Specimen Inventorum,'" *Studia Leibnitiana* 6, 1974, pp. 1-27.

Parsons, T., "Nuclear and Extranuclear Properties, Meinong, and Leibniz," *Nous* 12, 1978, pp. 137-51.

Perl, M., "Physics and Metaphysics in Newton, Leibniz and Clarke," *Journal of the History of Ideas* 30, 1969, pp. 507-26.

Peursen, C., *Leibniz: A Guide to His Philosophy*, trans. Hubert Hoskins (New York), 1970.

Philonenko, A., "Etude leibnizienne: Feuerbach et la monadologie," *Revue de Metaphysique et de Morale* 75, 1970, pp. 20-46.

——, "La Loi continuite et le principe des indiscernables, etude leibnizienne," *Revue de Metaphysique et Morale* 72, 1967, pp. 261-86.

Piat, C., *Leibniz* (Paris), 1915.

Pichler, A., *Die Theologie des Leibniz. I-II* (Munich), 1869-70.

Pickler, H., *Leibniz: Ein harmonische Gesprach* (Gray), 1919.

Piguet, J., "Un Fait dialectique: la science newtonienne," *Dialectica* 24, 1970, pp. 165-83.

Plantinga, A., *The Nature of Necessity* (Oxford), 1974.

——, "Which Worlds Could God Have Created?" *The Journal of Philosophy* 70, 1973, pp. 539-52.

——, "World and Essence," *The Philosophical Review* 74, 1970, pp. 461-92.

Politella, J., *Platonism, Aristotelianism and Cabalism in the Philosophy of Leibniz* (Philadelphia), 1938.

Popkin, R., "Leibniz and the French Sceptics," *Revue Internationale de Philosophie* 20, 1966, pp. 228-48.

Poser, H., "Zum logischen und inhaltlichen Zusammenhang der Modalbegriffe bei Leibniz," *Kant Studien* 60, 1969, pp. 436-51.

——, *Zur Theorie der Modalbegriffe bei G. W. Leibniz*, 1969.

Price, M., "Identity through Time," *The Journal of Philosophy* 74, 1977, pp. 201-17.

Priestley, F., "The Clarke-Leibniz Controversy," on *The Methodological Heritage of Newton*, ed. Robert E. Butts and John W. Davis (Toronto), 1970, pp. 34-56.

Radermacher, H., "Das Principium identitatis indiscernibilium des Leibniz," *Perspektiven der Philosophie. Neues Jahrbuch* 3, 1978, pp. 239-50.

Rather, L., and Frerichs, J., "The Leibniz-Stahl Controversy," *Clio medica* 5, 1970, pp. 53-67.

Reese, A., "Die Rolle der Historie beim Aufstieg des Welfenhauses 1680-1714," *Studia Leibnitiana* 2, 1970, pp. 78-80.

Reichenbach, H., "Die Bewegungslehre bei Newton, Leibniz und Huyghens," *Kant-Studien* 29, 1924, pp. 416-38.

Reimann, W., "Droit de Dieu, droit de l'homme, droit de l'etre dans la philosophie de Leibniz," *Archives de Philosophie* 34, 1971, pp. 231-43.

Reinhardt, L., "Leibniz, Causality and Monads," in *Akten des II. Internationalen Leibniz-Kongresses Hanover* (Weisbaden), 1972, pp. 173-82.

Rescher, N., "Contingence in the Philosophy of Leibniz," *The Philosophical Review* 61, 1952.

——, "The Contributions of the Paris Period (1672-76) to Leibniz's Metaphysics," in *Leibniz a Paris 1672-1676* (Weisbaden), 1978, pp. 43-53.

——, "Leibniz and the Plurality of Space-time Frameworks," in *Essays on the Philosophy of Leibniz*, ed. Mark Kulstad (Houston), 1977, pp. 97-106.

——, "Leibniz und die Vollkommenheit der Welten," in *Akten des II. Internationalen Leibniz-Kongresses Hanover* (Weisbaden), 1972, pp. 1-14.

——, "Leibniz' Conception of Quantity, Number, and Infinity," *The Philosophical Review* 64, 1955, pp. 108-14.

——, "Leibniz's Interpretation of his Logical Calculi," *Journal of Symbolic Logic* 19, 1954.

——, "Logical Difficulties in Leibniz' metaphysics," in *Essays in Philosophical Analysis*, ed. N. Rescher (Pittsburgh), 1969, pp. 159-70.

——, "Monads and Matter: A Note on Leibniz's Metaphysics," *Modern Schoolman* 32, 1955, pp. 172-75.

——, *The Philosophy of Leibniz* (Englewood Cliffs), 1967.

——, *A Theory of Possibility* (Oxford), 1975.

Richter, L., *Leibniz und sein Russlandbild* (Berlin), 1946.

Riley, P., "An Unpublished Lecture by Leibniz on the Greeks as Founders of Rational Theology: Its Relation to his 'Universal Jurisprudence,'" *Journal of the History of Philosophy* 14, 1976, pp. 205-16.

——, "An Unpublished manuscript of Leibniz on the Allegiance due to Sovereign Powers," *Journal of the History of Philosophy* 11, 1973, pp. 319-36.

Risse, W., "Die characteristica universalis bei Leibniz," *Studia Inter Filosofia* 1, 1969, pp. 107-16.

Robinet, A., "Le Discours de Metaphysique dans la vie de Leibniz," Revue Internationale de Philosophie 20, 1966, pp. 165-73.

——, "Grundprobleme der 'Nouveaux Essais,'" in *Erkenntnislehre* (Weisbaden), 1969, pp. 20-23.

——, "Leibniz, l'automate et la pensee," *Studia Leibnitiana* 4, 1972, pp. 285-90.

——, "Leibniz und Heidegger: Atomzeitalter oder Informatikzeitalter?," *Studia Leibnitiana* 8, 1976, pp. 241-56.

——, *Malebranche et Leibniz* (Paris), 1955.

——, "Du Nouveau sur la correspondance Leibniz-Des Bosses," *Studia Leibnitiana* 1, 1969, pp. 83-103.

——, "Premieres Reflexions sur les applications de l'informatique a l'etude des textes philosophiques," *Cirpho Review* 1, 1973, pp. 7-13.

Rodingen, H., *Aussage und Antweisung* (Meisenheim Am Glan), 1973.

Rodis-Lewis, G., "Un Lapsus de Leibniz," *Les Etudes Philosophiques* 4, 1976, pp. 495-96.

Rosenblatt, L., "A Reading of Leibniz," *The Independent Journal of Philosophy* 2, 1978, pp. 67-69.

Rowe, W., "Plantinga on Possible Worlds and Evil," *The Journal of Philosophy* 70, 1978, pp. 554-55.

Roy, O., *Leibniz et la Chine* (Paris), 1972.

Ruf, O., *Die Eins und die Einheit bei Leibniz* (Meisenheim Am Glan), 1973.

Russell, B., *A Critical Exposition of the Philosophy of Leibniz, with an Appendice of Leading Passages* (London), 1951.

——, *Introduction a la philosophie mathematique*, trans. G. Moreau (Paris), 1928.

Russell, L., "Gottfried Wilhelm Leibniz," in *The Encyclopedia of Philosophy*, ed. Paul Edwards (New York), 1967.

——, "Leibniz on the Metaphysical Foundations of Science," *Studia Leibnitiana* 9, 1977, pp. 101-10.

——, "Leibniz's Account of Phenomena," *Proceedings of the Aristotelian Society* 54, 1953-1954, pp. 167-86.

——, "Leibniz's Philosophy of Science," *Studia Leibnitiana* 8, 1976, pp. 1-17.

——, "Possible Worlds in Leibniz," *Studia Leibnitiana* 1, 1969, pp. 161-75.

——, "What is Living and What is Dead in the Philosophy of Leibniz," *Filosofia* 19, 1968, pp. 699-712.

Saame, O., *Der Satz vom Grund bei Leibniz: ein constitutives Element seiner Philosophie und ihrer Einheit* (Mainz), 1961.

Sanford, D., "Locke, Leibniz and Wiggins on Being in the Same Place at the Same Time," *The Philosophical Review* 79, 1970, pp. 75-82.

Savile, A., "Leibniz's Contribution to the Theory of Innate Ideas," *Philosophy* 47, 1972, pp. 113-24.

Saw, R., *Leibniz* (Middlesex), 1954.

Scarrow, D., "Reflections on the Idealist Interpretation of Leibniz's Philosophy," in *Akten des II. Internationalen Leibniz-Kongresses Hanover*, (Weisbaden), 1972, pp. 85-93.

Schapers, H., "Leibniz arbeiten zu einer Reformation der kategorien," *Zeitschrift fur Philosophische Forschung* 20, 1966, pp. 539-67.

Scharschuch, H., *Einfuhrung in die Monadologie Leibnizens* (Berlin), 1939.

Scheffler, S., "Leibniz on Personal Identity and Moral Personality," *Studia Leibnitiana* 8, 1976, pp. 219-40.

Schiedermair, H., *Das Phanomen der Macht und die Idee des Rechts bei Gottfried Wilhelm Leibniz*, 1969.

Schischkoff, G., "Die Gegenwartige Logistik und Leibniz," in *Beitrage zur Leibniz-Forschung*, ed. G. Schischkoff (Reutlingen), 1947, pp. 226-40.

———, "Das Leibniz Bild im Werke Kurt Hubers," *Zeitschrift fur Philosophische Forschung* 20, 1966, pp. 569-94.

Schlosser, E., *Die Rezensionstatigkeit von Leibniz auf mathematischen und physikalischen Gebiet* (Heidelberg), 1934.

Schmalenbach, H., *Leibniz* (Munich), 1921.

Schmidt, F., "Ganzes und Teil bei Leibniz," *Archiv fur Geschichte der Philosophie* 53, 1971, pp. 267-78.

———, "Die symbolisierten Elemente der Leibnizschen Logik," *Zeitschrift fur Philosophische Forschung* 20, 1966, pp. 595-605.

Schmidt, G., "Das ontologische Argument bei Descartes und Leibniz," *Analecta Anselmiana* 4, 1975, pp. 221-30.

Schmiedecke, A., "Leibniz' Beziehungen zu Zeitz," *Sachsische Heimatblatter*, 1970, pp. 217-22.

Schneider, H., "Justitia universalis," *Studia Leibnitiana* 2, 1970, pp. 236-40.

Schneiders, W., "Leibniz' doppelter Standpunkt," *Studia Leibnitiana* 3, 1971, pp. 161-90.

———, "Naturrecht und Gerechtigkeit bei Leibniz," *Zeitschrift fur Philosophische Forschung* 20, 1966, pp. 7-65.

Scholz, H., "Leibniz und die mathematische Grundlagenforschung," in *Jahresbericht der deutschen Mathematiker Vereinigung*, ed. E. Sperner, vol. 52, book 3, 1942, pp. 217-44.

———, Mathesis universalis (Basel), 1961.

Schrocker, A., "Leibniz' Mitarbeit an Etienne Chauvins Nouveau Journal des Scavans," *Studia Leibnitiana* 8, 1976, pp. 128-39.

Schulz, D., "Die Bedeutung der analytischen Urteilstheorie fur die Entwicklung des Rationalismus bei Leibniz," *Studia Leibnitiana* 3, 1971, pp. 115-35.

———, "Die Funktion analytischer saetze in Leibniz' fruehen Entwuerfen zur charakteristik," *Studia Leibnitiana* 2, 1970, pp. 127-34.

Schupp, F., "Hempel, Stegmuller und die Leibniz-Bedingung," *Studia Leibnitiana* 10, 1978, pp. 116-22.

Schwarz, R., "Leibniz's Law and Belief," *The Journal of Philosophy* 67, 1970, pp. 122-37.

Seeskin, K., "Is Existence a Perfection? A Case Study in the Philosophy of Leibniz," *Idealistic Studies* 8, 1978, pp. 124-35.

———, "Moral Necessity," *New Scholasticism* 51, 1977, pp. 90-101.

Serres, M., *Le Systeme de Leibniz* (Paris), 1968.

Sesan, M., "Leibniz und Cantemir," *Studia Leibnitiana* 2, 1970, pp. 135-39.

Sheldon, W., "Leibniz's Message to Us," *Journal of the History of Ideas* 7, 1946, pp. 385-96.

Sher, G., "Reasons and Intentionality," *The Journal of Philosophy* 66, 1969, pp. 164-68.

Sinisi, V., "Leibniz's Law and the Antimony of the Liar," *Philosophy and Phenomenological Research* 30, 1969, pp. 279-89.

Sleigh, R., "Leibniz on Individual Substances," *The Journal of Philosophy* 72, 1975, pp. 685-87.

———, "Leibniz on the Simplicity of Substance," in *Essays on the Philosophy of Leibniz* ed. Mark Kulstad (Houston), 1977, pp. 107-21.

Sommers, F., "Leibniz's Program for the Development of Logic," in *Essays in Memory of Imre Lakatos*, ed. R. S. Cohen, P. K. Feyerabend, and M. W. Wartofsky (Boston), 1976, pp. 589-615.

———, "Frege or Leibniz?" in *Studien zu Frege* Bd 3, 1976, pp. 11-34.

Spector, M., "Leibniz vs. the Cartesians on Motion and Force," *Studia Leibnitiana* 7, 1975, pp. 135-44.

Spisani, F., "The Influence of Leibniz on Italian Philosophy between the Seventeenth and Eighteenth Centuries," in *Akten des II. Internationalen Leibniz-Kongresses Hanover* (Weisbaden), 1972, pp. 293-95.

Spitz, L., "The Significance of Leibniz for Historiography," *Journal of the History of Ideas* 13, 1952, pp. 333-48.

Staab, W., "Die Leibnizsche Monadenlehre und die moderne Wissenschaft," *Philosophia Naturalis* 11, 1969, pp. 360-94.

Stack, G., "Leibniz and the Problem of Knowledge," *Darshana International* 7, 1967, pp. 81-94.

Stammler, G., *Leibniz* (Munich), 1930.

Stein, L., *Leibniz in seinem Verhaltnis zu Spinoza* (Berlin), 1888.

Stenius, E., "On the System of Leibniz," *Ajatus* 35, 1973, pp. 49-73.

Steudel, J., *Leibniz und die Medizin* (Bonn), 1960.

Stevenson, L., "Relative Identity and Leibniz's Law," *Philosophical Quarterly* 22, 1972, pp. 155-58.

Sticker, A., *Die Leibnizschen Begriffe der'Perzeption und Apperzeption* (Bonn), 1900.

Sticker, B., Alexander von Humbolt und die Einheit der Wissenschaft," *Studia Leibnitiana* 2, 1970, pp. 241-61.

Stieler, G., *Leibniz und Malebranche und das Theodicee-Problem*, (Darmstadt), 1930.

Stjazkin, N., *History of the Mathematical Logic from Leibniz to Peano* (Cambridge), 1969.

Strahm, H., *Die 'petites perceptions' im System von Leibniz* (Bern), 1930.

Strauss, M., "Die Huygens-Leibniz-Machsche Kritik im lichte Heutiger Erkenntnis," *Deutsche Zeitschrift fur Philosophie* 16, 1968, pp. 107-20.

Strong, E., *Procedures and Metaphysics: A Study in the Philosophy of Mathematical-Physical Science in the Sixteenth and Seventeenth Centuries* (Berkeley), 1936.

Struik, D., ed. *A Source Book in Mathematics, 1200-1800* (Cambridge), 1969.

Stuewer, R., ed., *Historical and Philosophical Perspectives of Science* (Minneapolis), 1970.

Swartz, R., "Leibniz's Law and Belief," *The Journal of Philosophy* 67, 1970, pp. 122-37.

Swinburne, R., "Whole and Part in Cosmological Arguments," *Philosophy* 44, 1969, pp. 339-40.

Tillmann, B., *Leibniz' Verhaltnis zur Renaissance im allgemeinen und zu Nizolius im besonderen* (Bonn), 1912.

Tonelli, G., "Early Reactions to the Publication of Leibniz' 'Nouveaux Essais' 1765," in *Proceedings of the 3. International Kant Congress, University of Rochester, March 30 - April 4, 1970*, ed. Lewis White Beck (Dordrecht), 1972, pp. 561-67.

———, "Leibniz on Innate Ideas and the Early Reactions to the Publication of the Nouveaux Essais (1765)," *Journal of the History of Philosophy* 12, 1974, pp. 437-54.

Totok, W., and Haase, C., ed., *Leibniz: sein Leben, sein Wirken, sein Welt* (Hanover), 1966.

Turch, D., "Leibniz's Theory of the Soul," *Southern Journal of Philosophy* 12, 1974, pp. 103-16.

——, "Die Substanz als metaphysische Hypothese—zum Problem der Methode in der Metaphysik von Leibniz," *Studia Leibnitiana* 2, 1970, pp. 12-29.

Tymieniecka, A., *Leibniz's Cosmological Synthesis* (Assen), 1964.

——, "Leibniz's Metaphysics and his Theory of the Universal Science," *International Philosophical Quarterly* 3, 1963, pp. 370-91.

Vaught, C., "The Identities of Indiscernibles and the Concept of Substance," *Southern Journal of Philosophy* 6, 1968, pp. 152-58.

Vendler, Z., "On the Possibility of Possible Worlds," *Canadian Journal of Philosophy* 5, 1975, pp. 57-72.

Vennesbuch, J., *G. W. Leibniz* (Bad Godesberg), 1966.

Verburg, P., "The Idea of Linguistic System in Leibniz," in *History of Linguistic Thought and Contemporary Linguistics*, ed. Herman Parret (New York), 1976, pp. 593-615.

Verhave, T., "Contributions to the History of Psychology. Leibniz on the Association of Ideas and Learning," *Psychological Reports*, 1967, pp. 11-16.

Vinci, T., "What is the Ground for the Principle of the Identity of Indiscernibles in Leibniz Correspondence with Clarke?," *Journal of the History of Philosophy* 12, 1974, pp. 95-101.

Voisin, J., "Leibniz et le calcul integral," *Revue Questions Scientifique* 138, 1967, pp. 233-46.

Vonessen, F., "Reim und Zahl bei Leibniz," *Antaios* 7, 1966, pp. 99-120.

Waley, A., "Leibniz and Fu Hsi," *London University School of Oriental Studies Bulletin* 2, 1921, pp. 165-67.

Walker, D., "Leibniz and Language," *Journal of the Warburg and Courtauld Institutes* 35, 1972, pp. 294-307.

Ward, A., *Leibniz as a Politician* (Manchester), 1911.

Wells, R., "Leibniz Today," *Review of Metaphysics* 10, 1956-57, pp. 333-49.

——, "Leibniz Today, II," *Review of Metaphysics* 10, 1957, pp. 502-24.

Werkmeister, W., *Der Leibnizsche Substanbegriff* (Halle), 1899.

Whittemore, R., "Dogma and Sufficient Reason in the Cosmology of Leibniz," *Tulane Studies in Philosophy* 2, 1953, pp. 103-22.

Wiedeburg, P., *Der junge Leibniz. Das Reich und Europa* (Wiesbaden), 1970.

Wiener, P., "G. W. F. Leibniz: On Philosophical Synthesis," *Philosophy East and West* 12, 1962, pp. 195-202.

——, "Leibniz's Project of a Public Exhibition of Scientific Inventions," *Journal of the History of Ideas* 1, 1940, pp. 232-40.

——, "Notes on Leibniz' Conception of Logic and its Historical Context," *The Philosophical Review* 48, 1939, pp. 567-86.

Wiggins, D., "On Being in the Same Place at the Same Time," *The Philosophical Review* 77, 1968, pp. 90-95.

——, "Identity, Designation, Essentialism and Physicalism," *Philosophia* 5, 1975, pp. 1-30.

——, *Identity and Spatio-temporal Continuity* (Oxford), 1967.

Wildermuth, A., *Wahrheit und Schopfung. Ein Grundiss der Metaphysik des Gottfried Wilhelm Leibniz* (Wintherthur), 1960.

Wilson, M., "Confused Ideas," in *Essays on the Philosophy of Leibniz*, ed. Mark Kulstad (Houston), 1977.

——, "Leibniz and Locke on 'First Truths,'" *Journal of the History of Ideas* 28, 1967, pp. 347-66.

——, "Leibniz and Materialism," *Canadian Journal of Philosophy* 3, 1974, pp. 495-513.

——, "Leibniz: Self-Consciousness and Immortality in the Paris Notes and After," *Archiv fur Geschichte der Philosophie* 58, 1976, pp. 335-52.

——, "Leibniz's Dynamics and Contingency in Nature," in *Motion and Time, Space and Matter. Interrelations in the history of philosophy and science*, ed. Peter K. Machamer and Robert G. Turnbull (Columbus), 1976, pp. 264-89.

——, "On Leibniz's Explication of 'Necessary Truth,'" in *Leibniz: A Collection of Critical Essays*, ed. Harry Frankfurt (New York), 1972, pp. 401-20.

——, "Possibility, Propensity, and Chance: Some Doubts about the Hacking Thesis," *The Journal of Philosophy* 68, 1971, pp. 610-17.

Wilson, N., "Individual Identity, Space, and Time in the Leibniz-Clarke Correspondence," in *The Philosophy of Leibniz and the Modern World*, ed. Ivor Leclerc (Nashville), 1973, pp. 189-206.

Wisdom, J., "Berkeley's Criticism of the Infinitesimal," *British Journal for the Philosophy of Science* 4, 1970, pp. 22-25.

Wolff, E., "Kant and Leibniz. Criticisme et Dogmatisme," *Archives de Philosophie* 30, 1967, pp. 231-55.

Wolff, H., *Leibniz. Allbeseelung und Skepsis* (Munich), 1961.

Woolhouse, R., "Leibniz's Principle of Pre-determinate History," *Studia Leibnitiana* 7, 1975, pp. 207-28.

Wren, T., "Leibniz's Theory of Essences: Some Problems Concerning their Ontological Status and their Relation to God and the Universal Harmony," *Studia Leibnitiana* 4, 1972, pp. 181-95.

Wundt, M., "Die geschichtlichen Grundlagen von Leibniz' Metaphysik," *Zeitschrift fur Philosophische Forschung* 11, p. 497.

Yost, R., *Leibniz and Philosophical Analysis* (Berkeley), 1954.

Zacher, H., *Die Hauptschriften zur Dyadik von G. W. Leibniz* (Frankfurt am Main), 1973.

Zempliner, A., "Gedanken uber die erste deutsche Ubersetzung von Leibniz' Abhandlung uber die chinesische Philosophie," *Studia Leibnitiana* 2, 1970, pp. 223-31.

——, "Leibniz und die chinesische Philosophie," *Studia Leibnitiana Supplementa* 5, pp. 15-30.

Zimmermann, K., *Leibnizens Grundlegung der Metaphysik in den dynamischen Untersuchungen* (Hamburg), 1938.

Zocher, R., *Leibniz Erkenntnislehre* (Berlin), 1952.

John Kish
The Johns Hopkins University

Indexes

Name Index

Subject Index

Citations Index

All citations in this collection have been indexed to the Gerhárdt edition of Leibniz's *Philosophische Schriften* whenever possible.

Citations taken from Gerhardt, *Leibniz: Mathematische Schriften*.

Citations taken from Couturat, *Opuscules et Fragments inédits de Leibniz* (Paris: 1903).

23	273
46	271
64	249, 250
66	250
85	223, 224
247	223
286	146
287	145
374	230
375	191
376	264
388	229, 230, 231
402	226
405	267
517	253
519	51
520	41
530	193

Citations taken from Grua, *Leibniz: Textes Inédits* (Paris: 1948).

GRUA	HOOKER
16	269
270	250
273	250
288	267
289	247, 267, 272
297	268
300	259, 268, 269
301	267, 271
303	257
305	255
311	262, 263, 270, 274
325	192, 277
333	267, 268
336	255
343	266
345	272
348	227, 270
351	255
353	262
358	113
360	268
383	262, 263
385	266
390	276
393	268
479	265
480	266
493	256
494	256, 269
536	245
608	253

Citations taken from the Prussian Academy Edition of *Leibniz: Sämtliche Schriften und Briefe* (Darmstadt and Leipzig: 1923-).

Citations taken from Dutens, *Leibniz: Opera omnia* (Geneva: 1768).

Citations taken from Foucher de Careil, *Nouvelles lettres et Opuscules inédits de Leibniz* (Paris: 1857).

Michael Hooker is President of Bennington College. He has taught philosophy at Harvard University and Johns Hopkins University. He is the editor of *Descartes: Critical and Interpretive Essays.*